HATTIESBURG

HATTIESBURG

An American City in Black and White

WILLIAM STURKEY

THE BELKNAP PRESS OF
HARVARD UNIVERSITY PRESS

Cambridge, Massachusetts
London, England

Printed in the United States of America

First Harvard University Press paperback edition, 2021
First printing

Library of Congress Cataloging-in-Publication Data

Names: Sturkey, William, author.
Title: Hattiesburg : an American city in black and white / William Sturkey.
Description: Cambridge, Massachusetts : The Belknap Press of Harvard University Press, 2019. | Includes bibliographical references and index.
Identifiers: LCCN 2018040469 | ISBN 9780674976351 (cloth : alk. paper) | ISBN 9780674248274 (pbk.)
Subjects: LCSH: African Americans—Segregation—Mississippi—Hattiesburg—History. | Whites—Mississippi—Hattiesburg—Attitudes. | African Americans—Mississippi—Hattiesburg—Public opinion. | Civil rights movements—Mississippi—Hattiesburg—History—Personal narratives. | Hattiesburg (Miss.)—Race relations—History.
Classification: LCC F349.H36 S78 2019 | DDC 305.8009762/18—dc23
LC record available at https://lccn.loc.gov/2018040469

For the black men, women, and children, including my ancestors, who experienced life in the Jim Crow South

Contents

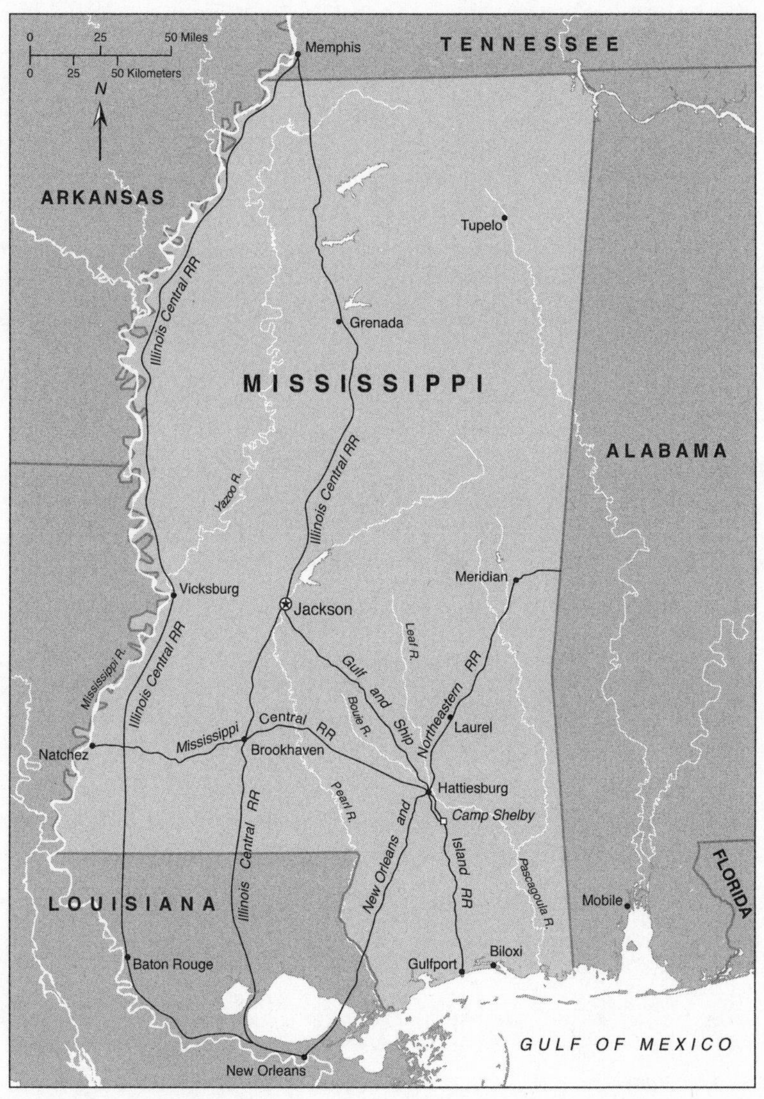

0
25
50 Miles
0
25
50 Kilometers
N
TENNESSEE
ARKANSAS
MISSISSIPPI
ALABAMA
LOUISIANA
FLORIDA
GULF OF MEXICO
Memphis
Tupelo
Grenada
Vicksburg
Jackson
Meridian
Natchez
Brookhaven
Laurel
Hattiesburg
Camp Shelby
Mobile
Biloxi
Gulfport
Baton Rouge
New Orleans
Illinois Central RR
Illinois Central RR
Illinois Central RR
Illinois Central RR
Yazoo R.
Mississippi R.
Leaf R.
Bouie R.
Pearl R.
Pascagoula R.
Gulf and Ship Island RR
Northeastern RR
Mississippi Central RR
New Orleans and Northeastern RR

Introduction

People of Spirit

It was a whole lot better than it is now because it's gone now.

—Hattiesburg native Richard Boyd, 1991

On the first weekend of every October, the old black downtown of Hattiesburg, Mississippi, hosts an event called the Historic Mobile Street Renaissance Festival. By that time of year, the summer heat has faded away from southern Mississippi and left the region with clear, sunny skies and temperatures in the mid-seventies. Mobile Street, a once thriving black commercial center now pockmarked with empty lots, returns to life. Festival organizers estimate that ten thousand people come to the event, an impressive number for a city of fifty thousand.

Saturday is the busiest day. Beginning early in the morning, the day features a full slate of events, including a gospel competition, a motorcycle show, a hip-hop contest, and the ever-popular Sho' Nuff Good Barbecue Cook-off. All day long, representatives from local organizations and churches sell artwork, clothing, raffle tickets, and plates of food, filling the warm autumn air with the smells of pulled pork, macaroni and cheese, greens, ribs, and fried catfish. In the afternoon, blues artists infuse the festival with the sound of electric guitars and deep, guttural lyrics. Kids scamper about the crowd, chasing one another between games of double-dutch and turns on inflatable playgrounds. Teenagers stroll down the paved road, holding hands with sweethearts and making plans for Saturday night. Adults gather in small groups along the cracked sidewalks, laughing, sipping sweet tea, and waving at friends and neighbors. The festival draws people of all ages and races to eat, dance, and help celebrate the history of

Hattiesburg's Mobile Street District. The weather is beautiful. The food is delicious. The music is fun. And the people are happy.[1]

A little park sits about a block south of the center of the festival. The park contains three benches, a handful of small trees, and a plaque commemorating the site as the former location of the Woods Guesthouse. Destroyed by fire in 1998, the guesthouse stood at 507 Mobile Street for over seventy years. The building served a variety of purposes during its time, but today it is remembered most often as the local headquarters of the 1964 Mississippi Freedom Summer, an epic, statewide civil rights campaign that captured America's attention and helped black Mississippians gain the right to vote. A second sign in front of the park indicates the site's number on the Hattiesburg Freedom Summer Trail, a guided audio tour of fifteen sites that were important to the civil rights movement in Hattiesburg.[2]

Hattiesburg, also known as the Hub City, abounds in civil rights history. Of over forty Mississippi towns involved in Freedom Summer, Hattiesburg hosted the greatest number of movement volunteers, and its Freedom Schools boasted the largest enrollment. Black Hattiesburgers participated at rates unheard of in other places. By one estimate, over three thousand local African Americans—about a third of the city's black population at the time—were active in the Freedom Summer. Those were powerful days in Hattiesburg. Local churches swelled with mass meetings. People who had never cast a ballot in their lives went to the courthouse to demand voter registration forms. Children as young as eight years old wrote letters to the president of the United States demanding their freedom. Grade-school dropouts helped plan an overthrow of the state Democratic Party. Regular folks turned into leaders. Some became heroes. They were, as one outsider later remembered them, "people of spirit."[3]

Freedom Summer itself was merely one act in a broader local movement. Hattiesburg was active throughout the 1960s. The city's civil rights era was filled with hundreds of marches, protests, sit-ins, and boycotts and tragically marred by arrests, beatings, and murder. Hattiesburg was the home of well-known freedom fighters such as Vernon Dahmer, Clyde Kennard, Dorie and Joyce Ladner, and the indomitable Victoria Jackson Gray, who in 1964 became the first woman in Mississippi history to run for United States Senate. During the 1960s, scores of nationally known activists passed through the city—Fannie Lou Hamer, Medgar Evers, Dick Gregory, Bob Moses, and Martin Luther King Jr., who spoke at Mt. Zion Baptist Church (a stop on the Hattiesburg Freedom Summer Trail) just days before he was assassinated in Memphis. The movement is etched in local lore. Locals know this history well, and they're proud of it. But it is not the history of the movement that draws people to Mobile Street every October.[4]

Scattered among the crowd at the Historic Mobile Street Renaissance Festival are dozens of elderly African Americans who grew up in the neighborhood. They started this event, and the day truly belongs to them. They seem to appreciate the celebration more than most. These men and women came of age during a time when black residents could not live, shop, or eat in other parts of town. Back then, the old black neighborhood was filled with homes, offices, drugstores, groceries, ice cream parlors, barbershops, dance halls, and restaurants. Back then, Mobile Street was not as empty as it is today.

Standing among the vacant lots and crumbling buildings, the elders share memories from that bygone era. They reconstruct Mobile Street as it once was, pointing out where the old stores stood and exchanging stories of the people who lived and worked in the neighborhood. They recall buying sodas at Dr. Hammond Smith's drugstore, working at Mrs. McLaurin's newsstand, or running errands for Mrs. Woods. The Smith Drug Store is closed, but the building remains for now. The same cannot be said of Mrs. McLaurin's newsstand; like the Woods Guesthouse and so many others, it too is gone. All that remains of these vanished structures are slabs of concrete or piles of brick.

Having worked so courageously during the civil rights movement to break down racial barriers, many of those elderly storytellers are local legends. Yet most of them agree that something was actually lost in those epic victories. Jim Crow had to go; there was no question about that. It was a horribly unjust society, and no one yearns for the ways black people were treated back then. But many of the elders also radiate a palpable nostalgia as they describe the old community. Through tear-streaked smiles, they recall the old community, carefully explaining that the neighborhood did not always look so decayed or feel so barren. The Mobile Street that these older folk knew once bustled with vibrant individuals and institutions. Their recollections reveal to younger folk that earlier generations of black people had built something special there, even within the constraints of Jim Crow. Once upon a time, Mobile Street had a soul.[5]

Established in 1880, Hattiesburg was a quintessential town of the "New South" that emerged after Reconstruction. Railroads—the definitive industrial mechanisms of post–Civil War Southern modernization—changed the nature of Southern life, opening Dixie's interior for rapid development and creating new jobs that brought people to places like Hattiesburg. Teeming with railroad tracks, sawmills, manufacturing shops, and rising downtowns, this New South offered unprecedented industrial opportunities for a historically agrarian population. Most Southerners remained in the countryside, but hundreds of thousands of others abandoned their ancestors' agricultural dreams in search of fresh opportunities.

White Southerners, their society defeated and upended, arrived in the developing towns hoping for renewed stability, better economic prospects, and an expansion of a racial order that protected and enhanced white supremacy. The white architects of this society developed Jim Crow in the subsequent transition from antebellum to modern. Racial segregation laws were pioneered on the railroads, and lynchings increased as the cities grew. To restore control, the white leaders of this New South institutionalized laws designed to consolidate opportunity and power, barring African Americans from full citizenship with new legislation that eliminated constitutional rights, limited access to public spaces, and restricted employment and educational opportunities. These laws were backed by fierce violence and humiliating customs of racial deference. Segregation, lynching, and exclusion cast long shadows over black freedom as African Americans were ferociously blocked from the finest promises of the New South.[6]

But thousands of former black slaves and their children also came to the cities, desperate to flee the farms where their ancestors had toiled. They too took the new jobs and converged in the growing urban spaces. Racial segregation limited their prospects in every walk of life but also helped form remarkable communities like the one that developed in Hattiesburg's Mobile Street neighborhood. The nature of Jim Crow knit African Americans into tight, self-reliant groups that struggled together in their churches, businesses, and schools to insulate themselves from the horrors of racial oppression and to provide better futures for their children. The roots of dramatic change were established during this process. The foundations of the churches that later became famous during the civil rights movement of the 1950s and 1960s were laid in the 1880s and 1890s, the very era during which Jim Crow was constructed.

Through a racial history of Hattiesburg, Mississippi, *Hattiesburg: An American City in Black and White* explores the forces that shaped race in the

American South during the era of Jim Crow. Like the Historic Mobile Street Renaissance Festival, this book is far more concerned with Jim Crow itself than with the more widely celebrated history of the civil rights movement, which, in fact, often eclipses a far more profound history of race in the American South. Jim Crow is frequently portrayed as an unbending system of racial apartheid that remained stagnant between Reconstruction and the civil rights movement. Or it is reduced to the well-known segregation statutes that affected public accommodations and education. But Jim Crow was far more complex. Such portrayals and simplifications frequently overlook key aspects of this particular form of racial apartheid and fail to uncover dramatic transformations in the racial realities of individuals, families, and cities that occurred within Jim Crow. To provide a more complete vision about black and white lives during the era of Jim Crow, this book explores a much deeper Southern racial history by looking beyond the most obvious forms of public segregation and traditional conceptualizations of a "movement," however long or short it may have been.

In search of this more complete vision, *Hattiesburg* traverses traditional chronological and racial boundaries to explore the diverse set of factors that transformed race during the era of Jim Crow. Of the many components of this approach, the most important to mention here is that this book, by necessity, is a biracial history. It investigates the perspectives of both white and black Hattiesburg residents, treating representative individuals, both black and white, as conscious historical actors responding to the opportunities, challenges, and constraints of life in the modern American South.

The white sections of this narrative are presented through the personal histories of several of Hattiesburg's leading white civic boosters and their families. These include a handful of leading businessmen, the town's founder, and a two-term mayor, all of whom came to Hattiesburg from elsewhere and for decades heavily influenced political and economic strategies and racial policies. While thousands of white citizens played important roles in Hattiesburg during Jim Crow, not all their stories can be included here. This book makes choices that may lead to obvious omissions, especially for local readers. Moreover, as a consequence of both available evidence and historical realities, the perspectives of white women and poor white citizens are not equal to those of affluent white men. After all, it was prosperous white men who most profoundly shaped Hattiesburg's trajectory. Their actions touched the lives of tens of thousands of people and outlined the framework of life in the Hub City for nearly a century.

In some cases, members of their families remain prominent local citizens to this day.[7]

Documenting white lives and black lives in Southern cities are two entirely different tasks. This is a result of Jim Crow itself. The practice of segregation and the geographies of black settlement have resulted in vastly fewer archival sources of African Americans' innermost thoughts and political and economic strategies. As in hundreds of other Southern cities, Hattiesburg has no longstanding wealthy black families who would have donated materials to historical archives. That fact, in Hattiesburg and elsewhere, is a result of the economic, political, and spatial limitations imposed upon African Americans during Jim Crow. Because of the absence of such documents as financial ledgers, meeting minutes, and newspaper records, the black sections of this narrative differ from the white sections in their ability to chronicle economic and political activity. Still, despite a dearth of traditional historical sources, the variety of methodologies used here makes possible a vivid recreation of black lives and perspectives.

The black chapters focus primarily on a local family named Smith. For decades, members of the Smith family played important roles in the Mobile Street District. The family first arrived in 1900, and for more than eighty years, they remained heavily involved in local black business, religious, educational, and civic organizations. Led by a formerly enslaved patriarch who raised four sons who became doctors, the Smith family was in many ways exceptional. Yet it was this very exceptionalism and the historical documentation that they left behind that makes the Smith family such an ideal lens through which to document black life in the Mobile Street District during the era of Jim Crow.

This alternating biracial narrative allows *Hattiesburg* to develop two themes crucial to understanding the changing nature of race in the American South during the era of Jim Crow. The first is to highlight black perspectives and actions. Black Southerners were never merely victims, even during the most violently repressive era of racial oppression. Rather than focusing solely on the atrocities committed against African Americans, of which there were so many, this book probes deeper into the framework of modern Southern life to explore how local African Americans responded to their present realities based on their experiences of the past and their expectations for the future. As grim as those realities may seem in hindsight, everyday African Americans in Hattiesburg constantly found and created new opportunities for themselves and their families, opportunities that produced both immediate and intergenerational results. Even at the nadir of black Southern life, thousands of African Americans experienced the greatest prospects anyone in their family had ever known.[8]

The second theme explores how local white leaders effected racial change in unintended and surprising ways. This does not mean that the city's white powerbrokers were not segregationists or white supremacists. They absolutely were, and they worked in tandem with state and regional authorities to craft a system of racial oppression that was both vicious and tragic. But they too struggled while trying to navigate the challenges and opportunities of life in the modern American South. By examining their perspectives and actions over the course of time, this book shows how local white leaders often inadvertently created changes within the local racial order. By incorporating the multifaceted perspectives of white Southerners, *Hattiesburg* demonstrates how renegotiations in modern Southern life created patterns of unanticipated racial consequences throughout what historian C. Vann Woodward famously called "the strange career of Jim Crow."[9] As they were in real life, the fortunes of the oppressors and the oppressed in this book are at once separate and intractably bound.

The following chapters alternate between white and black perspectives to tell the story of the rise and fall of Jim Crow in Hattiesburg, Mississippi. These synchronized narratives enable *Hattiesburg* to reveal three primary factors that created rhythmic fluctuations in the local racial order during the era of Jim Crow while also ultimately helping to frame its demise.

First, although often brutal, the process of post–Civil War Southern modernization created unprecedented mobility for African Americans. Most black Southerners stayed on farms in the early years of the New South, but millions of others arrived in the growing cities to take the jobs offered by industrialization. Some took jobs in railroads, sawmills, factories, and light manufacturing. Others held more traditional service jobs, working in domestic positions such as maids and laundresses that were clustered by urbanization. Although black Southerners typically received only the worst jobs in the New South, they took them willingly because of the social and geographical mobility offered by wage labor and urban work. Modernization brought black migrants to the growing cities of the New South and facilitated their movement within, throughout, and eventually beyond those urban spaces. That mobility offered increased levels of autonomy for millions of black Southerners while subsequently weakening white supremacy and control, especially over the African Americans who left the

South altogether. The white Hattiesburg sawmill owner who in 1917 "ran down to the station and begged the men not to leave [for Chicago]" had clearly lost an element of power.[10]

Second, the economy of the New South—deeply rooted as it was in its reliance on external capital and federal spending—created patterns of unintended racial consequences throughout Jim Crow. Hattiesburg's economic history embodies this longstanding dependence. Yankees, not Southerners, built the railroads and sawmills that ignited the Hub City's first boom. Reliant on external capital for Hattiesburg's initial growth, local white leaders throughout the twentieth century continuously asked—at times, even begged—Northern investors and the federal government for assistance. This reliance forced local white leaders to reconsider or alter components of the local racial order. It is certainly true that white Southerners were often quite successful in maintaining power and control over African Americans during the era of Jim Crow—hence the most visible targets of the civil rights movement: public segregation, voting laws, schools, and jobs. But this book looks beyond those obvious examples of racial discrimination to examine how white leaders' interminable pursuit of external support often resulted in subtler alterations to Jim Crow.

There were several dimensions to this. Most simply, new factories and federal government spending led to more jobs—and thus increased resources and mobility—for black residents. More complex were the political coalitions that had longstanding effects on local race relations. In an ironic twist, local white segregationists eventually found their political allies influenced by the very same black migrants who had used the mobility offered by Southern industrialization to move north, where they could vote. That expanding black political influence would haunt white Southerners in the years after World War II, when they suddenly found their racial order challenged by the "big government" and Northern influence upon which they so heavily relied. In Hattiesburg, the very same white leaders who lobbied the federal government for increased resources during the 1930s and 1940s spent much of their later years mired in a losing struggle to curb federal influence on local race relations. Jim Crow ultimately came undone when African Americans gained the ability to circumnavigate local racial power structures to access protection and equality from a federal government whose authority rapidly expanded between the 1930s and the 1960s.

The third major factor bearing upon the shift in the local racial order was racial discrimination itself. By pushing all African Americans into the margins of Southern life, the white architects of the New South helped foster the development of black communities that grew increasingly resourceful and influential. Restricted and excluded from virtually every aspect of Southern life, African Americans necessarily consolidated resources to develop their own societies and institutions that enriched black life behind the veil of Jim Crow. In many ways, these activities resembled a form of internal governance among a disfranchised people. And when we step back to see this era in a broader perspective, it becomes very clear that the organic origins of the civil rights movement in Hattiesburg and elsewhere lie in turn-of-the-century African American institution building and longstanding community-organizing traditions. Well before civil rights leaders such as Martin Luther King Jr., Rosa Parks, or Fred Shuttlesworth were even born, Atlanta's Ebenezer Baptist Church, Montgomery's Dexter Avenue Baptist Church, and Birmingham's Sixteenth Street Baptist Church functioned as crucial organizing spaces in Southern black communities. The memory of the sense of unity and cohesion that developed in those Jim Crow–era communities still sparks nostalgia among the elderly black men and women who tell their stories every October at the Historic Mobile Street Renaissance Festival. Tragically, the value and richness of those now hollowed-out communities are so often only appreciated in their absence.

Opening amid the rise of the New South from the destitution of the Civil War and Reconstruction, this book takes readers through approximately eight decades of black and white life in Hattiesburg to illuminate how these concurrent processes affected race during the era of Jim Crow. Ultimately, this narrative weaves Hattiesburg into the fabric of modern American life, using the city itself as a character in a story that looks beyond traditional narratives of segregation and civil rights to deliver a more complex and more nuanced historical examination of race in the American South.

CHAPTER ONE

Visionaries

> The Yankee has done a great many things that he should not have done, and left undone things that he should have done, but he has made the flowers bloom, the corn to tassel, homes to flourish and business prosper in this section.
>
> —*New Orleans Daily Picayune*, 1893

On a scorching summer afternoon in the year 1880, a burly, middle-aged, Confederate veteran named Captain William Harris Hardy took a lunch break in a dense Mississippi forest. The pathless woods stretched for miles in every direction, enveloping the captain under an endless canopy of pine needles. A few small homesteads dotted the forest, but no large group had ever settled the remote area, not even Native Americans, who had found little use for the land. A previous traveler once described the region as "a picture of desolation," noting, "Every day adds to the stagnation of the mind." And the forty-three-year-old Hardy had been in the forest for weeks, surveying the area for railroad construction.[1]

On that particular afternoon, Captain Hardy's lunch break was prompted by the sound of flowing water. Thinking that a river or waterfall would offer a brief respite from the monotony of the forest, Hardy walked toward the trickle and came upon a small creek. "The crystal clear water running over a white sandy bottom was a refreshing sight," he later recalled. On the creek bank sat a fallen log that Hardy used as a bench while eating his meal. Hot and tired, the captain took a moment to enjoy his break. He stretched his long legs and lit a cigar, smoking and thinking as he studied a map of the state.[2]

Hardy's employer, the New Orleans & Northeastern Railroad, was part of a European-owned railroad syndicate planning an ambitious new route between Cincinnati and New Orleans. Named for its two terminal cities, the Queen and Crescent City Route would move goods between the Gulf of Mexico and Ohio faster than any other railway. Cargo arriving in Cincinnati could then be dispersed on existing tracks throughout the Northeast, giving New Orleans rapid access to places such as New York, Philadelphia, and Boston. The route promised to greatly enhance Deep South commerce, but it would have to cut through approximately 150 miles of the dreadfully thicketed Piney Woods of southeastern Mississippi. In much of the region, the pine trees and undergrowth were so dense that one could not roll a ball more than ten yards without bumping a trunk. Surveying the area for railroad construction was a daunting assignment.[3]

But there was something about that place near the creek that struck Captain Hardy during his lunch. He lingered on the spot, studying his map, watching the water, and staring into the forest. After finishing his meal, the captain took a short nap on a bed of fallen pine needles before moving on through the woods. Hardy spent the ensuing months completing his work for the railroad, but he never forgot about that particular spot, and he later filed an application to purchase a plot of land near the creek. When his federal land grant was accepted in the spring of 1882, Hardy founded a new town near the site of his lunch. Ever the romantic, the captain named the settlement Hattiesburg in honor of his wife, Hattie.[4]

Captain Hardy was a self-made man. Born in 1837 in Lowndes County, Alabama, he first arrived in Mississippi in 1855 on the heels of a major setback. The young man was just one year shy of graduating from Tennessee's Cumberland College when a dreadful case of pneumonia forced him to withdraw from school. The cold air, a doctor advised him, could worsen his condition and possibly even lead to death. So the young student reluctantly rode home toward an uncertain future in the Alabama cotton belt. Hardy's family, who had paid his tuition by selling "everything on the farm that was not actually needed," was heartbroken. His mother cried at the news of his withdrawal. After a few shiftless weeks, Hardy traveled into Smith County, Mississippi, where he had a cousin who might be able to help the young man find a job.[5]

Like many southern sons who would never inherit great wealth, William Harris Hardy had seen higher education as a promising means toward a better future and was disappointed by having to withdraw from college. But Hardy was resilient. The bout with pneumonia may have forced him to

Captain William Harris Hardy, founder of Hattiesburg. (McCain Library and Archives, University of Southern Mississippi)

leave school, but it would not dictate his future. Diploma or not, the young social climber arrived in Mississippi determined to succeed.

During a horse swap, Hardy met a man who offered him a job running a local school. He accepted the position and taught for about a year. Hardy was the first teacher in that part of Smith County and proved popular among local families. But he did not want to be a teacher. Desiring greater social status and influence, Hardy arranged to apprentice at a local law office, and in less than a year, he managed to pass the state bar exam. He took a job at a firm in Raleigh, Mississippi, and after a few years, he opened his own practice.[6]

In the fall of 1859, Hardy met a young woman named Sallie Johnson at the Mississippi State Fair. "I had never in my life seen so beautiful a girl," he later recalled. "It was a case of love at first sight." After a brief courtship, the pair married the following year. Hardy was smitten with his new bride. Affectionate and warm, he doted on her constantly. By all accounts, they were madly in love. The young couple was just embarking on a promising new life together when the South seceded from the Union, and America went to war. Hardy was not a member of the wealthy plantocracy that owned most of Mississippi's slaves, but he believed in the Confederate cause and answered Jefferson Davis's call to protect the Southern way of life.[7]

Hardy had the stature and bearing of a born leader. Standing six feet, two inches tall, he weighed over two hundred pounds and possessed a booming voice that later earned him a reputation as an impressive orator. Those qualities helped the charismatic attorney recruit a force of eighty men primed to fight the Yankees. On May 31, 1861, Hardy was commissioned a captain in the Confederate Army, a post that paid him a respectable salary of $130 a month. He and his men were mustered into the 16th Mississippi Infantry and given the nickname the Smith County Defenders.[8]

The Smith County Defenders arrived in Manassas, Virginia, shortly after the First Battle of Bull Run. They served in the hottest theater of the Civil War, fighting in the grueling battles for Northern Virginia alongside legendary Confederate generals Robert E. Lee, Stonewall Jackson, and James Longstreet. The 16th was the only Mississippi regiment to participate in the celebrated Valley Campaign of 1862, when Stonewall Jackson's infantry divisions became the fabled "foot cavalry," gloriously routing Union forces up and down the Shenandoah Valley.[9]

But glory eluded those men in the following days. Although Captain Hardy missed much of the fighting due to illness, the rest of the Smith County Defenders saw far too much of the war. They fought at Antietam, Chancellorsville, Gettysburg, and the Battle of the Wilderness, four of the deadliest conflicts to ever occur on American soil. Nearly sixty thousand Confederate soldiers spilled blood during those haunting battles in the shadows of the Blue Ridge Mountains. Captain Hardy withdrew from the army before the end of the war, but the remaining members of the Smith Country Defenders were among the troops who surrendered with General Lee at the Appomattox Court House in April of 1865. The survivors trudged home to a broken society.[10]

Postwar Mississippi was a godforsaken place. The war had destroyed the state's infrastructure. Thousands of railroads, mills, factories, bridges, streets, and buildings had been demolished by Union and Confederate troops alike. The population itself was even more bereft. Mississippi's villages and towns were littered with widows, orphans, and broken men. Approximately one-third of white male breadwinners had been injured, crippled, or killed. According to one estimate, in 1866, the state spent one-fifth of its revenue on artificial limbs. The people were left poor and disillusioned. Some had lost everything—homes, warehouses, wagons, furniture, clothing, art, jewelry, and family heirlooms. In Hinds County alone, an estimated $25 million of property (nearly $370 million today) had been lost or destroyed. Fields lay barren. Barns were burned. In less than six years, Mississippi had lost more than half its pigs and approximately 44 percent of its livestock. In 1860, Mississippi's farms were collectively worth $190,760,367. A decade later, they were valued at just $65,373,261 and produced less than half as much cotton. As one historian recounted, Mississippi's "disbanded Confederate soldiers returned to their homes to find desolation and starvation staring them in the face."[11]

To make matters worse for the defeated Confederates, Union troops occupied the state. As part of the Fourth Military District of the occupied South, Mississippi was filled with the despised Yankee soldiers and Republican politicians whom locals scornfully dubbed scalawags and carpetbaggers. Northern Republicans had not only defeated Southerners in battle, now they were imposing new laws during this process of Reconstruction.

Led by a group nicknamed the Radical Republicans, the federal government passed three constitutional amendments designed to establish and protect the basic rights of newly freed African Americans. The Fifteenth Amendment gave black males the right to vote. Outnumbering whites in thirty-three of Mississippi's sixty-one counties at the beginning of 1870, recently emancipated black males elected dozens of African American legislators to national and state offices. During Reconstruction, Mississippi produced the first two black United States senators in American history—Hiram Revels in 1870 and Blanche K. Bruce in 1875. Black Mississippi communities also enjoyed scores of local political victories. In 1870, Mississippi's 117-member state legislature included thirty black elected officials. Three years later, fifty-five African Americans were serving in the Mississippi House of Representatives, with nine more in the state Senate.[12]

Thousands of white Mississippians resented the carpetbagging Republicans and despised any notion of black equality. White Mississippi Democrats yearned for the day when they could restore the old Democratic order and return to the days of total white supremacy. Some disgruntled whites used violence to reestablish racial control. Through paramilitary groups like the Ku Klux Klan, they terrorized black Mississippians and their Republican allies. But as a tactic for their reactionary agenda, violence had its limits. Organized attacks further validated the federal presence and offered the potential to attract even more federal involvement. While some Mississippi white supremacists went on the attack, a more careful contingent of white Mississippi Democrats, including William Harris Hardy, awaited a permanent restoration of local white political power. They were led by a man named Lucius Q. C. Lamar.[13]

Georgia native Lucius Quintus Cincinnatus Lamar had been a dedicated Confederate. Born in 1825, he had spent his twenties moving between Georgia and Mississippi engaged in a variety of careers, including attorney, college professor, and cotton planter. At the age of thirty-one, Lamar was elected to the United States House of Representatives from Mississippi's First Congressional District. He did not serve long. In 1860, Lamar resigned from the House to join the Mississippi Secession Convention. After helping draft Mississippi's Ordinance of Secession, he served as lieutenant colonel in the 19th Mississippi Infantry and was later the Confederacy's minister to Russia. Following the war, Lamar joined the faculty of the University of Mississippi and practiced law in Oxford. In 1872, he became the first Mississippi Democrat elected to Congress since secession.[14]

About a year after returning to Congress, Lamar performed a remarkable public gesture by delivering a lengthy eulogy for Charles Sumner, the abolitionist senator from Massachusetts who in 1856 had been famously assaulted in the Senate chamber by South Carolina's Preston Brooks. As one of the framers of Radical Reconstruction, Sumner was a longtime opponent of southern Democrats and a staunch advocate of black rights. When he died of a heart attack on March 11, 1874, the executive committee of the National Civil Rights Council recommended that black residents in "every city and town in the country drape their houses and churches in mourning." Needless to say, Sumner was not a popular man among most white Southerners.[15]

Nevertheless, just weeks after Sumner's death, Lucius Q. C. Lamar stood in front of his congressional colleagues and delivered a heartfelt tribute to his longtime adversary. "Charles Sumner in life believed that all occasion for strife and distrust between the North and South had passed away," Lamar told his fellow representatives. "Shall we not, while honoring the memory of this great champion of liberty, this feeling sympathizer with human sorrow, this earnest pleader for the exercise of human tenderness and heavenly charity lay aside the concealments which serve only to perpetuate misunderstandings and distrust, and frankly confess that on both sides we most earnestly desire to be one?"[16]

This was no small gesture. The former Confederate leader had stood in public to commemorate the life and career of a man who for over twenty years had been one of the South's most powerful political opponents. Lamar's impassioned speech reportedly drew tears from the eyes of both Democratic and Republican congressmen. The legend of Lamar's homage reached mythical proportions. One writer later recounted that Lamar's speech "touched the freezing hearts of North and South, unlocking their latent stores of kindly and generous feeling and kindling anew in them the fast-failing fires of love." Decades later, future president John F. Kennedy stressed the speech's importance in his Pulitzer Prize–winning book *Profiles in Courage*, writing, "Few speeches in American political history have had such immediate impact."[17]

But Lamar's speech was about more than rhetoric alone. The Mississippi congressman understood that Sumner's death presented a political opportunity for white southern Democrats. The war had been over for nearly eight years, and much of America had lost its taste for Reconstruction. Sumner himself even called for withdrawing federal troops. Lamar's eulogy posthumously glossed Sumner's stance toward reconciliation in a symbolic effort to help persuade Republicans that the South was ready to stand on its own. But the public acquiescence was also designed to serve Lamar's own ends; at home, the congressman would soon help lead an effort to eliminate black political power and remove the Republicans from office.

After the Civil War, William and Sallie Hardy moved to Paulding, Mississippi, where the captain resumed practicing law. Captain Hardy hated Reconstruction. Even worse than the humiliation of Northern occupation were the threats to the Southern racial order. Hardy ardently believed in the natural inferiority of African Americans and offered no repentance for slavery. In fact, he stressed its morality. "There was no place on earth," Hardy once wrote, "where the negro was treated so kindly as among the better class of Southern people during the days of slavery." According to Hardy, emancipation actually hindered the character of black Mississippians. "The 'new negro,'" he later claimed, "has not the general intelligence, nor the politeness and refinement, nor the industry, nor the love of truth and virtue, of the 'old negro'—the slave."[18]

Hardy was surrounded by like-minded allies. In 1871, groups of white citizens in nearby Meridian organized an attack on local black citizens. During the ensuing Meridian Race Riot—an extended two-year campaign of racial terrorism—local Klansmen murdered more than 170 African Americans. The widespread violence attracted the attention of the federal government and helped serve as a basis for the 1871 Ku Klux Klan Act, which was designed to disband the terrorist organization.[19]

Although the victims of the Meridian Race Riot were predominantly black, Hardy blamed local African Americans for instigating the violence. "The negroes were insolent and overbearing," the captain later recounted, "and white men and white women got off the sidewalk rather than be jostled or pushed off by half-drunken negroes." Hardy also cited dissident local black residents who, he claimed, assaulted a white sheriff, threatened to kill white citizens, and refused to help a white store owner extinguish a fire. There is no evidence that Hardy was directly involved in the violence at Meridian, but he clearly sympathized with the white murderers. Later in life, he called the Ku Klux Klan "a necessity of the times" and "a great boon to an impoverished people." Despite condoning violence, Hardy also recognized that widespread attacks could attract an even larger federal presence, a point reinforced by the federal response to the Meridian Riot. Real change required a political solution.[20]

In the meantime, tragedy reshaped the captain's life. In the late summer of 1872, Sallie, his beloved wife, contracted malaria and died after a miserable ten-day fight. After Sallie passed, Hardy moved to Meridian, where he continued practicing law and began writing editorials in the *Meridian Tri-Weekly Homestead*. Hardy's columns in the paper became increasingly brazen, denouncing federal occupation and Republican rule and calling for the impeachment of the Republican governor, Adelbert Ames, a native of Maine and former general in the Union Army. Hardy was not alone.

Across Mississippi, dozens of other local daily newspapers began similarly embracing a harder line against the state's Republicans.[21]

In the summer of 1875, the year after Lucius Q. C. Lamar delivered his eulogy to Charles Sumner, several Mississippi cities experienced acts of loosely organized racial violence. Rumors of black insurrection and fears of greater Republican control sparked small-scale skirmishes in Vicksburg, Yazoo City, and Friar's Point. Fearing outright revolt, Governor Ames began organizing the state militia, which further aggravated white Democrats. By late summer, some newspapers and white Democratic leaders were openly advocating outright rebellion. That October, the *Hinds County Gazette* told its readers that Governor Ames had raised a "Raiding Army" and quoted the governor as saying, "Hell must be inaugurated in Mississippi." "Ames is organizing murder, civil war, respite and anarchy," the *Gazette* warned its readers. "Let every white man arm and equip and be ready for action at a minute's notice."[22]

A week later, the *Hinds County Gazette* openly advocated violence to overthrow Republican rule. Referring to the Election Day of 1875 as "the grand battle," the *Gazette* asserted that "the imbeciles and thieves must be overthrown—good honest government must be restored" and that "every Democrat and Conservative in Hinds County should make his arrangements to devote to his country all the twelve working hours of the 2d day of November. Nothing should keep him from his voting place." Other Mississippi newspapers offered similar calls for political violence. The *Macon Beacon* told readers, "Every man should do his duty in the campaign." The *Jackson Clarion* reported, "Ames is organizing a war of races. . . . The time has arrived when the companies that have been organized for protective and defensive purposes should come to the front."[23]

That November, Mississippi Democrats reclaimed political power through widespread voter fraud and violence. Across the state, small paramilitary groups stuffed ballot boxes, seized armories, and intimidated Republican voters. The sheriff of Yazoo County so feared the power of these white supremacist renegades that he refused to call his regular militia against them to avoid the risk of open warfare. At West Point, white Democrats paraded two cannons through the streets. Two days later, Lowndes County Democrats pulled a twenty-four-pound cannon to the court house and fired it across town in broad daylight, "breaking and shattering the glass in adjacent buildings." As one historian has observed, the Democratic Party "had become as much a military as a political organization."[24]

Threats of violence kept thousands of black Mississippi voters away from the polls. As the *Hinds County Gazette* noted, "There was an immense deal of quiet intimidation. The blacks were given to understand that they must elect a better set of men to office." Real violence ensued as well. A dispatch from Columbus reported, "Every negro found on the streets was arrested and tack[ed] up. Four negroes refusing to be arrested were shot and killed." In other places, white Democrats used economic intimidation to keep black voters away from the polls. For example, in Aberdeen County, 190 prominent white landowners signed pledges not to enter into labor contracts with known Republican voters. "Whoever eats the white man's bread," the pledge declared, "must vote with the white man or refrain from voting at all."[25]

Lucius Q. C. Lamar served as the de facto orator of the Mississippi Revolution of 1875, as it came to be known. He spent that fall "rushing from meeting to meeting to meeting," wrote one historian, "arousing the wildest enthusiasm." "Lamar was the most popular speaker in the campaign of 1875," observed another historian. "Every community wanted him."[26]

Captain Hardy, who in 1873 had remarried a woman named Hattie Lott, later claimed that he hosted Lucius Q. C. Lamar in Meridian. Hardy revered the Mississippi statesman and later paid homage to this hero by naming his and Hattie's first son Lamar. Hardy also made his own contributions to the revolution. His editorials in the *Meridian Tri-Weekly Homestead* helped plant the seeds of local rebellion, and the captain spent the weeks before the election traveling to other counties to encourage groups of white citizens to mobilize against the Republicans. Years later, a family friend fondly remembered Hardy's influence in nearby Kemper County, where the captain appeared just before Election Day to inspire local residents to "prepare for action."[27]

Mississippi's well-armed Democrats swept the state elections of 1875. The violence and intimidation aimed at black voters was, of course, in violation of the Fifteenth Amendment. But the federal government, fatigued from fourteen years of war and occupation, stood idly by as white Democrats expelled black voters from the polls and retook political power in Mississippi. The results were implausible for a truly democratic election. In some places, Republican candidates counted fewer than ten votes among thousands of ballots. Even in majority-black counties, Democrats enjoyed enormous margins of victory. For example, in Yazoo County, where African Americans outnumbered white residents by approximately two thousand, the Republican Party received support on only seven ballots. The Mississippi Revolution of 1875 was a decisive assault in the war to restore white supremacy. "In the domestic history of Mississippi," wrote one of Lucius Q. C. Lamar's biographers in 1896, "the year 1875 is the supplement of 1861. It is the year of redemption, the year in which a great political revolution reclaimed the prize of state sovereignty." Collectively referred to as the Redeemers, white Mississippi Democrats had virtually eliminated black political power.[28]

Mississippi's Redeemers set the stage for similar Democratic uprisings across the South. During the election of 1876, political corruption ran rampant across Dixie as black voters were threatened with violence and ballot boxes were stuffed with illegal votes. Because of widespread fraud, electoral returns in South Carolina, Louisiana, and Florida were hotly contested, resulting in a nationwide controversy over the presidential contest between Republican Rutherford B. Hayes of Ohio and his Democratic opponent Samuel Tilden of New York. Tilden carried the entire South except for the disputed states of South Carolina, Louisiana, and Florida, which were worth a combined nineteen electoral votes. Those states, along with a disputed electoral vote in Oregon, held the key to the presidency. Tilden had a nineteen-point lead in the Electoral College. If he took even one of the contested Southern states, the Democrats would take the White House. If Hayes won all three, then he would become the nineteenth president of the United States.[29]

Sensing opportunity, Lucius Q. C. Lamar led Southern Democratic congressmen in brokering a deal. In exchange for Democrats conceding the election in the disputed states, Republicans agreed to withdraw the remaining troops from Dixie and to help fund the construction of a southern transcontinental railroad (which never fully came to fruition). South Carolina, Louisiana, and Florida went Republican, and Hayes won the presidency. The following year, the occupying troops left the South. Reconstruction was over, leaving Mississippi's white Redeemers free to craft a new society as they pleased.[30]

Like Lamar, many white Mississippi leaders were captivated by the possibilities of railroads. During most of the antebellum era, Mississippi cotton planters had relied primarily on steamboats to transport cargo up and down the Mississippi River. By the 1850s, however, cotton farms had spread farther into Mississippi's interior. Moving crops from the interior to the Mississippi River could be a complicated process requiring numerous modes of transportation. Transferring bales of cotton between wagons, docks, and boats could result in an over-handled and devalued crop. Moreover, the state's smaller inland rivers were prone to dramatic water level changes that could stall shipments. Railroads, unlike rivers, could provide reliable service virtually anywhere and deliver goods directly from the mill or the compress to the market. And so between 1850 and 1860, tracks slowly crept across the Mississippi landscape as the state's railroad mileage increased from 75 to 872. Then, of course, came the war.[31]

The completion of the First Transcontinental Railroad in 1869 marked the beginning of an American railroad renaissance. Between 1870 and 1890, America's railroad mileage increased from 52,922 to 163,597, an average of fifteen miles per day over twenty consecutive years. Roughly thirty thousand miles of these tracks were laid in the South. But Southerners did not control these new lines; Yankees and Europeans did. By one estimate, Northerners and Europeans controlled nearly 90 percent of Southern railroad mileage in the late nineteenth century. Railroads were extraordinarily expensive to build, and the former Confederacy was broke. With most of its wealth lost in the war and Emancipation and lacking the capital to build railroads on their own, Southerners, along with the federal government, sold or gave millions of acres of land to Northern and European industrialists to lay railroad tracks across the surface of the postwar South.[32]

Captain Hardy was one of thousands of Southerners who took jobs with the Northern- or European-owned railroad companies. Besides modernizing the region, railroads also offered exciting new opportunities for people like Hardy by extending prospects of prosperity beyond the plantation. Hard working and dependable, Hardy served the New Orleans & Northeastern Railroad in several capacities, including as surveyor of land for track construction, the job that sent him stomping deep into the Mississippi Piney Woods during the summer of 1880. He also worked as a general counsel, a part-time fundraiser, and even an engineer. The company was so impressed by Hardy's intellect and diligence that it placed him in charge of its most ambitious new project, the construction of a bridge across Louisiana's 630-square-mile Lake Pontchartrain.[33]

Railroad companies had for years dreamed of a bridge over Lake Pontchartrain to speed travel in and out of New Orleans. But such a bridge would have to cross approximately six miles of the lake. No one had ever before built a railroad bridge that far over water, let alone in the middle of the hurricane-ridden Gulf Coast South. News of the plan to bridge Lake Pontchartrain aroused skepticism among professional engineers and architects. The track, many argued, would surely collapse under the enormous weight of a locomotive.[34]

But Captain Hardy disagreed with the experts and set out to prove them wrong. Both engineering interests and personal pride were at stake. Many of the project's detractors held advanced engineering degrees and hailed from privileged backgrounds. As a self-educated college dropout from the Alabama Cotton Belt, William Harris Hardy was still trying to prove his mettle in a rapidly modernizing world. Just as when he rode down from the Smoky Mountains nearly thirty years before, Captain Hardy was determined to succeed against the odds.

To bridge Pontchartrain, Hardy designed a twenty-one-mile-long overpass that stretched more than three times the distance between the lakeshores. He intuitively realized that if the bridge's landed sections were fixed and immovable, they would help stabilize the overwater section and absorb some of the stress of a locomotive's weight. To support the overwater section, Hardy ordered more than fifteen million feet of lumber from a nearby creosoting factory. Because the lake averaged only ten to fifteen feet in depth, it was relatively easy to install railroad trestles on the lake bed. Hardy's Pontchartrain bridge was locked into place by inflexible landed foundations and supported underneath by a virtual underwater forest.[35]

His plan worked splendidly. On the evening of October 15, 1883, the first train to cross Lake Pontchartrain steamed into New Orleans. Captain Hardy was vindicated. The self-taught engineer had just fashioned the world's longest working railroad bridge. Built for approximately $1.3 million, the bridge offered an unprecedented path across Lake Pontchartrain, thus completing a crucial portion of the New Orleans & Northeastern Railroad's Queen and Crescent City Route. The new line trimmed shipment times, offered passengers easy access to the other side of the lake, and earned the captain and his employer a great deal of prestige. Decades later, New Orleans rum runners paid tribute to the captain by nicknaming the overpass "Hardy's Moonshine Bridge."[36]

A few months after the completion of Hardy's bridge, a train from Cincinnati arrived in New Orleans in just twenty-eight hours. For more than eighty years, steamboats had been delivering people and cargo between the Queen and Crescent cities. Paddlewheel engineers and captains had tirelessly chased speed records up and down the Mississippi and Ohio Rivers. But steamboats were no match for trains. With the completion of the Queen and Crescent City Route, a locomotive could travel from New Orleans to Cincinnati *and back* before a steamboat covered even half the distance between the cities—and only then if the steamboat traveled at record speed for two days, avoided snags and sandbars, and managed not to explode on the way, which many overworked steamboats were liable to do. Whereas Southerners had once been reliant on Mother Nature's natural highways, railroads allowed them to devise their own. Locomotives were the future, the backbone of a New South.[37]

Settlers arrived in Dixie's new railroad towns like sweet ants on a chocolate bar. Between 1880 and 1890, the populations of Atlanta, Chattanooga, and Little Rock nearly doubled. Birmingham grew from 3,086 to 26,178 residents. Richmond added nearly eighteen thousand people. And Memphis and Nashville together attracted over sixty-two thousand new residents. Between these larger cities grew hundreds of mid-sized railroad towns such as Meridian, Mississippi; Asheville, North Carolina; Knoxville, Tennessee; and Macon, Georgia. The railroads began to define life in Dixie as Southerners attached their lives to the tracks.[38]

The area around Captain Hardy's new town of Hattiesburg was chock-full with growth. As one local man recalled, "From New Orleans to Meridian was a beehive of activity. Literally thousands of people were employed." "Of all the little towns and villages located between Meridian and lake Pontchartrain," noted the *New Orleans Daily Picayune* a few years later, "Hattiesburg has advantages inferior to none." The Queen and Crescent City Route created unprecedented opportunities in the dense Mississippi Piney Woods, including Hattiesburg's first brush with fame.[39]

For a brief moment in the summer of 1889, Captain Hardy's young town became the epicenter of the international sports world when it hosted America's last bare-knuckle heavyweight boxing championship. Originally scheduled for New Orleans, the match between champion John L. Sullivan and challenger Jake Kilrain was moved to Hattiesburg when Louisiana governor Francis T. Nicholls forbade the bout under pressure from local citizens who objected to the brutality of bare-knuckle fighting. The fight's planners quickly enacted a backup plan.[40] A Mississippi sawmill owner (and future Hattiesburg mayor) named Charles W. Rich constructed a makeshift boxing ring on his property just outside Hattiesburg, and the fighters, trainers, managers, and a horde of spectators all secretly boarded a train in

New Orleans that whisked them across Lake Pontchartrain on Hardy's Moonshine Bridge and up the Queen and Crescent City Route to Rich's property. An estimated three thousand passengers paid $15 each for a spot on the train. Dozens more hid on the tops of passenger cars as stowaways, causing conductors to halt partway to throw them off. Those who paid got their money's worth. The epic match lasted seventy-five rounds, spanning two hours and sixteen minutes, before Kilrain's corner threw in the towel. Hundreds of newspapers recapped the momentous fight, and John L. Sullivan became America's first sports superstar. More significantly for the Mississippi Piney Woods, the match further demonstrated the tremendous potential of railroad travel.[41]

Hattiesburg was strategically located—and not only for fugitive fight promoters. Captain Hardy had founded his town at a major intersection of Deep South commerce and travel, within one hundred miles each of Jackson, Mobile, and New Orleans, three of the Deep South's most important cities—Jackson, Mississippi's state capital; Mobile, Alabama's largest port; and New Orleans, at the time the second-busiest port in the United States. Within twenty years of Hardy's backwoods lunch, major railroad lines from each city would run through downtown Hattiesburg; it was precisely this unique geographic potential that had caught the young surveyor's eye while studying his map in the summer of 1880. The surrounding forest offered additional advantages.[42]

Hattiesburg was birthed by railroads, but it was lumber that would make her boom. Captain Hardy had established his new town in the middle of one of America's last great untouched forests—the Mississippi "Piney Woods," part of the 250-million-acre longleaf pine–wiregrass ecosystem that once covered much of the southeastern United States. Billions of pine trees sprawled across the rolling hills of southeastern Mississippi, sprouting from the sandy orange soil and stretching up to 150 feet into the sky. The density of the virgin forest complicated Captain Hardy's railroad work, but it also captured the attention of nearly every lumberman in North America.[43]

The American lumber industry was on the brink of a major transformation. The vast forests of eastern white pine that once covered much of New England and the Great Lakes regions had been under assault since the colonial era, when the British Royal Navy had harvested the massive

Lumber harvesters with virgin longleaf pine, 1904. (McCain Library and Archives, University of Southern Mississippi)

200-foot-tall trees for use in their man-of-war battleships and restricted their removal for other purposes. After American independence, settlers on the frontier were free to use the sturdy northern pines to construct their homes and for products such as buckets, shelves, and trunks. Throughout the nineteenth century, eastern white pine supplied much of the timber for American growth.[44]

By the turn of the twentieth century, nearly two hundred years of harvest had exhausted many of the North's great pine forests. In 1896, the *Chicago Tribune* declared the forests of Michigan and Wisconsin "practically stripped," with Minnesota likely sharing a similar fate. "In from ten to fifteen years," the paper warned, "the last white pine forests in the United States will have disappeared." A growing conservationist movement argued that timber extraction had to be curtailed. But America still needed lumber. In fact, it needed it more than ever.[45]

As the century turned, electricity, the telegraph, and eventually the telephone brought millions of wires into an increasingly urbanized American landscape. Something was needed to hold those wires off the ground. Very quickly, engineers discovered that southern longleaf pine was the best wood for utility poles. Fire resistant, tall and narrow, but also heavy and strong, longleaf pine (also known as yellow pine) is capable of holding thousands of pounds of wires, lights, and metal clasps. To this day, it remains the most widely used lumber for wooden utility poles.[46]

Entire sections of the Mississippi Piney Woods—as well as vast tracts in Florida, Alabama, and other Southern states—were virtually reassembled in the frenzied metropolises of America. Turn-of-the-century city planners in places such as New York, Philadelphia, and Chicago hungered for yellow pine. The New York City Board of Electrical Control observed that their city looked like "a forest of tall poles." One historian estimates that in 1910, the Illinois Central Railroad delivered more than five hundred million feet of Southern lumber to Chicago alone. The popularity of longleaf pine timbers commanded the attention of America's lumber barons. Those able to extract and deliver large quantities of pine stood to make a fortune. As Kansas City lumberman R. A. Long declared, "No great body of timber has ever made or promises to make as good a percent of profit for its investors as has yellow pine."[47]

Mississippians had been harvesting small quantities of longleaf pine for decades, but the state's timber industry had always been limited by proximity to water. Before railroads, tree harvesters loaded the large trunks onto oxen-pulled wagons and then guided the large animals through the forest to the river, an extremely arduous task. But this was just the first step.[48] Once the logs reached the water, they were guided down shallow rivers by skilled raftsmen who walked along the shore using long poles to control the floating timbers. Those early lumber drives must have been quite a scene, featuring dozens of unkempt rivermen driving thousands of fallen trees down slow rivers like herds of cattle across the plains. By 1880, Mississippi raftsmen were regularly conducting log drives in southeastern Mississippi. There is an excellent chance that Captain Hardy witnessed one of these lumber drives during his months surveying land in the Mississippi Piney Woods. In fact, according to at least one source of local lore, a forest of felled longleaf pine timbers glided past him during his lunch break on that summer afternoon in 1880.[49]

Railroads made Mississippi lumbering safer and more efficient. Lumber transportation was never accident free (in fact, it remains one of the state's most dangerous industries), but the railroads gave timber harvesters more control. Rather than work at the whim of the weather and the river currents that frequently created deadly logjams, railroads allowed harvesters to neatly stack and secure their timber on freight cars. The trains also enabled harvest in places without rivers. That was important. Once tracks were laid, lumber from deep inside the Piney Woods could be shipped to virtually anywhere on the globe. Railroads opened Mississippi's interior for timber extraction, sparking an enormous lumber boom and creating new avenues of economic opportunity. If Mark Twain was accurate in once calling the Mississippi Basin the "Body of the Nation," then railroads became its arteries and veins, pumping longleaf pine timbers from Dixie's interior across America.[50]

Captain Hardy did not merely work for other people's railroads. He also planned one of his own. This new line was rooted in an old idea. For years, Mississippians had dreamed of a railroad that could deliver goods to a port city on the Gulf of Mexico. Believing that a Mississippi harbor could offer natural advantages over New Orleans and Mobile, a group of antebellum Mississippians, Jefferson Davis among them, planned a railroad through the interior of the state to the Gulf of Mexico that would give Mississippi planters and manufacturers direct access to the global marketplace (a particularly important consideration when secession became a genuine possibility). "Our position," asserted the road's commissioners in 1858, "compels us to be parties to the important transactions of which the Gulf of Mexico is the destined theatre. Let us sustain the part which nature seems to have designed for us." But the initial plan for this "Gulf & Ship Island Railroad" stalled during the war and Reconstruction.[51]

Thirty-two years after its initial conception, William Harris Hardy joined a group of decorated Mississippi Civil War veterans to revive construction of the Gulf & Ship Island. Wirt Adams, the company's new president, was the most well known of the group, having led the First Mississippi Cavalry at the battle of Shiloh and later become a brigadier general. Colonel William Clark Falkner, Gulf & Ship Island's vice president, was known for his role with the 11th Mississippi Infantry in Northern Virginia; at Manassas, wrote a dispatcher, his unit "covered themselves in glory" while helping form the line of defense that earned General Thomas Jackson the nickname "Stonewall."[52]

After the war, each man returned to positions of influence in Mississippi. Adams resumed life as a planter before entering public service as the state revenue agent and postmaster. Falkner, a renaissance man, rebuilt a house destroyed by federal troops, ran a plantation, organized a small railroad, and took what one writer described as a "self-assumed position of leadership in his own area of the state." Colonel Falkner also resumed a promising literary career. He published several successful novels, each of which later influenced his great-grandson and namesake, the novelist William Cuthbert Faulkner. The younger Faulkner, who returned the letter "u" to the family name, grew up telling teachers that he "wanted to be a writer like my great-granddaddy." In 1929, William Cuthbert Faulkner published the novel *Sartoris,* his first to feature the ghostly patriarch Colonel John Sartoris, a character based on his great-grandfather.[53]

Wirt Adams incorporated the new Gulf & Ship Island Railroad on March 4, 1882. Hardy, by then a well-reputed railroad man because of his experiences with the New Orleans & Northeastern, was recruited onto the board of directors the following year. Hardy instantly recognized the tremendous potential of the railroad. Shortly after joining the board of directors, he purchased land on the Mississippi coast and established a new town named Gulfport. The planned railroad was slated to run between Hardy's two new towns of Hattiesburg and Gulfport, passing through an area described by the *New Orleans Daily Picayune* as the "richest pine lumber section of the world." There was immense opportunity here. Hardy and his colleagues stood to make a fortune if they could finish the railroad connecting the virgin forest to the sea.[54]

The Gulf & Ship Island board of directors scrambled to finance their project. Although none of the primary officials on the board could access enough capital to finish the railroad on their own, they each offered important expertise or connections. Hardy and Falkner were both experienced with railroad finance and construction. Wirt Adams lacked his colleagues' railroad experience, but he did have important political connections. The group spent the next two years pooling resources, recruiting investors, selling bonds, and securing a mortgage. In 1884, the Gulf & Ship Island Railroad acquired a workforce when it signed an agreement with the Mississippi State Penitentiary board to lease the labor of hundreds of "able-bodied" prisoners, almost all of whom were black.[55]

In 1876, the year after Mississippi's white Democrats won their "Redemption," the state legislature passed the Leasing Act and another statute commonly known as the "Pig Law." The Pig Law specified that anyone convicted of stealing a commodity valued at $10 or more could be sentenced to up to five years in prison. Within two years, the state's prison population quadrupled, with black prisoners comprising approximately 85 percent of the inmates. The Leasing Act authorized the Mississippi Penitentiary to lease those prisoners to private firms.[56]

Companies and individuals had leased black laborers since slavery, but this new convict-lease system was different. In the antebellum era, slave owners expected their human chattel to be returned alive and in good working condition. After Emancipation, companies that leased black laborers had less incentive to provide proper food and healthcare; the burden of death belonged only to those black workers and their families. Access to food and shelter was inconsistent and medical attention was virtually nonexistent. Black workers were subject to excruciatingly long hours, back-breaking labor, and brutal punishments, including whipping meted out by mounted white overseers. Another common punishment was to put black workers in "sweat boxes," coffin-like cells with an air hole the size of a silver dollar, for days at a time. Runaway workers were beaten, tortured, or killed. In 1882 alone, starvation, disease, industrial accidents, and the sheer cruelty of overseers claimed the lives of 126 of Mississippi's 735 black convict-laborers.[57]

Construction of the new Gulf & Ship Island Railroad began in 1886. The initial progress was encouraging. By March of 1888, workers had laid twenty-two miles of track, graded another seventy miles of road, and cut enough ties for the next twenty miles. Amid a region saturated with Northern investors, the *Biloxi Herald* celebrated the possibility of a railroad built and owned by Mississippians. The new line, the paper delightedly told readers, "promises to be the crowning glory of grand southern enterprises." Weeks later, the *Herald* reported promising news of the growing local lumber industry. "The logging business is booming," the newspaper told readers. The railroad seemed on the cusp of fulfilling its promise.[58]

The string of setbacks that followed was sudden and unexpected. On May 1, 1888, Wirt Adams was killed in a street duel by a newspaper editor who had accused him of lying under oath. The death of Adams forced Hardy to assume a greater role in raising capital to help finance the railroad. Without additional capital, the railroad could not be finished, and Hardy spent the ensuing summer traveling to attract investors in New York and London. "I must not fail," Hardy wrote to his wife Hattie. "Everything is at stake." But Captain Hardy despised the metropolises of the North Atlantic and the wealthy men who controlled their banks, and he returned unsuccessful. Few details are known of his fruitless attempts to recruit investors, but the would-be fundraiser came home bitter and without having secured the much-needed capital to continue construction.[59]

In December of that same year, the Mississippi State Penitentiary Board of Control cancelled the railroad's convict-lease. Spurred by complaints from people living near the railroad construction, the penitentiary board launched an investigation into the railroad's labor practices. What they discovered was appalling. In a report to the state legislature, Mississippi Penitentiary superintendent W. L. Doss condemned the railroad for inhumane treatment of workers, subletting laborers without authority, failing to provide convicts with proper medical care, and falling behind on payments to the state. When the state recovered the black prisoners, the men were found with "only one suit of clothing," and even it was "not very good." Most importantly, hundreds of men working for the Gulf & Ship Island Railroad had gone missing. Some had escaped, but others had been killed by the overseers or by the work itself. A state House of Representatives investigating committee heard one witness testify that he had seen an overseer "club the convicts over when their legs were all swollen up, when they said they were not able to work." A former guard for the railroad later testified, "We saw enough of the brutal flogging business when the Gulf and Ship Island railroad was being graded with convict labor to last us the balance of our life." Over the course of less than three years, 225 of the black workers employed by the Gulf & Ship Railroad had died or disappeared. Between sixty and eighty men had perished in 1888 alone.[60]

Hardy dismissed the impact of the lease cancellation, waiving his right to appeal and insisting that he would finish the railroad anyway. "The Gulf and Ship Island Railroad [and] its success does not depend upon the convict labor and it will go on," he told the *Meridian News* just days later. To the *Biloxi Herald*, he said, "I hope to have my road opened to Hattiesburg by the 1st of June next, in time for the excursions to the seashore." But Hardy's bravado could not alter his reality. The railroad was in serious trouble.

Cheap black labor was essential to the initial plans, and the leaders of the Gulf & Ship Island Railroad simply could not finish their line without it. As a reporter later noted, "But for the howl that was made about the cruelties that were alleged to be practiced by the 'drivers' and overseers, the road would long since have been completed."[61]

The following autumn, Colonel Falkner, the railroad's vice president, was shot and killed in the streets of Ripley, Mississippi. Hardy was devastated. "I am so sad," he wrote to Hattie. "He was my best friend. Oh when will this flow of blood cease." Already limping toward completion, the Gulf & Ship Island Railroad had lost much of its leadership. With its management decimated, its finances floundering, and its workers gone, Hardy desperately tried to secure more investors. "I must have it built if I lose everything I have," he panicked in a letter to Hattie, "otherwise my reputation is ruined." Despite overtures to investors in Denver and Chicago, Hardy could not secure the necessary capital to continue, and the railroad fell into forfeiture. He and his fellow Confederates had failed, leaving the once-promising line lying unfinished in the forest. As it turned out, the Gulf & Ship Island Railroad needed a Yankee to complete the job.[62]

Four years later, in 1896, a Pennsylvanian named Joseph T. Jones assumed control of the Gulf & Ship Island Railroad. Nature had taken a toll. Because of "ravages of time and floods," reported one inspector, "I am told that the grading in most places had been practically washed away." Some portions of the road's track and bridges were usable, but much of the grading would have to be redone. Nevertheless, it still offered enormous potential. Mississippi's lumber boom was in its infancy, and a railroad from the Piney Woods to the coast promised to attract the attention of America's lumbermen. Conceptually, the idea for the line remained sound.[63]

A native Philadelphian, Joseph T. Jones had made his fortune in the short-lived western Pennsylvania oil boom. Having first struck oil in Venango County in 1867, Jones's Bradford Oil Company controlled five hundred wells by 1890. In 1895, Jones learned of the fledging Gulf & Ship Island Railroad through a railroad engineer who lived just across the Pennsylvania border in western New York. After a trip to Mississippi the following year, Jones organized the Bradford Construction Company to take control of Gulf & Ship Island Railroad. He and several Northern investors organized a new board of directors—which excluded Captain

Hardy—and hired a young Gulf Coast–based attorney named Eaton J. Bowers as the road's general counsel.[64]

Eaton J. Bowers and Joseph T. Jones were an interesting pair. Born two months after the end of the Civil War, Bowers was the son of a notoriously brutal Confederate veteran who hated Yankees, belonged to a Klan-like terrorist organization, and proudly told his son that he had killed Northerners during *and after* the war. But the son did not share his father's disdain for all things Yankee. Like many New South visionaries, the younger Bowers saw great opportunity in working with Northern capitalists.[65]

Unlike Captain Hardy's Confederate cohort, Jones possessed the finances to finish the Gulf & Ship Island Railroad. Through his Bradford Construction Company, Jones secured a $500,000 mortgage with the Manhattan Trust Company. According to one relative, he also spent at least $100,000 of his personal wealth to help complete the line. Jones's firm spent an additional sum of almost $200,000 to dredge a half-mile-wide channel and construct a one-hundred-yard-long dock into the Gulf of Mexico, thus fulfilling the longstanding dream of Mississippi's first deep-water port. Extending the railroad's original vision, Jones's firm laid new tracks all the way to Jackson, stretching the Gulf & Ship Island Railroad through approximately 150 miles of the Mississippi Piney Woods. Excitement returned to the forest.[66]

On August 27, 1900, the first train from Jackson pulled into the Gulfport Gulf & Ship Island depot at approximately two o'clock in the afternoon. With the road finished and the forest open for harvest, the possibilities for the local lumber industry seemed almost limitless. Even outsiders took note. The *Louisville Courier-Journal* proclaimed, "There is no question but this is the finest yellow pine region in the world, and that the building of this railroad will open it up to the markets at home and abroad." "Gulfport is on something of a boom," the *Washington Post* told its readers. "The fact that it is the terminal of the Gulf and Ship Island will make it an important lumber shipping point for years to come." The *Nashville American* similarly noted, "The road opens to the lumber trade a virgin pine forest. It is estimated that within the next five years more than a billion feet of timber will go to the North from cars hauled by this new line."[67]

The completed Gulf & Ship Island Railroad surpassed every speculator's wildest dreams. A 1902 report counted more than ninety sawmills along the line, collectively exporting "hundreds of millions of feet of lumber." In 1904, more than 225 million board feet of lumber were shipped from Gulfport. The *Wall Street Journal* called Gulfport the "leading Southern port in regards to lumber shipments." Two years later, the Gulf & Ship Island Railroad transported more than eight hundred million board feet of lumber and grossed approximately $2.5 million.[68]

Captain Hardy's sleepy coastal settlement at Gulfport became one of the busiest lumber ports in the world. Stories of the city's growth appeared in newspapers across the country. Ambitious locals began calling Gulfport the "Newport of the South." Hattiesburg, sitting along the Gulf & Ship Island Railroad, also grew rapidly. By 1900, more than four thousand people had arrived in Captain Hardy's young town. Dozens of other settlements—Howison, Wiggins, Maxie, McHenry, and McLaurin among them—formed along the tracks. As the *Hattiesburg Progress* noted in 1902, "Along the line of this road are prosperous villages, towns, and cities with churches, newspapers, factories and farms, where before were nought to be seen but unbroken pine forests, utterly worthless because there was no way of getting their product to the market."[69]

Gulf & Ship Island president J. T. Jones planned two beautiful new hotels, one each in Gulfport and Hattiesburg. The Great Southern Hotel in Gulfport opened first and quickly earned an impressive reputation. In 1906, a visiting writer from the *Atlanta Constitution* called it "without a doubt one of the best conceived and appointed hotels in the entire south." Painted pine green and adorned with dark-red terracotta roof tiles, the Great Southern stood over a beautiful Gulf Coast beach. Its immaculate grounds were covered with palm trees, man-made fishing ponds, a clay tennis court, and a sloping sandy walkway to the sea. Jones installed an orchestra that was soon regarded as one of the finest ensembles in the South. Visitors arrived from across the country to spend time in the beautiful hotel by the sea. The Great Southern Hotel was particularly popular among visiting lumber barons from Northern states such as Wisconsin and Illinois. Yankees filled the hotel lobby with their Northern accents. "Sitting in the hotel at Gulfport listening to the crowd of lumbermen conversing," observed a visiting *New York Times* reporter in 1901, "it is hard to realize that the stretch of water beyond is the Gulf of Mexico, and not Huron or Michigan."[70]

Joseph T. Jones became something of a local icon. He became enamored with the developing coastal city and began spending about half his time in Gulfport, investing heavily in the city's growth. The Pennsylvanian built an electric track between Gulfport and Biloxi that connected the two cities and increased local property values. He also helped develop the First

National Bank of Gulfport, a new golf course, and a local yacht club, helping lay much of Gulfport's infrastructure. Jones was one of Gulfport's greatest champions. His ambition and optimism inspired locals. "So vivid was the beautiful picture that he drew," reported the *Hattiesburg Daily Progress* of a 1902 Jones speech, "that it makes one's heart go pit-a-pat."[71]

On the evening of November 21, 1906, a prestigious group of Mississippi businessmen and politicians gathered in downtown Hattiesburg to celebrate the grand opening of the city's newest hotel. Built by Joseph T. Jones for just shy of $300,000, the beautiful five-story Hotel Hattiesburg served numerous purposes. In addition to hosting out-of-town guests, it also housed railroad ticket offices, a barbershop, and the city's finest restaurant. Soon considered one of the best guesthouses in the South, the Hotel Hattiesburg was the site of the most important local gatherings and celebrations. It was the fanciest place in town.[72]

Guests at the Hotel Hattiesburg's grand opening enjoyed an exquisite dinner of broiled Spanish mackerel, braised beef tenderloin, roasted duck, Saratoga potatoes, French peas, and strawberry ice cream. The renowned Great Southern Hotel Orchestra arrived from Gulfport to play a private show, entertaining the audience with a medley of the latest Ragtime hits such as "Dixie Blossoms" and "Vanderbilt Cup" and nostalgic Old South songs including "Take Me Back to Old Virginia" and "Massa's in de Cold, Cold Ground," eclectic musical selections that straddled time and place, symbolizing a reunification of old with new and North with South.[73]

The evening's guests included a collection of influential Mississippi leaders. In attendance were Governor James Vardaman, Congressman John Sharp Williams, and Congressman Eaton J. Bowers, the Gulf & Ship Island Railroad's general counsel, who in 1903 had won a seat in the United States House of Representatives. Also attending was Captain William Harris Hardy, who twenty-six years before had envisioned this modern city where these men now gathered. But Captain Hardy had been unable on his own to realize the full extent of his New South vision. That night, Hardy and the other Mississippi leaders gathered to toast the man who had—the Pennsylvanian Joseph T. Jones.[74]

According to the *Biloxi Herald*, Jones offered the most "pointed and stimulating" toast of the evening. The Northern businessman praised the region's rapid development and offered great hope for its future. He remembered his first impression of Gulfport as "the most uninviting spot for a city or a terminal that I had ever looked upon" and of southern Mississippi in general as a "poor spot." But how things had changed. By 1906, the Gulf & Ship Island Railroad had opened the forest for harvest and transformed Hattiesburg, Gulfport, and the small lumber towns between them into bustling centers of commerce and progress. "The possibilities of the state are far beyond the comprehension of the majority of the people," Jones praised. "The future of the state is so bright that words can not describe it."[75]

The men at the Hotel Hattiesburg's grand opening celebration must have been in a festive mood. The coming years would be kind to each of them. Their group included future judges, United States senators, and several individuals who would soon become quite wealthy. The most intimate details of the evening were unrecorded, but surely this was a night filled with toasts, handshakes, and hearty congratulations.

It would be interesting to know more about how the Mississippians interacted with the Pennsylvanian in their midst. Joseph T. Jones possessed one particular feature that none of them could have ignored. Anyone who saw Jones walk into a room or move about a party would have noticed a limp that hobbled the Northerner for the final fifty-two years of his life. In a region still full of men broken from the war, surely some locals would have contemplated the origins of that limp and wondered what the Pennsylvanian had been doing fifty years earlier when his entire generation went to war. Perhaps they already knew.[76]

Like William Harris Hardy, Joseph T. Jones had also once been a captain. And he had met Mississippians before. As commander of the H Company in the 91st Pennsylvania Infantry, Captain Jones had first crossed paths with Mississippians at Fredericksburg in December of 1862. Captain Hardy's Smith County Defenders had been on the field as well, at one point fighting only about a thousand feet away. Five months later, both companies would be at Chancellorsville, and that summer, each unit would march to Pennsylvania. While Joseph T. Jones was defending Little Round Top at Gettysburg, the Smith County Defenders were fighting in Picket's Charge, a bold but disastrous maneuver that felled half of the approximately 12,500 men who rushed desperately at Union lines. America was forever changed by these momentous battles, and every man who fought in them was forever changed as well. And both the 16th Mississippi and 91st Pennsylvania Infantries had been there, each desperately trying to blow the other off the face of the earth.[77]

Had Hardy not fallen ill, he and Jones would have met in battle. It is impossible to know if anyone mentioned those battles during the grand opening celebration at the Hotel Hattiesburg; one can only imagine how such a conversation might have gone. Regardless, forty-three years after Gettysburg, there sat Captains Jones and Hardy, two old veterans from opposing sides, toasting under the flag of the Army of Northern Virginia in a state whose people vowed to never forget.

Years later, a Mississippi governor fondly remembered the excitement of the railroad era. "Judge Hardy lived in an age when the possibilities of this country were unfolding themselves to the minds of men who had vision," the politician sentimentalized. William Harris Hardy indeed had a vision, but it was Joseph T. Jones who had the means. The men were drawn together by the promise of the New South. Hattiesburg needed them both.[78]

The Northern carpetbaggers who arrived during Reconstruction to protect the promises of Emancipation for Mississippi's freedpeople were persecuted, beaten, killed, and eventually run out of Dixie. But those who arrived in the wake of Reconstruction to lay the foundations of modernization were welcomed with open arms. Decades later, Samuel Holloway Bowers, Eaton J. Bowers's murderous grandson and cofounder of the notorious White Knights of the Ku Klux Klan, recalled, "The stable civilized carpetbagger movement, which I say was represented by Captain Jones and the Gulf & Ship Island Railroad, was able to make a coalition contact with responsible Southern lawyers."[79] If the Old South was about honor, then the New South would be about pragmatic profits. Principles would be redeemed elsewhere.

CHAPTER TWO

The Bottom Rail

When you marry, don't marry no farming man . . .
Everyday Monday, hoe handle in your hand . . .
When you marry, marry a railroad man . . .
Everyday Sunday, dollar in your hand!

—Lyrics from "Berta, Berta"

Turner and Mamie Smith arrived in Hattiesburg in the spring of 1900. Deeply religious and politically conscious, the black couple named their children to reflect their values. The oldest son, Charles Wesley, was named after the famous pioneer of Methodism. The second, Edwin Hammond, was named in honor of a preacher who had once inspired Turner. The third, Martin Luther, was named for the celebrated German theologian. And the fourth, Wendell Phillips, was named in honor of the famous Massachusetts abolitionist. Modest and discerning, Turner and Mamie worked hard, abstained from alcohol and tobacco, and spent hours each week in church. They never used physical punishment to discipline their children, choosing instead to lead by example. Turner also emphasized the importance of contributing to one's community. "Don't be a reprobate," he often told his children.[1]

Turner and Mamie had been teachers, and they fervently believed in the power of education. Edwin Hammond remembered the value that his father placed on books. "He would buy a book when you need clothes," the second son recalled. "He just [loved] books." Few Mississippians valued education more than Turner Smith. Learning had dramatically altered his own life, having enabled him years earlier to make his exodus from the cotton fields that haunted his lineage.[2]

Before cotton, the Magnolia State had disappointed generations of French, British, Spanish, and American settlers who learned that contrary to colonial myths, Mississippi contained neither secret stashes of gold and silver nor a climate amenable for growing tobacco and rice. But the state was ideal for growing cotton. Its short winters, abundant rainfall, and high average temperatures facilitated cotton growth like nothing ever seen in the Americas. With Eli Whitney's cotton gin, invented in the early decades of the First Industrial Revolution, the world's demand for cotton skyrocketed.[3]

It was cotton that brought most black people to Mississippi in the first place. In 1820, Mississippi produced approximately ten million pounds of cotton; by 1860, the annual crop exceeded 535 million pounds. With the rise of cotton came the arrival of hundreds of thousands of black slaves to harvest it. During those same forty years of cotton growth, Mississippi's black population increased from 33,272 to 437,404. Unlike other Southern slave states such as Maryland or Virginia, Mississippi's black population was not spread across a diverse array of occupations, racial categories, and social standings. Almost all black residents were slaves (99.8 percent in 1860), and almost all the slaves worked in the cotton fields or as plantation servants.[4]

Their days were filled with grueling labor. Enslaved cotton pickers spent much of their lives bent at the waist, towing burlap sacks through the fields, stopping at each plant to pluck the fluffy, white fibers from their stubborn encasings. Days in the fields left them with scraped wrists, cracked skin, cramping muscles, and backaches. Years in the fields left them with arthritis, gout, and warped spines. Some slaves spent their later years unable to stand straight, "their bodies bent in forced tribute to the cotton plant," writes historian Walter Johnson. Bondsmen were often underfed and poorly clothed. One former enslaved woman remembered competing with dogs for "mush and milk" and entering the fields on "many a frosty mornin' with rags tied 'round my feet." And of course, there were the masters and slave drivers who filled their lives with beatings, torture, rape, and death. The horrors of enslavement notwithstanding, picking cotton was—and still is—a tremendously difficult way to spend a life. But most black Mississippians knew little else. Even after Emancipation, sharecropping bonded them to the land.[5]

Sharecroppers were tenant farmers whose rent was paid to the landowner in the form of a share of the crop. In theory, the agreement seemed reasonable. After paying landowners a share, tenants were free to sell the remaining crop as they pleased. Theoretically, a poor tenant who could not otherwise acquire property might eventually save enough money from the profits of their leftover crop to buy their own land. But very few tenants ever achieved that goal. In reality, most sharecropping arrangements were designed to provide white landowners with cheap, controllable labor. White planters, many of whom brazenly referred to black sharecroppers as "their niggers," designed and controlled the system.[6]

In need of supplies to begin farming, many sharecroppers borrowed against future earnings to purchase seed, fertilizer, food, tools, and livestock, thus starting their tenancies already deeply in debt. As the seasons passed, high interest rates and subsequent borrowing needs set sharecroppers back even further. Some fell victim to unpredictable calamities such floods, droughts, insects, injuries, or sheer bad luck. Others were simply cheated. Landowners regularly altered scales, overpriced supplies, and modified existing contracts. Disputes were settled with intimidation and violence or in white-controlled courts. If a white landowner was able to convince a jury that a black tenant had entered into a sharecropping contract with the intent to commit fraud, the sharecropper faced imprisonment and a fine of up to $100. The landowner could then pay the fine, thus springing the tenant from jail while sinking the sharecropper even deeper into the landowner's indenture. Some landowners even arranged to have tenants arrested on fraudulent charges just to reestablish their debts. Even with a good crop, sharecroppers could end the year further indebted than when they started. A bad harvest could cripple a family for generations.[7]

Emancipated as a toddler, Turner Smith grew up the son of sharecroppers in Clarke County near Quitman. Like hundreds of thousands of other black Mississippians, Turner probably first went out into the fields as a young child. Starting with small peripheral jobs such as pulling weeds or carrying water, Turner would have experienced the tragic rites of passage of his lineage, task-by-task and year-by-year, until he was fully integrated into life as a cotton picker. Even as a boy, Turner would have understood the limitations of a lifetime in the fields; he had only to look at his parents and neighbors to understand the forlorn future that lay before him. Black sharecroppers found elements of happiness in their families and communities, but much of their lives were filled with punishing labor, hungry nights, and crushing poverty.[8]

Like most young black Mississippians, Turner had few educational opportunities. But he managed to attend school sporadically between the harvest seasons, and he slowly pieced together the ability to read and write.

When not in the fields, Turner found a measure of solace in books and literature. He loved reading, and at some point in his youth he found the gumption—and the gall—to envision education as a plausible escape from the cotton fields.[9]

One day, while driving a mule plow through a field, the seventeen-year-old Turner made a decision that would change his life. Although farm work was all he had ever known, Turner recognized the limitations of a lifetime of agricultural labor. On that day, filled with hope for a better future, Turner dropped the mule plow in the soil and walked away from the field, leaving behind the beast and his burden.[10]

For Turner Smith's parents, attending school was simply not an option. Fearing truancy, escape, or organized rebellion, antebellum Mississippi law forbade the teaching of slaves to read and write. Although some did find ways to learn subversively, most slaves remained illiterate. Upon Emancipation, thousands of black Mississippians clamored to learn to read and write. Literacy offered many advantages to freedpeople, especially the ability to inspect contracts, maintain financial records, write letters, cast ballots, and read the Bible and newspapers. Some saw literacy as a symbol of freedom simply because it was previously denied to them. As W. E. B. Du Bois suggested, "The very feeling of inferiority which slavery forced upon them fathered an intense desire to rise out of their condition by means of education."[11]

During Reconstruction, the Freedmen's Bureau organized a series of schools across the South. Recently emancipated black Mississippians demonstrated an eagerness to learn. In Natchez, where enrollment in Freedmen's Bureau schools grew by 600 percent in just nine months, an African American teacher reported that "there is manifested quite an eager desire to gain knowledge by the pupils. The rapidity in their studies is astonishing." In Jackson, a Freedmen's Bureau school teacher observed that their class was "composed exclusively of work hands" who came to classes after work on four days out of the week. Reports from Davis Bend described a population of African Americans "advancing rapidly in letters."[12]

Just days out of enslavement, freedpeople organized to build, maintain, fund, and protect their own schools. In his seminal study of Reconstruction, Du Bois estimated that the Freedmen's Bureau covered only half of school expenses; black communities made up the rest. In Vicksburg, black students began paying tuition after State Superintendent Joseph Warren accused them of having not "done enough" to support the school. In Macon, a teacher reported receiving "no other pay than that I obtained from the Freedmen." In Columbus, local African Americans raised $658 during a meeting and later volunteered to help guard the schoolhouse and homes of its teachers. When threatened with closures, black communities often organized to keep schools open. Superintendent Warren described one community that "had become obsessed at the prospect of losing their teachers and had raised some 25 dollars to give them." In Aberdeen, where Freedmen's Bureau school teacher Sarah H. threatened to end classes, African Americans responded by renovating the school. "They have made the room much more comfortable," Sarah reported. The following month, Sarah received additional support when one of the older girls in her class began to assist her with teaching duties. In some places, black Mississippians simply started their own schools.[13]

The African American legislators elected by black Mississippians during Reconstruction responded to their constituents' interest in education. In 1870, Mississippi's black elected officials helped establish the South's first public school system for African Americans. The schools were designed to be racially segregated but equally funded. Mississippi's first public school law required "separate free public schools for whites and colored pupils" with "the same and equal advantages and immunities under the provision of this act." It also mandated a minimum punishment of three months in prison and a $200 fine "whenever any county, municipal, corporation, or school district shall fail to provide separate schools for white and colored pupils, with the same and equal advantages" and stated, "Such persons so offending shall also be liable to an action for damages by the parent or guardian of the pupil so refused." According to the initial public school law, a black parent could sue a school district for racial discrimination.[14]

Teachers for Mississippi's black public schools were trained at a handful of local colleges for African Americans. Four such colleges existed by 1871: Tougaloo, Shaw, Alcorn, and the Haven Institute. Tougaloo College was founded just outside Jackson in 1869 with a $13,000 Freedmen's Bureau grant. Shaw University, later renamed Rust College, was established in Holly Springs by missionary groups. Alcorn State, named for a postwar Mississippi governor named James Alcorn (who fought for the Confederacy but advocated black education), was founded in Lorman. The Haven

Institute was organized by Methodists in Meridian. About a decade after it opened, Turner Smith became one of its pupils.[15]

After dropping his plow, Turner Smith walked some twenty miles to Meridian, where he enrolled in classes at the Haven Institute. Also known as Meridian Academy, the school was supported financially by the Methodist Church and managed by a group of former slaves, many of whom had been educated in Freedmen's Bureau schools. Although underfunded, the Haven Institute played an important role by helping train a cadre of desperately needed black public school teachers. By the late 1870s, Mississippi's black public school enrollment swelled to over one hundred thousand students. With only about two thousand teachers, classrooms were overcrowded and teachers overworked. Teaching in black public schools was difficult and low paying, but for Turner Smith, a lifetime in the classroom seemed infinitely more attractive than one in the cotton fields.[16]

Turner studied hard at the Meridian Academy and graduated with the qualifications to teach. He moved often in the following years, spending much of his twenties teaching in small Mississippi communities before taking a position across the border in Bladon Springs, Alabama. While there, Turner met another young teacher named Mamie Grove. The details of their courtship are lost to history, but the couple fell in love, and sometime in 1888, they were married. Turner was just shy of thirty; Mamie was twenty-two. Turner and Mamie spent their first few years of marriage in Alabama before moving back to Mississippi sometime between the summer of 1891 and the fall of 1894. In the years that followed, Turner took teaching jobs near Meridian and Ellisville, a small town located along the New Orleans & Northeastern Railroad.[17]

Mamie quit teaching when the children started coming. "The old man kept the family growing so fast that she had to give up teaching," one of the sons later joked. Charles Wesley was born first, in 1891. The next three boys followed in successive three-year increments. Born free to educated parents, Turner and Mamie's children would enjoy opportunities that would have been unimaginable to previous generations. But any sense of optimism must have been strewn with caution. Emancipation and Reconstruction had freed black Mississippians and provided new opportunities, but by the time Charles Wesley was born, Mississippi's white Redeemers had retaken control of state politics. The white Democrats made decisions that had devastating consequences for black public school teachers like Turner Smith.[18]

In 1876, Mississippi's Redeemers had inherited a state budget deficit of approximately $3,750,000. Part of the problem, they argued, was that the Reconstruction-era Republican government had allocated too many resources to African Americans. The Democrats quickly decreased spending, cutting annual state expenditures from approximately $1.4 million to $520,000. Black institutions, especially schools, experienced severe cuts. Resources were diverted, and the teacher pay was drastically reduced. In 1876, the average monthly salary of black teachers decreased from $53.45 to $38.54. Their salaries would steadily decline for the next thirty years.[19]

By the time Turner and Mamie had their first child in July of 1891, the average salaries of black teachers had dropped below $23 per month. As the family grew, Turner and Mamie realized that they could not support their growing family on Turner's declining wages. "I asked him once why he quit teaching," explained one of the sons. "And he said, 'I couldn't when the salary was getting smaller.'" Forced to give up teaching to find another way to support his family, Turner explored his options. He and Mamie saw an opportunity in Hattiesburg, then a young town sprouting in the Piney Woods. In search of a new foundation for their family, Turner, Mamie, and their four young sons arrived in the Hub City in the spring of 1900. Turner found work as a carpenter, and Mamie earned money by working as a laundress.[20]

The Smith family settled among a cluster of recent Hattiesburg arrivals. Their neighbors came from diverse backgrounds. Most in the community had come from somewhere in Mississippi, but a good number came from neighboring states such as Tennessee, Alabama, and Louisiana. Some arrived from even farther away—South Carolina, Virginia, Georgia, and Florida. An eighty-one-year-old woman who lived with her son was originally from North Carolina; another neighbor was from Texas. It is unknown when or how each of these people came to Mississippi. Some had probably arrived decades before as slaves. Others were new to the Magnolia State and had arrived recently by their own free will. Some could read, others could not. Some owned homes, others rented. They worked as cooks, preachers, laundresses, draymen, maids, and general laborers. The majority of men held positions that were in some way connected to the modernization of the New South—thirty-two-year-old Huston Thornton was a widowed railroad worker from Alabama; twenty-seven-year-old

J. H. Mintoe was a railroad fireman from Virginia; twenty-six-year-old Walter Williams was a railroad laborer from Georgia. Dozens more, including twenty-nine-year-old Louis Ward from Alabama, twenty-four-year-old Charles Bailey of Louisiana, thirty-year-old Mondes Ruffin from Georgia, and seventeen-year-old Wayne Bailey from Tennessee, worked in the local lumber industry.[21]

Hattiesburg's visionaries may have been white, but many of its workers were black. Mississippi itself was predominantly black. Between 1870 and 1900, Mississippi's black population grew from 444,201 to 907,630. With a white population of 641,200, Mississippi in 1900 had the highest percentage of black residents of any state in America. Most black adults still worked on farms (about 79 percent in 1900), but as the century closed, increasing numbers of black men and women left the fields. African American workers were essential to the railroads and lumber industry. The state simply could not modernize while leaving behind the bulk of its population.[22]

In the railroad industry, the worst jobs went to black men. In 1910, African Americans comprised only 1, 2, and 4 percent, respectively, of conductors, engineers, and foremen on Mississippi railroads. But African Americans were well represented in almost every other position in the railroad industry. Black firemen spent their days shoveling coal into fires. Black brakemen hopped between moving cars to turn heavy wheels that slowed trains. And black passenger car porters carried bags, changed linens, served meals, bussed tables, and shined shoes. Some even offered haircuts.[23]

In 1910 Mississippi, African Americans amounted to 97 percent of porters, 60 percent of both brakemen and firemen, and 87 percent of general railroad laborers. Performing the most unpleasant tasks, African American workers were essential to the spread and function of Mississippi's railroads. Hattiesburg, a convenient intersection of Deep South travel, was filled with these men.[24]

Even more found work in the local lumber industry. By 1910, Mississippi sawmills employed more than twelve thousand African Americans. Across the state, seven out of every ten sawmill employees were black; besides agriculture, no Mississippi industry employed more black men before World War II. Many sawmill owners and managers preferred black workers over white ones. "I would rather have one black man in a sawmill than two white men," one Southern lumberman noted. "All he wants is three square meals a day and his wage paid to him every Saturday night." As with the railroad industry, the most unpleasant jobs in the sawmills were reserved for African Americans. Derogatorily referred to as "nigger work," these jobs included sweeping sawmill dust, cleaning machines, and inspecting trees for defects.[25]

Some positions were more dangerous than others. Many black men worked as carriage operators, typically the most dangerous job in the sawmill. Carriage operators guided raw timbers into massive circular saws that sliced the logs into boards, often sending large, sharp shreds of wood hurtling through the industrial workspace. Flying chunks of wood left mill workers with splinters, bruises, cuts, and broken limbs—and this occurred even when the machinery was working properly. Carriage malfunctions could be even more hazardous. If a carriage gear or saw blade became damaged or bent, pieces of the machine could separate or break, pulling human appendages into the saw or sending parts of a steel blade buzzing across the shop floor.[26]

Black workers were also heavily involved in the operation of temporary logging railroads known as spur or dummy lines. Spur lines were short tracks laid by sawmills to deliver timbers from the forest to the mill. When an area was cleared of trees, sawmill workers simply moved the makeshift lines to another section of the forest. Hundreds of black workers served as graders or "road monkeys" for spur lines, moving and maintaining the temporary tracks. Hastily assembled spur lines presented the same dangers as railroad construction without many of the same minimum safety standards. Locomotives ran off tracks, steel rails separated or fell, and trees came down in the wrong places. Early Hattiesburg-area newspapers regularly contained reports of the deaths of black men operating spur lines in the forest. In 1898, a man named Bill Lloyd was decapitated by a runaway train on a dummy line near Hattiesburg. In 1903, a logging train ran over a black worker, "crushing his head, breaking one arm and doing internal injury." In 1912, a thirty-seven-year-old lumber employee named John Boyd was working just south of Hattiesburg when he fell between two timber trains and was crushed to death. Less than a week later, Ten-Mile Lumber employees Ernest Reed, Robert Walker, and Andrew Giller were killed in an explosion that reportedly "tore the bodies of all the victims to shreds."[27]

Jobs in Mississippi's growing naval stores industry were even less desirable. The products of naval stores include turpentine, tar, pitch, and rosin oil, all of which are rendered from the sap of pine trees. Turpentine is great for waterproofing cloth, manufacturing rubber, lighting oil lamps, polishing shoes, and disinfecting supplies; raw tar prevents rust and helps preserve underwater wood posts; pitch stops leaks; and rosin is used to produce soaps and floor wax.[28]

Naval stores workers, almost all of whom were black men, labored in camps deep inside the forest. Each camp included between fifteen and thirty crops, with one harvester working each crop. Crops consisted of approximately ten thousand boxes cut into the side of pine trees. Workers known as chippers would "tap" the trees by carving two or three six-inch-wide boxes into each tree. Tree sap, or "dip," flowed from the tree's marrow into these boxes and was collected by naval stores workers. Chippers kept a close eye on trees, which could stop bleeding their sap in less than a week. To maintain the flow of dip, chippers spent their days walking through the forest carrying long metal blades with hooked ends used to reopen healed trees. When the boxes filled, the accumulated dip was taken to a large still where it sat over a furnace. The heated dip produced a nose-burning vapor that collected in a chamber above the still. Turpentine was the resulting product of that cooled vapor. Rosin, pitch, and tar were produced from the byproducts of the excess dip.[29]

The naval stores industry imposed numerous hazards on workers. Turpentine harvesters spent days in the forest, hiking across dozens of acres and chopping and chipping into pine trees for hours on end. This exhausting labor left them with severe scrapes, blisters, and sores. The Mississippi forest offered additional challenges—heat, thick brush, and several species of well-camouflaged snakes whose venom could kill an adult human within a few hours. Moreover, men who worked turpentine stills were prone to illness. Short-term exposure to turpentine vapors can cause dizziness, nausea, and irritation to the skin, eyes, throat, nose, and lungs; prolonged exposure can lead to serious respiratory, kidney, and liver diseases. Furthermore, naval stores workers were highly susceptible to unfair working arrangements. Some chippers were cheated out of pay. Others were drawn into cycles of debt by shopping at isolated makeshift commissaries out in the forest. The work fostered the creation of a rough and dangerous lifestyle with a culture of its own. Frequently isolated from black communities, naval stores workers lived lives that were often nomadic, unpredictable, and violent. Fights, vagrancy, poverty, and instability were etched into their existence.[30]

Naval stores workers. (McCain Library and Archives, University of Southern Mississippi)

The early black jobs of Southern modernization—railroads, sawmills, and naval stores—were difficult and dangerous. There was little glory in these positions, and victims of accidents paid a steep price. Perilous days working on the railroads, in the sawmills, or out in the forest cost hard-working men fingers, limbs, and years of their lives. Each industry stole hundreds of husbands, brothers, and sons from their families. Many of the first generation of black workers to work these types of industrial jobs were not fully aware of the dangers that faced them when they accepted these positions. Although those who followed—and indeed, many of those who had pioneered these jobs—surely knew what lay ahead, thousands of black men took these jobs despite the severe hazards. Autonomy was key: all of these jobs offered an alternative to work on the farm.[31]

While railroad and sawmill work were dominated by men, black women found new jobs in the developing urban spaces of the New South. By 1910, nearly forty thousand black women in Mississippi (about 15 percent of all employed black women) were working in some type of domestic service job. These positions included cooks, nannies, maids, washerwomen, and general domestics, who did a bit of everything—caring for children, cleaning homes, washing clothes, and preparing meals. Black female domestics played an important role in the lives of white Mississippians by freeing privileged white women from household duties to participate in a culture of Southern white womanhood that was full of garden club events and society meetings. For some whites, the employment of black female domestic workers served as a cultural reminder of the fabled Old South plantations, where mythically happy enslaved black mammies ran Southern households. For others, the employment of a black female laborer symbolized an aspirational societal status. Even lower-class white families often employed black domestics in an effort to claim social or economic status.[32]

Domestic work offered numerous challenges for black women. The work was dirty and demeaning, the hours long, the pay low, and the expectations unrealistic. Their tasks included cleaning, cooking, changing diapers, doing yard work, and scores of other duties. There was also an important emotional component to in-home black female domestic labor. In addition to their daily tasks, black women were often expected to perform what one sociologist has dubbed "emotional labor," meaning they were supposed to care deeply about the daily lives and general well-being of white families. Although many black women formed sincere and rewarding bonds with white families, this emotional labor often added an exhausting and stressful component to an already difficult workload, which itself had to be borne along with black women's enormous responsibilities within their own families. Moreover, spending hours in the homes of white employers exposed black domestics to the possibility of mental, physical, and sexual abuse. Their experiences ranged widely. Some domestics were treated fairly; others were regularly underpaid, humiliated, beaten, or raped. Black domestics employed various methods of resistance and empowerment. They switched jobs, blacklisted dangerous or cruel employers, organized for better working conditions, and took extra food from white people's kitchens. Some simply quit.[33]

Many black women avoided the potential pitfalls of housework by taking jobs as laundresses. Washerwoman is, of course, a very old profession. But in turn-of-the-century Mississippi, the opportunities available to black laundresses were linked directly to urban development. Before the growth of Southern towns and cities, many black women did not have access to a large enough customer base to work only in laundry. A woman living in rural Mississippi might have had to walk dozens of miles each day to wash clothes (although some women did just that). Urbanization conglomerated customers and expanded the marketplace for laundresses, who could work for hundreds of families within a few square miles. The rise in the number of full-time black laundresses directly reflected the expansion of Mississippi railroads and the subsequent growth of its towns. In 1880, when Mississippi had approximately 1,120 miles of railroad track and five towns with populations over twenty-five hundred, there were fewer than three thousand full-time laundresses. Thirty years later, when the state had over 4,200 miles of track and twenty-nine towns over twenty-five hundred people, there were more than eighteen thousand full-time laundresses, 98 percent of whom were black. Mamie Smith was among their ranks.[34]

Laundresses usually had either one of two common arrangements. The first was to travel to clients' homes and work in the back or side yard. Using homeowners' wash pots, the women would boil clothes, rinse them, hang them on the line, starch them, and leave them on the line to dry. Some were paid extra to return later in the day to iron and fold the clothes. The other common arrangement was to take in laundry. Some black women had their own wash pot or even a small washing shack where they would boil, scrub, and hang clothes. In some cases, groups of women gathered at the home of a neighbor or friend to work together. Regardless of the arrangement, life as a laundress often allowed black women to limit potentially dangerous contact with white employers. This is not to say that the work was easy; black laundresses carried heavy loads across town, worked with scalding hot water and irons, and spent much of their day bent over. But the jobs did also offer a bit more control over their workspace and labor. And like the black male jobs of modernization, work as a laundress or domestic provided thousands of women with a way off the farm. Even in small towns, urban jobs offered an element of flexibility and mobility not available to most sharecroppers.[35]

When Turner and Mamie Smith arrived in Hattiesburg in 1900, the town itself was less than twenty years old, meaning that all of their adult neighbors had come from somewhere else. The details of their backgrounds are unknown, but it is safe to say that many of these black men and women—especially those from Mississippi, Alabama, and Louisiana—came from long lineages of fieldwork. The children and grandchildren of field slaves, these people took jobs that had not existed even two decades before. Racial discrimination limited them to hazardous and low-paying jobs, but the decisions of these black men and women to move to Hattiesburg and take these positions should not be reduced to mere victimization narratives. These people made choices based on lifelong experiences and new opportunities they believed existed within structural changes to Southern life. Regardless of the injustices of employment discrimination, these new positions often presented these black workers with the best opportunities they or anyone else in their family had ever encountered. Like Turner Smith, the black people who came to Hattiesburg in those early years were in some way dropping their own mule plows and walking away from the fields of their ancestors.[36]

Black Mississippians had complex relationships with the railroads. As much as the tracks created opportunities away from the farm, they also served to demarcate racial separation and inequality. In 1888, Mississippi's Democratic legislature passed a new law requiring railroads to "provide equal but separate accommodation for the white and colored races by providing two or more passenger cars for each passenger train or by dividing the passenger cars by a partition so as to secure separate accommodations." Racial segregation was not new to Mississippi—even the original 1870 public school law, proposed and supported by black legislators, called for "separate free public schools for whites and colored pupils." But that public-school statute was also designed to allow for "the same and equal advantages" for the separated races. The new laws of segregation, largely initiated on railroads, would create institutional racial disparities that characterized the emergent system of Jim Crow.[37]

In 1888, the State of Mississippi indicted the Louisville, New Orleans, & Texas Railroad for failure to comply with the new racial segregation ordinance. The railroad company protested, citing the economic inefficiency of state-mandated racial segregation. To fully comply with Mississippi's new law, the railroad would have to provide separate first-class cars for both white and black passengers. If one or both of the first-class cabins was only partially filled—a high probability in post-Reconstruction Mississippi—then the company would not be able to maximize profits on its first-class service. It would not make sense to maintain and pull two half-empty first-class cars when all first-class passengers could simply ride together in the same car. Furthermore, the law raised an important question about state-mandated segregation: What if Arkansas, Louisiana, Tennessee, and other Southern states all enacted different segregation laws? It would be nearly impossible for railroads to comply with different seating regulations at every state border. Facing a perpetual fine of $500 for each violation, the Louisville, New Orleans, & Texas Railroad challenged Mississippi's right to enforce segregation on a privately owned railroad.[38]

But the Mississippi Supreme Court upheld the law, arguing that previously established steamboat laws requiring equal accommodations for passengers on interstate carriers were not relevant to railroads. This new law, the supreme court contended, was a "matter respecting wholly commerce within a State, and not interfering with commerce between the States." The Louisville, New Orleans, & Texas Railroad appealed the ruling and in 1890 argued their case in front of the United States Supreme Court (which by then included Mississippi's own Lucius Q. C. Lamar) in the case *Louisville, New Orleans & Texas Ry. Co. v. Mississippi.* America's highest court agreed with the state. The statute "may cause an extra expense to the railroad company," the Supreme Court reasoned, "but not more so than state statutes requiring certain accommodations at depots, compelling trains to stop at crossings of other railroads, and a multitude of other matters confessedly within the power of the state." Justice Louis Harlan, one of the Supreme Court's two dissenters, sympathized with the railroad company and pointed to the potential difficulties of different seating regulations in each state. "If each State was at liberty to regulate the conduct of carriers while within its jurisdiction," he argued, "the confusion likely to follow could not but be productive of great inconvenience and unnecessary hardship."[39]

The 1890 Supreme Court decision upheld Mississippi's first formal Jim Crow segregation law. Because white Southern legislators had no desire to enact a difficult series of racial regulations, the new law did not create the "hardship" that concerned Justice Harlan. They merely wanted to elevate white passengers above all others. Although the law simply "strengthen[ed] an existing practice," as historian Neil McMillen has noted, it also established a broad precedent for racial segregation statutes. Black and white citizens could be separated in every aspect of life. In almost every Southern state, railroads came first. Within eighteen months of *Louisville, New Orleans & Texas Ry. Co. v. Mississippi*, nine other states passed railroad segregation laws, including Louisiana, which on July 10, 1890, passed the statute that was later famously challenged by Homer Plessy.[40]

About a week after the Supreme Court handed down *Louisville, New Orleans & Texas Ry. Co. v. Mississippi*, newly inaugurated Mississippi governor John M. Stone issued a proclamation calling for a state constitutional convention. Mississippians had for years debated about reforming the state constitution. The old constitution was written and passed during Reconstruction by Republican legislators who included "carpet-baggers, scalawags and negroes," as the *Atlanta Constitution* observed. Redeemers had firmly retaken power, but many white Democrats were offended by having to live under the laws established by the overthrown Republican government. Moreover, although African Americans had been effectively disfranchised since the Revolution of 1875, Mississippi's widespread voter suppression, rooted in intimidation and violence, directly violated the Fifteenth Amendment to the United States Constitution and was thus illegal. As Judge J. B. Chrisman of Lincoln County argued in 1890, "no man can be in favor of perpetuating the election methods, which have prevailed in Mississippi since 1875, who is not a moral idiot, and no statesman believes that a government can be perpetuated by violence and fraud."[41]

In August of 1890, white Mississippi legislators gathered at a constitutional convention to legally—and permanently—eliminate the black vote. Mississippians made little secret of their goal. "We came here to exclude the negro," convention president S. S. Calhoon flatly explained. Outsiders also understood the reason behind the gathering. "The most important work of the convention," observed the *Baltimore Sun*, "is to find some means of either reducing or neutralizing the negro vote without coming into conflict with the federal constitution." The *Washington Post* noted, "That purpose is to devise a way whereby, without fraud or violence, the minority may be enabled to govern the majority."[42]

Formally adopted in November of 1890, Mississippi's new constitution included measures designed to circumvent the Fifteenth Amendment. The new state constitution included a $2 poll tax, literacy tests, and an "understanding clause" for voter registration. The understanding clause was particularly important. Even if black citizens paid the poll tax, white registrars could prevent them from registering to vote through impromptu understanding-clause examinations requiring them to interpret sections of the Mississippi Constitution to the satisfaction of the registrar. The actual questions and answers mattered very little. All understanding-clause test takers were passed or failed at the discretion of the registrar—and the registrars were almost always white. So beginning in 1890, thousands of black Mississippians—even doctors, teachers, and former legislators—were rendered unqualified to vote, thus further securing white Democratic political control. Commonly known as "The Second Mississippi Plan" (the first being the Revolution of 1875), the new state constitution provided a model for other Southern states to similarly disfranchise African Americans between 1890 and 1908.[43]

The year 1890, a banner year for the institutionalization of Jim Crow in Mississippi, was also the year of Hattiesburg's first lynching. Newspaper reports indicate that on the evening of June 2, a black man named George Stevenson was being taken to prison for allegedly attempting to rape a white woman when a mob of "thirty or forty men" intercepted the prisoner and hanged him from a tree.[44]

On July 25, 1895, another white mob gathered in Hattiesburg. A black man named Tom Johnson had reportedly admitted (while already in custody) to killing a fifteen-year-old white girl and shooting at her sister and mother, who apparently recognized and identified the black assailant, thus leading to Johnson's arrest. As Johnson sat in his cell, a white mob marched to the local jail and demanded that the prisoner be turned over to them. The local sheriff refused but was quickly overpowered by the crowd. The horde stormed Johnson's cell and found the black prisoner waiting with a crowbar. Johnson was outnumbered; the crowd shot him, took his crowbar, and carried him to the scene of the alleged crime. One of the leaders of the mob, which by then numbered over a thousand people, told Johnson he was going to die and reportedly offered him the option of being hanged, shot, or burned alive. Johnson chose to be shot. He also indicated the men he wanted to do the shooting, but this was denied to him. Hundreds in the well-armed mob were anxious to blast atonement through their gun barrels into the black man's body. Someone tied Johnson's wrists between two close trees, leaving just enough slack for him to kneel down facing away from the crowd. Then Captain George Smith yelled "Fire!" and the volleys began. Tom Johnson was most likely killed by the first few shots, but bullet after bullet continued slicing through the air and into Johnson's flesh, reportedly lifting his "lifeless body from the ground." Estimates were that between five and seven hundred rounds had been fired. Johnson's mangled body, "riddled with buckshot," was left for his father-in-law to bury on the spot.[45]

Lynchings like that of Tom Johnson were increasing in the Magnolia State. White Mississippians had always used violence to harass, intimidate, and punish African Americans, but near the turn of the twentieth century, the attacks became increasingly vicious and ritualized. Lynchings were not merely concerned with retribution; some of the killings began to resemble hunting ceremonies, complete with hounds and photographs showing the killers alongside the dead. Women and children also frequently appear in lynching photographs, pointing and smiling at hanging, disfigured, or charred black bodies. As with Tom Johnson, it was common for mobs to continue mutilating bodies long after the point of death, enjoying the desecration of flesh, bone, muscle, and fat like a sport. The rituals sent chilling messages to African Americans: even in death, their bodies were not their own. In this New South, African Americans were denied the full range of citizenship rights that white people enjoyed, and they could be publicly disciplined at any time, without question or remorse.[46]

The next Hattiesburg lynching occurred on July 25, 1899, four years to the day since Tom Johnson had been killed. A black man named Henry Novels was accused of attacking a white woman named Rosaline Davis on a hot Saturday night, and he paid for his alleged crime by being tied to a tree and shot dead by an angry crowd.[47]

Turner and Mamie Smith arrived in Hattiesburg the following spring. The family spent their first years in Hattiesburg in a home on Jackson Street, a short road near the recently laid tracks of the Gulf & Ship Island Railroad. Turner was hired by white landlords to help build and maintain the small homes being constructed for the city's new black workers. Although Turner did not work for one of the railroads or in one of the sawmills, he made his living building the homes of those who did. Mamie worked as a laundress.[48]

Turner and Mamie had four more children after their move to Hattiesburg. The couple strove to protect their children from the brutal realities of Jim Crow, but as African Americans, their lives were shrouded by dangerous limitations. Race dictated where they could live, eat, work, sleep, and worship and determined the health of their children. Of the four babies born to Turner and Mamie after their move to Hattiesburg, only two lived past early childhood. The circumstances of those deaths are unknown. Many white families in that era also lost children, but black babies clearly faced distinct disadvantages. A daughter and son survived. The girl, born in 1903, was named Mamie for her mother. The son, born two years later, was named William Lloyd Garrison Smith after one of the most famous abolitionists in American history.[49]

Frugal and disciplined, Turner and Mamie worked hard and saved. Eventually, they were able to purchase a plot of land on Dewey Street. The couple built a four-bedroom house with a large living room. Mamie spent her time taking in laundry, while Turner continued working as a carpenter. Turner also managed to find a way to start teaching again, volunteering as a Sunday school instructor at the local black Methodist church.[50]

Turner and Mamie would spend the rest of their lives in that home on Dewey Street. Their home was filled with books, and they constantly encouraged their children to read, learn, and excel in school. Most of Hattiesburg's black children quit school when they were old enough to take jobs in town, but not the Smith kids. Turner and Mamie's children stayed in school and graduated. They learned to read and to reason. Most importantly, they learned how to survive in their environment, and they came to understand how faith, education, and hard work could help them cope with the restrictions of black life in Jim Crow Mississippi. Educational achievement took each of those children far. Four of Turner and Mamie's sons graduated from high school and college and eventually became doctors. Their daughter Mamie also graduated from college. She later became a teacher, just like her parents had once been.[51]

Turner and Mamie kept a piano in the living room of their home on Dewey Street. Sometimes in the evenings, the children would gather around the instrument to sing and dance. Turner rarely joined in. "He'd stand there and look at us," remembered Hammond, "and then go on to bed." No one will ever know what thoughts passed through Turner's mind as he headed to bed with the sounds of music filling his home. Born into slavery, his life was dramatically different from that of his parents. Turner and his family still lived under a system of severe racial oppression, but he and Mamie had managed to craft a more promising future in Hattiesburg and to provide their children with opportunities unimaginable to their ancestors. On these nights when the kids gathered around the piano, Turner would drift off to sleep with the sound of their singing voices echoing off the walls of the house that he and Mamie had built. Always hardworking and pragmatic, Turner could well have been thinking about the next day's work or worrying about his children's future. One can only hope that buried somewhere deep in his thoughts was a calming realization that none of his children would spend their lives picking cotton.[52]

Facilitated and defined by the spread of railroads, the rise of the New South created both restrictions and opportunities for African Americans. The processes of Southern modernization led to bleak outcomes, including racial segregation, lynching, and the disfranchisement of black voters—in short, the onset of Jim Crow. But along with those developments came structural changes that provided new jobs and unprecedented mobility. Uncertain of their futures but sure that a better life existed off the farm, thousands of African Americans came to Hattiesburg from farms and rural communities across Mississippi, Alabama, and Louisiana. For those black men and women, the view from the bottom rail looked far better than the one from the cotton field.

CHAPTER THREE

The Noble Spirit

> Northerners could come down in comfort and open the land indeed: setting up with their Yankee dollars the vast lumbering plants and mills in the Southern pine sections, the little towns which had been hamlets without change or alteration for fifty years, booming and soaring into cities overnight.
>
> —William Cuthbert Faulkner

Pennsylvania lumberman Fenwick Peck first came to Hattiesburg in the fall of 1896. At the time, Captain Hardy's young settlement of about fifteen hundred residents looked more like an old western frontier village than a burgeoning city of the New South. Its meager downtown featured a single hotel amid a handful of clapboard general stores, cobblers, and barbershops. The town had no electric lights, paved roads, or indoor plumbing. With no proper police department, public vagrancies such as street fights, untethered livestock, gambling, and prostitution were fairly common sights. To Scranton-native Fenwick Peck, a wealthy forty-two-year-old lumber tycoon who spent much of his time socializing in opulent homes and private clubs in New York City, Philadelphia, and Buffalo, the small village must have seemed tiny and backward. Surely a trip to Manhattan would have been far shorter and more luxurious than the thousand-mile journey to Hattiesburg. But such was the pull of Mississippi's budding lumber industry. Peck's arrival marked the beginning of rapid changes to come.[1]

By the time of Peck's initial visit, Hattiesburg was already showing potential, though its future prosperity was hardly assured. Joseph T. Jones had only recently acquired the Gulf & Ship Island Railroad, and the region's lumber trade had yet to fully blossom. The city itself, lacking resources and isolated in the Mississippi Piney Woods, lay in a precarious state. Just three years before Peck's trip, the entire town had almost burned down. Filled with rickety wooden buildings and lacking a decent water system or fire department, Hattiesburg in 1893 experienced a string of midnight fires. The first started at a hotel in January and burned for over an hour. The second ignited at a livery stable in August and destroyed approximately $3,000 worth of property, including nine horses whose charred remains were found among the ruins. "A witness of the conflagration says it was one of the most horrible sights he ever beheld," reported the *New Orleans Daily Picayune.* The most damaging fire occurred that autumn, when on October 11, a defective flue sparked a blaze that consumed more than two dozen buildings and caused over $75,000 in damages. "For a time," the *Daily Picayune* exclaimed, "it looked like the whole town was gone."[2]

The worst victim of the autumnal fire was the Wiscasset Sawmill, one of the city's largest employers. A virtual tinderbox, the Wiscasset was filled with freshly cut timber and gas lanterns but equipped with neither hoses nor sprinklers. The October fire tore through the mill, reportedly incinerating more than two million board feet of lumber and causing over $30,000 in damage. The Wiscasset's owners, lumbermen from nearby Meridian, were only partially insured and could not afford to rebuild, leaving hundreds of local men without jobs. Initially, the fire appeared to be a major setback for Hattiesburg. Fortunately for the young town, the blaze also sparked the attention of an opportunistic Yankee.[3]

About a year after the October fire of 1893, a Buffalo-based lumberman named Judson Jones Newman purchased the former site of the Wiscasset mill for $40,000. The veteran lumberman planned to build a larger and more modern sawmill. Completed in the spring of 1895, the J. J. Newman Lumber Company sawmill sprawled over approximately fifteen acres and was outfitted with the latest industrial technologies—new conveyors, electric lights, a sawdust exhaust system, and a modern, thirty-thousand-gallon automatic sprinkler system. All parties benefitted. Judson Jones Newman found a new source of timber to sell to his Northern clients, and Hattiesburg recovered hundreds of jobs. But Newman's interest in the mill that bore his name was short-lived; about a year and a half after the J. J. Newman Lumber Company opened, Fenwick Peck bought him out.[4]

Peck was a third-generation lumberman. His family had been involved with the timber trade since the 1830s, when his grandfather moved from Massachusetts to Pennsylvania to open a sawmill. Born in 1854, Fenwick entered the family business after graduating from seminary school in 1875.

He lived with his parents for much of his twenties, working closely with his father and uncle as he learned the trade. Fenwick's diligence and ambition impressed his relatives and colleagues. As a young man, he was known to spend his days supervising production in the forests and sawmills and his nights inspecting records in the company office. In 1887, Fenwick and his father formed the Lackawanna Lumber Company, which became the most successful venture in the family's history. Within five years, the firm's capital stock increased from $200,000 to $750,000. When his father died in 1895, Fenwick assumed control of the company. The following year, he accepted an invitation from Judson Jones Newman, who was an investor in a neighboring sawmill, to visit Mississippi. As part of their journey, the lumbermen traveled to Biloxi to meet with the superintendent of the recently reorganized Gulf & Ship Island Railroad. The implications of a railroad from the forest to the sea would have been obvious to all.[5]

Fenwick Peck (whose stepmother, coincidentally, was named Hattie) was intrigued by a number of factors in the Mississippi lumber industry. First and foremost was the availability of timber. Railroads were just beginning to open the region for harvest, and most of the forest was virgin. Second, land surrounding Hattiesburg was both flat and cheap. Having spent much of his career harvesting trees in the Poconos Mountains, Peck must have appreciated the low elevations of the Mississippi Piney Woods; his own house in Scranton sat at a higher elevation than the tallest peak in the entire state of Mississippi. And because that flat land was blanketed by trees, it was unattractive to most Mississippi farmers and thus available for purchase for as little as $1.25 an acre. Another factor was the absence of harsh winters. Unlike Pennsylvania, Mississippi hardly ever froze or experienced snow, meaning that full-scale production could continue year-round. Lastly, southern Mississippi presented the ambitious lumberman with an entirely new type of opportunity. For years, the Peck lumber companies had been paying expensive shipping rates to Northern railroads. In the sparsely developed Mississippi Piney Woods, Fenwick Peck realized that he could simply build a railroad of his own.[6]

Peck bought a controlling share of J. J. Newman Lumber and began injecting capital. He expanded the mill and acquired over six hundred square miles of forested land. The following year, Peck organized the Pearl & Leaf River Railroad. The company laid tracks between downtown Hattiesburg and the nearby town of Sumrall—about eighteen miles away—where Peck constructed another J. J. Newman Lumber sawmill. The Pearl

& Leaf River Railroad, Hattiesburg's third major line, traversed some of the richest pine forests in North America and attracted dozens more lumber investors to the Piney Woods. By the time the railroad changed its name to the Mississippi Central in 1904, twenty-six mills were operating along its tracks, and the firm was grossing approximately $300,000 in annual lumber freight revenue.[7]

Fenwick Peck's expansion of J. J. Newman Lumber spurred Hattiesburg's growth from a rural backwoods village into a modern city of the New South. As one local noted in 1898, "This is by far the largest industry in our town," observing that "by this mill alone fifteen hundred men, women and children are fed and clothed." When Peck first arrived in 1896, Hattiesburg was home to just over fifteen hundred people. A decade later, his firms alone employed more than sixteen hundred, and the town's population had increased to approximately nine thousand.[8]

Peck was merely one of several dozen wealthy Yankees to invest in Mississippi's burgeoning lumber industry. One historian has estimated that by 1905, Northern lumbermen had invested a total of over $24 million in Mississippi sawmills. Southerners also built sawmills, but even these, which

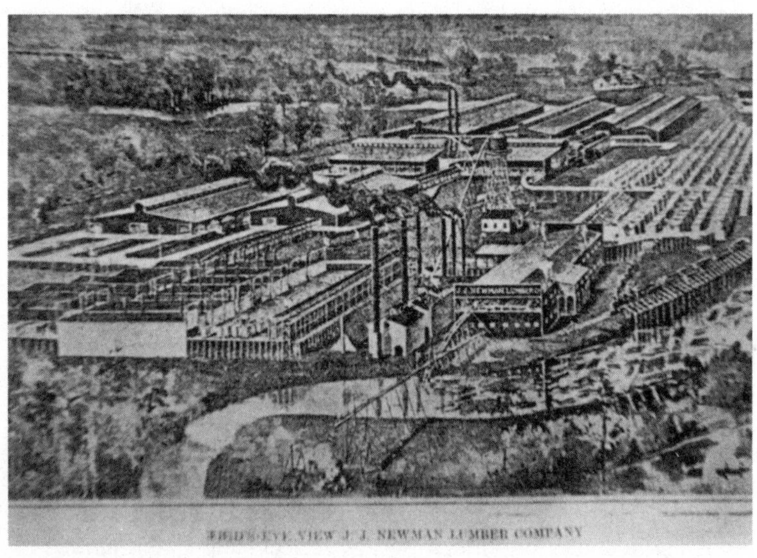

J. J. Newman Lumber Company sawmill. (McCain Library and Archives, University of Southern Mississippi)

were generally much smaller, needed railroads capitalized by Northerners to ship their timbers. In 1905, at least 120 sawmills were operating along the three major railroad lines that passed through Hattiesburg—the New Orleans & Northeastern, the Gulf & Ship Island, and the Mississippi Central—all of which were constructed by Northerners or Europeans.[9]

Over the following years, the global demand for longleaf pine skyrocketed, drawing sawmill builders to the Piney Woods like prospectors to a gold rush. By 1910, longleaf pine comprised over a third of all timber cut in the United States. Timber from the Piney Woods could be found in Philadelphia window frames, New York City utility poles, Chicago railway ties, and California homes. Moreover, longleaf pine was used in German railroad cars, Australian fishing boats, Uruguayan warehouses, and the Panama Canal. Lumber export records from the era show pine cargos leaving from the Gulf Coast to places as far flung as Barcelona, Copenhagen, Vera Cruz, Buenos Aires, Genoa, Montevideo, and Queenstown, New Zealand.[10]

When Captain William Harris Hardy took his lunch break in the summer of 1880, Mississippi's lumber industry employed 1,170 people and produced less than $2 million worth of products. Three decades later, a modernized state lumber industry provided thirty-seven thousand jobs and generated over $42 million worth of annual goods. Located deep in the Piney Woods at the intersection of three major railroads, Hattiesburg sat at the epicenter of the timber boom and offered more opportunities in lumber than anywhere else in the state. And so the people came, and Hattiesburg grew.[11]

For tens of thousands of white Mississippians, sawmill jobs offered a fundamentally different existence than life on the farm. As late as 1900, over 70 percent of white Mississippi men still worked in agriculture. Although some of these white farmers did quite well, the vast majority struggled. Like African Americans, thousands of white Mississippians worked as sharecroppers or tenant farmers. They too entered exploitative farm labor arrangements that led to cyclical poverty and instability. Everything depended on the harvest, which itself was never dependable. Natural disasters, falling cotton prices, a crooked landowner, and scores of other misfortunes could deliver tragic setbacks, negating thousands of hours of field labor. White farm families could work all year only to be left with nothing to show for their labor. "On a farm," explained the son of a white Hattiesburg migrant, "you didn't know if you were going to get anything or not."[12]

Sawmill work offered a more reliable exchange of labor and capital. Unlike on the farm, work always resulted in pay. Some sawmills had commissaries that overcharged for goods and drew workers into debt, but most mills paid wages, unimpressive though they often were. In 1910, Mississippi's sawmill employees were paid an average of $377 a year, far less than people working manufacturing jobs in the North. But those wages, however meager, paid rents, bought food, and clothed children. Most importantly, those wages freed them from the land and offered a sense of security and stability. The men who entered the mill each day left the mill each night confident that their labor would result in pay. Among a generation who had come of age in the wake of destroyed society, that peace of mind was no small thing.[13]

For whites, a life in the lumber industry could offer a number of lucrative possibilities. Some "would migrate from mill to mill," remembered one local sawmill worker, periodically changing jobs and employers in search of better wages. Others enjoyed upward mobility within individual companies. With the best jobs reserved for them, white workers could eventually obtain better-paid positions such as millwright, saw flier, sawyer, sizer feeder, or pipefitter. Some white sawmill employees advanced into managerial positions. Hundreds more worked as engineers, bookkeepers, administrators, or lumber dealers. With massive orders, it was common for mills to sell to one another. At the height of the boom, Hattiesburg had at least thirty lumber wholesale offices.[14]

Hattiesburg's sawmill workers arrived from a variety of locales. Most white migrants were originally from Mississippi or the bordering states of Tennessee, Alabama, and Louisiana. Smaller numbers arrived from other Southern states such as Texas, Georgia, or Virginia. The major difference between the black and white migrants was that some whites came from the North. Unrestricted by Jim Crow, dozens of white migrants arrived in Hattiesburg from places like Ohio, Illinois, Michigan, New York, Vermont, and parts of Canada. There was even one local family who came from Norway.[15]

The expansion of Mississippi's timber industry created thousands of additional jobs. Sawmills and railroads needed machine shops that specialized in metal parts of locomotive and sawmill equipment. In 1890, an enterprising man from Louisville, Kentucky, named George Komp arrived in Hattiesburg to organize one such firm. By 1905, his Komp Machine Works was the largest machine shop in the state. Hattiesburg was also home to the Davis & Company Foundry and Machine Shop and the Watkins Machine and Foundry Shop. Dozens of other companies manufactured timber products such as wagon wheels, cabinets, and doors. Hattiesburg also had a few smaller non-timber-related firms, including the Hattiesburg Compress, the Dixie Mattress Company, Swift and Company's Packing House, and the Meridian Fertilizer Company. Over the years, these smaller companies combined with sawmills and railroads to offer thousands of additional wage-labor jobs that drew people to Hattiesburg.[16]

These industrial jobs were often dangerous and unpleasant. The dangers of sawmill work were visible in the population. "If you were sitting in a car beside the street," recalled an early Hattiesburg migrant, "chances are that one man out of every five that passed by you either had one leg or one eye or one arm or fingers gone, or something of the sort, from working in a sawmill." Railroad work was also hazardous. In 1911, the Mississippi Railroad Commission reported 1,072 injuries and 83 deaths. Other industrial jobs offered a litany of dangers. Machinists lost fingers, wood workers inhaled sawdust, and fertilizer employees breathed chemicals. Yet even with the hazards, these wage-labor jobs offered many white workers the best opportunities they had ever known.[17]

The wages paid by Hattiesburg's new firms cascaded across town. The workers and their families needed basic goods and services such as sugar, butter, yeast, bacon, haircuts, and shoe repairs, and as Hattiesburg expanded, hundreds of entrepreneurs opened new businesses that catered to the workers and their families. Reliant on sawmill workers as customers, the livelihoods of these merchants were also intimately connected to the lumber boom. In 1903, the employees at J. J. Newman Lumber spent an estimated $30,000 a month in downtown stores. Hattiesburg's swelling population also needed schools, churches, hospitals, banks, and legal services, creating demand for teachers, preachers, doctors, bankers, and lawyers.[18]

One of Hattiesburg's first attorneys was none other than its founder, Captain William Harris Hardy, who first moved to town in the fall of 1899. His wife Hattie had died of uremia four years before and never lived in the city that bore her name. But the captain once again found love. In the spring of 1900, the sixty-three year-old Hardy married a much younger woman named Ida May, and the pair settled together in a new house near Hardy's downtown law office. They had two children in Hattiesburg before moving to the Mississippi coast six years later, where Hardy accepted a judgeship. He spent the final decade of his life living near the coast before succumbing to a heart attack in February of 1917 at the age of eighty. (Joseph T. Jones, the man who more than anyone had fulfilled Hardy's vision, died in Buffalo earlier that same winter.)[19]

Dozens of other white professionals and entrepreneurs moved to Hattiesburg and established prosperous lives. Dr. T. E. Ross came on horseback from Neshoba County to open Hattiesburg's first hospital. William Sion Franklin (W. S. F.) Tatum arrived in 1893 and erected a new sawmill along the tracks of the New Orleans & Northeastern Railroad. John McLeod came from Purvis and opened a large downtown department store. Thomas Smiley Jackson moved from McComb to open a shoe store and then later a grocery. Louis Faulkner left a teaching career in Pennsylvania to take a managerial position with the Mississippi Central Railroad. Perhaps the greatest success story was that of Paul Johnson, who migrated to Hattiesburg from Scott County to work at the J. J. Newman Lumber sawmill. Johnson used his wages to put himself through law school in Jackson and eventually returned to Hattiesburg in 1903 to start a law practice. He went on to a prominent career that included several judgeships, two terms as a United States congressman, and a victorious campaign for the governorship of Mississippi in 1939.[20]

Most of the migrants did not envision great wealth or affluence; they just wanted a better future for their families. In Hattiesburg, sharecroppers who had struggled with the unpredictability of farm life could find consistent wages; people who had once run dying country stores could open thriving downtown groceries; underpaid and overworked rural teachers could take salaried positions as clerks or managers; and families who had struggled for generations could break cycles of poverty to provide better opportunities for their children. Whether they were worn-down farmers, laid-off rivermen, country doctors, or Northern transplants, between 1890 and 1910, approximately fourteen thousand white migrants poured into Hattiesburg and its environs. Together they crafted a new society.[21]

During the first decade of the twentieth century, Hattiesburg transformed into Mississippi's fastest growing and most modern city. Local businessmen replaced the downtown's fire-prone clapboard buildings with multistory brick storefronts. City officials used increased tax revenues to erect utility poles and install new sewage and water systems. Police and fire departments, established in 1903 and 1904, respectively, helped clean up the city streets and protect against fire. Dozens of other new facilities enriched local culture and commerce. By 1905, Hattiesburg's downtown included a city hall, a court house, an opera house, and scores of new businesses, including six hotels, a bottling works, a billiard hall, and dozens of restaurants, groceries, drugstores, laundries, tin shops, barbershops, and butchers. "From a dense pine forest, much of which twenty-five years ago had never been seen or traversed by man, to one of the wealthiest, most populous and prosperous sections of the state," bragged a local newspaper editor in 1905, "such is the record of Hattiesburg, typical of the New Era of the New South."[22]

In 1906, Hattiesburg received its first tall building when Gulf & Ship Island Railroad proprietor Joseph T. Jones opened the five-story Hotel Hattiesburg. Featuring a barbershop, a train depot, and the city's finest restaurant, the new guesthouse quickly became the crown jewel of Hattiesburg's growing downtown. Over the next three years, the construction of two additional large buildings—the five-story Ross Building and the six-story Carter Building—provided a modest skyline. Between the rising structures stood rows of two- and three-story brick storefronts, newly paved streets, and the bustle of a thriving modern downtown. "Hattiesburg, the beautiful Queen of the Pine Belt is in all respects the model city of the state," raved a Jackson writer in 1907.[23]

The earliest available images of Hattiesburg come from postcard photographs taken during this era. The images depict horse-drawn carriages clopping up and down muddy streets, white businessmen in dark suits and bowler hats shuffling between banks and offices, white women wearing high-waisted white dresses and broad straw hats strolling through downtown, and casually dressed laborers loading wagons or climbing ladders. "Hattiesburg is a beautiful city," read one of the postcards. "We have fine streets, big industries, high buildings, [and] pretty girls."[24]

These migrants carved new residential neighborhoods out of the forest. Most of the new homes were modest, one-story dwellings with small front and back porches where locals could briefly escape the southern Mississippi heat. The most affluent whites—successful entrepreneurs, high-ranking sawmill employees, lawyers, and doctors—lived in extravagant, two- and three-story homes featuring manicured lawns, wraparound front porches, second-story balconies, and backyard quarters for black servants.[25]

Front Street looking South from Palace Restaurant, Hattiesburg, Miss.

Downtown Hattiesburg in the early 1900s. (McCain Library and Archives, University of Southern Mississippi.)

Affluent white residents led efforts to build beautiful new churches. Whereas Hattiesburg's original churchgoers once met in rickety clapboard structures, the expanding congregations of the early twentieth century built themselves elaborate cathedrals. The congregation of the Main Street Methodist Church financed a red-brick Gothic-revival structure, complete with pointed arches, parapet gables, rose-colored stained-glass windows, and a three-story bell tower. Not to be outdone, members of the Main Street Baptist Church soon thereafter relocated into a brick church featuring gaudy, Greek Corinthian columns and a large sanctuary capped by a fabulous glass-dome ceiling. Across Hattiesburg, brick and mortar replaced wood and nails as the migrants settled into new lives and built permanent places of worship.[26]

Hattiesburg's white leaders parlayed the city's economic growth into improved educational opportunities for white children. The city's first school was built with a $15,000 bond measure passed in 1893, and a series of smaller neighborhood schools followed. By 1909, Hattiesburg had seven schools serving 1,300 white pupils. As with housing and jobs, local whites consolidated the best educational opportunities among their own children. Not only were black students excluded from white schools, at one point the Hattiesburg Board of Education also considered a proposal to provide a separate school for "Italian, Syrian and Russian Jew children." Hattiesburg was never home to a large number of European migrants, but the proposal, which never came to fruition, indicates the importance of ensuring that only local white American children enjoyed the best advantages. All local black schools were severely underfunded. In 1911, city officials opened a new 21,000-square-foot downtown high school, complete with electric lights and an eight-hundred-person auditorium. For most of the next fifty years, thousands of white adolescents enjoyed school lessons, track and field competitions, class plays, oratorical contests, literary societies, choir concerts, and candy sales in their lively new high school. No black student ever attended.[27]

In 1910, local municipal leaders entered Hattiesburg into a statewide competition to house the newly planned Mississippi Normal College for teachers. Competing against several other cities, Hattiesburg's civic leaders lobbied hard to convince the Mississippi Normal College board that their town was the best site for the college. These efforts were bolstered by resources provided by the city's Northern benefactors. Fenwick Peck's J. J. Newman Lumber Company offered to donate an additional 640 acres to the campus, and his Mississippi Central Railroad promised to construct a spur line to deliver building materials. When representatives from the Mississippi Normal College board visited Hattiesburg, they were hosted at Joseph T. Jones's Hotel Hattiesburg, where they enjoyed a sumptuous dinner of shrimp cocktail, baked snapper, beef tenderloin, French coffee, and imported cheeses. The college board came away impressed and named Hattiesburg as the site of the new school. Mississippi Normal (now the University of Southern Mississippi) opened in 1912 with 227 white students.[28]

That same autumn, Hattiesburg officials held a contest to nickname their rapidly growing town. A local man won a small amount of gold for his suggestion of "the Hub City," a moniker that remains to this day. Soon thereafter, the Henry L. Doherty & Co. utility company donated a fifty-foot "Hub City" electric sign that locals erected atop the new, five-story Ross Building. Lit by 1,400 electric lights, the $3,000 sign was first illuminated during a ceremony on Thanksgiving night in 1912. The Hattiesburg High School Glee Club sang "America the Beautiful" as thousands of locals gazed up at the beaming new fixture. A *Hattiesburg News* editorial promised readers that the sign was the "one thing in which Hattiesburg beats the world," predicting that "globe trotters will tell about this sign to the far ends of the earth." One reporter, remembering the town's humble origins, observed, "The people are now catching a vision seen by that noble spirit, the founder of Hattiesburg, Captain W. H. Hardy."[29]

Life in the Hub City was not without its challenges. In 1906 and 1908, the city was hit by a pair of natural disasters. The hurricane of 1906 came ashore near Biloxi and traveled all the way to Kentucky, killing over 130 Gulf Coast–area residents, knocking down acres of trees, and causing tens of millions of dollars in damages. Two years later, a cyclone tore through the Piney Woods, killing approximately 150 people. That same spring, J. J. Newman Lumber experienced the second of two major fires, which led to temporary layoffs and threatened to displace the economic backbone of Hattiesburg.[30]

But the people of Hattiesburg persevered. Flooded streets were cleared and fallen homes rebuilt. When the cyclone hit, locals helped erect temporary tents for the homeless and raised thousands of dollars in aid. The fires at J. J. Newman were particularly worrisome because each blaze presented Fenwick Peck, who was fully insured, with an opportunity to rebuild his mill elsewhere. But local officials successfully lobbied the firm to stay in Hattiesburg, offering to help rebuild the mill and guaranteeing multiyear tax breaks to keep J. J. Newman in the Hub City. Each incarnation of the sawmill was larger and more technologically advanced than the last, ensuring new opportunities that continued to draw thousands more white migrants based on the strength of the booming lumber industry and the promise of life in the Hub City of the New South.[31]

Those lives were filled with the basics of modern America—Coca-Cola, trolley cars, and Sears catalogues—and capped by the distinct customs that characterized white communal life in Hattiesburg. On Saturday mornings, local whites shopped at downtown stores, stopping in the streets to wave and chat with friends and neighbors. On warm Sundays, large crowds of Hattiesburgers in their best suits and dresses congregated on the downtown shores of Gordon's Creek, standing in bunches to watch the baptisms of their children. On summertime weekday evenings, hundreds of whites headed out to the ball fields, gathering on the sidelines to watch lumber company baseball clubs compete in spirited contests. At Christmastime, crowds of white customers shopped late into the evenings, taking advantage of extended store hours to buy toys for their children and splurge on their sweethearts. Every Fourth of July, Hattiesburg's white business leaders adorned the downtown in red, white, and blue banners for the city's annual Independence Day parade. On those summer days, hundreds of local whites assembled in throngs several rows deep along the city streets, waving miniature American flags as they watched a parade of merchants compete for the annual prize of Best Company Float. As Hattiesburg grew, the new migrants congregated to establish new traditions that came to define their modern lives.[32]

Not all of their acts were performed with such a blithe spirit. On June 4, 1902, a black Hattiesburg convict named Will Smith picked his lock while working on a downtown chain gang and fled into the nearby forest. Although leasing convicts to private companies had been outlawed, in large part because of the practices of the Gulf & Ship Island Railroad, the state and many municipalities still used convict labor for public works projects. News of Will Smith's escape spread quickly through Hattiesburg, galvanizing local whites into action. Led by a team of bloodhounds, a party of white residents chased Smith six miles into the forest before they caught him and returned the prisoner to his chains. For many, the chase was like a sport, an exciting haul into the woods after a runaway black convict. "The chase was a beautiful one," enthused a reporter from the *Hattiesburg Daily Progress*. "That nigger ran, that nigger flew, that nigger tore his shirt in two."[33]

Another hunt occurred the following day. On June 5, 1902, a white woman named Mrs. Gardner reported to her husband that she had been raped by a biracial man on the Pearl & Leaf River Railroad (the original name of Fenwick Peck's Mississippi Central Railroad). Mrs. Gardner did not know her alleged rapist; the only clue she could provide was his mixed race. This left a lot of possibilities. White men had been fathering children with black women for generations, and Mississippi at the turn of the century was home to approximately ninety thousand people of mixed race (approximately 10 percent of all non-whites). Nevertheless, as word of the assault spread through town, dozens of local whites formed a makeshift posse to hunt down the mixed-race perpetrator. Their purpose was no great mystery. "If found," the *Hattiesburg Daily Progress* flatly told readers, "he will very likely be lynched."[34]

As reported in the *Hattiesburg Daily Progress*, the mob was a few hours into their search when Mrs. Gardner's husband, Ed, caught sight of a mixed-race man named Walter Bankhead and inexplicably identified him as his wife's attacker. Despite Bankhead's pleas of innocence, the white men delivered their black prisoner to the jail, where Mrs. Gardner confirmed Bankhead as her accused attacker. The crowd then returned home to rest and spread word of the impending lynching. Later that evening, a three-hundred-person mob arrived at the Hattiesburg jail to kill Walter Bankhead in what would have been Hattiesburg's fourth lynching.[35]

But in the hours since his arrest, Walter Bankhead, who claimed to have a reliable white alibi, had gained an important ally. Hattiesburg sheriff Thomas Batson resolved to uphold law and order by protecting the prisoner's right to stand trial. Knowing that a mob was forming, Batson asked state officials to send two companies of militia to guard the prisoner. When the mob arrived at the jail that evening, they were turned back by the militia. Soon thereafter, Bankhead was transferred to Jackson to await trial. Although few doubted Bankhead's guilt, some locals reluctantly recognized the sheriff's obligation to uphold the law. "If, without overriding the law, the negro could have been put to death," the *Hattiesburg Daily Progress* asserted, "[the sheriff] would not have objected in any way."[36]

Five days after Walter Bankhead was nearly lynched, another black man named Will Dantzler confessed to raping Mrs. Gardner. Dantzler tried to retract his confession the next day, but his fate was sealed when Mrs. Gardner positively identified him as her attacker (her second positive identification that week). Will Dantzler was convicted of rape on June 30, 1902, and executed a month later by a jailhouse trapdoor hanging. Bankhead's whereabouts at the time were unknown.[37]

The following summer, Sheriff Batson was powerless to stop an even larger mob from killing a black prisoner. On an August night in 1903, five hundred people armed with "crowbars, axes, picks, and sledge-hammers" broke into the Hattiesburg city jail and pulled accused murderer Amos Jones from his cell. Sheriff Batson once again tried to intervene but was grabbed and bound. Members of the mob then tied a rope around Amos Jones's neck and dragged the black prisoner a half mile to a wooden bridge over Gordon's Creek. According to at least one report, Jones was dead by the time the assembly reached the creek. Nevertheless, the mob strung his body high on a telegraph pole and "emptied their revolvers into it."[38]

Between 1890 and 1910, white Mississippians lynched nearly 350 African Americans. The victims were usually accused of rape or murder and were killed by hanging, shooting, or both. Others were beaten to death. Some were burned alive. In 1901, a group of whites operating along the Gulf & Ship Island Railroad just south of Hattiesburg captured a black man, tied him to a stake, and watched him burn to death. As in the case of Amos Jones, it was common for members of a mob to shoot or maim bodies well past the point of death. In some cases, white Mississippians collected souvenirs from the corpses, carving a nose, an ear, a tongue, or a penis from the body of the alleged perpetrator.[39]

Though it is hard to fully explain such violence, it is crucial to keep in mind that lynchings of this type were not antiquated relics of the antebellum South. Although the South had a long history of mob violence, these turn-of-the-century lynchings—defined by race and characterized by spectacle and participatory violence—were modern acts conducted within the broader context of the rise of the New South. Mississippi's bloodiest era of lynching occurred during the very same years of its initial industrialization and urban growth. Like the railroads and sawmills, lynchings were part of a societal transition. Turn-of-the-century lynchings served as a slight "revolt against modernity," writes historian Amy Louise Wood, that helped define and strengthen the racial and social boundaries of a society in transition.[40]

The pressing need for those racial boundaries was constantly reinforced by contemporary perceptions of African Americans, especially black men, as vicious, immoral criminals who did not deserve or could not properly manage access to the same opportunities as whites. Southern public discourse regularly included discussions of what white Southerners perceived to be the diminishing character of African Americans. Black freedom, they often argued, needed to be held in check. "Every year," the *Hattiesburg Daily Progress* told readers in 1902, "the negro becomes more unreliable and more worthless." "The black 'mammies' and the 'uncles' and the sturdy young bucks and wenches of slavery time have vanished, supplanted by the present generation of worthless degenerates," wrote the *Saturday Evening Eye*.[41]

In 1905, hundreds of white Hattiesburgers packed the city's new auditorium to watch Thomas Dixon's play "The Clansman." The play, adopted from a novel of the same name that also served as the basis for the 1915 film *Birth of a Nation*, depicted Southern Reconstruction as an era in which recently emancipated African Americans raped, robbed, and killed innocent white Southerners until heroic members of the Ku Klux Klan overthrew Republican rule and disfranchised black voters. A local reviewer called the play "so much better than expected" and "a triumphal answer to the negrophiles, the negro-lovers, the advocates of either social or political equality."[42]

This anti-black rhetoric was common among leading political figures. James Vardaman, Mississippi's governor between 1904 and 1908, unabashedly promoted anti-black sentiment in extraordinarily racist editorials and speeches throughout his career. "The negro," read one, "made greater moral and intellectual progress as a race during the period of slavery in America than he has ever accomplished before or since." Vardaman referred to the black man of the new generation as a "lazy, lying, lustful animal which no conceivable amount of training can transform into a tolerable citizen" and openly defended the practice of lynchings. If ever faced with a "Negro fiend," Vardaman noted, "if I were a private citizen I would head the mob to string the brute up, and I haven't much respect for a white man who wouldn't." The owners of the Hattiesburg *Daily News* admired Vardman's political rhetoric and leadership so much that they offered him the princely sum of $7,500 a year to become the newspaper's executive editor when his term as governor ended.[43]

In media, literature, plays, and politics, Mississippi society at the time was inundated with messages of African American degeneracy. The point was constant and clear. For many whites, one of the challenges of the transition to modernity was living among a black population that was believed to be not only naturally inferior but also rapidly losing its capacity to function in a changing society. In response, hordes of white people in Hattiesburg and elsewhere worked together to perform their perceived civic duties of controlling and punishing African Americans through the daily rituals of Jim Crow and brutal acts of violence.

The next Hattiesburg lynching occurred on August 4, 1905. That evening, a thousand-person mob broke into the city jail and dragged out two black prisoners, Kid George and Ed Lewis. Earlier that day, George and another black man had escaped a local chain gang by stealing the revolver of their overseer and shooting the white guard. That afternoon, George was shot in the ear while trying to flee into the countryside and jailed along with Lewis, a black business owner who was accused of helping George remove his shackles. At nine o'clock that night, the mob used a makeshift battering ram to break into the city jail and remove the men from their cells. Some in the mob suggested that they start a fire to burn the black men alive, but that proposal was declined in favor of a more traditional lynching. The crowd marched the two men to a bridge, placed a noose around each of their necks, and then pushed them off the side, snapping their vertebras near the neck and killing them within seconds. "Those who were armed then proceeded to riddle the bodies with bullets," reported one local writer.[44]

The 1905 lynching created a local controversy. Shortly after the murder, a contingent of Hattiesburg citizens organized a mass meeting to discuss the barbarity and illegality of mob violence. Led by several ministers and civic leaders, the group passed a series of resolutions denouncing mob violence as "savage and inhuman." One local writer called the lynchers "cowards of the lowest type." But responses were mixed. Another newspaper printed a very different editorial. "*The Daily Progress*," asserted the city's largest newspaper, "is not going to offer any apologies to the outside world for what was done in the city last night. . . . Those who perform the task are not to be condemned." Three months later, four men were arrested for their participation in the murders, but each was quickly released, and none ever faced serious criminal charges.[45]

Twelve days after the initial 1905 lynching, the second escaped black convict was captured in a small turpentine camp about forty-five miles southeast of Hattiesburg. As this news spread, another lynch mob convened at a downtown depot in hopes of apprehending and killing the accused man. But Hattiesburg's sheriff managed to evade the mob by personally taking custody of the prisoner and requesting a special military company to help deliver the fugitive to Jackson by bypassing the normal stop at Hattiesburg. That year, white Mississippians lynched twenty African Americans, an average of one every eighteen days. The murders of black residents in 1905 occurred more often than major holidays, full moons, or the first of each month—far too regularly to be considered abnormal parts of modern life in the Magnolia State.[46]

On March 12, 1900, Captain William Harris Hardy's future wife, Ida May, founded an organization called the Hattiesburg United Daughters of the Confederacy (UDC). Established in the couple's living room with thirty-eight charter members, the UDC helped lead local efforts to commemorate the lost Confederate cause. The UDC's sibling organization, the Sons of Confederate Veterans (SCV), had been founded four years earlier, though that group played a lesser role in local commemorative activities. Men built the town, but it was women who shaped its memory. In addition to their common mission, the two organizations shared the same infamous namesake: officially, they were known as United Daughters of the

Confederacy Nathaniel Bedford Forrest Chapter #422 and Sons of Confederate Veterans Nathan Bedford Forrest Camp #1353.[47]

Nathaniel Bedford Forrest made for an interesting choice as a namesake. Hailing from a modest background, Forrest accumulated a fortune in the Memphis slave markets. By the time the South seceded, the self-made businessman was worth an estimated $260,000 (over $4 million in 2018 dollars), nearly all of it derived from the slave trade. With an intense hatred toward Yankees and the threat they represented to his livelihood, Forrest joined the Confederate Army and quickly earned a legendary reputation on the battlefield. Despite having little formal training, he became one of the Civil War's most dangerous combatants. He reportedly killed more than two dozen Union soldiers and survived several horses being shot out from under him. Forrest's battlefield prowess earned him widespread accolades as he rose from enlisted private to brigadier general in just over a year, a feat unmatched by any other soldier on either side of the war.[48]

But the bursts of emotional adrenaline that made Forrest such an imposing warrior also limited his leadership. Anxious to fight and kill, he never fully grasped the tactical role of cavalry within the broader strategic movements of an army. And although his ferocity made him a phenomenal leader of deadly charges against ground forces, it also left him prone to reckless decisions. In April of 1864, Forrest ordered the murder of 292 surrendered black soldiers at Fort Pillow, Tennessee, in one of the worst crimes of the Civil War. "The slaughter was awful," wrote one Confederate sergeant to his sister. "The poor deluded Negroes would run up to our men, fall upon their knees, and with uplifted hands scream for mercy, but they were ordered to their feet and then shot down. General Forrest ordered them shot down like dogs." The murder of black soldiers may have brought Forrest some temporary personal satisfaction, but the massacre also galvanized both black and white Union soldiers. It was a powerful reminder of why they fought. For the rest of the war, black Union troops would often cry out "Remember Fort Pillow" before making a charge.[49]

Forrest had a hard time swallowing defeat. He never lost his passion for the Confederate cause, and for a brief time he even considered riding to Mexico to conduct guerilla attacks from across the border. Forrest did not enact his Mexico plan, choosing instead to settle down to become a farmer and make attempts at building railroads. But he did continue to promote white supremacy and resist black freedom by helping organize and lead America's original Ku Klux Klan, a paramilitary offshoot filled with other bitter Confederate veterans who organized terrorist attacks against recently emancipated African Americans. Forrest was the Klan's first Grand Wizard, and he is often credited with introducing the organization into Mississippi. More than anything, Forrest became a powerful symbol of white resistance to black citizenship and equality. As one of his biographers wrote, "As the Klan's first national leader, he became the Lost Cause's avenging angel, galvanizing a loose collection of boyish secret social clubs into a reactionary instrument of terror still feared today." Both the Hattiesburg Sons of Confederate Veterans and United Daughters of the Confederacy decided on Forrest as the namesake for their commemorative organizations. As one of the most notorious white supremacists in American history, he called to them like no one else.[50]

Hattiesburg's UDC was part of much larger trend. The national UDC, established four years before Ida May Harris's chapter in Hattiesburg, had a membership by 1912 of over eighty thousand. The national UDC conducted a number of activities, including hosting annual meetings, holding reunion suppers, raising money for monuments and veteran retirement homes, and planning educational programs. Many of these efforts were rooted in historical mythmaking to promote present-day political agendas. As historian C. Vann Woodward observed, "One of the most significant inventions of the New South was the 'Old South.'" White advocates of the Lost Cause of the Confederacy nostalgically stressed the morality and superiority of the Southern antebellum way of life. White Southern women, they argued, were more civilized, honorable, feminine, and morally adept than their Northern counterparts. Of course, many of these revisions centered on the war, which they refused to call the "Civil War," preferring instead terms such as the "War Between the States" or even the "War of Northern Aggression." The origins of that war, this new generation argued, were not grounded in agrarian slavery but rather in the superiority of white Southern people and their quest to secure states' rights and protect their way of life against invasive Northern political, cultural, and economic systems. Across the South, the UDC led the new charge to redefine the cultural and historical memory of their defeated society and its Lost Cause of the Confederacy. It was quite like—and was often directly connected to—various cultural components of their Christian beliefs.[51]

Education was particularly important to the Hattiesburg UDC. In 1908, the UDC helped publish a special issue of the *Hattiesburg Daily News* (which had acquired the *Hattiesburg Daily Progress* the year before) that included an insert called "Our Women in the War," which helped local whites learn more about the role of women in supporting the Confederate war effort. Members of the Hattiesburg UDC could also be found inside classrooms checking that the proper textbooks were being used, hanging Confederate flags and portraits of generals in classrooms and offices, and sponsoring student essay contests. It was essential to them to pass along an appreciation of this Confederate heritage to the next generations of white students. To that end, they offered small rewards to white students who wrote the finest essays celebrating the Lost Cause and encouraged young students to learn about and share stories of family members who fought for the Confederacy. In some classrooms, show-and-tell turned into neo-Confederate symposiums, with young students proudly rehashing the contributions of their Confederate ancestors. In later years, the senior class at Hattiesburg High School was known for putting on plays with alternative endings to the Civil War, including one fictional final scene in which white students in black-face makeup played enslaved African Americans joyously celebrating a Confederate victory in the "War Between the States."[52]

The Hattiesburg Daughters were also involved with a number of national initiatives. Representatives from the Hattiesburg UDC regularly attended Confederate reunions in cities across the South, hosted statewide UDC meetings, and helped raise money to purchase and preserve Beauvoir, a house on the Mississippi coast that was the last home of Jefferson Davis and later became a retirement home for Confederate veterans and their wives. In 1906, the local Daughters also played a major role in organizing the national convention of the United Daughters of the Confederacy at Gulfport, where they helped secure the funding and approval to erect a new Confederate monument at Arlington National Cemetery.[53]

Like lynching, Lost Cause commemorative efforts were not merely antiquated relics of a bygone society. Confederate tributes operated as symbolic devices used against the backdrop of a transition to a new society that was extremely dependent on Northern investment. Remember that the capital foundations of Hattiesburg's growth were provided by Yankees and Europeans, especially the Pennsylvanians Joseph T. Jones and Fenwick Peck. As some historians have suggested, this embrace of the Lost Cause during a moment of widespread Northern investment may have served as a tool for Southerners to ease the sting of Northern reliance. "Glorification of the Old South," wrote historian James Cobb, "was at least in part a psychological device, designed to help humiliated southerners hold their heads up as they accepted much-needed investment capital from their Yankee conquerors." As they took the sawmill and railroad jobs provided by Northerners, thousands of white Hattiesburgers huddled en masse in the shadows of marble Confederate monuments as a final cultural memory of Southern resistance.[54]

But that embrace of the Lost Cause also held an additional meaning. In commemorating the Lost Cause through their erection of monuments and their celebration of the barbarous Nathaniel Bedford Forrest, white Hattiesburgers were also helping to shape a modern white supremacy by paying homage to a failed nation whose primary objective was the maintenance of black slavery. And this message was not only enacted to promote lessons of racial hierarchy among white residents. Consider the view of Hattiesburg's black men and women. Although UDC members incorrectly argued that the defense of slavery was only loosely connected to the war, no black citizens could have fully detached the incessant Confederate hagiography from the peculiar institution that created its wealth. The commemorations were haunting reminders of a horrific society that had held their ancestors captive. Yet local whites seemed so proud and nostalgic.[55]

Hattiesburg's white migrants seemingly embodied change and modernity, embracing industrial opportunities and new lives in the rising tide of modern America as they moved further away from the annihilated antebellum system. Yet as Southern journalist W. J. Cash once wrote, "If the war had smashed the Southern world, it had left the essential [white] South mind and will . . . entirely unshaken." Nearly fifty years later, the conquered Confederate cause still lived in their imagination. They crafted their new society in the cultural mold of the old, honoring their Lost Cause and stressing the immorality of African Americans to develop a novel ethos that helped assuage the humiliation of dependence on their former enemies while also promoting the violent white supremacist tactics that undergirded Jim Crow. Through politics, violence, culture, and history, the racial principles of the Old South were adapted to protect and enhance the white supremacy of the New South.[56]

In 1908, local whites celebrated the formation of a new county. For years, Hattiesburg's new migrants had wanted to break free from Perry County, a relatively unimportant and sparsely populated antebellum county in which the Hub City had been founded. As early as 1889, the superintendent of

Perry County schools complained to his supervisor that the people of Hattiesburg "have recently prevailed themselves of the provision of law and declared the town of Hattiesburg a separate school district, and secured teachers with a view to providing higher education than is afforded by the common schools in the county." Locals temporarily created a separate judicial district, but it was not until 1908 that a new county, with Hattiesburg as its seat, was officially formed. During the process of choosing a name, political wrangling and old grudges eliminated the name "Hardy County" from contention. But local white leaders were eventually able to settle on a name of which they could be proud. On January 6, 1908, Forrest County officially became Mississippi's newest territory.[57]

Two years later, the Hattiesburg UDC unveiled a marble Confederate monument erected beside the new Forrest County Courthouse. Dedicated to the "honor and memory of those who wore the gray," the monument stood three stories tall and featured an armed Confederate soldier standing guard over a fellow infantryman and a Confederate heroine. The statue's unveiling attracted an estimated eight thousand attendees to downtown Hattiesburg and reportedly brought tears to the eyes of nearly everyone in the crowd. One reporter called the ceremony the "greatest event in Hattiesburg history." Another assured readers that "Forrest County, a mere baby in the state's great sisterhood of counties, has started off right."[58]

CHAPTER FOUR

A Little Colony of Mississippians

> Others may be found to do his work, in a way and at a price, but the negro's "place" cannot be filled. . . . And the South will miss them when they are gone, and don't you forget it.
>
> —*Hattiesburg News*, December 7, 1916

In the spring of 1910, the Smith family was living in a little rented home about a mile from downtown Hattiesburg. Turner, who turned fifty-one that year, was still working as a carpenter. His job did not pay particularly well, but he managed to supplement his earnings with a variety of entrepreneurial projects. At times, he rented a small plot of land to grow vegetables and potatoes that he peddled to neighbors. For a few years, he operated a little shop called Smith's Store that sold dry goods such as flour, salt, and sugar. Resourceful and proud, Turner worked hard to provide his family with a level of financial security. The Smith family remained relatively poor, but the additional income did enable Mamie to quit working as a laundress, freeing her to spend the bulk of her time tending to the couple's home and six children.[1]

That May, the Smith family children ranged in age from five to seventeen. The four middle children were enrolled in classes at a little wooden schoolhouse located about a quarter mile from their home. The oldest son was working with his father while saving for college. The youngest boy was not yet old enough to attend school. All the Smith children were expected to excel in the classroom. Turner and Mamie filled their house with books and strove to create an environment in which learning was cherished. The former teachers supplemented their children's school lessons with home instruction on history, civics, and politics, and the Smith children entered school "way ahead of the other folks," explained the second son, Hammond.[2]

Sometime between 1910 and 1914, Turner and Mamie bought a house on Dewey Street, about two blocks away from their first home in Hattiesburg. With eight occupants, the four-bedroom house was fairly cramped, but the family made do with the space they had. The daughter, Mamie, had a room to herself, and the five boys shared bedrooms or slept on the porch when it was warm. To provide inexpensive meals for their family, Turner and Mamie grew their own vegetables, kept a milk cow, and bought sacks of rice in bulk. "We always had a garden and things like that," remembered Hammond. "So we did all right."[3]

The Smith family lived in a rapidly growing black neighborhood known as the Mobile Street District. Named for the road that traverses its center, the Mobile Street District lies in a roughly 500-acre floodplain near the confluence of the Bouie and Leaf Rivers. Because periodic flooding rendered the area undesirable to whites, black migrants were free to settle the area. The neighborhood's early boundaries were framed by rivers and rails—the Bouie and Leaf Rivers to the north and east and the tracks of the Mississippi Central and Gulf & Ship Island Railroads to the south and west. In 1910, the vast majority of Hattiesburg's 4,357 black residents lived in or near the Mobile Street District.[4]

Most residents of the Mobile Street District lived in single-story rental homes traditionally known as "folk" or "shotgun" houses. These one- or two-room wooden structures were characterized by a front-gable roof, slim panel doors, vertical windows, and narrow wooden siding. Some homes stood on stacks of bricks or large rocks to help protect against flooding. Each home, even the frailest shotgun house, also had a porch. Perhaps considered luxuries in some contexts, porches were vital to poor black people living in southern Mississippi. Covered by flat-shed roofs, porches offered escape from the heat, platforms to perform chores, and additional areas for families and neighbors to congregate. A handful of black residents owned larger homes—two-story bungalows with front and back porches or shotgun houses with added rooms.[5]

Most black men in the neighborhood worked as wage laborers in one of the city's sawmills, railroads, or light manufacturing shops—firms such as J. J. Newman Lumber, the New Orleans & Northeastern Railroad, or Komp Machinery. Like their working-class white counterparts, many black families were drawn to Hattiesburg by the promise of wage labor. Black men were almost always paid less than white men, and their work was often irregular and susceptible to layoffs. But Hattiesburg in the early twentieth century was one of the best places in the region for black men to find wage-labor jobs.

Years later, the sons and daughters of early migrants recalled the appeal that Hattiesburg held to their fathers. Ariel Barnes remembered that her father "just kind of followed the work," and "found more work here [in Hattiesburg] than where he came from." Richard Boyd told an interviewer that his family came from Enterprise, Mississippi, so his father could work at J. J. Newman Lumber. Sarah Ruffin's dad moved his family from Selma, Alabama, to take a job at the same mill. Marie Washington Kent, whose family arrived in 1911, remembered, "My father was employed at J. J. Newman Lumber Company, many years." Nathaniel Burger, whose family came from Brookhaven, remembered the prominence of black sawmill workers in Hattiesburg. "As a boy coming here around five or six years old," Burger recalled, "all I realized was that the mills were manned by blacks." At times, as many as half of the city's black males worked in sawmills. They typically earned between $1.10 and $1.35 per day, with some of the more senior black employees earning up to $4.[6]

Employees of J. J. Newman Lumber Company. (McCain Library and Archives, University of Southern Mississippi)

Nearly all black women were limited to employment in some form of domestic service. They worked as maids, nannies, cooks, laundresses, or some combination thereof. In some of the more fortunate families like the Smiths, wives, mothers, and sisters did not need to work outside the home. But even these women filled essential roles as caregivers in their own families. Many also engaged in informal commercial exchanges, such as peddling produce or styling hair, to earn extra money. Some women worked multiple jobs to provide for their families.[7]

Other black men and women were employed in a variety of service or general-labor jobs typically reserved for African Americans, positions such as waiter, drayman, servant, street sweeper, bricklayer, or gardener. These difficult jobs usually paid less than $2 per day. Many black workers moved between positions, changing jobs whenever a conflict or new opportunity arose. Regardless of the field, most black labor was connected by the common themes of low pay and dirty work. Every day across Hattiesburg, black men and women cleaned, lifted, stocked, shoveled, swept, cooked, loaded, changed, ironed, and served. Their cheap labor undergirded much of the city's economic foundation and enabled many of its daily operations.[8]

Many black families benefitted from wages earned in these jobs, but in the broader scope of society, most black labor was designed to enhance the social and economic superiority of whites. White-owned firms profited from hiring inexpensive black workers to perform the most dangerous and dirty jobs. Individual white families benefitted through their ability to hire cheap cooks, landscapers, maids, and childcare providers. Even the city itself capitalized from black labor by hiring poorly paid African Americans to dig trenches, construct sewers, and sweep streets. African Americans were pushed into these types of jobs by stringent racial job discrimination. With few exceptions, black men were ineligible for managerial positions in sawmill or railroad firms. Black women were usually limited to teaching as the only viable employment alternative, but that job paid even less than domestic work and required more education than most of them had.

Although over 70 percent of black Hattiesburg adults could read and write, less than 2 percent had completed high school. The city did not even have a black high school. There was a public school for African Americans, but it offered only eight grades and was severely underfunded and overcrowded. Whereas the best white school met in a brick building with electricity and running water, the black school was housed in a windowless wooden structure with neither. The gap in pay between black and white teachers was significant. In 1910, white teachers in Mississippi earned an average monthly pay of $42.38; their black counterparts earned only $20.52 per month—despite the fact that black teachers were often responsible for far more students. In Hattiesburg at the time, black classrooms averaged seventy-five students compared to about forty in white ones. "I don't see how you could keep that many people quiet, let alone teach them," recalled Hammond Smith of his time as a student in the little wooden schoolhouse.[9]

Black parents who wanted to send their children to high school needed to make special arrangements for their kids to be educated in another county. Turner and Mamie Smith did precisely that, sending their oldest children to a residential high school located over one hundred miles away. But the Smith kids were exceptions. Most black families did not send their children to high school, either because they could not or because they saw little point in sending their kids away for a high school degree that would most probably not alter their prospects for employment. Many poor black families sent their kids to school only until they were old enough to start earning money. "Most children, they didn't go when they got big enough to work," Hammond explained.[10]

A girl named Osceola McCarty attended the little wooden schoolhouse alongside some of the youngest Smith children. The offspring of a rape, Osceola lived with her grandmother and aunt, both of whom worked as laundresses. The McCarty family struggled financially, particularly because Osceola's grandfather had been killed years before in a sawmill accident. Tragedy struck again when Osceola's aunt was diagnosed with a fibrous tumor. The subsequent surgery left the aunt bedridden and unable to work. With her aunt ailing, it fell upon young Osceola to help her grandmother provide for the family. The twelve-year-old girl dropped out of school in the sixth grade, trading the pencils and paper of a student for the iron and washboard of a laundress, the first job in a domestic service career that would span more than seventy years. Such was the reality for many of Hattiesburg's working black poor. Their poverty and lack of education benefitted local white residents, who paid very little for domestic-service work.[11]

The various structural limitations of black life were reinforced by hundreds of laws and regulations that further outlined Jim Crow. The most obvious of these was public segregation. African Americans were barred from shopping in stores, eating in restaurants, and accessing many public amenities and services. Some stores did allow black customers, but African American shoppers did not enjoy the same basic consumer rights as whites. Policies varied by store. In many cases, black customers could not return goods, try on merchandise, use restrooms, enter the front door, or ask clerks to wrap their purchases. All interactions with white shopkeepers presented the risk of mistreatment. Some shop owners refused to accept payment directly from the hands of black customers, insisting that bills or coins be placed on the counter and slid over. Other merchants were simply rude and disrespectful.[12]

Segregation extended to virtually every realm of public life, blocking African Americans from partaking in many of the basic pleasures of modern life in Hattiesburg. For local black citizens, there would be no extended downtown Christmas shopping hours, baptisms in Gordon's Creek, lumber company baseball games, or entries into the Hub City's annual Fourth of July Parade. The city's tax revenues did not pave their streets, install electric lights in their neighborhoods, maintain their cemeteries, or provide their homes with water.

African Americans were also expected to abide by countless customs of racial submission. By law or by tradition, black people were required to perform a repertoire of deferential social gestures—stepping off sidewalks to let white people pass, avoiding eye contact with white people, refraining from arguing with white people, and silently enduring an endless barrage of casual but degrading insults. Whites hardly shied away from such customs. Some reveled in them, relentlessly calling black men and women "boy," "girl," or "nigger" and constantly seeking to publicly humiliate African Americans. "If you were on the sidewalk and there were three or four white boys coming," remembered Constance Baker, who moved to Hattiesburg in 1914, "they would scatter themselves out so you would have to get off the pavement to pass them. Or maybe they might push you off the pavement, if you didn't get off." African Americans learned these expected public behaviors at a young age and lived with them all their lives. "I just came up sort of knowing what it was," remembered Ariel Barnes of black life in Hattiesburg. "We would meet white girls on the street, and we just knew to move over," Barnes told an interviewer.[13]

Black people also lived with the constant possibility of criminal accusations, which could lead to fines, arrests, or even death. Crime was a major component of life in the black neighborhood. Dozens of rogue African American men and women were engaged in various sorts of criminal activity, especially bootlegging, assault, and burglary that victimized other African Americans. In 1907, the murder of a black Hattiesburg banker named Ed Howell drew widespread media attention.[14]

Of course, Hattiesburg's white neighborhoods also experienced their fair share of crime, including bootlegging, assault, rape, burglary, and murder. But racial stereotypes and judicial discrimination subjected even the most law-abiding African Americans to criminal scrutiny. Very few black residents enjoyed due process of the law. They could not testify against whites, serve on juries, or hire a black defense attorney, meaning that mere accusations could result in swift convictions and punishments. Consequences varied. For some, the accusation of an offense such as swearing in public might result in a fine of a few dollars. For others, charges of assault or robbery could lead to prison. Those convicted of the rape or murder of a white person were usually executed if not lynched beforehand.[15]

Every component of Jim Crow was reinforced by the threat of violence. All black Southerners understood from an early age that violations of racial norms could result in physical punishments ranging from impromptu public whippings to death. Many had experienced or witnessed violence firsthand. All of them had heard the stories about lynching. Some no doubt heard the lynchings themselves. Early residents of the Mobile Street District lived within earshot of the downtown bridge over Gordon's Creek, the spot where Amos Jones had been killed by five hundred white people in 1903 and where Kid George and Ed Lewis had been "swung into eternity" by a thousand-person mob in 1905. In each of these murders, the white mobs shot hundreds of rounds of bullets into the dead black men's hanging corpses. Many residents of the Mobile Street neighborhood would have been able to hear the shooting from their homes. There is no telling what other sounds of the lynchings they heard—the screams, the cheers, the march of the mob, or the loud banging noises created by the makeshift battering ram that the white crowd used in 1905 to extract the black prisoners from jail. The terror is hard to imagine.[16]

Even if they managed to avoid the worst interactions with whites, all black men, women, and children felt the weight of the oppression. Physicians now know that prolonged exposure to intense fear and stress can weaken immune systems, cause cardiovascular damage, and lead to ulcers. Contemporary research has shown that as late as the 1960s, African Americans living in the Jim Crow South experienced higher rates of hypertension, premature death, and infant mortality than their white counterparts, even those with a similar economic status (this is, of course, in addition to having far less access to professional healthcare). Formalized segregation conspired with the daily customs of Jim Crow to create an omnipresent culture of white supremacy that ground relentlessly into the bodies and souls of black people.[17]

Every Sunday, the Smith family walked about two blocks to attend services at St. Paul Methodist Church. Organized in 1882, St. Paul was one of Hattiesburg's oldest churches, black or white. For most of its first forty years, the congregation met in a small, twenty-three-foot-tall wooden structure located near the tracks of Fenwick Peck's Mississippi Central Railroad, which for many years demarcated the southern boundary of the black community. Commonly known as the "church on the hill," St. Paul rested on some of the highest elevated land African Americans could purchase at the time, giving it an important role for a population that lived in a floodplain. For decades, the church served as a refuge for people escaping rising waters during the rainy seasons of early spring and late summer.[18]

Not all black Methodist churches were part of the African Methodist Episcopal (AME) Church, an African American denomination that broke away from the Methodist Episcopal Church (MEC) in 1816 because of racial discrimination and conflicts over slavery. Other African American Methodist–based denominations formed, most notably the Christian Methodist Episcopal (CME) Church and the African Methodist Episcopal Zion (AMEZ) Church, but in the early twentieth century, most of Mississippi's black Methodist churches, including St. Paul, remained part of the MEC. Much of this allegiance was a legacy of the Reconstruction era, when Northern Methodist missionaries came to the South and helped build schools for African Americans, including institutions such as Rust College and the Haven Institute, where Turner Smith matriculated. Former bondsmen like Turner Smith remained forever loyal to the Methodist Church and the Republican Party for their role in Reconstruction. As one of his sons later explained to an interviewer, Turner Smith "had three loves: his family, the Methodist Church, and the Republican Party."[19]

Regardless of denomination, black churches were the most important component of the Mobile Street District. By 1910, the neighborhood was home to five major congregations—St. Paul Methodist, Mt. Carmel Baptist, Zion Chapel African Methodist Episcopal, St. James African Methodist Episcopal, and True Light Baptist, all located within a mile of each other. With little access to other public spaces, African Americans poured their resources into the churches. They did not yet have the means to build stone or brick structures, but in an era when few black homes had electricity or heat, each of the city's major wooden black churches had both.[20]

Black Hattiesburgers were deeply religious. Their Christianity was a legacy of their enslaved ancestors whose faith in God and heaven helped them navigate difficult lives. Fifty years after Emancipation, the offspring of those bondsmen invoked God and the Bible at virtually every gathering and meal. Prayers, church services, and multi-day revivals offered not only courage and hope but also brief respites from the realities of life under Jim Crow. Many never looked or felt better than they did when they were praying and singing together in the churches. Every Sunday in Hattiesburg, black women and men who normally dressed in tattered work clothes donned clean white dresses and freshly pressed suits. People who spent their days cleaning outhouses or making fertilizer led Sunday school classes and directed choirs. And folks who were called "boy" or "girl" or "nigger" in the street became "sir" or "ma'am" or "Reverend" within the sanctuaries of their community.[21]

The church buildings were also important sites of community organizing. People used the pulpits to announce local initiatives, explain the need for collections, or offer community updates. Each church was home to dozens of clubs and societies—missionary organizations, pastors' wives groups, and community choirs that organized a variety of social activities and charitable initiatives. Because African Americans had such restricted access to other large venues, churches were usually the only places where even secular groups could meet. Hattiesburg's black churches were busy almost every day. Beyond the standard religious services, funerals, and weddings, Hattiesburg's black churches hosted scores of concerts, lectures, debates, club meetings, suppers, and schools.[22]

In addition to Turner Smith's role as a Sunday school teacher at St. Paul Methodist, he also belonged to an organization known as the Howell Literary Club. Named for Ed Howell, the black banker who was murdered in 1907, the Howell Literary Club was an interdenominational organization that met in local black churches after regular Sunday services. "This club has brought the different denominations together more than any other organization in the history of this city," said a 1908 newspaper report. Like every other component of black life, the meetings of the Howell Literary

Club were packed with religious observances, including invocations, prayers, scripture readings, and church choir performances. But their gatherings also featured a variety of secular activities, including lectures and debates covering such issues as the value of industrial education or the morality of child labor. Several reports from the era list Turner Smith as a participant in the debates.[23]

Excluded from so many aspects of broader public life, the black men and women of Hattiesburg had little choice but to construct a parallel society of their own. Barred from the local white Commercial Club, black business owners started the Negro Progressive Business League. Ridiculed and ignored in white newspapers, local African Americans published *The Weekly Times* and the *Beacon Light.* Unable to trust white-owned banks, black entrepreneurs established the People's Bank and the Magic City Bank. Ineligible to play on lumber company baseball teams, black Hattiesburgers formed their own squad, which competed against teams from nearby black communities. New schools and large department stores were beyond their capacity, but African Americans managed to craft a mirroring black society in the Mobile Street District, complete with businesses, hotels, offices, social clubs, and restaurants. "Mobile Street was our city," remembered one resident of the neighborhood. "Mobile Street supplied the needs of our community."[24]

An emerging group of black businessmen led the construction of this parallel society. Hattiesburg's black laborers may not have earned much, but they still needed basic goods and services. And because black people faced such severe discrimination in white-owned stores, many had no choice but to shop in black-owned businesses. In fact, some preferred to shop among their own race. In black-owned stores, they were more likely to enjoy basic consumer rights and a modicum of dignity. Black business owners did not operate in an open market. Jim Crow may have limited their earning potential, but it also helped ensure a large, concentrated customer base. A growing number of black consumers led to a growing number of black businesses.

As Hattiesburg grew, dozens of ambitious black entrepreneurs and professionals opened new shops and offices in buildings that ranged in size from one-room wooden shacks to a three-story brick building completed in 1906. Most of these entrepreneurs came from small Mississippi communities near Hattiesburg. Notable early black business leaders Gaither Hardaway, Samuel Carmichael, and Timothy S. Thigpen each came from small towns located within seventy-five miles. Others came from bordering states. Furniture salesman Stephen Kinnard and restaurateur Noah Shackelford were from western Alabama. The city's first black doctor, Dr. James Randall, arrived from Louisiana. Frank Sutton, often regarded as the neighborhood's best tailor, moved to Hattiesburg from South Carolina.[25]

Like their working-class customers, most of the entrepreneurs originally came to Hattiesburg for wage-labor jobs before saving enough to open their own businesses. Gaither Hardaway started off as a sawmill worker before opening his own barbershop and later a successful grocery store. Noah Shackelford began his life in Hattiesburg as a cook in a white-owned hotel before opening his own barbeque joint and later a skating rink and a dance hall. Richard McBride first worked as a day laborer before becoming manager of a black guesthouse named the Glenmore Hotel. John Bradley (J. B.) Woods arrived in the late nineteenth century to work for the New Orleans & Northeastern Railroad before starting a successful black grocery store. Most formal storefronts in the Mobile Street District were owned by men, but black women also operated a small number of hairdressers, restaurants, and boarding houses. White investors owned a handful of the early shops.[26]

Turner and Mamie Smith lived near the heart of the Mobile Street District. If the couple stepped out of their home in 1910 and walked about two blocks east, they would have passed three grocery stores, two tailor shops, two restaurants, a barbershop, a laundry, a butcher, the Magic City Bank, and a two-story drugstore on the corner of Seventh and Mobile Streets, the epicenter of the black downtown. If the couple then turned south onto Mobile and proceeded three additional blocks, they would have passed another five grocery stores, five restaurants, three barbershops, two butchers, two tailors, two pool halls, a cobbler, a hotel, a printing company, a general store, Noah Shackelford's skating rink, a dance hall, Stephen Kinnard's furniture store, a drugstore, a bicycle shop, and a clothing store—all within five blocks of their home. Dozens more groceries, butchers, pressing clubs, tailors, and barbershops were scattered throughout the neighborhood.[27]

In 1908, Hattiesburg's black businessmen formed an organization called the Negro Progressive Business League. Founded to "unite, foster and promote the Negro business interests of this the city and suburbs," the organization met monthly to discuss neighborhood events and to socialize (though it left few records). It was common for groups to form based on employment, socioeconomic status, or church membership. The black sawmill employees at J. J. Newman Lumber tended to work, live, and socialize among one another. So too did the black waiters at the Hotel Hattiesburg, who formed their own social club that met on days off work. Railroad porters in Hattiesburg and elsewhere were known to form tight social bonds. And most of the city's black female teachers lived together in black-owned boarding houses. Other groups of women formed through cooperative working arrangements—especially laundry—and church membership.[28]

Hattiesburg's early black organizations left little trace of the overt activism that occurred in larger Southern cities such as Atlanta or New Orleans—with one notable exception. In 1914, a committee of black entrepreneurs drafted a "Bill of Complaints" addressing conditions on segregated railroad cars and sent copies to the superintendents of each of the three major railroads that passed through Hattiesburg—the Gulf & Ship Island, the New Orleans & Northeastern, and the Mississippi Central. There is no record of the companies' responses, but for the era, the protest itself was certainly a bold maneuver.[29]

This Bill of Complaints was part of a one-day national protest named Railroad Day, organized by Booker T. Washington, who by that time was the most influential African American in the United States. Born into slavery in 1856, Booker T. Washington argued that an industrial- and agricultural-based education was crucial to the advancement of African American character and work ethic. He won the support of many white Southern leaders in the 1890s by advocating a vision of racial advancement focused on African American self-improvement, morality, and institution building, as opposed to the immediate civil rights promoted by Northern intellectuals such as William Monroe Trotter and W. E. B. Du Bois. Although Washington tactfully used his influence to quietly advocate for increased civil rights and a cessation of lynching, many of his contemporaries strongly criticized him as an "accomodationist" whose approach to racial uplift, wrote Du Bois, "practically accepts the alleged inferiority of the Negro."[30]

This debate has been largely overblown in terms of its applicability to most African Americans at the time, but it is important to note here because all available evidence indicates that members of Hattiesburg's black entrepreneurial class strongly supported Booker T. Washington and his approach to racial uplift. Bear in mind that many were the sons and daughters of former bondsmen (if not former slaves themselves), living in a state where the governor publicly advocated lynching black people. Having come of age during an era of horrific violence, they had very little reason to believe that overt demands for racial equality would result in increased civil, social, or political rights. In fact, their experiences would have suggested that violence—perhaps even death—was a more likely result of public activism. Du Bois and his allies were absolutely correct in noting that African Americans were fundamentally limited by racially discriminatory social, economic, and political constructs, but many black Southern leaders at the time were more immediately concerned with survival.

Hattiesburg's most visible Washington supporter was the barber Timothy S. Thigpen. Thigpen and his brothers, one of whom named a son Booker T. Thigpen, played instrumental roles in helping establish the alternative black society in the Mobile Street District through their involvement with several local businesses and organizations and their roles at St. Paul Methodist Church. It was Timothy Thigpen who in 1903 began self-publishing the Mobile Street District's first black newspaper, *The Weekly Times*, which closely subscribed to and routinely defended Washington's principles. When *Chicago Broad Ax* editor Julius Taylor criticized Washington in 1907, Thigpen responded with a heated editorial. "Brother Taylor is wrong," wrote the Hattiesburg publisher. "He lets his prejudice against Dr. Washington lead him to accuse wrongfully, men who have been the moulders [*sic*] of race sentiment in this country. Editor Taylor, with his talent and his paper should lay aside his prejudice against Dr. Washington and help him when he is in the right and cease his useless yawping." In a later editorial, Thigpen noted, "We of the South are tired of theorizing from the Northern Negro who knows nothing about the conditions in the South." For Thigpen and his colleagues, racial progress was best accomplished by sidestepping the already lost battles for civil rights and developing one's own community.[31]

Alongside churches and businesses, mutual aid and Freemasonry societies also served as important avenues of self-help and economic uplift. The Mobile Street District was home to five such groups in the 1910s—the locally-based Sons and Daughters of Gideon and the Industrial Toilers of America, and branches of the national Odd Fellows society, the Knights of Pythias, and the Stringer Grand Lodge of Free and Accepted Masons, the largest black Masonic order in Mississippi. Dubbed by one black Southern newspaper as "one of the largest, wealthiest and most aggressive organizations in the country," the Stringer Grand Lodge by 1907 included more than eleven thousand members and controlled over $166,000 in assets. That year, the organization held its annual meeting in Hattiesburg's Mobile Street District, attracting approximately one thousand African Americans "from all parts of the state."[32]

Black mutual aid societies, also commonly referred to as beneficial or benevolent societies, operated essentially as insurance cooperatives. Weekly or monthly dues entitled members to health, unemployment, and death benefits. Some societies even offered retirement pensions. Masonic orders, which were often closely affiliated with mutual aid societies, were generally designed to enhance the professional, moral, and spiritual development of black men. Some branches also had auxiliary groups for women. In Hattiesburg and elsewhere, these organizations often met and conducted their activities in secret. Several local black leaders belonged to numerous orders at once. For example, Timothy S. Thigpen was not only the founder of the Industrial Toilers of America, but also a member of the Odd Fellows and Knights of Pythias. Membership was often stratified by socioeconomic status and/or religious affiliation, but the core of their mission also included a variety of community-based service projects and self-help initiatives.[33]

The dues collected by these organizations were used to fund social activities and to provide various forms of insurance, medical care, scholarships, loans, and financial aid to black families and institutions. The ability of these groups to accumulate and distribute resources effectively helped subsidize the low wages paid to African Americans and provide some access to welfare and insurance services for black men and women. Pioneered by Hattiesburg's first wave of black business leaders, Masonic societies would play a major role in local black life throughout the Jim Crow era. The local Stringer Grand Lodge remains active to this day.

Throughout the early twentieth century, churches, work-based social groups, and a variety of mutual aid and Freemasonry societies formed the pillars of black communal life in Hattiesburg, offering not only a sense of belonging but also important economic benefits and avenues of civic participation. The "collectivist ethos" of these organizations, to use the phrase of historian Robin Kelley, was necessitated by the racial segregation and oppression that characterized black life in the Jim Crow South. The very same forces that restricted African Americans in the South also pushed them together and led to the creation and expansion of black communal institutions and traditions that helped them navigate life in a very dangerous society. For some, these community groups facilitated an escape from that society altogether.[34]

At about noon on December 7, 1916, one hundred black employees at Hattiesburg's J. J. Newman Lumber sawmill received their biweekly paychecks and walked out of the mill. When the whistle blew signaling the end of lunch, the rough sheds, box factory, and docks remained unmanned and were forced to cease operations for the rest of the day. White employees at the mill, who "announced that it would be impossible for them to continue their work without assistance from the negroes," managed to keep the planers and kilns operating for a few hours, but the entire mill shut down the following day and remained closed for two weeks. The black workers never returned. By the time J. J. Newman finally reopened, they had already left for Chicago.[35]

An exodus had begun that autumn. In October, between one hundred fifty and two hundred black Hattiesburgers boarded a special midnight train to Chicago. On December 11, another group of thirty-seven left. During the next month, additional groups of thirty-one and forty also went north. The following spring, other large groups of thirty, twenty-eight, eighty, one hundred twenty, and one hundred forty-seven left Hattiesburg for the Windy City. "It was considered 'fashionable' to go," reported one migrant. "Anybody that had any grit in his craw, went." Over the span of about sixteen months, an estimated 2,500 African Americans—roughly half the city's black population at the time—packed up and left Hattiesburg for good.[36]

It was cheaper to go in groups. Railroad companies offered discounted rates for ten or more passengers. Migrants could save as much as $8 apiece for traveling in such groups. Travel groups formed from existing social structures in the Mobile Street District. Like the men who walked out of J. J. Newman Lumber, many of the migrants organized moves with coworkers. Others migrated with members of their churches. In less than two years, Mt. Carmel Baptist Church lost 550 of its 700-member congregation. One pastor discouraged members of his church from leaving, only to join them later in Chicago when they offered to pay for his move. At least two other congregations made similar arrangements for their preachers to join them up North.[37]

With the Great War grinding European migration to a halt and Northern factories still in need of labor, black Southerners were recruited to work in manufacturing jobs in Northern cities. Intrigued by the promise of jobs and a life outside the Jim Crow South, hundreds of thousands of African Americans left Dixie forever. For black Mississippians, Chicago was the most common destination. Migrants from the Magnolia State comprised a large share of the fifty-thousand-plus African Americans who flocked to Chicago between 1916 and 1918.[38]

For many black Mississippians, the move to Chicago was highly influenced by an African American newspaper named the *Chicago Defender*. Founded in 1905 by Georgia native Robert Sengstacke Abbott, the *Defender* commanded attention with brazen headlines such as "100 Negroes Murdered Weekly in United States by White Americans" and scathing critiques of Jim Crow. Black Southerners, living in places where newspapers typically ignored local or national black news, were attracted to the *Defender*'s broad scope and militant attitude. By 1918, the *Defender* had more than eighty thousand subscribers outside of Chicago. Pullman porters and other railroad employees delivered large stacks of the *Defender's* weekly national edition to black neighborhoods across the New South.[39]

The *Defender* was immensely popular with black folks in southern Mississippi. A Hattiesburg barber named Robert Horton often bought between forty and fifty copies of the *Defender* and sold them to his customers at cost "just for the sake of distributing the news of a 'fearless paper,'" he explained. One report noted that black Hattiesburgers "grab the *Defender* like a hungry mule grabs fodder." "Men in business sell them without profit," wrote a National Urban League official of black Hattiesburgers. "It is passed around until it is worn out." In nearby towns, there were stories of even illiterate African Americans carrying copies of the *Defender* "simply because it was regarded as precious."[40]

The *Defender* played an important role in helping spark migration. It published dozens of articles advocating black migration and even set a date—May 17, 1917—for what it called "The Great Northern Drive." Black people in Hattiesburg sat in the shops of their community and discussed articles from the *Defender*, having "semi-public discussions" about life in the South, one migrant described, and "[bringing] up the reasons for wanting to leave." Some actually wrote to the *Defender* itself to ask questions about jobs, train tickets, or housing. "I am a yellow Pine Lumber inspector," one Hattiesburg man wrote to the newspaper. "My job pay me well but as my wife and Children are anxious to come north I would try and get a job." The *Defender*, noted the Urban League, "which unquestionably stimulated the movement, is in large measure responsible for the popularity of Chicago." Some local whites accused the paper of "ruining Hattiesburg."[41]

The communal culture of the Mobile Street District was also crucial to people's decisions to move. During return visits to Hattiesburg, recent migrants regularly stopped into local barbershops and grocery stores to see old friends and tell them about jobs, schools, and housing in Chicago. According to one observer, these barbershop discussions "were as effective as labor agents in seducing labor." Locals were also influenced by letters from friends who had already moved to Chicago. "Letters were passed around and read before large groups," reported a 1919 study on the black migration. "A woman from Hattiesburg is accredited with having sent back a letter which enticed away over 200 persons." Another Hattiesburg migrant named Mr. Holloway reported that he and his wife had received two letters per week from friends who had moved to Chicago. "All made them anxious to come," he explained upon his arrival in the Windy City.[42]

Many business owners in the Mobile Street District also left. Stephen Kinnard, the Mobile Street furniture salesman and head of the Howell Literary Club, moved to Chicago, where he took a position with a life insurance company. Former hotel manager Richard McBride also moved to the Windy City, where he worked as a hotel cook. Restaurateur Noah Shackelford sold his barbeque business on Mobile Street to open a new restaurant on Chicago's South Side. Even Timothy S. Thigpen, the avid supporter of Booker T. Washington, ignored Washington's advice to "cast down your bucket where you are" and went to Chicago, where he took a job in printing.[43]

The *Hattiesburg News*, which did not typically run stories about the black community, paid close attention to the departures. Many local whites were deeply concerned about the loss of the city's black labor force. "No body of men can be found," the paper cautioned readers, "who will work as long and at as small wages and do it as uncomplainingly, in forrests and lumber camps and the mills of the South as the negro does." "[White] Housekeepers are not taking at all kindly to the activities of the labor agents," another article noted, "and are trembling lest they will soon have to build their own fire in the kitchen stoves on wintry days and cook breakfast."[44]

Placing the blame on "oily-tongued labor agents," white Hattiesburg officials took measures to stop the departures. They searched the city for traveling labor agents and issued fines to anyone they suspected of recruiting workers for Northern firms without a proper license. Hattiesburg's mayor instructed the police to monitor the local railroad depots and break up any large crowds of African Americans and "make inquiries of the negroes found there as to their businesses." In Chicago, some of the black migrants reported that white officials actively tried to keep African Americans away from the railroad ticket offices and that private employers of domestic laborers often withheld pay if they suspected a worker might leave.[45]

The *Hattiesburg News* reassured white readers that the departures would soon end and promised the return of black migrants. The black migrants, they argued, were victims of corrupt labor agents who made false promises of jobs and housing in Chicago. "Negroes who have been carried away from Hattiesburg in hundreds by labor agents to work in northern states are not finding the labor conditions as represented," a reporter claimed. Some African Americans, the paper asserted, were "'caught in the trap' and anxious to return to their homes here, but are unable to get away." "Chicago is not as fond of the members of the black race as oily tongued New Orleans labor agents have led the negroes to believe," another local report noted. Weather was the subject of another common argument. "They are helpless before the elements," the paper insisted. One story told of a "strong, healthy negro" who had been warned by a doctor to "Go back South. . . . You'll die if you stay here." "Cold climate," the story explained, "tends to have that kind of an effect on negroes." Other writers concluded that the black migrants would return simply because of how much they would miss the South. One unsubstantiated report claimed that when "the lights of Hattiesburg began fading in the distance," some of the departing migrants began "jumping through windows, or off onto the platform, so anxious were they to get off that train." The *Hattiesburg News* ultimately predicted that "the exodus . . . will teach the negroes who leave to appreciate the South more."[46]

Of course, the papers were wrong. Hattiesburg's black men and women kept leaving, and local whites could do very little to slow their departure. At one point, one of the local sawmill owners reportedly became so desperate to keep his black workers that he "ran down to the station and begged the men not to leave his place, offering more money." "The negroes refused," reported a witness. Those black men would never again abide by the white sawmill owner's demands or the rules of the Jim Crow society from which they fled.[47]

The greatest irony in these exoduses was that white Hattiesburgers had done so much to lay the groundwork for the migrations. The sawmills and the railroads that they had so welcomed—and that first brought black workers into the city—were the very firms that ultimately provided those black workers with the resources (wages) and the transportation (railroads) to leave. None of the black men who left the J. J. Newman Lumber Sawmill in December of 1916 had very deep roots in Hattiesburg. Those over the age of twenty-one were older than their employer; those over the age of thirty-two were older than Hattiesburg itself. This meant that they had come from elsewhere. The opportunity of lumber work had drawn them from other labors and enabled them to envision a very different life. As the black sociologist E. Franklin Frazier once noted, "Some of the men had their first glance of the world beyond the plantation or farm when they worked in sawmills, turpentine camps, or on the roads." The development of the New South offered a great many things. For hundreds of thousands of African Americans, its greatest gift was to provide a mode of exodus from the lands where their ancestors had been enslaved.[48]

Chicago was rife with all sorts of its own racial problems—including a major race riot in 1919—but many Hattiesburg migrants were enthralled by the opportunity to escape Jim Crow Mississippi. In explaining the reasons for leaving, most cited low pay, poor schools, and the threat of violence. "They say that we are fools to leave the warm country and how our people are dying in the east," one Hattiesburg migrant explained. "Well I, for one, am glad that they had the privilege of dying a natural death. That is much better than the rope and torch. I will take my chances with the northern winter." Another Mississippi migrant simply explained, "I just want to be somewhere where I won't be scared all the time." One Hattiesburg man, grateful to escape the daily indignities of Jim Crow, told an Urban League official that in Chicago, "for the first time in his life he had felt like a man."[49]

Anxious to flee Jim Crow, thousands of black Hattiesburgers quit their jobs, abandoned their belongings, and sold their homes. "Men who had spent their lives buying homes gave them away for a trifle," a report noted. "Negroes have almost given away what few holdings they may have gotten together after hard years of work and are leaving on every train," reported the *Hattiesburg American*. Chicago became such a common word in the

Mobile Street District that black people began simply referring to it as "Chi." "The people got the Northern fever," testified one migrant, "just like they got religion."[50]

For some, the act of migration was indeed spiritual. When a group of 147 Hattiesburg migrants crossed the Ohio River at Cincinnati, they bowed their heads in silent prayer, thanking God for delivering them out of the South. After a brief moment of silence, the group broke out in song, their voices jubilantly echoing throughout the train car: "I done come out of the land of Egypt, ain't that good news" and "I'm looking now across the river, where my faith will end in sight." Men on the train took out their watches and stopped them at 10:30, the exact moment when they crossed the Ohio River. One woman even went so far as to claim that she could tell the difference in the air on the Ohio side of the river. They were the children and grandchildren of slaves—some were former slaves themselves—and many still viewed the North as a mythical land of freedom. The migration itself was a spiritual journey away from the horrors of their ancestral lives in the South.[51]

In Chicago, Hattiesburg migrants helped one another find jobs and housing. One couple from Hattiesburg bought a large, seven-room house and offered short-term lodging for new migrants. Their boardinghouse was constantly filled with recent arrivals from the Hub City who stayed with them while searching for permanent housing and jobs. Capable of hosting up to twenty-one guests at a time, the woman estimated that during the winter of 1917–18, she hosted nearly seven hundred boarders from Hattiesburg and other nearby towns in southern Mississippi.[52]

For many, the culture of communal self-help that had developed in the Mobile Street District transferred easily to Chicago. Hundreds of Hub City migrants chose to live together in the Windy City, developing a distinct community of Hattiesburg migrants in Chicago near the corner of Rhodes Avenue and 35th Street. The Urban League reported, "There is in Chicago a little colony of Mississippians from Hattiesburg principally, which has been transplanted so completely as to retain practically all of its customs and mores." The people from Hattiesburg, the report noted, settle among one another because "they are desirous of helping each other." "We stick by one another," one of the migrants told an interviewer.[53]

Robert Horton, the Hub City barber who had sold the *Defender* from his shop in Mississippi, opened a new barbershop in Chicago named the

Hattiesburg Barbershop. Sitting in the middle of over 150 families from Hattiesburg, the shop retained many of its old customers and social functions. It was a site of gathering, reunion, and gossip. "At the barbershop," an Urban League representative observed, "it is possible to meet all old friends from home or learn of their whereabouts." Fellow Hattiesburg migrants Noah Shackelford and Timothy S. Thigpen lived and worked less than six blocks away. Various other Hattiesburg migrants started a coal and wood company, a deli, and a pool room. There were also at least three church congregations comprised primarily of Hattiesburg migrants and an organization called the Hattiesburg Social Service Club.[54]

The crux of that cohesiveness was birthed in Hattiesburg's Mobile Street District, where the black population forged a variety of institutional, social, economic, and religious structures to help navigate Jim Crow. Transferred across more than eight hundred miles, people who had lived, worked, and worshipped together continued to operate within existing communal structures and traditions in Chicago. When asked why they remained together in the Windy City, one of the Hattiesburg migrants simply explained, "I guess it's because they made us stick together down there."[55]

Back in Hattiesburg, the departures sparked several significant developments. First, local white leaders began paying more attention to the condition of African Americans. As a correspondent for the *Defender* reported, "White people are paying more attention to the race in order to keep them in the South." The fundamental characteristics of Jim Crow remained unchanged, but the 1920s would see numerous examples of local white leaders supporting black community initiatives. This increased interest led them to work with local black community leaders. Businessmen and clergy who remained in the Mobile Street District increasingly began to serve as intermediaries between working-class African Americans and white city leaders who were interested in making token gestures to help curb the exodus. In 1919, the *Hattiesburg American* (previously the *Hattiesburg Daily News*, which had changed its name early in World War I) even started a new series on local black life titled the "Colored Column," marking the first time in Hattiesburg history that the city's largest newspaper included regular discussions of life in the Mobile Street District. This fairly short-lived column was by no means revolutionary, but along with the increased support of black community initiatives, it represented a growing recognition of the concerns of an oppressed but much-needed black population that had proven it could at any time simply pack up and leave.[56]

The second development was that many local firms raised wages to try to keep black workers. According to a national study conducted by the scholar Emmet J. Scott, a former aide to Booker T. Washington, the average wages in Hattiesburg sawmills increased from $1.10 per day to "$1.75 and $2" during World War I. Another historian recently estimated that statewide industrial wages for African Americans increased between 10 and 30 percent. African Americans still worked in the city's worst jobs and earned far less than their white counterparts, but they also earned more than they had before the departures.[57]

The third and most important result of the departures was that the city decided to build a black high school in the Mobile Street District. In 1919 or 1920, William H. Jones, principal of the local black school, was invited to address a contingent of the city's leading white businessmen at a banquet concerning the status of Hattiesburg's black school district. From this meeting, local white leaders urged Hattiesburg citizens to pass a $75,000 bond to build a new high school for African Americans. Subsidized by the Rosenwald Fund, a national foundation that supported the improvement of black schools, Hattiesburg's first high school for black students opened in September of 1921. William Jones decided to name the new school Eureka, meaning "I have found it." Shortly after Eureka opened, a story in the *Los Angeles Times* featured Hattiesburg's new black high school in an article titled "Schools Stop Negro Exodus," which concluded, "[White] Citizens here say the school has undoubtedly served to stabilize colored labor."[58]

These new developments helped generate a resurgence in the local black population. In the wake of the departures, thousands of new black migrants came to Hattiesburg to take wage-labor jobs, start new businesses, and send their children to the new school. "The town has been almost depopulated of Negroes and repopulated again," reported the Urban League of Hattiesburg. "The towns were first drained of the available laborers," observed the black historian Carter G. Woodson in 1930. "Then the farm Negroes were brought in to take the places vacated by those who had left for Northern points." Woodson concluded, "Especially was this the case in cities like Birmingham and Hattiesburg." Despite losing more than half its members,

Hattiesburg's black population over the long run continued to grow steadily.[59]

Turner and Mamie Smith left behind no record of their thoughts about leaving Hattiesburg, but amid such a massive exodus, they must have considered the possibility. That was another effect of the departures: from that point forward, all local black men and women were presented with the possibility of leaving the Hub City. Of course, a variety of factors influenced individual and family decisions. Turner and Mamie had plenty of reasons to stay. One was that they were a bit older; Turner was fifty-seven years old when the exodus began in 1916 and probably believed that he had a lesser chance than a younger man of finding work in Chicago. Additionally, he and Mamie had a built a life in Hattiesburg. After moving for years between teaching jobs and careers, they had bought their own home, had established themselves among the congregation at St. Paul, and were still helping support their children. Some members of the Smith family did eventually leave the South, but Turner and Mamie stayed in Hattiesburg for the rest of their lives.

In the mid-1920s, after years away in school, the two eldest Smith sons, Charles and Hammond, completed their education and returned to Hattiesburg. Upon their return, they encountered an even larger and more vibrant Mobile Street District than the one they had left nearly a decade before. They re-joined the congregation at St. Paul Methodist Church and soon thereafter started businesses of their own on Mobile Street, integrating themselves into the city's black business community and leadership class.

CHAPTER FIVE

Broken Promises

> The man who expects to live until the timber is exhausted must think that he has a very long lease on life.
>
> —*Hattiesburg Daily Progress*, 1902

No white Hattiesburg migrant found greater success than William Sion Franklin Tatum. Like many arrivals to the Hub City, W. S. F. Tatum came from an exceedingly difficult background. Born in 1858 into a struggling Tennessee farm family, his childhood was beset by the Civil War and its tragic aftermath. Tatum's family lived only about twenty miles from the site of the Battle of Shiloh, where more than twenty-three thousand men were felled in the spring of 1862. One of his earliest childhood memories was of two aunts, both of whom had husbands fighting in the battle, rushing into the yard of his boyhood home "crying and wringing their hands." The following year, the young boy lost his mother to disease. At the age of five, W. S. F. was held up to his mother's deathbed and instructed to "kiss his dying mother goodbye." He was six when the war ended, leaving behind a defeated and deprived region where Tatum spent the remainder of his youth.[1]

As the son of a widowed farmer, W. S. F. was needed to work in the fields as a child and rarely attended school. At the age of six, he was already "dropping corn and throwing cotton," and by eight he was driving the plow. Eventually, Tatum's father opened a small general store where W. S. F. worked through much of his adolescence. In 1879, Tatum was still working for his father when he met a local girl named Rebecca O'Neal at a holiday party. The pair began exchanging letters, which led to in-person visits and eventually marriage in the summer of 1881. When Rebecca became pregnant, Tatum arranged with his father to take over the family store, which he ran for the next eleven and a half years. Although they struggled at times, the store left them better off than most.[2]

W. S. F. Tatum. (McCain Library and Archives, University of Southern Mississippi)

Sometime in 1892, Tatum learned of a promising new lumber town named Hattiesburg sprouting deep in the Mississippi Piney Woods. Having previously dabbled in the timber trade by selling logs on the land next to his store, Tatum was intrigued by the future prospects of the Southern lumber industry and journeyed about three hundred miles to inspect the area. He liked what he saw and decided to move his family to southern Mississippi. With the help of capital provided by his in-laws, Tatum bought a 2,200-acre plot along the tracks of the New Orleans & Northeastern Railroad and erected a sawmill.[3]

Struggling against "many anxious days and nights," W. S. F. slowly built a local lumber empire. The family lived frugally and used extra earnings to expand the company's holdings. Tatum also made a shrewd entrepreneurial move by constructing a company town named Bonhomie near his sawmill. Employees of Tatum Lumber traded wages or borrowed against future pay in exchange for goods at the overpriced commissary (which some employees spitefully dubbed a "robbissary"), thus enabling their employer to profit off the very wages he paid them. As the local timber trade grew, Tatum Lumber did extremely well. Over the following years, the firm went on to acquire more than forty thousand acres and employ up to four hundred workers at a time. W. S. F. made a fortune. Having once earned $500 a year working for his father, Tatum by 1916 was worth more than $930,000 (nearly $20 million today). He became the city's wealthiest resident and a two-time mayor.[4]

Thomas Smylie Jackson was another white Hattiesburg migrant who found prosperity near the turn of the century. The son of a prominent slave-owner, T. S. Jackson was born in Amite County, Mississippi, one year before the Civil War ended. Emancipation freed much of his father's wealth and labor, forcing Jackson and his brothers to work in the fields. When asked later in life, Jackson classified the work as being "so hard he didn't care to refer to it." With six brothers, Jackson could not count on inheriting his father's land, and so he pursued other interests. Soon after marrying his childhood sweetheart, he opened a little general store, and for a while he operated a small cotton gin.[5]

T. S. Jackson was in his mid-thirties when Hattiesburg started to boom in the early 1900s. At the time, virtually every newspaper in the region was gushing about the promise of this new city located deep in the Piney Woods. Wondering what opportunities might exist in the growing young town, Jackson examined Hattiesburg's business community and discovered a need for a shoe store. In 1902, he moved his family to Hattiesburg and opened a new downtown shop. Soon thereafter, Jackson sold his shoe store and invested in a wholesale grocery company. This was a wise decision. Merchants Grocery Company filled the city's growing need for a wholesale grocer. The company grew quickly. Within a few years, it moved into a new downtown building, expanded its cold-storage facilities, built warehouses in surrounding towns, and eventually added a cornmeal mill and mixed feed plant. As a founding partner, Jackson emerged as one of Hattiesburg's leading white businessmen and most affluent citizens.[6]

Louis Faulkner traveled much further on his journey into the ranks of Hattiesburg's white elite. Born in 1883, the Pennsylvania native started his adult life as a teacher but was quickly drawn out of the classroom by more lucrative opportunities. After just one year of teaching, the young man took an engineering job with a West Virginia railroad company. Faulkner was no engineer, but the line needed smart, educated men and offered him an entry-level position. This initial experience enabled Faulkner to secure a position with the Buffalo & Susquehanna Railroad, a syndicate of logging railroads operating in northern Pennsylvania and western New York. One of the Buffalo & Susquehanna Railroad's best clients was the Pennsylvania lumber magnate Fenwick Peck.[7]

Peck was in the process of expanding his recently established Mississippi Central Railroad and needed experienced railroad men to oversee his growing operations in Mississippi. In 1905, Louis Faulkner secured one of these positions and moved south to work in the Mississippi Central's office at Brookhaven. Over the subsequent years, he advanced in the company from level man to resident engineer to division engineer and eventually chief engineer. In 1912, he was promoted to general manager of the Mississippi Central, a job that brought him and his wife, Vera, to Hattiesburg. The Faulkners bought a house, had a baby, and began settling into comfortable lives among Hattiesburg's prominent whites.[8]

Hattiesburg may have been founded by Captain Hardy and capitalized by Northerners, but local life was shaped by prominent white residents like W. S. F. Tatum, T. S. Jackson, and Louis Faulkner. Each man touched the city in different ways. Tatum was the primary benefactor of the Main Street Methodist Church, a major supporter of several local educational initiatives, and a patron of the Hattiesburg YMCA. T. S. Jackson was a longtime deacon in the Main Street Baptist Church and heavily involved with the Rotary Club and the Red Cross. Louis Faulkner was a Sunday school superintendent, deacon at the First Presbyterian Church, and a major supporter of the local Boy Scout troop. These prominent men participated in a variety of local initiatives based on their own particular values, interests, and goals. There was one group, however, that drew them all together: the Hattiesburg Chamber of Commerce.[9]

Originally established as the Commercial Club in 1906, the Hattiesburg Chamber of Commerce operated with the stated goal to "promote the civic, economic and social welfare of the people of Hattiesburg and vicinity." The organization typically included between 150 and 250 dues-paying members, but its leadership for decades was dominated by a core of about four dozen prominent white men.[10]

W. S. F. Tatum, T. S. Jackson, and Louis Faulkner each played crucial roles. Jackson was a founding member and served as its president between 1909 and 1911 and then secretary-manager throughout most of the 1920s.

Faulkner served as president in 1920 and remained on the executive board for nearly twenty years. Tatum never formally headed the organization, but for decades he was a dues-paying member who worked very closely with the organization, especially during his mayoral terms. In 1929, his oldest son, West, was elected Chamber of Commerce president. Another son later served as vice president.[11]

Comprised of an elite body of white men—bankers, politicians, businessmen, and the editor of the *Hattiesburg American*—the Hattiesburg Chamber of Commerce exerted influence over virtually every aspect of local life, ranging from municipal expenditures to local elections to media coverage. It was the Chamber of Commerce that convinced Fenwick Peck to rebuild J. J. Newman Lumber in the Hub City after the fires of 1903 and 1908; that helped persuade the Mississippi Normal College board to locate the state's new teacher school in Hattiesburg; that wrote a report advising white employers how to handle the mass departures of black workers in 1917 and 1918; that used personal connections in 1917 to help convince General Leonard Wood to establish an Army training base just outside the city. And it was the Hattiesburg Chamber of Commerce that scrambled to save the city in the mid-1920s when things suddenly took a turn for the worse.[12]

For most of the early migrants, life in Hattiesburg revolved around wages. By 1920, Hattiesburg's manufacturing establishments were paying a combined average of $86,500 per month in wages, approximately one-third of which came from J. J. Newman Lumber. Thousands of workers and their families carved lives out of those wages. Wages paid for coffee, milk, flour, sugar, coats, shoes, and coal. Wages provided for church donations, doctor visits, haircuts, and clean laundry. Wages bought Coca-Colas, ice cream floats, hats, and stationery. Perhaps most importantly, wages funded the unforgettable moments that enriched their working-class lives—weddings, anniversaries, graduations, vacations, and the births of their children. Most people in Hattiesburg did not have much, but whatever they did have was provided by those wages. Earned hour-by-hour and day-after-day, the wages of the New South were a foundation, a promise, even an identity. But then something went horribly wrong.[13]

On January 2, 1924, officials at the Hattiesburg J. J. Newman Lumber Company sawmill announced the termination of the third shift, meaning hundreds of layoffs and the reduction of the company's payroll by about a third. Newman was not alone. Other mills experienced similar layoffs or closed entirely, leading to a decline of wages and commercial activity that started pulling Hattiesburg's economy into a downward spiral.[14]

The origins of Hattiesburg's recession were far less complex than that of the major recession that eventually affected the rest of the United States. As one resident later explained, "We would have had a depression here in the late 1920s [even] if all of the rest of the world had been prosperous." Hattiesburgers could find the roots of their economic woes in the areas just outside the city. All they had to do was take a walk in the woods. Vast swaths of the forest were simply gone.[15]

There had been prior warnings. As early as 1903, an official for the Gulf & Ship Island Railroad told the *Wall Street Journal*, "The forests are being rapidly destroyed and a period will soon be reached when the operation of the road will be unprofitable." Three years later, the conservationist Gifford Pinchot stood with National Lumber Manufacturers' Association president N. W. McLeod and cautioned American lumbermen that "there is less than twenty years supply of Yellow Pine in the South." President Theodore Roosevelt, among many others, also chimed in. "If the present rate of forest destruction is allowed to continue," Roosevelt warned the American Forest Congress in 1905, "a timber famine is obviously inevitable." Some Southern lumber firms did practice conservation. Near the turn of the century, a group of Alabama lumbermen proposed minimum price scales to ensure fair competition and to encourage conservation, and more than three hundred sawmills in Georgia, Florida, and South Carolina agreed to run at two-thirds capacity.[16]

But there was little conservation in southern Mississippi. Most of the Northern lumbermen who came to Mississippi tore through the Piney Woods with the discretion of a lawnmower. Trees that had survived untouched for hundreds of years were chopped down or bled for their sap. Lumber railroads used large cranes known as skidders to pull fallen timbers through the forest like dragnets, trampling young saplings in their path. The railroads ensured access to every patch of forest, and steam technology offered unprecedented levels of production.[17]

The sawmills harvested lumber at astonishing rates. At its height, the J. J. Newman Lumber Company produced approximately 200 million board feet of lumber per year. To put that into perspective, 200 million board feet is enough timber to erect a three-foot-tall wooden fence around the entire coastline of the United States of America, including Alaska and Hawaii. And that was merely one year in one sawmill. J. J. Newman was Mississippi's most productive sawmill, but by 1910, the state had over sixteen hundred others. Between 1905 and 1925, those sawmills produced more than forty-five billion board feet of lumber. At some point, they were simply bound to run out of trees.[18]

New trees could be planted, but virgin forests like the one Captain Hardy traversed in the summer of 1880 are irreplaceable. Even if the sawmill companies had immediately begun planting trees (which they did not), it would have taken a hundred years or more for the new trees to grow as large as the ones they cut down. According to a 1929 study conducted by the Mississippi State Forestry Commission, an eighty-year-old longleaf pine forest can produce up to 33,500 board feet per acre. At forty years old, a forest can produce about 11,000 board feet per acre. At twenty, the potential productivity plummets to approximately 1,000 board feet per acre. In describing the old forest, one resident remembered, "When I was a boy it wasn't anything unusual to see a log that was six feet in diameter, or eight feet, or something like that." To this day, the people of the Mississippi Piney Woods have never again seen longleaf pines that size.[19]

By 1930, Mississippi's original longleaf pine forest had been reduced from 11.7 million to 2.6 million acres. One of the last great forests east of the Mississippi River, the Mississippi Piney Woods had essentially been destroyed in just over three decades. Lumber production rapidly declined. In 1925, Mississippi's lumber industry produced more than 3.1 billion board feet. By 1932, that figure dropped to roughly 531 million feet—an 83 percent decrease in only seven years.[20]

Ultimately, Northern lumbermen like Fenwick Peck cared little about the Mississippi Piney Woods or the sustainability of its forests. Peck owned sawmills in three other states. When the trees were felled, he was prepared to simply move on to the next forest. It was a classic case of cut-out and get-out, a cruel but common tactic that left behind heartbroken communities and destroyed forests across America. "When the timber was gone," Hattiesburg native Buck Wells bitterly remembered, "they folded up their carpetbags and left." For the sawmill workers of the Piney Woods, a way of life hung in the balance.[21]

In 1923, workers at Hattiesburg's J. J. Newman Lumber sawmill earned nearly $360,000 in wages. When the layoffs went into effect the following year, the payroll dropped to just over $236,000. This payroll remained about the same for the next five years, but by 1930, it was clear to virtually everyone that the mill would soon cut out. In 1929, T. S. Jackson predicted that "the Newman Lumber Company at Hattiesburg has only about two and one-half years cut." "We will have a thousand men seeking employment," Jackson warned his colleagues. The final years at J. J. Newman Lumber were characterized by declining hours and widespread layoffs. Many of the employees who were lucky enough to keep their jobs were forced to travel up to fifty miles to work. But even these unsteady arrangements lasted only a few years. In 1935, after forty-one years of operation, J. J. Newman Lumber shut its doors for good.[22]

There was a time in early Hattiesburg history when up to one-fourth of the city's population either worked at J. J. Newman Lumber or lived with someone who did. As one local historian noted, for some Hattiesburg boys, "working for the Newman Lumber Company had been ordained from childhood." That opportunity was never again to be. And Newman was just one example. Layoffs occurred in every sawmill, and many closed. In a short span of time, the nearby firms of Ferguson Lumber, James Hand Lumber, Helen White Lumber, Love Lumber, Nortac Manufacturing, Red Creek Lumber, and the Major-Sowers Saw Mill Company all ceased production. Precise employment figures for each mill are unavailable, but the closing of Major-Sowers alone cost Hattiesburg approximately three hundred jobs. Even Tatum Lumber would eventually cut out, leaving about four hundred men with no work. In Hattiesburg, the closing of the mills signified the start of the Great Depression. "They cut all the timber," remembered Henry Watson, the son of a J. J. Newman employee. "That brought the Depression, that made a depression. There wasn't nothing else for nobody to do. It just wasn't no more jobs."[23]

The timber decline affected virtually every other industry, especially the logging railroads, which were also hurt by the emergence of automobiles. Rapidly losing revenue, the Gulf & Ship Island Railroad sold out to the Illinois Central in 1925. The Mississippi Central Railroad, whose annual lumber freight declined from over 500,000 tons in 1925 to less than 175,000 tons by 1931, laid off hundreds of workers and ended passenger service on some existing routes. Dozens of other timber-related companies laid off their workers or closed for good. The closing of the Hattiesburg Veneer Plant left behind $75,000 in lost payroll. The layoffs affected almost every local business. Merchants who had for years depended on sawmill workers as customers suddenly found their revenues slashed.[24]

As the 1920s wore on, signs of the oncoming depression could be seen across Hattiesburg. Jobless men from nearby lumber towns began entering the Hub City, camping under railroad bridges and begging for food at people's back doors. According to the son of a local attorney, some doctors and lawyers were forced to begin accepting "potatoes and hams and turnip greens" in exchange for medical and legal services. Downtown stores that had operated for decades held liquidation sales and closed for good. The Hotel Hattiesburg, for decades the city's finest guesthouse and restaurant, was hit by a string of robberies and ultimately defaulted on its taxes in the late 1920s. The Hub City even lost its semi-pro baseball team, the Pinetoppers, whose owners moved the club to Baton Rouge when they could not meet payroll because of declining attendance. In one of the cruelest incidents of the era, the body of a dead white infant was discovered floating amid piles of wood in Gordon's Creek during the fall of 1928. A coroner's report revealed that the poor child's head had been crushed before the body was dumped into the creek. The murder was not necessarily related to the recession, but it was impossible to ignore the context. Tragedies mounted as the promises of the New South came undone.[25]

The Chamber of Commerce mobilized to save Hattiesburg. The worst of the sawmill layoffs would not come until the 1930s, but by the close of the 1920s, it was clear that if the town were to survive, it needed to replace the declining number of jobs in the lumber industry. "Unless Hattiesburg brings new industrial plants, new capital, more payrolls, increasing your taxable values, the result is sure," T. S. Jackson warned his Chamber of Commerce colleagues. "Hattiesburg, the city that you love so well, will no longer be prosperous, but will decline from year to year until we will be like unto a deserted saw mill town."[26]

Such a solution would require outside help. Although the Chamber of Commerce was composed of Hattiesburg's wealthiest white citizens, this group did not possess the capital to establish new industries on its own. "There are few business men in Hattiesburg who are clear of debt," explained one local banker. "We do not possess wealthy citizens." Like the previous generation of white developers operating in southern Mississippi, this group also desperately needed the help of Yankees.[27]

Not all the news was bad. There were a few promising recent developments. As lumber production declined, a small number of innovative companies began finding new ways to produce timber products. By the late 1920s, Hattiesburg's manufacturing community had added several newer companies, including a creosoting plant, a pine felt plant, and several sawmills that converted production to naval stores.[28]

The Hercules Powder Company was the largest and most important of these new manufacturers. A Delaware-based chemical firm that opened a large factory in Hattiesburg in 1923, Hercules actually benefitted from the destruction of the Mississippi Piney Woods. They were most interested in Mississippi's tree stumps. The company helped pioneer a steam-solvent process that produced turpentine by collecting and distilling the vapor from leftover sap found in the stumps. "You could see for yourself that literally billions of old stumps were available," explained a company official of the region's appeal. Hercules purchased cut-over land from J. J. Newman Lumber for as little as 75¢ an acre and established a new plant about a mile from downtown Hattiesburg. The company employed over four hundred workers through much of the Great Depression.[29]

The new firms offered some jobs but had a fairly limited effect on the local economy. Their combined workforces never approached the number of people once employed at J. J. Newman Lumber, let alone the total number of other laid-off sawmill employees. Moreover, their impact was also stymied by an expanding labor pool. As dozens of sawmills cut out across the Mississippi Piney Woods, thousands of laid-off workers poured into Hattiesburg from dying lumber towns across the region. Hattiesburg's population expanded by more than 40 percent during the 1920s. The Hattiesburg Chamber of Commerce sought to not only replace the lost sawmill jobs but to add as many new positions as possible to help meet the growing demand for work.[30]

Seeking to attract external investors, the Chamber of Commerce worked to promote the desirability of the region and its population. The organization formed a publicity committee that spent $750 to publish fifteen thousand copies of a sixteen-page pamphlet titled "Introducing Hattiesburg: 'The Hub' of South Mississippi," which was mailed to businesses and municipal leaders across the United States. Dedicated to "disseminating plain facts," the publication outlined Hattiesburg's merits as a potential site for new industries. The brochure highlighted Hattiesburg's strategic geography and climate and showcased the local workers, schools, railroad lines, highways, retail stores, and churches. Each description was accompanied by a serene image depicting life in Hattiesburg.[31]

Hercules Powder Company. (McCain Library and Archives, University of Southern Mississippi)

The Chamber of Commerce formed a bevy of committees to execute its mission. Along with the publicity committee, other committees included municipal affairs, industrial affairs, county affairs, mercantile, agricultural, airport, conventions, building, canning plant, local finance, federal soldiers home, and the brick, tile, and pottery factory committee—each charged with formulating proposals to solicit external investment capital. Various other impromptu committees were formed to work with specific companies. And several additional ad hoc committees hosted visiting potential investors or traveled to special events such as industry or trade conventions.[32]

From afar, the early Chamber of Commerce committee work appears both desperate and dull. The organization's records are filled with dozens of far-reaching proposals and unsolicited correspondence, including an initiative to persuade Detroit automaker Henry Ford to establish a vocational training school in Hattiesburg; an effort to convince a Navy official that Hattiesburg would be an ideal location for a naval air base; a proposal for a federally funded narcotics farm; a political lobbying campaign designed to convince the state legislature to appropriate $950,000 for new facilities at the state normal college; and a series of schemes aimed at securing new industries such as a silk-weaving plant, a hosiery manufacturer, and a garment factory. None of these came to fruition. At best, they were overly ambitious. At worst, they resembled begging.[33]

The most desperate appeal of the era came from F. W. Foote, president of the Hattiesburg First National Bank. During an effort to raise capital to subsidize a new factory, Foote decided to ask J. J. Newman Lumber Company president Fenwick Peck to invest $3,000. To ensure the appropriateness of such a request, Foote asked Louis Faulkner to review his appeal to Peck. Faulkner, by then a high-ranking employee of Peck's Mississippi Central Railroad, was as well positioned as any Hattiesburg resident to correspond with Peck. The two men regularly exchanged letters and even Christmas gifts; in fact, Faulkner had received Peck's Christmas gifts of a pair of neckties just a few weeks prior to Foote's request. With Faulkner's blessing, Foote submitted his request to Peck, confessing, "It is always embarrassing to me to be appointed to call on friends for money." There is no record of Peck's reply, but he appears to have chafed at the request, even going so far as to scold Hub City residents during his annual trip to Hattiesburg the following year for what he perceived to be a lack of local initiative. "The great trouble with people in south Mississippi," Peck chided a local audience, "is that they sit around on a gallery and say what ought to be done without showing any disposition to do it."[34]

The Hattiesburg Chamber of Commerce did try to achieve some things on its own. Most visibly, it worked hard to inject the city with a sense of optimism. The editor of the *Hattiesburg American*, himself a dues-paying member of the Chamber of Commerce, invited his colleagues to contribute reassuring updates about the organization's program for economic recovery. Even in the midst of the recession, locals on almost any day could pick up a copy of the *Hattiesburg American* and find encouraging stories about the city's bright future.[35]

The most concerted attempt at optimism occurred in 1928, when the Chamber of Commerce helped publish a special "Club and Achievement Edition" of the *Hattiesburg American*. With the headline "City and County Move toward Destiny of Greatness," the issue fondly retold the story of Hattiesburg's emergence from a "struggling village" to a "rapidly growing industrial center." Dozens of feature articles invoked the "dream" of Captain William Harris Hardy and his sagacious visions for the future of southern Mississippi. T. S. Jackson composed a special article outlining the contributions of the Chamber of Commerce. Other leading white men contributed pieces on the city's history, growth, and promising future.[36]

That same year, members of the Chamber of Commerce sold municipal bonds to finance the construction of a new downtown hotel. In their minds, this new venture would impress visiting potential investors and help Hattiesburg "become a tourist center." W. S. F. Tatum, several of his children, and Louis Faulkner were all major investors. Opening in 1929, the Forrest Hotel was an impressive nine-story brick tower featuring chevron-and-lozenge molding and four large, open-winged eagles that adorned each corner of the building's top floor. It was indeed a beautiful building, but the hotel did not help boost the local economy in the way the Chamber of Commerce had envisioned. The construction jobs were only temporary, and the hotel did not reach even a 50 percent occupancy rate for its first ten years. During its first five years of operation, the company lost an average of $15,500 per year.[37]

During that same autumn of 1928, W. S. F. Tatum responded to popular demand by announcing his candidacy for mayor of Hattiesburg. Having previously held and then lost reelection to that same office, Tatum ran unopposed. Many locals saw Tatum's own financial success as a model for the entire city. In their view, his rise to prominence from a country-store owner to major industrialist epitomized the ingenuity, resolve, and innovation that Hattiesburg needed if it was to restore its once promising future. "He had the vision to see opportunities and the courage to seize them," the *Hattiesburg American* editorialized. "The story of Mr. Tatum's success . . . points the way to useful achievements to others." Just days after W. S. F. Tatum's victory, his oldest son, West, was elected as the new president of the Chamber of Commerce.[38]

By the time of Tatum's election in December of 1928, the Chamber of Commerce did finally have one promising lead. Since the previous summer, the organization had been engaged in serious talks with an Arkansas firm named the Tuf-Nut Garment Manufacturing Company. Tuf-Nut, which had recently opened branch factories in McComb, Mississippi; Wichita, Texas; and Columbia, Tennessee, was looking to add another plant. The company anticipated that the new factory would employ approximately two hundred people (mostly women) and provide a total annual payroll of "about $120,000." This factory alone could not save Hattiesburg, but at that point, this was the city's most promising proposition. When T. S. Jackson called a meeting to examine the "financial and moral standing" of the Arkansas company, he emphasized to his colleagues that "this is the most important meeting that has been called since I have been secretary of the Chamber of Commerce." After a thorough investigation of the company, including a trip to Little Rock by T. S. Jackson, members of the Hattiesburg Chamber of Commerce decided to proceed with negotiations.[39]

Just three days after Tatum's mayoral victory, Tuf-Nut Garment Manufacturing president R. A. Nelson visited Hattiesburg. Understanding that Hattiesburg was somewhat desperate, the Tuf-Nut president negotiated from a position of strength. According to the *Hattiesburg American*, Nelson "made it clear that he was in Hattiesburg by invitation and not to beg or solicit but to make a business offer."[40]

After meeting with the Chamber of Commerce board of directors, Nelson attended a town-hall meeting at which he presented the company's terms. To locate a new factory in Hattiesburg, Tuf-Nut required the city to raise $75,000 in capital stock subscriptions and procure a two-story brick building of at least 22,500 square feet. Hattiesburg leaders tentatively agreed to the terms. W. S. F. Tatum and his son West vowed to finance the new factory building at an estimated cost of $35,000, and several other prominent white men, including Louis Faulkner, signed pledge cards vowing to help raise $75,000 of capital stock. The stock, they estimated, would provide 7 percent dividends after three to five years.[41]

As Christmas approached, members of the Chamber of Commerce scurried to secure stock subscriptions. Individuals pledged whatever they could afford and urged friends and neighbors to do the same. Four days after R. A. Nelson's visit, a crew of thirty "volunteer stock salesmen" met at the Chamber of Commerce's downtown offices to participate in an organizing session and pep rally before pouring out in a citywide canvassing effort. Each man was armed with a book of $125 stock certificates and backed by the economic and moral pretext that all sales would help save their beloved city.[42]

By December 22, the Chamber of Commerce had secured a reported $40,000 in pledges, more than half the total amount of capital stock required to underwrite the factory. Pleased with their effort, the organization decided to take a Christmas break before making what West Tatum dubbed one "final charge to victory." "The good old 'Hattiesburg Spirit' still lives and wins," he said encouragingly.[43]

But then a dramatic event occurred that threatened to disrupt their entire campaign. On the day after Christmas, amid an epic public-relations campaign to recruit new industries by highlighting the merits of their city, the Hattiesburg Chamber of Commerce suddenly found itself forced to contend with a lynching.

At about midnight on December 26, approximately a dozen white men knocked on the front door of a black man named Emmanuel McCallum. A twenty-eight year-old laborer at a local garage, McCallum lived with his wife Mary and daughter in a small black neighborhood just south of downtown Hattiesburg. Mary answered the door to find the group of white men demanding entrance in the name of the law. She probably knew these men were lying, but she was powerless to deny them entry. The intruders stormed through the house and found McCallum sleeping in his undershorts. They dragged him from the home, pulled him into one of their two cars, and sped off into the night.[44]

Six weeks earlier, Emmanuel McCallum had helped a thirty-eight-year-old white clothing merchant named William D. Easterling pull a car out of a ditch. Easterling, who hailed from a long legacy of farmers, had been one of the ambitious white migrants who left behind a life on the farm to pursue opportunity in the Hub City. He had arrived in Hattiesburg during the lumber boom and opened a successful downtown clothing shop. The business had done well, enabling Easterling to purchase a modest home in one of Hattiesburg's middle-class white neighborhoods. By the time of his roadside encounter with McCallum, Easterling had owned the store for more than eleven years.[45]

The precise details of this roadside exchange are unavailable, but the interaction led to some type of conflict, probably related to payment, that ultimately resulted in the black man striking the white man. Easterling reported the incident to the local sheriff, and McCallum was arrested. But then Easterling refused to press charges, resulting in the eventual release of McCallum. The black man left town for a few days to let tensions calm before eventually returning to his job at a garage on Main Street.[46]

Over the next several weeks, Easterling began harassing the black mechanic. He twice appeared at the Main Street garage, where he tried to convince McCallum's white boss to let him take custody of the black employee. On another occasion, he and an unidentified group of white men arrived on McCallum's doorstep only to be rebuffed by a collection of black men waiting with guns. McCallum appealed to local officials for protection, but the authorities appear not to have taken any steps to ensure his safety. When another group of white men appeared at the McCallum home on the night after Christmas in 1928, there were no black men waiting with guns to drive them away.

The white men drove McCallum to a nearby gravel pit and tied a noose around his neck. They slung the other end of the rope over a low pine-tree branch and began to pull. Of two common methods to kill someone by hanging, this is the least humane. Because McCallum was lifted rather than dropped, the noose did not kill him by instantly breaking his neck, as in jailhouse executions. Instead, McCallum dangled alive from the branch, struggling to breathe as he stared out into the faces of his killers. Losing oxygen, he slipped out of consciousness and then died of asphyxiation.

McCallum's body was found the next morning still hanging from the tree. A group of bystanders gathered to look at the corpse. When a photographer from the *Hattiesburg American* arrived to snap a picture, someone in the crowd reportedly said, "It ought to be against the law to take pictures of anything like that." A local law enforcement official joked, "He's a good nigger now." Later that day, a coroner's jury visited the scene of the lynching and returned a verdict of "death at the hands of parties unknown."[47]

Two days after the lynching, the Hattiesburg Chamber of Commerce called an emergency meeting of local citizens to address the murder. A downtown auditorium swelled with "between 125 and 150" of the city's most "honest, law-abiding, God-fearing, determined men," reported the *Hattiesburg American*. A group of local white ministers condemned the killing. The all-white Hattiesburg Ministers Association issued a statement reading, "The Christian sensibilities of our community have been outraged by an atrocious murder disguised as a lynching." Reverend Joseph Smith of the Main Street Baptist Church demanded justice. "I am painfully tired of these perfunctory verdicts of coroners' juries," he said. "I want the cowardly, cringing, white-livered, yellow-blooded scoundrels arrested and convicted."[48]

The Chamber of Commerce resolved to act. Well-versed in committee work, the organization formed a special committee to respond to the lynching. Louis Faulkner was selected to serve as its chairman. The committee passed a series of six resolutions, including an official condemnation of the act, a formal recording of the town's "sense of shame," a pledge to underwrite "the expenditure of any funds necessary for the apprehension and conviction of the guilty parties," and a call for a special grand jury investigation. These resolutions were published in the *Hattiesburg American*, and copies were sent to various city leaders and to Mississippi governor Theodore Bilbo, a notorious white supremacist who routinely defended the practice of lynching throughout his political career. (There is no record of his response.) The Chamber of Commerce also began collecting donations to pay for McCallum's funeral. Then they announced an effort to raise a reward of several thousand dollars for information leading to the "apprehension and conviction" of the men who killed Emmanuel McCallum.[49]

By the late 1920s, anti-lynching sentiment among white civic leaders was not especially unusual. Religious groups, including the YMCA and YWCA, commonly criticized the immorality of mob violence, and even a handful of the state's white politicians condemned the practice. Much of their rhetoric, though, was motivated by national efforts to pass anti-lynching legislation that would expand the jurisdiction of federal investigators to investigate Southern lynchings. If lynching became a federal crime, then white Southern prosecutors, sheriffs, and grand juries would no longer be able to protect participants in lynch mobs by declaring lack of evidence or simply ignoring murders. And because the cases would fall under federal jurisdiction, investigations would be led by federal agents and trials would take place in federal circuit courts as opposed to Southern county courthouses, where all-white juries regularly acquitted murderers despite often overwhelming evidence. Anti-lynching legislation was eventually defeated. But one bill—the Dyer Bill—did pass the House of Representatives, alarming some Southern politicians enough to compel them to speak out against lynching in an effort to curb mob rule and thereby limit the need for federal intervention.[50]

The Hattiesburg Chamber of Commerce, however, had other concerns. Emmanuel McCallum was the fourth man to be lynched in Hattiesburg during the 1920s, but none of the earlier murders had drawn such a widespread public response. Regardless of any personal attitudes toward lynching, Chamber of Commerce leaders worried about how their city's image would affect their pursuit of external capital. By the end of 1928, Hattiesburg's leaders understood that potential investors did not want to send executives, products, and capital to unstable communities susceptible to mob rule. Nor did potential investors want to hire murderers to run their new factories. From the perspective of the Chamber of Commerce, lynching was simply bad for business.

Prominent members of the Hattiesburg Chamber of Commerce explained how the murder negatively affected their efforts to save the Hub City. "I have told interested people that they would find the Hub City as educational center, a cultural center, a moral, law-abiding community," T. S. Jackson lamented. "This terrible crime has upset everything the Chamber of Commerce has done for the last five years." Louis Faulkner echoed a similar sentiment. "We might as well cease all stockraising efforts, stop our work to build a bigger Hattiesburg," Faulkner said, "unless we can build a better Hattiesburg and make this town safe." A *Hattiesburg American* editorial reinforced the concern: "Recognition of the fact that law and order is the primary requirement of community life means that as Hattiesburg's Chamber of Commerce seeks for new factories, it also seeks to strengthen the moral fibre of the community." "Commercial growth and moral advancement," the paper stressed, "go hand in hand."[51]

Hattiesburg judge Robert S. Hall answered the Chamber of Commerce call for a special grand jury investigation. At that time in Mississippi, grand juries were still used to investigate unsolved crimes or public complaints. West Tatum, just days away from assuming the presidency of the Chamber of Commerce, was appointed foreman of the grand jury. Members of the grand jury spent four days poring over evidence and interviewing forty-two witnesses in their search to uncover the identity of the "parties unknown."[52]

These responses drew a great deal of attention in the national media. Mississippi was infamous for its racial violence, and many outsiders viewed these actions as promising signs of a possible decline of lynchings in the Magnolia State. An Associated Press story about the promised reward for information leading to conviction was carried in dozens of newspapers across the country. Other coverage highlighting the efforts of the Hattiesburg Chamber of Commerce appeared in major media outlets such as the *New York Times*, the *Los Angeles Times*, the *Washington Post*, the *Atlanta Constitution*, and African American newspapers in Chicago, Baltimore, Indianapolis, Pittsburgh, Philadelphia, and New Orleans. In a special editorial, the *New York Times* highlighted a segment from a *Hattiesburg American* editorial and praised local residents for "beginning to take up that State's lynching habit from an angle typical of the age in which we live." Even the *Chicago Defender*, one of the nation's boldest critics of white Southerners, applauded the effort in Hattiesburg. "Time was when Mississippi led America in the drive for the yearly lynch record and was proud of it," editorialized the *Defender*. "It is inspiring to see those same white people up in arms and obviously serious about catching the persons responsible. Mississippi may be making progress toward civilization after all."[53]

Locally, the *Hattiesburg American* similarly praised the grand jury investigation. On January 10, it ran the headline "Grand Jurors Condemn M'Callum Lynchers" and celebrated West Tatum as a "worthy successor" to the presidency of the Chamber of Commerce. Judge Hall congratulated members of the grand jury for their efforts, telling them, "your searching investigation will make lynchers think twice before they take a human life and will go a long way toward checking mob violence in this part of the state." The *Hattiesburg American* concluded that "the mass meeting of outraged citizens, the strong charge of Judge Hall, the searching and determined investigation of the grand jury and its stinging condemnation of this lynching—all these mark important steps in the molding of an overpowering public sentiment against mob murders."[54]

But they did not take the final and most important step. No one was ever indicted for the murder of Emmanuel McCallum, a fact that reveals a sobering incongruity between public sentiment and legal action. At least one suspect could have been identified without question. Mounds of evidence pointed to the involvement of William Easterling. Testimonies provided by Hattiesburg sheriff Bud Gray and McCallum's employer Charlie Ross offered a clear motive and indicated at least three separate incidents in which Easterling had tried to abduct Emmanuel McCallum. Yet Easterling was neither arrested nor charged.[55]

It is also worth scrutinizing the role of the Chamber of Commerce, especially the organization's purported reward for the "apprehension and conviction" of the killers. At least one media outlet reported that the organization was prepared to offer a reward as high as $20,000. Such an amount is preposterous. In fact, it is extremely doubtful that the organization ever intended to issue any reward at all. Even if it wanted to, the Chamber of Commerce simply did not have the money. One member pledged $1,000, but a closer look at the organization's records reveals that it was broke. When the reward was offered, the organization had less than $130 in its bank account, the same account it had overdrawn by $100 the year before. And even if it could have somehow miraculously raised several thousand dollars in a week, the possibility that the Chamber of Commerce would have used this money as a reward in a murder case, especially in the middle of its efforts to raise money for Tuf-Nut capital stock, is unimaginable, as is the chance that it would ever have handed over such a large reward to a black informant, should one have come forward. In the end, the Hattiesburg Chamber of Commerce was far more concerned with appearances than justice.[56]

But the murder did carry some consequences for one of its likely perpetrators. Although William Easterling never faced a murder charge, his role in the McCallum lynching appears to have dramatically altered his life. Within days of the grand jury investigation, Easterling suddenly sold the clothing store that he had owned for over eleven years. Little is known about the details of the sale, but the timing certainly suggests a connection to the murder. The sale was announced in a front page story in the *Hattiesburg American*, which reminded readers of Easterling's initial dispute with McCallum. The story also reported that Easterling was leaving Hattiesburg for good. This turned out to be inaccurate; though he may have left for a brief period, Easterling soon returned to Hattiesburg, where he lived until his death in 1971. He worked a variety of jobs over the following years, but he never again owned his own store. That part of his life was over.[57]

On the day before Easterling sold his store, the *Hattiesburg American* announced the return of Tuf-Nut president R. A. Nelson. The Chamber of Commerce had completed its stock-raising effort soon after the New Year and was ready to sign a deal with the company. By mid-January, everything seemed in place. During the visit, Nelson and Mayor W. S. F. Tatum visited prospective sites for the new Tuf-Nut factory. On January 16, the *Hattiesburg American* told readers that the factory would open within three months. Nelson did not sign the final agreement during this trip, but the *American* assured readers that he would return "in about 10 days, when formal commitments will be signed."[58]

But Nelson never did return, and Hattiesburg never got its new Tuf-Nut factory. After stringing the city along over the ensuing weeks and months, Tuf-Nut informed the Chamber of Commerce in April it was no longer interested in establishing a new factory in Hattiesburg. Company officials explained that they were concerned about expanding too quickly and had decided to slow down. It is unknown if any other factors affected their decision. In any case, the Hattiesburg Chamber of Commerce had failed in its first serious attempt to attract a major new employer.[59]

Regardless of the reasons behind Tuf-Nut's retreat, the local reaction to the McCallum murder offers two important lessons related to the future of the relationship between economic development and racial violence in Hattiesburg. First, the local response to the lynching clearly demonstrated an awareness of outside perception and an understanding that racial violence could undermine efforts to attract jobs. Second, although some white citizens would have sympathized with Easterling's actions, virtually all local white residents would have come to understand that such acts of violence that threatened to put "a stain upon the fair name of Forrest County," as the grand jury concluded, could jeopardize their own standing in the community. Although Easterling was never indicted, his financial fate did serve as a clear deterrent for any citizen, especially businessmen, who did not want to risk social and or financial ostracism for their role in a lynching.[60]

The lynching of Emmanuel McCallum was the last of its kind in Hattiesburg. Other African Americans were later murdered by white assailants, and in the late 1960s, a black civil rights leader was assassinated by a group of Klansmen, several of whom were later convicted of murder. But the classic form of New South lynching—premeditated and unprosecuted mob-based capital punishment—never again occurred in the Hub City. The ending of this type of lynching in Hattiesburg was not the result of black activism or any type of moral or religious crusade. Nor did it necessarily represent a major alteration to the socioeconomic underpinnings of Jim Crow. Rather, this change was a product of the economic realities facing white Hattiesburg leaders. Although their reaction to the McCallum murder left much to be desired, it also clearly indicated that whites who engaged in the most severe acts of racial violence could face consequences. Offenders might not be imprisoned, but they also could not count on the complete immunity of previous eras.[61]

Little is known about how local African Americans felt about the lynching investigation of Emmanuel McCallum. Over half a century later, Hammond Smith remembered, "They had a big investigation and all this. But they ended up doing nothing." Yet Smith also remembered the McCallum murder as Hattiesburg's "last lynching." The fear of a lynch mob could never be fully dissipated for most African Americans. All black Mississippians grew up hearing stories of lynch mobs. And lynchings did continue in other parts of the state. During the 1930s, fifty African Americans were lynched in Mississippi. Nevertheless, in Hattiesburg, the nature of racial violence had clearly changed since the era when thousand-person mobs gathered to publicly torture and kill black people.[62]

Hattiesburg's next opportunity to secure a major new employer did not come again until the fall of 1932. Just weeks before company officials visited the city, a white man named J. P. Lee shot and killed a black man named Leroy Ward in southern Forrest County. After a short investigation, Lee, a notorious bootlegger, was arrested and charged with murder. During the subsequent trial, Lee's four-man defense team argued that he had killed the black man to defend his wife from an attempted rape. The team contended that Lee was defending white womanhood and "applauded his manhood and chivalry," wrote a *Hattiesburg American* reporter. Toward the end of the trial, Lee's wife even testified that she was actually the one who fired the bullet that killed Leroy Ward.[63]

But the all-white jury did not believe the self-defense argument. Three black men were also allowed to take the stand to testify that they had seen the white man shoot the black victim in cold blood. After deliberating for forty-one hours and twelve minutes, the jury returned a guilty verdict and recommended that the white defendant, Lee, spend the rest of his life in prison for the murder of the black victim, Leroy Ward. (We can be fairly certain that a black man convicted in a similar case would have received the death penalty.)[64]

Just days after the conviction, the *Hattiesburg American* ran an editorial congratulating the city for its commitment to justice across racial lines. "The conviction of JP Lee," the paper editorialized, "constitutes a tribute to the justice and impartiality of the jurors. Every person in Forrest County should be righteously proud of the manner in which justice is being administered."[65] At the national level, the Associated Negro Press ran a bulletin that appeared in African American newspapers across the country: "The verdict of the jury after deliberating some 40 hours came as a surprise to many who yet feel that a white man in this section can kill a Negro without punishment."[66]

Several writers documenting the civil rights era have incorrectly claimed that the first convictions in Mississippi of whites for the murder of blacks occurred during the 1960s. To those scholars and many others, it is inconceivable that such convictions could have happened earlier. Perhaps some rural hamlet somewhere in the state did previously convict a white man of killing a black man, but in all likelihood, J. P. Lee was the first white person convicted of murdering an African American in Mississippi since Reconstruction. This might defy common stereotypes about the absolutism of Mississippi Jim Crow, but the verdict is more understandable when viewed within the context of the 1928 McCallum murder and the city's economic goals. Not all future whites accused of killing African Americans would be convicted. And in this particular case, J. P. Lee's shoddy reputation as a bootlegger surely eased the racial barriers to conviction. But all things considered, J. P. Lee was white, and Leroy Ward was black, meaning that this verdict, as the Associated Negro Press observed, "was history making."[67]

CHAPTER SIX

Those Who Stayed

I'm glad I stayed now, I think. I think I made the right decision.

—Dr. Hammond Smith, 1982

In the fall of 1924, Hammond Smith, Turner and Mamie's second son, returned home for good. Hammond had first left Hattiesburg in 1915 to attend Alcorn Agricultural & Mechanical College, an all-black institution that also offered a residential high school for black youths who came from places like Hattiesburg that had no secondary school for African Americans. Located near the Mississippi River in the town of Lorman, Alcorn sits about 130 miles northwest of Hattiesburg. To get there, Hammond took a train from Hattiesburg to Jackson, where he spent the night before catching another train to the small town of Harriston. From Harriston, he then took a "wagon train" about fifteen miles through the forest to the isolated campus. Distance and cost limited trips home. During Hammond's first two years at Alcorn, the young man was unable to visit his family over Christmas. But he and his older brother, Charles, also a student at Alcorn, did return to Hattiesburg every summer to live with their parents and to earn tuition money by working as general laborers.[1]

Hammond stayed at Alcorn for college. He participated on the debate team and demonstrated a natural talent for both science and English. One professor suggested he become a journalist, but Hammond decided on another path. During his years at Alcorn, Hammond took occasional trips to nearby Natchez, where he shopped at a black-owned drugstore. Hammond was impressed by the druggist and intrigued by the role a black pharmacist could play in an African American community. The position commanded not only a great deal of respect but also the opportunity to become an entrepreneur. "I wanted to get in something where I could go into business for myself," Hammond later explained.[2]

Hammond's ambition was a byproduct of his upbringing. His father had constantly stressed the importance of financial independence to his children. "Don't hire yourself out," Turner frequently told them. "You're not going to get anywhere like that." This philosophy was deeply rooted in Turner's own life experiences. The son of sharecroppers, he understood how unfair labor arrangements with white bosses could hold black families in perpetual debt. Having escaped the sharecropper's life by becoming a teacher, he later found his financial future shackled again, this time by the racially imbalanced budget cuts of post-Reconstruction white Redeemers. Understandably, these experiences led Turner to believe that true liberation required financial independence from white people. As Hammond remembered of his youth, "I had it instilled in me to go in business." As a pharmacist, he could open his own drugstore, thus becoming a respected entrepreneur like the black druggist he admired in Natchez.[3]

Hammond was further motivated to open his own store by an incident involving his younger brother Martin Luther. While shopping at a white-owned Hattiesburg drugstore, Martin Luther once had a nasty exchange with a white pharmacist for allegedly not saying "please" when placing an order. The white man behind the counter chastised the young black customer in a threatening manner. "He thought he was going to have to fight his way out of there," Hammond recalled of the episode. "If they treated him like that, I know they treated others like that." Hammond's motivation was as profound as it was straightforward—black customers at his drugstore would be treated with dignity.[4]

After receiving his bachelor of science degree from Alcorn in 1921, Hammond enrolled in pharmacy school at Meharry Medical College in Nashville, Tennessee. Founded in 1876, Meharry was the second black medical school established in the United States (the first being Howard in Washington, DC). Working nights to pay tuition, Hammond excelled at organic chemistry and physics while also serving as chairman of the auditing committee in the Pharmaceutical Department. He graduated on May 22, 1924, almost a year to the day after his older brother Charles received his medical degree from the same institution. Hammond worked in Meridian for about six months before returning to Hattiesburg later that fall. He was twenty-nine years old.[5]

Shortly after Hammond returned, his father gave him and his brother a little two-story building located in the heart of Mobile Street. Hammond did not know when or how his father had acquired the property, but the purpose aligned with Turner's principles of self-sufficiency and financial independence. The idea was for Hammond to operate a drugstore on the first floor and Charles to see patients on the second. The building was invaluable to each brother's career. Strict racial regulations disqualified them from working in any white-owned drugstore or medical office, and without their own building, there was no guarantee that either could have practiced medicine in their hometown. Without an office of their own, the brothers might have been forced to find another place to work.[6]

In 1925, Hammond bought his first stock of pharmaceuticals on credit and opened Smith's Pharmacy at 606 Mobile Street. Charles started his new practice upstairs. With their education completed and careers established, the Smith brothers entered new phases of their lives. In 1926, Charles married a Mississippi woman named Myrtle and soon started his own family. Two years later, Hammond wed Lucille Trotter, the daughter of a Methodist minister from Meridian. Each son purchased a home on Dewey Street, the same road where their parents lived. Charles and Myrtle lived next door to Turner and Mamie; Hammond and Lucille lived just down the road.[7]

Like many African Americans of his generation, Hammond Smith considered leaving the Jim Crow South. His personal and professional connections would have eased the transition to a new city. In Chicago, Hattiesburg-related black social networks lasted well into the 1960s, even as the "little colony of Mississippians" eventually dispersed throughout the city. (The Chicago-based Hattiesburg Social and Civic Club continued meeting until at least 1966.) Hammond's medical school connections would have offered an extensive professional network—Meharry graduates lived and worked all over the United States—and virtually every American city needed black doctors. Two of Hammond's younger brothers who also became doctors did eventually leave Mississippi for Ohio and California. Hammond himself came close to doing just that; he considered Ohio seriously enough to travel to Columbus to take the state pharmacy licensure exam. But Hammond did not like the cold, and he believed that opportunities existed for him in Hattiesburg. Ultimately, he decided to stay.[8]

While Hammond and Charles were away at school, Hattiesburg's black community underwent several significant changes. Most noteworthy was its growth. After a brief decline during the departures of the late 1910s,

Hattiesburg's black population rapidly expanded once again in the 1920s. Between 1920 and 1930, the city's black population grew by about 40 percent, from 4,937 to 6,811.[9]

Like their predecessors, the new black migrants were pulled to the Hub City by the promise of wage-labor jobs. Sawmill layoffs were on the horizon, but the increased wages that were paid to black sawmill workers in the wake of the departures continued to draw black workers to Hattiesburg. Other wage-labor positions could be found in municipal service jobs, in small local manufacturing companies, and among the city's countless positions typically reserved for black men—general laborer, painter, porter, or deliveryman. Black women's work was less diverse; as in previous eras, nearly all employed black women worked in some type of domestic service.[10]

As the sawmills began to decline, several hundred black workers moved into positions relatively new to Forrest County. The Hercules Powder Company, which opened in 1923, employed up to two hundred African Americans throughout most of the 1920s. Other black workers found jobs in sawmills that were converting to naval stores products. And as Hattiesburg slipped into a recession, a growing number of African Americans began working in agriculture. Large sections of the cutover forest were converted to farmland, leading to an unprecedented number of black agricultural workers in Forrest County by 1930. As before, black jobs tended to be more difficult and lower paying than those held by whites. But not all black workers were completely impoverished. There also existed a growing black middle class of entrepreneurs and professionals. And even some of the black sawmill and railroad employees owned their own homes. By the close of the 1920s, more than 35 percent of black Hattiesburgers were homeowners, a rate unmatched anywhere else in the state.[11]

The influx of black migrants in the early 1920s contributed to the growth of three additional black neighborhoods. The first, a settlement of about two hundred residences, developed near the banks of the Leaf River next to J. J. Newman Lumber. Many referred to the neighborhood as "Newman's Quarters" because of the large proportion of residents who worked at the sawmill. Another black neighborhood of about the same size grew about a mile and a half south of downtown. A third and smaller black community named Palmer's Crossing developed just outside the Hattiesburg city limits. Each of these newer black neighborhoods would continue to expand throughout the 1920s and 1930s, adding their own schools, small business communities, and churches.[12]

Most black life, however, remained concentrated in the Mobile Street District. By the time the Smith brothers returned to Hattiesburg, the black downtown was home to more than 720 black residences and over fifty black businesses, highlighted by a variety of grocery stores, butchers, tailors, barbers, cobblers, boarding houses, and cleaners. By 1925, the black downtown also included a black dentist, a black jeweler, a black life insurance company, and a black funeral home. When Hammond and Charles returned, the neighborhood already had two black-owned drugstores and doctor's offices, meaning that the Smith brothers were the third African Americans in each of their professions to open shop in the Mobile Street District. With a ratio of one black doctor for every 2,270 citizens in 1930, Hattiesburg's black community exceeded the national average of 3,125 and was significantly better than Mississippi's total ratio of 14,221 African Americans for every black doctor.[13]

Along with a growing number of black churches, professional organizations, social clubs, and Masonic lodges, the Mobile Street District had by then also added a vital new community institution—the Eureka High School. Built by a citywide bond passed in 1920, Eureka High School was constructed over the site of the old dilapidated wooden building where the Smith family children first attended school. The new two-story brick structure featured electric lights, a heating system, washrooms, an auditorium, and a domestic science annex. The new school sat on the corner of Sixth and New Orleans Streets, just a block away from the heart of the Mobile Street business district.[14]

Eureka provided a new generation of local black students with the best educational opportunities anyone in their family had ever experienced. For a black school in 1920s Mississippi, Eureka offered an impressive curriculum that included English, African American and American history, Latin, geography, algebra, biology, chemistry, and home economics. The vast majority of students did not finish high school (Eureka's early graduating classes were as small as fourteen), but while enrolled, black youths enjoyed the support of a cadre of dedicated teachers who worked hard to provide one of the best secondary educations available to black Mississippians. Several of Eureka's early graduates matriculated at colleges such as Alcorn or Tougaloo. Nathaniel Burger, class of 1928, earned a master's degree at Cornell University and returned in 1940 to serve as principal of his alma mater.[15]

Eureka's academic curriculum represented merely a sliver of the institution's broad contributions to the local black community. The school's new auditorium immediately became an important site for communal gatherings. Throughout the 1920s, thousands of black residents of all ages poured into Eureka for a wide range of community events, such as organizational meetings, choir concerts, and church services. Some of the South's leading black preachers and educators visited Eureka to deliver sermons and lectures on such topics as "Evolution or Devilution" and "The Comparison of the American Negro's Progress with the Other Colored Races of the World." Eureka also hosted an annual summer institute for black Mississippi teachers and several annual meetings of statewide black fraternal and professional organizations. Local African Americans also used the building to house a community library and to host movie nights. Musical concerts were the most popular events at Eureka. In addition to the school's own glee club, Eureka frequently welcomed traveling black choirs from across the South. On three separate occasions during the 1920s, the auditorium hosted the world-famous Williams Jubilee Singers of Holly Springs, Mississippi. Several concerts even attracted local white residents, who sat in a segregated section of the auditorium. Mrs. West Tatum, the wife of W. S. F. Tatum's oldest son, encouraged white citizens to attend concerts at Eureka. "The conduct of the students is remarkably good," she told an interviewer in 1925, "and would be a lesson to many of the white students."[16]

Many programs at Eureka were chronicled in the pages of the *Hattiesburg American*, which by the 1920s had begun integrating updates from the Mobile Street District into local news coverage. But even this unprecedented attention offered mixed results. News from the black community was almost always relegated to back pages and did not typically include any discussion of the social lives or achievements of African Americans. Rather, stories about the black community focused almost exclusively on efforts to improve African American morality or health, which suggests that much of the news from the Mobile Street District was actually written for the benefit of white readers who were concerned about the behavior of the black men and women who shared their city. Nonetheless, positive stories from the black community represented a major change from previous eras when African Americans only appeared in the local press as victims or criminals. Beginning in 1926, one local black merchant was even allowed to start placing ads in the *Hattiesburg American*.[17]

Despite some positive alterations in the social fabric, racial disparities proliferated, even in the brightest spots of black life. Though Eureka High School was one of the best black schools in Mississippi, its facilities and resources were still vastly inferior to those of the local white high school. In fact, part of the money allocated to building the black school was used to purchase secondhand textbooks from the white school, which then used those proceeds to buy new books for white students. Hattiesburg's black teachers earned a fraction of the salaries paid to their white counterparts. During the 1922–1923 school year, the principal and teachers at the white high school earned annual salaries of $2,700 and $1,246, respectively; the black principal and faculty at Eureka were paid $1,000, and $453.[18]

And of course, there was the violence. Lynchings occurred with far less regularity than they had twenty years before, but they were still fairly common in the early 1920s, not ending until the lynching of Emmanuel McCallum in 1928. In 1921, a group of white men abducted a black prisoner named Arthur Jennings from the Hattiesburg jail, hanged him from a tree branch, and then shot his body full of bullets. Two years later, a young man named John Gray was taken from police custody by a group of white men and shot to death in retribution for defending a black woman who was being sexually assaulted by a white man. His body was found abandoned in a ditch, and no one was ever officially questioned or arrested.[19]

Although certainly the most extreme, lynching was just one of the many common acts of racial violence that tainted black life in the Jim Crow South. African Americans were routinely verbally abused, threatened, and assaulted. Any conflict with a white person carried dangerous implications. For school children, walking home through the wrong neighborhood could mean a busted jaw, a blackened eye, or a concussion from an unseen brick. Black women and girls also faced the common threat of sexual assault. At the time, white men in Mississippi were not prosecuted for raping black women, and every black girl had to learn strategies to avoid potentially dangerous situations. One of the great challenges in this endeavor was that the only jobs available to most of them—domestic work—often left them the most vulnerable. Many parents allowed their daughters to work only for white families whom they already knew and trusted or encouraged them to work in an alternative setting to avoid having to enter white people's homes. Still, the nature of Jim Crow ensured that black residents faced great risks almost every day. Black women and their families had little course of action to seek justice for a rape. And black men could be killed for trying to stop sexual assaults—as John Gray's family knew all too well.[20]

In addition to continuities within Jim Crow, the 1920s also saw a disturbing new development—the expansion of the Hattiesburg Ku Klux Klan. This was part of a national trend. Sparked by a rise of post–World War I xenophobia toward Catholic and Jewish immigrants and Northern anti-black sentiment following the Great Migration, the Ku Klux Klan experienced a major revival in the 1920s. Many Klan members were also motivated by what they perceived to be a decline in American morals during the Roaring Twenties and joined the organization to help promote and police civic and religious morality. Unlike the Reconstruction-era Klan, this new version existed in virtually every corner of the United States and even some parts of Canada. With a membership estimated to be as high as five million, the Klan of this era was more organized, better funded, and much larger than previous incarnations.[21]

In Southern cities like Hattiesburg, Klan members were also heavily influenced by the immensely popular film *Birth of a Nation*. The highest-grossing motion picture to that point in American history, *Birth of a Nation* depicted the original Reconstruction-era Ku Klux Klan as the heroic saviors of Southern white society from the terrors of Reconstruction, a message that closely aligned with core concepts of the Lost Cause that white Southerners had been promoting for decades. When *Birth of a Nation* opened in Hattiesburg in 1916, a *Hattiesburg News* editorial read, "Every student at the Normal College; every girl at the Woman's College; every pupil of the high grade schools of the city; every young man and young woman in Forrest County ought to see that show. . . . They can learn more in those three hours from looking at that panorama of the Civil War than they get from any book." The paper concluded, "It is the greatest play ever put upon the screen."[22]

Inspired by Klan nostalgia and the call of civic duty, hundreds of white Hattiesburgers joined the White Knights. By December of 1923, the white supremacist organization claimed over five hundred members. The Hattiesburg Klan left behind very few organizational records, but the nature of other Southern branches suggests that the local Klan would have drawn its membership from church congregations and white Masonic lodges. It could also be expected that dues-paying members would have included predominately middle-class white men—including businessmen, politicians, and clergy—as well as ladies auxiliary branches. In Hattiesburg, the Klan also had a junior division that offered free membership to teenage boys.[23]

As in the rest of the country, Hattiesburg's Ku Klux Klan expanded its targets beyond African Americans to include immigrants, communists, feminists, homosexuals, and virtually anyone who did not adhere to their deeply conservative values. The Hattiesburg Klan targeted anyone it deemed a criminal or moral deviant, including bootleggers, cheating spouses, and even people who left their animals out in the sun too long. Any white person who stepped out of line could face the Klan's wrath. One young white man who grew up in Hattiesburg during this time remembered once "smooching" with a girl in a park when "all of a sudden two of the Ku Klux Klan stuck their heads in my automobile and wanted to know what I was doing." The most extreme example of Klan violence toward whites occurred in the summer of 1921, when a group of seventy-five masked Hattiesburg men abducted and lynched a white man who had been convicted of murder.[24]

Throughout the 1920s, the Hattiesburg Klan openly published editorials and advertisements in the *Hattiesburg American* and held public initiation ceremonies at downtown parks. At one such event, they charged one dollar admission and raffled off a new Studebaker. Other typical Klan activities included speaking in churches, marching downtown in full regalia, posting warning signs against bad behavior, protesting racy films, chartering special trains to attend regional Klan rallies, and leading various public events, such as the 1923 flag dedication ceremony at the all-white Main Street High School. The organization enjoyed such widespread public acceptance that in 1924, the sheriff of Forrest County deputized local Klansmen to investigate bootlegging in the Mobile Street District. This brand of Klansmen did not need sheets; they had badges. One can only imagine the terror among African Americans created by such widespread acceptance and public visibility of the white supremacist terrorist organization.[25]

Soon after the Smith brothers returned to Hattiesburg, they joined an organization named the Hattiesburg Negro Business League, the local branch of the National Negro Business League. Established by Booker T. Washington in 1900, the National Negro Business League was founded to advance black commercial development by cultivating a vast network of

America's leading black businessmen. Under Washington's guidance, the organization spread into nearly every black enclave in the United States. By the time Washington died in November of 1915, the National Negro Business League included more than six hundred branches and between forty thousand and fifty thousand members.[26]

The National Negro Business League remained active well after Washington's death. During the 1920s, its annual meetings continued to draw hundreds of African Americans from across the county, including influential figures such as Washington disciples Emmett Scot and Robert Moton, North Carolina–based insurance magnate Charles Clinton Spaulding, *Chicago Defender* publisher Robert Abbott, Brotherhood of Sleeping Car Porters president A. Philip Randolph, and the nationally known black educator Mary McLeod Bethune. Attendance and membership began to decline later in the decade, but the league continued for years to provide a major forum for America's leading black business leaders.[27]

Perhaps the organization's most important function, however, was its role in developing subsidiary groups such as the National Negro Insurance Association, the National Negro Bankers Association, the National Negro Finance Corporation, the Associated Negro Press, and hundreds of city and state divisions, including the Hattiesburg Negro Business League, one of twelve branches of the Mississippi Negro Business League. Led by Charles Banks of Mound Bayou, a banker whom Booker T. Washington once called "the most influential negro business man in the United States," the Mississippi Negro Business League held its own additional meetings in rotating locations across the state.[28]

When the Smith brothers joined, the Hattiesburg Negro Business League was led by a man named Gaither Hardaway. Born near Enterprise, Mississippi, in 1878, Hardaway arrived in Hattiesburg near the turn of the century to work in one of the local sawmills. He first appears in local records in the 1900 census as a twenty-one-year-old sawmill worker living in a little rented home with six other African Americans. Hardaway's job at the time would have required long hours and paid him very little, but for a man of his race in that time and place, he would go on from there to great success.[29]

Within a few years of moving to Hattiesburg, Hardaway married a woman named Minnie and moved in with her and her father. Soon thereafter, he decided to leave his sawmill position to explore other options in the city's growing black business district. Hardaway worked a few odd jobs before taking a position in a barbershop on Mobile Street. A few years later, he took over the barbershop of Timothy Thigpen (the local black newspaper man and Booker T. Washington supporter) when Thigpen migrated to Chicago. Hardaway operated his shop at 417 Mobile Street over the next few years. He even briefly lived in the shop during the months between Minnie's death and his marriage to his second wife, Lillie.[30]

Sometime between 1918 and 1920, Hardaway sold his barbershop to purchase a grocery store on the corner of Seventh and Mobile Streets. Business took off in the early 1920s as the city's black neighborhood experienced a new phase of rapid growth. Eventually known simply as "the Groceryman," Hardaway enjoyed a prime location in the heart of Mobile Street and created a broad customer base by offering a free delivery service. His success enabled him to buy a new home and a small office building adjacent to his store. It was he who in 1926 became the first local black merchant to begin regularly placing advertisements in the *Hattiesburg American*.[31]

Like many local business owners, black or white, Hardaway parlayed entrepreneurial success into civic leadership. In addition to serving as president of the Hattiesburg Negro Business League, Hardaway was a member of the executive committee of the National Negro Business League, a deacon at the Mt. Carmel Baptist Church, a grand almoner in the Order of the Eastern Star Freemasonry lodge, chairman of the Colored Auxiliary of the local Red Cross, chairman of the Colored Committee of the local Salvation Army, and Hattiesburg's representative to a statewide black leadership organization known as "The Committee of One Hundred." Formed in Jackson in 1924, the Committee of One Hundred was composed mostly of black clergy, businessmen, and educators who encouraged racial uplift through morality, religion, civic duty, and the development of black businesses. This organization remained active through the end of World War II and in later years served as a gateway to NAACP membership.[32]

By the late 1920s, members of the Hattiesburg Negro Business League regularly participated in a variety of statewide organizations that helped develop professional and social networks among black leaders across Mississippi. There were numerous examples. Charles Smith belonged to the Mississippi Medical and Surgical Association of Negro Doctors. Hammond Smith joined a preexisting organization of black pharmacists. E. W. Hall, the city's most successful black funeral home director, was a member of the Mississippi Funeral Directors and Embalmers Association. Several local teachers were leading figures in the Mississippi Association of Teachers in Colored Schools, which in 1924 began holding annual summer training programs at Eureka High School. Alongside preexisting fraternal orders and mutual-aid societies, these professional organizations increasingly drew together African American leaders from different communities across Mississippi. Like the Committee of One Hundred, many of their members would later form the vanguard of post–World War II NAACP membership. This was not yet the civil rights movement, but these were the people who developed the institutions and networks that later made possible civil rights activism in Mississippi.[33]

The Hattiesburg Negro Business League essentially operated as the black version of the Chamber of Commerce. Like the all-white Chamber of Commerce, it drew together leaders from different religious denominations into an influential civic organization that guided local black life. With at least fifty members by 1927, the Hattiesburg Negro Business League supported the activities of local churches and schools, conducted annual Christmastime food and clothing drives, led Emancipation Day celebrations each January, organized neighborhood beautification initiatives, and planned countless school fundraisers, health education programs, lectures, and concerts. They even raised money for needy African Americans in other communities. When the Mississippi River flooded in 1927, the Hattiesburg Negro Business League collected cash, food, and clothing to send to displaced African Americans in the Mississippi Delta.[34]

The Hattiesburg Negro Business League also at times successfully solicited financial and material assistance from whites. President Gaither Hardaway was particularly effective in convincing white wholesale grocery companies to donate food and/or cash to the annual Christmastime charity drives. In 1927, Merchants Grocery, Hattiesburg Grocery, and Mohler Brothers Coffee provided a combined forty sacks of corn meal, one hundred pounds of sugar, a barrel of flour, and twenty-five pounds of coffee that were rationed into hundreds of Christmas baskets and distributed to needy black families. On several other occasions, local white merchants gave cash to support causes led by the league. At other times, Hardaway worked with the all-white Lions Club to secure boxes of toys for poor black kids during Christmas. He also led a survey of local black youths that helped convince white YMCA administrators to sponsor a baseball league for black boys. Eventually, Hardaway and his colleagues even convinced white city officials to pave Mobile Street.[35]

Perhaps Hardaway's most intriguing interracial project was conducted through an organization named the Colored Upbuilding League. Headquartered in Hardaway's office, the Colored Upbuilding League launched a program in 1929 to build a training center for black female domestic workers. After convincing a local white realtor to give them a plot of land, the group raised money from white and black benefactors to construct a "model community house" where young black women learned skills such as cooking, cleaning, and sewing. Black women who were trained in the model home then registered with the organization's employment bureau, which helped them find jobs. Although by contemporary standards this effort to usher black women into domestic service was highly questionable, the effort must be considered within the context of 1920s Mississippi, when most black women in Hattiesburg were fated to end up as domestic workers anyway, a hard-and-fast reality that was beyond their control. At the very least, this program offered room and board during a period of formal training, as well as the opportunity to directly connect with potential employers.[36]

John Bradley (J. B.) Woods, the black grocer who sold his store to Gaither Hardaway, also worked with local white businessmen on projects designed to benefit the black community. Like Hardaway, J. B. Woods was initially drawn to Hattiesburg near the turn of the century by the promise of wage-labor jobs. A native of Greenville, Mississippi, he had begun his life in Hattiesburg as an employee of the New Orleans & Northeastern Railroad before leaving that position to open the grocery store on Mobile Street.[37]

After selling his grocery store to Hardaway, Woods purchased a two-story brick storefront just a few blocks down Mobile Street and opened a new grocery store. He and his wife Ella lived in a small home in the back of the store. Over the following years, Woods, along with Ella and later his second wife, Lenon, earned his living operating a series of businesses out of the storefront, including a grocery, dressmaker shop, barbershop, and boarding house. The building burned down in 1998, and the lot is now occupied by a little park commemorating the old storefront as the local headquarters of the 1964 Mississippi Freedom Summer.[38]

J. B. Woods died in 1944, two decades before his old building played that crucial role in the civil rights movement. But the legacy of political activism in that building was rooted in his life's work. As early as 1921, J. B. Woods began hosting political meetings in his store on Mobile Street. It is unknown who else was involved, but for years, Woods and several other local

African Americans met in the building to read and discuss race stories and political developments covered in the *Chicago Defender.* Woods himself was politically active. During the 1920s and 1930s, he served as the chairman of the Forrest County Republican Executive Committee and served as a delegate to the Republican National Conventions of 1924, 1932, and 1936.[39]

Little is known about Woods's internal political ambitions. As a black Republican living in Jim Crow Mississippi, he was a disfranchised official of an unelectable party. His influence was so scant that local whites appear to have barely noticed his political activities. Still, Woods participated in politics to the utmost of his ability, hobnobbing with other black leaders at political functions across the country and claiming a political leadership role in the only ways available to him. Though one cannot know precisely what Woods sought to accomplish, the building he owned on Mobile Street was the site of political engagement since at least 1921. When his former wife Lenon decided to open her doors to civil rights organizers in the 1960s, she was building on a long-term legacy of political leadership operating out of that structure. Of course, all of that lay in the years to come.

During the 1920s, J. B. Woods was most influential in Hattiesburg through his role in the Zion Chapel A.M.E. Church and a series of collaborations with black and white business leaders. Whereas Gaither Hardaway worked with the Lions Club, Woods partnered with several white organizations during the Christmas season to help raise money and toys for needy black families. He also promoted events at Eureka High School, served on the Negro Welfare Committee during World War I, led the effort at Zion Chapel A.M.E. to construct a new brick church, and worked with a local white businessman to open a black movie theater. In 1930, he helped convince members of the Hattiesburg Chamber of Commerce to sell land to a group of black ministers for the construction of a new playground for black children. And in 1932, he worked with a special city relief committee to run an unemployment office for African Americans out of his building on Mobile Street.[40]

White leaders did not leave behind records explaining their rationale for participating in interracial initiatives that provided benefits to the black community, but it is fairly easy to recognize several potential motivations. Surely, some of them were genuinely interested in helping poor black residents, perhaps out of a sense of paternalism or genuine sympathy. But their involvement in such projects also offered potential benefits to the white community. To start, local white leaders concerned with black outmigration were motivated to maintain their labor force. Small overtures and acts of charity were designed not only to offer relief but also to improve African Americans' attitudes toward local race relations. Black businessmen such as Gaither Hardaway and J. B. Woods served as intermediaries between leading whites with resources and poor blacks with needs. In addition, programs such as the Colored Upbuilding League's school for black domestics benefitted whites by training cheap workers for employment in white homes. Lastly, any sort of charity, education, or health program offered the potential to elevate black behavior and morality, thus improving society as a whole in the eyes of a white population that subscribed to stereotypes of black degeneracy and filth.

Regardless of incentive or strategy, none of these efforts directly threatened white supremacy or required white citizens to make any major racial concessions. The programs did, however, hold the potential to offer tangible benefits for local African Americans. Individuals such as Gaither Hardaway and J. B. Woods used these efforts to expand leadership roles and societal influence. And the black community itself was given greater access to resources and an increased stake in society. "The negroes of Hattiesburg form an integral part of this community," noted one member of the Chamber of Commerce in a 1929 editorial. "Mississippi negroes should be able from time to time to offer worth-while suggestions for the common good. Certainly they should be encouraged to do so."[41]

Consider the other view as well. Hattiesburg Negro Business League president Gaither Hardaway may not have left behind memoirs, speeches, or writings that would have better illuminated his own views toward whites, but his perspective can be inferred from his lived experiences. Born in Mississippi the year after Reconstruction ended, Hardaway was in all likelihood the son of former slaves. He came to Hattiesburg during the city's initial lumber boom and found both opportunity and oppression. As Hardaway rose through the social ranks of the black community, he also lived through the everyday experiences of Jim Crow and bore witness to several extraordinary acts of racial violence that occurred less than a mile from where he lived and worked. Six black men were lynched in Hattiesburg after his arrival, and even if he did not see the murders or the bodies, it is quite likely that he heard the shooting. At the very least, he was aware of the killings.

Gaither Hardaway's outlook was shaped by years of fear and persecution. But by the early 1930s, Hardaway also enjoyed a level of civic influence unimaginable just a decade before. Like all African Americans, he would have been required to abide by the basic regulations of Jim Crow, including customs of submission and deference in his interactions with whites. It would have been very dangerous for a black man of that era in Hattiesburg to publicly criticize racial segregation or demand increased civil rights. As the son of another member of the Committee of One Hundred later told an interviewer, "Had blacks pushed in the 1920s like they did in the 1960s, they would have been slaughtered." As with J. B. Woods, no one will ever know Hardaway's innermost ambitions or his thoughts toward white citizens. To fully consider how a man living under those circumstances might have measured change and progress across the difficult years of a life lived in Jim Crow Mississippi, we need only recognize the realities of his lived experiences.[42]

In small black Southern communities, Jim Crow ensured that all black people experienced the same forms of social, educational, and economic discrimination. Rich or poor, black people had no choice but to live, shop, dine, and worship among themselves. And because middle-class blacks were excluded from participating in all-white organizations such as the Chamber of Commerce, the only form of leadership they could claim lay in membership in statewide networks and programs they developed to benefit people in their own communities. If viewed at the communal level, this type of activity constituted a parallel form of local government in the black neighborhood.

Certainly, there were undocumented conflicts, jealousies, and social and professional slights, but in the broader sense of society, Jim Crow bonded them together out of necessity. "What was good for one was good for all, and what was bad for them was bad for all," said the son of a local minister whose family moved to Hattiesburg in 1919. "That was the kind of unity that we had at that particular time."[43]

Although men held the official titles in local business and religious organizations, most daily activities in the Mobile Street District were organized and led by black women. Living in a patriarchal society, women did not have the same formal opportunities for community leadership through fraternal organizations or groups such as the Hattiesburg Negro Business League. But involvement in local churches enabled them to carve out unique niches where they could develop leadership roles, exert societal influence, and provide for the welfare of community members.

By 1930, Hattiesburg was home to eighteen black churches—nine Baptist, six Methodist, one Presbyterian, and two branches of the Christ's Sanctified Holy Church. Regardless of denomination, all Southern black churches included female leadership bodies. Methodist churches had boards of stewardesses, and Baptist churches had deaconesses who advised male leaders and helped lead the congregation. Black churches also had an endless array of female-led organizations that oversaw the congregation's daily activities and charitable drives. Black women directed choirs, provided food, played the organ, collected clothing for needy families, organized recitals, plays, debates, and lectures, and served as secretaries and treasurers. The most influential women in local black churches tended to be the wives of the city's leading black businessmen, professionals, and teachers, in part because many of them did not hold formal jobs and therefore had more time to dedicate to organizing activities.[44]

Several interdenominational women's groups met separately outside of the churches. In the mid-1920s, an organization named the Colored Neighborhood Society met weekly in the homes of its members to pray, sing, discuss scripture readings, and share cake, cookies, and punch. Almost all reports of their activities included a rendition of the song "Swing Low, Sweet Chariot," an old slave spiritual that many members likely learned from their mothers and grandmothers. The meetings closed by taking a collection that was donated to a particular cause or needy local family. Ella Woods, the first wife of J. B., was a prominent member of the group.[45]

Other black women participated in a variety of organizations that were affiliated with local churches. These included groups like the Women's Social Club, the Poro Club (whose members sold Poro-brand cosmetology products), the Silver Moon Social Club, the Mah-Jong Social Club, and the Negro Women's Federation. Like many of the church groups, these organizations conducted initiatives for the benefit for local African Americans. These female-led organizations also held recreational events that were important to the social lives of many black women. Excluded from the debutante balls, garden clubs, and fashion shows of the white community, Hattiesburg's black women came together in these clubs to craft their own traditions and establish their own standards of respectability and status. They held bridge parties, luncheons, birthday celebrations, dances, cake walks, and health programs, and they hosted tea parties for new graduates of Eureka High School.[46]

Much of what is known about the activities of black Hattiesburgers in the 1920s and 1930s actually comes from the pages of the *Chicago Defender.* Because so many aspects of Southern black life were excluded from mainstream newspapers, nearly all of the major Northern black newspapers printed special updates from Southern black communities in their national editions. This type of coverage enhanced the national popularity of Northern black newspapers, especially the *Chicago Defender,* which by 1929 had an estimated weekly circulation of nearly eighty thousand *outside* Chicago. Pullman Porters brought copies of the newspaper on trips into Dixie and passed them along to individuals who sold the papers in the barbershops and grocery stores of Southern black neighborhoods.[47]

The *Defender* was immensely popular in the Mobile Street District. Black residents who wanted to include updates could send announcements of social events or personal milestones to Amanda McGee, Jessie Brunson, or Curtis Mitchell, local black women who compiled and submitted reports to the paper. Additional news from the Mobile Street District appeared more sporadically in newspapers such as the *Baltimore Afro-American,* the *Philadelphia Tribune,* the *Pittsburgh Courier,* the *New York Amsterdam News,* and the *Cleveland Call and Post.*[48]

Major Hattiesburg stories such as the lynching of Emmanuel McCallum received front-page coverage in the *Defender.* But thousands of smaller stories from Hattiesburg were also mentioned in nearly every national edition of the Chicago paper throughout the 1920s and 1930s. The *Defender* covered graduations, birthday parties, bridge parties, automobile accidents, dances, organizational meetings, dinner-party menus, retirement parties, engagement parties, people's vacations, and visits between Hattiesburg and Chicago.[49]

Upon their return, Hammond and Charles Smith fell into the ranks of black leadership in the Mobile Street neighborhood. They joined the Hattiesburg Negro Business League and immersed themselves in its activities, including the annual Christmas food and toy drives and the Emancipation Day celebrations. In 1929, Charles was elected secretary of the Hattiesburg Negro Business League.[50]

The Smith brothers played essential roles in the continuously developing Mobile Street District. As an African American doctor, Charles was known by virtually every black person in town. He served thousands of patients and performed a wide range of medical procedures ranging from treating small cuts to delivering babies. Hammond was also widely known. His drugstore in the heart of the Mobile Street commercial district was an important source for medicines and everyday products such as perfumes, tobacco, razor blades, hair pomade, and sanitary napkins. The Smith Drug Store also sold gum and candy and operated a soda fountain that was immensely popular among the students who attended Eureka High School just around the corner.[51]

Both brothers quickly assumed leadership roles at St. Paul Methodist Church, where their family had belonged since arriving in Hattiesburg in 1900. Shortly after returning to Hattiesburg, Charles was elected to the church's board of trustees. Hammond joined him in later years. When St. Paul was badly damaged in 1927, the brothers helped arrange a temporary meeting space in the Eureka High School auditorium and one of the black Masonic lodges on Mobile Street until a new church could be completed. In 1930, St. Paul's congregation moved into a beautiful new brick church that is still in use today. Charles's and Hammond's names appear on a stone plaque attached to the northeast corner of the church.[52]

In later years, St. Paul would develop a reputation as an "elitist church," according to one member, because it was led primarily by professionals, teachers, and business owners. But this was not yet the case in the late 1920s. The eight men who joined Dr. Charles Smith on the St. Paul board of trustees in 1930 represented a diversity of socioeconomic backgrounds. Among their ranks were a funeral home director, a grocer, a porter, a janitor, a laborer at J. J. Newman, a service station attendant, and a railroad worker.[53]

Members of the Smith family were frequently mentioned in the *Chicago Defender.* Charles and Hammond regularly appeared as participants in local community events, and their wives, Myrtle and Lucille, received mention through their roles in the Women's Home Missionary Society and Phyllis Wheatley Club of St. Paul Methodist Church. The family also appeared in the *Defender* as attendees of local celebrations, bridge parties, and church services, thus chronicling the basic components of their social lives in the Mobile Street District. The two eldest sons and their wives were the most visible, but nearly all members of the Smith family appeared in *Defender* updates from Hattiesburg, even Charles's two young boys, Charles Jr. and Grover.[54]

The most widely covered Smith family story came in 1932, when Turner and Mamie's only daughter, Mamie, became engaged to a Clarksdale dentist named Arthur Gipson. After finishing courses at Tougaloo College in Jackson and Knoxville College in Tennessee, the younger Mamie Smith had accepted a teaching job in Clarksdale, Mississippi, where she met Dr. Gipson. The pair were engaged in August of 1932 and traveled to Hattiesburg to celebrate their coming nuptials.[55]

Mamie's engagement party was probably the largest celebration her parents ever held at their home on Dewey Street. Turner and Mamie ordered special announcements and sent them to friends and family, who arrived at the Smith home on the evening of Friday, August 19. After the introduction of the engaged couple, guests were treated to games of bridge, a three-person musical recital, and cake and ice cream. The local correspondent for the *Baltimore Afro-American* called the party "one of the loveliest social events of the summer." Mamie and her husband married less than a month later in the Smith family home and spent their honeymoon traveling through Florida before returning to Clarksdale, where they started a family. Over the years, Mamie and her children—Mamie, Arthur Jr., and Hammond—returned often to Hattiesburg to visit her parents and brothers on Dewey Street.[56]

In the year that Mamie became engaged, Turner and Mamie celebrated their forty-fourth year of marriage. He was seventy-three; she was sixty-six. By then, their children were all nearly grown and gone. Martin Luther, the third son, had finished medical school and was practicing in nearby Laurel. Wendell, the only son who did not become a doctor, was working as a clerk at Hammond's drugstore. The youngest boy, William Lloyd Garrison Smith, was enrolled in medical school. City directories indicate that Turner kept working through the 1930s, but his age would surely have slowed him down. Considering his work ethic, he probably never completely retired. Very few black people of his generation did. They worked until they died, which is part of the reason many of them died so young. But Turner and Mamie still had some years left. With the help of their children, they would both far surpass the average life expectancy of black southerners born in any era.

As Turner and Mamie faded into a quiet life on Dewey Street, their two oldest boys, Charles and Hammond, emerged as local black leaders, developing their businesses and taking active roles in the organizations and institutions cultivated by previous generations. Although their race would always limit their position in Hattiesburg society, in the Mobile Street District, they were able to build rich and meaningful lives. In the years to come, those lives would be profoundly eventful.

CHAPTER SEVEN

Reliance

> Nobody wants Mississippi to become a beggar at the government's back door but other states are being helped by the federal relief commission and there is no reason why this state should not be included in the project.
>
> —*Hattiesburg American,* November 1, 1932

In October of 1932, white Hattiesburg leaders held an epic Golden Jubilee Festival to celebrate the city's fiftieth anniversary. For six consecutive days, thousands of locals braved unseasonably cold and rainy weather to attend a series of commemorative events. On Monday, city representatives initiated the festivities with a ceremonial lighting of the "jubilee light" and opening of a temporary "Golden Jubilee Museum." On Tuesday, members of the Rotary Club reviewed highlights of Hattiesburg history at a special luncheon. That Wednesday, the Exchange Club offered a similar recital, and the *Hattiesburg American* published a special twenty-eight-page "Golden Jubilee Edition." Thursday was "Hattiesburg Day" in all local white schools. Students received historical programs during their chapel periods and attended afternoon pep rallies. Later that night, local merchants sponsored a fashion show and an outdoor concert. The next day, the State Teachers College marching band led a parade from downtown to the college, where Mississippi governor Martin S. Conner (a Hattiesburg native) dedicated the school's new athletic field. That evening, the governor and his wife attended an elegant party and dance at the Forrest Hotel. The following morning, they were among over four thousand spectators who watched the State Teachers College football team defeat Spring Hill College twelve to zero.[1]

The *Hattiesburg American* brimmed with optimism, suggesting throughout the week that lessons from the city's past should inspire confidence in its future. Wednesday's commemorative edition was filled with articles highlighting proud moments in the city's history—Captain Hardy's lunch break in the forest, the completion of various railroads and sawmills, the construction of new churches and schools, and the contributions of organizations like the United Daughters of the Confederacy and the Hattiesburg Chamber of Commerce. This past glory, the paper insisted, not only offered a blueprint for future prosperity but practically assured it. "Hattiesburg, striding city of the past, well founded by the pioneers who settled this part of Mississippi looks forward confidently to an era of future expansion and development which will outdistance all achievements of the past," one reporter wrote.[2]

Despite the optimism, Hattiesburg in the fall of 1932 was in very poor shape. That year, Mississippi produced its lowest timber yield since 1889. From a high of approximately forty thousand workers in the mid-1920s, Mississippi sawmills by 1932 employed less than thirteen thousand men. Most of Hattiesburg's lumber wholesale offices had closed, and all the local sawmills had begun laying off workers. J. J. Newman was in its eighth year of layoffs and on the verge of closing for good. Tatum Lumber, the city's second largest sawmill, had by then also started laying off workers; it too had only a few years left. Hundreds of sawmills across the region had already ceased operations. Over the previous six years, at least 450 sawmills had cut out of the Piney Woods, leaving behind a "scenery of stumps, [and] 'ghost' lumber towns," observed one local. The people of the Piney Woods were heartbroken. "Where once saws hummed a ceaseless song along hundreds of miles of railroads traversing South Mississippi," a local writer noted, "today the mills still in operation are few and far between." That autumn, even the relentlessly optimistic *Hattiesburg American* finally admitted, "The forests are dead as an industry; almost gone as a possible source of income and revenue."[3]

The decline of the timber trade represented only one component of a broader statewide economic collapse. Agriculture, still the state's most valuable industry and largest employer, experienced a similarly rapid decline. Several factors—including unprecedented international competition, overproduction in the American South, and the emergence of synthetic fibers such as rayon—combined to drive down cotton prices throughout the late 1920s. Between 1923 and 1931, the price of cotton plummeted from a high of 31¢ per pound to a low of just 6¢. In 1920, Mississippi farms were worth nearly $790 million. A decade later, they were valued at less than $570 million. Of course, all of this occurred amid a disastrous global economic collapse.[4]

By the fall of 1932, Mississippi was mired in its worst financial crisis since the end of the Civil War. With farmers struggling and sawmills closing, state tax revenues were dramatically slashed, dragging an already poor state even deeper into poverty. Between 1928 and 1932, Mississippi's assessments declined by more than $80 million and the state's debt spiraled to over $50 million (the city of Hattiesburg itself had outstanding bonds totaling over $2.3 million). Financial destitution could be seen across Mississippi. People defaulted on their taxes. Retailers closed shops. Manufacturing firms ceased production. There were some wealthy planters and merchants who continued to do well, but most working-class Mississippians, both white and black, suffered tremendously. The state had been very poor since the Civil War, but the economic recession of the 1920s and 1930s charted an unprecedented path of almost unthinkable destitution. Between 1929 and 1933, the state's per capita annual income dropped from $285 to $131.[5]

In the Mississippi Piney Woods, thousands of people were desperate for work. During the week of Hattiesburg's Golden Jubilee Festival, an advertisement for part-time temporary highway jobs drew an estimated fifteen hundred applicants from Forrest County alone. At the time, only about fifteen thousand males lived in Forrest County, which suggests that roughly one out of every ten males in the county applied for those jobs. And that does not even factor in young, elderly, or disabled males, or those who simply took one look at the applicant line and walked away. In the coming years, every such advertised position drew large crowds of applicants, including hundreds of migrants who poured into Hattiesburg from the dying sawmill towns of southeastern Mississippi.[6]

Competition for work could be fierce. Some traditionally black jobs—especially on the railroads—became so desirable that whites were willing to kill for them. The early 1930s saw the outbreak of a racially based shooting spree in southern Mississippi over positions such as brakeman and fireman. During the summer and fall of 1931, four black brakemen and firemen were shot on the job. One particularly unfortunate man named Frank Kincaid survived a shooting that August only to be killed in November. Black railroad workers Turner Sims and Aaron Williams were shot a month later. By the autumn of 1932, the *Hattiesburg American* counted fifteen black Mississippi firemen and brakemen who had been wounded or killed by gunfire during the previous year.[7]

There were some jobs in Hattiesburg. Throughout much of the 1930s, the Hercules Powder Company and Tatum Lumber each employed up to four hundred people at a time. Additionally, a few dozen smaller companies combined to offer several hundred more jobs. Most of these positions, however, were fairly unstable. Employees could never be certain how many hours would be available or how long the jobs would last. Thousands of local jobholders worked only part time, experienced roving layoffs, or earned too little to fully provide for their families. In 1933, workers at Tatum Lumber earned only 15¢ per hour over ten-hour workdays. Even people with jobs still scrambled to earn extra wages however they could.[8]

These laborers resembled what contemporary scholars would label a "precariat"—a "precarious proletariat" made up of blue-collar workers who moved between a variety of temporary jobs to earn a living. Some people worked part time for a number of firms at once. Others performed farm work for daily pay. Hundreds more hopped on railroad cars or hitchhiked in search of out-of-town jobs. Local youths delivered boxes of groceries and newspapers to help their parents. Families raised chickens and pigs and grew their own vegetables. People sold sweet potatoes, pecans, and homemade quilts by the roadside. Some traded produce or performed odd jobs in exchange for services. Many local lawyers and doctors were forced to accept payment in goods such as milk or corn in lieu of cash. The people of Hattiesburg scraped and saved to survive an era of instability and uncertainty. The only clear truth was that the Hub City needed more jobs.[9]

Between 1929 and 1932, the Hattiesburg Chamber of Commerce exhausted virtually every imaginable possibility in its search for new industries. Their far-reaching efforts included proposals to secure a fish hatchery, a disabled soldiers home, a garment factory, a tire and tube factory, a denim factory, a canning plant, a fireplace heater factory, a battery plant, a hospital, a cattle farm, a vocational school, and a furniture factory. On several occasions, J. J. Newman Lumber Company president Fenwick Peck mentioned the possibility of establishing a paper plant, but neither this nor any of the aforementioned proposals ever came to fruition. A new downtown library built through a combination of municipal bonds, individual donations, and corporate sponsorships and a new movie theater built by the Saenger Theatre Company of New Orleans provided several dozen temporary jobs and enhanced local public life, but the Chamber of Commerce in 1932 had not yet been able to attract any significant new employers. "Results have been disappointing," admitted T. S. Jackson in a 1931 memo.[10]

T. S. Jackson himself was not doing very well. His health was failing, and as he lost his capacity to work, his income was rapidly diminishing. By the close of the 1920s, his primary source of income was the salary he received as secretary of the Chamber of Commerce. But even this job soon exceeded his capabilities. In 1930, illness kept him from several meetings; by the autumn of 1932, he had been forced to resign. Jackson's colleagues were worried. At one Chamber of Commerce meeting that fall, a close friend noted that Jackson was "ill in bed, and in need of the money." Thomas Smiley Jackson held on for another fifteen months before dying peacefully in his sleep on January 8, 1934. "Few if any citizens believed as strongly, or asserted their faith as emphatically in this community as did Mr. Jackson," the *Hattiesburg American* memorialized.[11]

Jackson's contemporaries W. S. F. Tatum and Louis Faulkner were doing much better. Tatum's sawmill was on the verge of cutting out, but the wealth he had built in previous decades sustained him and several generations of his family throughout the Great Depression. He and many of the city's leading white men tried to help the poor by giving generously to charities. Tatum was never known for treating his sawmill employees very well, but throughout his life, he gave hundreds of thousands of dollars to organizations such as the Main Street Methodist Church, the Hattiesburg YMCA, Mississippi Women's College, and Millsaps College; he even gave a large donation toward construction of a church in Santiago, Cuba. "He holds his wealth in trust for the less fortunate of his fellows," one contemporary noted of Tatum, "and his life has been filled with good deeds."[12]

Louis Faulkner, who weathered the recession through his position with the Mississippi Central Railroad and a variety of small investments, also poured much of his energy into helping less fortunate citizens. He sent checks to the Red Cross, the Bible Society, the Salvation Army, the American Legion, Palmer Orphanage, Hattiesburg High School, Mississippi Normal College, Mississippi Women's College, Hattiesburg Boys Brotherhood, Mississippi Children's Home Society, the YMCA, and the Lion's Club Doll and Toy Fund. Faulkner was also heavily involved in the local Boy Scout troop and the First Presbyterian Church, and he played an instrumental role in building the new football field at the State Teachers College, which bore the name Faulkner Field in his honor.[13]

Despite some examples of interracial cooperation in the 1920s, most Hattiesburg charity drives were strictly segregated by race. The *Hattiesburg American*'s inventive 1932 "Church and Charity" campaign, for example, which bolstered downtown commerce by donating advertising revenues to church charities, was open "to every white church or organization." No black congregations or businesses could apply. In fact, there is very little evidence of cooperation between white and black churches, even those of the same religious denomination. And the charitable programs of organizations such as the local YMCA and the Boy Scouts were generally open only to white citizens. Personal donations also reflected this trend. Although Louis Faulkner donated money to help the all-white Prentiss High School purchase new marching band uniforms, for example, he did not respond to a request from the all-black Prentiss Normal Institute for help rebuilding its grist mill. The black students might not get enough to eat, but those white kids sure would look sharp in their new uniforms.[14]

In 1931, this commitment to segregated charity created a controversy that drew national attention to Hattiesburg. In January of that year, the local branch of the Red Cross received a grant from the national organization to distribute goods to poor families "without food, clothing, and fuel," explained the chapter's chairman. "No hungry person will go unfed," promised the organization's Mississippi field representative, "no family needing food, clothing, medical supplies or fuel will go unattended in Forrest County." Operating out of an office in City Hall, the Red Cross campaign started well. In the first month, the organization received over twenty-five hundred applications for assistance and provided food vouchers and clothing to approximately five hundred families. For a few weeks, the effort looked promising. But then the Red Cross encountered a series of challenges.[15]

The first challenge was that some families applying for relief did not actually live in Forrest County. The second was that some applicants were fraudulently exaggerating their poverty or the size of their families to receive additional food vouchers. Although impossible to completely eliminate dishonest requests, local residents helped out by verifying the residences and economic conditions of the families. The third problem—the one that threatened to completely undermine all local Red Cross efforts—was that some of the families applying for relief were black.[16]

Poor Hattiesburg whites, themselves in desperate need of charity, were appalled by the idea of having to wait in the same lines and be served at the same counters as African Americans. Some even threatened violence, promising to beat up needy black applicants who came to City Hall for help. The objections did not come only from the poor. Middle- and upper-class white women—presumably members of the United Daughters of the Confederacy who met in City Hall—also issued complaints about the presence of poor black men and women in the building. "The droves of negro applicants to the Red Cross . . . was embarrassing to ladies who visited the City Hall on business and otherwise," explained a statement from the mayor's office.[17]

White Hattiesburgers wanted the Red Cross to adhere to the racial regulations of their society, but the national Red Cross had a nondiscrimination policy and refused to segregate its charity. As the field worker Margaret Butler-Bishop explained to the *Hattiesburg American* in 1931, the Red Cross "knows no race, creed or color lines: hunger and suffering are universal and the organization's policy is to deal with all needy alike."[18]

Mayor W. S. F. Tatum decided to offer the Red Cross an ultimatum: either quit serving African Americans or vacate City Hall. When the organization once again refused to discriminate, Tatum ordered the eviction of the Red Cross from its City Hall offices. On the afternoon of Thursday, February 12, his workmen moved the organization's supplies and office furniture to a public sidewalk, where it sat outdoors for several hours before the manager of the new Saenger Theatre provided access to some extra storage space. A notice explaining the eviction read, "No nigger should be fed while a single white man, woman or child is hungry."[19]

Even as their society crumbled around them, white Hattiesburgers held tight to their society's racial order as if it were the last remaining promise of the New South. In destitution or in wealth, Jim Crow ensured racial superiority for even the most deprived whites. As the *Philadelphia Tribune* observed of the incident, "Even the gnawing pains of hunger are unable to make the white people of that God-for-saken section forget their white supremacy."[20]

The Red Cross eviction was indicative of how white Hattiesburgers tried to maintain a sense of normalcy during the economic crisis. In a society filled with job loss, poverty, and uncertainty, local white residents embraced longtime traditions to help manufacture optimism through the preservation of their way of life. Not only did they continue following the customs of racial segregation, they also went to church, sent their kids to school, celebrated holidays, and attended community events such as garden club meetings, dances, football games, and the 1932 Golden Jubilee Festival. "Cares will be forgotten," the *Hattiesburg American* ensured readers of the commemoration, "as all contemplate the gift of years and envisage the possibilities of the future."[21]

The optimism surrounding the Golden Jubilee Festival was not entirely unfounded. Just two months before, the Hattiesburg Chamber of Commerce had been contacted by the Fantus Factory Locating Service of Chicago. Fantus was scouting potential new factory sites for a Chicago-based company, Reliance Manufacturing. In operation for over twenty years, Reliance Manufacturing was a well-established company with a national reputation. Its "Big Yank" work shirts were sold in hundreds of J. C. Penney stores. This possibility represented a major opportunity. A Chamber of Commerce committee estimated that a new Reliance factory could bring approximately five hundred jobs and an annual payroll of over $250,000 to Hattiesburg.[22]

Two months after the initial contact, the Hattiesburg Chamber of Commerce invited Reliance officials to visit the Hub City during the Golden Jubilee Festival. This was, of course, no coincidence. In fact, it is likely that the festival would have looked very different if not for the out-of-town guests. Perhaps it might not have occurred at all. In any case, the Chamber of Commerce members did everything they could to impress the visiting Chicagoans. They nicknamed that Wednesday "Reliance Day" and placed a two-page advertisement in the *Hattiesburg American*'s "Golden Jubilee Edition" welcoming the Chicago businessmen to the Hub City. "Today is your day," the advertisement told the Northerners. "The city is yours!"[23]

In addition to an original Reliance Committee (one of the few committees ever chaired by Mayor Tatum), the Hattiesburg Chamber of Commerce formed three additional committees just to oversee the visit. Louis Faulkner chaired the Reliance Welcoming Committee, and two smaller committees organized a luncheon and dinner. Reliance officials were feted with an official welcoming ceremony, a tour of the city, meetings with white civic leaders, and several small ceremonies. On the evening of "Reliance Day," 175 local white businessmen paid 50¢ each to attend a banquet at the Hotel Hattiesburg in honor of their Chicago guests. Louis Faulkner served as toastmaster.[24]

All local citizens were asked to participate in the courtship of Reliance. Several newspaper articles provided details about the visit, and an editorial in the *Hattiesburg American* urged residents to "clean-up of premises, both private and public." "Unsightly debris and trash, fallen fences and decaying refuse ought to be hauled away and dumped out of sight," the editorial instructed. Any locals who encountered the visiting Chicagoans were encouraged to act friendly and upbeat. Coffee was to be poured with extra care and soda served with a cheerful smile. Homeowners were directed to fly flags and place welcome signs. And everyone was advised to lift their chin and walk with a sense of pride. "Some folks will be embarrassed by the vacant store buildings in the business district," the *American* acknowledged, but "every town has vacant store buildings and Hattiesburg probably has fewer of them than any city its size in the South."[25]

Like the visiting Tuf-Nut officials from a few years before, Reliance Manufacturing Company representatives understood that Hattiesburg was desperate for jobs and negotiated from a position of strength. The Chicago-based firm made several requests, including multiyear tax exemptions, an annual subsidy, and the construction of a new factory building that Reliance could lease rent free for twenty years. The building was the most burdensome requirement. To complete such a facility, the city needed to raise at least $75,000.[26]

Debate ensued within the Chamber of Commerce, but it does not appear that the group ever seriously considered rejecting Reliance. With outstanding municipal bonds totaling more than $2.3 million, the city was in no position to underwrite the building, but several prominent local businessmen quickly vowed to cover construction costs. Mayor Tatum offered to loan the Chamber of Commerce $30,000, and several other white businessmen, including Louis Faulkner, collectively contributed $25,000. The rest of the building was financed by smaller investments, local bonds, and a mortgage with the First National Bank of Hattiesburg whose president was a member of the Chamber of Commerce. An additional noteworthy benefit of constructing a factory was that all the work was contracted to local companies, including some owned by members of the Chamber of Commerce. Financing the building also presented intriguing investment opportunities. In the final deal, each major investor agreed to exchange their share of the building for equivalent shares of stock in Reliance Manufacturing.[27]

After several months of negotiations and visits, the Hattiesburg Chamber of Commerce in April of 1933 sent representatives to Chicago to sign the contract with Reliance. The organization had finally realized its longtime dream of bringing a major new employer to Hattiesburg. For weeks, news of the deal dominated the front pages of the *Hattiesburg American*. No one thought the factory alone could save Hattiesburg, but it did promise hundreds of jobs that would help many local families. When the factory opened that October, thousands of people, including both of Mississippi's United States senators, attended the dedication ceremony in downtown Hattiesburg. "This building," a Chamber of Commerce representative told the audience, "is an expression of your humanity." Only white people were allowed to work there.[28]

The other great source of optimism during the autumn of 1932 was the upcoming presidential election. White Hattiesburgers were eager to cast their votes for Franklin Delano Roosevelt, the charismatic Democratic governor of New York, and they hoped the rest of the country would join them in doing so. Mississippi was solidly Democrat and had been ever since the Revolution of 1875, when the Republican carpetbaggers were removed from power. The party of Lincoln would not carry the Magnolia State; there was no drama there. But since 1892, the national Democratic Party had nominated just one successful presidential candidate, and even that victory had been something of a fluke. Virginia Democrat Woodrow Wilson won the 1912 election only because former president Teddy Roosevelt had split the Republican vote with his progressive "Bull Moose Party." Wilson was barely reelected in 1916 (he would have lost if just 3,800 more Californians had voted Republican), and Republican candidates had taken each presidential election since 1920.[29]

By the autumn of 1932, however, nearly every corner of the United States had been pulled into the depths of the Great Depression, and many Americans were ready to remove Republican president Herbert Hoover. Although widely recognized as a great humanitarian before his presidency, Hoover seemed oblivious to the realities facing American families during the depression. He rejected most proposals for direct assistance to the unemployed and was continuously vilified for his inability—even outright refusal—to offer more aid to America's poor. The public demonized him for his lack of action, dubbing their ramshackle shantytowns "Hoovervilles" and calling the sheets of newsprint that they used for warmth "Hoover Blankets."[30]

Hoover's popularity plummeted further in the summer of 1932, when a group of World War I veterans known as the Bonus Army was violently evicted from their makeshift camp in Washington, DC, where they had gathered to demand early payment of their service bonuses. Images of American troops scuffling with World War I veterans appeared in newspapers across the country, drawing the ire of an already aggravated populace. The fiasco was not entirely Hoover's fault. The military officials who performed the eviction were largely responsible for the ugly result, and many Americans—including Franklin Roosevelt—did not support the veterans' demands (which included a petition signed by 513 veterans from Forrest County, Mississippi). But as with the depression itself, widespread national sentiment concluded that Hoover should have handled the situation with greater tact. "If Governor Roosevelt had been president," insisted the *Hattiesburg American*, "U.S. troops never would have been called out against the Bonus Expeditionary Force. Hoover is going to get the royal boot of the veterans and other thousands of voters who side with them on the basic issue."[31]

Like many Americans, most white Hattiesburg voters wanted the federal government to undertake more direct actions to help mitigate the effects of the recession. White Hattiesburgers were a proud people who believed that their society had been built by innovative visionaries who used ingenuity and grit to construct a modern society from the devastation of the Civil War. But these hardworking people also believed themselves to have been victimized by timber mismanagement and other economic factors beyond their control. The white working-class people of Hattiesburg did not want handouts; they just needed jobs. And Roosevelt's "New Deal" promised to use the resources of the federal government to help put them back to work. On November 8, 1932, over 91 percent of Hattiesburg voters cast their ballots for Franklin Roosevelt.[32]

Roosevelt and his New Deal captured Hattiesburg's attention. When Roosevelt took to the airwaves that spring with his "fireside chats" that explained his new policies, white Hattiesburgers gathered in groups around radios to hear his plans to save America's economy. "When Roosevelt was making his famous fireside chats," remembered local white resident Buck Wells, "then you couldn't find a soul that had a radio that his whole family wasn't wrapped up in it."[33]

In Hattiesburg, the meaning of the New Deal extended beyond economics or politics. The ambitious programs became a part of residents' culture and society, offering to many an essential foundation for hope. "That's what the people needed," Wells explained. "They needed a leader that could tell them to hang in there that help was coming." Locals followed New Deal programs religiously. The *Hattiesburg American* began running a daily syndicated column titled "New Deal Doings" and carried various news of the New Deal in every single issue for over seven years.[34]

The anti-statism that characterized Southern political thought in other historical moments was not widely espoused in the 1930s. In reality, such sentiments were only consistently employed in response to issues related to race. The New Deal included several anti-discrimination measures, but it nevertheless functioned quite well within the racial hierarchy of the Jim Crow South. White Southern legislators and civic officials controlled the distribution of New Deal benefits, enabling them to discriminate by steering jobs and funding projects to disproportionately benefit white residents. White Hattiesburgers enthusiastically welcomed massive government expansion and federal influence into their lives. When it came to the New Deal, there was little talk of "states' rights" in southern Mississippi.[35]

One of the first New Deal programs, the Civilian Conservation Corps (CCC), seemed tailor-made for the Piney Woods. The CCC was designed to remedy both unemployment and decades of environmental abuse by providing federally funded conservation jobs to young men to improve parks, plant trees, build rural roads, and protect the forest from fires, insects, and disease. This environmental relief program quickly became one of the most popular and successful New Deal initiatives, employing approximately 2.5 million Americans in nine years and planting an estimated 570 million trees.[36]

The CCC was enormously popular in Hattiesburg. "We had a jillion of them in this area," recalled one local man of the CCC workers. Throughout the 1930s, the *Hattiesburg American* printed dozens of stories detailing the organization's activities and advertising CCC jobs. "Pine tree seedlings today are basking in the balmy spring sunshine, stretching their leafy little arms skyward—and growing in terms of dollars and cents daily," the *American* noted. Interested locals could even visit CCC camps during intermittent open houses.[37]

Mississippi's thirty-four CCC camps employed white men almost exclusively. Despite African Americans' historical predominance in the Mississippi lumber industry, black workers comprised only 1.7 percent of Mississippi's CCC workers. If not for an antidiscrimination clause in the original CCC bill, there very well might have been none.[38]

Another New Deal program, the National Recovery Administration (NRA), also benefitted many local white residents. The NRA was designed to support good domestic manufacturing jobs by endorsing companies that paid minimum wages and offered reasonable hours for their employees. The endorsement was typically made by the inclusion of a special NRA blue eagle logo printed on the packaging of NRA-backed goods. Across the country, consumers knew that products stamped with the blue NRA logo were manufactured by hardworking Americans who labored in fair conditions.[39]

The new Reliance Manufacturing Company was Hattiesburg's largest NRA shop. Though the Supreme Court eventually ruled the NRA unconstitutional, in two years, the program helped boost Reliance sales across the country. In the first quarter of 1934, the company broke all previous sales records, which benefitted both employees and investors connected to the Hattiesburg shop. Other companies, some of which were not even eligible for NRA membership, included the blue eagle logo in their advertisements. And the *Hattiesburg American* regularly printed the image in the corner of its front page, even months after the program ended. People in Hattiesburg were excited about the New Deal.[40]

There were some critics among prominent local white men. Both Louis Faulkner and W. S. F. Tatum were fiscal conservatives who usually identified as Republicans and later levied major criticisms at federal spending and involvement in local affairs. Tatum in particular was critical of the effects of the Social Security Act on his payroll. No one knows how the men voted in the 1932 presidential election, but it is clear that they cast aside whatever reservations they may have held to become very involved in overseeing New Deal spending. Ironically, the New Deal's most vocal local critics participated heavily in managing improvement projects in Hattiesburg, especially after Roosevelt announced the formation of the Works Progress Administration (WPA).[41]

Enacted in 1935 as part of Roosevelt's "Second New Deal," the WPA was essentially a massive expansion of the CCC. The organization hired millions of unemployed men and women to complete a wide range of construction, maintenance, and art projects that helped beautify America's landscape and improve the nation's infrastructure. The scope was colossal. During its existence, the WPA paid nearly $10 billion in wages to over eight million workers who built or repaired over 650,000 miles of roads, nearly 78,000 bridges, over 937,000 traffic signs and 35,000 public buildings, and thousands of swimming pools, airports, golf courses, sidewalks, viaducts, curbs, and gutters. To that date, the WPA was the largest known public works program in the history of human civilization.[42]

Federal WPA spending was unevenly distributed among states. Politically powerful states such as New York, Ohio, Pennsylvania, Massachusetts, and Illinois were among the nation's leaders in per capita WPA expenditures, while less influential states such as Mississippi ranked near the bottom (Mississippi tied with Alabama for thirty-sixth place). Nonetheless, the federal grants contributed greatly to Mississippi's economy and infrastructure. During the 1930s, the WPA employed as many as 48,690 Mississippians at one time and provided over $41.5 million in wages while funding thousands of new roads and community initiatives that ranged from park beautification and school lunches to public health programs. Like many white Southerners, Hattiesburg's civic leaders worked to maximize their access to federal resources and ensure that the windfalls of federal spending disproportionally benefitted whites. The Hattiesburg Chamber of Commerce led the charge.[43]

Just six weeks after President Roosevelt signed the legislation creating the WPA, Louis Faulkner proposed a widely supported motion that the Hattiesburg Chamber of Commerce "take an active part in getting some of the money which is being appropriated by the Government for certain projects." This motion marked a pivotal change for the Hattiesburg Chamber of Commerce. The organization never stopped its pursuit of new industries, but it did shift its focus from recruiting private firms to accessing federal grants. Over the following years, the Chamber of Commerce essentially operated as a local clearinghouse for federal spending, soliciting and distributing WPA funding and other federal resources to local public works projects that provided thousands of jobs and helped improve the city's infrastructure.[44]

Depending on the nature of the project, WPA funding proposals were typically submitted to state or federal officials by the Hattiesburg Chamber of Commerce or the Forrest County Board of Supervisors. After an initial grant of $22,204 (part of a large statewide WPA distribution), they very quickly gained access to greater resources. On November 6, 1935, local officials announced approval of a federal grant totaling $272,306 to support street paving and road repair. That same day, the state's WPA Women's Work Division announced funding for several library positions in Hattiesburg. And two weeks later, the city of Hattiesburg received notice of a

$30,000 WPA grant to begin construction on a new 3,700-seat athletic gym for Hattiesburg High School. The federal grants delivered new employment opportunities. By the end of 1935, the *Hattiesburg American* estimated that the WPA and other New Deal programs had created over forty-five hundred jobs in the region. The paper dutifully recognized the importance of the New Deal itself, but it also celebrated the role played by the Chamber of Commerce in accessing those federal dollars. The newspaper's editor, himself a member of the chamber, called 1935 "one of the most successful years in the history of the civic body."[45]

Over the next five years, dozens of WPA-funded projects provided thousands of jobs for local workers, both white and black, and millions of dollars for improvements to the city's infrastructure. Projects included widening streets, building a new post office, digging new sewer lines, clearing debris from creeks, erecting utility poles, grading a new airport runway, and improving parks and public spaces. As part of the WPA Writer's Project, a bevy of local scholars and writers were paid to research the city's history and document its flora and economy. Their notes were collected and deposited in the state archives (where they remain today) and used to help produce a book titled *Mississippi: The WPA Guide to the Magnolia State*, part of a national WPA series on each state.[46]

Another major WPA-backed project was the restoration of Camp Shelby. The establishment of Camp Shelby in 1917 had been one of the Hattiesburg Chamber of Commerce's greatest early achievements. When the United States entered World War I, the Hattiesburg Chamber of Commerce sent representatives to New York City in an attempt to convince National Guard officials to select Hattiesburg as a site for one of the Guard's new bases. Competing with dozens of similar groups from across America, the Hattiesburg faction could never secure a meeting. But the organization realized that it held a tremendous advantage. George McHenry, an Ohioan who had moved to Mississippi to start a sawmill along the Gulf & Ship Island Railroad, was an old military buddy of General Leonard Wood (with whom he had served during the Spanish-American War), and he used his personal connection to convince General Wood to visit the Hub City. Upon visiting Hattiesburg and meeting with local citizens, Wood ultimately selected the Hub City as one of the final two sites for National Guard bases. The camp was named in honor of Revolutionary War hero Colonel Isaac Shelby of Kentucky. During World War I, Shelby hosted up to forty thousand troops and employed thirty-five hundred workers at a time, briefly providing an enormous boost to the local economy. But the camp was abandoned shortly after the war, and its land had been reclaimed by the forest.[47]

Fifty days after President Roosevelt established the WPA, the Hattiesburg Chamber of Commerce formed a "Camp Shelby Committee" to solicit federal grants for the restoration of the old military base. For this effort, they appealed directly to the military. In 1935, the Chamber of Commerce hosted the influential general William L. Grayson, taking him out to visit the camp and hosting him at a lavish banquet at the Hotel Hattiesburg. And in 1937, Louis Faulkner led a small contingent of Chamber of Commerce officials to Atlanta to meet with Army General George Van Horn Moseley, commander of the Fourth Corps Area. Grayson and Moseley each endorsed the reestablishment of Shelby, leading to a number of different grants provided by the WPA and the National Guard to help restore the old military base.[48]

Between 1935 and 1940, the WPA and National Guard spent an estimated $80,000 per year to pay for labor and supplies to reestablish Camp Shelby as a suitable military base. For reasons unknown, Forrest County officials also used convict laborers at Shelby. Together, the convicts and the WPA workers cleared foliage, regraded roads, and erected utility poles, putting the camp into "spick span shape," observed a local writer, by the time a small contingent of troops was scheduled to arrive for training in the summer of 1937.[49]

In February of that same year, the new Hattiesburg High School gym opened to great fanfare with a double-header basketball contest between the boys' and girls' teams of Hattiesburg and Purvis High School. The girls lost the opening game 30–15, but the boys prevailed in the nightcap, dispatching Purvis 32–17. A large crowd, "distended with pride," wrote one reporter, turned out to see the new WPA gymnasium, whose total cost expanded to approximately $50,000. The gym was a great boon to the white community. Over the following years and decades, it hosted countless games, graduations, baccalaureates, assemblies, theatrical performances, and a broad range of other events. City officials even let white people from other nearby communities use the gym for basketball games. Several other smaller WPA grants were used to maintain trees and shrubs on the Hattiesburg High School campus and purchase new paint and blackboards for classrooms, making the all-white school a much nicer place to learn. No black student was ever allowed to attend or use the federally funded gym.[50]

Throughout the 1930s, the Hattiesburg Chamber of Commerce continuously steered most federal spending toward projects that only benefitted whites. There were several components to this unbalanced distribution. Individually, whites received most of the jobs provided by New Deal programs such as the CCC and WPA. In 1939, white public relief workers in Forrest County outnumbered African Americans five-to-one in a city where African Americans comprised roughly 35 percent of the population. Some black workers did receive public relief jobs, but the concept of "nigger work" existed even in the era of the Great Depression. Black WPA workers were typically relegated to tasks such as ditch digging, sewer clearance, general labor, and spraying pesticide.[51]

Black women were almost completely excluded from WPA opportunities. Their white female counterparts were generally limited to such positions as librarian, secretary, researcher, or writer, but white women, many of whom were widowed or married to unemployed men, still accounted for approximately 17 percent of public relief employees in Forrest County. Black women comprised less than 2 percent and were restricted almost exclusively to childcare positions. Certainly, white women tended to be more educated and thus more qualified for these types of jobs. But the black community also included several female college graduates and high school teachers, none of whom were given the opportunity for WPA jobs. Perhaps the most nonsensical example of this disparity was the employment of white women by the WPA Writer's Project to conduct research about the black community. Clearly, some of the black women who actually lived in that community could have provided a better perspective. In fact, some of the basic information reported about local black churches was inaccurate.[52]

Beyond individual jobs, the greatest discrepancies of New Deal–era relief could be seen in the management and dispersal of federal grants. Proposals made by the all-white Hattiesburg Chamber of Commerce and Forrest County board of supervisors were not designed to improve or benefit the black community. Some of the grants helped improve public spaces that explicitly barred all black people. Black Hattiesburgers did not benefit from WPA spending on Hattiesburg High School or the State Teachers College because those institutions did not accept black students or allow black citizens to use their facilities. The same can be said of some of the local parks and libraries that received funding from New Deal programs. And although some black men worked in the road-building projects, most streets selected for improvement were not located in the black community. Of course, this was precisely how many whites believed WPA funding should be managed. As in past eras, local whites took the opportunities provided by others and consolidated them among members of their own race.[53]

In Hattiesburg, increased WPA spending was accompanied by a brief glimmer of industrial hope. The mid-1930s saw the creation of several hundred new job opportunities. By the spring of 1937, Reliance Manufacturing employed somewhere between 550 and 600 local white workers—almost exclusively women—who worked eight-hour shifts and earned an average of about $12 per week. This was no great fortune. But even $12 per week offered a significantly greater income than the average Mississippian earned during the Great Depression. Reliance jobs had an especially significant impact on the hundreds of white female employees who might otherwise have held no job at all. These earnings helped support hundreds of white families, who in turn contributed to the local economy by spending their wages in local stores. Reliance Manufacturing also contributed directly to Hattiesburg's economy by purchasing an estimated $100,000 per year in supplies and equipment from local retailers.[54]

Another northern company opened a new factory in 1935. Recruited through the efforts of the Chamber of Commerce and a loan underwritten by W. S. F. Tatum, a New York–based company opened the Hattiesburg Pioneer Silk Mill that September. By 1937, Pioneer Silk employed over 250 workers who earned an average of about $10 per week. That fall, Pioneer Silk was one of several factories featured in a *National Geographic* article titled, "Machines Come to Mississippi." The local white woman who saw her picture in one of America's most popular magazines was no doubt thrilled.[55]

According to a WPA study, by the end of 1937, Hattiesburg had nearly forty industrial employers offering jobs for approximately twenty-five hundred workers. The largest employers and their approximate workforces were as follows: Reliance Manufacturing, 550–600; Tatum Lumber, 400; Hercules Powder Company, 400; Pioneer Silk, 250; Meridian Fertilizer, 105; and Gulf States Creosoting, 50. Several additional firms, such as the Gordon-Van Tine Tire Company, Hattiesburg Brick Works, Clinton Lumber, Hub City Ice, and the Weldmech Steel Products Company each employed between twenty-five and forty-five people. And dozens of smaller firms employed fewer than twenty-five people.[56]

In addition to paying wages, Hattiesburg's largest employers offered further benefits for local white workers. Reliance Manufacturing provided employees with a nonprofit cafeteria, tennis and basketball courts, and a "Dixie Club" filled with couches, game tables, and a small library. Employees and their families accessed these amenities on lunch breaks, after work, and on weekends. The Dixie Club included a dance hall that hosted Saturday night socials and a variety of fundraisers. Reliance employees also formed their own Employees Mutual Benefit Society that provided healthcare and wage subsidies in case an employee fell ill and could not work.[57]

Pioneer Silk provided similar benefits. The firm's white employees also enjoyed access to a clubhouse with reading and music rooms. Pioneer Silk provided local white organizations with access to the club and even offered to pay to have the space cleaned after events. Like Reliance, Pioneer employees enjoyed access to a subsidized cafeteria whose deficits were absorbed by the New York–based company.[58]

In 1937, the Delaware-based Hercules Powder Company also built a beautiful new clubhouse for employees. Its first floor contained a company store, a restaurant, and a barbershop. The second floor included reading and music rooms with velvet-covered couches, a billiard room, and "one of the most expensive and most modern bowling alleys in Mississippi," noted the *Hattiesburg American*, which dubbed the club "one of the most modern structures in [the] state." Hercules employed both black and white workers, but only whites were allowed full access to the club.[59]

Nevertheless, despite federal aid and some new jobs, Hattiesburg at the close of the 1930s was far from saved. The Chamber of Commerce did virtually everything it could to increase federal funding and recruit new industries, but the organization simply could never come close to replacing the lost wages of the vanished sawmill jobs. By 1940, Forrest County sawmills employed only 284 men, a number whose significance becomes especially clear by recalling that J. J. Newman Lumber alone had once provided approximately twelve hundred jobs. New companies like Reliance and Pioneer Silk helped the local economy but could not possibly satiate the demand for good jobs. Moreover, the potential benefits of new manufacturing firms were mitigated by a constant stream of migrants looking for work. Between 1930 and 1938, an estimated six thousand people came to the Hattiesburg metropolitan area in search of jobs, boosting the population by about 25 percent. Local merchants might have been quite satisfied with the population increase, but the flood of jobseekers far outpaced the number of new positions offered by either the federal government or private enterprise.[60]

Another problem was that not all the jobs lasted. After only three years of operation, Pioneer Silk closed in the summer of 1938. Several weeks later, Tatum Lumber closed after forty-five years of operation. After years of struggling to replace jobs, Hattiesburg over three months in 1938 lost an additional five hundred jobs and approximately $325,000 in annual wages. Unless Hattiesburg could find some way to "provide able-bodied people with work," the *Hattiesburg American* predicted that autumn, "people will go on the relief until relief stops and then they will have to move away to more fertile fields." The city still faced a precarious future.[61]

Many who could not access steady work struggled to survive and were forced to rely on the kindness of others. In 1939 alone, the local Red Cross branch reported 6,913 visits in a county of fewer than thirty-five thousand residents. Hattiesburg swelled with panhandlers and hoboes who slept under bridges or formed large camps on the outskirts of town, periodically skulking into the city to beg at people's back doors for jobs and meals. "There was never a day during the Depression that people didn't come by our house for a handout," one local man remembered. Describing his childhood in the 1930s, Presley Davenport recalled that "they would come to the back door of our house, and mama would always give them something to eat. They'd come to the back door and knock." Dorothy Musgrove, echoing these memories of home life during the recession, added, "and you know you would fix them a plate of food, whatever you had." Soup lines stretched far down city streets. "I remember people standing in line," Musgrove recalled, "all the way a block toward Main Street and around the corner for assistance from the federal government."[62]

By 1938, approximately one-third of Hattiesburg's labor force was either unemployed, partially employed, or employed by federal New Deal programs. The decline of total wages across Mississippi illuminates the bleakness of the state economy at the end of the 1930s. Between 1919 and 1939, the total amount of wages earned by Mississippians decreased from $51 million to just over $27.1 million. Deflation accounts for much of the decline, but the greatest factors were job loss, bankruptcies, and closures.[63]

Like many cities, Hattiesburg was struggling mightily even with the aid of the federal government and new jobs provided by northern firms such as Reliance and Hercules. It is difficult to imagine Hattiesburg in the 1930s without all the outside aid. In fact, by 1940, the federal government was by far the largest employer of white men in both Hattiesburg and Forrest County. Almost completely reliant on outsiders, Hattiesburg at the close of the 1930s still found itself hapless and depressed, with no permanent solution in sight.[64]

CHAPTER EIGHT

Community Children

> My life has been made much, much fuller by attending Eureka between 1935 and 1938. I never would have gone to college. I never would have been a professional man if I hadn't attended Eureka.
>
> —Dr. Isaac Thomas, Eureka High School Class of 1938

On Tuesday, May 1, 1934, the Hattiesburg Negro Business League threw a celebration of its own. At about noon, black shop owners closed their businesses and teachers released children from school so that all could participate in the opening parade of the 1934 "Negro Fair." Two black marching bands, one from Hattiesburg and another from nearby Laurel, led a procession of black residents through the city streets. People with cars adorned their vehicles in ribbons and signs and drove slowly behind the bands. Hundreds more marched on foot, following the convoy from downtown Hattiesburg to the campus of Eureka High School, where the crowd gathered underneath a big-top tent for a series of prayers and speeches marking the opening of the fair.[1]

This Negro Fair was organized to raise money for a new park for local black youths. Black business owners sought to transform a lightly used section of the Mobile Street District into a recreational area containing tennis and basketball courts, a baseball diamond, a multipurpose athletic field, a cinder track, and playground equipment. This idea had been in development for several years. In 1930, the grocer J. B. Woods and several black ministers approached the Hattiesburg Chamber of Commerce with a proposal to buy and develop land for a new park. Four years later, a grant from a New Deal program called the Civil Works Administration (CWA) was expected to help pay for landscaping and playground equipment, but that financial support fell through when the CWA was dissolved in March of 1934. Soon thereafter, the Hattiesburg Negro Business League resolved to raise the money on their own.[2]

Open every afternoon and evening between May 1 and May 4, the 1934 Negro Fair featured a variety of fundraising events. Local artisans and cooks erected small booths where they sold handicrafts and plates of food. Several local choirs, including the Eureka High School Glee Club, performed ticketed concerts in the Eureka High School auditorium. On the final day of the festival, several members of the black community staged a minstrel show.[3]

Wednesday was "White Citizens Day" at the Negro Fair. An estimated fifty white residents attended a special chicken dinner prepared by local black women and enjoyed an evening concert at the Eureka High School auditorium. A local white judge delivered a speech "thanking the leaders among the colored population for their example in avoiding conflict with the law," reported a journalist in the *Hattiesburg American*. The *American* supported the fair throughout the week, calling it a "worthy enterprise" and labeling the event a "success." The local black correspondent for the *Chicago Defender* went so far as to call the fair "one of the outstanding events in the history of this city."[4]

The 1934 Negro Fair raised approximately $110—not enough to complete the park, but a good start nonetheless. Over the following months, the Hattiesburg Negro Business League partnered with other black organizations to secure additional funding through individual donations, church collections, community rallies, and contributions from various social clubs and mutual-aid societies.[5]

After two years of fundraising, the effort at last proved successful. The new community park officially opened on June 2, 1936, with tennis matches, ball games, and a ceremonial parade of local black youths who would grow up playing on those grounds. The original facilities have since been replaced, but the park remains in use today at the corner of New Orleans and Ninth Streets in Hattiesburg's Mobile Street District. It was initially placed there by black men and women who led an extended, multipronged community-organizing effort during the middle of the Great Depression. That community loved its children.[6]

Hammond and Charles Smith played key roles in the playground effort. No direct details of their contributions are documented, but both brothers were heavily involved in the Hattiesburg Negro Business League. Hammond was secretary of the organization in 1934, and Charles was elected chairman the following year. Both were involved in a statewide professional organization called the Mississippi Medical Surgical Association of Negro Doctors, and they were influential at St. Paul Methodist Church, the "congregation on the hill" where their family had belonged since arriving in Hattiesburg in 1900.[7]

In 1934, Turner Smith turned seventy-five and Mamie sixty-eight. Turner was still listed in city directories as a carpenter, but he and Mamie appear in few other records from that era. Although each had at least a decade more life to live, their most active days were behind them. But they were enveloped by family. Three of their children had moved away, but the fourth son, Wendell, still lived at home. Charles and his wife, Myrtle, lived next door with their four children—Charles Jr., Grover, and the twin girls Myrtle and Sarah. Hammond and his wife, Lucille, who never had children, lived just four doors down. Now led by a younger generation, the Smith family stood out in the Mobile Street District for their professional success and leadership. They were pillars of the community.[8]

The economic recession of the 1920s and 1930s did not affect Hammond Smith as badly as it had most Hattiesburg residents. Everyone struggled in some way, but Hammond's drugstore provided him and his family with a stable foundation during these hungry times. Owning a drugstore was one of the most financially lucrative opportunities available to black Mississippians during the early decades of the twentieth century. According to a 1935 study, Mississippi's black drugstore owners generated, on average, nearly three times the income of grocers and far more revenue than restaurateurs. In addition to filling prescriptions, Hammond Smith also cashed checks, sold tickets to local events, and retailed the essential products of daily life—razor blades, perfumes, shoe polish, hair pomade, pipes, chewing gum, candy, sodas, and ice cream. "I got along better than the physicians in those days . . . because I had so many things to sell," Hammond recalled. "I'm not saying that it didn't hurt, but I got along pretty good."[9]

Hammond and Lucille lived fairly comfortable lives throughout the 1930s. Like all local African Americans, they remained subject to the racial ordinances and customs of Jim Crow, but their lives also appear to have been much more pleasurable than were the lives of most working-class whites. They owned their own home and never struggled to feed or clothe themselves. Hammond was even able to afford to hire help in his store. "I always had two or three people working," he remembered of the depression years. The couple led active social lives, spending much of their time in church, with family, or at various parties, celebrations, meetings, picnics, and bridge tournaments. They also regularly took vacations to the Gulf Coast or traveled to other parts of the state to see relatives. In late October of 1933, the couple went to Chicago for the 1933 World's Fair. The timing of their trip would have placed them at the "Century of Progress Exhibition" near the arrival of the famous *Graf Zeppelin*, the largest airship in the world until construction of its successor, the *Hindenburg*.[10]

Of course, Hammond and Lucille Smith were exceptions for the era. Most of Hattiesburg's working-class black men and women struggled mightily. Their challenges were rooted in the broader trends of job loss that affected the entire city. Local black workers were not as negatively affected by the practice of "last hired, first fired" that characterized depression-era black economic inequality in other parts of America. Despite some examples of whites taking black jobs, racially segregated fields of employment generally survived the financial crisis. Domestic work remained an almost exclusively black occupation, and large percentages of black men were always employed by local firms and the city's municipal departments. What did change in the 1930s was that even the most menial black jobs became increasingly difficult to acquire. Few white men were ever going to clean a Hattiesburg city sewer, but as the sawmills cut out, unemployed African Americans flooded the city's labor pool, making even the least desirable wage-labor jobs harder to find. During the 1930s, the city's black male unemployment rate ranged between 20 and 30 percent.[11]

As with working-class whites, low pay and unstable labor arrangements led to the expansion of a distinct class of roving laborers who spent their days moving between entry-level, low-paid jobs such as construction worker, general laborer, deliveryman, or servant. Several black men also began working on nearby farms for daily wages. Very few black Hattiesburgers ever worked permanently in agriculture, but farm jobs on the outskirts of town offered seasonal employment for some.[12]

It is impossible to cite any precise income figures for the local black male precariat, but their earnings in the mid-1930s likely ranged somewhere between Mississippi's average per capita annual income of $177 in 1935 and about $400, roughly the amount a general laborer could earn working sixty-hour workweeks at Tatum Lumber over the course of a year. Income could vary widely depending on a variety of factors. One truth remained constant:

nearly all of Hattiesburg's working-class black men performed physically demanding and dangerous jobs for extremely low wages. Of course, this was not exactly a new development.[13]

Black women in 1930s-era Hattiesburg actually experienced relatively low rates of unemployment; because their jobs paid so little, they were essentially recession proof. Even amid the worst financial catastrophe in modern American history, thousands of white Hattiesburg families could still afford to hire black women as maids, cooks, nannies, and laundresses. A handful of black women started their own businesses or became teachers, but most were prevented from pursuing any other avenue of employment. Even well-educated black women were not eligible to work as secretaries or typists in white-owned offices. And fewer than twenty local black women ever secured one of the federally funded jobs provided by the New Deal. Also remember that black women were not allowed to work at the Reliance Manufacturing factory that opened in 1933. These restrictions left thousands of working-class black women with no other choice than to work in domestic service for very little pay. With an unemployment rate of only about 10 percent toward the end of the 1930s, black women were at once the most highly employed and the most severely disadvantaged segment of Hattiesburg's population.[14]

Part of the reason for such statistically low rates of unemployment among black women was that roughly 40 percent simply did not participate in the city's labor force. Married women—more than 70 percent of local black women over the age of fifteen—had advantages. Some, including Lucille and Myrtle Smith, did not have to work, because their husbands earned enough income to provide for the family. Others chose not to work because the wages were so low. Many wives and mothers concluded that it was far more logical to spend their time maintaining a family garden or sewing clothes for their children than cleaning a white person's house for just a few dollars per week. Most unmarried black women did work, but few lived alone. The Mobile Street District included dozens of boardinghouses and female-led intergenerational units where single women lived together.[15]

Joblessness and poverty affected people of all races, but black Hattiesburgers were further disadvantaged by unequal access to New Deal benefits. Despite provisions restricting racial discrimination, white Hattiesburgers enjoyed vastly more access to programs like the CCC and WPA. In a city where black people comprised roughly one-third of the population, the white-to-black ratio in public emergency-work jobs was roughly five-to-one for men and nine-to-one for women. And because African Americans had been systematically disfranchised and blocked from participation in city government, nearly all local WPA grants were used to fund projects that only benefitted whites.[16]

Consider, for example, the vastly different nature of Hattiesburg's two youth recreation projects. As the Hattiesburg Negro Business League scrambled to raise a few hundred dollars for a new park, the city's white civic leaders secured federal grants totaling over $50,000 to construct a new gymnasium for the white school. White people from neighboring towns were allowed to use the WPA gym, but no black team was ever allowed to take the court. Despite some modest examples of interracial cooperation in the 1920s and 1930s, local white leaders demonstrated very little willingness to include African Americans in any meaningful federal relief program. There were too many parks, schools, roads, and gardens to fully measure these disparities, but thousands of local whites clearly enjoyed disparate access to federal support.

Poor black people in Hattiesburg lived extraordinarily difficult lives. Black children who grew up in Hattiesburg during the depression later remembered the adversities of the era. Clearese Cook, whose father took to the rails in search of out-of-town jobs, remembered days when her family could not afford flour or shortening and times when she "had to wear the same dress five days a week." Douglas Conner, whose father worked at J. J. Newman Lumber until the mill closed, remembered "times when we had only bread and water to eat." Constance Baker, the daughter of a black carpenter, remembered her father struggling to find work and occasionally having to accept used goods in exchange for his services. One white woman paid him for a job with "an old piano and an old quilt." When asked about the depression, the black washerwoman Osceola McCarty told an interviewer, "You just couldn't get no food hardly." One particularly heartwrenching story from the era occurred during the summer of 1932, when two hungry black children aged ten and six appeared at Hattiesburg City Hall and began singing, hoping "that they would collect a few cents with which to buy food," reported the *Hattiesburg American*.[17]

The poverty of the era ravaged the psyche of many. Some turned to larceny; just about every major store in the Mobile Street District appears to have been robbed at one point (though whether the thieves were black or white is often unknown). Others turned to alcohol. Bootlegging was common in the region, and consumers had access to all sorts of moonshine or hooch, which helped them detach from the stressful realities of their environment. Douglas Conner remembered the way his father used to drink. "He would be sober enough to go to work and do his job," Conner explained, "but during off-duty hours, except when he was sleeping, he was constantly drinking. I don't believe I ever saw him completely sober a day in his life." Similar testimonies about alcoholism are scarce, but we can be certain that Conner's father was not alone. Hattiesburg's working-class white community experienced its own share of crime, alcoholism, and vagrancy, but black life, with its immense racial disadvantages and disproportionate punishments for violations of social norms, was almost always more stressful. The fact that most local African Americans lived in a floodplain only added to their vulnerability and their challenges.[18]

As difficult as their lives were, it is also important to remember that working-class black Hattiesburgers were a resilient and well-callused population. Most had struggled with poverty all their lives. Some, including Turner Smith, had once been enslaved. Many black families responded to the continuing challenges of the 1930s as they always had—by embracing traditions of self-help and community organizing that had characterized black life in the Mobile Street District for decades. Working-class black families maintained side gardens and kept chickens or even cows to provide food for their families. "I don't know of a single person out in that neighborhood that didn't have a garden and hogs and chickens and all those kinds of things," remembered Ralph Woullard Jr. of growing up black in the area just south of Hattiesburg. Some people made their own clothing or shoes. Even the poorest black families strove to instill a sense of pride and self-sufficiency in their children. Speaking of the pride of his mother, Douglas Conner related that she never let any of her kids accept food from another family, "even if we were hungry." Clearese Cook took an after-school job as a domestic worker during junior high school so that she could buy fabric to make her own dresses. "That was one thing that was taught in my family growing up," Cook later told an interviewer. "A sense of pride." For black families like the Cooks, the notion of "a sense of pride" represented intergenerational principles of self-sufficiency to survive poverty on their own terms.[19]

The city's black poor were not entirely on their own. Throughout the 1930s, they received a variety of aid from dozens of community institutions and organizations. In spite of widespread economic challenges—or perhaps because of them—black communal activity expanded at unprecedented

Table 8.1 Black Hattiesburg Organizations during the 1930s (Church affiliations denoted in parentheses)

Benevolent	Fraternal	Professional	Religious	Social	Youth
Civic Improvement Association	Afro-American Sons and Daughters	Forrest County branch of the National Association of Negro War Veterans	Boys Unit (St. Paul)	Afro-American Society	Colored Youth Forum (Mt. Carmel)
Colored Citizens Welfare League	Elks	Hattiesburg Negro Business League	Ladies Aid Society (St. Paul)	Art and Industrial Club	Girls Reserves
Home Guards (St. Paul)	Royal Zophangs	Poro Agents	Pastor's Wives Club	Chain of Friendship Club (Presbyterian Church)	Luxis Club
Missionary Society (Mt. Carmel)			Pulpit Aid (Zion Chapel AME)	Friendship Club	Negro Boys and Girls Improvement Association
Missionary Society (Zion Chapel AME)			Union Choir Service	Galaxy Federated Club	PTA
Mother's Club				Happy Hearts Social Club	
Mothers' Jewels Band (Zion Chapel AME)				Hattiesburg Social Service Club [Chicago]	
Queen Esther Circle (St. Paul)				Hercules Social Club	
Welfare Club (True Light)				Jolly Five Social Club	
Willing Workers Club (Mt. Carmel)				Just Us Club	
Women's Federation Club				Mah-Jong Social Club	
Women's Foreign Missionary Society (St. Paul)				Peanut Social Club	
				Phyllis Wheatley Social Club	
				Rescue Club (Mt. Carmel)	
				Silver Moon Social Club	
				Social King's Club	
				White Rose Social Club	
				Women's Social Club	

rates during the Great Depression. In addition to churches, Hattiesburg in 1936 was home to more than forty black community organizations, including fraternal orders, social clubs, interdenominational religious groups, professional societies, and neighborhood improvement associations. Working together through interconnected, multilayered networks, these groups led a variety of initiatives designed to improve the lives of local black citizens. The 1934 Negro Fair was just one example among thousands of black community initiatives in the 1930s.[20]

The best-documented community programs were led by the Hattiesburg Negro Business League. Even during the recession, Mobile Street sustained a vibrant downtown business community filled with shops, including a confectionary and ice cream parlor, a dental office, a movie theater, an auto mechanic shop, an insurance company, a jewelry repair shop, a beer garden, a black-owned filling station, and numerous funeral parlors, doctors' offices, barbershops, groceries, tailor shops, and restaurants. Local black business owners worked through the Hattiesburg Negro Business League to orchestrate charitable projects that benefitted other members of their race.[21]

The regular activities of the Hattiesburg Negro Business League included fundraising drives to aid needy children, annual Christmastime toy drives, a "Poor Folks Christmas Fund," and a variety of charity football games, luncheons, and rallies. Additionally, black businessmen often organized parallel relief organizations when African Americans were excluded from citywide relief programs. For example, the grocer Gaither Hardaway led a Colored Division of the Salvation Army and a Colored Auxiliary of the local Red Cross. The year after Mayor Tatum evicted the Red Cross from City Hall for serving African Americans, Hardaway led a month-long effort of the Colored Auxiliary that raised $165. After a similar initiative in 1933, local Red Cross chairman J. C. Fields praised Hardaway's leadership, telling the *Hattiesburg American*, "We appreciate the splendid membership and interest the Hattiesburg and Forrest county colored people have always given in the past." Fellow grocer J. B. Woods similarly created a black version of a citywide relief program, during much of the 1930s operating an unemployment office for black workers out of a building he owned on Mobile Street.[22]

Additional forms of aid were disbursed through churches. By the mid-1930s, Hattiesburg was home to twenty-five black churches. Due to a diverse array of denominations in black communities, the Hub City actually had more black churches than white ones. The city's African American denominations included thirteen Baptist, seven Methodist—three AME, three MEC, and one CME—one Presbyterian, one Christ's Sanctified Holy Church, and three Pentecostal Churches of God.[23]

Hattiesburg's three oldest black churches—St. Paul Methodist, Mt. Carmel Baptist, and Zion Chapel A.M.E.—formed the bedrock of communal life of the Mobile Street District. Initially established during the 1880s in rickety wooden buildings, each church had since relocated into large brick structures located within a half mile of one another near the center of the black downtown. In addition to being the oldest churches in the black community, St. Paul, Mt. Carmel, and Zion Chapel were also the largest. Precise congregation numbers are not available for each year, but a report from 1937 indicates that St. Paul and Zion Chapel each had about five hundred members. It is safe to assume that Mt. Carmel, which added new wings in the 1920s to accommodate a growing population, had at least as many congregants. By the mid-1930s, True Light Baptist Church had also grown quite large, with a membership of about 350. Approximately one-fourth of all local African Americans belonged to one of the city's four largest congregations. Nearly all of Hattiesburg's most influential black leaders belonged to one of the original three.[24]

Whereas smaller churches often only met biweekly and were guided by itinerant preachers, Hattiesburg's largest black churches met at least twice per week and were led by full-time pastors who lived in homes provided by the congregation. Pastors at the big churches changed every few years, but they always held active roles in the community, working closely with local organizations and participating in community events such as fairs, sporting contests, and neighborhood fundraisers. Moreover, they were among the regular customers of the city's barbershops, groceries, and restaurants. To residents of the Mobile Street District, pastors were at once religious leaders, neighbors, and friends.[25]

The city's largest black churches were also guided by deacons and boards of trustees who controlled financial and personnel decisions. Pastors served as temporary figureheads, but deacons and trustees held the most influence. Local black businessmen featured prominently in the leadership of the city's largest African American churches. Hammond and Charles Smith served on the board of trustees at St. Paul, Gaither Hardaway was a longtime deacon at Mt. Carmel Baptist, and for over thirty years, J. B. Woods was among the leading members at Zion Chapel. Entrepreneurs and professionals guided church governance, but most congregants were among the city's working-class black population. Although a handful of blue-collar workers did serve as deacons or trustees, most working-class black men and women contributed to church life by participating in Sunday schools and choirs, volunteering for church-related events and organizations, and making small donations to collection plates as their finances allowed. People in every church gave to help those who struggled. "If we knew that somebody was having a hardship, we shared with them," remembered the son of a local pastor. "What I mean by 'we,' I'm talking about the community."[26]

As they had in earlier decades, black women continued to play crucial leadership roles in every single church. There were several layers to their involvement. Informally, black women oversaw logistical support for nearly all church events—suppers, revivals, weddings, funerals, choirs, parties, holiday celebrations, and special commemorations, such as Women's Day or Grandparent's Day. It was women who arranged flowers, placed Bibles in the pews, set out candles, washed pastors' robes, and cleaned church floors. The largest churches included formal organizations that performed these services—such as the Pulpit Aid of Zion Chapel or the Ladies Aid of St. Paul.[27]

Black church women also occupied formal leadership roles by serving on stewardess or deaconess boards or belonging to women's missionary societies. Most black women's missionary societies were local branches of state and national missionary societies that in some cases predated the Civil War. Many American missionary societies worked for international causes, but in most Southern black communities, these groups focused primarily on aiding the local poor. The largest black missionary societies in Hattiesburg included St. Paul's Foreign Missionary Society, Home Guards, and Queen Esther Circle; Mt. Carmel's Missionary Society and Willing Workers Club; and Zion Chapel's Missionary Society and Mothers' Jewels Band. Operating within prescribed gender roles of the era, they led Bible study classes, provided instruction on women's hygiene and childcare, and helped plan activities in local schools. Because these organizations usually charged monthly dues, their membership was typically limited to the wives and relatives of the city's leading black business and professional men. Lucille and Myrtle Smith, Hammond and Charles Smith's wives, both belonged to the St. Paul Women's Foreign Missionary Society.[28]

In addition to forming their own organizations, local black churches worked together constantly. In the fall of 1931, six of Hattiesburg's largest black churches—St. Paul Methodist, Mt. Carmel Baptist, Zion Chapel A.M.E., True Light Baptist, Mt. Bethel Baptist, and Mt. Zion Baptist—formed an interdenominational organization named the Union Choir Service. Led by local businessman Paul Weston, the Union Choir Service raised money for charity by holding monthly singing competitions at one of the member churches. Held after regular Sunday services, the events began with a scripture reading and congregational singing before moving on to the competition. During the competition, each of the six church choirs would perform two or three traditional spirituals. A collection basket was circulated through the crowd during each performance, allowing audience members to vote for the best choir based on the amount of money they donated. Whichever church collected the most money during their performance was declared the winner. The winning church choir went home with the bragging rights, and all the money went toward the same causes. A report from November of 1934 indicates a total collection of $20.80, a modest amount but quite enough to help feed and clothe some needy families.[29]

On Thanksgiving Day of 1934, the Union Choir Service worked in conjunction with the Hattiesburg Negro Business League to publish the inaugural issue of *The Union Messenger*, the city's first black newspaper in over twenty years. *The Union Messenger*, its editors explained, sought "to bring to the public a clean and clear cut paper . . . [that] will meet the long needs of the city for a colored newspaper." Thanking the support of local ministers and business leaders, the newspaper encouraged "the full cooperation of the 7000 Negroes of this city." That inaugural issue was filled with dozens of community updates and advertisements. "Go Forward," encouraged an advertisement sponsored by several local black businesses, including the office of Dr. Charles Smith and the Smith Drug Store.[30]

Religious and business organizations predominated over local life, but more than a dozen other women's clubs formed in black Hattiesburg by the 1930s offered the greatest level of interconnectivity between community organizations. Although often affiliated with churches, women in these groups worked with a wide variety of peers, ranging from close friends and neighbors to women from other parts of town or even other cities. Many women belonged to several clubs at once. Lucille and Myrtle Smith both belonged to the Phyllis Wheatley and Women's Federated Clubs, meaning that each belonged to at least four community organizations.[31]

Rooted in the late nineteenth century, the African American clubwomen's movement spread through every sizeable black community in the United States during the early 1900s. By 1916, the National Association of Colored Women (NACW) counted over fifteen hundred affiliated branches. But even this official count captures only part of black women's involvement in clubs. Countless numbers of black women joined informal non-NACW affiliates. After all, it does not take much effort to organize a group of friends or neighbors and attach a name to it. Some clubs operated with well-defined sociopolitical objectives. Others just gathered on weekends to socialize. The NACW affiliates are best known, but black women's clubs were diverse. Hattiesburg was home to all kinds.[32]

America's most visible black clubwomen's organizations participated in community-based initiatives such as running orphanages, supporting schools, teaching domestic service courses, and advocating racial uplift across socioeconomic classes. The NACW, which later changed its name to the National Association of Colored Women's Clubs, adopted the motto "Lifting as We Climb," a slogan that reflected their shared vision of racial uplift as a broad mission of black advancement. Generally speaking, the organization was guided by the philosophy that improvements to the education and behavior of lower-class African Americans offered universal benefits to the race as a whole. Like their counterparts in places such as New York City and Washington, DC, Hattiesburg's most visible black clubwomen worked toward racial uplift by designing community projects focused on improving public health, education, childrearing, and domestic skills.[33]

Religious groups and women's clubs were not exclusively limited to African Americans. Similar organizations played analogous roles in Hattiesburg's white community. White men controlled local politics and business activities, but white women actively influenced society through involvement in a variety of church missionary groups and women's clubs that aided pastors, raised money for charity, ran public health projects, and supported local schools. The biggest difference between black and white women's clubs, however, was that white women's clubs enjoyed support from local companies and access to publicly funded institutions. Many of the activities conducted by white women, such as college scholarship drives and library book donations, were impractical for African Americans, who could neither attend the State Teachers College nor borrow books from the local library. White women belonged to a community with far greater access to federal benefits, municipal support, and wealth, and the activities of their clubs reflected their social privilege.[34]

But black women's clubs did also organize a variety of purely social activities. In addition to running daycares and teaching home economics courses, the lives of black clubwomen in the 1930s were filled with parties, cake walks, hikes, picnics, ice cream socials, beauty pageants, and dances. Hammond, Lucille, Charles, and Myrtle Smith were all featured prominently in social news from the Mobile Street District. They hosted dinners, attended parties, and participated in bridge tournaments.[35]

The social lives of Mobile Street residents were documented by local women, who sent neighborhood updates to national black newspapers such as the *Chicago Defender*, the *Baltimore Afro-American*, and the *Pittsburgh Courier* for inclusion in the "Mississippi" sections of their national weekly editions. The *Baltimore Afro-American* and the *Pittsburgh Courier* were each sold in the Mobile Street District during parts of the 1930s, but the *Chicago Defender* always remained the most popular Northern black newspaper in the neighborhood. Between 1930 and 1939, the *Defender* published at least four hundred updates from Hattiesburg's Mobile Street District. It is impossible to gauge exactly how many local African Americans read the *Defender* each week, but the newspaper was clearly important for many people in the neighborhood. In 1936, a reporter for the *Defender* interviewed Hattiesburg grocer J. B. Woods at the Republican National Convention in Cleveland, writing, "He says people in his town are strong for *The Chicago Defender* and feel lost without it."[36]

Black women's clubs stereotypically included middle- and upper-class women, but Hattiesburg was also home to a small number of clubs led by working-class women. For example, Reponzia Washington, the wife of a sawmill worker and carpenter, was a leader in the Social Kings Club. Verda Mott, whose husband was a truck driver, was president of the Mah-Jong Social Club. Numerous groups of working-class black men and women participated in a variety of groups that outlined the parameters of their social lives.[37]

In 1936, a group of black male employees at the Hercules Powder Company formed their own organization called the Hercules Social Club. These men lived difficult lives and occupied rigidly segregated and dangerous jobs that placed them in close proximity to toxic and explosive chemicals. Black employees at Hercules were not even allowed to enter the plant through the same entrance as white workers, let alone use the company's new clubhouse. But even these low-paid and excluded men developed a group identity based on their common employer.[38]

Members of the Hercules Social Club left behind no explanation of their particular goals or vision, but its leadership suggests that these working-class men ascribed great importance to their roles within the group. The club's business manager, twenty-eight-year-old Roosevelt Fox, was a former railroad laborer; its chairman, twenty-five-year-old Albert Washington, had an eighth-grade education; its treasurer, fifty-four-year-old Steve Gould, was an Alabama native supporting a family of seven; its secretary, Robert Richardson, lived with his wife and infant daughter in a tiny rented shack; its vice-president, thirty-four-year-old Hattiesburg resident Houston Haney, had a seventh-grade education and lived with his wife, mother, niece, and two daughters in a little rented shotgun home; and its president, Muffy McCoy, lived with his wife in the left side of a split shotgun house that was only large enough for a single window. One can only speculate what this club meant to these men. They were all poor, black, and disfranchised, living in Great Depression–era Mississippi. But as leaders in the Hercules Social Club, they carried impressive titles in front of their names. And they gathered with their families on every fourth Friday night at eight o'clock to play cards, sing, and talk, enjoying precious respite from lives that were otherwise filled with little respect and very difficult days. Race and socioeconomic status framed the parameters of their working-class lives, but did not extinguish their sense of communal belonging or in any way eclipse their humanity.[39]

On weekend nights, the dance halls and makeshift juke joints of the Mobile Street District filled with more raucous activities. By the mid-1930s, Hattiesburg's black downtown was home to drinking establishments such as the Red Circle Beer Garden and the Love Garden of Joy, as well as dozens of informal bars operated out of stores and private homes. Although Mississippi extended prohibition even after the repeal of the Volstead Act in 1933, a 1934 state law did authorize the sale of light wine and beer—but not hard liquor—in some venues. Regardless, state liquor laws mattered little in the unregulated juke joints that operated near Mobile Street. On weekend nights, hundreds of working-class black men and women gathered in those spaces to gamble, drink, and dance late into the night. "They used to say that they lived for Saturday night," remembered one local of the neighborhood's reputation. "That's when they whooped it up and had a real good time."[40]

The black revelers who frequented these juke joints and dance halls bore witness to some remarkable American musical history. Hattiesburg's Mobile Street District, located in close proximity to New Orleans, had for decades been a hotbed of black musical talent. Jazz pioneer Jelly Roll Morton appeared in Hattiesburg nearly twenty years before most people in New York City or Chicago had ever heard of him. As early as 1907, the neighborhood had its own group—the Hattiesburg Big Four String Band—that played to both black and white audiences across the region. This rich tradition continued throughout Jim Crow. The list of musicians known to have performed in the Mobile Street District in the 1930s includes Robert Johnson, Little Brother Montgomery, Cooney Vaughn, Hattiesburg natives Gus Perryman and Mississippi Matilda, and the Edgewater Crows, who performed a popular song called the "Mobile Street Stomp" in homage to the local black business community. In 1936, a white music producer from Jackson came to Hattiesburg to record a group known as the Mississippi Jook Band. According to *Rolling Stone* magazine, their tracks "Barbeque Bust" and "Dangerous Woman" represented the first recorded evidence of "fully formed rock & roll guitar riffs and a stomping rock & roll beat."[41]

The most popular events in the Mobile Street District were the Friday night football games played by the Eureka High School Tigers. In 1936, the Tigers moved to a new home field located at the recently completed recreational park in the Mobile Street District. That fall, the Tigers enjoyed their best season to that point in school history. Appropriately dressed in orange and black, the Tigers won all ten of their games by a combined score of 146–6 on their way to winning the Big Eight Conference championship (Mississippi's toughest conference for black schools).[42]

The Eureka Tigers captured the city's adoration. "Everybody loved Eureka football games," remembered class of 1938 graduate Isaac Thomas. "Hattiesburg used to be booming with celebrations after the football games," recalled another black resident. Even white people started coming. Eureka games were regularly advertised in the *Hattiesburg American* and included a "special section" reserved for white spectators. Ruby Cook, a white girl who grew up in Hattiesburg during the 1920s and 1930s, frequently attended Eureka games with her future husband and their friends. In fact, the couple's first date was at a Eureka Tigers game. Mrs. Cook remembered the stadium "wrapped up with people, black and white." "It was bigger than Hattiesburg High," she recalled. "They had a little old drum major. . . .

Eureka High School football team, 1941. (McCain Library and Archives, University of Southern Mississippi)

That kid could stand and put his feet on the ground and his head on the ground backwards and twirl his baton."[43]

Eureka was the Big Eight Conference champion again in 1937 and produced strong teams in each of the following years. The best team in school history was probably the 1940 squad, which went unbeaten and was named Mississippi state champion. That December, the Tigers were given the honor of hosting the Pine Bowl Classic, an annual exhibition game played between championship teams from different Southern states. On Christmas Day of 1940, Eureka hosted Haywood High School from Brownsville, Tennessee. The Tigers jumped out to an early lead before eventually losing their momentum and falling by a score of 13–6.[44]

Football occupied a half dozen or so evenings in the fall, but Eureka High School played a major role in local black life throughout the year. During the 1930s, Eureka hosted an endless variety of adult education classes, summer teacher workshops, organization meetings, lectures, and concerts. At one point in the early 1930s, Eureka hosted an estimated eighteen hundred attendees during the annual statewide meeting of the Afro-American Sons and Daughters, Mississippi's largest black fraternal organization. People from the community were in the building all the time. Eureka was a site of constant activity and a beacon of communal pride.[45]

As should be expected, Eureka High School received far fewer financial resources than the all-white Hattiesburg High School. During the Great Depression, the state of Mississippi spent about half the national average on per pupil school expenditures. Black students were particularly disadvantaged. During the 1929–30 academic year, Mississippi spent an average of $31.33 on white students and only $5.94 on black ones. Per capita expenditures offer a useful contrast, but because these calculations typically do not account for additional expenses such as transportation, electricity, water, and administrative costs, they do not fully measure the totality of racially based educational inequalities. Critical, too, is the fact that black schools did not have comparable access to benefits provided by the New Deal. Between 1935 and 1937, New Deal programs allocated approximately $8 million to white school buildings in Mississippi and $400,000 to black school buildings, a particularly stark comparison considering that African Americans still comprised roughly half of the state's population.[46]

The disparities in Forrest County were not quite as unequal as the state averages. Figures from each year are not readily available, but in 1940, the county spent an average of $37.84 on white students and $18.20 on black students. Despite this inequity, $18.20 actually represented about three times the state average for per-pupil spending on African American students. As late as 1939, 30 percent of Mississippi counties still did not even have a high school for black students. Hattiesburg actually had one of the best black educational systems in the state. Students in grades one through six were split between three schools: the Third Ward School, the Sixteenth Section School, and Eureka. All local black students who continued beyond sixth grade went to Eureka.[47]

Eureka opened the 1937 academic year with an enrollment of 822 students guided by a faculty of fifteen. Principal J. W. Addison had taught math at Eureka since the school opened in 1921 and had recently been promoted. Henry Whisenton, a graduate of Tougaloo College, was the assistant principal and football coach. Alfred Todd, a graduate of the Tuskegee Institute, taught history and served as assistant football coach. All the other teachers were women: Ruby Henry, Vera Spencer, Laura McLaurin, Marie Washington, Rubye Watson, Rosa Hines, Estelle Jenkins, Rhoda Mae Hopkins, Rhoda Tademy, Grace Love, Sarah Clark, and Pennie Lee Cole, who later married Mr. Todd. Most of the female teachers were single and over the age of thirty, with at least two years of college experience. At least three of the twelve were Hattiesburg natives. Pennie Lee Cole, Marie Washington, and Rosa Hines were second-generation Hattiesburgers whose fathers had worked for one of the railroads or at J. J. Newman Lumber.[48]

Eureka's curriculum included basic subjects—English, social and vocational civics, health, general mathematics and algebra, science, American government, economics, and history. Some teachers also offered a variety of electives based on their expertise. Marie Washington, for example, taught Latin. Former student Douglas Conner also remembered black history classes featuring lessons on Frederick Douglass, Booker T. Washington, W. E. B. Du Bois, and Marcus Garvey. Female students learned domestic science in a small annex in back of the school. Many of the girls learned to make the very dresses they wore to school at the school itself.[49]

Most black Hattiesburg youths did not finish high school, but they did generally remain enrolled in school longer than the average black Mississippian. Hattiesburg was among the state's leaders in rates of school attendance and literacy among African Americans. Many of those who did graduate—usually less than forty per year—went to college. "There have gone out of the [Eureka] high school of Hattiesburg quite a number of young men and women who have gone to colleges," observed a local white WPA researcher in 1936. The Eureka alumni who attended college seem to have felt well prepared by their experience at the school. Douglas Conner, salutatorian of the 1939 class, remembered having been "fortunate to have had dedicated teachers who demanded performance." Conner, who later became a doctor, was particularly encouraged by Mr. Whisenton, who, he remembered, "inspired in me a love of science which was so essential for my later medical training." Isaac Thomas, a 1938 graduate who also became a doctor, credited his greatest professional accomplishments to the teachers at Eureka and the education he received there. "If it hadn't been for the encouragement of the instructors there at Eureka like Mrs. Clark, Mrs. Love, Professor Todd, Professor Whisenton, Mrs. Washington, Mrs. Tademy," Thomas told an interviewer in 1994, "I don't know what I would have done."[50]

Eureka teachers were compassionate and devoted. They were also strict and demanding. They dressed formally for classes and required colleagues and pupils alike to refer to them as "Professor," "Miss," or "Missus." They were also harsh disciplinarians. Back then, there was little debate about corporal punishment in Southern public schools. Eureka teachers used switches, straps, and paddles to strike students who violated the rules. "The strap was the road then," remembered one former student. "You just had to obey." Another Eureka graduate remembered an incident when Principal Addison overheard a student disrespect a teacher. Without asking any questions, Principal Addison stormed into the classroom and whipped the student. "He came in taking off his belt," the observer recalled. Cora Jones, a longtime seventh grade teacher, developed a particularly frightening reputation as a harsh disciplinarian. Douglas Conner recalled that she "taught with the aid of a thick strap." Isaac Thomas remembered that Miss Jones had a special chair that she called "the electric chair." When students misbehaved, Thomas explained, Miss Jones would "make them sit in the chair and whup them with the left hand."[51]

Extracurricular activities at Eureka closely reflected communal values of racial uplift and self-help. In 1931, black students at Eureka formed an organization named the Negro Boys and Girls Improvement Association. Advised by their teachers and the pastors of Mt. Carmel Baptist and St. Paul Methodist churches, the Negro Boys and Girls Improvement Association included approximately eighty students dedicated to improving the "physical, mental and moral" health of black youths in the community. They invited guest speakers, organized efforts to improve school grounds, and held fundraising concerts. They somehow convinced the internationally renowned Celestin's Original Tuxedo Jazz Orchestra to play at one such event. In 1935, another group of Eureka students successfully organized a fundraising effort to build a new hedge around the building.[52]

For years, Eureka also had an active Luxis Club, which was essentially the black version of the YMCA-supported Hi-Y clubs for white youths. Led by high school students aged fifteen and older, members of the local Luxis Club contributed to local black life by sponsoring speaking engagements at the school, leading exercise programs, and participating in statewide meetings. In 1936, Eureka hosted several hundred student leaders during the Thirteenth Annual Assembly of the Mississippi High School Luxis Clubs. Among the attendees at that 1936 conference was a high school student named Gladys Noel, who later, as Gladys Noel Bates, became famous for her civil rights activism, especially in 1948 when she and NAACP attorney Thurgood Marshall sued the state of Mississippi over racially unequal teacher salaries.[53]

Located just a block from Mobile Street, Eureka was a direct extension of the community. From elementary to high school, Eureka students were immersed in the community-organizing traditions of the Mobile Street District. The young people experienced all the normal school-age rites of passage—building new friendships, taking exams, attending dances, falling in love. But even beyond the school lessons and social activities, Eureka students also learned important lessons about how to behave in their community and navigate life in the Jim Crow South. These messages reinforced lessons that black youths learned at home and church and helped provide crucial pathways toward community membership.[54]

For students, the community must have also at times seemed like an extension of Eureka. As former student Ralph Woullard Jr. recalled, "All of the teachers lived in the community." Principal Addison lived directly across the street. Students interacted with Principal Addison not only in Eureka's hallways but in virtually every corner of their neighborhood. In 1938, one unfortunate student skipped school to go to the movies only to find Mr. Addison perched next to him in the theater. Students saw their teachers all the time—at churches, concerts, lectures, sporting events, grocery stores, barbershops, and even in their own living rooms. Deeply respected and influential in the community, black teachers were ubiquitous role models and sources of guidance.[55]

The Eureka Parent Teacher Association (PTA) also played an essential role in supporting students. One of the most interesting aspects of the Eureka PTA is that it included some adults who were neither parents nor teachers. The roster of PTA captains from the 1937 Christmastime fundraising drive included a diverse set of individuals: Jennie Brown, the wife of a local auto mechanic, was in her early fifties and had a fifteen-year-old son; Frank Calloway was a local janitor in his late twenties who was married and had a five-year-old child; beautician Brookie Young was in her mid-twenties and married to a much older night watchman who had four daughters of his own; railroad employee Isiah Reed and his wife, Maggie, were the parents of a ten-year-old daughter; Janie Stringer was a single woman in her mid-thirties who had no children and worked at one of the local black-owned funeral homes; Myrtle Smith was a captain in the 1937 drive. Along with Principal Addison and teachers Susie Neal and Cora Jones, this group in 1937 raised a reported $371.91 in support of the school, thus helping alleviate some of the racially imbalanced school funding discrepancies. Other PTA activities included collecting baskets of food and clothing, hosting benefit concerts in the school auditorium, and organizing a school brass band.[56]

Local adults also helped plan numerous school lunches, theatrical performances, proms, and birthday and graduation parties. "The baccalaureate was held at the school and it was always packed," recalled one student. The school was widely supported. Virtually all black community organizations were somehow affiliated with Eureka, either by holding events at the school or organizing programs to benefit the school. Examples of these activities include a 1938 movie night sponsored by local churches, the formation of a Colored Youth Forum by members of the Mt. Carmel Baptist Church, a beauty pageant for black girls run by the Mt. Carmel Missionary Society, an effort by local businessmen to purchase curtains for the auditorium, and the inclusion of several girls in crafting and artwork contests at the annual meeting of the state Women's Federated Club.[57]

Eureka was more than just a school. It was a communal rallying point, and the children who attended that school were reared not only by their relatives but also by their teachers, neighbors, and other members of the community. "It's not like today where you only look after your children," remembered class of 1937 graduate Veola Chase. "It was more like a family setting. . . . All of the children were community children."[58]

It might be difficult to imagine how black children who grew up in Hattiesburg during the Great Depression could have felt optmistic about their futures. Most people in their community were desperately poor, and members of their race were treated as second-class citizens and excluded from many of the opportunities available to whites. All the black children of that era suffered through the difficulties of daily life during Jim Crow. "Day after day I lived with segregation," remembered Douglas Conner years later. "It was a part of my community; it was a part of my life. Being black meant a life of subordination, a life of limited goals and expectations."[59]

But just as memorable to Conner and to many of his peers was the support and guidance they received from the adult leaders of their community. Much of that support is obvious—the 1934 Negro Fair, PTA drives, school programs, and fundraisers. Less obvious—yet just as important—were the ways in which local black leaders acted as sources of guidance and role models for impressionable young black students like Douglas Conner.

When Conner's parents divorced because of his father's drinking, Conner moved in with relatives who lived down the street from members of the Smith family. Conner at a young age was impressed by Dr. Charles Smith. Walking by Dr. Charles Smith's house almost every day, Conner came to see the black physician as a model of how to obtain success and happiness within the constraints of Jim Crow. "I saw a black man who seemed to have material success, and I dreamed it might be possible for me too," remembered Conner of Dr. Smith. "As I passed his house on my way to and from school, I would see his fine home, his finely manicured lawn, and I would say to myself: 'My goodness, that's the way to live.'" Writing in 1985—nearly fifty years after graduating from Eureka High School—Conner reflected, "I often recall how Dr. Charles Smith had been my role model simply by being there as I walked to school in Hattiesburg. . . . Deep down, I think I am following in Dr. Smith's footsteps."[60]

Hammond Smith, whose store was located around the corner from Eureka, offered similar inspiration for some of the community's children. In an interview conducted fifty-six years after Isaac Thomas graduated from Eureka High School, Thomas remembered one particular day when he walked into the Smith Drug Store "to buy me a cone of cream. I walked in and I saw the license on the wall, saw the diplomas and things. Alcorn College and Meharry Medical College. And I just made up my mind then I wanted to be a pharmacist."[61]

Arvarh Strickland, a black Hattiesburg native who grew up during the 1930s and 1940s, remembered the value of local black leaders and community institutions such as Eureka High School and St. Paul Methodist Church during his youth. At Eureka, Strickland explained, "We developed pride, we acquired ambition, and above all, we learned to dream and to appreciate the dreams others had for us." At St. Paul Methodist, Strickland remembered finding "sympathetic audiences to listen" and a forum where "I was given my first opportunities to lead." "At St. Paul," he recalled, "I was somebody, as were we all."[62]

Strickland, who went on to become an esteemed professor of history at the University of Missouri, later in life referred to the older generation of "role models and mentors" in the Mobile Street District as "the bridges that carried us over." In Hattiesburg, the men and women who operated as these bridges were people like Charles and Hammond Smith and the other black men and women of their community who worked together through their churches and various organizations to help provide a sense of belonging, propriety, and hopefulness among an incredibly disadvantaged population. And these men and women became all the more empowered in the 1940s, when the Depression's grip finally weakened and Hattiesburg's economy suddenly surged.[63]

CHAPTER NINE

Salvation

> There are growing out of Camp Shelby's presence substantial benefits to the entire state which should be consolidated and husbanded by the whole people, thus enabling the federal government, which pressing its armament program in Mississippi, incidentally to make fuller contribution to the economic life of the state.
>
> —David P. Cameron, chairman of the Hattiesburg Camp Shelby Cooperative Association, November 10, 1940

The men began appearing at Camp Shelby on a warm September Sunday, weary and uncertain, but desperate to work. They came by the thousands, gathering in large crowds on the sandy orange hillsides near the employment office. The tattered workers arrived however they could. The roads leading to the camp were filled with the creaking of rust-bitten vehicles, and the highway was "jammed with cars, trucks, bicycles, and anything else that would roll," wrote a local reporter. Some arrived on railroad cars and then hitchhiked or walked the final ten miles between downtown Hattiesburg and Camp Shelby. One man came all the way from Rhode Island, traveling across a thousand miles of America's backroad byways in search of a job in the Mississippi Piney Woods. The workers arrived from at least seventeen different states, but most were locals from the dying lumber towns of southern Mississippi. A large black man had walked from near Prentiss, making the entire forty-mile trek without proper shoes. Blood soaked through the makeshift bandages covering his aching feet. He said his last meal had been a hamburger the night before. He needed a job. They all did.[1]

An estimated five thousand men arrived at Camp Shelby on Sunday, September 15, 1940. Their presence drew dozens of opportunistic locals to the forest. Adults erected makeshift drink and sandwich stands; black and white boys peddled peanuts, candy, and newspapers. Some of the poor men could not afford even the cheapest indulgences. As a local writer noted, the members of this "grim army" were "battling old man depression and his step-son unemployment." With nowhere to sleep, the nomadic workers huddled around makeshift campfires or lay down on soft patches of grass. Some pulled branches off young pine trees and used the prickly limbs as cover from the chill of the night. Others spent much of the evening shooting dice for spare change. As dusk faded into darkness, the anxious men closed their eyes, desperately hoping to find work in the morning.[2]

That summer, America began earnestly preparing for war. In response to political and military developments in Asia and Europe, the United States Department of War began placing massive orders for hundreds of thousands of new aircraft, artillery, engines, guns, jeeps, and countless other war-making materials. In September, President Franklin Roosevelt signed into law the Selective Service Act of 1940, authorizing the first peacetime draft in American history. Across the nation, dozens of old military bases were activated and enlarged to train the troops. On September 6, Mississippi governor and Hattiesburg native Paul B. Johnson authorized the transfer of Camp Shelby from the state national guard to the federal government, an act one writer appropriately dubbed "the most significant event in the history of Hattiesburg."[3]

On Friday, September 13, the Fourth Army Corps announced an $11 million building program to reconstruct Camp Shelby into a major military installation capable of accommodating forty-two thousand troops. J. A. Jones Construction, a large firm from Charlotte, North Carolina, won the bid to refurbish the camp. The initial plans called for 318 mess halls, 50 repair shops, 37 warehouses, 36 administration buildings, 19 infirmaries, 5 fire stations, a 2,000-bed hospital, a post office, a telegraph building, a bakery, a laundry building, and an ice plant. And that was merely the first wave of construction. Over the ensuing five months, the federal government spent an estimated $22 million (over $375 million today) to reestablish Camp Shelby.[4]

Well-capitalized and desperate for labor, J. A. Jones Construction announced wage scales that dwarfed pay rates across the region. At a time when few workers in the Deep South earned more than a couple of dollars per day, J. A. Jones offered $1.25 per hour for bricklayers, $1 per hour for experienced carpenters, and 40¢ per hour for general laborers. In 1939, Mississippi's average annual income was only $204. With a job at Camp

Camp Shelby. (McCain Library and Archives, University of Southern Mississippi)

Shelby in September of 1940, an experienced bricklayer could expect to exceed that figure in just over three weeks.[5]

On September 18, the War Department expanded its initial request, asking Shelby's capacity to be increased from forty-two thousand to fifty-two thousand troops. Thousands more workers arrived at the base. On October 1, nearly six thousand individuals were working at Shelby. Two weeks later, the workforce exceeded ten thousand. By the end of the month, more than twelve thousand laborers were working at the camp. By then, those workers were joined by approximately eight thousand Army troops. The last day of October was a payday for both workers and troops. Their combined total wages and salaries topped more than $1 million, by far the biggest payday to that point in Hattiesburg history.[6]

News from Camp Shelby buzzed through Hattiesburg. On the morning after men began arriving on the hillside, the *Hattiesburg American* started running a daily front-page column titled "Shelby Briefs" that detailed the building program and forthcoming troop arrivals. The next day, the Hattiesburg Chamber of Commerce called a special meeting in City Hall to discuss "Co-ordination of plans for handling the additional population." In the coming weeks, tens of thousands of well-paid workers and troops were scheduled to arrive in Hattiesburg, all in need of meals, lodging, clothing, prescriptions, toiletries, and entertainment. "Every merchant should plan immediately for any changes or expansions in his business," the Chamber of Commerce advised local business owners.[7]

Shelby's mobilization delivered immediate benefits for Hattiesburg's economy. Within the first forty days of construction, local merchants expanded their hours and hired additional salespeople. Hotels and homeowners rented thousands of rooms to workers and troops and their families. Nearby farmers and local laundry services were swamped with orders. Tool and building suppliers cleared their inventories. A Jackson-based developer announced plans to build a $500,000 apartment complex for soldiers. The Mississippi Central Railroad invested $200,000 to resume its defunct passenger service between Hattiesburg and Camp Shelby. The WPA announced road-paving and airport projects to support camp logistics. The Army ordered the construction of updated water and sewer systems. At local electric and gas companies, business spiked. After years of struggle, the entire city was suddenly inundated with new jobs, wages, and revenues.[8]

In one way or another, virtually all Hattiesburgers stood to benefit from Camp Shelby. Even teenage white girls, who were ineligible for most of the new jobs, became involved. That autumn, Paramount Studios invited white girls to the camp to serve as extras in newsreels. The girls were instructed to "look pretty, smile and wave their hands to soldiers" aboard a departing train. What a thrill it must have been for them to know that they might soon appear on movie-theatre screens across the United States.[9]

Perhaps there was one local man who did not appreciate Shelby's rise, but he had good reason to be sour. That autumn, Charles "Pinky" Rohm was set to begin his first season as the head coach of Hattiesburg High School's varsity football team. Having recently completed one of the most brilliant football careers in the history of Louisiana State University, Coach Rohm was a nationally known gridiron star who brought with him high expectations for Hattiesburg High. But just days into the 1940 season, Coach Rohm suddenly lost a starting guard and a pair of running backs to the Camp Shelby labor force, and his team was pummeled 42–0 by McComb

High School in their first conference game. The Tigers struggled that autumn, but the rest of Hattiesburg came roaring back to life.[10]

The Hattiesburg Chamber of Commerce responded immediately to Shelby's mobilization. The organization had already formed a "Camp Shelby Committee," but the level of activity in the autumn of 1940 warranted the formation of an entirely new organization—the Mississippi Camp Shelby Cooperative Association. This body was directed by veterans of the Hattiesburg Chamber of Commerce. Longtime Chamber of Commerce officials Louis Faulkner and West Tatum (the oldest son of W. S. F. Tatum) served on the executive committee and directed one of the subcommittees. The Mississippi Camp Shelby Cooperative Association had a number of important goals, but its most pressing objective was to maximize the economic benefits of federal spending for local white residents. One of its first goals was to convert a federal program designed to aid African Americans into one that would exclusively benefit whites.[11]

About a year earlier, in August of 1939, the Hattiesburg Housing Authority announced the procurement of a $744,000 loan from the federal government to construct separate low-income housing units for white and black residents. The city's initial request for $1 million yielded a loan offer of only $600,000. But Hattiesburg's mayor and the head of its housing authority worked for weeks with their congressional representative William Colmer, a New Deal Democrat who assumed office in 1933, to increase the loan by lobbying members of the United States Housing Authority. Their effort was helpful. Upon learning of the larger loan, the chairman of the Hattiesburg Housing Authority thanked Congressman Colmer for his "splendid cooperation," which was "greatly appreciated by all concerned here in Hattiesburg."[12]

This low-income housing loan was made available through the passage of the Housing Act of 1937. This act, also known as the Wagner-Steagall Housing Act, created the United States Housing Authority (USHA) to provide loans for cities to demolish slum neighborhoods in order to construct "low-rent housing" for "families of low income" who did not otherwise have access to "decent, safe, and sanitary dwellings." With interest rates as low as 3 percent and repayment periods as long as sixty years, USHA loans were affordable to even the poorest municipalities. Cities were required to raise 10 percent of construction costs, but that capital could be secured through another loan with a private bank. Once completed, USHA housing projects were subsidized by the federal government to ensure low housing costs. The USHA was unique among earlier New Deal housing legislation (most notably the National Housing Act of 1934) in that it catered to low-income renters as opposed to insuring the mortgages of buyers.[13]

The black housing complex known as Robertson Place was the only major federally funded New Deal–era project designed specifically to aid black Hattiesburgers. The project was slated for construction in the Royal Street Neighborhood, one of the city's smaller black neighborhoods located just south of downtown. The plan was to raze a section of decrepit black rental homes to clear space for the construction of twenty two-story brick buildings containing six apartments each, thus providing housing for 120 black families who would pay monthly rents between $9 and $15.75. This was highly significant. For the first time in their lives, hundreds of the city's poorest black residents would be given the opportunity to live in affordable brick housing with indoor plumbing.[14]

Capitalized at $398,000, Robertson Place also offered numerous benefits to several groups of local white residents. The first white Hattiesburgers to benefit were landowners who sold sections of their property for exorbitant prices to the Hattiesburg Housing Authority. Lots occupying the future site of Robertson Place were sold by local white businessmen for as much as $100 each. Retired real estate mogul George William Kamper sold his lots to the authority for $840. It is difficult to accurately gauge property values in that neighborhood in 1939, but it is clear that these were not valuable properties. Lots owned by the city sold for an average of only $12.06, and monthly rents in the neighborhood rarely topped $8. Landlords might have turned meager profits over several months or years, but these dilapidated properties did not generate much revenue. Nonetheless, it was the flow of capital that told the real story: the federal government loaned money to the Hattiesburg Housing Authority, which used that very same capital to buy slum properties from white landowners at inflated prices. There is nothing about the sales that reveals obvious corruption, but it is worth bearing in mind that many people involved in USHA transactions—including the head of the Hattiesburg Housing Authority, the mayor, and several landowners—were personally acquainted through church affiliation or membership in one of the city's civic organizations, including the Chamber of Commerce. At best, these deals unfairly advantaged sellers.[15]

The Robertson Place project also benefitted local white construction firms that built the apartments. The white-owned Newton & Glenn

Contractors won the initial bid with a construction estimate of $299,950. The white-owned architecture firm of Landry and Matthes received the contract to design the buildings. And the white-owned Southern Glass & Builders Supply Company was hired to install culverts. The contracts benefitted the owners and employees of these firms at a time when good work was hard to find. Between April and August of 1940, Newton & Glenn Contractors employed an average of 150 men who earned nearly $45,000 in wages. The racial composition of their workforce is unknown, but six decades of local employment history suggests that white men at the very least occupied the most desirable positions.[16]

On September 5, 1940, Frank Glenn of Newton & Glenn Contractors reported that his firm expected to finish Robertson Place well ahead of the scheduled completion date of January 25, 1941. But when the Shelby development erupted in the forest less than two weeks later, local white leaders began to consider alternative arrangements for the black housing project. Remember that the Hattiesburg Housing Authority had applied for the USHA grant under the premise that it would build low-income housing for both blacks and whites. Nonetheless, in mid-September of 1940—after the grant had been received, the slum properties cleared, and the housing project nearly finished—several members of the Hattiesburg Chamber of Commerce led an effort to procure the apartments for white families instead of black ones.[17]

The prospect of "converting the Robertson Place negro housing project into apartments for white families" was first discussed at the Hattiesburg Chamber of Commerce public meeting in City Hall on September 17, 1940. As the housing project neared completion over the following months, members of the Chamber of Commerce continued working in private to secure Robertson Place for white families only. Their argument was that the homes could be used by enlisted men who were coming to Shelby for training. This point had some merit; Hattiesburg did not have enough housing to accommodate the onslaught of thousands of military families. But even this approach demonstrated a clear racial bias. No one ever spoke of transforming the white USHA housing project into military housing. Nor was there ever any talk of reserving Robertson Place for black troops, despite the fact that African American units were mentioned in virtually every notice of the forthcoming troop arrivals. They knew black troops were coming. In fact, during that same fall of 1940, the Hattiesburg Rotary Club held a special meeting to discuss "the problem of Negro soldiers."[18]

In December of 1940, West Tatum sent letters to the Hattiesburg Housing Authority, the United States Housing Authority, and commanding officers at Camp Shelby to inquire about "the possibility of working out some proposition wherein we might get the consent of the Washington authorities to use this [Robertson Place] during the life of Camp Shelby as a place for the families of the enlisted men." Tatum also encouraged Congressman Colmer to contact the United States Secretary of the Navy Frank Knox to advocate on behalf of the Hattiesburg housing authority.[19]

Their efforts did not look promising. In late January, the chairman of the housing committee of the Mississippi Camp Shelby Cooperative Association reported that "the attempt to convert the negro Housing Project, now nearing completion, had not been successful." On February 3, Representative Colmer received a direct response from United States Secretary of War Henry Stimson, declaring that the USHA "takes the position that the houses should be occupied by the persons for whom they were intended." Still, members of the housing committee of the Mississippi Camp Shelby Cooperative Association continued with their efforts. After failing to convince military officials to advocate on their behalf, they tried to secure an endorsement from local black leaders for the conversion, but this tactic also failed to produce any results. Next, they unanimously approved a motion to try to secure an "executive order" that would transfer Robertson Place from the USHA to the War Department "for the use of low income whites." This somewhat preposterous effort to secure an "executive order" to transfer the USHA-funded housing project to the War Department never came to fruition.[20]

In March of 1941, the Hattiesburg Housing Authority began selecting black tenants to occupy the Robertson Place apartments. The white housing project, named Briarfield, opened later that same year. Local white leaders, who at the time were consumed with other issues related to Camp Shelby's mobilization, do not appear to have been overly distraught at their failure to convert the federally funded housing project from black to white. In hindsight, however, this inability to exert local authority over the disbursement of federal resources foreshadowed political conflicts that would soon give them great cause for concern.[21]

The Camp Shelby labor force peaked in early 1941 with an estimated seventeen thousand workers. In less than six months, the workers erected over

14,000 platform tent frames, 400 mess halls, 80 warehouses, 50 repair shops, 50 administration buildings, 34 mail kiosks, 32 recreation buildings, a 2,000-bed hospital, 50 miles of paved roads, 85 miles of water line, 60 miles of sewer line, and 181 miles of electric wiring. By the end of February, Army officials estimated that Shelby could comfortably house over sixty-five thousand troops.[22]

By February of 1941, the Hub City was in the midst of what the *Hattiesburg American* was already calling the "biggest boom in [Hattiesburg] history." Businesses thrived as consumer demand skyrocketed. Between September of 1940 and February of 1941, at least sixty-six new businesses opened. Other economic indicators such as bank deposits, postal receipts, building permits, land values, and money orders also dramatically increased. In March of 1941, a report from the *Mississippi Business Review* showed that Hattiesburg led the state in economic growth by a wide margin. As a longtime Chamber of Commerce official observed that February, "[Shelby] has created boom conditions in Hattiesburg and all of our people have received substantial benefits." This was still nine full months before the United States officially entered World War II. The boom was just beginning.[23]

Most of the seventeen thousand workers left for other jobs when Shelby was completed in March of 1941, but they were quickly replaced by tens of thousands of troops. In March, Shelby was home to approximately thirty-five thousand soldiers. By August, there were over fifty thousand, meaning that Camp Shelby was by then the second-largest training base in the United States behind North Carolina's Fort Bragg. Four months later, the United States officially joined the war.[24]

During World War II, Camp Shelby hosted an average of fifty thousand troops at a time with a high of about seventy-five thousand soldiers. Because most GIs stayed only long enough to prepare for battle, Shelby experienced constant turnover. All told, approximately 750,000 troops passed through Camp Shelby during the war. Hattiesburg in 1940 was a town of only about twenty-one thousand people. Its civilian population grew during the war, but the number of soldiers at Shelby during World War II always exceeded Hattiesburg's population. In fact, Shelby during the war housed more people than any city in the state except for Jackson. Many troops spent weekends in other nearby cities such as Birmingham, Gulfport, Mobile, or New Orleans, but Hattiesburg absorbed the brunt of their arrival.

Throughout World War II, the people of Hattiesburg found both major challenges and immense opportunities created by the presence of hundreds of thousands of well-paid troops and their families.[25]

Many of the challenges were predictable. Everything was very crowded, especially local businesses and schools. The city increased municipal tax rates to expand roads and build new public bathrooms, but during the war it also struggled at times to provide basic public services such as electricity and public transportation. The young male soldiers also attracted hundreds of bootleggers, gamblers, and prostitutes, unsavory characters who helped spread illegal activities and triggered what one writer called a "spectacular rise in venereal disease." The troops also exacerbated conflicts over the city's blue laws, which prohibited most entertainment venues, particularly movie theatres, from operating on Sundays. And as might be expected, the young, adrenalized men often drank too much, started fights, played pranks, cat-called women, and caused a variety of other commotions. At times, the soldiers' behavior created quite a nuisance for local residents. But these challenges paled in comparison to the economic benefits provided by the troops and their government pay.[26]

Through its Mississippi Camp Shelby Cooperative Association, the Hattiesburg Chamber of Commerce took the lead in managing relations between the city and the camp. Soon after the first troops arrived in the fall of 1940, the organization treated roughly sixty Army officers to a "get acquainted" steak dinner at the Forrest Hotel. Several members helped officers find rental homes for their families. And the organization worked with the WPA to produce a pamphlet titled *A Serviceman's Guide to Hattiesburg and Area,* which provided a brief overview of the city's history, local sights of interest, and directions to churches and recreational areas. "I doubt it there is a camp in the United States where a better relationship exists than that between the officers and enlisted men of Camp Shelby and the citizens of Hattiesburg," bragged the Chamber of Commerce president at the end of 1940.[27]

Soldiers were transported between Hattiesburg and Shelby by trains, busses, taxis, and private drivers. During the war, as many as eight thousand-person trains ran from Shelby to Hattiesburg each day. But even these large trains struggled to meet the demand. A Vermont soldier reported that "an awful mob" awaited each train and that he sometimes had to wait up to one and a half hours to secure a spot onboard. With the trains overcrowded, hundreds of busses and taxis also transported soldiers between the base and town. The high demand allowed taxi drivers to inflate prices. According to one soldier, a Hattiesburg taxi driver charged him and four friends $6 (the equivalent of nearly $90 today) to drive just ten miles. Along with taxis, hundreds of opportunistic locals with private vehicles began providing rides between the base and town. Resident Ben Earles recalled that "everybody that had an automobile could make . . . a small fortune at that time." Because many soldiers wanted to go down to the Gulf Coast on their days off, weekends were particularly lucrative. "They would give you fifty, seventy-five dollars, a hundred dollars to take a carload of them down to Gulfport on the weekend," Earles noted. The Gulf of Mexico is only about sixty miles south of Camp Shelby, meaning that an efficient driver could earn more for a half-day of driving than the average Mississippian did in a month.[28]

Local businesses filled with tens of thousands of new customers. "As soon as they could get out of camp," remembered local woman Dorothy Musgrove of the troops, "they was coming to spend." Every store and restaurant was packed. Earles recalled that "you could go downtown in Hattiesburg and the line might be a block or two long to get into a restaurant, and the picture shows, and everything else." As another local named J. S. Finlayson remembered, "Some nights you couldn't hardly walk on the sidewalks for the soldiers were so thick. They'd surge up and down the streets and go to the ice cream parlors and everything they could to get a little entertainment." "Hattiesburg was incredibly crowded at the time," said a soldier from Los Angeles. "You had to wait in line to go to the restaurant, to go to the show, everything." Businesses barely had to advertise. Some did, but all they really needed to do was to keep the lights on, the shelves stocked, and the plates of food coming to the tables.[29]

In addition to business growth, Camp Shelby also provided new financial opportunities for thousands of people who took jobs on the base. During the war, about five thousand civilians worked at Shelby. Men predominated in jobs such as construction, maintenance, and transportation, but hundreds of women also found work as nurses, secretaries, typists, cashiers, librarians, dieticians, cooks, telephone operators, and office managers. Local resident Jeanette Coleman explained that "many women got their first job working at Camp Shelby." Some of Shelby's female employees had worked before, but few had ever earned as much income. Eweatha Royse was employed at the Woolworth's Dime Store when she learned she could earn $16 more per month working as an office manager at Shelby. "They thought I was making it up," she remembered of telling her friends about the pay rates. "It was like nothing I had ever experienced before. Being so young, it was a great opportunity." Betty Cooley, who worked in one of the finance offices at Shelby, remembered earning up to $120 per month. "I could put gas in the car," remembered Cooley, "and I could buy new clothes."[30]

Even kids got jobs. Every morning during the war, between forty and fifty boys as young as eight years old rode trucks out to Camp Shelby to spend the day selling copies of the *Hattiesburg American*, the *New Orleans Times-Picayune*, and magazines such as *Collier's*, *Life*, and *Liberty*. The most enterprising boys found additional ways to earn money by selling greeting cards and metal clothes hangers. Soldiers were always interested in purchasing cards to mail home. And because of metal rationing, the Army only issued cardboard hangers, which created an underground market for metal hangers that sold for as much as a quarter apiece. Some of the working youths also received leftover groceries or even discarded watches and dress suits from soldiers departing for the war. Bobby Chain, a future Hattiesburg mayor, remembered that he earned as much as $2 per day working as a thirteen-year-old paperboy at Shelby. "Two dollars a day at that time would buy all the clothes I needed and a little spending money," remembered Chain. "Couldn't make that much around town." Jimmy Mordica, who sold newspapers and metal hangers, earned enough to buy a $250 used car at the age of fourteen.[31]

Hattiesburg's wealthiest citizens, especially prominent members of the Chamber of Commerce, were uniquely positioned to enjoy additional profits from Shelby's mobilization. Some of the primary beneficiaries were those who invested in the Forrest Hotel. Completed in 1929 with the goal of attracting tourists to the region, the Forrest Hotel was funded by a group of longtime city leaders, including Louis Faulkner, W. S. F. Tatum, and several of Tatum's sons. But few tourists occupied the hotel during the early 1930s. The company lost money in each of its first five years of operation. The worst year occurred in 1932, when Louis Faulkner was serving as company president. That year, the Forrest Hotel Corporation lost nearly $18,000 (the equivalent of over $300,000 in 2018 dollars). In 1940, the hotel's fortunes suddenly reversed with the arrival of tens of thousands of troops and workers. That year, the Forrest Hotel earned a profit of $28,690, by far the largest in company history. Even better years followed. In both 1943 and 1944, the hotel earned annual net revenues of over $107,000 (over $1.45 million today) due to unprecedented occupancy rates during the war. Louis Faulkner and the Tatums all profited handsomely.[32]

The Tatum family also benefitted from a massive uptick in the consumption of natural gas. In 1934, W. S. F. Tatum and his sons started a firm named the Wilmut Gas and Oil Company. The company was always profitable, but wartime mobilization escalated its gross revenues to new heights, as is amply shown by comparing sales reports from different years for the period between February 20 and March 20. Between February 20 and March 20, 1936, Wilmut Gas sold $12,844 worth of product. Over the same period in 1938, the company's gross sales totaled $14,619. Then came the war. During those same weeks in 1941 and 1944, Wilmut's gross revenues increased to $33,368 and $28,625, respectively. Net revenues are unknown, but the firm's gross revenue and total cubic feet of gas sold more than doubled during the war.[33]

The fate of Louis Faulkner's concrete business was also dramatically altered by World War II. Founded in 1915, Faulkner Concrete for years generated nearly all its revenue through contracts with Louis Faulkner's employer, Fenwick Peck's Mississippi Central Railroad. In 1936, Faulkner Concrete was a profitable company with twenty-one employees, but in over twenty years of operation, it had never expanded significantly. Federal contracts obtained during the New Deal and World War II changed its fate. Detailed monthly revenues are not available, but records show that Faulkner Concrete received government contracts at Shelby during both the WPA-sponsored refurbishment in the late 1930s and the War Department's complete overhaul that began in 1940. Soon thereafter, Faulkner Concrete began acquiring other firms as it rapidly expanded from a small local business into one of the largest companies of its type in the state. In 1941, Faulkner Concrete acquired the Mississippi Concrete Pipe Corporation. In 1943, the firm purchased another concrete firm in Meridian, charting a course of growth that lasted for over twenty years.[34]

As a longtime leader in the Hattiesburg Chamber of Commerce, Louis Faulkner was well-positioned to receive federal contracts. In fact, it was Faulkner who in 1937 led a delegation of local businessmen to Atlanta to meet with Army officials about securing WPA funds to begin restoring Shelby in the late 1930s. When Army officials from the Fourth Corps began planning Shelby's expansion in September of 1940, they directly referenced using Faulkner Concrete as a client. The details of the selection are unknown, but clearly Faulkner's company held an advantageous position.[35]

Ironically, in the years after the war, Faulkner and several members of the Tatum family became some of Hattiesburg's most vocal opponents of federal spending and overreach. As early as July of 1944, W. S. F. Tatum's son Frank wrote a letter to Congressman William Colmer—the New Deal Democrat who helped the city secure the USHA housing project that Tatum's brother tried to convert from black to white—expressing concerns over "postwar planning" and advocating "the elimination of all bureaus and government spending where possible." Tatum stressed that "this government or any other government cannot carry on at the high rate it has been carrying on." As we will see, Louis Faulkner similarly went on to become one of the city's most strident critics of excessive federal spending and overreach into local affairs.[36]

Faulkner and the Tatums did not become rich solely because of federal spending during World War II. They were social elites prior to the war and would have remained so even without the financial windfalls of Shelby's mobilization. But they benefitted from federal wartime spending as much as anyone else in Hattiesburg. And it is also worth recalling that Faulkner and several Tatums were instrumental in overseeing WPA spending during the New Deal era. It makes complete sense that local elites worked to obtain relief for their struggling city and managed to profit from the enormous level of federal wartime spending. The inconsistencies lie in their later critiques of many of the same federal mechanisms that had benefitted their own private interests.

Among white Hattiesburgers, the most common financial benefit of Shelby's mobilization was the revenues generated by wildly inflated rental rates. Throughout the war, thousands of local homeowners converted houses, rooms, shacks, and even closets into rental units for soldiers and their families. People rented virtually every possible space. Some units were so small that soldiers and local media alike called them "rabbit pens" or "chicken houses." In some cases, homeowners hung little more than a blanket to partition bedrooms into two or three units that were rentable by the weekend or even just the evening. Before Shelby's mobilization, Hattiesburg had an estimated eight hundred rental units. By October of 1944, there were over ninety-one hundred.[37]

People took advantage of the troops, especially married soldiers who desired a bit of privacy with their families before heading off to war. Young couples flooded the rental market. "It was very common for homeowners here in town . . . to rent a room to some guy that had just gotten married and was about to go overseas," remembered Bobby Chain. Soldiers and their lovers were so desperate for places to stay that some even offered to "'sleep on the porch if you have a place for us,'" recalled one local woman. Thousands of officers and other men with families rented entire houses or apartment units during the war.[38]

To maximize revenues during the wartime housing shortage, Hattiesburg's new landlords charged troops as much as possible. Rental rates increased both suddenly and substantially. In October of 1940, one local couple was forced out of a rental property they had occupied for thirteen years when the monthly rent suddenly increased from $6 to $30. When looking for a new home, the couple, who earned $46 per month, encountered another rental where the monthly rate had jumped from $6 to $50. Even the "rabbit pens" and "chicken houses" went for as high as $15 per month. Rents increased so much that even some of the soldiers struggled to afford housing. And some landlords increased their revenues by charging exorbitant prices for basic services such as water or access to a telephone or a stove. "In Hattiesburg," one Colorado soldier bitterly recalled, "you probably had to pay to walk across the lawn."[39]

By 1944, Forrest County landlords were earning an estimated $3,808,500 (nearly $52 million today) in annual rental income—roughly thirteen times the rental revenue earned in the county before the war. Local and federal officials had previously tried to control rent inflation through voluntary suasion. As early as September of 1940, the *Hattiesburg American* pleaded with "landlords and property owners" not to abuse the "present supply-and-demand emergency." But these efforts influenced the market very little. In June of 1942, the national Office of Price Administration (OPA) declared Hattiesburg one of sixty "defense rental areas" where "voluntary efforts had failed." In June of 1942, the OPA ordered that rents be reset to rates in April of 1941, and at one point the *Hattiesburg American* even published a chart detailing how much rent could be applied to servicemen based on rank. But landlords throughout the war consistently overcharged tenants and found ways to evade OPA price controls through a variety of schemes, the most common of which was to inflate charges for other goods and services. In one particularly egregious example, a landlord who rented a furnished home for $75 per month required tenants to pay $300 upon occupancy to purchase the furniture. When the tenants left, the landlord then paid $50 to reacquire the furniture only to inflict the same scheme on the next tenant. The estimate of $3,808,500 in annual rental income does not include all the extra revenue earned by Hattiesburg landlords who were intent on pinching every dollar possible from the troops.[40]

Local churches also experienced significant financial windfalls. Camp Shelby had its own chapels and military chaplains, but many soldiers were interested in joining more established and traditional congregations. *A Serviceman's Guide to Hattiesburg* included the locations and schedules of the city's largest churches. Many of the churches advertised like businesses, placing regular advertisements in the *Hattiesburg American* that encouraged visiting white troops to join their congregation for Sunday services. Local pastors also held special events for soldiers both on and off the base. And several major churches organized soldier's lounges or held informal gatherings to help entertain the troops.[41]

Soldier-church relationships were mutually beneficial. Many young men facing the prospect of war desperately needed spiritual guidance and appreciated the opportunity to join established faith communities. Churches also fulfilled social interests. Because very few young women attended one of the twenty-two chapels at Camp Shelby, male soldiers often attended church-sponsored social mixers and private dinners to meet members of the opposite sex. The wives of soldiers were similarly drawn to female-led church organizations.[42]

From the churches' perspective, soldiers presented a tremendous financial opportunity. The young men who sat in the pews every Sunday helped fill collection plates and contribute to various church initiatives. The full scale of their economic impact is immeasurable, but one study of Hattiesburg during the war has shown that between 1940 and 1946, the city's six white Baptist churches increased their net worth from $234,000 to $420,000. The net worth of Main Street Baptist alone grew from $67,500 to $186,000. Though some of this economic growth was a result of the city's improving economy, the presence of more than seven hundred thousand troops clearly helped swell the coffers of nearly every congregation during World War II.[43]

None of this is to suggest that Hattiesburgers did not also contribute to the war effort. Local residents supported troops in a variety of ways. They helped build and staff a federally supported Soldiers' Service Center and two new United Service Organizations (USO) buildings, welcomed white troops into local organizations such as the YMCA and American Legion, and allowed white troops to use recreational facilities such as the Elks Club, the new Hattiesburg High School gymnasium, and Reliance Manufacturing's Dixie Club. The *Hattiesburg American* ran two almost-daily columns, "Shelby Briefs" and "Shelbyettes," that included news about the soldiers and their families who were stationed at the base. There were also countless examples of local residents inviting troops into their homes for "dine-ins" and cook-outs. And thousands of residents attended football scrimmages between Army Divisions or participated in an endless number of suppers, parades, concerts, lectures, parties, balls, and dances held for the troops. With young male soldiers vastly outnumbering their female counterparts, Hattiesburg camp liaisons and the local Girls' Service Organization made arrangements for busses to transport women from nearby towns into the camp for social events. Promised one such program committee in 1942, "Dates will be provided for those who do not bring their dates." So many couples formed during these co-recreational activities that one local woman joked that "Hattiesburg ended up as the mother-in-law of the army."[44]

The people of Hattiesburg also contributed significantly to the broader national war effort. They bought war bonds, grew victory gardens, donated to the Red Cross, collected scrap metal, rationed every staple imaginable—from pork to gasoline—and, of course, sent many of their own young men to fight in the war. Hattiesburg did not have a large industrial defense plant, but there were some smaller local manufacturers, such as Komp Manufacturing and Reliance Manufacturing, that produced ammunition and parachutes for the military. As in many towns across the United States, Hattiesburgers embraced a national sense of duty in support of the war effort. "I had never seen patriotism of that magnitude before or since," remembered local woman Gloria Coleman. "They felt real privileged to be able to do the small things that we could do to help."[45]

Ultimately, however, the story of World War II in Hattiesburg is the story of how wartime mobilization saved the town's economy. This was widely recognized and appreciated by locals who lived through the wartime boom. "Hattiesburg prospered . . . because of the money and all from Camp Shelby," Dorothea Musgrove remembered. "Then come along World War II, and it boomed," said local man Harmon Strickland of Hattiesburg during the war. "I remember that very well. It was just a different world to live in here." Ben Earles and his wife took jobs as a safety engineer and a nurse during the war. More than thirty years later, Earles recalled that "between us, we saved enough money to build this house, during the first two years of the war."[46]

It is impossible to fully measure the aggregate economic impact of the wartime boom on Hattiesburg, but a 1946 survey conducted by the Chamber of Commerce reveals the scope of local economic growth. In 1935, Hattiesburg banks had approximately $5.4 million in deposits and cleared roughly $45 million worth of transactions. In 1945, local banks counted over $29 million in deposits and cleared over $154.5 million in transactions. Inflation explains some of this increase, but Camp Shelby's mobilization was by far the greatest factor in Hattiesburg's explosive economic growth during World War II. Camp Shelby did not merely boost Hattiesburg's economy; during the war years, Camp Shelby essentially was the local economy.[47]

Few places in Mississippi—or the entire South for that matter—experienced the economic benefits of a military base as large as Camp Shelby. The state had thirty-six other wartime military installations, but only Keesler Air Force Base in Biloxi offered similar economic benefits to the surrounding population. Nonetheless, wartime mobilization created new opportunities for thousands of workers across Mississippi, especially those who took industrial jobs on the coast at the Ingalls Shipyard or worked for one of the smaller manufacturers scattered throughout the state. "Anybody that wanted to leave home and work," remembered one local man, "they could work in the shipyard if they kept their nose clean." Between 1939 and 1947 the state added 750 new industrial establishments, twenty-five thousand workers, and nearly $103 million in payroll. In total, the state's per capita income tripled between 1940 and 1946.[48]

Throughout all those years, white voters in Hattiesburg and across Mississippi ardently supported the national Democratic Party. All of Mississippi's congressmen and senators were Democrats, and President Franklin Roosevelt was enormously popular in Hattiesburg and across the state. As local man Buck Wells recalled, "Everybody in the South thought Roosevelt was just the greatest thing that ever lived." In 1940, Franklin Roosevelt won 93 percent of the vote in Forrest County and more than 95 percent of the vote in Mississippi. Roosevelt lost a few Forrest County supporters in 1944, but still captured a commanding 87 percent and 93 percent, respectively, of the local and statewide vote. Yet toward the end of the war, Mississippi's most ardent Democrats began to experience several problems with the National Democratic Party that would ultimately lead them to abandon the party during the 1948 presidential election. It should not come as a surprise that these problems were related to race.[49]

On June 25, 1941, President Franklin Roosevelt signed Executive Order 8802, barring racial discrimination in national defense industries and creating the Fair Employment Practices Committee (FEPC) to enforce the policy. This action was largely spurred by growing national black influence in labor unions, such as the Congress of Industrial Organizations (CIO), the American Federation of Labor (AFL), and the Brotherhood of Sleeping Car Porters, which expanded in the 1930s largely because of pro-labor legislation passed during the New Deal. The FEPC was only lightly enforced during the war, but the order nonetheless represented a symbolic gesture from the federal government that, if enforced, offered the potential to use federal authority to thwart racial segregation.[50]

Soon after the end of the war, several national Democratic leaders, including Roosevelt's successor, President Harry Truman, began advocating for a permanent and more comprehensive FEPC. This advocacy grew in response to expanding national black political influence during and immediately after World War II. During the war, hundreds of thousands of African Americans left the Jim Crow South to take jobs in defense industries. Between 1940 and 1950, the number of black people living in New York, Pennsylvania, Illinois, California, Ohio, Michigan, and New Jersey increased by 72 percent. In the North, black migrants could exercise voting rights previously denied to them in the South. Because of the growing number of black voters, Northern political candidates from each major party began increasingly expressing support for civil rights initiatives.[51]

The prospect of the FEPC mortified white Southern Democrats. Although there had been some racial concessions in the New Deal, white Southern Democrats had used their legislative influence to ensure local control of federal grants and exclude black farmworkers and domestic laborers from programs such as Social Security. They were major supporters of the New Deal, but only so long as any new federal program enabled them to maintain local control over access to resources. The FEPC endangered their ability to do so by prohibiting racial segregation in federal defense-related contracts, meaning that black Southerners might gain direct access to federal resources.[52]

During and after the war, Mississippi legislators offered more boisterous opposition to the FEPC than politicians from any other state in America. While filibustering against the FEPC in 1945, Mississippi senator Theodore Bilbo dubbed the program "a damnable, Communist, poisonous piece of legislation," adding, "Some Catholics are linked with some rabbis trying to bring about racial equality for niggers." "The Negro race is an inferior race," insisted Mississippi's other senator, James Eastland, who suggested that the Communist Party was "exploiting the Negroes by making special promises such as FEPC, such as social equality, such as racial amalgamation." In 1947, Mississippi congressman John Rankin promised white supporters, "I will take the floor the first hour, if necessary, and tear to shreds the arguments of the opposition who are attacking you and who are pushing those vicious measures that are calculated and designed to stir up trouble for you such as the anti-poll tax bill, the dishonest anti-lynching bill . . . and the communistic FEPC bill." The following year, Rankin's congressional colleague William Colmer told a Hattiesburg audience that the FEPC was a "vicious program" designed to "reduce the people of this country to an inferior race and make of our anglo-saxon heritage a mockery." In Hattiesburg, the *Hattiesburg American* ran a series of anti-FEPC editorials with titles such as "Nature of the Beast" and "Evils of FEPC."[53]

Senator Bilbo successfully ran for reelection in 1946. In a one-party state, he did encounter some challenges from more moderate Democrats who did not condone his public usage of the term "nigger" or his call over the radio that summer for "every red-blooded Anglo-Saxon in Mississippi to resort to any means to keep Negroes from the polls." But Bilbo still won the primary by a significant margin. In a five-man race to determine which Democrat would run unopposed that November, Bilbo carried 51 percent and 53 percent of the vote in Mississippi and Forrest County, respectively.[54]

Bilbo did not, however, return to the Senate. For months, his return was delayed by senatorial opposition to his extreme anti-black rhetoric and an investigation into improper usage of campaign finances. During that time, the Mississippi statesman was diagnosed with oral cancer and then experienced a series of medical complications that ultimately led to his death of "a progressive heart failure" in August of 1947.[55]

That November, five Democrats ran in a special election to decide Bilbo's replacement. This contested race, which featured two of the state's sitting congressmen, was decided by a series of internal state political factors and regional allegiances. But the nominees were not all that different in terms of their broader political goals. Each of the five viable candidates openly opposed the FEPC and vowed to fight federal intrusion into state Jim Crow laws. Ultimately, a forty-six-year-old attorney named John Stennis won the Senate seat, a post he would hold until 1989.[56]

Mississippi congressman John Rankin finished fifth in the special election of 1947, but offered one of the most historically perceptive observations of the challenge facing white Mississippi leaders in the years immediately after the war. In a speech given about a month before the election, Rankin told voters, "Mississippi has more at stake in this race than she has had in a senatorial contest since Reconstruction."[57]

Consider Rankin's point within the broader context of Hattiesburg's history. Hattiesburg had undergone several major transformations in the years between Captain Hardy's lunch and the end of World War II, but Congressman Rankin's notion of a historical continuum is appropriate. There was indeed a fundamental pattern that stretched across each era of Hattiesburg history. From the end of Reconstruction to the end of World War II, white Hattiesburg leaders had always relied on their ability to procure external resources and consolidate the dividends of such resources among white residents. This dynamic was central to their economy and form of governance. By the late 1940s, however, that authority was being threatened by the very same Democratic Party that had not only helped save their city but that they themselves had so ardently supported.

CHAPTER TEN

A Rising

> The background and history of my town is very important to me, because I feel it played the major part in my decision of what I wanted to do in life. It is just an average town, but there is one exception, it is owned and operated almost wholly by Negroes.
>
> —Nineteen-year-old future civil rights icon
> Victoria Jackson (Gray), 1945

Hammond Smith described World War II as "my big years." "Anybody could make it back then," he remembered, "if you could get the stuff to sell." The Smith Drug Store was so busy during the war that Hammond started keeping later hours and hiring extra help. "At one time," he recalled, "I was working somewhere around fifteen people." Business was good to the family. In the spring of 1942, he and Lucille added a major addition to their house.[1]

By the time of Shelby's mobilization in 1940, the Smith Drug Store had been a staple in the Mobile Street District for over a decade and a half. Eureka High School students congregated at the store during lunch breaks, after school, and on the weekends. One Eureka student later compared the environment at the drugstore to the teenage hangout in the popular television show *Happy Days*. "One thing that I remember so vividly," recalled another Eureka student who grew up in the 1940s, "was the Smith Drug Store and the smell of the drugstore and the ice cream." The drugstore played a vital role for thousands in the community, offering a vital place to buy toiletries, tobacco, and candy and to gather and socialize. Virtually everyone in the community knew of the Smith Drug Store and understood its central role in the Mobile Street District. When black soldiers started arriving in Hattiesburg in the early 1940s, they too were quickly acclimated to its role.[2]

During World War II, black soldiers comprised a small minority of troops stationed at Camp Shelby. Throughout the war, Army officials were challenged by segregation ordinances in Southern towns that housed major military bases. A lot of black men—approximately 10 percent of the Army—served in the war, but they had to be trained and housed separately from white soldiers, thus inherently limiting the number of black troops that could be trained at any Southern base. Even with the country engaged in a state of total war, Southern segregationists prioritized local racial protocols over military concerns. Some Southern cities and states forcibly resisted the presence of any black troops at all. Officials in Georgia, for example, rejected black enlistees at "exceedingly high" rates, according to the Army, for vaguely diagnosed disorders such as "psychoneurosis" or "inadequate personality." Other white segregationists resisted the presence of black troops from the North who they feared might not be familiar with Southern Jim Crow laws and customs. And in some places, white officials expressed concerns over certain types of black servicemen, especially officers, combat troops, and military police. At Camp Shelby, black military policemen were not allowed to carry firearms.[3]

The precise number of black troops stationed at Shelby each year of the war is difficult to measure, but several reports from the summer of 1941 indicate the presence of just over two thousand black troops, approximately 4 percent of the roughly fifty thousand men stationed at Camp Shelby at the time. Although the percentage of black men in the Army expanded during the war, the number of black men stationed at Shelby remained relatively small. If the 4 percent ratio is applied to Shelby's total troop numbers throughout the war, then the number of black troops stationed at Shelby during World War II would have averaged about two thousand, with a total of approximately thirty thousand. Very few stayed longer than a few months, but their presence was incredibly important to the Mobile Street District.[4]

In a city of about seventy-five hundred mostly poor African Americans, the arrival of thousands of well-paid black troops presented enormous economic opportunities for local black business owners. As in the white community, the black restaurants and shops of Mobile Street experienced a sudden surge during the war. In fact, because black soldiers were required to abide by local segregation laws, African American servicemen often had no choice but to eat, shop, worship, and sleep in black-owned establishments. The Chamber of Commerce's *Serviceman's Guide to Hattiesburg* included separate sections for black churches and "Negro Recreation Centers."[5]

Black merchants barely had to advertise. Any African American soldier who visited Hattiesburg was immediately directed toward Mobile Street. Black servicemen on leave flooded the neighborhood. "I can just recall as a little girl going down Mobile Street," remembered Iola Williams. "I thought there must have been a million soldiers on Mobile Street because everywhere you looked, you saw a soldier." "I never saw so many," remembered local resident Albert Hopkins of the uniformed troops. "Every time you looked, you just saw a sea wave of brown."[6]

Dozens of new businesses opened. In 1939, the Hattiesburg city directory listed thirty black-owned restaurants and grocery stores; by 1946, there were seventy-nine. Moreover, considering the nature of the black neighborhood's informal economy, thousands of other unrecorded transactions must have occurred involving people selling plates of food, taking in laundry, and converting small homes into restaurants and juke joints. "Hattiesburg was really exciting during World War II," reminisced Iola Williams. "Mobile Street had anything your heart desired." "Mobile Street was busting with people, with black businesses," said local man Charles Brown of Hattiesburg in the 1940s. "It was a mecca."[7]

Vernon Dahmer, a future civil rights leader, opened his first grocery store just outside of town during the war. "We were enjoying a wartime economy," remembered his son Vernon Dahmer Jr. "People had money. Camp Shelby . . . was booming." During the war, Dahmer also operated an icehouse and a gristmill and later added a filling station and small sawmill. Like many black businessmen before him, Dahmer's rising prosperity translated into an expanding leadership role in the black community. Although he is best remembered today for his activism during the 1960s, it was actually in 1944 and 1945 that Vernon Dahmer's name first began appearing on the rosters of local black organizations alongside individuals such as Hammond Smith and Gaither Hardaway.[8]

Milton Barnes, another businessman, experienced a similar trajectory. The son of a widowed domestic worker, Barnes first arrived in Hattiesburg as a child in the 1920s. Like many poor black kids, he dropped out of school as a young teenager to help provide for his family. He worked a variety of jobs, including time in a local laundry company and a stint at the Hercules

Powder Company, where he briefly belonged to the Hercules Social Club. As legend has it, Barnes became a sole proprietor sometime in 1938 or 1939 when he won the title to a small laundry firm in a game of craps.[9]

The war facilitated the growth of Barnes Cleaners from a small firm into one of the city's largest laundry companies, largely because of a deal Barnes struck with some of the Army units stationed at Camp Shelby. This success later enabled Milton Barnes to open a second business named the Embassy Club, a bar and music hall that operated just outside city limits in the black neighborhood of Palmer's Crossing. The Embassy Club, later renamed the Hi-Hat Club after a fire in 1958, served as a major stop on the Chitlin' Circuit, a series of Southern black music halls that operated during the final decades of Jim Crow. The list of artists who played at Milton Barnes's clubs includes legends such as James Brown, Otis Redding, Sam Cooke, Al Green, Ray Charles, and Ike and Tina Turner. Much of that lay ahead. The essential thing to understand here is that Barnes's first business emerged during World War II. And like Dahmer, it was during this era that he first began appearing on the rosters of black community organizations alongside figures such as Hammond and Charles Smith.[10]

Jesse Brown, a Hattiesburg native born in 1926, became a national black celebrity in the late 1940s. During the war, he was one of the young people employed by Hammond Smith. He also worked at Camp Shelby for a summer and later found employment as a server at the all-white Holmes Club. After graduating as salutatorian of Eureka High School's class of 1944, Brown used the money he saved working during World War II to help pay his first year's tuition at Ohio State University. He left Ohio State after only two years to join the Navy, and in 1948 became the first black naval aviator in the history of the United States. To this day, he remains a beacon of pride for hundreds of thousands of African Americans, especially black servicemen.[11]

Shelby's mobilization created a host of financial opportunities for African Americans. Jimmy Fairley, the son of a turpentine worker and sharecropper, first came to Hattiesburg from Collins, Mississippi, to work as a cement finisher at Shelby. Twenty years later, he became president of the local NAACP. Lee Owens Jr. came to Shelby from a cotton farm near Natchez to unload cement cars. "When I left home," Owens remembered, "I was making fifty cents a day; $2.50 a week." At Shelby, he started off making 75¢ per hour and eventually worked his way up to a dollar. "I thought I was rich at the time," Owens recalled. Isaac Gray, an eighteen-year-old Hattiesburg native, was earning 30¢ an hour as a laborer when he took a job in the laundry at Shelby. "They were paying more than there was anywhere around here," he said of his decision to take the job. Clearese Cook's father also did "cement work" at Shelby. Years later, she remembered that her father's new job enabled her family to purchase "a whole set of school books." "When the Camp Shelby opened up," she explained, "it made a difference in our family, and not only our family, other black families."[12]

Shelby's rise also created new financial opportunities for black female domestic workers. The arrival of hundreds of thousands of troops and laborers completely transformed the local market for domestic labor. Local whites, who for decades had benefitted from cheap black labor, suddenly found themselves forced to compete for the services of black domestic workers. The outside troops who came from places such as California and Ohio were willing and able to outspend local whites for black women's services. Black women's labor roles remained static during the war, but their compensation generally improved.[13]

Laundry work in particular paid more than before. During World War II, the number of black-owned cleaners tripled, and the wages earned by employees of those cleaners increased by up to 50 percent. Individuals and small groups of washerwomen also enjoyed increased compensation. Longtime local laundress Osceola McCarty claimed that white troops paid anywhere from "five to ten or fifteen or twenty dollars" for a "bundle of clothes." "I got so much work," McCarty recalled, that "I just give some of it to my friends, get them—beg them—to take work for me so I could have a little rest."[14]

Many black women took jobs working directly on the base. Osceola McCarty preferred to work at home, but she remembered "so many people" who went "to the camp where they can make some money." Hattiesburg native Richard Boyd recalled the flood of black domestics to Shelby. "Women who had been doing domestic work would go to Camp Shelby and work for, you know, scales wage," Boyd recalled. "They were getting paid just like the men. Anybody that could go out there and make that kind of money naturally wasn't going to do domestic work where they made maybe ten or fifteen dollars a week."[15]

Future civil rights leader Victoria Jackson Gray was among the black women who took a job at Shelby during the war. Later a nationally known voting rights activist, Gray was just a teenager when she took a job at Shelby. In addition to better pay, she was also drawn to Shelby by improved working conditions. According to Gray, black women working at the base experienced better treatment than those who worked in town. "Out there, people were treated humane," she recalled. Several women who worked at Shelby organized a new social group called the Camp Shelby Civil Service Laundry Club.[16]

White employers responded to these developments in a number of different ways. Frank Tatum actually wrote to Congressman John Rankin to suggest that the Army compel German prisoners of war (of whom there were about three thousand at Shelby) to work in the camp's laundry facilities so that black women would be forced to return to jobs in town. Of course, this outlandish suggestion far exceeded the Army's authority and never came to fruition. Most private white employers and large firms simply responded by raising wages to compete for black labor. Black workers in a variety of professions experienced wage increases during the war. Richard Boyd, who took a job with Hercules Powder in 1941, explained that "economically, the camp had a great effect upon Hattiesburg because working conditions got better here in town because of the conditions out there. The employment situation got three hundred percent better." Not all local African Americans experienced sudden, great financial gains, but Shelby's mobilization created better opportunities for many.[17]

Like whites, local black homeowners also rented rooms to traveling workers and soldiers. Most black families did not own homes large enough to rent out extra rooms, but many of those who did converted their homes into makeshift boardinghouses. Precise rental figures for black neighborhoods are unavailable, but records from the black USO indicate at least ten thousand housing referrals over six years through that organization alone. In all likelihood, there were at most a few hundred rentals available at any given time, and most of these were probably very cramped. Arvarh Strickland remembered his grandmother renting three spare rooms that "were fitted out with several beds that would sleep from two to five men in each room. My grandmother presided over this enlarged household as if the men were her sons." Presumably, she also earned a significant amount of extra income by boarding up to fifteen men at a time.[18]

Along with new financial opportunities, the arrival of thousands of black troops and laborers also created a number of challenges. First, Eureka High School became extremely overcrowded. Within two years of Shelby's mobilization, Eureka's enrollment soared from about eight hundred to approximately thirteen hundred. All city schools were congested, but as the *Hattiesburg American* observed, "overcrowding was worse [at Eureka] than in any other school." At one point during the war, the seventh-grade classroom alone had 117 students.[19]

The increased enrollment was due to several factors. Soldiers and workers alike brought along many of their children and wanted to enroll them in school. Changing economic conditions also played a role. With better jobs and wages, many local black families could afford to send their children to school later into their teenage years before they had to join the workforce. Of course, another major reason for overcrowding was a shortage of black classrooms, teachers, and resources. Eureka was initially designed to serve a much smaller population, and black schools were given far fewer resources than white schools. On average, the state of Mississippi in 1942 spent $47.95 and $6.16, respectively, on white and black students, a gap that was actually wider percentage-wise than it had been a dozen years before. As before, black teachers were paid far less than their white counterparts, yet they were often charged with instructing more pupils. The city did erect and maintain a small school for the children of Japanese American soldiers, but black educational facilities were not expanded until after the war.[20]

In 1940, a Eureka alumnus named N. R. Burger (class of 1928) returned to Hattiesburg to lead his alma mater. Under Burger's energetic leadership, Eureka teachers and students worked with the local community to endure the challenges of overcrowding. One of their solutions was to conduct classes in two shifts, one in the morning (7:30–12:30) and one in the afternoon (1:00–4:00). School administrators recruited additional teachers from the local black community, sought volunteer help, and raised money for extra desks and to convert parts of the auditorium into makeshift classrooms. Despite the challenges, Eureka successfully continued its mission of community-based education throughout World War II. "It was a village," remembered one of the students who attended Eureka during the war. "And that whole village there raised that child."[21]

Other major challenges stemmed from the arrival of thousands of black troops into a rigidly segregated society. Racially related incidents began occurring almost immediately after Shelby's mobilization. In December of 1940, two white police officers shot two black soldiers during a late-night melee outside a Mobile Street beer hall. Thankfully, both servicemen survived.[22]

Most racial conflicts were less violent, but they were commonplace nonetheless. Throughout the first winter of troop arrivals, the Hattiesburg

Police Department was inundated with complaints about black soldiers on city busses. The rules on the busses were clear: black people were required to allow white passengers to board first, and all passengers were expected to sit or stand in the corresponding "white" or "colored" section of the bus. Some drivers also required black passengers to pay at the front and then enter the bus at the rear door. All of these rules were challenged by the influx of passengers during Shelby's mobilization. Even though the city expanded bus services, thousands of new people began riding the busses. As both "white" and "colored" sections filled beyond capacity, passengers of all races began spilling across the designated racial boundaries. To manage this issue, Hattiesburg city police ordered the local bus company to erect partitions that more clearly "designated separate compartments for negro and white passengers" and threatened to fine any drivers who failed "to keep the white and colored passengers in the sections designated for them." The chief of police also insisted that segregation laws applied to taxis. "We will not tolerate carrying of mixed loads—colored and white—passengers, in any of the taxi cabs," he insisted. Such policies only further aggravated an already overburdened transportation system, but they helped maintain rigid racial segregation policies, so local white leaders fought to enforce them despite the difficulties.[23]

Black troops also experienced regular problems with Hattiesburg police and white residents. Numerous black soldiers reported beatings at the hands of local police and threats to arrest any black soldier who strayed into a white neighborhood. The Hattiesburg chief of police noted that "we expect negro soldiers to stay in the negro section." In June of 1941, five black soldiers were arrested for a vaguely defined offense related to "disrespect for a white woman." Other black soldiers reported various forms of harassment. "Twice, whites have driven up beside me and told me to get of[f] the highway," said Technical Sergeant William Brown. In another incident, a black soldier at Camp Shelby pulled a switchblade to help convince a white supervisor to stop calling him "nigger." And at one point, local police tried to restrict the sales of the *Chicago Defender* and other African American newspapers from Northern cities because of the messages of racial equality advocated in the black press.[24]

Despite these examples of racial conflict, Hattiesburg during World War II was relatively peaceful. Bear in mind that none of these disturbances were novel conflicts for a Jim Crow society. And far worse examples of racial violence occurred in other parts of the state and nation. In October of

1942, black teenagers Charlie Lang and Ernest Green were hanged from a bridge in Shubuta, Mississippi, about sixty miles away. Five days later, a black man named Howard Wash was lynched in neighboring Jones County. The following year, racially related violence occurred at military bases in Georgia, Louisiana, Texas, Kentucky, Kansas, Pennsylvania, and California, as well as at Camp Van Dorn in Centreville, Mississippi. That same summer, thousands of Americans were involved in race riots in Detroit, Los Angeles, Harlem, and Beaumont, Texas, that resulted in the deaths of at least fifty people. By comparison, the racial incidents that occurred in wartime Hattiesburg were mild.[25]

The local black community deserves much of the credit for this peace. In fact, the nature of the black community in the Mobile Street District was one of the primary reasons that Shelby received as many black troops as it did. When placing black troops, Army officials always had to consider how black soldiers would interact with local populations. Vibrant black neighborhoods like Hattiesburg's Mobile Street District offered the ability to absorb black soldiers into well-established African American communities, thus helping avoid racial conflicts that might stem from the presence of black troops in white neighborhoods.[26]

Hattiesburg's black community mobilized rapidly to welcome black troops into their neighborhoods. "The black soldiers were welcomed into the homes and hearts of the people of this community," remembered Arvarh Strickland. The city's black churches, businesses, civic organizations, and social clubs participated in virtually every aspect of supporting black troops. There are countless examples. Local women organized a program called "Home Hospitality" that invited soldiers into private homes and churches for Sunday suppers once per month. Community groups organized meal preparation events to provide home-cooked meals for soldiers, especially those soon headed overseas. Business leaders created a separate employment office and separate bus station on Mobile Street for African Americans. When local men were drafted, the Eureka High School Marching Band escorted the new inductees to the bus station "to the blare of martial music," reported the *Hattiesburg American*. Community leaders also hosted numerous health programs and social activities both on and off the base. For black soldiers, Hattiesburg was not an ideal place to train, but the support of the black community greatly increased their quality of life. As the *Baltimore Afro-American* reported of Shelby in February of 1942, "Soldiers on this post are beginning to feel at home."[27]

Local African Americans were also very involved in supporting the war effort. Members of the black community appointed "Negro Air Raid Wardens" and devised civil defense strategies for each section of the city's black neighborhoods. N. R. Burger served as the black community's "chief of defense" and helped organize "defense training classes" at Eureka High School. Thousands of local African Americans also participated in largescale war bond and Red Cross drives organized by the city's leading "Colored business and professional men," wrote the *Hattiesburg American*.[28]

The war bond drives were particularly impressive. In October of 1943, fifty-two community leaders divided Hattiesburg's black neighborhoods into twelve sections, each represented by a "captain" and "staff" who worked to raise donations for the Mississippi War Fund and United Welfare Organization. By running sales booths, canvassing potential donors, and collecting money at local churches, these volunteers managed to sell a reported $18,000 in war bonds in just three months. The following January, community members celebrated their contributions with a "rousing rally" that included a rendition of "Let My People Go" and other traditional African American spirituals performed by the Eureka Glee Club. Eureka principal N. R. Burger planned to print the names of all donors on a large blackboard, but he ran out of space.[29]

Successful war bond drives continued throughout the war, drawing extensive coverage in the *Hattiesburg American* and praise from local white leaders. Banker and Chamber of Commerce official G. M. McWilliams wrote that "our negro citizens in Forrest county are perfecting a strong and efficient organization looking toward the enlistment and participation of every colored resident of Forrest county in the purchase of war bonds." Although local whites repeatedly applauded the black community for its support of the war, none of them appear to have publicly observed the irony of a disfranchised population helping fund a war for democracy.[30]

The Hattiesburg Negro Business League seems to have been curiously absent from the wartime community initiatives, but the cast of actors included nearly all the old leaders from the black business organization. Longtime Hattiesburg Negro Business League members such as Gaither Hardaway, J. B. Woods, Hammond and Charles Smith, and Paul Weston (the restaurateur and director of the Union Choir Service) each played major roles in wartime community initiatives. Other participants included dozens of local clergy, various women's groups, and an emerging younger generation of leaders, including the businessmen Vernon Dahmer and

World War II–era Human Relations Committee. (McCain Library and Archives, University of Southern Mississippi)

Milton Barnes and the principal N. R. Burger. As in previous eras, community organizing was led by an upper tier of black businessmen and was heavily supported by churches, women's clubs, students, and the general black population. These well-established community-organizing traditions expanded during the war, leading to the development of an entirely new set of organizations related to the local black war effort. The largest of these new groups included the Colored Health Committee, the Colored War Loan Committee, the Human Relations Committee, the Negro Civic Welfare Association, and the Negro USO Committee.[31]

Led by Paul Weston, the Negro Civic Welfare Association was founded in August of 1941 "to clean up Mobile street for the benefit of the residents and negro soldiers at Camp Shelby." This organization resembled several preexisting community groups that had operated in the 1930s, but there was one major difference in their approach. In addition to funding their own neighborhood beautification projects, the Negro Civic Welfare Association also requested that white Hattiesburg city officials make civic improvements in the Mobile Street District in the name of the war effort.[32]

Two months after its formation, the Negro Civic Welfare Association presented a "six-point program" to white city officials, asking the city to provide street cleaning, more police protection, an enforced curfew, the appointment of a black truant officer, the installation of street lights, and new stop signs. Earlier generations of black leaders had previously asked for and received some resources to improve Mobile Street, but this request represented a compelling new tactic for appealing for additional resources based on the broader war effort. It is not clear exactly how many of these requests were fulfilled, but the neighborhood did indeed get new stop signs by the end of 1941. The Negro Civic Welfare Association was active through 1946, organizing health programs, planning neighborhood beautification projects, sponsoring visiting speakers and choirs, conducting youth programs, and coordinating neighborhood parades and ceremonies. The organization first met at the Smith Drug Store before moving its meetings to the new black USO in the spring of 1942.[33]

On March 22, 1942, black Hattiesburgers celebrated the grand opening of the finest black USO center in the United States of America. Very few of the roughly three hundred black USO centers that operated during World War II were housed in new buildings. Most were established in existing spaces that were converted during the war or in hastily built temporary cement-block buildings. The black USO in Hattiesburg was much more impressive. A T-shaped white clapboard building, the Hattiesburg black USO was constructed on East Sixth Street, kitty-corner from Eureka High School, about a block from Mobile Street. The building contained men's and women's locker rooms, a library, a writing room, a lounge, several meeting rooms and offices, a snack bar, and an auditorium with a stage large enough to accommodate band concerts and weddings. News of the opening of the Hattiesburg black USO was covered by the Associated Negro Press and announced in nearly every major black newspaper in the country. The *Atlanta Daily World* called the building "One of the most modern U.S.O. Centers in the United States."[34]

Construction of Hattiesburg's black USO was funded by a grant provided by the Federal Works Agency (FWA), an umbrella organization of federal public works projects formed in 1939 that oversaw domestic defense building programs during the war. The USO is a nonprofit organization separate from the federal government, but during World War II, many of the organization's structures were built and maintained with federal money. During the war, Hattiesburg was home to five USO centers, four for white troops and one for African Americans. Three of the white USO centers operated in existing structures. The fourth was built with another grant from the FWA for approximately $150,000. The black USO in the Mobile Street District cost about $41,000.[35]

Most USO expenses were provided by the national organization, but daily operating costs were also subsidized by local communities. When the Sixth Street USO opened, black Hattiesburgers were asked to raise $1,000 to help fund programming. Led by a committee of black entrepreneurs, including Paul Weston, Gaither Hardaway, and Hammond Smith, the original African American USO Committee canvassed local black neighborhoods to collect donations from businesses, churches, social clubs, and individuals. They received an impressive amount of support. On two occasions, the *Hattiesburg American* published lists of contributors to the black USO. The lists included not only local business owners, teachers, and clergy, but also hundreds of working-class people and even children who donated amounts ranging from a nickel to several dollars to help support USO activities. The committee exceeded its fundraising goal in about a month and celebrated the accomplishment with a concert at Zion Chapel A.M.E. Church.[36]

The Sixth Street USO fell under the authority of Hattiesburg's broader U.S.O. Management Committee, which, of course, was led by longtime members of the Chamber of Commerce. W. S. F. Tatum's son Frank was the chairman. Frank Tatum occasionally spoke at the black USO and regularly received financial reports and program schedules detailing activities in the building. He also worked to ensure that the city's USO centers operated in strict accordance with Mississippi's racial ordinances. When the question arose about which USO Japanese American troops should patronize, Tatum consulted with two local attorneys to provide support for barring them from the white USO centers because "the Mongolian race is classified as colored."[37]

Although the black USO was overseen by an all-white management committee, virtually every single activity that occurred in the club was organized by African Americans. As in churches, men held the highest formal positions on the USO advisory board, but women organized and executed most USO activities. These female organizers were led by an impressive staff. The initial "director of Negro work" was a woman named Aquilla Matthews, a professor of music at Southern University in Baton Rouge, Louisiana, who quit her teaching job in the spring of 1942 to work at Hattiesburg's black USO. The bookkeeper was Goldie Walker, a graduate of Jackson College and the Tuskegee Institute who worked for the local branch of the Universal Life Insurance Company. And the leaders of the USO-based Volunteer Service Organization and Girls Service Organization were longtime Eureka teachers Iva Sandifer and Miss Cora Jones, the notoriously tough disciplinarian known for placing misbehaving students in her "electric chair." The seven-member USO Women's Advisory Board consisted of three additional teachers and the wives of several black businessmen, including Dr. Charles Smith's wife, Myrtle.[38]

The black women who ran the Sixth Street USO unleashed the full force of a fifty-year-old community organizing tradition. During roughly sixteen hundred days of operation, the black USO was supported by 40,261 volunteer hours—an average of twenty-five volunteer hours per day over the course of four and half years. Local black church and clubwomen worked constantly in the USO. They maintained and cleaned the building, planted flowers and shrubs around the perimeter, collected silverware and plates for meals, crafted decorations and fliers, cooked meals, organized the library, managed invitations and visits, oversaw finances, and provided logistical support for nearly every activity. "The [USO] club," bragged a souvenir pamphlet, "boasts of having the finest type of womanhood doing volunteer work."[39]

The USO offered a wide variety of daily activities: game nights consisting of whist, croquet, checkers, ping-pong, bridge, bingo, and dominoes; classes on typewriting, shorthand, "Negro history," ballroom dancing, and photography; Bible discussion groups and Vesper services; volleyball and softball matches; fashion shows and Easter egg hunts; wiener roasts and chicken dinners; movies and concerts; and socials and dances. People even held weddings there. The women who ran the center also distributed religious literature, provided sewing and counseling services for troops, operated the library, and helped workers and soldiers secure transportation and room and board. By the time the black USO services ended in the summer of 1946, administrators counted a total of 386,676 participants in USO activities and services (including repeat attendees). Hattiesburg's black USO was busy all day, every day, even on Sunday.[40]

Celebrities passed through Hattiesburg's black USO. In July of 1942, an estimated twenty-five hundred people packed the USO auditorium to hear legendary black activist and educator Mary McLeod Bethune deliver a speech in which she advocated "equal opportunity for participation in all phases relating to human welfare and to the war program." A correspondent for the *Chicago Defender* reported that Bethune's speech "greatly inspired the huge audience." About two weeks later, world-famous Olympic champion Jesse Owens visited the new black USO as part of his duties as an assistant community recreation organizer for the Federal Security Agency. He stayed in the Mobile Street District for several days at the home of local teacher Edward Tademy.[41]

In December of 1943, boxers Joe Louis and Sugar Ray Robinson, the heavyweight and welterweight champions of the world, appeared at Shelby to participate in exhibition bouts and deliver talks on physical fitness. Louis Armstrong also passed through town on several occasions to perform for both black and white audiences. Bluesman B. B. King was not yet well known, but he too performed at Camp Shelby while stationed there as a member of the Army during the winter of 1943–44. During that same winter, the Harlem Globetrotters held a public scrimmage against black troops at Camp Shelby.[42]

The black USO was built primarily for troops but was widely used by local residents. Military purposes notwithstanding, the USO offered a new building where the people of the Mobile Street District could access services and host events. Local black residents also had access to the writing room, library, auditorium, snack bar, and meeting rooms. In fact, some of the classes held at the USO, especially typewriting and shorthand, were reserved for civilians only. The women who ran the building kept track of civilian participation. To offer one example, in January and February of 1943, civilians accounted for 14,620 of the 70,100 visitors (roughly 20 percent) to the black USO.[43]

The black USO formally ended services in 1946, but the local black community continued using the structure as a library, meeting space, dance hall, and auditorium. For a number of years, it hosted Eureka High School's junior and senior proms. Usage ebbed and flowed over the years, but the black USO in the Mobile Street District has generally played an important role in that neighborhood since its opening. Having survived numerous floods and a devastating tornado in 2013, the Sixth Street USO to this day remains widely used. Most recently, the building has been renovated into an impressive African American Military History Museum that regularly hosts book club meetings, educational programs, exercise classes, speeches, and commemorations in honor of local black history and military veterans of all races. Initially constructed in 1942, it is the only surviving USO in the United States built solely for black troops.[44]

Turner Smith died in his home on Sunday, May 7, 1944, the year he would have turned eighty-five. Born into slavery, Turner had obtained an education as a free man and married a woman with shared values with whom he raised six successful children. He was an ardent Methodist, Republican, and educator, and for over forty years, he was an active and respected member of Hattiesburg's black community. Turner's funeral was held at St. Paul Methodist Church on May 10, 1944, and he was laid to rest at River View Cemetery, one of Hattiesburg's two black graveyards. A gracious article in the *Hattiesburg American* memorialized Turner as "one of the pioneer negro citizens of this section" who "won the respect of both races for his work in religious and community enterprises."[45]

At one point during the war years, Hammond Smith was working in his drugstore when a young woman entered to tell him a surprising story about his father. "I want to tell you about your daddy, Mr. Smith," the woman told Hammond. "I see him getting on the bus, and he don't wait for the white folks to get on."[46]

Turner by that time was in his eighties. When he needed to go somewhere, one of his sons usually drove him, but he sometimes took the city bus. Hammond recalled instances when his father had refused to pay his fare in protest for having to enter the back of the bus, but this was the first time he had heard of his father violating racial protocols by boarding the bus before white people. "I didn't know what they might do to him," remembered Hammond upon hearing the story. "I knew that if any of them hit him, it was going to be a big fight, and they was going to kill him."[47]

No one will ever know precisely when or why Turner started refusing to let whites board the bus in front of him. Perhaps this was a conscious act of racial defiance, a bold final stance by a proud old black man whose entire life had been confined by strict racial boundaries. Perhaps he was simply too tired to wait. As with many components of his life, one can only speculate what that defiance meant to him in that place and time.

Having always told his children "Don't be a reprobate," Turner would have been proud of his sons' community leadership during and after the war years. Both Hammond and Charles made great contributions to local black life. Hammond catered to thousands of troops and their families, wiring money, pouring fountain sodas, selling toiletries, cashing checks, and continuing to play a major role in the local black business community. In 1942, he began serving as an advisor to several new community health clinics for local black residents and troops. He also served as chairman of the Business and Professional Committee of the Colored Red Cross, belonged to the original black USO, and for a time hosted meetings of the Colored War Loan Committee at his shop. Of course, he and his wife Lucille continued their roles as leaders among the congregation at St. Paul Methodist Church.[48]

Dr. Charles Smith was also heavily involved. He helped organize Red Cross and war bond drives, served as an advisor for new branches of the Forrest County Health Center, and played a prominent role in the Human Relations Committee, an organization founded during the war to help manage relations between black soldiers and local residents. It is worth remembering too that Dr. Smith was one of only three black doctors in a city with an African American population of roughly seventy-five hundred. This position alone required heavy involvement in the black community, as he provided medical services for thousands of local African Americans.[49]

On September 9, 1946, Hammond and Charles Smith were among the founding members of the Forrest County NAACP. Early organizational records are sparse, but several local historians have noted that the original members included the entrepreneur Vernon Dahmer, grocery store owners Benjamin Bourn and Robert and Constance Baker, and Reverend James H. Ratliff, the pastor of True Light Baptist Church since 1927, who served as the first NAACP president. Membership of the Forrest County NAACP has fluctuated wildly over the years, especially during its first decade, but the organization has remained continuously active ever since its founding.[50]

This local NAACP growth was part of a much larger trend. Between 1940 and 1946, national NAACP membership grew from approximately 50,000 to 450,000 members. These numbers declined at times, especially in the 1950s, but the NAACP in the years immediately after World War II became larger and more influential than at any point in its prior history. Led by legendary black activists such as Ella Baker, Walter White, Roy Wilkins, and Thurgood Marshall, the NAACP of the postwar era waged a far-reaching and intensive legislative fight for increased civil rights and school desegregation, all of which culminated in the 1954 Supreme Court decision *Brown v. Board of Education*.[51]

The wartime surge in NAACP membership was one of several oncoming challenges to Southern Jim Crow. During the war, the black newspaper the *Pittsburgh Courier* advocated a national campaign called "Double V," which represented the need to fight for democracy on both its fronts—not only abroad, but also at home. Millions of African Americans envisioned a similar victory related to their wartime service and the Allies' philosophy of a war purportedly fought to rid the world of fascism in the name of democracy. The contradictions between this wartime message of self-determination and Southern Jim Crow were widely observed across the globe, most famously by the Swedish sociologist Gunnar Myrdal.[52]

Although white segregationists successfully maintained most components of Jim Crow during the war, there were some encouraging signs of potential change for African Americans and their allies. In 1941, the FEPC (Fair Employment Practices Committee) represented a symbolic—if only superficially enforced—gesture of federal authority over regional racial discrimination. In 1944, the Supreme Court decided in *Smith v. Allwright* that all-white primaries—a tactic of disfranchising African Americans by requiring primary participants to be members of political parties that banned African Americans—were unconstitutional. Jim Crow remained, but these challenges to white supremacy were threating enough to generate concern among white Southern segregationists, especially over the notion of a permanent FEPC. The worst of the vitriol was spewed by Mississippi senator Theodore Bilbo, in his plea during the 1946 primaries for "every red-blooded Anglo-Saxon in Mississippi to resort to any means to keep Negroes from the polls." Some black Mississippians did vote in the 1946 primary, but the threat of violence limited African American political participation to only a few sites. Hattiesburg was not one of them.[53]

Shortly after the war, Hammond and Charles Smith and several other local black leaders formed a group to encourage black voter registration. Hammond had actually been trying to register to vote for years. Beginning in 1934, he attempted to register to vote every year when he paid his annual property taxes at the courthouse, but was repeatedly turned away based on the grounds that his interpretations of the Mississippi Constitution were inadequate. It is unknown how many other African Americans tried to register to vote during the 1930s and early 1940s, but the years after the war saw the emergence of a new group that began pushing more aggressively for voting rights.[54]

Voter registration appealed to local African Americans for a variety of reasons. First, at its most basic level, these tax-paying citizens simply wanted to exercise their constitutional right by participating in the democracy. Second, if African Americans could vote, then they could play a larger role in shaping decisions that affected their communities. Local black leaders had for decades essentially operated a parallel form of governance in the black community. Access to the ballot would allow them to exert much broader societal influence. They probably did not imagine a program of rapid neighborhood equalization, but participation in the political process would offer the opportunity to advocate for improved infrastructure in their neighborhoods and increased funding for their schools. Moreover, voting would allow them to vote for county sheriffs, circuit clerks, and tax assessors who could offer more equitable treatment toward African Americans.

The black men and women who tried to register in late 1940s were continually rebuffed by longtime Forrest County circuit clerk Luther Cox. In office since 1935, Cox showed no intention of allowing significant numbers of African Americans to vote. He asked potential black registrants unanswerable questions such as "What do you mean by due process of law?" and "What does the Mississippi Constitution say about titles to land, land sales?" Remember that the Mississippi Constitution of 1890 included an "understanding clause" that empowered local registrars to decide who was qualified to register to vote. In Hattiesburg and elsewhere, the questions and answers mattered very little; it was the race of the applicants that dictated their eligibility. Cox was less educated than either Charles or Hammond Smith, but his power as the local registrar enabled him to make on-site decisions about individuals' qualifications to vote. Cox made little attempt to hide the absurdity of this process. At times, he ridiculed black applicants with such ridiculous questions as "How many bubbles are in a bar of soap?"[55]

In response, Hammond, Charles, and thirteen other local black men did something that no black Mississippian had ever done. In the spring of 1950, they hired a sixty-five-year-old white attorney named T. Price Dale to sue Cox for racially based voter discrimination in violation of the Fifteenth Amendment of the United States Constitution. Their case, *Peay et al. v. Cox*, was filed in federal court on April 11, 1950.[56]

The fifteen African American appellants in *Peay et al. v. Cox* represented a cross-section of traditional local black male community leadership:

Hammond Smith was a self-employed druggist and his brother Charles was a doctor; Reverend Isaac Peay was the pastor at Mt. Zion Baptist Church; Reverend Charlemagne Payne was the pastor at St. Paul Methodist Church; Reverend John H. Mayes was the pastor at Sweet Pilgrim Baptist Church; Dr. Theodore Fykes was a black dentist; Clifford Kelly, Joe Knox Jr., and Ratio C. Jones were teachers; Alfonso Clark owned a funeral home; Benjamin Bourn and R. H. Howze owned grocery stores; and Milton Barnes was a laundry and nightclub owner. The only outliers were the two oldest men in the group, Berry L. Neal and Joe Knox Sr., both of whom were retired laborers who had lived in Hattiesburg for decades. Ranging in age from thirty-four to sixty-nine, the plaintiffs in *Peay et al. v. Cox* represented the full scope of the history of black economic opportunity in Hattiesburg.[57]

A team of twenty-two local white attorneys came to the defense of Luther Cox. The judiciary was filled with sympathetic white segregationists. Federal judge Sidney C. Mize, a native white Mississippian appointed to southern Mississippi's Fifth Circuit Court in 1937, dismissed the case based on the grounds that the plaintiffs should first appeal to the State Election Commission. In response, the appellants' attorney filed suit in the United States Court of Appeals Fifth Circuit, which reversed Mize's decision to dismiss the suit so that it could "remain pending in the district court for a reasonable time to permit the exhaustion of State administrative remedies."[58]

Peay et al. v. Cox never proceeded much further, but the case did attract the attention of the national black press and support from the NAACP. While the case remained pending in 1952, NAACP special counsel Thurgood Marshall examined affidavits filed by black Forrest County residents and called for the Department of Justice to conduct "an immediate investigation of these complaints." Marshall and the NAACP, however, did not prioritize *Peay et al. v. Cox*, in part because the organization's attorneys were preoccupied by other cases, including *Brown v. Board of Education*, and also because the Hattiesburg registrar assured the Department of Justice that he would stop discriminating against African Americans. Cox specifically agreed to stop asking the question about bubbles in a bar of soap. He did indeed allow a few African Americans to register—including Hammond Smith in 1954—but continued to deny most black applicants. There is no evidence that Cox ever rejected a white applicant. In fact, the United States Department of Justice later found that dozens of illiterate whites, even some who could not even write their own name, were allowed to register.[59]

The plaintiffs in *Peay et al. v. Cox* did not file another appeal, because in addition to attorney fees, further action would have required them to pay $100 to appeal to the county circuit court and then an additional $500 to appeal to the Mississippi Supreme Court. Obviously, they had no reason to believe that any court in the state would require a circuit court clerk to start registering black voters.[60]

In 1953, Thurgood Marshall submitted another round of affidavits from Forrest County to the Department of Justice, prompting the federal government to resume its investigation of Luther Cox. But Cox's strategic decision to allow a handful of African Americans to register effectively convinced the Federal Bureau of Investigation (FBI) that he was no longer systematically discriminating against all black voters, and so in 1955, the FBI dropped its investigation. That year, only sixteen African Americans were registered to vote in a county with 7,406 African Americans over the voting age of twenty-one.[61]

Although *Peay et al. v. Cox* did not win black Hattiesburgers the right to vote, it nevertheless represented a watershed moment in the tactics of local black leadership. For decades, Hattiesburg's black leaders had worked within the constraints of Jim Crow to mobilize neighborhood resources and appeal to local white authorities in efforts to improve conditions in the black community. *Peay et al. v. Cox* offered a fundamentally different approach. With the lawsuit, black leaders in the Mobile Street District were attempting to circumvent local and state authority in a direct appeal to the federal government for civil rights.

Hammond and Charles Smith and their fellow plaintiffs left behind no explanation of their decision in 1950 to challenge Mississippi's sixty-year-long processes to disfranchise black voters, but clearly something had changed. Much has been written about how American involvement in World War II helped expose contradictions between the Allied fight for democracy and the realities of Southern Jim Crow. This is true. But disfranchised African Americans did not necessarily need a war for democracy to reveal to them that their rights were being violated. Millions of Southern black men and women knew this all along. Turner Smith certainly did. So did J. B. Woods, the local black grocer who regularly attended Republican National Conventions in the 1920s and 1930s. Those men knew of the Fifteenth Amendment and the rights supposedly guaranteed to them by the Constitution. Had they not died within three weeks of one another in the spring of 1944, it is highly likely that Turner Smith and Woods would have been co-appellants in *Peay et al. v. Cox.*

The greatest advantage held by the new generation was not necessarily one of enhanced perspective but rather one of increased economic independence. Although World War II–era black community organizing resembled the methodologies of previous generations, it was also uniquely bolstered by federally funded projects—especially the black USO and the Robertson Place apartments—and new economic opportunities created by Camp Shelby's mobilization. Consider these developments within the broader scope of Hattiesburg's racial history. Local white city leaders had always controlled black access to external resources. But during the 1940s, massive federal spending—all of which was also supported and enjoyed by local whites—created greater financial independence and new paths to federal resources that helped facilitate more aggressive appeals to the federal government for civil rights. As one of Hammond Smith's employees later told an interviewer, the plaintiffs in *Peay et al. v. Cox* were all "more or less independent professional men." *Peay et al. v. Cox* was a loss, but they were far from the end of their fight.[62]

In October of 1954, Hammond completed a major renovation of the Smith Drug Store. That autumn, he held a large ceremony to celebrate the reopening and to commemorate the store's twenty-ninth year in business. The event received coverage in the *Hattiesburg American*, which cited Hammond's estimate that he had filled nearly 500,000 prescriptions since first opening in 1925. Hammond placed an advertisement below the feature article, inviting all to the store's reopening and offering door prizes, souvenirs, and free toys and balloons for the children. The advertisement also included a portrait of Hammond. A black leader in the city for nearly three decades, Hammond had never before had his picture in the local paper.[63]

Sometime in the following year, Hammond and Charles Smith began meeting with a man named Medgar Wiley Evers in a back room of the Smith Drug Store. In 1954, Medgar Evers was appointed the NAACP's first full-time Mississippi field secretary. Part of his job included increasing membership and coordinating activities and communication among NAACP branches across the state. It was in this capacity that he began meeting with the Smith brothers in 1955.[64]

Community members in the remodeled Smith Drug Store, 1955. N. R. Burger is second from right. (McCain Library and Archives, University of Southern Mississippi)

Medgar Evers began working closely with members of the Forrest County NAACP. Local black leaders helped introduce Evers to other members of the Mobile Street District. Over the following years, Evers regularly appeared in Hattiesburg. Besides meeting with local NAACP leaders, he also spoke at St. Paul Methodist Church, helped organize a youth chapter of the local NAACP, and constantly encouraged local black men and women to try to register to vote. In 1957, he collected affidavits from local black residents whose voter registration applications had been denied and arranged for the pastor of True Light Baptist Church to speak in Washington, DC, before the Senate Subcommittee on Constitutional Rights. The men and women of the Forrest County NAACP who helped facilitate these efforts were small in number. But they used their status as community leaders to operate within well-established community organizing traditions to create a space that allowed for a much more extensive resistance against Jim Crow when the movement finally came.[65]

CHAPTER ELEVEN

Crying in the Wilderness

You have been a "voice crying in the wilderness," but I believe that you are going to be well pleased with the following.

—Mississippi judge Tom P. Brady to Louis E. Faulkner, July 18, 1955

October 8, 1949, marked a day of transition in Hattiesburg. On that Saturday afternoon, hundreds of local white citizens gathered beneath a cloudy sky at Oaklawn Cemetery for the burial of W. S. F. Tatum. Having first arrived in Hattiesburg in 1893 "looking for pine trees," Tatum had for more than fifty years played an enormous role in shaping local life. He was a two-time mayor, a major municipal investor, and a benefactor of dozens of white churches, schools, and civic organizations. When news of Tatum's death became public, Hattiesburg's mayor issued a special proclamation declaring a "day of mourning" and ordered the closure of all municipal offices to commemorate the passing of Hattiesburg's preeminent pioneer.[1]

Meanwhile, a celebration raged across town. That Saturday marked homecoming at Mississippi Southern College. Festivities began that morning with a parade that "splashed color" across the downtown, noted one reporter. Thousands of local residents filled downtown sidewalks and crowded into the windows of office buildings to watch the lively procession. Student organizations competed for prizes awarded to the most attractive or most inventive parade floats. The Kappa Alpha fraternity received an award for a float featuring a pretty female student sitting in a champagne glass filled with balloons made to look like bubbles. Chi Omega won the sorority prize for a float adorned with twelve hundred homemade golden paper flowers.[2]

Filled with cheer and vigor, the day-long fete featured student and alumni lunches, campus tours, open houses at the student lounge and the Pan-Hellenic Council, an afternoon tea at the Home Economics Department, smokers hosted by an athletic booster club and the Hattiesburg Junior Chamber of Commerce, two dances, and, of course, the football game. That evening, ten thousand raucous fans watched the Mississippi Southern College Southerners dismantle the McMurray College Indians by a score of 55–32.[3]

The featured guest of the 1949 Mississippi Southern College Homecoming Ceremony was the enormously popular Mississippi governor Fielding Wright. Wright led the morning parade and attended that evening's football game. A longtime politician from the Mississippi Delta, Wright was lieutenant governor in 1946 when the governor died and left him the office. Wright was reelected the following year, bucking a longstanding state political trend by becoming the first governor-elect from the Delta region in over thirty years. In Forrest County, he even beat out Hattiesburg native Paul B. Johnson Jr. in that summer's primary.[4]

Governor Wright was not a racial demagogue in the mold of Theodore Bilbo, but like all the state's leading politicians of the time, he was an ardent and outspoken white supremacist. As with the senatorial campaign of 1947, each major gubernatorial candidate ran on a platform vowing to maintain Mississippi's racial hierarchy amid perceived threats to Jim Crow.

In Governor Wright's 1948 Inaugural Address, he criticized what he considered to be "anti-Southern legislation" proposed by Northern Democrats. According to Wright, these included the "FEPC, anti-lynching legislation, anti-poll tax bills, and now the anti-segregation proposals." These proposals, Wright charged, promised to "eventually destroy this nation and all the freedoms which we have long cherished and maintained."[5]

By 1948, white Southern segregationist Democrats did indeed have cause for concern. On February 2, 1948, President Harry Truman delivered a civil rights message to Congress, calling for federal anti-lynching legislation and greater protections for African Americans' civil and voting rights. Northern Democrats were joined by Republican leaders in the North and West who also advocated for increased civil rights for African Americans. Later that summer, the Republican Party national platform included calls for anti-lynching legislation, the abolition of poll taxes, the end of racial segregation in the armed forces, and federal legislation to ensure that "equal opportunity to work and to advance in life should never be limited in any individual because of race, religion, color, or country of origin."[6]

Bear in mind that none of this was particularly radical. Every component of these proposals fell within the basic framework of constitutional

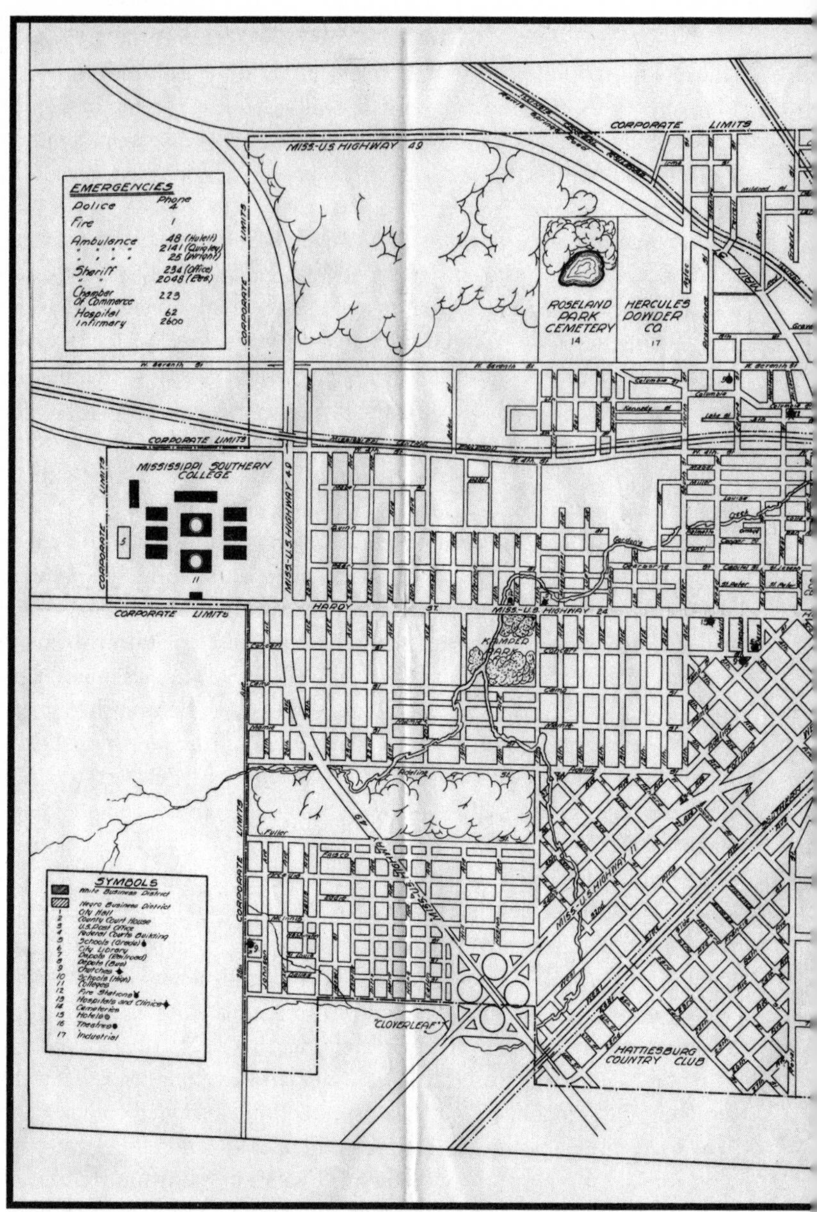

Map of Hattiesburg, 1946, produced by the Hattiesburg Chamber of Commerce. The "White Business District" is indicated with heavy cross-hatching, and the "Negro Business District" with light cross-hatching.

(McCain Library and Archives, University of Southern Mississippi)

NOTE: This map is not drawn to any scale and should not be used for measuring, or scaling distances. For Tourist's Only.
CHAMBER OF COMMERCE MAP OF
HATTIESBURG, MISSISSIPPI.
FORREST COUNTY
ESTIMATED POPULATION 40,000
No Scale
April 1946
LEAF RIVER
MISS-U.S. HIGHWAY 11
MISS.-U.S. HIGHWAY 49
BOUIE
RIVER AVE.
CORPORATE LIMITS
LIMITS
Mississippi Central Railroad Yards
Southern Railway Yards
LEGEND
City / Mileage / Via Route
Ackerman 139 11&45
Aberdeen 203 11&45
Biloxi 82 49&90
Bogalusa, La 59 11
Baton Rouge, La 154 24 or 11
Bogalusa, La 64 24
Brookhaven 83 49&84
[Brookhaven] 97 24&51
[Brookhaven] 80 42&84
Bude 104 24&84
Batesville 244 49&51
Birmingham, Ala 243 11&80
Covington, La 87 11
Columbia 28 24
Collins 27 49
Canton 114 49&51
Clarksdale 246 49
Columbus 176 11&45
Corinth 285 11&45
Durant 150 49&51
Gulfport 70 49
Grenada 205 49&51
Greenwood 185 49
Greenville 215 49&82
Hammond, La 109 11
Hazlehurst 107 49, 84&51
Holly Springs 287 49, 51&7
Houston 207 11&15
Jackson 162 49, 84&51
[Jackson] 90 49
Lucedale 51 24
Lumberton 25 11
Laurel 29 11
Macon 148 11&45
Meridian 87 11
Mobile, Ala 90 24
[Mobile, Ala] 148 49&90
McLain 50 24
McComb 71 24
Monticello 60 42&84
[Monticello] 65 49&84
Magee 47 49
Memphis, Tenn 332 49, 36&51
[Memphis, Tenn] 307 49&51
[Memphis, Tenn] 332 49, 51, 7&78
New Orleans, La 127 11
[New Orleans, La] 149 49&90
New Augusta 15 24
Natchez 141 24
[Natchez] 145 42&84
[Natchez] 148 49&84
Newton 89 11&15
Pascagoula 104 49&90
[Pascagoula] 99 24&63
Purvis 15 11
Poplarville 38 11
Picayune 63 11
Prentiss 48
Philadelphia 118 11&15
Pontotoc 232 11&15
Slidell, La 89 11
Tylertown 51 24
Vicksburg 131 49&80
Wiggins 55 49
Waynesboro 60 11&84

rights already guaranteed to American citizens. The problem was that the federal government had not genuinely protected the individual liberties of black Southerners since the 1870s. This civil rights advocacy of the 1940s was significant because it symbolized the greatest support for Southern black rights by Northern politicians since Reconstruction.

There were several factors behind the timing of such support. First and foremost was the plain fact that Jim Crow–era disfranchisement was an undeniable contradiction to the foundations on which American democracy was purported to have been built; this basic detail cannot be overlooked. Black people in the Jim Crow South were expected to pay taxes and abide by laws without having any ability to vote for representatives who might serve their interests.

Second was the expanding political influence of a Northern black electorate. The black migration that began in the 1910s accelerated once again during World War II, bringing hundreds of thousands of new black voters into Chicago, Detroit, New York City, and elsewhere. During the 1940s, nearly three hundred thousand African Americans left Mississippi alone. These newly enfranchised black voters helped elect several African Americans to Congress and increased pressure on Northern white politicians to support black civil rights in the North and South. Any white politician running for a major office in New York, for example, needed to consider the potential effects of the black vote.[7]

Another factor was the glaring hypocrisies on the international stage between the rhetoric of American democracy and the realities of Southern Jim Crow. As the United States claimed to be the world's greatest purveyor of freedom and democracy during the early years of the Cold War, Southern racial violence, disfranchisement, and segregation threatened to undermine the country's purported commitment to liberalism and self-determination. Southern Jim Crow created an obvious conundrum with global implications: if people within America's own borders could not vote because of their skin color, then how could people in the nations of Africa, Asia, and South America possibly view the United States as the world's leading democracy?[8]

A fourth major factor was the collection of racially progressive precedents—especially the FEPC (Fair Employment Practices Committee), the "Black Cabinet," anti-discrimination clauses in New Deal programs, and *Smith v. Allwright*—that were enacted during the Roosevelt Administration. New Deal policies often worked in sync with Southern Jim

Crow, but in the postwar years, Northern New Deal Democrats, including Eleanor Roosevelt, continued to expand their vision of a greater federal role in enhancing individual freedom and opportunity in American life. As the reach of the federal government continued to broaden through the 1930s and 1940s, there appeared to be significant national interest in supporting the basic civil rights of African Americans. Of course, white Southern segregationists viewed these developments as serious threats to the foundations of institutionalized white supremacy.[9]

Less than two weeks after President Truman's civil rights address, Mississippi governor Fielding Wright called a meeting of state legislators and other influential white leaders. With approximately five thousand "true white Jeffersonian democrats" in attendance, the meeting opened with rebel yells, Confederate flag waving, and a loud rendition of "Dixie," the Confederate States of America's unofficial national anthem. The group denounced all components of President Truman's civil rights message to Congress and adopted a resolution warning the National Democratic Party that Mississippi legislators would "make every effort within the party to defeat such proposals," even if they had to "nominate our own candidate for president and vice president and throw our electoral vote to those men," asserted House Speaker Walter Sillers.[10]

Eight days later, on February 20, fifty Southern Democrats in the United States House of Representatives met in Washington, DC, where according to the Associated Press, they "declared war today on President Truman's civil rights program" and adopted their own resolution expressing concern over "an invasion of the sovereignity [*sic*] of the states." The following day, Democratic leaders from ten Southern states gathered in Jackson, where they also adopted resolutions outlining a break with the national Democratic Party and the formation of a new "States' Rights" political party. After decades of unflinching loyalty, these white Southern Democrats stood ready to abandon the political party of their forebears.[11]

Despite Governor Wright's warning that federal overreach threatened "to tear down and disrupt our institutions and our way of life," by the late 1940s, nearly two decades of federal spending had saved Mississippi from utter destitution and generated the best economic conditions in the history of the state. First came the New Deal of the 1930s and 1940s, which created tens of thousands of jobs and injected an immeasurable amount of capital into the state's payroll and infrastructure. Then came the federal wartime spending of the 1940s, which created unprecedented statewide economic growth. Although most of Mississippi's wartime boom was concentrated at Camp Shelby, Kessler Field in Biloxi, and the Ingalls Shipyard in Pascagoula, the economic benefits of wartime mobilization touched every corner of the state. Smaller military installations and federal contracts boosted the economy of several additional cities. And thousands of Mississippians flocked to Camp Shelby and the shipyards on the Gulf Coast for temporary jobs. Between 1940 and 1946, Mississippi's annual per capita income nearly tripled, increasing from $218 to $605. Mississippi remained one of the poorest states in America, but federal spending over the preceding decades ensured a level of stability unimaginable just twenty years earlier during the onset of the Great Depression.[12]

It is important to understand that the Southern dogma of states' rights as it was employed in 1948 was both a ruse and a logical fallacy. Beyond issues related to race, Southern Democrats showed little concern over federalism or Northern involvement in Southern affairs. In fact, many of them and their constituencies had not only supported the New Deal of the 1930s but had also actively sought to expand federal programs and spending in their states. Furthermore, no white Southern elected official could accurately claim to represent the entire citizenry of their state. African American residents comprised enormous portions of the population in every state in the Deep South and factored into the calculations that determined the number of congressional representatives each state was assigned. Yet most black people were completely blocked from political participation. In reality, Southern states'-rights politicians represented the rights and interests of white residents only. State sovereignty was of little concern to states'-rights advocates in 1948. The real concern was the ability of white Southerners to maintain white supremacy by continuing to violate the constitutional rights of African Americans.[13]

In any case, during the 1948 presidential election, white Southern Democrats formed a new political party called the States' Rights Democrats and left the national Democratic Party for the first time in a presidential election since Reconstruction. Also known as the Dixiecrats, these white Southern legislators nominated South Carolina governor Strom Thurmond for president and Mississippi governor Fielding Wright for vice president.[14]

As might be expected, the Dixiecrats were enormously popular among white Mississippi voters, carrying 87 percent of the popular vote in the 1948 presidential election. They performed even better in Hattiesburg. Local attorneys Stanton Hall and Dudley Conner helped lead a get-out-the-vote campaign, and the *Hattiesburg American* offered free transportation to the polls while encouraging local whites to cast ballots "against indignities proposed against the South." A record turnout in Forrest County supported the Dixiecrat ticket with over 90 percent of the vote.[15]

Although the Dixiecrats captured approximately one-fifth of the popular vote in the South, the party ultimately failed to achieve its broader goals. Struggling to secure financial contributions and develop broad grassroots support, the Dixiecrats won only four Southern states in the general election—Mississippi, South Carolina, Alabama, and Louisiana—and did not significantly alter the 1948 Democratic Party platform. Nonetheless, the movement was important for several reasons. Representing the first time since Reconstruction that the South had not voted solidly Democratic, the Dixiecrat movement demonstrated an unprecedented level of partisan flexibility in the region. Remember that Democratic president Franklin Roosevelt of New York had carried at least 93 percent of the popular vote in Mississippi during each of the previous four elections. No Democratic presidential candidate has ever again approached such broad support in the Deep South. The Democratic Party recaptured each of the Dixiecrat states in 1952, but the Dixiecrat revolt of 1948 symbolized a clear fracture in the New Deal political coalition of the 1930s and 1940s.[16]

The Dixiecrat movement also demonstrated once again the immense political capital available to white Southern politicians who explicitly resisted any threat to Jim Crow. In hindsight, it is easy enough to condemn the Dixiecrats' most famous racial demagogues. But we must not forget the people who voted for them. In the late 1940s, it would have been obvious to any Southern politician that hysteria and hardline defiance created widespread political appeal among white voters. As the South prepared to enter its most prosperous era, white Southerners stood ready to defend racial supremacy. In Hattiesburg and elsewhere, the most defiant politicians—Fielding Wright among them—were regarded as heroes. And as heroes, they were invited to events like the Mississippi Southern College Homecoming.[17]

Less than three weeks after the war ended, the Hattiesburg Chamber of Commerce launched an initiative called the "Post-War Development Fund" to avoid what the *Hattiesburg American* labeled a potentially "disastrous post-war slump." With Shelby demobilizing, the organization once again turned its attention to recruiting new manufacturing firms. Previous experience in pursuing industries had shown that interested firms might require the city to provide land, buildings, tax credits, equipment, or subsidies. The Chamber of Commerce postwar development fund was conceived in anticipation of these expenses. The plan was to collect enough capital from local businesses to purchase $75,000 worth of United States Treasury Bonds. The bonds were a conservative yet lucrative investment. They promised to generate yearly interest and could be sold as needed to obtain liquid capital.[18]

The effort to attract new industries was widespread across Mississippi. Aided by a newly formed Mississippi Agricultural and Industrial Board, dozens of cities across the state successfully attracted new industries in the years after World War II. The Magnolia State never became a major manufacturing center, but it did enjoy significant industrial growth. In 1939, Mississippi had 1,235 manufacturing establishments that paid a total of $27.1 million in wages. Eight years later, the state had 1,985 firms that paid $116.2 million in wages. By 1954, Mississippi's manufacturing establishments numbered 2,252 with a total payroll of $188.8 million. In a state with an essentially static population over those same years, the wages paid by manufacturing establishments increased by an inflation-adjusted factor of three.[19]

Similar growth occurred throughout the South. Much of that development took place in major cities such as Atlanta or Birmingham, but industrial growth also touched hundreds of mid-sized Southern towns that attracted new industries by offering state-supported development bonds, tax exemptions, and the promise of cheap labor. Between 1939 and 1954, the number of manufacturing establishments in the six Southern states of Mississippi, Alabama, Arkansas, Georgia, Louisiana, and Tennessee expanded from 11,391 to 21,756, a 90 percent increase that created over 466,000 jobs in all corners of those six states.[20]

The Hattiesburg Chamber of Commerce, its members flush from the wartime boom, met its goal for the postwar development fund in less than two months. "It was [an] appropriate and proper time to put on a drive," explained the Chamber of Commerce president, "as practically every business house in Hattiesburg had prospered tremendously from the activities of Camp Shelby." Contributions ranging between $5 and $1,500 poured in from every type of business—bakeries, groceries, restaurants, banks, contractors, theatres, chain stores, cleaners, law offices, doctor's offices, and automobile dealers. In less than sixty days, the campaign closed with

Board of directors of the Hattiesburg Chamber of Commerce, 1947. Louis Faulkner is seated in the lower-right-hand corner. (McCain Library and Archives, University of Southern Mississippi)

$91,886.50 "to be used EXCLUSIVELY," noted a Chamber of Commerce report, "in the development of industrial and agricultural activities." The organization purchased $75,000 in United States Treasury Bonds and invested the remainder in two local banks.[21]

The growth of Hattiesburg's postwar development fund was enabled almost entirely by federal spending. New Deal programs notwithstanding, the federal government between 1940 and 1945 poured tens of millions of dollars into Camp Shelby, creating thousands of local jobs and paying the salaries of hundreds of thousands of troops who spent their earnings across the city. The white business owners who profited most handsomely from this economic boom then contributed a portion of their profits into a fund that was used to purchase federally insured treasury bonds.[22]

Before Shelby mobilized in 1940, the Hattiesburg Chamber of Commerce was powerless to save the city's crumbling economy. As the *Hattiesburg American* bluntly observed of the prewar era, "The Chamber of Commerce was broke." Then came Shelby's salvation. "This community," observed the local paper in 1945, "has been blessed, economically, as few others in the nation have been blessed."[23]

In 1946, the Chamber of Commerce went to work with over $93,000. Members identified a number of strategies to secure future prosperity: establishing Camp Shelby as a permanent military training center, recruiting new industries, developing more local farms, and establishing a new airport. Despite their best efforts, most of these goals failed to come to fruition.[24]

Camp Shelby demobilized in 1946 and did not again play a significant role in the local economy for nearly fifty years. The federal government did spend roughly $3 million in 1953 to prepare the site for troop training during the Korean War, but the base was never activated for deployments. And although Shelby became a permanent military establishment in 1956, it did not host a large number of troops until the late twentieth century. During the Vietnam War, only one brigade deployed from Shelby. In more recent years, Shelby has once again become a major military installation, offering similar benefits to Hattiesburg as it did during World War II. But for most of the postwar era, Camp Shelby remained a "ghost town," as one National Guardsman dubbed the site in 1947. As the 1940s came to a close, it became clear that new jobs and revenues would have to come from elsewhere.[25]

The effort to recruit new industries also met limited success. The Chamber of Commerce spent much of the late 1940s gauging the interest of dozens of companies across the United States. In 1947, the organization sent representatives on a long road-trip through Tennessee, Missouri, and Illinois to meet with officials from some thirty companies about plans for future plant locations. The Hattiesburg representatives seemed optimistic, but nearly all of these interactions appear to have been nothing more than courtesy meetings. Attracting new industries in the postwar era was more difficult than they had anticipated. Their challenges were rooted in a combination of increased competition and lack of capital.[26]

With virtually every Southern city interested in attracting new firms, Hattiesburg promoters were often simply too late. On several occasions, Chamber of Commerce representatives met with company officials only to learn that the particular firm was already in negotiations with cities such as Pine Bluff, Arkansas; Gulfport, Mississippi; Monroe, Louisiana; Greenville, Mississippi; Savannah, Georgia; Dallas, Texas; or, in one case, "a little town in Alabama."[27]

The other major problem was that companies required too much of the city. Increased competition for factories led to increased subsidies, tax credits, land, and buildings required by companies. None of these requirements was necessarily new. In fact, the Chamber of Commerce's postwar development fund was created in anticipation of such requests. But the organization was not prepared to contend in the highly competitive postwar era. They simply did not have the capital.[28]

In 1947, the Hattiesburg Chamber of Commerce entered negotiations with the National Gypsum Company, a wallboard manufacturing firm based in Buffalo, New York. National Gypsum was seeking a site for a new factory that would annually employ over 450 people and contribute an estimated $2 million to the local economy. But the firm also asked the city of Hattiesburg to donate land for the new factory and provide at least $2.5 million to subsidize half the construction costs. Hattiesburg's entire operating budget in 1946 was only $207,805, and the city already had a bonded indebtedness—for libraries, schools, parks, and sewers, among other public projects—of over $1.4 million. After some talk of a municipal bond referendum, the organization ultimately realized it could not proceed. Even with their postwar development fund, this was simply far beyond their range of affordability.[29]

Such limitations prevented Hattiesburg from developing into a major industrial center, but the city was able to add some jobs. In 1946, the Chamber of Commerce used portions of the postwar development fund to organize a small farming cooperative that marketed agricultural products. In addition, the economic recovery of the war years enabled the foundation or expansion of several small firms, including Hattiesburg Concrete Products, Dixie Pine Products, American Sand & Gravel Company, Burkett Sheet Metal Works, Gilkey's Welding and Boiler Works, and Roby & Anderson Machine Works. Other jobs were offered at automobile service stations, grocery stores, cleaners, electric companies, building contractors, plumbing firms, and retail stores. And the city still had some larger employers from the prewar era that expanded during and after the war. These existing firms were their greatest asset.[30]

For most of the late 1940s and 1950s, Hattiesburg's largest employer was the Reliance Manufacturing Company. Having first opened its Hattiesburg plants in 1933, the Chicago-based firm profited handsomely during World War II with orders for over sixteen million units of clothing that were manufactured in over twenty plants across the country. In 1943, Reliance built a second Hattiesburg factory, known as the "Freedom Plant," to help meet demand.[31]

Buoyed by wartime growth and a strong postwar domestic economy, production at Reliance expanded throughout the late 1940s. The Hattiesburg plants were so inundated with orders that they struggled to find enough employees. Reliance managers erected employment booths at local grocery stores and operated busses to transport workers from nearby towns. By the time Reliance celebrated its fifteenth anniversary in 1948, the company employed approximately eight hundred people and provided an annual payroll of over $1 million. For hundreds of young women, a position at Reliance was the first—perhaps the only—job they had ever held. One did not need any significant amount of training or skill to procure a desirable entry-level job at the factory. The only requirement was that one needed to be white.[32]

Hattiesburg's second-largest employer during the postwar era was the Hercules Powder Company, the Delaware-based firm that first arrived in 1923. Hercules profited during the war by selling munitions to the Allies. The company continued growing after the war with the production of explosives and naval stores products such as turpentine, pine oil, and rosin. In 1950, Hercules invested approximately $1.5 million in the Hattiesburg plant to expand production of toxaphene, a highly toxic insecticide that was later banned in the United States. The dangerous products manufactured in Hattiesburg may have been hazardous to the environment and to public health, but they also provided over 650 local jobs through the 1960s.[33]

Unlike Reliance, Hercules employed large numbers of both white and black workers, all of whom belonged to the AFL-CIO affiliate Hattiesburg Chemical Workers Local No. 385. Although white and black employees belonged to a single union, this type of interracial labor organizing did not signify any significant threat to local segregation ordinances. In fact, the first incarnation of the union held racially separate meetings. The national AFL-CIO eventually convinced locals to abandon that practice, but black and white employees continued using separate entrances and restrooms, playing on segregated softball teams, and participating in separate social clubs. Interracial unionization and Jim Crow were not inherently incompatible.[34]

Nevertheless, the union did help facilitate a handful of examples of racial progress. Longtime African American Hercules employee Richard Boyd credits the union with his ability to become the "first black man to get and hold an operating position at Hercules," a promotion he received in 1954, his fourteenth year with the company. Such cases, however, were rare. Most of the plant's roughly two hundred-plus black employees held menial jobs and enjoyed far fewer opportunities for advancement than did their white counterparts.[35]

Jobs at Hercules were at once dangerous and desirable. White and black workers who had survived the Great Depression in America's poorest state rushed to take positions handling dangerous chemicals because those positions offered stable work and decent wages. "That job at Hercules was supreme back in those days," remembered Huck Dunagin, who worked at the plant between 1933 and the 1970s. Though the local union did not add much in terms of occupational safety, a nine-day strike in 1946 helped raise wages. By the late 1940s, wages at Hercules ranged from $0.67 to $1.38 per hour; employees who worked full-time at Hercules could thus earn between $1,580 and $2,870 per year. At the time, Mississippi's average per capita income was $609. In the Southeast region, the average per capita income was $885; in the United States, it was $1,247. Even by national standards, Hercules workers were relatively well paid.[36]

The most exciting development in postwar Hattiesburg was the rapid expansion of Mississippi Southern College. Originally founded in 1910, the college changed its name from State Teachers College to Mississippi Southern College in 1940 to reflect the school's transformation from a small teaching institute to a fully accredited college. Enrollment at the school declined briefly during World War II, but then it exploded during the 1940s and 1950s. From a low enrollment of roughly three hundred undergraduates in 1945, the student body expanded to approximately two thousand by 1950 and nearly five thousand by the end of the decade.[37]

Mississippi Southern's growth was enabled by the GI Bill, the widely popular federal program that provided educational grants and low-interest loans to veterans. During the 1946–47 academic year, GI Bill–related expenditures accounted for an estimated $700 million of the roughly $1 billion the federal government spent on higher education. One historian of World War II veterans' education has estimated that the program funded the higher education of approximately 450,000 veterans who otherwise would not have attended college. By 1947, veterans accounted for nearly 70 percent of all male college undergraduate students.[38]

The GI Bill fundamentally changed the student body at Mississippi Southern. Women had once comprised a large majority on the campus.

During the 1935–36 academic year, for example, only 22 percent of students were men. Two decades later, men accounted for up to 63 percent of undergraduates. "Mississippi Southern College as it was known when I became president, had very few men students," recalled school president R. C. Cook. "With the 1946–47 session, we began to get a large number of GI students." Of course, this growth only included white male veterans. Most of Mississippi's roughly eighty-five thousand black World War II veterans were also eligible for GI Bill benefits, but none of them were permitted to enroll at Mississippi Southern or any of the state's other white institutions.[39]

The federally funded GI Bill provided enormous benefits to Mississippi Southern and a new generation of white students, enabling thousands of male students from working-class families to attend college. Their presence strained the campus's residential and academic capacities, but also facilitated rapid growth of the school. Mississippi Southern responded to expanding enrollments by securing housing facilities from Camp Shelby and arranging for busses to transport students. The wave of new pupils justified curriculum expansion. Student demand led to new programs and departments, including a business school, departments of biology, speech and hearing, and physical education, and a graduate program in education. With such a rapid influx of students, the school successfully lobbied the state for additional funds that helped maintain constant growth throughout the 1950s. President Cook also expanded Greek life to include national sororities and fraternities, revamped the school's marching band, and hired a full-time director to run the school's athletic program, which joined the National Collegiate Athletic Association (NCAA) in 1952. The increased enrollments remade the small teachers' school into a large college with division-one sports. As President Cook later observed, "the influx of GI students changed the whole nature of the school."[40]

In the postwar years, Mississippi Southern emerged as a central part of local life. The Hattiesburg Chamber of Commerce was thrilled with the growth of the college. Rising enrollments brought thousands of educated residents to town, expanded retail opportunities, and created new jobs. The school also helped enhance a sense of community. Football games and homecoming parades were terrific for local boosterism and communal spirit, even among those who did not attend the college. Local white residents also benefitted from access to a large campus library and the beautiful on-campus park, Lake Byron, both of which had been financed by New Deal projects in the 1930s. As Mississippi Southern grew, the Hattiesburg Chamber of Commerce increasingly incorporated the college into its activities and programming. The organization even reserved a spot for President Cook and his successor on its board of directors.[41]

Although the Hattiesburg Chamber of Commerce was never able to fulfill its most ambitious industrial dreams, by the early 1950s, the city's economy stood on solid ground. People who needed work could generally find it. Less than 25 percent of local adults held high school diplomas, but most people did not need an extensive education to earn a living wage in Hattiesburg. Thousands of men and women found blue-collar jobs at Reliance, Hercules, or in one of the city's smaller manufacturing firms, service stations, restaurants, and retailers. In 1950, the city's unemployment rate was 4.5 percent, and the median individual income was $1,578, roughly 50 percent higher than the state average. Local African Americans were blocked from many opportunities, but even their median individual income of $1,028 was the highest for a non-white population of any city in the state.[42]

The economic story of Hattiesburg in the postwar era was one not of explosive expansion but rather of slow and steady growth. Hattiesburg was not a bustling Southern metropolis in the model of Nashville or Dallas, but it was a place that offered opportunity for thousands of working-class people. So once again, people came. Between 1940 and 1950, the city grew from 21,026 residents to 29,474, an increase of over 40 percent. Most of these folks had lived through the depression and the war and were quite happy to find stability in postwar Hattiesburg. They worked hard, went to church, sent their kids to school, and continued to abide by the rules of a rigidly segregated society. Those who violated the rules faced severe consequences.[43]

Louis Faulkner was infuriated by the Supreme Court's 1954 *Brown v. Board of Education of Topeka* decision. Faulkner, a native Pennsylvanian and longtime Republican, was not a typical homegrown white Southern segregationist. But since arriving in Mississippi in 1905, he had become an ardent defender of Southern Jim Crow. As a longtime member of the Chamber of Commerce, deacon of Hattiesburg's First Presbyterian Church, and leader in a variety of local organizations ranging from the Boy Scouts to the Rotary Club, Faulkner enjoyed a great deal of local influence. When federal policies threatened white supremacy, he sought to expand that influence far beyond local affairs.

Faulkner's first major gripe was with the FEPC, the World War II–era executive order designed to prevent companies that practiced segregation from receiving defense contracts. When some members of the national Democratic Party began floating the idea of establishing a permanent FEPC after the war, Faulkner used his platform as a leader in the First Presbyterian Church to voice his opposition to any organization that supported the FEPC, including churches. Faulkner's own company, Faulkner Concrete, and his employer, the Mississippi Central Railroad, had both received federal contracts during the New Deal and World War II; he had no real grievance over federal spending or influence when it benefitted him. The source of his agitation lay in the suggestion that white Southerners should be required to share the spoils of federal money with African Americans.

In 1947, Faulkner "urged withdrawal of the Southern Presbyterian church from the Federal Council of Churches of Christ (FCC)," reported the *Hattiesburg American*, because the FCC "had 'committed more than 27,000,000 church members to FEPC legislation.'" In the following years, Faulkner constantly attacked the FCC (which in 1950 became the National Council of Churches [NCC]), delivering scores of speeches, writing hundreds of letters, and publishing numerous anti-NCC op-eds in the *Hattiesburg American*. Like many segregationists of his era, Faulkner positioned his critiques within the framework of the postwar Red Scare. Increasingly paranoid about the influence of non-Southerners, Faulkner in 1950 ceased all donations to national organizations based on growing suspicion of their support for civil rights or socialism.[44]

The *Brown* decision in May of 1954 intensified Faulkner's activism. That July, Faulkner received a copy of an anti-*Brown* letter written by a Jacksonville businessman to an NAACP official. Faulkner was "so well impressed" by this letter that he mimeographed a thousand copies and "mailed them to the Governors, Attorney Generals and other officials of several southern states, and to a large number of ministers and other church officers." This was the first of many efforts to distribute segregationist literature. Between 1954 and 1960, Faulkner essentially operated as a one-man clearinghouse for hundreds of segregationist pamphlets and essays. He had many allies.[45]

No state mounted a more venomous response to *Brown* than Mississippi. The state's politicians seemingly scrambled to outdo one another with extraordinarily racist and cataclysmic rhetoric that went so far as to suggest the possibility of another civil war. "Negro education and interracial comity," stated Congressman John Bell Williams, "suffered their most damaging setback since the War Between the States." Congressman William Winstead argued that the decision would retard educational progress in the South "for at least half a century." Mississippi senator James Eastland launched into a bitter, hour-long tirade on the Senate floor, accusing members of the United States Supreme Court of being "brainwashed" and promising "The South will retain segregation."[46]

Louis Faulkner's mailing campaign placed him in touch with a number of Mississippi's leading segregationist voices, including Congressman Williams and Senator Eastland. In addition to distributing segregationist literature, Faulkner also worked to challenge the NAACP Legal Defense Fund's tax-exempt status as a nonprofit organization. Beginning in 1955, he wrote dozens of letters to high-ranking public officials, including administrators at the United States Treasury Department, the governor of Mississippi, White House chief of staff Sherman Adams, the commissioner of the Internal Revenue Service, and FBI director J. Edgar Hoover, urging these officials to investigate the NAACP Legal Defense Fund and revoke the organization's nonprofit status. None of these requests produced the desired results, but Faulkner was continuously encouraged by his fellow Mississippi segregationists. "You are certainly doing fine work," Eastland wrote to Faulkner, "and the position which you take is the right one."[47]

The motivations behind Faulkner's crusade are curious. Apart from his angst over the school desegregation ruling, Faulkner in 1954 lived in relative ease and comfort. Having turned seventy-one that year, the longtime city leader was slowly retreating into retirement. He had given up his seat on the Hattiesburg Chamber of Commerce board of directors and was in the process of grooming his son-in-law to replace him as the head of Faulkner Concrete, which had rapidly expanded since securing federal contracts during the New Deal and World War II. He and his wife of over forty years lived in a beautiful, 6,000-square-foot home they had built in the 1920s. And his daughter and son-in-law lived just two blocks away with his grandchild. Life was seemingly good for Louis Faulkner. Nevertheless, he spent his final years on earth engaged in an obsessive fight against a school desegregation ruling that bore no practical consequences for his own life.[48]

With limited influence at the federal level, Mississippi segregationists employed several new strategies to fight desegregation. Their first tactic, which actually predated the *Brown* decision, was to provide more funding for black public schools in a preemptive attempt to ward off a broad federal mandate. During the late 1940s and early 1950s, Mississippi officials built new black public schools (with construction of a new black high school in Hattiesburg beginning in 1949) and raised black teacher salaries in an attempt to show that segregated schools could be equal. Between 1946 and 1953, the state spent an unprecedented $11 million on black public schools.[49]

Yet broad racial disparities remained. Despite increased funding for black schools, Mississippi never came even remotely close to equalizing segregated schools. Even if state legislators insisted that funds be proportionately distributed between black and white schools, local white superintendents and school boards still allocated far more resources toward white schools. The $11 million spent on black schools between 1946 and 1953 paled in comparison to the $30 million spent on white schools during that same period.[50]

This half-hearted school equalization program continued after the *Brown* decision. In another case known as *Brown II*, the United States Supreme Court in May of 1955 ordered school districts to desegregate "with all deliberate speed," language that was designed to alleviate potential social upheavals if states were forced to instantaneously restructure their public school systems. *Brown II* gave some segregationists hope that they might be able to continue avoiding school desegregation by equalizing school funding. But disproportionate public school funding continued. As late as 1962, Mississippi's average per-pupil expenditure was still nearly four times higher for white students than for black ones.[51]

The second tactic to combat desegregation was the creation of a statewide investigative unit named the Mississippi State Sovereignty Commission, which surveilled any group or individual advocating civil rights or desegregation. "The duty of the commission," read the enacting legislation, was "to protect the sovereignty of the State of Mississippi, and her sister states, from encroachment thereon by the Federal Government." To conduct its mission, the state-funded Sovereignty Commission employed full-time investigators, worked with local law enforcement officials, and even hired African American informants. The organization was particularly concerned with the NAACP because of its central role in the *Brown* decision. Anyone with suspected NAACP ties was subject to intensive investigation and potential retribution.[52]

The third and most proactive approach toward resisting desegregation was led by the Citizens' Council, a grassroots organization. Founded on July 11, 1954, the Mississippi Citizens' Council was organized by a man named Robert Patterson as a vehicle for white segregationists to "stand together," in Patterson's words, "forever firm against communism and mongrelization." The Citizens' Council was led by middle- and upper-class white professionals who primarily used economic pressure to restrict civil rights activism. As one of its founding members explained, "It is the thought of our group that the solution to this problem may become easier if various agitators and the like be removed from the communities in which they now operate. We propose to accomplish this through the careful application of economic pressures." The council, which exchanged intelligence and received financial support from the Sovereignty Commission, hounded suspected civil rights activists through financial penalties. Among other activities, the organization instructed banks to deny loans, employers to terminate employees, and wholesalers to cut off supplies to anyone accused of advocating civil rights. The Citizens' Council touched virtually every corner of the state. Sixty thousand Mississippians joined in the first year alone. Within two years, the organization counted over eighty thousand dues-paying members in Mississippi and had spread to all parts of the South.[53]

The Hattiesburg Citizens' Council was founded at the downtown courthouse on the night of March 22, 1956. The inaugural meeting was announced in a front-page story in the *Hattiesburg American.* One hundred people attended the first meeting, a turnout that disappointed attorney Dudley Conner, who concluded that with dues as low as $5, the local Citizens' Council "should have at least 5,000 members." Another early member, businessman M. W. Hamilton, explained the essence of the organization's racially based motivations. "The black race," Hamilton later told an interviewer, "in our opinion hadn't advanced to the point where they could contribute anything to the schools." "The white race," he claimed, "is probably ten thousand years ahead of them in intelligence."[54]

The Citizens' Council promoted its message publicly but operated subversively. Although the Hattiesburg Citizens' Council left behind no public membership rolls, newspaper accounts reveal the names of some members: attorney Dudley Conner was the first president; another attorney, Thomas Davis, served as vice president; real estate agent Dennis Frost was the treasurer; and postal clerk David Reed was the secretary. Luther Cox, the longtime Forrest County circuit clerk infamous for asking black voter registrants about bubbles in a bar of soap, was also among the original members. The composition of other Citizens' Councils suggests that most members were middle- to upper-class white citizens, the same demographic that would have belonged to the Kiwanis, the Rotary Club, or the Chamber of Commerce. Unlike those other civic organizations, however, the Citizens' Council operated almost entirely in secret.[55]

Louis Faulkner's name does not appear on any Citizens' Council rosters, but an abundance of evidence suggests he was a member. Faulkner not only helped distribute Citizens' Council literature, he also regularly corresponded with high-ranking Mississippi Citizens' Council officials, including the organization's founder, Robert Patterson, and its most notorious member, Judge Tom P. Brady, whose 1954 segregationist pamphlet "Black Monday" is widely credited with inspiring the creation of the Citizens' Council. Later in life, Brady was labeled by *Time* magazine as "the philosopher of Mississippi's racist white Citizens' Councils" and recognized by the *New York Times* as the "intellectual godfather of the segregationist Citizens Council movement." Brady and Faulkner often exchanged letters and appear to have been fairly close acquaintances. In fact, they had known each other for decades; during the 1920s, Brady's father worked for Faulkner as legal counsel of the Mississippi Central Railroad.[56]

As the Citizens' Council spread, Mississippi became increasingly deadly for civil rights activists. In May of 1955, voting rights activist Reverend George Lee was killed in a drive-by shooting in Belzoni, Mississippi. In August of the same year, voting rights advocate Lamar Smith was shot and killed in Brookhaven, Tom P. Brady's hometown. That November, one of George Lee's allies, Gus Courts, was also shot and almost killed in Belzoni. Other African Americans murdered that year include Emmett Till, Timothy Hudson, and Clinton Melton. The final three were not killed explicitly in retaliation for civil rights activities, but it is impossible to ignore the context. Rumors of a "death list" floated among the state's NAACP leaders. Any black civil rights activist operated under a pall of fear.[57]

The Citizens' Council always denied involvement in violence, but at the very least, the organization helped identify and publicize targets. When Louis Faulkner came across copies of a Jackson-based pro–civil rights newspaper named the *Eagle Eye*, for example, he took it upon himself to distribute copies to white segregationists across the state. Arrington High, the

Eagle Eye's publisher, was later arrested and committed to the Mississippi State Lunatic Asylum, where he lived for five months before being smuggled out of the state in a casket. Most cases of retribution cannot and should not be accredited to any single Citizens' Council member, but the organization's affiliates clearly played a vital and active role in spreading information about civil rights activists. Members of one branch claimed that "the Council is not an anti-negro organization, but that it is opposed to radical outside elements who are attempting to break down the Southern way of life." Virtually all of their activities, however, were designed to hurt native black Mississippians.[58]

Repercussions in Hattiesburg were generally less severe. Locally, the broadest consequence was probably a decline in membership of the Hattiesburg NAACP from 110 in 1955 to 25 in 1956, then 20 in 1957. Deterrents were obvious. People were concerned about job loss, informal economic sanctions, and violence. The threat of violence was nothing new to black Southerners, but the long reach of the Sovereignty Commission and the Citizens' Council elevated the risk of racially subversive activities.[59]

Those who remained in the Hattiesburg NAACP tended to be either entrepreneurs or ministers, who were less susceptible to economic repercussions. Milton Barnes, owner of Barnes Cleaners and the Embassy Club, led the organization for much of the late 1950s. Other entrepreneurial members included Hammond and Charles Smith, Vernon Dahmer, grocer Benjamin Bourn, newsstand owner Lillie McLaurin, grocer Annie B. Howze, and several local black teachers. This small group also included the pastor of each of the four largest churches in the Mobile Street District—George Williams of St. Paul Methodist, James Chandler of Mt. Carmel Baptist, W. D. Ridgeway of True Light Baptist, and W. H. Hall of Zion Chapel A.M.E.[60]

The involvement of ministers offers interesting implications for local NAACP activities. Although the organization counted only twenty official members in 1958, it was supported by at least several hundred local residents. One did not necessarily need to formally belong to the NAACP to support its cause. In 1958, several disgruntled members of Mt. Carmel Baptist told a Sovereignty Commission investigator that Reverend James Chandler had been passing around a collection plate in support of the NAACP. When these particular members objected, Chandler "had them thrown out of the church," read the Sovereignty Commission report.

Chandler also organized an ad hoc budget committee that in some unknown way managed the funds raised in support of the NAACP. This type of activity suggests that the NAACP was supported by potentially hundreds of members at Mt. Carmel, which rebuilt in 1953 to accommodate eight hundred people. It is not known if Chandler's contemporaries at St. Paul Methodist, True Light Baptist, and Zion Chapel A.M.E employed similar fundraising tactics. If they did, then the actual number of NAACP supporters in the Mobile Street District could have numbered in the thousands.[61]

Financial independence helped insulate clergy and entrepreneurs but did not leave them completely immune to retribution. In 1957, Reverend W. D. Ridgeway of True Light Baptist Church traveled to Washington, DC, where he testified in front of a Senate subcommittee about voting rights. According to Mississippi NAACP field secretary Medgar Evers, when Ridgeway returned to Hattiesburg, a man arrived at his home to inform him that his car was being repossessed. Soon thereafter, Ridgeway's son-in-law was suddenly denied a previously arranged loan to purchase a home. That same year, local NAACP leader Milton Barnes lost the license to sell beer in his club. The following year, the club burned down in an unsolved fire. There is no evidence directly connecting the Citizens' Council to either event, but let each reader consider the delicate balance between context and coincidence.[62]

Although most activities of the Hattiesburg Citizens' Council remain unknown, there were at least two definitive victims—one white, one black—whose lives were ruined in retaliation for challenging racial segregation. The first was a white man named P. D. East. Born in 1921, East grew up in the Piney Woods near Hattiesburg. After briefly serving in the military during World War II, he took a job as a railroad ticket agent before being hired to manage the newsletter produced by the union at the Hercules Powder Company. In 1953, he started his own newspaper, called the *Petal Paper*, in Petal, a small township in the northeast part of Hattiesburg.[63]

At first, the *Petal Paper* was fairly popular among locals. Desiring to "keep everyone happy," East focused on local events and profiles of community leaders. He wrote about the local football team and church events, and included a "Citizen of the Week" in every issue. His theory for running a successful local paper was simply to "mention everyone's name." "Had Joseph Pulitzer established a prize for 'Pleasing Everyone,'" East recalled, "I feel certain I'd have won it twice in the same year." In its first year, the

Petal Paper had nearly two thousand subscribers and almost forty advertisers. But then East began discussing school desegregation.[64]

East was not drawn into the school desegregation issue by the *Brown* decision but rather by a statewide referendum in December of 1954 to close Mississippi's public schools. The referendum, which passed by a majority of two to one, would have allowed the state legislature to "abolish public schools" and use the saved expenditures to subsidize tuition for white students to attend private schools. East, who never publicly endorsed *Brown*, labeled the amendment "a black mark against the state," editorializing that "whenever we are forced to pay taxes for private education we are just that much closer to a dictatorship." East's editorials generated immediate backlash. One store owner who advertised in the *Petal Paper* told East, "Well, I sure won't advertise in any paper that's against the school amendment. Anybody who wants niggers to go to school with my children, I won't do business with." Soon after East printed his editorial, the man and several other advertisers pulled their support.[65]

East lost additional supporters with a string of editorials that increasingly drew the ire of local white residents. Some people were unhappy when he labeled Abraham Lincoln's death "unfortunate." Others cancelled subscriptions or pulled advertisements after East criticized the acquittal of the two men who killed fourteen-year-old Emmett Till in another part of the state. East also received angry letters from disgruntled readers after he suggested that heaven was not racially segregated. And he received even more flak for making the simple observation that only eight of Forrest County's twelve thousand African American citizens were registered to vote. "In the state of Mississippi," East wrote, "a Negro asking to register to vote is about like asking Satan for a drink of water."[66]

East's greatest offense occurred in March of 1956 when he published a parodic advertisement known as the "Jack-Ass Ad" that mocked the formation of the Hattiesburg Citizens' Council. In a searing editorial, he referred to the group as the "Citizens Clan" and warned locals against the travails of "fear," "ignorance," and "mass insanity." Subsequent editorials further mocked the organization, calling it the "Ku Klux Council" and the "Bigger and Better Bigots Bureau," while charging the council with responsibility for a slew of violent public incidents directed against local African Americans. When a seventeen-year-old boy was randomly beaten unconscious by a group of white youths in May of 1956, East editorialized, "We do not believe that Council members were in any way involved, but we believe that with the organization of such an outfit, certain unintelligent, bigoted, inferior whites feel something resembling guardian-angel protection of their existence."[67]

Retribution came swiftly. By autumn of 1956, East had lost every single one of his local advertisers and his circulation had fallen from a high of nearly two thousand to just nine. The Citizens' Council, he later learned, had warned local merchants against advertising in his paper. During this time, he also experienced constant harassment and social ostracism. People whom he had known since childhood stopped speaking to him in public and inviting him to social functions. Strangers delivered threats via phone, mail, and daily interpersonal interactions. His wife was followed. He bought a gun for self-defense. He developed an ulcer and a drinking problem. With the loss of advertisers and subscribers, he fell deeply into debt. His wife left him. The Citizens' Council kept a large file on him and reported his activities to the Sovereignty Commission. "We have a full file on East's activities," reported a Citizens' Council official to the Sovereignty Commission. Rumors spread of a price on his head. "They're going to kill you," warned a member of his family. East eventually fled the state.[68]

The second victim of the Hattiesburg Citizens' Council was a black man named Clyde Kennard. Born on June 12, 1927 (he was delivered by Dr. Charles Smith), Kennard grew up on his grandmother's farm in Eatonville, a small rural settlement located just north of Hattiesburg. He spent much of his youth working on the farm and attending the tiny local black school. In 1945, he left Hattiesburg to join the United States Army. While enlisted, Kennard served in Korea, obtained his GED, and took courses at the all-black Fayetteville State Teachers College while stationed at Fort Bragg in North Carolina. After his honorable discharge in 1952, Kennard enrolled at the University of Chicago.[69]

In 1955, Kennard returned to Mississippi to help his mother run the family farm. Desiring to continue his education, Kennard applied for admission to Mississippi Southern College. A self-described "segregationist by nature," Kennard might have applied to a black college if one had been located closer to his home. But the nearest black college was located more than an hour away in Jackson. When Kennard called Mississippi Southern to ask for an application, he "stated that he was a negro," reported the registrar, and thus never received the form. Kennard then visited the campus, where he met with the school's new president, William D. McCain, who informed Kennard that applicants to Mississippi Southern needed to secure "five recommendations from former alumni in Forrest County," which was, of course, a virtually impossible task for any African American applicant at that time. Kennard submitted his application anyway, but was rejected on the grounds that he had submitted an incomplete file. Kennard dropped the issue and spent most of the next three years helping run his family farm.[70]

Mississippi Southern president William McCain was a white supremacist neo-Confederate who idolized Confederate general and Ku Klux Klan pioneer Nathaniel Bedford Forrest. He hung a portrait of Forrest in his office and changed the school's mascot from the Yellow Jackets to "General Nat." "Hopefully," McCain once wrote, "General Nathan Bedford Forrest whose courage and valor gave this County its name will continue to inspire victory over adverse circumstances and good citizenship." Committed to preserving segregation, McCain joined the Hattiesburg Citizens' Council and worked with the segregationist organization when Kennard once again decided to apply for admission to Mississippi Southern.[71]

Between 1955 and 1958, Clyde Kennard helped run his mother's farm and worked as a general laborer for a downtown department store. He also became increasingly involved in the local NAACP. Vernon Dahmer, who lived near Kennard in Eatonville, helped introduce the former serviceman to the organization. Kennard attended local NAACP meetings and served as advisor for an NAACP Youth Council in nearby Palmer's Crossing. After he was denied the opportunity to register to vote in 1957, Kennard was one of several local African Americans who completed affidavits for Mississippi NAACP field secretary Medgar Evers. In 1958, he decided to reapply to Mississippi Southern College.[72]

That November, Kennard telephoned Mississippi Southern registrar Aubrey Lucas to request five applications for himself and four other African Americans for the upcoming winter semester. Lucas, whose black maid was acquainted with Kennard and reported him to be "well educated" and "very intelligent," told the black applicant he could only send him one application. If there were indeed four other interested prospective black students, none of the rest called to ask for an application. Kennard acted alone. He did not even ask the NAACP for help, but the organization and several national black media outlets did closely follow his case.[73]

In response to Kennard's 1958 application, the Hattiesburg Citizens' Council worked with the Sovereignty Commission to launch a major investigation into Clyde Kennard. Sovereignty Commission investigators examined his public and Army records, interviewed dozens of acquaintances, checked his credit report, examined property transactions, searched for any potential FBI records, and even hired a former FBI agent to investigate Kennard's activities in Chicago. The goal of this extensive investigation was to uncover some past transgression that might serve as grounds to reject Kennard's application. Regardless of his credentials, Mississippi Southern College officials had no intention of ever voluntarily admitting Kennard. But they and other segregationist leaders were concerned about having to wage a legal battle against the national NAACP. Despite searching far and wide for some major character flaw, the Sovereignty Commission found no damning evidence in Kennard's past. Even the white people they interviewed uniformly endorsed his character and intelligence.[74]

Dudley Conner, the head of Hattiesburg's Citizens' Council, suggested that Kennard could be killed. According to a Sovereignty Commission investigator, "Mr. Connor [*sic*] stated that Kennard's car could be hit by a train or he could have some accident on the highway and nobody would ever know the difference." Conner was not alone. That December, the head of security at Mississippi Southern was approached by a group of unnamed individuals who suggested planting dynamite in the starter of Kennard's vehicle.[75]

The Sovereignty Commission decided not to follow these suggestions. Instead, it recruited a group of influential black Hattiesburgers—principals N. R. Burger, Clarence Roy, and Alfred Todd and local pastor Reverend Ralph Woullard (a Sovereignty Commission informant)—to meet with Kennard to convince the prospective student to withdraw his application. One interesting item of note is that each of the black principals "brought into the conversation their need for a Negro Junior College in that area." "The inference was inescapable," noted the Sovereignty Commission investigator, "that they were attempting to bargain in a subtle manner." In any case, this meeting achieved its intended result. Kennard withdrew his application. But he was not yet finished.[76]

The following autumn, Clyde Kennard once again applied to Mississippi Southern. Unable to procure the required five letters of recommendation from local alumni, Kennard instead submitted five letters from "professional people who live in my community, and have at least the equivalent of a degree from Mississippi Southern College." "As a Negro," Kennard argued in his application cover letter, "I feel that these people would be in a much better position to attest to my moral character." After receiving a call from President McCain, the Sovereignty Commission opened another investigation and explored the possibility of once again recruiting the ad hoc "negro committee" to speak with Kennard. This time, however, local actors took more initiative. Because their actions were planned in secret, there is no record of which individuals were responsible for each action. What follows is a description of the basic facts.[77]

Less than two weeks after McCain learned of Kennard's intention to reapply, the office manager of the Forrest County Cooperative, where Kennard conducted business, filed a $4,300 claim against Kennard based on an unsubstantiated breach of contract. After Kennard refused to transfer a deed of trust to the co-op, representatives from the co-op seized and sold all the hens on Kennard's farm. Soon thereafter, the Southern Farm Bureau Insurance Company cancelled the insurance policy on Kennard's automobile.[78]

McCain invited Kennard to meet with him in his office on the morning of September 15, 1959. At the meeting, Kennard steadfastly refused McCain's requests to withdraw his application. After a twelve-minute meeting, Kennard was "ushered out of a side door," reported the Sovereignty Commission, to avoid members of the media who had gathered outside McCain's office. When Kennard arrived at his automobile, he encountered two local policemen who claimed to have seen the vehicle speeding earlier that morning. The policemen arrested Kennard on the charges of reckless driving. Once at the jail, the thirty-two-year-old veteran learned that he was also being falsely charged with illegal possession of whiskey. Clyde Kennard did not drink.[79]

Upon making bail, Kennard drove to Jackson, where he conferred with NAACP field secretary Medgar Evers, who helped arrange legal counsel for Kennard's defense. The trial was a sham. Kennard was convicted of all charges and lost subsequent appeals. The convictions provided the grounds for Mississippi Southern to reject any further applications from Kennard based on moral depravity. And yet he persisted. Over the following months, Kennard published two letters in the *Hattiesburg American* outlining the reasons why he should be admitted to Mississippi Southern. "The question," he stressed in one letter, "is whether or not citizens of the same country, the same state, the same city, shall have equal opportunities to earn their living, to select the people who shall govern them, and raise and educate their children in a free democratic manner." During these months, he also continued his work with the local and statewide NAACP.[80]

On Sunday, September 25, 1960, Clyde Kennard was rearrested on false charges that he helped orchestrate the theft of $25 worth of chicken feed from the Forrest County Cooperative. A nineteen-year-old black man named Johnny Lee Roberts, whose car was spotted leaving the scene of the crime, identified Kennard as a co-conspirator. Roberts later recanted this testimony on numerous occasions, most openly in 2005 when he told a reporter that Kennard "wasn't guilty of nothing." Nonetheless, the accuser's testimony in 1960 provided adequate evidence for a jury to deliberate for just ten minutes before finding Kennard guilty of burglary. Roberts, who actually committed and admitted to the burglary, received a suspended sentence. Kennard was sentenced to seven years in prison. NAACP-led efforts to overturn his conviction at the state level were unsuccessful, and a federal judge sent the case back to the Mississippi Supreme Court.[81]

While in prison, Kennard contracted stomach cancer. In June of 1962, a physician gave Kennard a mere 20 percent chance of living longer than five years and recommended immediate parole for the sake of survival. Despite pressure from the NAACP and other advocacy groups, officials at the Parchman State Penitentiary not only refused parole but continued forcing Kennard to perform hard labor in the fields surrounding the prison. Dying of stomach cancer, Kennard was forced to work for at least six months after his diagnosis. Whenever he collapsed of exhaustion, other inmates dragged him back to his bed. Clyde Kennard was finally released in January of 1963. On July 4, 1963, he died of stomach cancer at the age of thirty-six.[82]

Clyde Kennard and Mississippi Southern president William McCain stand as remarkable contrasts to the accessibility of opportunity for black and white residents of Hattiesburg in the postwar era. Whereas Kennard was a humble, hard-working veteran of the Korean War who spent much of his time in service to others, McCain was an arrogant plagiarist who was later discredited by the American Historical Association for submitting portions of a student's master's thesis as his own work. Yet McCain was white, and Kennard was black; one enjoyed full access to the finest opportunities available in the postwar era, while the other was imprisoned for merely suggesting that he too deserved an opportunity. In arguing his case for admission to Mississippi Southern in 1958, Clyde Kennard wrote, "What we request is only that in all things competitive, merit be used as a measuring stick rather than race." But such a stance contradicted the essence of Jim Crow. Race trumped merit, and individual dignity provided no additional safety. The consequences for people like Clyde Kennard were devastating and tragically unfair.[83]

Louis Faulkner passed away of a chronic heart condition on January 16, 1961, at the age of seventy-seven. For over fifty years, he and his colleagues in the Chamber of Commerce and other organizations had tried to increase their access to resources provided by Northerners and the federal government while mitigating the effects of outside influence on the local racial hierarchy. When outside forces appeared to threaten the foundations of white supremacy, they howled about federal overreach and "states' rights," while trying to suppress local attempts at black advancement. Paradoxically, they also appealed to federal officials for help in maintaining their society's racial order. In 1955 and 1956, FBI director J. Edgar Hoover felt compelled to explain in letters to Louis Faulkner that it was "not within the province" of the FBI to make judgments over the tax status of the NAACP Legal Defense Fund.[84]

The hysteria of white segregationists over the FEPC and the *Brown* decision created a powerful and dangerous backlash, but their fight to maintain Jim Crow still contained one fundamental flaw: the continued denial of black voting rights. Black disfranchisement was central to Jim Crow because it undercut African Americans' ability to influence social policies and resource allocation by voting. But such systematic and blatant disfranchisement always left open the possibility that federal legislators might take seriously the continuous violations of the Fifteenth Amendment. The burden to prove those violations, however, lay with black Southerners. In 1950, black Hattiesburgers had first attempted to prove these constitutional violations with the case *Peay et al. v. Cox*. The early 1960s presented another opportunity. Just months before Louis Faulkner died, FBI agents arrived at the Forrest County Courthouse to check "on voting," noted a Sovereignty Commission report, "and voting registration of negroes."[85]

CHAPTER TWELVE

When the Movement Came

> My involvement is something I can never forget. It was on a Sunday. Doug Smith and Charles Glenn stopped by the house. . . . And they came by and told us that there was a movement starting in Hattiesburg.
>
> —Hattiesburg native Daisy Harris Wade, 2001

In March of 1962, two young black men named Hollis Watkins and Curtis Hayes appeared in the Mobile Street District. Both just twenty years old, Watkins and Hayes were the first native Mississippians hired as full-time staff members in the Student Nonviolent Coordinating Committee (SNCC, pronounced "snick"), a young civil rights organization founded in April of 1960. In the evenings, the young men stayed a few miles outside of town at the home of local NAACP leader Vernon Dahmer. During the daytime, they walked through Hattiesburg's black neighborhoods, "knocking on doors," said Watkins, and "talking with people" about registering to vote.[1]

Watkins remembered black Hattiesburgers as somewhat reluctant, yet also more receptive than people in McComb, where the young men had tried to organize voter applicants the previous year. All black Mississippians, especially those living in McComb, had good reason to fear violent or economic retribution in response to political activity. The punitive activities of the state-sponsored Citizens' Council and Sovereignty Commission led one white Mississippian to conclude, "Mississippi comes as near to approximating a police state as anything we have yet seen in America." When Watkins and Hayes were organizing in McComb, several young people were beaten, jailed, and then expelled from school for participating in a sit-in. About a month later, a voter registration activist named Herbert Lee was shot and killed.[2]

In describing his first impression of Hattiesburg, Watkins remembered that "fear permeated the community." "But the more I began to meet and talk with people," he said, "then I saw that the fear did not seem to be as deep as it was in other areas, and especially among people who seemed to have been a little bit more educated . . . among people who were business people." According to Watkins, Hattiesburg's black business leaders and professionals were crucial in helping ignite political activity among members of the local black community. "I think part of it also had to do with especially the business people realizing that their economic stability was not dependent upon the white community," Watkins recalled nearly five decades later, "but was dependent upon being backed and supported from the black community."[3]

Hattiesburg's black business community peaked in the early 1960s. With a growing population and improving local economy, the Mobile Street District during the 1950s filled with dozens of additional groceries, barbershops, salons, restaurants, cleaners, funeral homes, and hotels. Three generations of entrepreneurs conducted their business in the neighborhood. The oldest businesses, most notably the Smith Drug Store and Lenon Woods's guesthouse, had been in operation since the mid-1920s. Many in the next generation had gotten their start during the war years. And a

Mobile Street in the 1960s. (McCain Library and Archives, University of Southern Mississippi)

younger set, which included more women, operated shops that had opened since the 1950s. A large portion of the younger shop owners had spent their youths in that community, attending local black schools and churches and patronizing shops in the Mobile Street District.[4]

By 1960, Hattiesburg was home to roughly 11,200 African Americans, most of whom were working class. Although many local families had deep roots, this was not a static population. Hattiesburgers of all races were constantly coming and going. The postwar economic boom combined with the realities of Jim Crow to create a second major wave of black outmigration. Between World War II and 1960, the number of African Americans living in Mississippi declined by about one hundred thousand.[5]

Despite this statewide decline, the total number of African Americans living in Mississippi's cities actually increased significantly. Urban growth was part of a broader statewide trend that included both black and white residents. Cities and towns simply offered more opportunities and higher pay. Mississippi residents of any demographic—man or woman, black or white—could expect to earn about twice as much annual income if they lived in an urban setting. By 1960, one-third of black Mississippians lived in a town or city.[6]

Black Hattiesburgers were relatively poor compared to many other Americans, but economic conditions in the city's black community had never been better. In 1960, Hattiesburg's black population had an unemployment rate below 6 percent and a median family income of $2,431 (just over $20,000 today), the highest of any urban black community in the state. Decades of severe racial discrimination created racially stratified socioeconomic conditions across Hattiesburg, but the city's black population was generally more prosperous than previous generations in the same community. And most lived in far better conditions than nearly all black Mississippians who still worked in agriculture.[7]

The best jobs for working-class African Americans were available only to men. The Hercules Powder Company, by far the city's largest employer of black men, offered the highest wages. "We were all poor," remembered Anthony Harris, the son of a Hercules employee, "but nobody knew we were poor because we sort of had basic things." "We didn't always get what we wanted," Harris said, "but we never went without something that we needed." The Hercules jobs were actually pretty good. It was fairly common for the wives of Hercules employees not to work outside the home and for their children to finish high school or even college.[8]

Hundreds of other black men worked at Meridian Fertilizer, the municipality of Hattiesburg, or one of the city's automobile service stations or concrete companies, positions that paid less than Hercules but offered steady wages. Other blue-collar black men held positions such as deliveryman, porter, driver, landscaper, painter, waiter, or butler, historically black jobs that paid very little.[9]

Working-class black women enjoyed far fewer opportunities. Many would have been terrific candidates for jobs at Reliance Manufacturing, the city's largest employer of women. Reliance was so desperate for female laborers that for years the company operated busses to transport female employees from as far as forty miles away. Meanwhile, thousands of black women with lifetimes of sewing experience lived within blocks of Reliance's two factories. But local segregation ordinances prevented Reliance from hiring black women. These restrictions protected the best female factory jobs for white women and helped ensure that black women had few opportunities for employment beyond domestic work.[10]

In 1960, roughly 75 percent of black women in the Hattiesburg labor force worked in domestic service, one of the few options available to black women as a result of their exclusion from other employment opportunities. This dearth of alternatives conspired to suppress the wages of black women. On average, working black women in Mississippi cities earned only $761 per year (about $6,265 today), roughly 40 percent of the average annual income earned by black men in cities. Because of such limitations, nearly half of Hattiesburg's adult black women chose not to participate in the labor force. Most of these women lived with their husbands or other relatives and performed household labor that benefitted their own families.[11]

Local black life continued to revolve around black institutions and community programs, especially churches. The oldest churches in the Mobile Street District remained the most important. Of Hattiesburg's twenty-four black churches in 1960, St. Paul Methodist, Mt. Carmel Baptist, True Light Baptist, and Zion Chapel A.M.E. still had the largest and most influential congregations. Their physical structures had been remodeled and rebuilt over the years, but the origins of each congregation dated back to at least 1904.[12]

In addition to regular services, marriages, and funerals, local black churches hosted a variety of events—social gatherings, organizational meetings, dinners, concerts, revivals, and dozens of other activities. At times, they were havens from the storm, both literally and figuratively. When the

Leaf and Bouie Rivers flooded in the spring of 1961, black churches helped house the approximately four thousand African Americans displaced by the rising waters. "The churches was like the glue," remembered a young man who grew up attending St. Paul Methodist in the 1950s, "the cement, the foundation, the conscience of our community."[13]

By 1962, Hammond and Charles Smith had become the preeminent elders at St. Paul Methodist. When a new cornerstone was laid that year, the Smith brothers were the first two names listed on the marble plaque listing the board of trustees. Hammond and Charles, who turned sixty-eight and seventy-one that year, were the last remaining members of their nuclear family still living in Hattiesburg. The fourth-oldest brother, Wendall, had died of unspecified causes in 1954 at the age of fifty-four. Two other brothers, Martin Luther Smith and William Lloyd Garrison Smith, were practicing medicine in Muskegon, Michigan, and Los Angeles. Their sister, Mamie, lived in Clarksdale with her husband. And their mother, Mamie, had died in 1956, the year she would have turned ninety.[14]

Hammond and Charles were less active than in previous years, but remained stalwarts in their community. They were both still working and involved in the W. M. Stringer Grand Lodge and the local black Boy Scout troop. Community leaders for over forty years, the Smith brothers remained prominent local figures. But they were aging. In the postwar era, members of a younger generation emerged as the predominant community leaders.[15]

By 1960, Eureka principal N. R. Burger, also a member of St. Paul Methodist, had become the most visible black leader in the Mobile Street District. Throughout the early 1950s, Burger's role as the city's leading black educator created an important role for him as a liaison between local black educators and white Hattiesburg officials who were interested in resisting federally mandated school desegregation by improving black schools. Obsessed with the *Brown* decision, white civic leaders approached Burger in the 1950s for nearly all matters related to local public education. In 1958, Burger was one of the three black educators asked to help dissuade Clyde Kennard from applying to Mississippi Southern College.[16]

Burger, who held degrees from Alcorn State and Cornell University, was one of the most respected black educators in the state. Soon after the passage of *Brown v. Board of Education*, he was one of several black Mississippi leaders invited to meet with the governor about school segregation. Burger never publicly supported or condemned the *Brown* decision, positioning himself as an apolitical educator who merely wanted to improve black schools by maximizing access to resources. This stance enabled him to convince local white leaders to provide additional funding to support black Hattiesburg schools. "If you proposed something," Burger explained of working with the white school board in the 1950s, "and you could prove that it was needed, you got it."[17]

Supported by state funds, Hattiesburg between 1949 and 1953 built a new high school and two new elementary schools for African Americans. The black high school—Royal Street High School—opened for the 1950–51 school year, replacing Eureka, which became a junior high school only. Expansion of black schools, which was accompanied by simultaneous improvements to white schools, was long overdue. No new black school had been constructed since the 1920s, a thirty-year gap during which Hattiesburg's black population quadrupled. In the 1940s alone, enrollment at Eureka nearly doubled.[18]

Although the state NAACP routinely criticized Mississippi's half-hearted school equalization program, black public education did improve in the years after *Brown*. Between 1954 and 1962, the average salary of black Mississippi public school teachers increased from $1,244 to $3,236. Several municipalities also spent money to renovate or expand black schools. In Hattiesburg, both Eureka Junior High School and Royal Street High School (whose name changed in 1958 to Rowan High School) underwent significant renovations in 1960. Principal Burger oversaw these improvements and served as the public face of black educational initiatives. He even wrote several articles about school improvements that were published in the *Hattiesburg American*.[19]

Even in light of these improvements, Hattiesburg's black and white public schools remained severely unequal. The local school board was never going to provide resources to black schools without offering even greater resources to white schools. Therefore, building renovations and teacher-salary increases at black schools were always accompanied by better improvements at white schools. Black schools still received less financial support per pupil and substandard supplies, including hand-me-down textbooks from white schools. As late as 1961, Hattiesburg spent an average of $115.96 per year on each white pupil and $61.69 on each black pupil. White residents paid more in taxes, but education was stratified by race, not income. The poorest white student still had an opportunity to attend a better school than the wealthiest black pupil.[20]

It is also worth noting that black teachers, even with their pay raises, were closely monitored to suppress their academic and political freedoms. Their in-class curriculums were often monitored, and they were subject to termination for belonging to the NAACP or any other civil rights organization. And of course, their lives were also limited by the racial discrimination that affected all African Americans. Principal Burger was allowed to register to vote, but his wife Addie, who taught civics, was not.[21]

Nevertheless, the schools that were built in the 1950s did become important institutions in the black community. Like Eureka in previous eras, these new schools fostered the intellectual and social development of a new generation of students and provided communal gathering spaces for the local black residents. The 1960 renovations at Rowan High School included new chemistry and physics laboratories, a cafeteria, a football stadium, band and music rooms, and a new auditorium. Under the guidance of Principal Burger and community partners like the local Parent Teachers Association, Rowan High School quickly developed into one of the best black high schools in the state. And like Eureka in previous eras, the institution served as an important site for all members of the black community, hosting countless sporting events, meetings, concerts, fundraisers, graduation ceremonies, and lectures.[22]

When Hollis Watkins and Curtis Hayes arrived in Hattiesburg, they entered a community with deep institutional roots dating back roughly eighty years. The Mobile Street District was by no means a glamorous place. In fact, one activist from New York City later described the neighborhood as "rundown." But that community's wealth lay not in the shimmering new cars and towering skyscrapers that characterized prosperity in other parts of America but rather in the institutions and traditions that had for decades framed local black life. From the Howell Literary Club to the Hattiesburg Negro Business League to the Union Choir Service to Eureka High School, the people of that community had for generations organized to help each other navigate the difficulties of black life in the Jim Crow South. To Watkins and Hayes, these longstanding institutions and social networks would prove indispensable to their efforts to draw local people into a national mass movement. The forces that brought the pair to Hattiesburg in the first place were the result of another interconnected set of processes.[23]

Between 1955 and 1963, Medgar Wiley Evers served as the first NAACP Mississippi field secretary. Born in Decatur, Mississippi, in 1925, the World War II veteran spent most of his career focused on voting rights. This focus predated his employment with the NAACP. Inspired by the 1944 *Smith v. Allwright* decision that eliminated the white primary, Medgar and his brother Charles first registered to vote near their home town in 1946. Threats of violence prevented the brothers from casting ballots in that year's election, but Evers remained an active voting rights advocate for the rest of his life.[24]

After using the GI Bill to graduate from Alcorn State in 1952, Evers was hired by a black physician named T. R. M. Howard to work for the Magnolia Mutual Insurance Company in Mound Bayou, Mississippi. In addition to running Magnolia Mutual, Dr. Howard was the most aggressive black voting rights advocate in the state. The year before hiring Evers, Howard founded a political organization, the Regional Council of Negro Leadership (RCNL), which held annual "Freedom Day" rallies where well-known Northern black political leaders stressed the importance of voter registration to crowds of up to ten thousand people. The organization also investigated incidents of racial violence, organized selective buying campaigns to protest racial discrimination, and worked closely with journalists from several national black media outlets to report race news from Mississippi. Among its members, the RCNL also served as a conduit into the NAACP. Evers first started working with a local NAACP branch within weeks of starting at Magnolia Mutual.[25]

In 1954, Evers applied to law school at the University of Mississippi. His application was denied. After consulting with representatives from the national NAACP, the young insurance salesman decided against appealing the decision. But the national NAACP officials were so impressed by Evers that they decided to hire the charismatic young black professional as the organization's first Mississippi field secretary. Medgar and his wife, Myrlie, who was hired as his secretary, opened their first office in Jackson on January 23, 1955.[26]

The Evers's duties included investigating incidents of racial violence and discrimination and expanding statewide NAACP membership, a particularly difficult task considering the anti-*Brown* backlash led by Mississippi's Citizens' Councils and the Sovereignty Commission. Between 1955 and 1958, Mississippi's NAACP membership declined from 4,026 to 1,436. Such a decline was quite typical across the South. Between 1955 and 1958, the NAACP lost nearly fifty thousand members and 246 branches in the South. "It is not the lack of interest," Medgar reported, "but fear."[27]

During these same years, Evers helped investigate and publicize virtually every major race story in Mississippi. In 1955, he played a major role in investigating the famous murder of fourteen-year-old Emmett Till, as well as the murders of black Mississippians George Lee, Clinton Melton, J. E. Evanston, and Timothy Hudson. Evers also produced hundreds of reports detailing financial harassment of NAACP members, voter registration denials, and miscellaneous examples of racial discrimination, including the case of Hattiesburg's Clyde Kennard. Evers was devastated by the Kennard case. He attended the Kennard trials in Hattiesburg and was at one point cited for contempt of court for an outburst in response to Kennard's 1960 conviction for stealing chicken feed. Years later, Myrlie Evers called the Clyde Kennard case "one of the long wracking pains of Medgar's years as Mississippi field secretary."[28]

Medgar and Myrlie spent countless hours typing reports, compiling financial data, and dispatching memos to NAACP offices and various sympathizers across the country. During their first three years on the job, Medgar and Myrlie mailed more than seventy-five hundred reports, newsletters, and memos—an average of twenty-one pieces of mail per day over three consecutive years. Despite declining NAACP membership in Mississippi, the Evers's work helped reinforce the resolve of a core of deeply committed members. As longtime Evers ally Aaron Henry of Clarksdale recalled, "The years from 1956 to 1961, although relatively calm, marked significant advancement for us."[29]

Medgar's most vital activities occurred outside the office. He spent much of the late 1950s driving across Mississippi in his Oldsmobile, armed with a .38 Smith & Wesson Special in the glove compartment. His NAACP mileage reports read 13,372 in 1955, 12,775 in 1956, and 16,622 in 1957. These trips took Medgar to all corners of the state, where he met with small but deeply committed groups of men and women who retained their NAACP membership in spite of the repressive actions of the Citizens' Councils and Sovereignty Commission.[30]

Few details of these meetings were ever recorded. Most occurred in private homes, black-owned businesses, or churches. In Hattiesburg, these meetings were held in the back room of the Smith Drug Store. The Smith brothers also helped welcome Evers as a speaker at St. Paul Methodist Church. Evers was encouraged by the nucleus of local leaders who remained committed to the organization. "It is most heartening to see," he reported to the national NAACP at the end of his first year, "in the face of tremendous difficulty, the increased interest Negroes have shown in our fight for freedom in a state where the word freedom is used mythically as it pertains to the Negro."[31]

Voting rights comprised the core of that "fight for freedom." Desegregation, especially in schools, was a highly visible national imperative that sent white Southern segregationists into a frenzy. But most black Mississippi NAACP members were actually far more concerned about gaining access to the ballot. As Hattiesburg police chief Bud Gray reported of a 1958 Hattiesburg NAACP meeting, "the negroes are staying away from the subject of Integration and are only talking about Voting."[32]

Evers wanted to connect local Mississippi leaders not only to the national organization but also to each other. Throughout his time as Mississippi's NAACP field secretary, Evers helped develop a network of homegrown NAACP leaders across the state. This was essential. "Medgar knew the importance of their communicating with each other," remembered his close friend and ally Ed King. To cultivate such a network, Evers held rotating regional meetings several times per year across Mississippi. Along with the annual statewide meeting in Jackson, these gatherings drew together courageous NAACP leaders from across the state. More specifically, these events helped develop strong alliances between local NAACP leaders such as Amzie Moore of Cleveland, Aaron Henry of Clarksdale, C. C. Bryant of McComb, and Vernon Dahmer of Hattiesburg. "Those were people," remembered Ed King, "who sort of had said, 'when the fullness of time comes I'll be ready.'"[33]

The fullness of time came in 1960. A twenty-five-year-old man named Bob Moses arrived that year at the home of Amzie Moore, a longtime Evers ally since their days working with the RCNL in the early 1950s. Bob Moses was not a native Southerner. He came from Harlem, inspired by the wave of sit-ins that originated in Greensboro, North Carolina, in February of 1960 and spread across the South that spring. In less than three months, an estimated fifty thousand black and white protestors had participated in sit-ins and other public demonstrations in direct defiance of racial segregation ordinances.[34]

Moses was captivated by this massive wave of civil disobedience. "I could feel how they felt just by looking at those pictures," he explained. A teacher, Moses left New York that summer to work with Martin Luther King Jr.'s Southern Christian Leadership Conference (SCLC) and SNCC, the national student organization formed in the wake of the sit-in movement.[35]

After a few slow weeks in Atlanta, Moses became dissatisfied with the tedious pace of office work. He wanted to become more directly involved with grassroots organizing, and he shared this ambition with his mentor Ella Baker, a longtime NAACP leader who played a central role in the formation of SNCC. Sympathetic, Baker and another SNCC activist, Jane Stembridge, suggested that Moses work to expand SNCC's influence in Alabama, Louisiana, and Mississippi. With a list of NAACP contacts provided by Baker, the young activist traveled by bus to Deep South cities such as Talladega, Birmingham, New Orleans, Shreveport, Clarksdale, Gulfport, Biloxi, and Cleveland, Mississippi, where he met Amzie Moore. Moses stayed longer with Moore than with anyone else.[36]

Like most members of Medgar Evers's Mississippi NAACP network, Amzie Moore was focused on voting rights. He had been politically active since at least 1936, when he first joined the Republican Party. Moore recognized that the sit-ins of 1960 represented an unprecedented form of direct action and became interested in incorporating this momentum into the fight for black voting rights in Mississippi. According to Moses, Moore viewed his arrival as an "opportunity of capturing this sit-in energy." According to Moore, Moses and the SNCC activists "had more courage than any group of people I've ever met."[37]

During the time that Moore hosted Moses, the NAACP veteran introduced the young activist to members of his church and a river of allies who passed through his home. Moses later described "a steady stream of people coming in and out of Amzie's house." Through these introductions, Moses came to realize that "Amzie was connected throughout the state." Although Moses could not possibly have fully grasped the deep history and expanse of this Medgar Evers–led NAACP network, it was through these existing NAACP-based relationships that SNCC began to operate in Mississippi the following year.[38]

Moses left the South to fulfill his teaching duties in New York but returned to Mississippi the following summer. Upon his return, Moore suggested that Moses travel south to work with NAACP leader C. C. Bryant of McComb. While working in McComb, Moses started recruiting local African Americans into SNCC. It was there that he met Hollis Watkins and Curtis Hayes, the most enthusiastic pair of recruits. As word of SNCC's presence spread, other members of the state NAACP network expressed interest in hosting SNCC activists. Sometime in late 1961 or early 1962, Hattiesburg NAACP leader Vernon Dahmer contacted his NAACP allies in

McComb to request that SNCC send workers to Hattiesburg. Watkins and Hayes arrived in Hattiesburg in March of 1962 with $50 to help fund a new voting rights project named the Forrest County Voters League.[39]

Watkins and Hayes did not arrive alone. In January of 1960, a pair of FBI agents appeared at the Forrest County courthouse to inquire about local voter registration procedures. By then, former Forrest County circuit clerk Luther Cox (the man known for asking how many bubbles are in a bar of soap) had been replaced by a new registrar, Theron Lynd. The thirty-nine-year-old son of an oil company distributor, Lynd was a graduate of Mississippi State College who had returned to Hattiesburg after graduation to work as an office manager for the same company that employed his father. He first tried to become circuit clerk by running against Cox in 1955, but lost badly. Shortly after Cox died in December of 1958, Lynd won a special election to become the new Forrest County circuit clerk.[40]

Theron Lynd could be a very threatening man. He was enormous. Standing six-foot-three-inches tall and weighing more than 320 pounds, he towered over the desk where people applied to register to vote. Virtually everyone who encountered him mentioned his size. Even the *Hattiesburg American* in 1959 commented, "Forrest County now has perhaps the biggest circuit clerk in Mississippi" before listing his height and weight.[41]

Over subsequent years, Lynd's physique and bold refusals to register black voters earned him national recognition as a caricature of backwards Southern racism. In 1962, CBS aired a nationally broadcast television special titled "Mississippi and the 15th Amendment" that showed clips of Lynd on the steps of the Forrest County Courthouse and dubbed him "one of the most powerful men in America." But Lynd's size was merely an extraneous physical characteristic. There was nothing particularly unique about his refusal to register black voters. Like his predecessor, Theron Lynd was merely one of several hundred Southern registrars who used the guise of literacy tests to disqualify black citizens from voting. Had Lynd not been the circuit clerk, another white person would have held the same office and used the same tactics to deny black voters. And although CBS emphasized his power, in reality, Lynd reported to the Hattiesburg Citizens' Council and the Mississippi State Sovereignty Commission, both of which maintained a file on him. Both organizations seemed pleased with his activities. In 1960, the president of the Hattiesburg Citizens' Council told a

Sovereignty Commission investigator that they were "very proud of the way the Circuit Clerk is handling the voter registrations." But Theron Lynd and his allies ultimately met a challenge they could not overcome.[42]

The root of that challenge lay in the continuous attempts of black Hattiesburgers to register to vote. African Americans had been trying to register to vote in Hattiesburg for decades. Hammond Smith first tried in 1934. There are few records of other early attempts, but it is implausible that Hammond acted completely alone. Soon after World War II, he and several leading black professionals created an organization named the Committee of One Hundred "to promote Negro registration in Forrest County." And in 1950, Hammond and his brother Charles were among fifteen local black plaintiffs who filed suit against the Forrest County registrar for voter discrimination in the case *Peay et al. v. Cox*. Because of the national attention garnered by the case, some local black leaders, including Hammond Smith and Nathaniel Burger, were allowed to register to vote to avoid accusations that all black people were prevented from voting. Most black applicants, however, continued to be denied. A 1955 study of voter registration in Mississippi found that only 16 of 7,406 age-eligible black Hattiesburgers (0.2 percent) were registered to vote.[43]

But they kept trying. In 1956, Reverend W. D. Ridgeway of True Light Baptist Church attempted to register with seventeen others, all of whom were denied. In 1957, local funeral-home director Rush Lloyd attempted to register, but was denied. That same year, Clyde Kennard was told "no reason" when he asked why he was not allowed to register. The next year, grocer Benjamin Bourn, a plaintiff in *Peay et al. v. Cox*, was turned away. Reverend John Barnes of the St. Paul Methodist Church estimated that between 1952 and 1959, he tried "to register about four times each year." In 1959, Barnes was part of a group that recruited a very light-skinned black woman to register as a "test case." After the light-skinned woman successfully registered to vote, Barnes and thirteen other African American applicants were turned away on the very same day. Reported a Sovereignty Commission investigator in 1960, "Reverend Barnes on East Fifth Street in Hattiesburg has been trying to register pretty regular and Lynd has been trying to keep him from it."[44]

The courage of these black voter applicants cannot be overstated. Few could have fully imagined the extensive inner workings of Hattiesburg Citizens' Council and the Mississippi State Sovereignty Commission, but they all certainly understood the severe consequences that confronted black activists. Black voting rights advocates in other parts of the state had been killed. And the persecution of local figures such as the white newspaper man P. D. East and Clyde Kennard offered concrete examples of the dangers facing black activists. Nevertheless, they persisted with no definitive guarantee of victory or even survival.

The profiles of Hattiesburg's black voting rights leaders in the 1950s resemble those of earlier generations of community leaders—clergy, business people, and teachers. These leaders did not act alone; their activism was bolstered by all members of the community. No one was ever completely immune to violent or economic reprisals, but business leaders and clergy did enjoy a modicum of financial independence that was made possible by the black women and men who shopped in their stores and populated their congregations. Not everyone was directly supportive, of course. But there were hundreds of unnamed people who helped make their activism possible.[45]

The importance of failed voter registration attempts lay in the ensuing processes of documentation. Every denial of a black voter applicant could be used as evidence to build a case detailing the long, systematic history of discrimination against black voters. In the years after *Peay et al. v. Cox* in 1950, dozens of rejected black applicants described their inability to register in notarized affidavits and sworn testimonies. This body of evidence continued to expand when Medgar Evers became the Mississippi NAACP field secretary. Whenever black Hattiesburgers were denied the right to vote, Evers arranged for them to complete affidavits that were notarized by local businessman Paul Weston, a longtime community leader who was former president of the Union Choir Service, editor of the 1930s-era black newspaper *The Union Messenger*, and president of the Negro Civic Welfare Association. Weston is not remembered today as a leader in the struggle for voting rights in Hattiesburg, but as the local black notary, he helped ensure that witnesses could complete authenticated legal testimonies.[46]

In 1957, Evers helped arrange for Reverend W. D. Ridgeway of True Light Baptist to testify in front of a Senate subcommittee on constitutional rights. Two years later, Reverend John Barnes also traveled to Washington, DC, to testify in front of a House judiciary subcommittee on constitutional rights. "Some continue to make attempts to register and will continue to do so," Barnes insisted, "but we need the Federal Government on this matter."[47]

Ridgeway and Barnes testified during hearings that led to the passage of the Civil Rights Acts of 1957 and 1960, the first two major pieces of federal civil rights legislation passed since Reconstruction. Others who spoke at these hearings included hundreds of advocates and opponents of federal civil rights legislation, including a full range of black and white citizens: Republicans and Democrats, Northerners and Southerners, and lawyers, registrars, and politicians.[48]

The primary issue at play during these hearings was a question over the validity of claims of voter discrimination. Although the Fifteenth Amendment to the United States Constitution, ratified in 1870, prohibited racially based voter discrimination and thereby rendered Jim Crow–era voter suppression tactics unconstitutional, the onus to prove such discrimination always fell upon the disfranchised. Despite abnormally low percentages of registered black voters across the South (0.2 percent in Forrest County in 1955), white Southern congressmen relentlessly questioned the legitimacy of African American witnesses to voter discrimination, even among activists who had been attacked—in one case, shot with shotgun pellets—as retribution for voting rights activism. Throughout these proceedings, black Southerners bore the burden of proving what should have been obvious violations to their constitutional rights—which, of course, made them even more vulnerable to violence and harassment at home.[49]

Throughout the legislative process, white Southern politicians successfully limited the scope and effectiveness of the 1957 and 1960 Civil Rights Acts. Contemporaneous commentators and modern historians alike have criticized these acts for failing to include enforcement mechanisms to oversee school desegregation and end voter discrimination. Senate majority leader Lyndon B. Johnson, who was largely responsible for both bills' compromises and passages, likened the 1957 Civil Rights Act to "half a loaf" of bread and acknowledged the bill was "just a beginning." NAACP leader Roy Wilkins labeled the act "a small crumb from Congress." The *Chicago Defender* called the 1957 Act "crippled," lamenting that "this legislation proves to be much weaker than we had previously expected." The Civil Rights Act of 1960 is even less acclaimed. It is not even mentioned in some histories of the civil rights movement and has been characterized by one historian as "at best, the smallest of steps forward—and it may have even have been a step back." Despite such critiques, however, both acts significantly affected the future of black voting rights in the South.[50]

Because the Civil Rights Act of 1957 was stripped of any ability to enforce school desegregation, the bill focused almost exclusively on voting. The legislation created a Commission on Civil Rights to "investigate allegations in writing under oath or affirmation that certain citizens of the United States are being deprived of their right to vote and have that vote counted by reason of their color, race, religion, or national origin." It also created a new Civil Rights Division in the United States Department of Justice to be led by a new assistant attorney general for civil rights.[51]

The symbolism of the 1957 Civil Rights Act, which was named "Best Achievement of 1957" by the NAACP, was also important. Southern voting rights activists interpreted the measure as a sign that the federal government might actually help enforce the Fifteenth Amendment. As Medgar Evers observed less than a month after its passage, "Denial of the right to register, not the right to vote, could be the first occasion for our calling upon the civil rights commission for aid." The commission's actual accomplishments over the ensuing years are debatable, but if nothing else, the law offered some promise of federal intervention for voting rights activists.[52]

White Southern politicians also limited the effectiveness of the 1960 Civil Rights Act, resulting in a jumbled piece of legislation that included obscure provisions, ranging from court procedures to the education of children of servicemen, that did not remedy the obvious limitations of the 1957 act. But there was one key component of the 1960 act that has been consistently underappreciated by historians. Title III required all election officials to retain copies of any voting-related records for twenty-two months and deliver copies of these documents to the attorney general of the United States upon request. This clause gave the Department of Justice direct access to the voter registration procedures of white Southern registrars, creating an unprecedented ability to investigate local voting procedures. President Eisenhower signed the Civil Rights Act of 1960 into law on May 6. On August 11, the United States attorney general requested permission to examine voting records in Forrest County, Mississippi.[53]

Advised by local white attorneys, Theron Lynd requested and was granted an extension to produce voter registration records. When he then refused to turn over records early the next year, the Department of Justice filed suit. Lynd managed to further delay federal access to his voting records with the help of a segregationist district court judge named William Harold Cox, who failed to issue a court order requiring that Lynd share the records. The

Department of Justice then appealed this inaction to the United States Fifth Circuit Court of Appeals. Based on the strength of the testimonies offered by sixteen local black witnesses, the Fifth Circuit Court of Appeals reversed Judge Cox's inaction, ordering Lynd to open his records for inspection and citing him for criminal and civil contempt.[54]

Forrest County was one of nineteen counties in Alabama, Georgia, Louisiana, and Mississippi where the federal government pursued voter discrimination cases between the passage of the Civil Rights Act of 1960 and the end of 1962. This was a political fight, but not necessarily a partisan one. When Democratic president John F. Kennedy assumed office in January of 1961, his attorney general, Robert Kennedy, essentially followed the same course of action as Republican president Dwight Eisenhower's attorney general William P. Rogers. Neither administration was particularly impressive in their support of black civil rights, but each was for various reasons concerned about the inability of black people to vote. In the end, the greatest effect of the Civil Rights Acts of 1957 and 1960 was to provide new tools to investigate suspected violations of the Fifteenth Amendment. White Southerners responded with commentaries about states' rights and defending their way of life, but these blustery political dogmas were merely rhetorical cover for their means of maintaining white supremacy by violating the constitutional rights of African Americans.[55]

Between 1961 and 1965, Lynd's case followed a long and winding path through the federal court system. Although this lengthy timeline allowed Lynd to deny hundreds more black voters, it also enabled the Department of Justice to continue compiling evidence, especially after gaining access to Forrest County voter registration records that revealed clear patterns of racial discrimination.

Ultimately, the most damning proof of Lynd's voter discrimination was not the continual denial of black voter applicants but rather the registration of comparably unqualified white voters. Personal interviews and examinations of voter registration records revealed that both Lynd and his predecessor, Luther Cox, had not rejected a single white voter applicant before 1960. In fact, white applicants were registered through an almost entirely different procedure. They were asked to interpret different sections of the state Constitution than African Americans, and they were offered assistance when they struggled. White people could also register with one of Lynd's staff members, whereas black applicants could only apply through Lynd himself. Some white citizens registered to vote without having to complete any application or literacy test at all. Others passed the literacy test despite the fact that they were completely illiterate. This was discovered through interviews with registered white voters and in registration records where white voters had signed their application by leaving the mark "X."[56]

Despite the lawsuit, Lynd continued to discriminate. Between February of 1959 and March of 1962, he did not allow a single African American to register to vote. But every denial provided further evidence of voter discrimination. As white Southern registrars like Theron Lynd continued to perform their duty of denying black voters, they also contributed to mounting evidence that Southern counties were violating the Fifteenth Amendment. And therein lay the problem for Theron Lynd.[57]

Hollis Watkins and Curtis Hayes arrived in Hattiesburg in March of 1962, just days before the Department of Justice filed its appeal in the case of Theron Lynd. Hattiesburg was particularly appealing to SNCC because of the Lynd case, which itself was a consequence of preexisting local black activism and federal inquiries. Years later, when Hattiesburg native and legendary civil rights activist Joyce Ladner was asked, "How does the movement get into Hattiesburg?" she responded, "Mr. Dahmer invited Curtis Hayes and Hollis Watkins to Hattiesburg."[58]

Watkins and Hayes operated in Hattiesburg between March and September of 1962. In the evenings, they performed chores and slept at Vernon Dahmer's farm. During the days, they moved through Hattiesburg speaking with members of the black community. Their primary objective was to convince local African Americans to attempt to register to vote. Every effort to register, even if unsuccessful, promised to provide further evidence of the need for federal intervention to protect black voting rights in Forrest County.[59]

To mobilize potential black voters, Watkins and Hayes needed the help of black community leaders. Reports of their initial reception vary widely, but some members of the black community were quite receptive to the pair. Watkins later remembered that Vernon Dahmer provided the names of local NAACP members who might serve as allies. Watkins cited the grocer Benjamin Bourn, an NAACP member and plaintiff in *Peay et al. v. Cox*, as particularly helpful. Because of these contacts, Watkins remembered, "it was not hard, for example, to get a church to have a voter registration meeting." The initial meetings were not large. The first attracted only "somewhere between eight and ten people," Watkins recalled. At these meetings, Watkins and Hayes led "freedom songs," described the goals of their movement, and trained people how to complete voter registration forms.[60]

All told, between April 18 and August 10, 1962, 103 local African Americans attempted to register to vote. Not all of these attempts should be credited solely to Watkins and Hayes or SNCC, but the young men were certainly instrumental in expanding the number of black Hattiesburgers who tried to register. One unique aspect of their approach was the inclusion of larger numbers of working-class people in addition to traditional black community leaders. Watkins and Hayes wanted to convince any and all African Americans—regardless of their employment, personal history, or social standing—to attempt to register to vote.[61]

Of the 103 who attempted, only nine were allowed to register. But every attempt mattered. Each added to the total. Some of the people who were denied later testified against Theron Lynd on behalf of the Department of Justice. And two years later, examples of voter discrimination from Hattiesburg in the spring of 1962 were cited during congressional debates that eventually led to the passage of the 1964 Civil Rights Act. But for black Hattiesburgers, there was also something larger at play.[62]

During that spring, Watkins and Hayes met a thirty-five-year-old black woman named Victoria Jackson Gray. The granddaughter of a black lumberman who came to Hattiesburg decades earlier, Gray grew up during the 1920s and 1930s in Palmer's Crossing, the predominantly black community located just outside of town. Among Gray's strongest memories of those formative years was living in a deeply religious community guided by black business owners who, she recalled, "were committed to education." She was particularly influenced by her grandfather, who always stressed financial independence and forbade his children from working for white people. Gray left Hattiesburg several times throughout her early life, but she always returned. She spent part of her childhood in Detroit before returning to Hattiesburg, where she attended high school and worked at the laundry in Camp Shelby during World War II. After graduation, Gray briefly attended Wilberforce University in Ohio and then traveled extensively with her military husband. But when the marriage ended in the late 1950s, she again returned to Hattiesburg, where she sold Beauty Queen cosmetic products. "By the time the Movement came along," Gray said, remembering her meeting of Watkins and Hayes in 1962, she had become "an independent businesswoman."[63]

Victoria Gray initially joined the movement in a "supportive role," according to her, but she quickly became Watkins and Hayes's most effective local ally. She was a woman who "didn't intend to be left on the sideline," Watkins remembered. "She was one of them that [said], 'hey look, this is where I am, this is what I think, this is what I feel, I am willing to do this.'" "If it need to be done," he explained of her attitude, "I'm going to do it."[64]

Gray helped lead efforts to aid the young voter registration workers. She helped convince her brother to provide an office space in his radio shop on Mobile Street, and she organized what she labeled "a telephone tree" to ensure that at least one person per day prepared a meal for Watkins and Hayes. She also arranged for Watkins and Hayes to speak and hold meetings at her church, and she used her job as a door-to-door saleswoman to recruit additional participants. "As I went from place to place for my business," she remembered, "I talked about those young people and why it was important for us to support them."[65]

In 1962, Victoria Gray tried to register to vote on three separate occasions—April 23, June 15, and July 30. She was rebuffed each time by Theron Lynd, but the records and experiences of those failed attempts proved useful the following September when she testified against Lynd as a witness for the United States Department of Justice in the Fifth Circuit Court of Appeals.[66]

When Watkins and Hayes left Hattiesburg that September, Victoria Gray assumed much of the leadership of the local movement. By that time, Gray had worked extensively with a number of civil rights organizations, including SNCC, the NAACP, and Martin Luther King Jr.'s SCLC. In fact, soon after meeting Watkins and Hayes, Gray traveled to Dorchester, Georgia, to attend an SCLC "Citizenship School," where she was trained to run civics-based adult education programs. Much has been made of organizational rivalries in the civil rights movement, but these mattered little to people like Victoria Gray. "I didn't have an organizational affiliation," she explained. "I just worked with whoever was working."[67]

Throughout late 1962 and into 1963, a movement escalated in Hattiesburg. The old black churches were central. "Everything came through the churches," Victoria Gray said. Not all pastors or deacons were interested in civil rights activities; everyone had their reasons. But local movement people pushed many clergy into activism. Whenever a pastor was hesitant, Gray recalled, "the congregation would push the minister" until he let local activists make announcements about civil rights activities. Most who heard the announcements did not heed the call. But slowly over the months, a growing number of people began trickling into the "Freedom House" on Mobile Street to ask about learning how to become a registered voter.[68]

Several factors drew people into the movement. The radical rhetoric and potential for broad societal change inspired many. "When SNCC people came to Hattiesburg, Mississippi," Victoria Gray remembered, "they represented just one more kind of movement, a way for folks to get a better life." Voting rights might have provided the spark of the expansion of the local movement, but many who joined this movement began to expand their goals beyond the right to vote. Some even had the audacity to imagine a world without Jim Crow. For them, this was a revolution, an opportunity to escape the system of racial apartheid that had framed their entire lives. For the true believers, this opportunity to pursue freedom was life altering. Victoria Gray used to make a distinction between "people [who] were in the Movement" and "people, who the Movement was in them." "Once it gets in you," she explained of joining the movement, "it's in there forever."[69]

Others who joined the local movement were inspired by the broader national context of the Southern civil rights movement. "The Race Beat," as many journalists labeled the media phenomenon of Southern black protest in the 1950s and 1960s, flooded American public life. Major events across the region—the Montgomery Bus Boycott, the desegregation of Little Rock Central High School, the Sit-In Movement of 1960, the Freedom Rides of 1961 and 1962, the desegregation of the University of Mississippi in 1962, and scores of other highly visible events—signified increasing domestic and international support for the civil rights of African Americans. The Mississippi press often overlooked or omitted major stories, but news of civil rights filtered into the consciousness of African Americans in virtually every corner of the South.[70]

Black Hattiesburgers were also inspired by several uniquely local factors. Victoria Gray and Vernon Dahmer were inspirational leaders with strong personalities who helped draw people into the movement. Locals were also aware of the Theron Lynd case, which for years drew front-page coverage in the *Hattiesburg American* and regular attention in national newspapers such as the *New York Times*, the *Washington Post*, the *Chicago Tribune*, the *Los Angeles Times*, and the *Chicago Defender.* Hattiesburg had never seen such widespread national attention. Of course, local African Americans did not consume all the coverage, but they saw members of the media flooding their town. Reporters were all over the city; CBS filmed the nationally syndicated television special about black voting rights in Hattiesburg. And the Department of Justice sent teams of attorneys into town to interview witnesses. Most importantly, everyday African Americans began to see real results. In 1962, Theron Lynd, facing a court order, actually began allowing some black people to register to vote. Most were still denied, but after decades of disfranchisement by local officials, access to the American democracy had never seemed more within reach.[71]

Some activists were drawn into the movement by tragedy. Younger activists such as Joyce Ladner of Palmer's Crossing cited the famous murder of Emmett Till as a major source of inspiration. Born in the early 1940s, she and her sister Dorie were among what she labeled "the Emmett Till generation," an entire cohort of young black Southerners who grew up with the image of Till's lifeless body "etched in my generation's consciousness," Ladner explained. Other locals were spurred into action by a number of other injustices, including the plight of their own community member Clyde Kennard. On January 28, 1962, locals gathered at the St. Paul Methodist Church for an NAACP-sponsored Clyde Kennard Day rally. The following year, his tragic death broke the hearts of black people across the United States, especially those in his hometown.[72]

The most stunning tragedy of all occurred on the night of June 11, 1963, when Medgar Evers was shot and killed in his driveway just hours after President John F. Kennedy called for the legislation that would become the Civil Rights Act of 1964. "When Medgar Evers was killed," remembered local beautician Peggy Jean Connor, "I was determined to get deeper involved in the struggle."[73]

Soon thereafter, Connor walked across the street from her beauty shop on Mobile Street to the movement headquarters in Lenon Woods's guesthouse. She began attending mass meetings and was soon convinced by Victoria Gray to attend a training in Dorchester, Georgia, where she spent a week learning how to teach citizenship classes. When Connor returned, she began holding citizenship classes at her home church, True Light Baptist.[74]

In July of 1963, Theron Lynd was found guilty of civil contempt and served with an injunction to register forty-three African Americans. Even so, he continued denying most black applicants. Local white supremacists bolstered his brazen refusals with efforts to further suppress the black vote. Anyone who attempted to register to vote faced violent or economic reprisals, especially in the wake of a 1962 state law requiring newspapers to print names of voter registration applicants. But the people in the movement did not stop. Between July and September of 1963, an additional 125 African Americans tried to register to vote. Slowly but inexorably, the movement expanded. By the end of 1963, Connor remembered "having mass meetings every night."[75]

As the local movement spread and federal pressure on Lynd intensified, SNCC sent additional staff members to Hattiesburg. By the end of 1963, Hattiesburg had become the site of SNCC's most active project in Mississippi. Black Hattiesburgers and SNCC activists started a movement newspaper named *Voice of the Movement* that was distributed at local churches and businesses, announcing movement activities and encouraging people to attend. The Hattiesburg movement had for years been smoldering. That January, it exploded.[76]

On the night of January 21, 1964, hundreds of people gathered at St. Paul Methodist Church. No official attendance records are available, but one attendee described the scene as having "every seat filled, every aisle packed, the doorways jammed." That night, the audience heard a remarkable lineup of speakers—Ella Baker, John Lewis, Mississippi NAACP president Aaron Henry, and Charles Evers, the older brother of Medgar Evers and his successor as the NAACP's Mississippi field secretary. Other activists in attendance included Bob Moses, Fannie Lou Hamer, Howard Zinn, James Forman, Amzie Moore, Hollis Watkins, and dozens of lesser known Mississippi activists. Several dozen white ministers from across the United States also sat in the crowd. Most attendees were local black people in the Hattiesburg movement.[77]

The night was electrifying. In "a singing, foot-stomping session," the lively audience sat together in a sanctuary of hope, chanting, singing, and listening as speaker after speaker reaffirmed the righteousness of their movement. "This is a fire that water won't put out," Charles Evers told the crowd. Ella Baker insisted, "We are not fighting for the freedom of the Negro alone but for the freedom of the human spirit." The meeting lasted well past midnight. Toward the end, locals led calls of "Freedom" echoed

Mass meeting at St. Paul Methodist Church, 1964. (McCain Library and Archives, University of Southern Mississippi)

by responses of "Now" before the crowd joined together in an affirmational rendition of "We Shall Overcome." On that January night in 1964, Hattiesburg's St. Paul Methodist Church was the epicenter of America's civil rights movement.[78]

Years later, Hammond Smith spoke briefly about attending civil rights meetings at his home church, but offered few details. Imagine that night from his perspective. Hammond's family had belonged to St. Paul Methodist since arriving in Hattiesburg over sixty years before, when he was just five years old. He had spent countless hours in that church—he had grown up there—but he had never before seen a night like that.

Hammond was not among those asked to speak on that evening. He was a longtime leader of that church but not of this new movement; most of the famous younger activists probably had no idea who he was. To the visitors, he was just another old man in the crowd. But SNCC's voting goals, however revolutionary they may have seemed in the 1960s, were not new to Hammond. He had been fighting for the right to vote for nearly thirty years, asking for a registration form every year when he paid his taxes and in 1950 joining the lawsuit *Peay et al. v. Cox* to challenge black disfranchisement in Hattiesburg. Hammond Smith is not typically recognized as one of the leaders of Hattiesburg's dynamic civil rights movement. But Hammond and his family quite literally helped build that church in which memory and promise now so potently coalesced. Anyone who attended that powerful meeting on the night of January 21, 1964, had only to examine the church cornerstone to see the record of an older generation of community leaders who built the spaces that housed this burgeoning movement that would ultimately help set black people free.[79]

The next morning, approximately one hundred people arrived at the Forrest County Courthouse for a demonstration they called Freedom Day. Under a steady morning rain, protestors paraded around the courthouse, "singing, clapping and stomping," read a local report, and carrying signs with messages about voting and freedom. "We are trying to get more people registered to vote," explained SNCC representative Lawrence Guyot. "The only way this can be done is with federal intervention."[80]

Theron Lynd sat inside waiting, as small groups of local African Americans entered his office to attempt to register to vote. He resisted, limiting the number of black applicants to four at a time and closing the office for lunch. The protestors took a short break during Lynd's lunch but returned in the afternoon. Despite Lynd's delays, thirty-six African Americans applied to vote on that day, the largest number of black voter applicants of any single day to that point in Hattiesburg history.[81]

The *Hattiesburg American* published an editorial titled "Ignore Agitators," accusing "outsiders" of trying to "provoke city policemen into arresting them, thus obtaining publicity for themselves" and "seeking to steam things up with a demonstration against wrongs that don't exist." The local newspaper was particularly bothered by the presence of white ministers who came to Hattiesburg from across the nation, claiming that these clergy seemed "more interested in fighting social and political wrongs, real or imagined, than in preaching the Gospel." Of course, this was a lie. The violations to black voting rights were both real and obvious.[82]

The white clergy who participated in the Hattiesburg Freedom Day arrived from cities across the country: New York City; Chicago; Washington, DC; Kansas City; Berkeley, California; Lincoln, Nebraska; Cleveland, Ohio; Boulder, Colorado; Beloit, Wisconsin. Nearly all were Presbyterian, Episcopal, or Jewish. They represented just a small segment of thousands of white American religious leaders drawn into the civil rights movement by the events of 1963, especially the violent protests in Birmingham, Alabama, and the murder of Medgar Evers in Jackson, Mississippi. That June, the National Council of Churches established a Commission on Religion and Race to help facilitate activism among clergy interested in aiding the Southern black freedom struggle. To the chagrin of white Hattiesburg leaders, white clergy from all corners of America remained in town through the end of 1966.[83]

As Freedom Day demonstrators marched around the courthouse, local police stared on, unsure of how to react. They formed a barrier around the courthouse and ordered marchers to disperse but were essentially powerless to do much else about the demonstration. Journalists and cameras were everywhere. "The front porch and steps of the courthouse bristled with television cameras," reported the *Hattiesburg American*. ABC and NBC sent television crews to capture any violent disturbance like those that had occurred in other Southern cities. For a city deeply worried about its image because of a constant pursuit of new employers, violence would have been a tremendous embarrassment. And so the police acted mostly with restraint.[84]

A handful of people were arrested, and one man was beaten in a jail cell, but the day was otherwise free of mass arrests and violence. During the largest public civil rights demonstration to that point in the city's history, local police stood by in relative passivity. Ironically, in their quest to maintain peace, they inadvertently helped create what one historian has insightfully labeled "the first state-protected civil rights demonstration in the history of Mississippi." The lack of arrests and violence should not be considered as part of a moderate approach, but rather the response of an otherwise oppressive society forced to abandon traditionally violent tactics by the courage of the oppressed and the gaze of the media.[85]

Pickets around the courthouse lasted through April. Local officials did eventually seek to quell the protests through an injunction and arrests. By April 14, sixty-seven people, including local activists, white ministers, and SNCC workers, were incarcerated. But new activists arrived to take their place. Insiders and outsiders flocked to the Hattiesburg movement. By May, over two hundred white clergy from outside Hattiesburg had participated in the demonstrations. Between January and April, black Hattiesburgers made over five hundred attempts to register to vote.[86]

The black institutions of the Mobile Street District provided infrastructure for the movement. As local activist Raylawni Branch recalled, "During the civil rights time, if it had not been for Mobile Street, there wouldn't have been a base." Lenon Woods's guesthouse served as the headquarters for both SNCC and the Council of Federated Organizations (COFO), an umbrella organization of several Mississippi civil rights groups. The Hattiesburg NAACP operated out of a television repair shop co-owned by J. C. Fairley, president of the Hattiesburg NAACP during the early 1960s, and Glodies Jackson, the brother of Victoria Gray. The Hattiesburg Ministers Project, a subgroup of the National Council of Churches, operated out of an old black grocery store on Mobile Street. Mass meetings took place in local black churches. Planning sessions occurred virtually everywhere—street corners, cafes, beauty shops, and front porches. Visiting activists ate meals and bought newspapers on Mobile Street. They cashed checks and purchased sodas at the Smith Drug Store. "It was all there on Mobile Street," Branch recalled.[87]

The black school system was the one local black institution that was less involved with movement activities than in earlier community-organizing initiatives. During previous years, virtually all major community organizing involved black educators and local schools. Hundreds of local black students joined the movement, but because of concerns over relationships with the white-controlled school board, the school facilities themselves were largely unavailable for civil rights activities. "I helped when I could under the circumstances," Principal Burger later offered. Despite this reluctance, few locals were heavily critical of Burger, probably because they sympathized with his difficult position running a public institution or felt that he had contributed to local black life in so many other ways that he deserved some level of immunity.[88]

In July of 1964, the Hattiesburg Freedom Summer opened with an Independence Day picnic at Vernon Dahmer's farm. The Mississippi Freedom Summer, appropriately dubbed by one historian as "easily the most spectacular and sustained single event in recent civil rights history," was a statewide protest involving over a thousand mostly white activists from across the United States who arrived in the Magnolia State to join the black freedom struggle. In addition to drawing a great deal of media coverage with their presence, they spent their days in Mississippi canvassing potential black voters and teaching alternative educational institutions known as Freedom Schools. During that summer, Hattiesburg hosted over eighty volunteers, who lived among members of the black community.[89]

The local movement had been escalating for years, but the protests that rocked Hattiesburg in the summer of 1964 challenged Jim Crow in unprecedented fashion. That summer, an estimated three thousand local black citizens—roughly one-third of the city's black population—participated in the movement. All summer long, black Hattiesburgers congregated with white volunteers on dusty street corners, wooden porches, and cracked sidewalks, talking politics and holding impromptu planning sessions. The activists worked every day, organizing protests and meetings, canvassing potential voters, drafting memos, and teaching Freedom Schools. It was a transformative experience for all. Neither the white volunteers nor their black hosts had ever lived in such interracial conditions. In some cases, a summer volunteer was the first white person to ever set foot in a black host's home. In the evenings, they ate supper together and shared stories from their hometowns. On hot weekend nights, they crammed into the small homes and smoky rock-and-roll clubs of the black community to play cards, listen to music, and dance, taking brief respites from the otherwise pensive and dangerous moments that filled their summer. The activists were threatened regularly by indignant local white residents. Some were attacked; several had their cars shot at.[90]

Freedom Schools were perhaps the most inspirational feature of Hattiesburg's Freedom Summer. Before classes even started, 575 students preregistered to attend one of the six Freedom Schools held in local black churches. Most who attended the Freedom Schools were black youths between the ages of five and eighteen, but a few older folks also came. On opening day, one of the first arrivals was an eighty-two-year-old black man. When someone asked him why he was there, he explained that he wanted to "learn more in order to register to vote."[91]

Freedom Schools were profoundly liberating for black youths who had grown up in Jim Crow. In Freedom School, young black students studied African American history, read black magazines such as *Ebony* and *Jet*, and learned about the civil rights movement. Those lessons helped the students connect their own struggles to a rich tradition of African American resistance and to black heroes of the past. Ninth-grader John Wesley compared his evolving vision of freedom to the life of Frederick Douglass. "Freedom is more than a big bunch of words," he wrote. "Freedom meant so much to Frederick Douglass that he was beaten for it. He believed that every Negro should be free." For many students, attending Freedom School was a transformative experience that altered their expectations for the future. As fifteen-year-old Albert Evans asserted, "Today I am the world's footstool but tomorrow I hope to be one of its leaders. By attending freedom school this summer I am preparing for that tomorrow."[92]

Many of the black youths who arrived for Freedom School could not wait to share their voices. Almost immediately, they organized student newspapers and filled them with essays, poems, and stories that offered scathing testimonies of life in Jim Crow Mississippi. A thirteen-year-old boy named Larry wrote about the frustration of not being able to sit in downtown restaurants. Ten-year-old Mattie Jean Wilson told a story about her brother's fight with a bus driver over sitting in the back of the bus. Another young girl wrote a fictional story about a ten-year-old black boy who was pulled from his house and lynched for staring too long at a white girl. An eleven-year-old student named Lynette York wrote a letter to Mississippi governor Paul B. Johnson Jr. explaining that she was going to Freedom School because she wanted "to be a first-class citizen." Lynette just wanted a fair opportunity in life, the chance, as she put it, to one day "be a part of history."[93]

Over the ensuing six weeks, an estimated one thousand black students attended the Hattiesburg Freedom Schools, dwarfing all attendance expectations. The students came to the churches in droves, filling those hallowed spaces to the rafters with an unbridled sense of hope. So many students came that the schools ran out of space, forcing administrators to cut off registration. But the black youths of Hattiesburg would not hear of it. They went back to their neighborhoods and told their friends about Freedom School, promising to unlock side doors and open basement windows to allow more pupils to sneak in.[94]

Across Hattiesburg, hundreds of black youths spent much of their summers in those classrooms, singing, growing, and dreaming. In Freedom School, the cruel lessons of Jim Crow were replaced with remarkable possibilities for the future. They translated lessons into social activism, conducting their own sit-ins, producing movement newspapers, attending mass meetings, and encouraging their elders to attempt to register to vote. Nine-year-old Glenda Funchess, now a local civil rights attorney, remembers Freedom School as "training for us to go to the next level, whether it was integrating the public library, integrating the zoo, integrating the public schools."[95]

About a week after the Freedom Schools opened, a group of five civil rights activists—two black women and three white men—were walking through one of Hattiesburg's black neighborhoods when an ivory-colored pickup truck with no license plates began to follow them. The women lived in town, but none of the white men had been in Hattiesburg long. Two of the white men were college students from Oberlin College and Stanford University who were in town just for the summer. The third white man was Arthur Lelyveld, a fifty-one-year-old rabbi from Cleveland, Ohio, who had been in Hattiesburg for only three days. At approximately 11:30 in the morning, the group was taking a break from canvassing voters when the pickup truck started creeping behind.[96]

After trailing the activists for about two blocks, the truck slowed to a stop. Two white men jumped from the truck's cabin and charged toward the activists. An older man brandishing a tire iron reached Lelyveld first. The older man raised the metal rod into the air and crashed it onto the upper right side of Lelyveld's face, opening a large gash just above the rabbi's eye. Blood spurted from the wound, splattering over Lelyveld's face and shirt. A younger man from the truck arrived an instant later and struck the Oberlin student over the back of the head with a thin piece of steel, opening a nasty wound on the activist's skull. The attacker then turned to the Stanford student, knocking him to the ground and punching and kicking him. When a notepad fell from the volunteer's pocket, the attacker ripped out a sheet of paper, crumbled it into a tight ball, and tried to shove the wad of paper into the young man's mouth, all the while screaming, "Eat this . . . you nigger lover!"[97]

After the attackers sped off, the victims collected themselves and began hobbling toward the nearby Morning Star Baptist Church, a hub for movement people. Someone covered the gash over Lelyveld's eye with a cotton gauze pad, and the Cleveland rabbi took a seat on a metal-lattice bench. Bloody and stunned, he sat still, looking off into the distance and trying to explain what happened while friends helped clean the other men's wounds and debated what to do next.[98]

A photographer from New York City named Herbert Randall was walking nearby. Just the day before, Randall had been joking with Rabbi Lelyveld. Explaining his mission for that summer, the photographer playfully told the rabbi, "If you go out and you get your butt beat, I will come down there and photograph you and . . . that's really good publicity. This will go all over the world and that will help." The pair was supposed to go out together the following morning, but the rabbi had left early. When Randall heard the commotion at Morning Star, he rushed over to find Rabbi Lelyveld sitting with his arms draped over the back of the bench and "bleeding profusely." Dazed and soaked in blood, the rabbi looked up at Randall and said softly, "Go ahead, photographer. Take the picture."[99]

Herbert Randall's photograph of the bleeding Rabbi Arthur Lelyveld was sold to United Press International and reprinted in newspapers across the country. Accounts of the attack appeared in the *Los Angeles Times*, the *Washington Post*, the *Chicago Tribune*, and dozens of smaller newspapers across the nation. The attention helped pressure local officials into working with the FBI to investigate the attack. Eventually, the white assailants from the ivory-colored truck were identified and arrested. Those men probably had no idea that their attack would generate such widespread publicity in a world that existed outside their own. Nor did they know that Rabbi Lelyveld's son Joseph was a reporter for the *New York Times* who would write follow-up stories for days. Those attackers were acting in accordance with a long tradition of violence in southern Mississippi. Racially related violence was as old as Hattiesburg itself. But by the summer of 1964, the old tactics were losing their edge. Even the most brutal methods of racial control had the potential to actually strengthen the resolve and effectiveness of people in the movement. Like many locals, the attackers were probably stunned when they were each convicted of assault and fined $500 and received ninety-day suspended jail sentences. The end of Jim Crow was washing over them like a tidal wave. And there was simply nothing they could do.[100]

Conclusion

Changes

> The changes has been so great . . . The job market has increased. Blacks are in management on jobs. We don't have to go to the windows anymore. We can walk through the front door to be served. We can sit in a restaurant wherever we feel we want to sit. . . . We're moving into the neighborhoods wherever we want to live. And I can go to the bank, and there's a black girl and a white one, and there's one sitting over here as vice president of the bank.
>
> —Daisy Harris Wade, 2000

Between 1962 and 1968, the Hattiesburg civil rights movement revolutionized race in the Hub City. Through dozens of public demonstrations and countless acts of individual resistance, local African Americans excised Jim Crow from their society. By the end of the decade, the most visible signs of Jim Crow had been vanquished. Formal racial segregation in public spaces ended. Schools and hospitals desegregated. Black people gained the ability to register to vote, serve on juries, obtain jobs in previously segregated companies, and purchase homes outside traditionally black neighborhoods. The police force hired black men. In 1965, a white man was convicted of raping a black woman for the first time in Hattiesburg history. "Five years ago nothing would have been done about that case," noted a bailiff who served at the trial. "The civil rights movement had something to do with it all right." That same autumn, the University of Southern Mississippi admitted its first black students. These changes by no means completely erased racial problems or reconciled historical racial advantages, but they did indeed signify the end of Jim Crow.[1]

None of this was easy. Despite new federal legislation, especially the Civil Rights Act of 1964 and the Voting Rights Act of 1965, which barred racial discrimination in public places and empowered the Department of Justice to oversee local voter registration practices, the onus of extricating Southern society from the grip of Jim Crow fell upon the shoulders of everyday local black citizens. Many white segregationists refused to follow federal law unless compelled by overwhelming demonstrations or legal action. Black citizens, now armed with new legislative tools, committed themselves to the painstaking processes of eliminating Jim Crow from every corner of the South. These black citizens worked outside the purview of reporters and news cameras to demand equal opportunities.

There was never a time in Southern history when black people were not active. From organizing through churches and pouring resources into black schools, African Americans had always gotten together within their communities to help improve the lives and prospects of their fellow black citizens. But in Hattiesburg and elsewhere, the nature of black activism in the 1960s was inherently different from the activism of previous eras: the civil rights movement of the 1960s directly targeted and successfully overthrew Jim Crow. In this regard, although historians have argued for broader conceptualizations of the civil rights movement beyond the 1960s, local black activists engaged in 1960s-era protests typically consider the activism of that era distinct.

Consider the view of local people. Virtually all black Hattiesburgers who participated in the movement of the 1960s conceptualized precise points of origin. In later describing the movement, local activists such as Victoria Gray and Daisy Harris Wade used language such as "by the time the movement came" and "when this movement started in 1964," respectively, definitively positioning the beginning of their movement in the 1960s. To Daisy Harris Wade, the movement began on a specific day—Hattiesburg Freedom Day on January 22, 1964. For Victoria Gray, the movement began when she started working with SNCC activists in the spring of 1962. To local participants, the wave of extraordinary activism of the 1960s constituted a distinct civil rights movement.[2]

This does not mean that they did not recognize the movement of the 1960s within the broader context of local black community organizing traditions. Virtually all leaders in Hattiesburg's civil rights movement cited the importance of earlier institutions and communal values that predated the 1960s. Some cited Eureka High School; others pointed to the black business community. All noted the churches. When Victoria Gray was a high schooler in 1945, she wrote an essay about the influence of the local black business community in shaping, as she wrote, "My decision of what I wanted to do in life." In a 2002 interview, Gray continued to credit lessons passed down by her grandfather and neighbors that helped shape her worldview. In interviews conducted as late as 2011, Daisy Harris Wade, a graduate of the Eureka High School class of 1949, similarly cited her experiences as a student at Eureka in the 1940s and the importance of the old black churches in shaping her life before the movement. But those experiences were part of another era. The civil rights movement, however similar or deeply entwined it was with the efforts of the past, represented something entirely different: the rapid expulsion of Jim Crow from their society.[3]

Local movements were also largely shaped by black people's changing view of the potential of federal action. In the 1960s, African Americans more than ever came to believe in the possibility of circumnavigating oppressive local and state governments to gain access to federal protections, both old and new, that they had never enjoyed. As Hattiesburg reverend John M. Barnes stressed to the Senate Judiciary Subcommittee on Constitutional Rights in 1959, "We need the Federal Government on this matter. The officials of Forrest County will continue to deny colored people the right to register and vote unless they are required to do so." With the Department of Justice pursuing its case against Theron Lynd and the explosion of civil rights activism across the American South, black Hattiesburgers became increasingly active in their fight against Jim Crow. Reporters, cameras, and dozens of outside volunteers undergirded the potential effectiveness of local activism. As local African Americans gained increasing confidence in federal authority, the Hattiesburg movement flourished.[4]

It is also important to understand that black people were essential in pushing the federal government toward a greater commitment to protecting black civil rights. This increasing commitment was not only the result of growing black political constituencies and their allies in the North, but also from black Southern activists. The events in Selma, Alabama, on March 7, 1965, often receive credit for the passage of the 1965 Voting Rights Act. But that legislation was, in reality, a consequence of over a decade of black Southern political activism that documented blatant violations of the Fifteenth Amendment. When United States Attorney General Herbert Brownell testified in 1956 to the Senate Judiciary

Committee considering civil rights legislation, he read a 1952 affidavit completed by a black Hattiesburg voter registration applicant and cited the case of *Peay et al. v. Cox* as "one illustration" of black Southerners being denied the right to vote. In Hattiesburg and elsewhere, thousands of black activists spent years laying the groundwork to prove the necessity of additional enforcement mechanisms to help guarantee basic constitutional rights. After more than seventy years of racially based voter discrimination, the federal government finally provided these mechanisms with the Voting Rights Act of 1965.[5]

In the years after the Civil Rights Act of 1964 and Voting Rights Act of 1965, everyday African Americans shouldered the burden of desegregating Southern society. When racially segregated public schools were formally outlawed by the 1964 Civil Rights Act, it was black children and their parents who weathered the difficult processes of desegregating previously all-white schools. During that fall, Mississippi enacted a plan known as "freedom-of-choice" desegregation that for the first time in Hattiesburg history allowed students of any color to attend any public school in the municipal school district.[6]

In Hattiesburg, only black students crossed the old racial boundaries by desegregating previously all-white schools. This was a risky and challenging maneuver for black families, who faced job loss, social ostracism, violence, and any number of informal economic sanctions. For the students themselves, this was at times "a harrowing experience," noted Daisy Harris Wade's son Anthony, who desegregated one of Hattiesburg's public schools as an eighth-grader in 1966. Black youths experienced daily harassment from both peers and teachers.[7]

Glenda Funchess, a former Hattiesburg Freedom School student who entered a previously all-white school in 1967 at the age of thirteen, remembered regular chants of "nigger, nigger, nigger" and white children who refused to sit at lunch tables with black students. There were countless acts of racially based harassment and humiliation. Funchess recalled one such incident in which her white peers destroyed an essay she wrote for class because the paper focused on Martin Luther King Jr. In another episode, a white girl who sang in the school choir one day broke into tears because, as she explained to the choir director, "My parents are coming, and they're gonna see me standing next to Glenda." Tormented, attacked, and isolated, young black children endured the difficult process of pioneering school desegregation. Because of these challenges, at the beginning of the 1966–67 academic year, fewer than 3 percent of black Mississippi public school students were attending previously segregated white schools.[8]

Freedom-of-choice remained until 1969, when the United States Supreme Court decided in *Alexander v. Holmes County* to order Mississippi to develop alternative plans for desegregation. Many white families responded to school desegregation by moving to suburbs or enrolling their children in predominantly white private academies or parochial schools that were supported by state-funded tuition grants. In Hattiesburg, the Citizens' Council first announced its plan to form an all-white private school in the summer of 1965.[9]

Although formal public school segregation ended in 1964, Mississippi's schools as a whole have never truly integrated. As late as 2015, Mississippi had forty-four active school desegregation cases pending with the Department of Justice. In the thirty years after the *Alexander v. Holmes County* decision, white enrollment in Hattiesburg public schools declined from 55 percent to 11 percent. White families either relocated to the outskirts or sent their kids to more racially homogenous private schools. As of the 2017–18 school year, African Americans comprised approximately 91 percent of students enrolled in the public schools of Hattiesburg, a metropolitan area that is roughly 68 percent white. There is no reason to expect that Hattiesburg-area public schools will ever represent the racial demographics of the local population, but they are at least desegregated and provide black students with an opportunity to finish high school. Despite the lingering problems of educational inequality that affect thousands of public school districts across the nation, African American political participation helps give black residents a voice in electing representatives to the school board. The biggest difference between Jim Crow and now is that so many more black students have a chance to learn and succeed before their society systematically crushes their dreams.[10]

During the same autumn of 1964 that Hattiesburg schools desegregated, local civil rights activist Victoria Gray became the first black woman in Mississippi history to run for the United States Senate. Backed by an integrated independent political party known as the Mississippi Freedom Democratic Party (MFDP), Gray ran against incumbent John Stennis in the 1964 Democratic Primary and lost by a large margin of 153,572 to 4,249.[11]

The year 1964 marked the beginning of immense changes in black political participation in Mississippi. Gray was one of an unprecedented number of African American candidates who ran for state or local office in that year. As nationally syndicated columnist Robert G. Spivack observed, the 1964 Mississippi Democratic primaries featured "the largest number of Negro candidates for major office in Mississippi since Reconstruction." Black voters have played a major role in the state Democratic Party ever since, especially because so many white segregationist Democrats left the party after the passage of the 1964 Civil Rights Act. During that autumn's presidential election, Republican candidate Barry Goldwater, an Arizona senator whose vote against the 1964 Civil Rights Act earned him the endorsement of the Mississippi Citizens' Council, became the first Republican to win the state of Mississippi since Ulysses S. Grant in 1868 during Reconstruction.[12]

Over the ensuing years, black Hattiesburgers continued to expand local black political participation. Daisy Harris Wade remembered "stages" of growth, estimating 10 percent involvement of the black community "when the ministers were here" in January of 1964. By Freedom Summer, Wade estimated "about fifty percent." And then "about seventy-five or eighty percent of the people were involved one way or the other" by the early spring of 1966. These rough estimates provided by an activist reflect the growing numbers of registered black voters in Hattiesburg during the mid-1960s.[13]

On June 16, 1965, the United States Court of Appeals finally ruled in the Theron Lynd case. The federal court enacted specific limitations on Lynd's ability to deny voter applications and required an immediate review of 350 "application forms of those rejected Negro applicants who applied during his tenure in office and who are not now registered." Less than two months later, on August 6, 1965, President Johnson signed into law the Voting Rights Act of 1965, which provided the federal government with unprecedented authority to oversee voter registration in places like Forrest County, where African Americans had for decades been systematically disfranchised. Nearly a century after the ratification of the Fifteenth Amendment, black people in Forrest County could finally register to vote. In March of 1964, there were 196 black residents of Forrest County registered to vote. Roughly three years later, that figure soared to 5,467.[14]

Local movement activists led a charge to inform the newly enfranchised black electorate. Through community newspapers such *The Voice of the Movement* and the Forrest County NAACP's *Freedom Flashes*—both of which were produced in black-owned businesses in the Mobile Street District—black political leaders encouraged their neighbors to register to vote and provided updates on local political activities. In 1966, movement leaders compiled a "political handbook for the black people of Forrest County," a sixteen-page pamphlet explaining the duties of various city and state elected officials and encouraging local black voters to consider whether the current elected officials truly represented their best interests.[15]

Ever since African Americans regained the right to vote, white conservative Mississippi politicians have taken steps to limit their political power. In 1966—the year after the passage of the Voting Rights Act—white Mississippi legislators redrew the state's five congressional districts to split potential black voting blocs. In addition to recurrent gerrymandering, white Mississippi legislators since 1966 have employed a range of tactics to curtail the influence of the black vote. They have diluted black political power by expanding at-large voting across districts, changed the process of electing supervisors in countywide elections, altered nominating procedures for school district trustees, reformed primary elections, and switched some positions from elected to appointed. As former Mississippi civil rights attorney Frank Parker observed in 1990, "Outright denial to black Mississippians of the right to vote, now prohibited by federal law, was replaced with these more subtle strategies to dilute and cancel out the black vote." Conservative white Mississippians, who have now fully switched to the Republican Party, continue to work to weaken the power of black votes. Jim Crow ended, but black people have had to fight relentlessly to maintain access to the ballot box. Most recently, white conservatives have used new voter identification laws to target black voters. Even in post–Jim Crow Mississippi, there is no indication that they will ever cease their continual assaults on black voting rights.[16]

Nonetheless, black people embraced and defended new political activities. They fought virtually every plan designed to limit their political power, a battle that included two victorious cases involving Hattiesburg civil rights leaders—*Connor v. Johnson* and *Fairley v. Patterson*—that reached the United States Supreme Court. As early as 1967, black Mississippians elected twenty-two African Americans to local offices. By the late 1980s, Mississippi led the United States of America in the number of elected black officials with 646.[17]

Hattiesburg activists attacked all components of Jim Crow. Soon after the passage of the Civil Rights Act of 1964, local activists launched a series of demonstrations to desegregate public facilities. When thirty-five-year-old Dorothea Jackson was removed from a bus that August for refusing to give up her seat, the remaining twenty black passengers stood up and walked off the bus, spurring a boycott that ended segregated seating on city busses. Two days later, a half dozen Freedom School students and their teacher strolled through town during an impromptu desegregation tour. In a single afternoon, the group targeted the local public library and the local Kress Stores. The library closed to avoid having to allow black kids to borrow books, and a waitress at the Kress Store refused to serve the interracial group. Shortly thereafter, a police officer arrested the Freedom School teacher. But the library demonstration helped spur a larger response that later desegregated the library. The arrested teacher later won a lawsuit against the Kress Corporation.[18]

Most places, especially national chain stores, desegregated relatively peacefully as white onlookers silently watched racial segregation crumble. Other venues desegregated only after the threat of a lawsuit based on the new Civil Rights Act of 1964. Protestors were regularly beaten and arrested, but they nonetheless continued to mount desegregation campaigns throughout the duration of the local movement. Through the persistence of local activists and the support of new laws, Hattiesburg institutions desegregated.[19]

Hattiesburg's white leaders, deeply concerned about the optics of violent resistance, objected to the protests but advocated peace. Most local white citizens heeded the *Hattiesburg American's* warning that "violence would only play into the hands of the leaders of these extremist groups," but some white citizens just could not bring themselves to operate peacefully. When a group of thirty-five local African Americans and four Northern civil rights activists launched a sit-in at Lea's Restaurant in January of 1965, a group of unidentified local white terrorists burned a cross in front of a school in one of the black neighborhoods. When protests continued over the ensuing days, several local white men attacked the demonstrators. All told, local movement leaders reported twelve beatings during the last two weeks of January in 1965.[20]

But the freedom fighters persevered. Backed by the support of a branch of the Delta Ministry, which operated an office out of Lenon Woods's guesthouse on Mobile Street, civil rights workers who had been attacked pressed charges, completed affidavits, and publicized the violence to hundreds of supporters across the country. Ultimately, these reports helped lead to the arrest of several perpetrators.[21]

The aid of outside activists was crucial to carrying this fight forward, but it was primarily local African Americans who led efforts to expel Jim Crow. By August of 1965, a visiting white Presbyterian minister from Minnesota reported, "We feel so good about the progress here that we are beginning to look toward the time when our presence in Hattiesburg will no longer be needed."[22]

At about 2:30 in the morning on January 10, 1966, Klansmen laid siege to the home of voting rights activist Vernon Dahmer and his family. Two of the attackers ran toward the house under the cover of gunfire and tossed gasoline-filled containers through the windows followed by a flaming cloth that ignited the containers. As the fire spread, the Klansmen fired a continuous stream of bullets into the home. Vernon Dahmer leaned against his front door, returning fire as he could while his wife Ellie, ten-year-old daughter, and two sons, aged twelve and twenty, scrambled to escape the burning house. After Ellie managed to pop out a back window, the family fled into a barn located behind the house. Vernon Dahmer saved his family that night, but later succumbed to severe burns to his head, upper body, and arms. He was fifty-seven years old when he died on the afternoon of January 10, 1966.[23]

Local white leaders condemned the crime. The Chamber of Commerce issued a statement "condemning the tragic acts of violence against the Vernon Dahmer family" and urging "all of the law enforcement agencies to pursue with diligence their efforts to bring all of the perpetrators of this unconscionable crime to their justice." The Forrest County Board of Supervisors and Hattiesburg City Council issued a similar statement, calling for the "prosecution of the person or persons guilty of this tragic and deplorable crime" and creating a Dahmer Family Fund of Forrest County to help the family rebuild their home and pay for additional expenses. The *Hattiesburg American* rebuked the "revolting, cowardly crime" committed by "terrorists," editorializing that "the crime against them must be punished."[24]

Despite such sentiments, it is worth remembering that Vernon Dahmer had long been fighting these very same institutions—local white government officials, business leaders, and the press—for basic voting rights for African Americans. Although these groups expressed remorse for his death in 1966, white businessmen and city leaders had for years played key roles in fighting against black civil rights. The Hattiesburg Citizens' Council had helped publicize the names of local civil rights activists and closely monitored their behavior. Led by the city's elite white citizens, the local Citizens' Council had been responsible for framing Dahmer's friend and ally Clyde Kennard six years earlier and had for years been working to suppress black activism to protect white supremacy. The longtime enemies of civil rights activists shared a level of complicity in all attacks against activists. It certainly did not help that the *Hattiesburg American* published Dahmer's home address in the newspaper after his son applied to register to vote. Local white leaders had not operated on the side of Vernon Dahmer and his allies; only after his death did they publicly demonstrate sympathy toward him and his causes. Black people always bore the burden of the sins of their oppressors.[25]

Nonetheless, Vernon Dahmer's death signaled a sea change in the local movement. Just two days after Dahmer's murder, the *Hattiesburg American* published a fifteen-point list of requests submitted by local African American civil rights leaders. These included hiring more black police officers and firefighters, appointing African Americans to the school board, immediately desegregating all public facilities, fully complying with the 1965 Voting Rights Act, providing equal access to health services, adding paved curbs and new street signs to black neighborhoods, and using courtesy titles toward African Americans in the local press. There were no definitive deadlines for meeting these "requests," but the goals of black activists received unprecedented attention in the local media and from city officials. The Chamber of Commerce called a special meeting on January 12 to discuss the requests and formulate a plan to raise money for a reward leading to the apprehension of Dahmer's killers. Seventeen days after the Dahmer murder, the Chamber of Commerce actually held a meeting with local black leaders—including two of the original plaintiffs in *Peay et al. v. Cox*—to talk about grievances. Not all issues were resolved, but each attendee signed a statement declaring that the gathering was held in "an atmosphere of friendly mutual respect and understanding."[26]

When white Hattiesburg leaders wavered on responding to these requests, African Americans mobilized to aggressively pursue their goals. Beginning with a march on the morning of Dahmer's funeral, more black people joined the movement than ever before. "At the death of Mr. Dahmer in '66, the numbers grew," remembered Daisy Harris Wade. "I would say about seventy-five or eighty percent of the people were involved one way or the other." As one of the last few remaining clergy from the Delta Ministry reported in March of 1966, "The work here in Hattiesburg has fallen mostly into the hands of the local people now."[27]

In the months and years to follow, local African Americans expanded their voter registration campaigns and sit-ins to include protests designed to completely expel racial segregation from their society. In 1967, they executed a widespread boycott that successfully pressured downtown stores to hire more African Americans. They also secured federal funding from the national Office of Economic Opportunity to run eight Head Start centers that provided local black women with good jobs teaching young African American students.[28]

Black community activism did not operate entirely without conflict. In fact, the boycott of 1967 was supported by a militant group known as "The Spirit" that formed in the wake of Vernon Dahmer's murder. The members protected local black churches and NAACP officials, but also helped enforce the boycott by issuing warnings to any black person who shopped in a white store. Additionally, the local NAACP experienced regular infighting that led to the expulsion of several of its leaders. Some local NAACP members believed that working-class activists had been excluded from the process of formulating the "requests" sent to white city officials. Even in their differences, however, black people overthrew Jim Crow, ending the systematic racial segregation and disfranchisement that had for so long limited black life in Hattiesburg.[29]

In 1968, the state of Mississippi charged eleven Klansmen with murder and/or arson for their involvement in the death of Vernon Dahmer. The terrorists who murdered Dahmer belonged to sect of nearby Klansmen led by a violent and deranged white supremacist named Samuel Holloway Bowers. Prior to the 1964 Freedom Summer, Bowers warned his followers, "The events which will occur in Mississippi this summer may well determine the fate of Christian civilization for centuries to come." Members of this group were also involved in the famous Freedom Summer murder of civil rights activists Michael Schwerner, James Chaney, and Andrew Goodman in nearby Neshoba County. It was later discovered that Bowers ordered the murders of both Michael Schwerner and Vernon Dahmer as part of a campaign of guerrilla terror designed to stymie civil rights activism in Mississippi.[30]

In 1967, Bowers was one of seven Klansmen convicted of federal charges for conspiring to violate the civil rights of Schwerner, Chaney, and Goodman. Several members of the group had also been indicted on federal charges related to the murder of Vernon Dahmer, but these charges were later dismissed. Nonetheless, these federal indictments represented the first time that Mississippi Klansmen had been charged or convicted for anti–civil rights violence. The federal government was finally working to do something to protect black people from racialized violence in Mississippi.[31]

The local indictments for murder and/or arson represented an unprecedented commitment by the State of Mississippi to prosecute Klansmen who attacked civil rights activists. As a Hattiesburg reporter noted in 1968, "A remarkable facet of the state indictments and subsequent developments is that generally speaking citizens of the area appear to feel that something was needed in the way of action more stringent than the federal conspiracy charges." "Yet only a few years ago," the reporter observed, "such a move would have meant political suicide for the prosecutors and public ostracism."[32]

Hailing from a longtime Mississippi family, the Klansman Samuel Bowers carried with him a deep sense of family history that informed his violent actions. In interviews conducted in the early 1980s, Bowers sought to contextualize his role in maintaining the tradition of white supremacy in Mississippi. According to Bowers, his great-grandfather had been a Confederate soldier who engaged in "nightriding in order to recover Southern civilization" during Reconstruction. Representing the next generation was Bowers's grandfather, Eaton J. Bowers, the Gulf Coast lawyer who in the 1890s served as general counsel of the Gulf & Ship Island Railroad for the Pennsylvanian Joseph T. Jones. Labeling his grandfather "outstanding and brilliant," Bowers cited his role in helping establish the Gulf & Ship Island Railroad as part of "a pattern in American history" between a "responsible carpetbagger movement . . . which I say was represented by Captain Jones and the G. & S.I. Railroad" that allowed for Northern and federal economic involvement in the South as long as white Southerners were allowed to "hold the black people down." When Bowers became concerned that Northerners were no longer upholding their end of the bargain, he launched his violent crusade to maintain white supremacy, or, in his words, "to preserve Christian Civilization."[33]

With the help of a Klan informant and the FBI, local prosecutors managed to secure the convictions of four men involved in the Dahmer murder. This did not include all the perpetrators. It is unknown exactly how many people were involved, but the original complaint filed by the FBI included fourteen names. Local prosecutors were constantly challenged by racially prejudiced jurors and witness and jury tampering by Klansmen. Moreover, it is fair to question their commitment to justice. None of the convicted men served more than ten years in prison. Each was released early.[34]

Between 1967 and 1970, Samuel Holloway Bowers was tried four times without being convicted. During the May 1968 trial, a single juror blocked conviction after twenty-two hours of deliberation, resulting in a mistrial. Bowers did serve time in federal prison for violating the civil rights of the other people he helped kill, but he remained free for some thirty-two years after the murder of Vernon Dahmer. After years of various efforts to reopen the Dahmer case, Bowers was finally tried and convicted in 1998 at the age of seventy-four. "It shows that Mississippi has changed," reflected former Freedom School student Glenda Funchess after the conviction in 1998. Today, Ms. Funchess is a civil rights attorney in downtown Hattiesburg.[35]

The historic Mobile Street neighborhood still sits in the shadows of downtown Hattiesburg. On most days, the neighborhood is an empty shell of its former self. The ravages of natural disasters and neglect have taken down most of the buildings. The flood of 1974 inundated the entire neighborhood and displaced thousands of people. Subsequent rains, winds, and other adverse weather events have eroded much of the neighborhood. In 2013, a tornado tore through the Mobile Street District, taking down the neighborhood's tallest structure, a 107-year-old three-story building, and causing major damage to the now-abandoned Eureka High School and the old Sixth Street USO, which is now an African American Military History Museum. The rest of the neighborhood is filled with empty patches of grass where other buildings caught fire, flooded, or collapsed, and were never rebuilt.[36]

Mt. Carmel Baptist Church still stands proudly on the corner of Seventh and Mobile, right across from where Gaither Hardaway ran his grocery store. Its congregation, however, has since moved. Mt. Carmel now meets in what used to be a white church. True Light Baptist has similarly moved into a former white church that was vacated when its congregation moved into a church farther from downtown. Ironically, the black congregations now meet in buildings left vacant by those who left to get away from them. St. Paul Methodist remains in place to this day, filled with a proud congregation that does much to remember the church's history. Not everyone knows the significance of the names etched in the church's stained-glass windows. The writing on one of those windows reads, "In Memory, Turner Roger Smith & Mamie Grove Smith, By Children."[37]

Hammond Smith passed away in 1985 at the age of ninety. His brother Charles had passed years earlier, in 1971, at the age of seventy-nine. In today's South, Hammond and Charles Smith probably would not live in that black community. Nor would they even own their stores. Most likely, they would work at the Hattiesburg Clinic or a local pharmacy and live in one of the town's more prominent areas. They almost certainly would not live near Mobile Street. In today's South, Hammond and Charles could live, shop, and eat wherever they wanted. The destruction of everyday Jim Crow is a major victory of the civil rights movement. But that very system of Jim Crow, which limited black opportunities and was so oppressive and so deadly, also gave birth to the very communities that brought into being the movement that eventually killed it.[38]

Black people still own businesses and work throughout the city. But since the destruction of Jim Crow, the number of homegrown small black businesses has drastically declined. Hammond Smith's pharmacy probably couldn't survive today against the CVS stores and the Walgreens that dot the city and accept dollars from all races. Thousands of black Hattiesburgers now work and shop in two large Walmart stores on either end of the city. Black people are now free to spend their time and money as they please. That is no small thing. But decades ago, their time and dollars would have cycled through their own communities rather than into the bank accounts of multimillion-dollar corporations. Those dollars would have gone into the hands of the people who ran the groceries, cafes, and barbershops of that once vibrant community.

Since integration, Hattiesburg itself has sprawled miles away from its historic center. Thousands of residents, both white and black, have packed up their lives and moved away from the core. Commerce followed. Some of America's largest chain stores now dot Hardy Street for miles beyond the old city core. The migrants left a decaying downtown in their wake; there are still a few places to eat and drink, but downtown Hattiesburg is no longer the center of local commerce. A downtown association draws people back into the city center for concerts, plays, farmer's markets, and festivals. It is also leading an effort to reverse the outmigration by encouraging people to move downtown. But such efforts are merely the beginning stages of an effort to reverse outmigration processes underway since the end of Jim Crow. In the years after the 1960s, racial progress flipped the city inside out, leaving an old historic core for the black residents who cannot afford or choose not to move and some white residents who populate the older white neighborhoods.[39]

So much has changed. But the legacy of a racially disputed past hangs above the Hub City. Hattiesburg celebrates its civil rights history and even has plans to refurbish Eureka High School into a local civil rights museum that could be added to the Hattiesburg Freedom Summer Trail. But on most days, and in more subtle ways, the city also honors the white supremacists who worked most devotedly to tear the races apart. The county still bears the name Forrest, after the murderous Civil War general and Ku Klux Klan pioneer. And, of course, its Confederate monument stands tall next to the courthouse; never mind the fact that the city was founded more than ten years after the Civil War ended. The state flag contains the old Confederate battle flag in its upper left-hand corner. When the University of Southern Mississippi removed it from campus following the murder of nine black people in Charleston by a white supremacist in 2015, local white neo-Confederate boosters camped on the edge of campus waving Confederate flags in protest. One of them was a former member of the Citizens' Council in the 1960s; it is hard to take seriously his cries of "heritage not hate" when you know he belonged to an organization that sponsored racial terrorism. At the very least, Mississippians' refusal to remove Confederate flags and monuments represents the privileging of one people's heritage over that of others. It also signals the assurance that this seemingly eternal struggle over race will continue to pollute the lives of millions to come. Despite so much change, many Southerners today insist on passing down the sins of their ancestors to their offspring. But some do share a vision that one day this American cancer of racism might end.[40]

African Americans in the South have more opportunities now than they ever had. But losses were embedded within those iconic victories. Hollowed-out neighborhoods now sit in the former sites of bustling black downtowns; the entire American South is filled with those once-rich spaces, and some African Americans still occupy them. Most of those residents are poor, and although they can now ride in the front of the bus, one cannot help but wonder how many opportunities are actually theirs. Few black communities are as capable of self-sustenance as they once had been. The decline of Jim Crow was a victory of the movement. But it ultimately led to the fall of hundreds, perhaps thousands, of extraordinarily resilient black communities where a people lived and grew together within the confines of Jim Crow.

Archival Abbreviations

Beech Papers	Robert Beech Papers, 1963–1972, WHS
CoC	Hattiesburg Area Chamber of Commerce Records, USM
Cooper Collection	Forrest Lamar Cooper Postcard Collection, MDAH
Evers Papers	Medgar and Myrlie Evers Papers, MDAH
Faulkner Papers	Faulkner (L. E.) Papers, USM
FBR	Records of the Field Offices for the State of Mississippi, Bureau of Refugees, Freedmen, and Abandoned Lands, 1865–1872, record group 105, National Archives Building, Washington, DC
G&SI Papers	Gulf & Ship Island Railroad Minute Book Collection, USM
HHP	Hattiesburg Historical Photographs, USM
Howard Papers	Dr. T. R. M. Howard Papers, Vivian G. Harsh Research Collection of Afro-American History and Literature, Chicago Public Library, Chicago, IL
Martin Papers	Gordon A. Martin Jr. Collection, Archives and Special Collections, J. D. Williams Library, University of Mississippi
MCRR Collection	Mississippi Central Railroad Collection, USM
MDAH	Mississippi Department of Archives and History, Jackson, MS
Moore Papers	Amzie Moore Papers, 1941–1970, WHS
MSSC	Records of the Mississippi State Sovereignty Commission, MDAH
NAACP/mf	*Papers of the National Association for the Advancement of Colored People* (Bethesda, MD: University Publications of America Microfilm, 1991)

NUL	Records of the National Urban League, Library of Congress Manuscript Division, Washington, DC
Sanborn	Sanborn Maps Company Ltd., Digital Sanborn Maps, 1867–1970 (Ann Arbor, MI: ProQuest)
SNCC-M	Student Nonviolent Coordinating Committee Papers, 1959–1972 (Sanford, NC: Microfilming Corp. of America, 1981)
SNCC Papers	Student Nonviolent Coordinating Committee Records, 1959–1972, King Center, Atlanta, GA
Tatum Papers	Tatum Family Business Records, USM
USM	University of Southern Mississippi Libraries Special Collections, Hattiesburg, MS
USM-OH	University of Southern Mississippi Center for Oral History and Cultural Heritage, Hattiesburg, MS
W&H Hardy Papers	Papers of William H. Hardy and Hattie Lott Hardy, USM
W&S Hardy Papers	Papers of William H. Hardy and Sallie J. Hardy, USM
WHS	Wisconsin Historical Society, Madison, WI
WPA-Forrest	Works Project Administration Historical Survey, MDAH

Notes

Introduction

Epigraph: Richard Boyd, interview by Charles Bolton, Hattiesburg, MS, August 29, 1991, transcript, USM-OH.

1. Observations made by author on October 1, 2011; and 2011, 2012, 2013, 2014 and 2015 Historic Mobile Street Renaissance Festival Schedule of Events, in author's possession. For more on the Historic Mobile Street Renaissance Festival, see: http://mobilestreetfestival.com/.
2. "Fire Destroys Historic Hotel," *Hattiesburg American*, September 18, 1998, copy in folder 1, Woods Guest House Collection, USM.
3. Arthur Reese, "Freedom Schools—Summer 1964," *The Detroit Teacher*, December 1964, 4. The figure of three thousand is taken from Herbert Randall and Bobs M. Tusa, *Faces of Freedom Summer* (Tuscaloosa: University of Alabama Press, 2001), 7; and Barbara Schwartzbaum, interview by author, July 9, 2010, New York, NY. For more on Freedom Summer, see John Dittmer, *Local People: The Civil Rights Struggle in Mississippi* (Urbana: University of Illinois Press, 1994), especially 215–271.
4. For more on the history of the local civil rights movement, see Patricia Michelle Boyett, *Right to Revolt: The Crusade for Racial Justice in Mississippi's Central Piney Woods* (Jackson: University Press of Mississippi, 2015).
5. Observations made by author on October 1, 2011.
6. See Barbara Young Welke, *Recasting American Liberty: Gender, Race, Law, and the Railroad Revolution, 1865–1920* (New York: Cambridge University Press, 2001); Howard N. Rabinowitz, *Race Relations in the Urban South, 1865–1890* (New York: Oxford University Press, 1978); and Amy Louise Wood, *Lynching and Spectacle: Witnessing Racial Violence in America, 1890–1940* (Chapel Hill: University of North Carolina Press, 2009).
7. For a general history of Hattiesburg, see Benjamin Morris, *Hattiesburg, Mississippi: A History of the Hub City* (Charleston, SC: The History Press, 2014); and Kenneth G. McCarty Jr., ed., *Hattiesburg: A Pictorial History* (Jackson: University Press of Mississippi, 1982).

8. Historian Rayford W. Logan was the first to attach the term "nadir" to the period in African American history between 1877 and 1901. Historians have since offered numerous arguments in favor of extending this period, sometimes far into the twentieth century. See Rayford W. Logan, *The Negro in American Life and Thought: The Nadir, 1877–1901* (New York: Dial Press, 1954).
9. C. Vann Woodward, *The Strange Career of Jim Crow* (New York: Oxford University Press, 1955).
10. "Ran down . . ." quoted in Charles S. Johnson, "Migration Study," 15, part 1, box 86, folder: Migration Study Chicago Interviews, NUL.

1. *Visionaries*

Epigraph: "Hattiesburg: A Thriving Mississippi Town on the Northeastern Railroad," *New Orleans Daily Picayune*, May 1, 1893, 6.

1. This scene is reconstructed from William H. Hardy to Hattie Lott Hardy, May 9, 1880, Meridian, MS, box 1, folder 1, W&H Hardy Papers; "Judge William Harris Hardy," 13–22, box 2, folder 8, W&H Hardy Papers; and Toney Arnold Hardy, *No Compromise with Principle: Autobiography and Biography of William Harris Hardy in Dialogue* (Saddle Brook, NJ: American Book-Stratford Press, 1946), 217–232. "A picture of . . ." quoted on 519. J.F.H. Claiborne, "A Trip Through the Piney Woods," in Franklin L. Riley, ed., *Publications of the Mississippi Historical Society*, vol. 9 (Oxford, MS: Printed for the Society, 1906).
2. Hardy, *No Compromise with Principle*, "crystal clear" quoted on 218.
3. "Bridging Lake Pontchartrain," *New York Times*, November 1, 1881, 1; and "Our New Railroads," *The Daily Picayune*, October 16, 1883, 4. For more on the Queen and Crescent City Route, see Burke Davis, *The Southern Railway: Road of the Innovators* (Chapel Hill: University of North Carolina Press, 1985), 182–187; and Robert Adam Ellis, "Working Through a Forest of Change: An Environmental, Labor, and Social History of the Greater Hattiesburg, Mississippi Area, 1880–1910" (master's thesis, University of Southern Mississippi, 2005), especially 7–33.
4. "Judge William Harris Hardy," 13–22, box 2, folder 8, W&H Hardy Papers; Hardy, *No Compromise with Principle*, 218–232; Federal Land Grant made to William H. Hardy, May 10, 1882, box 2, folder 11, HHP; "Bridging Lake Pontchartrain," *New York Times*, November 1, 1881, 1; and Ellis, "Working Through a Forest of Change," especially 7–33.
5. Hardy, *No Compromise with Principle*, 29–43.
6. Ibid., 29–43.
7. Ibid., 42–57, quoted on 57. Examples of Hardy's affection for Sallie are seen throughout his letters to her, all of which can be found in box 2, W&S Hardy Papers.

8. "Register," "Company Muster-In Roll," and "Officers Pay Account (June 1–June 30, 1862)," Compiled Service Records of Confederate Soldiers Who Served in Organizations from Mississippi, 16th Infantry, Go–Hi, roll #242, National Archives.
9. William H. Hardy to Sallie Hardy, Manassas, VA, August 21, 1861, box 2, W&S Hardy Papers; William Hardy to Sallie Hardy, April 22, 1862, Gordonsville, VA, box 2, W&S Hardy Papers; and William Hardy to Sally Hardy, September 7, 1862, Camp near Frederick, MD, box 2, W&S Hardy Papers. For a discussion of the early Civil War in Virginia, see Edward Ayers, *In The Presence of Mine Enemies: War In the Heart of America, 1859–1863* (New York: Norton, 2003).
10. For more on the Civil War experiences of the Mississippi 16th Infantry, see Robert G. Evans, ed., *The Sixteenth Mississippi Infantry: Civil War Letters and Reminiscences* (Jackson: University Press of Mississippi, 2002). Hardy left the military in October 1864. William Hardy to Sallie, October 15, 1864, Bivouac near Lafayette, GA, box 2, W&S Hardy Papers.
11. James W. Garner, *Reconstruction in Mississippi* (Baton Rouge: Louisiana State University Press, 1968, orig., 1901), 122–146, one-third, one-fifth, $25 million, and 44 percent statistics taken from 122–125, quoted on 122; and Donald B. Dodd, ed., *Historical Statistics of the States of the United States: Two Centuries of the Census, 1790–1990* (Westport, CT: Greenwood Press, 1993), farm values and cotton statistic found on 201. The available capital for investment was even more limited considering that from 1860 to 1870, the number of farms increased from 42,840 to 68,023.
12. Hiram Revels was appointed to the US Senate by the Mississippi State Senate, and he served for just over one year. See Eric Foner, *Reconstruction: America's Unfinished Revolution, 1863–1877* (New York: Harper & Row, 1988); and Vernon Lane Wharton, *The Negro in Mississippi, 1865–1890* (New York: Harper & Row, 1947), especially 172–180.
13. Stanley F. Horn, *Invisible Empire: The Story of the Ku Klux Klan, 1866–1871* (Montclair, NJ: Patterson Smith, Reprint Series in Criminology, Law Enforcement, and Social Problems, 1969, originally published in 1939); and Allen W. Trelease, *White Terror: The Ku Klux Klan Conspiracy and Southern Reconstruction* (Baton Rouge: Louisiana State University Press, 1995, orig., 1971), especially 287–301.
14. Edward Mayes, *Lucius Q. C. Lamar, His Life, Times and Speeches* (Nashville, TN: Publishing House of the Methodist Episcopal Church South, 1896); and Wirt Armstrong Cate, *Lucius Q. C. Lamar: Secession and Reunion* (Chapel Hill: University of North Carolina Press, 1935).
15. "Every city . . ." quoted in "Death of Senator Sumner," *New York Times*, March 12, 1874, 1. For more on Sumner, see David H. Donald, *Charles Sumner*

and the Coming of the Civil War (New York: Knopf, 1960); and David H. Donald, *Charles Sumner and the Rights of Man* (New York: Knopf, 1970).

16. Lamar's eulogy is quoted from Thomas Brackett Reed, Rossiter Johnson, Justin McCarthy, and Albert Ellery Bergh, eds., *Modern Eloquence*, vol. 8 (Philadelphia, PA: John D. Morris and Company, 1900), 767–773.
17. Edward Mayes "touched the . . ." quoted in Dunbar Rowland, *History of Mississippi: The Heart of the South*, vol. 2 (Chicago, IL: S. J. Clarke Publishing Co., 1925), 179; and John F. Kennedy, *Profiles in Courage* (New York: Harper & Row, 1964, memorial ed., orig., 1956), quoted on 174 and 173, respectively.
18. Captain William Harris Hardy, "Reconstruction in East and Southeast Mississippi," *Publications of the Mississippi Historical Society*, vol. 4, 1901, 105–132, quoted on 132.
19. The 174 number is taken from Julius E. Thompson, *Lynchings in Mississippi: A History, 1865–1965* (Jefferson, NC: McFarland & Co., 2007), 12. For more on the 1871 Meridian Race Riot, see Allen W. Trelease, *White Terror: The Ku Klux Klan Conspiracy and Southern Reconstruction* (Baton Rouge: Louisiana State University Press, 1995, orig., 1971), 290–293; and Stephen Cresswell, *Rednecks, Redeemers, and Race: Mississippi after Reconstruction, 1877–1917* (Jackson: University Press of Mississippi, 2006).
20. Hardy quoted in Dunbar Rowland, *History of Mississippi: The Heart of the South*, vol. 2 (Chicago, IL: S. J. Clarke Publishing Co., 1925), 169; and "a necessity . . ." and "great boon . . ." in Hardy, "Reconstruction in East and Southeast Mississippi," 131.
21. Hardy, *No Compromise with Principle*, especially 111–137; and obituary clippings found in Oversize Materials box, folder 2, W&S Hardy Papers.
22. Garner, *Reconstruction in Mississippi*, 375–381; and "Ames and His Raiding Army," *Hinds County Gazette*, October 13, 1875, 1.
23. "The Meeting at Auburn," *Hinds County Gazette*, October 20, 1875, 1; and *Macon Beacon* and *Jackson Clarion* quoted in Garner, *Reconstruction in Mississippi*, 373 and 383, respectively.
24. Wharton, *The Negro in Mississippi*, 194; Henry B. Whitfield to E. Pierrepont, November 6, 1875, reprinted in Bond, ed., *Mississippi: A Documentary History*, "breaking and shattering . . ." quoted on 136–137; and Nicholas Lemann, *Redemption: The Last Battle of the Civil War* (New York: Farrar, Straus and Giroux, 2006), "had become . . ." quoted on 119.
25. "The Mississippi Case," *Hinds County Gazette*, January 5, 1876, 4; and "Our Late Election," *Hinds County Gazette*, November 17, 1875, 1. For pacts of economic discrimination, see Garner, *Reconstruction in Mississippi*, especially 393–394, quoted on 393.
26. Soon-to-be ousted Republic governor Adelbert Ames dubbed Lamar the "orator" of the Democrats. See Blanche Ames, *Adelbert Ames, 1835–1933:*

General, Senator, Governor, the Story of His Life and Times and His Integrity as a Soldier and Statesman in the Service of the United States of America throughout the Civil War and in Mississippi in the Years of Reconstruction (New York: Argosy-Antiquarian, LTD, 1964), 413; Claude G. Bowers, *The Tragic Era: The Revolution after Lincoln* (New York: Blue Ribbon Books, 1940, orig., 1929), quoted on 455; and Garner, *Reconstruction in Mississippi*, quoted on 375.

27. Toney Hardy, *No Compromise with Principle*, 108–163; "Memorial of Hattie L. Hardy," box 2, folder 9, W&H Hardy Papers.
28. Mayes, *Lucius Q. C. Lamar*, quoted on 329. For more on the results of the 1875 election, see Garner, *Reconstruction in Mississippi*, 395–401, Yazoo County statistic on 395. There are widespread arguments for the lack of government intervention. It is certain, however, that the federal government was informed of the fraud and intimidation. During the months before the election, Mississippi Republicans warned of impending violence. They also reported Election Day intimidation and voter fraud directly to US Attorney General Edwards Pierrepont, but received no federal assistance. See Lemann, *Redemption*, especially 135–209; Wharton, *The Negro in Mississippi*, 181–198; and Cresswell, *Rednecks, Redeemers, and Race.*
29. For more on the Compromise of 1877 and Lamar's centrality to the agreement, see C. Vann Woodward, *Origins of the New South, 1877–1913* (Baton Rouge: Louisiana State University Press, 1971 edition, orig., 1951), 1–50; C. Vann Woodward, *Reunion and Reaction: The Compromise of 1877 and the End of Reconstruction* (New York: Oxford University Press, 1991, orig., 1951); C. Vann Woodward, "Yes, There Was a Compromise of 1877," *Journal of American History* 60, no. 1 (June, 1973): 215–223; and Michael Les Benedict, "Southern Democrats and the Crisis of 1876–1877: A Reconsideration of *Reunion and Reaction*," *Journal of Southern History*, 46 (November 1980): 489–524.
30. The sources cited in the previous note support this interpretation. Some Republicans were impeached, while others, including Governor Ames, resigned or served the final years of their terms.
31. See John F. Stover, *The Railroads of the South, 1865–1900: A Study in Finance and Control* (Chapel Hill: University of North Carolina Press, 1955), 3–15; Aaron W. Marrs, *Railroads in the Old South: Pursuing Progress in a Slave Society* (Baltimore, MD: Johns Hopkins University Press, 2009); Davis, *The Southern Railway*, especially 118–127; and "Third and Fourth Annual Reports of the Railroad Commission of the State of Mississippi for the Years Ending September 30, 1888 and 1889," 16, MDAH. For more on early Southern railroad debates, see Craig Miner, *A Most Magnificent Machine: America Adopts the Railroad, 1825–1862* (Lawrence: University Press of Kansas, 2010), especially 156–171.

32. National railroad mileage statistic taken from John F. Stover, *History of the Illinois Central Railroad* (New York: Macmillan Publishing Co., 1975), 172–174; Stover, *The Railroads of the South, 1865–1900*, 190 and xviii, respectively, for Southern railroad mileage and percentage controlled by Northerners, and 130–134 for construction costs; William C. Harris, *Presidential Reconstruction in Mississippi* (Baton Rouge: Louisiana State University Press, 1967), especially 23–24 for railroad costs; and Nollie W. Hickman, *Mississippi Harvest: Lumbering in the Longleaf Pinebelt, 1840–1915* (Jackson: University Press of Mississippi, 1962), especially 68–100. For more on state and federal land policies and Northern investment, Paul Wallace Gates, "Federal Land Policy in the South, 1866–1888," *Journal of Southern History* 6, no. 3 (August 1940): 303–330.
33. "Judge William Harris Hardy," box 2, folder 8, W&H Hardy Papers; and "Bridging Lake Pontchartrain," *New York Times*, November 1, 1881, 1. For more on Southern attorneys working for Northern-owned railroads, see William G. Thomas, *Lawyering for the Railroad: Business, Law, and Power in the New South* (Baton Rouge: Louisiana State University Press, 1999).
34. "Judge William Harris Hardy," box 2, folder 8, W&H Hardy Papers; and "Bridging Lake Pontchartrain," *New York Times*, November 1, 1881, 1. For more on Hardy's Moonshine Bridge, see Davis, *The Southern Railway*, 186–187.
35. "Judge William Harris Hardy," box 2, folder 8, W&H Hardy Papers; and "Bridging Lake Pontchartrain," *New York Times*, November 1, 1881, 1; and Toney Hardy, *No Compromise with Principle*. For more on Lake Pontchartrain's historical dimensions, see Robert W. Hastings, *The Lakes of Pontchartrain: Their History and Environments* (Jackson: University Press of Mississippi, 2012), especially 163–167.
36. "Through From Meridian," *The Daily Picayune*, October 16, 1883, 4; "Opening of the New Orleans and Northeastern," *Chicago Tribune*, October 17, 1883, 3; "Current Comment," *Washington Post*, July 4, 1883, 2; "The New Orleans and Northeastern," *Chicago Tribune*, September 21, 1882, 7; and Davis, *The Southern Railway*, 186–187.
37. "Fast Running on a Railroad," *New York Times*, February 25, 1884, 5. For more on the role of steamboats in the Mississippi River Valley, see Walter Johnson, *River of Dark Dreams: Slavery and Empire in the Cotton Kingdom* (Cambridge, MA: Harvard University Press, 2013), especially 73–150. The estimate of steamboat speed is based on the record-setting time of the *R. E. Lee* in 1870.
38. US Bureau of the Census, *Census of the Population: 1890*, vol. 1, *Population*, part 1 (Washington, DC: Government Printing Office, 1895), 378–388. For more on the social impact of the spread of Southern railroads, see Edward L. Ayers, *The Promise of the New South: Life after Reconstruction* (New York: Oxford University Press, 1992), especially 3–33.

39. Statistics taken from "Third and Fourth Annual Reports of the Railroad Commission of the State of Mississippi for the Years Ending September 30, 1888 and 1889," 16 and 55; S. G. Thigpen, *A Boy in Rural Mississippi & Other Stories* (Kingsport, TN: Kingsport Press, 1966), quoted on 116; and "Hattiesburg: A Thriving Mississippi Town on the Northeastern Railroad," *New Orleans Daily Picayune*, May 1, 1893, 6.
40. "Sullivan Deposits His $5,000," *New York Times*, April 16, 1889, 8; "Preparing for the Fight," *New York Times*, July 2, 1889, 5; "Before the Battle," *Chicago Daily Tribune*, July 7, 1889, 9; and "Victor and Vanquished," *Chicago Daily Tribune*, July 10, 1889, 2. Mississippi's governor had also forbidden the fight, but his order was ignored until August, when both fighters were indicted for its violation. "Indictments Found," *New York Times*, August 15, 1889, 2; and "Jake Kilrain Dies; Fought Sullivan," *New York Times*, December 23, 1937, 21.
41. "Victor and Vanquished," *Chicago Daily Tribune*, July 10, 1889, 2; and Richard Hoffer, "Fisticuffs John L. Sullivan & Jake Kilrain in the Brawl that Started it All," *Sports Illustrated*, May 6, 2002.
42. "Judge William Harris Hardy," box 2, folder 8, W&H Hardy Papers.
43. Robert Kral, "Pinus palustrus," in Flora of North America Editorial Committee, eds., *Florida of North America North of Mexico*, vol. 2, *Pteridophytes and Gymnosperms* (New York: Oxford University Press, 1993), 386–387; "A Study of the Effect of Fire on Longleaf Pine," box 105, folder 2, Bilbo (Theodore) Papers, USM; and Hickman, *Mississippi Harvest*, 2–3.
44. F. Andrew Michaux and Thomas Nuttall, *The North American Sylva; or A Description of the Forest Trees of the United States, Canada, and Nova Scotia* (Philadelphia, PA: J. Dobson, 1842), 160–166.
45. "Doom of the White Pine," *Chicago Daily Tribune*, July 26, 1896, 33. Also see, Robert Kral, "Pinus strobus," in *Florida of North America North of Mexico*, vol. 2, *Pteridophytes and Gymnosperms*, 379–380; and William Cronon, *Nature's Metropolis: Chicago and the Great West* (New York City: Norton, 1991), 148–206.
46. Stephen Kern, *The Culture of Time and Space: 1880–1918* (Cambridge, MA: Harvard University Press, 2003, orig. 1983); and David E. Nye, *Electrifying America: Social Meanings of a New Technology, 1880–1940* (Cambridge, MA: MIT Press, 1990). For more on longleaf pine and utility poles, see Edwin B. Kurtz, Thomas M. Shoemaker, and James E. Mack, *The Lineman's and Cableman's Handbook* (New York: McGraw-Hill, 1997, orig., 1955), 7.1.
47. Nye, *Electrifying America*, "forest of tall poles" quote on 47–48; James E. Fickle, *Mississippi: Forests and Forestry* (Jackson: University Press of Mississippi, 2001), five hundred million statistic on 80; and Long quoted in Nollie W. Hickman, "Mississippi Forests," in Richard Aubrey McLemore, ed., *A History of Mississippi*, vol. 2 (Hattiesburg: University & College Press of Mississippi, 1973), 214.

48. Fickle, *Mississippi: Forests and Forestry*, especially 50–64; and Hickman, *Mississippi Harvest*, especially 1–120.
49. For more on rafting, see Hickman, *Mississippi Harvest*, 17 and 106–113. In 1932, the *Hattiesburg American* reported that Captain Hardy observed floating timber rafts during his lunch, but there is no definitive evidence to support the claim. See "Memories Stirred in Many by Golden Jubilee Play, Some High Spots Are Noted," *Hattiesburg American*, October 15, 1932, 1.
50. Twain's *Life on the Mississippi* opens with a vignette titled the "Body of the Nation," which was previously published in the February 1863 edition of *Harper's Magazine*.
51. "Address of the Commissioners of the Gulf and Ship Island Railroad," delivered in Jackson, MS, June 7, 1858, reprinted in "Address of the Commissioners of the Gulf and Ship Island Railroad" (Jackson: Mississippi Steam Power Press Print, 1858), quoted on 16.
52. Civil War records taken from Rowland, *History of Mississippi*, vol. 2, 22–27 and 44–51, "covered themselves . . ." quoted on 45–46; and Donald Philip Duclos, *Sons of Sorrow: The Life, Works, and Influence of Colonel William C. Falkner, 1825–1889* (San Francisco, CA: International Scholars Publications, 1998).
53. "The Gulf and Ship Island Road," *New York Times*, March 14, 1883, 4; "Minutes of April 16, 1884 Meeting," Gulf & Ship Island Railroad Minute Book, 13–15, G&SI Papers; "Minutes of February 11, 1886 Meeting," Gulf & Ship Island Railroad Minute Book, 76–77, G&SI Papers. Biographical sketches taken from Rowland, *History of Mississippi*, vol. 2, 22–27 and 47–51; Arthur F. Kinney, ed., *Critical Essays on William Faulkner: The Sartoris Family* (Boston, MA: G. K. Hall, 1985); Donald Philip Duclos, *Sons of Sorrow*, "self-assumed" quoted on 96; and Philip Weinstein, *Becoming Faulkner: The Art and Life of William Faulkner* (New York: Oxford University Press, 2010), especially 73–77.
54. "Judge William Harris Hardy," box 2, folder 8, W&H Hardy Papers; Hardy, *No Compromise with Principle*, 229–240; "The Gulf and Ship Island," *The Daily Picayune*, November 12, 1884, 6; and Federal Writers' Project, *Mississippi: A Guide to the Magnolia State* (New York: Hastings House, 1946, orig., 1938), 192–197.
55. Various Minutes and Records found in Gulf & Ship Island Railroad Minute Book, copy of convict-lease agreement on 31, G&SI Papers.
56. See Ruby E. Cooley, "A History of the Mississippi Penal Farm System, 1890–1935: Punishment, Politics, and Profit in Penal Affairs" (master's thesis, University of Southern Mississippi, 1981), especially 12–16.
57. 1882 death rate taken from David M. Oshinsky, *"Worse Than Slavery": Parchman Farm and the Ordeal of Jim Crow Justice* (New York: Free Press, 1997), 46, "sweat boxes" quoted on 44–45. For more on conditions of Southern convict-labor, see Walter Wilson, *Forced Labor in the United States* (New York:

International Publishers, 1933), especially 68–83. For more on convict-lease labor, see Edward Ayers, *Vengeance and Justice: Crime and Punishment in the Nineteenth Century American South* (New York: Oxford University Press, 1984), 185–222; and Douglas A. Blackmon, *Slavery by Another Name: The Re-Enslavement of Black Americans from the Civil War to World War I* (New York: Anchor Books, 2009).

58. Minutes of December 7, 1886 Meeting," Gulf & Ship Island Railroad Minute Book, 76–77, G&SI Papers; "Repealing the Exemption Law," *The Biloxi Herald*, February 11, 1888, 1; "Gulfport Gossip," *The Biloxi Herald*, March 17, 1888, 1; and "Gulfport Gossip," *The Biloxi Herald*, April 7, 1888, 8.

59. William Harris Hardy to Hattie Lott Hardy, London, England, July 11, 1888, box 1, folder 2, W&H Hardy Papers. Dozens of letters from Hardy's New York and London trips to his wife Hattie can be found in box 1, folders 2–3 of the Hardy Papers.

60. "Biennial Report of the Board of Control, Superintendent, General Manager and Other Officers of the Mississippi State Penitentiary, for the years 1888 and 1889," J. F. Sessions, Chairman, quoted on 23, MDAH; 225 statistic taken from "The Convict Lease Appealed," *The Biloxi Herald*, December 15, 1888, 5; "Convicts on a Railroad," *New York Times*, December 4, 1888, 2; testimonies quoted in Andrew English, *"All Off for Gordon's Station": A History of the Early Hattiesburg, Mississippi Area* (Baltimore, MD: Gateway Press, 2000), 60 and 61, respectively; James Lemly, *The Gulf, Mobile, and Ohio: A Railroad That Had to Expand or Expire* (Homewood, IL: Richard D. Irwin, Inc., 1953), death rate statistics on 290; and Cooley, "A History of the Mississippi Penal Farm System, 1890–1935," especially 18–20.

61. Hardy statement to the *Meridian News* taken from "Mr. Hardy's Statement," *The Clarion-Ledger*, December 13, 1888, 2; "The Gulf and Ship Island Railroad," *Biloxi Herald*, December 15, 1888, 5; and "but for the howl . . ." "Pine Lands," *Louisville Courier Journal*, August 12, 1899, 2.

62. "An Era of Tragedies," *Washington Post*, August 28, 1900, 4; "Death of Col. W. C. Falkner," *The Clarion-Ledger*, November 14, 1889, 4; William Harris Hardy to Hattie Hardy, New York City, November 7, 1889, box 1, folder 3, W&H Hardy Papers; William Harris Hardy to Hattie Hardy, New York City, November 8, 1889, box 1, folder 3, W&H Hardy Papers; and William Harris Hardy to Hattie Hardy, Chicago, IL, June 27, 1891, box 1, folder 4, W&H Hardy Papers.

63. Inspector M. M. Evans quoted in *Sixth Biennial Report of the Railroad Commission of the State of Mississippi for the Two Years, Ending June 30, 1897* (Jackson, MS: The Clarion-Ledger Print, 1898), 15.

64. Michael A. Leeson, *History of the Counties of McKean, Elk, and Forest, Pennsylvania* (Chicago, IL: J. H. Beers & Co., 1890), Jones biographical sketch found on 369–370; Melodia B. Rowe, *Captain Jones—the Biography of a*

Builder (Hamilton, OH: Hill-Brown Printing Company, 1942); Henry W. Black, *Gulfport: Beginnings and Growth* (Bowling Green, KY: Rivendell Publications, 1986), 14–15; "Mrs. J. T. Jones Dies; Noted for Charity," *New York Times*, March 13, 1931, 21; "Pointed and Stimulating," *Biloxi Daily Herald*, November 26, 1906, 1; and Minutes of August 17 and August 18, 1896 Meetings, Gulf & Ship Island Railroad Minute Book, 154–155, G&SI Papers.

65. Rowe, *Captain Jones*, especially 232–234; Samuel Holloway Bowers, interview by Debra Spencer, recording, October 24, 1983, Jackson, MS, MDAH; and 1900 U.S. Census, Hancock County, Population Schedule, Bay St. Louis, sheet 5, dwelling 91, family 91, Eaton J. Bowers, digital image, Ancestry.com, accessed June 18, 2014.

66. Minutes of August 18, 1896, and June 7, 1897, Meetings, Gulf & Ship Island Railroad Minute Book, 154–155, G&SI Papers; $100,000 statistic taken from Rowe, *Captain Jones*, 141; "Minutes of June 7, 1897 Meeting," Gulf & Ship Island Railroad Minute Book, 186–187, G&SI Papers; and "Minutes of May 3, 1902 Meeting," Gulf & Ship Island Railroad Minute Book, 246, G&SI Papers. For more on the Gulf & Ship Island Railroad, see Stover, *History of the Illinois Central*, 293–295; Hickman, *Mississippi Harvest*, 66–86; Fickle, *Mississippi Forests and Forestry*, 75; Hickman, "Mississippi Forests," in McLemore, ed., A *History of Mississippi*, vol. 2, 215; and John Ray Skates, "Hattiesburg: The Early Years," in *Hattiesburg: A Pictorial History*, ed. Kenneth G. McCarty Jr. (Jackson: University Press of Mississippi, 1982), 5–11.

67. "Pine Lands," *Louisville Courier Journal*, August 12, 1899, 2; "An Era of Tragedies: History of the Gulf and Ship Island Railroad," the *Washington Post*, August 28, 1900, 4; and "New Railroad Line to Mexican Gulf," *Nashville American*, September 1, 1900, 4.

68. "hundreds of millions . . ." quoted in "Mississippi's New Seaport," *Nashville American*, November 30, 1902, 18; 225 million statistic from "Gulf & Ship Island Railroad," *Wall Street Journal*, July 14, 1905, 8; "leading . . ." quoted from "Gulf & Ship Island," *Wall Street Journal*, October 22, 1904, 7; 800 million from "Another Road to Gulfport," *Wall Street Journal*, October 27, 1906, 3; and $2.5 million statistic from "Gulf & Ship Island's Year," *Wall Street Journal*, September 25, 1907, 6.

69. By 1902, the *Hattiesburg Daily Progress* routinely referred to Gulfport as the "Newport of the South"; US Bureau of the Census, *Census of the Population: 1910*, vol. 2, *Population, Alabama-Montana* (Washington, DC: Government Printing Office, 1913), 1046–1047; and "Capt. Hardy Ought to Have No Opposition," *Hattiesburg Daily Progress*, July 22, 1902, 2.

70. "Gulfport Mississippi," *Atlanta Constitution*, March 11, 1906, E2; and "Sitting in the hotel . . ." quoted in Wardon Allan Curtis, "Labor for Lumber Camps: A Would-be Man Stealer Tells How Unsophisticated Sailors Fooled Him," *New*

York Times, June 9, 1901, SM20. This description of the Great Southern Hotel is drawn from historical postcards produced between 1902 and the late 1940s found in Postcard Collection, USM. For more on the Great Southern Hotel Orchestra, see Lawrence Gushee, *Pioneers of Jazz: The Story of the Creole Band* (New York: Oxford University Press, 2005), 66.

71. "So vivid . . ." quoted from "Great Will Be Gulfport," *Hattiesburg Daily Progress*, June 27, 1902, 2; and Jones's Gulfport contributions are taken from "Mrs. J. T. Jones Dies; Noted for Charity," *New York Times*, March 13, 1931, 21; Black, *Gulfport*, 9–52; "Captain Jones Dies at Buffalo Home," *Hattiesburg American*, December 6, 1916, 1; and "Mississippi's New Seaport," *Nashville American*, November 30, 1902, 18.
72. Sheet 8, Hattiesburg, MS, March 1910, Sanborn Maps Company Ltd., Digital Sanborn Maps, 1867–1970; and McCarty, ed., *Hattiesburg*, 30–31.
73. "Menu from the Banquet Celebrating the Opening of the Hotel Hattiesburg," "Hotel Hattiesburg Grand Opening Musical Program," and "Hotel Hattiesburg Opening: A List of Toasts," all found in box 1, folder 3, HHP.
74. "Hotel Hattiesburg Opening: A List of Toasts," box 1, folder 3, HHP.
75. "Pointed and Stimulating," *Biloxi Daily Herald*, November 26, 1906, 1.
76. "Pointed and Stimulating," *Biloxi Daily Herald*, November 26, 1906, 1. Jones's wound is described in Leeson, *History of the Counties*, 369–370.
77. Rowe, *Captain Jones*; and Leeson, *History of the Counties*, 369–370. The positioning and movements of the 91st Pennsylvania Infantry and 16th Mississippi Infantry during the battles of Fredericksburg, Chancellorsville, and Gettysburg can be found in Colonel Vincent J. Esposito, chief ed., *The West Point Atlas of American Wars*, vol. 1, 1689–1900 (New York: Frederick A. Praeger Publishers, 1959), maps 72 a & b, 86, and 98 a & b, respectively. For more on Company H of the Pennsylvania 91st Regiment of Volunteers, see the Pennsylvania Volunteers of the Civil War website, www.pa-roots.com/pacw/infantry/91st/91stcoh.html.
78. Hardy, *No Compromise with Principle*, 308; Rowe, *Captain Jones*, 259–260; and Theodore G. Bilbo, "Judge William Harris Hardy" Memorial Dedication Speech, January 6, 1929, Gulfport, MS, transcript in box 2, folder 1, W&H Hardy Papers.
79. Bowers, interview.

2. *The Bottom Rail*

Epigraph: "Berta, Berta" was an early twentieth-century work song commonly sung by black laborers, especially prisoners, in the Deep South. For more, see Ted Goia, *Work Songs* (Durham, NC: Duke University Press, 2006), especially 200–224.

1. E. Hammond Smith, interview by Orley B. Caudill, Hattiesburg, MS, April 8, 1982, transcript, USM-OH.

2. Smith, interview.
3. Observations made at the gravesite of Turner Roger Smith, River View Cemetery, Hattiesburg, MS, on June 25, 2014. According to one of his sons, Turner, who was born in 1859, never spoke about slavery, but the children understood that he had been enslaved as a child. For a general overview of early Mississippi history, the cotton gin, and Mississippi migration, see Angela Lakwete, *Inventing the Cotton Gin: Machine and Myth in Antebellum America* (Baltimore, MD: Johns Hopkins University Press, 2003); Charles D. Lowery, "The Great Migration to the Mississippi Territory, 1798–1819," *Journal of Mississippi History* 30 (August 1968): 173–192; Richard Aubrey McLemore, ed., *A History of Mississippi* (Hattiesburg: University & College Press of Mississippi, 1973); and Westley F. Busbee Jr., *Mississippi: A History* (Wheeling, IL: Harlan Davidson, Inc., 2005).
4. "Statistics of Cotton and Internal Commerce," in Stewart Bruchey, *Cotton and the Growth of the American Economy, 1790–1860* (New York: Random House, 1967), Mississippi cotton statistics on 18; US Bureau of the Census, *Census of the Population: 1820*, vol. 1 (Washington, DC: Gales & Seaton, 1821), 30; US Bureau of the Census, *Census of the Population: 1860*, vol. 1, *Population* (Washington, DC: Government Printing Office, 1864), 270; and enslaved statistic taken from Donald B. Dodd, *Historical Statistics of the States of the United States: Two Centuries of the Census, 1790–1990* (Westport, CT: Greenwood Press, 1993), 49.
5. Walter Johnson, *River of Dark Dreams: Slavery and Empire in the Cotton Kingdom* (Cambridge, MA: Harvard University Press, 2013), quoted on 174; and Lillie Williams quoted in Andrew Waters, ed., *Prayin' to Be Set Free: Personal Accounts of Slavery in Mississippi* (Winston-Salem, NC: John F. Blair, 2002), 65.
6. Neil McMillen, *Dark Journey: Black Mississippians in the Age of Jim Crow* (Urbana: University of Illinois Press, 1990), 111–153, "their niggers" quoted on 141.
7. For more on sharecropping, see Leon F. Litwack, *Trouble in Mind: Black Southerners in the Age of Jim Crow* (New York: Vintage, 1998), 114–178; Pete Daniel, *The Shadow of Slavery: Peonage in the South, 1902–1969* (Urbana: University of Illinois Press, 1972); and McMillen, *Dark Journey*, 111–153.
8. Smith, interview.
9. Ibid.
10. Ibid.
11. W. E. B. Du Bois, *Black Reconstruction in America: An Essay Toward a History of the Part Which Black Folk Played in the Attempt to Reconstruct Democracy in America, 1860–1880* (New York: Russell & Russell, 1935), 637. For more on the struggle of enslaved and newly emancipated African Americans to gain

literacy, see Heather Williams, *Self-Taught: African American Education in Slavery and Freedom* (Chapel Hill: University of North Carolina Press, 2005); and Christopher Span, *From Cotton Field to Schoolhouse: African American Education in Mississippi, 1862–1875* (Chapel Hill: University of North Carolina Press, 2009).

12. Josephine L. Nicks, quoted in "Teacher's Monthly School Report, For the Month of October 1866," Teachers' Monthly School Reports, October 1865–November 1868, roll 1, M 1907, FBR; "Report of Schools," Mississippi Natchez District, October, 1866, & "Report of Schools," Natchez District, July 1867, Miscellaneous Reports Sent to the Assistant Commissioner, March, 1866–October, 1868, roll 37, M 1907, FBR; "Monthly Report of Freedmen's School at Jackson, County of Hinds, State of Mississippi, for the month of December 1865, Teachers' Monthly School Reports, October 1865–November 1868, roll 1, M 1907, FBR; and Janet Sharp Hermann, *The Pursuit of a Dream* (New York: Oxford University Press, 1981), Davis Bend quote on 183.

13. "Half" estimate taken from Du Bois, *Black Reconstruction in America*, 648; Joseph Warren, "Letter to the Colored People of Vicksburg," December 15, 1865, Letters Sent from Superintendent, vol. 1 (49), July–December, 1865, roll 1, M 1907, FBR; "Monthly Report of Freedmen's School at Macon, County of Noxubee, State of Mississippi for the Month ending July 31st, 1866," Teachers' Monthly School Reports, October 1865–November 1868, roll 1, M 1907, FBR; Williams, *Self-Taught*, $658 statistic on 93; "had become obsessed . . ." quoted in Joseph Warren, "Letter to Rev. George," May 16, 1866, Letters Sent from Superintendent, vol. 2 (50), January–June, 1866, roll 1, M 1907, FBR; "if the colored people do not . . ." quoted from Joseph Warren, "Letter to Miss May," November 29, 1865, Letters Sent from Superintendent, vol. 1 (49), July–December, 1865, roll 1, M 1907, FBR; and "they have made . . ." quoted in "Monthly Report of Freedmen's School at Aberdeen, County of Monroe, State of Mississippi for the month ending June 30th, 1866," Teachers' Monthly School Reports, October 1865–November 1868, roll 1, M 1907, FBR; and "Monthly Report of Freedmen's School at Aberdeen, County of Monroe, State of Mississippi for the month ending July 31st, 1866," Teachers' Monthly School Reports, October 1865–November 1868, roll 1, M 1907, FBR.

14. "Mississippi School Law," *Hinds County Gazette*, April 20, 1870, 1; Vernon Lane Wharton, *The Negro in Mississippi*, especially 243–247; Stuart Grayson Noble, *Forty Years of the Public Schools in Mississippi, With Special Reference to the Education of the Negro* (New York: AMS Press, 1918); and Charles C. Bolton, *The Hardest Deal of All: The Battle over School Integration in Mississippi, 1870–1980* (Jackson: University Press of Mississippi, 2005), especially 3–13.

15. For more on the establishment of Mississippi's first African American colleges, see Edward Mayes, *History of Education in Mississippi* (Washington, DC: Government Printing Office, 1899), especially 259–277, $13,000 statistic on 259; Josephine Posey, *Against Great Odds: The History of Alcorn State University* (Jackson: University Press of Mississippi, 1994); and Wharton, *The Negro in Mississippi, 1865–1890*, especially 250–255.
16. Jay Samuel Stowell, *Methodist Adventures in Negro Education* (New York: The Methodist Book Concern, 1922), especially 129–133 for the Haven Institute; and Noble, *Forty Years of the Public Schools in Mississippi*, 139 and 141, respectively, for enrollment and teacher statistics.
17. Smith, interview; and 1900 U.S. Census, Perry County, Mississippi, Population Schedule, Hattiesburg, sheet 16, dwelling 457, family 508, Smith family, digital image, Ancestry.com, accessed August 13, 2013.
18. 1900 U.S. Census, Perry County, Mississippi, Population Schedule, Hattiesburg, sheet 16, dwelling 457, family 508, Smith family, digital image, accessed August 13, 2013, Ancestry.com; and Smith, interview.
19. State Financial figures taken from James W. Garner, *Reconstruction in Mississippi* (Baton Rouge: Louisiana State University Press, 1968, orig., 1901), 320–321. White teachers' salaries were also cut, but not nearly as much as those of African Americans, leading to increasing pay disparities. By 1910, white instructors were earning twice the salary of their African American counterparts. Teacher salaries taken from Noble, *Forty Years of the Public Schools in Mississippi*, 141–142; Charles Bolton, *The Hardest Deal of All*; Horace Mann Bond, *The Education of the Negro in the American Social Order* (New York: Octagon Books, 1970, orig., 1934), 92–97; and McMillen, *Dark Journey*, especially 72–108.
20. Noble, *Forty Years of the Public Schools in Mississippi*, 141–142; Turner Smith quoted in Smith, interview; and 1900 US Census, Perry County, Mississippi, Population Schedule, Hattiesburg, sheet 16, dwelling 457, family 508, Smith family, digital image, accessed August 13, 2013, Ancestry.com.
21. These examples are taken from census records of Hattiesburg's Third and Fourth Ward taken in 1900.
22. Dodd, *Historical Statistics of the States of the United States*, 49–50; and US Bureau of the Census, *Census of the Population: 1900*, vol. 13, *Occupations* (Washington, DC: US Census Office, 1902), 316 and 318.
23. US Bureau of the Census, *Census of the Population: 1910*, vol. 4, *Population Occupation Statistics* (Washington, DC: Government Printing Office, 1913), 480. For more, see Joseph Kelly, "Organized for a Fair Deal: African American Railroad Workers in the Deep South, 1900–1940 (PhD diss., University of Toronto, 2010).

24. *Census of the Population: 1910*, vol. 4, *Population Occupation Statistics*, 480. As railroad historian Theodore Kornweibel argues, "So long as railroads could replace them with blacks, white firemen had to accept inferior pay, compared to firemen outside the South, and think long and hard about risking their jobs by striking." For more on African American railroad workers, see Theodore Kornweibel Jr., *Railroads in the African American Experience: A Photographic Journey* (Baltimore, MD: Johns Hopkins University Press, 2010), especially 62–167 for black railroad jobs, quoted on 68–69; and Eric Arnesen, *Brotherhoods of Color: Black Railroad Workers and the Struggle for Equality* (Cambridge, MA: Harvard University Press, 2001), especially 116–150.
25. Southern lumberman S. S. Henry quoted in Robert Adam Ellis, "Working Through a Forest of Change: An Environmental, Labor, and Social History of the Greater Hattiesburg, Mississippi Area, 1880–1910," (master's thesis, University of Southern Mississippi, 2005); and *Census of the Population: 1910*, vol. 4, *Population Occupation Statistics*, sawmill employment statistics found on 480. For more on African Americans in the Southern lumber industry, see William P. Jones, *The Tribe of Black Ulysses: African American Lumber Workers in the Jim Crow South* (Urbana: University of Illinois Press, 2005).
26. Nollie W. Hickman, "Black Labor in the Forest Industries of the Piney Woods, 1840–1933," in *Mississippi's Piney Woods: A Human Perspective*, ed. Noel Polk (Jackson: University Press of Mississippi, 1986), 79–91; S. G. Thigpen, *A Boy in Rural Mississippi & Other Stories* (Kingsport, TN: Kingsport Press, 1966), especially 176–206; and Osceola McCarty, interviews by Shana Walton, Hattiesburg, MS, February 22 and 23, 1996, transcript, USM-OH.
27. Bill Lloyd taken from Gilbert H. Hoffman, *Steam Whistles in the Piney Woods: A History of the Sawmills and Logging Railroads of the Forrest and Lamar Counties, Mississippi*, vol. 1 (Hattiesburg, MS: Longleaf Press, 1998), 106–178; "Run Over by Log Train," *Hattiesburg Daily Progress*, May 9, 1903, 1; John Boyd drawn from "Negro Man Fell Between Cars; Was Killed," *Hattiesburg News*, November 14, 1912, 1; and "Explosion Sends 4 To Instant Death," *Hattiesburg News*, November 20, 1912, 1.
28. In 1910, African Americans comprised 94 percent of Mississippi turpentine workers. *Census of the Population: 1910*, vol. 4, *Population Occupation Statistics*, 480. For more on the history of naval stores in the American South, see Robert B. Outland II, *Tapping the Pines: The Naval Stores Industry in the American South* (Baton Rouge: Louisiana State University Press, 2004).
29. This description of Piney Woods turpentine harvesting is taken from an account of a former African American Piney Woods turpentine worker named Tom Walley and various oral histories with turpentine workers conducted by historian Gilbert Hoffman. See Thigpen, *A Boy in Rural Mississippi & Other Stories*,

176–206; Hoffman, *Steam Whistles in the Piney Woods*, especially 79–82; and Outland II, *Tapping the Pines.*

30. Thigpen, *A Boy in Rural Mississippi & Other Stories*, 176–206; Hoffman, *Steam Whistles in the Piney Woods*, especially 79–82; and Outland II, *Tapping the Pines.* For a description of black life in the camps, see McCarty, interview; Henry Watson, interview by Michael Vaughn, Piave, MS, June 4, 1997, transcript, USM-OH; Jones, *The Tribe of Black Ulysses*, especially 60–88; Ellis, "Working Through a Forest of Change," 93–94; and Giles Oakley, *The Devil's Music: A History of the Blues* (Cambridge, MA: Da Capo Press, 1997, orig., 1976). In 1909, 91 percent of Mississippi turpentine workers were wage earners. *Census of the Population: 1910*, vol. 9, *Manufacturers Reports by States*, 630.
31. For more on the appeal of the city to rural black farmworkers, see Lorenzo J. Greene and Carter G. Woodson, *The Negro Wage Earner* (New York: AMS Press, 1970, orig., 1930), especially 48–123.
32. *Census of the Population: 1910*, vol. 6, *Population Occupation Statistics*, 481. For more on the role of black female domestic workers in Southern Jim Crow culture, see Grace Elizabeth Hale, *Making Whiteness: The Culture of Segregation in the South, 1890–1940* (New York: Random House, 1998), especially 85–119; Tera W. Hunter, *To 'Joy My Freedom: Southern Black Women's Lives and Labors after the Civil War* (Cambridge, MA: Harvard University Press, 1998), 105; and Micki McElya, *Clinging to Mammy: The Faithful Slave in Twentieth-Century America* (Cambridge, MA: Harvard University Press, 2007).
33. For more on the nature of African American domestic work, abuse, and resistance, see Hunter, *To 'Joy My Freedom;* and Rebecca Sharpless, *Cooking in Other Women's Kitchens: Domestic Workers in the South, 1860–1960* (Chapel Hill: University of North Carolina Press, 2010); Jacqueline Jones, *Labor of Love, Labor of Sorrow: Black Women, Work, and the Family, from Slavery to the Present* (New York: Basic Books, 2010, orig., 1985), especially 103–130; and Danielle L. McGuire, *At the Dark End of the Street: Black Women, Rape, and Resistance—A New History of the Civil Rights Movement from Rosa Parks to the Rise of Black Power* (New York: Knopf, 2011). The term "emotional labor" typically refers to contemporary service-industry jobs such as waitress or nurse, but it also applies to the labor of black domestic workers who were required to perform a wide range of personal service tasks for intimately acquainted employers. See Arlie Russell Hochschild, *The Managed Heart: Commercialization of Human Feeling* (Berkeley: University of California Press, 1983).
34. "Third and Fourth Annual Reports of the Railroad Commission of the State of Mississippi for the Years Ending September 30, 1888 and 1889," 16, MDAH; US Bureau of the Census, *Census of the Population: 1880*, vol. 1, *Population* (Washington, DC: Government Printing Office, 1883), town populations on 233–237 and laundress statistic on 766–767; *Thirteenth Biennial Report of the*

Railroad Commission of the State of Mississippi for the Two Years Ending June 30, 1911 (Nashville, TN: Brandon Printing Company, 1911), 1910 railroad mileage on 82; *Census of the Population: 1910*, vol. 2, *Population, Alabama-Montana*, 1024; and *Census of the Population: 1910*, vol. 4, *Population Occupation Statistics*, 280–281.

35. McCarty, interviews.
36. Although tenant farming data for Hattiesburg proper is unavailable, there were only 142 black tenant farmers in the county in which Hattiesburg was located (which accounted for 0.1 percent of Mississippi black tenants). Very few of them, if any at all, could have lived within the city limits. *Census of the Population: 1910*, vol. 6, *Agriculture Reports by State Alabama-Montana*, 872 and 874.
37. *Louisville, New Orleans & Texas Ry. Co. v. Mississippi*, 133 US 587–595 (1890); "Mississippi School Law," *Hinds County Gazette*, April 20, 1870, 1; and Vernon Lane Wharton, *The Negro in Mississippi*, especially 243–247.
38. *Louisville, New Orleans & Texas Ry. Co. v. Mississippi*, 133 US 587–595 (1890).
39. *Louisville, New Orleans & Texas Ry. Co. v. Mississippi*, 133 US, Harlan quoted on 594.
40. Ibid.; McMillen, *Dark Journey*, 291–295, quoted on 291; and *Plessy v. Ferguson*, 163 US 537 (1896). Historical memory has painted *Plessy v. Ferguson* as the transformative case in deciding the legality of compulsory railroad car segregation, but as the *Washington Post* noted during the *Plessy* proceedings, "The practical questions at issue in the case have already been decided in favor of the validity of the law involved." See "Capital Chat," *Washington Post*, April 14, 1896, 6. Furthermore, the Plessy case was different in that it actually involved the question of a railroad conductor's ability to racially classify an individual and thus determine where they should sit. Contrary to common belief, a favorable outcome would not have had an impact on customary or legal segregation practices regarding all African Americans across the South. For a broader discussion, see Stanley J. Folmsbee, "The Origin of the First 'Jim Crow' Law," *Journal of Southern History* 15, no. 2 (May, 1949): 235–247; Charles A. Lofgren, *The Plessy Case: A Legal-Historical Interpretation* (New York: Oxford University Press, 1987); Stephen J. Riegel, "The Persistent Career of Jim Crow: Lower Federal Courts and the 'Separate but Equal' Doctrine, 1865–1896," *American Journal of Legal History* 28, no. 1 (January, 1984): 17–40; Barbara Young Welke, *Recasting American Liberty*, especially, 249–375; Lofgren, *The Plessy* Case, especially 44–60; and Mark Elliot, *Color-Blind Justice: Albion Tourgée and the Quest for Racial Equality from the Civil War to Plessy v. Ferguson* (New York: Oxford University Press, 2006), especially 262–295.
41. "A New Constitution," *Jackson Clarion-Ledger*, November 6, 1889, 1; "The Convention Called," *Atlanta Constitution*, March 12, 1890, 3; "carpet-

baggers . . ." quoted from "Sovereign Mississippi," *Atlanta Constitution*, March 4, 1890, 1; and J. B. Chrisman quoted in Bradley G. Bond, *Mississippi: A Documentary History* (Jackson: University Press of Mississippi, 2003), 171.

42. "We came here . . ." quoted in McMillen, *Dark Journey*, 41; "The Mississippi State Constitutional Convention," *Baltimore Sun*, August 15, 1890, 2; "The Mississippi Convention," *Washington Post*, August 29, 1890, 4; and Wharton, *The Negro in Mississippi, 1865–1890*, 199–215.

43. Mississippi Constitution of 1890, Article XII, Sec., 244; *Williams v. State of Mississippi*, 170 US 213 (1898); and "Mississippi's New Constitution," *Chicago Daily Tribune*, November 5, 1890, 4. The Mississippi Constitution of 1890 can be found through the Mississippi History Now website using the following link: http://mshistorynow.mdah.state.ms.us/articles/103/index.php?s=extra&id=270. Also see McMillen, *Dark Journey*, 38–48; V. O. Key, *Southern Politics: In State and Nation* (New York: Knopf, 1949), 531–643; and Michael Perman, *Struggle for Mastery: Disfranchisement in the South, 1888–1908* (Chapel Hill: University of North Carolina Press, 2001), 70–90. Mississippi was not the first state to rewrite its constitution after Reconstruction, but it was a pioneer in designing the new Jim Crow–era suffrage laws designed to circumvent the Fifteenth Amendment.

44. "Overtaken by Party of Lynchers," *Washington Post*, June 3, 1890, 1; and "Attended to Him," *Nashville American*, June 3, 1890, 1.

45. This narrative is reconstructed from corresponding reports in "Probably Burned at the Stake," *New York Times*, July 26, 1895, 2; "Probably Lynched," *Nashville American*, July 26, 1895, 1; "lifeless body . . ." quoted in "How Johnson Was Lynched," *New York Times*, July 28, 1895, 19; "riddled with buckshot" quoted in "Lynching of Tom Johnson," *Atlanta Constitution*, July 27, 1895, 1; "A Black Fiend," *Atlanta Constitution*, August 1, 1895, 5; and Ellis, "Working Through a Forest of Change," 57–58.

46. Julius E. Thompson, *Lynchings in Mississippi: A History, 1865–1965* (Jefferson, NC: McFarland, 2007), 36 and 49. See Hale, *Making Whiteness*, especially 199–239; Amy Louise Wood, *Lynching and Spectacle: Witnessing Racial Violence in America, 1890–1940* (Chapel Hill: University of North Carolina Press, 2009); and James Allen, *Without Sanctuary: Lynching Photography in America* (Santa Fe, NM: Twin Palms Publishers, 2000) for more on the importance of lynching and the spectacle of violence.

47. "Negro Was Tied to a Tree and Shot," *New York Times*, July 26, 1899, 2. This Associated Press report also appeared in the *Los Angeles Times*, the *Washington Post*, and the *Baltimore Sun* on July 26, 1899.

48. Smith, interview; US Bureau of the Census, *Census of the Population: 1900*, Perry County, Mississippi, Population Schedule, Hattiesburg, sheet 16,

dwelling 457, family 508, Smith family, digital image, accessed August 13, 2013, Ancestry.com; and 1909 *Hattiesburg City Directory*, USM.

49. 1909 *Hattiesburg City Directory*, USM; and 1 US Bureau of the Census, *Census of the Population:* 1910, Forrest County, Mississippi, Population Schedule, sheet 6A, dwelling 144, family 153, Turner Smith, digital image, Ancestry.com, accessed August 24, 2013.
50. *Polk's Hattiesburg City Directory, 1918* (R. L. Polk, 1918), 382–384; 1920 US Census, Forrest County, Mississippi, Hattiesburg, sheet 13A, dwelling 211, family 268, Turner Smith, digital image, Ancestry.com, accessed August 14, 2013; and Smith, interview. Beginning with the 1910 census, Mamie is no longer listed as having an occupation. This is also reflected in city directory entries over the next two decades.
51. Smith, interview; *Census of the Population: 1910*, vol. 2, *School Attendance on 1040 and Literacy on 1047*; and "Marriage Announcement 3," *Chicago Defender*, August 20, 1932, 6.
52. Smith, interview.

3. *The Noble Spirit*

Epigraph: William Cuthbert Faulkner, "Mississippi," in *William Faulkner: Essays, Speeches, Public Letters*, ed. James B. Meriwether (New York City: Modern Library, 2004, orig., 1965), quoted on 20–21.

1. Sheets 1 and 2, Hattiesburg, MS, March, 1895, Sanborn; *American Biography: A New Cyclopedia*, vol. 10 (New York City: American Historical Society, Inc., 1922), 45–47; Horace Hayden, Alfred Hand, and John Jordan, eds., *Genealogical and Family History of the Wyoming and Lackawanna Valleys, Pennsylvania*, vol. 2 (New York City: Lewis Publishing Co., 1906), 181–183; Andrew English, *"All Off for Gordon's Station": A History of the Early Hattiesburg, Mississippi Area* (Baltimore, MD: Gateway Press, 2000), 66–70; and Gilbert H. Hoffman, *Steam Whistles in the Piney Woods: A History of the Sawmills and Logging Railroads of Forest and Lamar Counties, Mississippi*, vol. 1 (Hattiesburg, MS: Longleaf Press, 1998), 1–10.
2. Sheet 1, Hattiesburg, MS, July, 1890, and sheet 1, Hattiesburg, MS, March, 1895, Sanborn; "Hopeless Hattiesburg," *New Orleans Daily Picayune*, January 17, 1893, 2; "An Arkansas Robber Wreaks Vengeance," *New Orleans Daily Picayune*, August 29, 1893, 11; "Fire at Hattiesburg," *New Orleans Daily Picayune*, October 12, 1893, 2; and "Disastrous Fire Destroys Twenty-five Business Houses," *New Orleans Daily Picayune*, October 13, 1893, 6.
3. Wiscasset Mill information taken from sheet 1, Hattiesburg, July 1890, Sanborn. See "Southern New Items," *The Savannah Tribune*, April 7, 1894, 4, for two million board feet and $30,000 statistics.

4. Hoffman, *Steam Whistles*, $40,000 on 3; sheet 2, Hattiesburg, March 1895, Sanborn; sheet 4, Hattiesburg, April, 1898, Sanborn; and "Account Ledger: 1895–1896," Newman Lumber Company Records, box 1, USM.
5. *American Biography*, 45–47, graduation date and financial statistics on 46; *Genealogical and Family History of the Wyoming and Lackawanna Valleys*, 181–183; William Richard Cutter, ed., *New England Families. Genealogical and Memorial* (New York: Lewis Historical Publishing Co., 1913), 700–713; 1880 U.S. Census, Lackawanna County, Pennsylvania, Inhabitants Schedule, Blakely, page 8, dwelling 82, family 95, Fenwick Peck, digital image, Ancestry .com, accessed December 19, 2014; and "Prominent Visitors," *Biloxi Herald*, November 21, 1896, 1.
6. Hoffman, *Steam Whistles*, 1–45; and Nollie W. Hickman, *Mississippi Harvest: Lumbering in the Longleaf Pine Belt, 1840–1915* (Jackson: University Press of Mississippi, 1962), 180–183 and 88–101.
7. The figure of six hundred square miles is from Hickman, *Mississippi Harvest*, 181; "MCRR Annual Report (1905)," box 117, folder 2, sub-series J: Annual Reports, series II, MCRR Collection; *Tenth Biennial Report of the Railroad Commission of the State of Mississippi for the Years Ending June 30, 1905* (Nashville, TN: Brandon Printing Co., 1906), 132–136; and Hoffman, *Steam Whistles*, 1–45.
8. "By this mill alone . . ." from Otis Robinson, "Facts about Hattiesburg," box 3, folder 1, HHP, 23; 1,200 taken from Hoffman, *Steam Whistles*, 17; "Pearl & Leaf River Railroad Annual Report (1903)," 63, box 117, folder 1, MCRR Collection; and sheet 1, Hattiesburg, October, 1906, Sanborn.
9. Paul Wallace Gates, "Federal Land Policy in the South, 1866–1888," *Journal of Southern History* 6, no. 3 (August 1940): 320; $24 million from Nollie W. Hickman, "Mississippi Forests," in Richard Aubrey McLemore, ed., *A History of Mississippi*, vol. 2 (Jackson: University Press of Mississippi, 1973), 214; and 120 from Hickman, *Mississippi Harvest*, 177.
10. US Bureau of the Census, *Census of the Population: 1910*, vol. 10, *Manufacturers Reports for Principal Industries* (Washington, DC: Government Printing Office, 1913), 503; *Transportation by Water, 1916* (Washington, DC: Department of Commerce, Government Print Office, 1920); and *The Lumber Trade Journal: An International Lumber Paper*, October 15, 1916, 12, 43–44.
11. Paul Wallace Gates, "Federal Land Policy in the South, 1866–1888," *Journal of Southern History* 6, no. 3 (August 1940): 320; $24 million taken from Nollie W. Hickman, "Mississippi Forests," in *A History of Mississippi*, vol. 2, ed. Richard Aubrey McLemore (Jackson: University Press of Mississippi, 1973), 214; US Bureau of the Census, *Census of the Population: 1880*, vol. 2, *Manufacturing* (Washington, DC: Government Printing Office, 1883), 141; *Census of the Population: 1910*, vol. 9, *Manufacturers Reports by States*, 630.

12. US Bureau of the Census, *Census of the Population: 1900*, vol. 13: *Occupations* (Washington, DC: US Census Office, 1902), 316; and Buck Wells quoted from interview with Lawrence Knight, Hattiesburg, MS, April 24 and 28, 1997, transcript, USM-OH.
13. *Census of the Population: 1910*, vol. 9, *Manufacturers Reports by States*, lumber industry wage statistics on 630.
14. J. S. Finlayson, interview by Chester Morgan, Hattiesburg, MS, May 16, 1973, transcript, USM-OH; Ben Earles, interview by R. Wayne Pyle, Hattiesburg, MS, June 28 and 29, 1979, transcript, USM-OH; and 30 from Hickman, *Mississippi Harvest*, 198.
15. These examples are taken from 1900 U.S. Census, Perry County, Mississippi, Population Schedule, Hattiesburg, sheet 16, dwelling 457, family 508, Smith family, digital image, Ancestry.com, accessed August 13, 2013.
16. Rowland, *History of Mississippi*, vol. 4, 434–435 for Komp; Eva Pittman, interview by Chester Morgan, Hattiesburg, MS, August 24, 1973, transcript, USM-OH; Finlayson, interview; "Lumber Industries," box 10688, folder: Forrest County Agriculture," Series 447: Historical Research Material, 1935–1942, WPA-Forrest; "Assignment #17—Agriculture-Horticulture," box 10687, folder: Forrest County Agriculture, WPA-Forrest; "A New Industry," *Hattiesburg Daily Progress*, May 6, 1903, 1; sheets 1–3, Hattiesburg, April, 1898, Sanborn; sheets 1–8, Hattiesburg, April, 1903, Sanborn; and sheets 2–7, Hattiesburg, MS, October, 1906, Sanborn.
17. "If you . . ." quoted from Earles, interview; and *Thirteenth Biennial Report of the Railroad Commission of the State of Mississippi for the Two Years, Ending June 30, 1911* (Nashville, TN: Press of the Brandon Printing Company, 1911), 94.
18. Hoffman, *Steam Whistles*, $30,000 statistic on 17.
19. Toney Arnold Hardy, *No Compromise with Principle: Autobiography and Biography of William Harris Hardy in Dialogue* (Saddle Brook, NJ: American Book-Stratford Press, 1946), 260–270, 308; US Bureau of the Census, *Census of the Population: 1900*, Perry County, Mississippi, Population Schedule, Hattiesburg, sheet 8, dwelling 143, family 148, Captain Hardy, digital image, Ancestry.com, Accessed September 21, 2014; Melodia B. Rowe, *Captain Jones—the Biography of a Builder* (Hamilton, OH: Hill-Brown Printing Co., 1942), 259–260; and "Capt. Jones Dies at Buffalo Home," *Hattiesburg News*, December 6, 1916, 1.
20. T. E. Ross Jr., interview by Orley Caudill, Hattiesburg, MS, February 24, 1975, transcript, USM-OH; "Tatum Family History (1924)," box 464, folder 19, Tatum Papers, USM; John McLeod background is pieced together from various newspaper clippings and files found in the McLeod Department Store Records at USM; T. S. Jackson, "Glimpses of the Past: When I Was Twenty-One,"

Hattiesburg American, January 29, 1929, 4; "L. E. Faulkner Services Set for Wednesday," *Hattiesburg American*, January 17, 1961, 1; "Final Tribute Paid to L. E. Faulkner," *Hattiesburg American*, January 19, 1961, 9-A; and Johnson biographic information taken from Margaret Boutwell, "Assignment #27: The Bar," May, 1937, box 10687, folder: The BAR, WPA-Forrest.

21. Over 11,733 people lived within the Hattiesburg city limits, and about 9,000 more settled in the surrounding county. *Census of the Population: 1910*, vol. 2: *Population, Alabama-Montana*, 1023, 1046–1047.
22. Contracts for municipal work can be found in boxes 1–3, Hattiesburg Municipal Records, USM; Sewer Installation Payroll, box 173, folder 19, Hattiesburg Municipal Records, USM; Jody Cook, "Hub City Historic District National Register of Historic Places Inventory—Nomination Form," April 30, 1980, Hattiesburg, MS, U.S. Department of the Interior Heritage Conservation and Recreation Service; Hattiesburg Department of Planning & Community Development, "Historic Hattiesburg: The History & Architecture of Hattiesburg's First Neighborhoods," box 1, folder 1, Hattiesburg Department of Urban Development Collection, USM; "Early Transportation and Communication," box: 10688, folder: Industry, WPA-Forrest; early privilege tax records taken from box 169, folder 22, Hattiesburg Municipal Records; "History of the Hattiesburg Police Department," box 173, folder 18, Hattiesburg Municipal Records; sheets 2–6, Hattiesburg, April, 1903, Sanborn; various Hattiesburg postcards from the Cooper Collection; Reagan L. Grimsley, *Hattiesburg in Vintage Postcards* (Charleston, SC: Arcadia Publishing, 2004), especially 11–54; and Gaines Dobbins quoted in Roberson, "A History of the 'Hattiesburg American,'" 35–36.
23. Sheets 1, 4, & 5, Hattiesburg, October, 1906, Sanborn; "Early Transportation and Communication," box 10688, folder: Industry, WPA-Forrest; Cook, "Hub City Historic District"; John Ray Skates, "Hattiesburg: The Early Years," in *Hattiesburg: A Pictorial History*, ed. Kenneth G. McCarty Jr. (Jackson: University Press of Mississippi, 1982), 5–11; *Hattiesburg Area Historical Society Newsletter* 10, no. 2 (Fall 2007), 1–2; and Dunbar Rowland, ed., *Encyclopedia of Mississippi*: vol. 1 (Atlanta, GA: Southern Historical Publishing Association, 1907), quoted on 852.
24. Hattiesburg postcards found in Cooper Collection, "Hattiesburg is . . ." quoted from item 1318, box 107, folder 1.
25. Sheets 2–6, Hattiesburg, March 1910, Sanborn; "Historic Hattiesburg," box 1, folder 1, Hattiesburg Dept. of Urban Development Collection; and Cooper Collection.
26. Grimsley, *Hattiesburg in Vintage Postcards*, 55–60; "A Brief History of the New Church Building, Main Street M. E. Church, South, Hattiesburg, Mississippi," box 256, folder 10, Tatum Papers; various Hattiesburg postcards, Cooper

Collection; Cook, "Hub City Historic District," 6; and personal observations made on December 13, 2009 and June 15, 2011.

27. Robinson, "Facts about Hattiesburg," box 3, folder 1, HHP, 49–53; "Report on City Schools," March 22, 1909, box 167, folder 14, Hattiesburg Municipal Records; "Historic Hattiesburg," box 1, folder 1, Hattiesburg Dept. of Urban Development Collection; item 1367, box 107, folder 1, Cooper Collection; "Aliens in Separate Schools," *New York Times*, October 17, 1907, 1; and "A Barbarous Body," *The American Israelite*, October 24, 1907, 4.
28. "Tatum Family History (1924)"; Chester M. Morgan, *Dearly Bought, Deeply Treasured: The University of Southern Mississippi, 1912–1987* (Jackson: University Press of Mississippi, 1987), especially 1–40; and Chester M. Morgan, *Treasured Past, Golden Future: The University of Southern Mississippi* (Jackson: University Press of Mississippi, 2010).
29. "The Slogan Sign Celebration Thursday," *Hattiesburg News*, November 25, 1912, 1; "Thousands Thrilled When Slogan Sign Stands Illuminated against Sky," *Hattiesburg News*, November 29, 1912, 1 and 4; "Hattiesburg's Slogan Sign," editorial, *Hattiesburg News*, November 29, 1912, 4; and item 1391, box 107, folder 1, Cooper Collection.
30. "News from Cut Off Towns: Loss of Life Small, but Property Damage Heavy and Widespread," *New York Times*, September 29, 1906, 3; "Gale Brings Ruin to Cities on Gulf," *Chicago Daily Tribune*, September 28, 1906, 1; standing timber figure taken from Federal Writer's Project of the Works Progress Administration, *Mississippi: A Guide to the Magnolia State* (New York: Hastings House, 1946, orig., 1938), 197; "Many Are Dead in Mississippi," *Atlanta Constitution*, April 25, 1908, 1; "Relief Work," *Louisville Courier-Journal*, May 1, 1908, 4; "Losses by Fire," *New York Times*, March 18, 1908, 14; and Hoffman, *Steam Whistles*, 16–34.
31. "Many Are Dead in Mississippi," *Atlanta Constitution*, April 25, 1908, 1; "Relief Work," *Louisville Courier-Journal*, May 1, 1908, 4; and Hoffman, *Steam Whistles*, 16–34 for more on the Newman fires and reconstruction.
32. This description is constructed using the following images from the Hattiesburg Historical Photographs Collection: "Baseball Park," box 1, folder 5, "Baptism in Gordon's Creek," box 1, folder 5, "O'Ferrall's Store Fourth of July Float," box 1, folder 4, "Parade on Main Street," box 2, folder 10; also Captain George A. Stevens, interview by Orley B. Claudill, April 27, 1976, transcript, USM-OH; and Wells, interview.
33. "The Dogs Ran Him Down," *Hattiesburg Daily Progress*, June 5, 1902, 4.
34. "Assaulted the Woman," *Hattiesburg Daily Progress*, June 6, 1902, 4. The percentage of mixed-race blacks is taken from McMillen, *Dark Journey*, 19, and Donald B. Dodd, ed., *Historical Statistics of the States of the United States:*

Two Centuries of the Census, 1790–1990 (Westport, CT: Greenwood Press, 1993), 49–50.

35. "Negro Captured," *Hattiesburg Daily Progress*, June 7, 1902, 4; "Mob Came Near Lynching Negro Innocent of Crime," *Atlanta Constitution*, June 13, 1902, 5; "The Sheriff and the Soldiers," *Hattiesburg Daily Progress*, June 9, 1902, quote on 2; "Walter Bankhead, the Rapist Narrowly Escapes Death," *Hattiesburg Daily Progress*, June 9, 1902, 4; "Militia Stopped a Mob," *American Citizen*, June 13, 1902, 4; and "Evils of the Mob," *Hattiesburg Daily Progress*, June 14, 1902, 3.
36. "Mob Came Near Lynching Negro Innocent of Crime," *Atlanta Constitution*, June 13, 1902, 5; and "The Sheriff and the Soldiers," *Hattiesburg Daily Progress*, June 9, 1902, quote on 2.
37. "Confessed the Crime," *Hattiesburg Daily Progress*, June 13, 1902, 4; "Denies It Now," *Hattiesburg Daily Progress*, June 14, 1902, 4; "Mob Came Near Lynching Negro Innocent of Crime," *Atlanta Constitution*, June 13, 1902, 5; "Dantzler on Trial," *Hattiesburg Daily Progress*, June 30, 1902, 4; "Dantzler Will Hang," *Hattiesburg Daily Progress*, July 1, 1902, 4; "Dantzler Will Hang," *Hattiesburg Daily Progress*, July 2, 1902, 4; "Will Dantzler Pays Penalty," *Hattiesburg Daily Progress*, August 1, 1902, 4; and "For Assault Negro Hangs," *Atlanta Constitution*, August 2, 1902, 12.
38. This narrative is drawn from "Negro Shoots M. M. Sexton and Is Lynched by Mob," *Hattiesburg Daily Progress*, August 10, 1903, 4; quotes taken from "Dragged Negro to Death," *New York Times*, August 9, 1903, 1; and "Dead When Hanged," *Nashville American*, August 9, 1903, 14.
39. Julius E. Thompson, *Lynchings in Mississippi: A History 1865–1965* (Jefferson, NC: McFarland & Co., 2007), 36 and 49; "Assaults Woman; Burned at Stake," *Atlanta Constitution*, November 5, 1901, 5; "After Confession," *Nashville American*, November 5, 1901, 7; and McMillen, *Dark Journey*, 224–253.
40. Amy Louise Wood, *Lynching and Spectacle: Witnessing Racial Violence in America, 1890–1940* (Chapel Hill: University of North Carolina Press, 2009), quoted on 10; Crystal N. Feimster, *Southern Horrors: Women and the Politics of Rape and Lynching* (Cambridge, MA: Harvard University Press, 2009); and W. Fitzhugh Brundage, *Lynching in the New South: Georgia and Virginia, 1880–1930* (Urbana: University of Illinois Press, 1993).
41. Captain William Harris Hardy, "Reconstruction in East and Southeast Mississippi," *Publications of the Mississippi Historical Society*, vol. 4, 1901, 105–132, quoted on 132; "The Degeneracy of the Negro," *Hattiesburg Daily Progress*, June 26, 1902, 2; and "A Monument to the South's Old-Time Negroes," *Saturday Evening Eye*, November 4, 1905, 1.
42. "'The Clansman'; An Appreciation," *Saturday Evening Eye*, December 2, 1905, 9.

43. "Jefferson on the Negro," *The Issue*, March 21, 1908, 3; "lazy . . ." quoted in James C. Cobb, *The Most Southern Place on Earth: The Mississippi Delta and the Roots of Regional Identity* (New York: Oxford University Press, 1992), 147; "If I . . ." quoted in David M. Oshinsky, *'Worse Than Slavery': Parchman Farm and the Ordeal of Jim Crow Justice* (New York: Free Press, 1996), 91; and "Vardaman as an Editor," *Baltimore Sun*, August 19, 1907, 11.
44. "Two Negroes Lynched by Mob," *Saturday Evening Eye*, August 5, 1905, 1; "Two Negroes Lynched," *Washington Post*, August 5, 1905, 1; and "Negro Kills Convict Guard," *Atlanta Constitution*, August 5, 1905, 3.
45. "Those Mass Meetings," *Saturday Evening Eye*, August 12, 1905, 1; "Rev. J. E. Carpenter's Address at Mass Meeting Monday Night," *Saturday Evening Eye*, August 12, 1905, "savage and inhuman . . ." quoted on 8, and *Hattiesburg Daily Progress* editorial quoted in Address by Rev. J. E. Carpenter, August 7, 1905, reprinted on 9; "cowards of . . ." quoted in "Mob Violence," *Saturday Evening Eye*, August 12, 1905, 2; and "Developments in Lynching Case," *Saturday Evening Eye*, November 18, 1905, 10.
46. "Will Horn Tells Interesting Story," *Saturday Evening Eye*, August 19, 1905, 9; "To Protest a Negro," *Nashville American*, August 18, 1905, 5; "It Raineth Alike," *Saturday Evening Eye*, August 26, 1905, 2; "Militia Ordered to Guard a Prisoner," *Louisville Courier-Journal*, August 18, 1905, 1; "Horn Case Goes to Supreme Court," *Saturday Evening Eye*, December 9, 1905, 3; and "Score of Lynchings," *Washington Post*, January 2, 1906, 9.
47. "U.D.C. Founded 30 Years Ago," *Hattiesburg American*, October 26, 1932, 1; and Tressie Graham Mangum and Mary Clement Perry, "United Daughters of the Confederacy, Nathaniel Bedford Forrest Chapter #422," in *The History of Forrest County, Mississippi*, Hattiesburg Area Historical Society Volunteers (Hattiesburg, MS: Hattiesburg Historical Society, 2000), 78–79.
48. Jack Hurst, *Nathan Bedford Forrest: A Biography* (New York: Knopf, 1993), financial statistic on 64.
49. Unnamed Confederate soldier quoted in James W. Loewen and Edward H. Sebesta, eds., *The Confederate and Neo-Confederate Reader: The "Great Truth" about the "Lost Cause"* (Jackson: University Press of Mississippi, 2010), 207; Thomas Jordan, and J. P. Pryor, *The Campaigns of General Nathan Bedford Forrest and of Forrest's Cavalry* (Cambridge, MA: Da Capo Press, 1996, orig., 1868). For a good analysis of Forrest's shortcomings as an officer, see David Powell, *Failure in the Saddle: Nathan Bedford Forrest, Joe Wheeler, and the Confederate Cavalry in the Chickamauga Campaign* (El Dorado Hills, CA: Savas Beatie, 2010), especially 199–227; and Richard L. Fuchs, *An Unerring Fire: The Massacre at Fort Pillow* (Cranbury, NJ: Associated University Press, 1994).

50. For more on Forrest's role with the Klan in Mississippi, see James W. Garner, *Reconstruction in Mississippi* (Baton Rouge: Louisiana State University Press, 1968, orig., 1901), especially 338–339; and Hurst, *Nathan Bedford Forrest*, quoted on 6. It is worth noting that Forrest, as self-made slave trader, revered cavalryman, and pioneer of postwar resistance, could appeal to numerous cultural aspects of the Old and New South and thus serve as a bridge between chronological eras and even white social classes.
51. David W. Blight, *Race and Reunion: The Civil War in American Memory* (Cambridge, MA: Belknap Press of Harvard University Press, 2001), statistics on 272–274.; and C. Vann Woodward, *Origins of the New South, 1877–1913* (Baton Rouge: Louisiana State University Press, 1971; orig., 1951), quoted on 154–155. Karen L. Cox, *Dixie's Daughters: The United Daughters of the Confederacy and the Preservation of Confederate Culture* (Gainesville: University Press of Florida, 2003); W. Fitzhugh Brundage, *The Southern Past: A Clash of Race and Memory* (Cambridge, MA: Belknap Press of Harvard University Press, 2005); and Charles Reagan Wilson, *Baptized in Blood: The Religion of the Lost Cause, 1865–1920* (Athens: University of Georgia Press, 1980).
52. Special insert celebrating the role of women in the Confederacy found in *Hattiesburg Daily News*, April 16, 1908; Cox, *Dixie's Daughters*, 118–140, especially 130 for specific Hattiesburg examples; and "Emily Cook's Hattiesburg High School Memory Book, Parts 1, 2, and 3," box 2, folders 4–6, Cook (Joseph Anderson) Family Papers, USM.
53. "Old Home of Jefferson Davis is Sold to Sons of Veterans for Ten Thousand Dollars," *Atlanta Constitution*, October 17, 1902, 5; "Gates Wide Open," *Louisville Courier-Journal*, June 14, 1905, B1; "Honor Confederate Dead," *Washington Post*, December 30, 1906, 12; and Mangum and Perry, "United Daughters of the Confederacy, Nathaniel Bedford Forrest Chapter #422."
54. James C. Cobb, *Industrialization and Southern Society, 1877–1984* (Lexington: University Press of Kentucky, 1984), quote on 14; and Gaines M. Foster, *Ghosts of the Confederacy: Defeat, the Lost Cause, and the Emergence of the New South, 1865 to 1913* (New York: Oxford University Press, 1987).
55. Grace Elizabeth Hale, *Making Whiteness: The Culture of Segregation in the South, 1890–1940* (New York: Random House, 1998), especially 43–119.
56. W. J. Cash, *The Mind of the South* (New York: Vintage Books, 1941), 105.
57. H. J. Holmes, "Reports of County Superintendents," in *Biennial Report of the State Superintendent of Education to the Legislature of Mississippi, for the Years 1888 and 1889* (Jackson: R. H. Henry, State Printer, 1890), 223–225; John H. Long, ed., *Mississippi: Atlas of Historical County Boundaries* (New York City: Simon & Schuster, 1993), 1 and 62; *Laws of the State of Mississippi*, Special Session, January 2, 1906–April 21, 1906 (Nashville, TN: Brandon Printing Company, 1906), 174–175; and Frances W. Griffith, "History of Forrest

County," and Lois Hunt, "The Formation of Forrest County," box: 10688, folder: Forrest County Formation, WPA-Forrest.

58. "Greatest Event in Hattiesburg History," *Hattiesburg News*, October 13, 1910, 1.

4. *A Little Colony of Mississippians*

Epigraph: "The Negro and the South," *Hattiesburg News*, December 7, 1916,

1. E. Hammond Smith, interview by Orley B. Caudill, Hattiesburg, MS, April 8, 1982, transcript, USM-OH; 1909 *Hattiesburg City Directory*, USM; 1910 U.S. Census, Forrest County, Mississippi, Population Schedule, sheet 6A, dwelling 144, family 153, Turner Smith, digital image, Ancestry.com, accessed August 24, 2013.
2. Smith, interview; and "Report on City Schools," March 22, 1909, box 167, folder 14, Hattiesburg Municipal Records, USM.
3. *Hattiesburg Polks City Directory, 1914* (Memphis, TN: R. L. Polk & Co., 1914); Smith, interview; and 1920 U.S. Census, Forrest County, Mississippi, Hattiesburg, sheet 13A, dwelling 211, family 268, Turner Smith, digital image, Ancestry .com, accessed August 14, 2013.
4. US Bureau of the Census, *Census of the Population: 1910*, vol. 2, *Population, Alabama-Montana* (Washington, DC: Government Printing Office, 1913), 1060; Jesse Oscar McKee, "The Residential Patterns of Blacks in Natchez and Hattiesburg and Other Mississippi Cities" (PhD diss., Michigan State University, 1972); and Hattiesburg Department of Planning & Community Development, "Historic Hattiesburg," box 1, folder 1, Hattiesburg Department of Urban Development Collection, USM.
5. Hattiesburg Department of Planning & Community Development, "Historic Hattiesburg: The History & Architecture of Hattiesburg's First Neighborhoods," box 1, folder 1, Hattiesburg Department of Urban Development Collection, USM; sheets 15 & 16, Hattiesburg, MS, March 1910, Sanborn; and *Hattiesburg Polk's City Directory, 1914* (Memphis, TN: 1914).
6. Ariel Barnes, interview by Priscilla R. Walker, Hattiesburg, MS, January 6, 1995, transcript, USM-OH; Richard Boyd, interview by Charles Bolton, Hattiesburg, MS, August 29, 1991, transcript, USM-OH; 1920 U.S. Census, Forrest County, Mississippi, Population Schedule, Hattiesburg, 17A, dwelling 365, family 408, Nelson Boyd, digital image, Ancestry.com, accessed August 24, 2013; Sarah Harris Ruffin, interview by Fannie Cole Dickerson, Brooklyn, NY, November 23, 1995, transcript, USM-OH; 1930 U.S. Census, Forrest County, Population Schedule, Hattiesburg, sheet 10A, dwelling 198, family 237, Douglas Harris, digital image, Ancestry.com, accessed August 4, 2014; Marie Washington Kent, interview by M. L. Beard, Grenada, MS, June 16, 1995, transcript, USM-OH; N. R. Burger, interview by R. Wayne Pyle, Hattiesburg, MS, May 11, 1982, transcript, USM-OH; and S. Johnson,

"Migration Study," box 86, folder: Migration Study Mississippi Summary, part 1, F. Research Department, 1916–1963, NUL. This collection includes a number of interviews in which African American lumber workers indicated their pay in Hattiesburg.

7. *Census of the Population*: 1910, vol. 2, 1023 and 1046–1047; and vol. 1, 607; and Jones, *Labor of Love, Labor of Sorrow,* 103–130.
8. *Census of the Population*: 1910, vol. 2, 1023 and 1046–1047; 1909 *Hattiesburg City Directory;* and Lorenzo J. Greene and Carter G. Woodson, *The Negro Wage Earner* (New York: AMS Press, 1970, orig., 1930), especially 48–144.
9. *Census of the Population*: 1910, vol. 2, 1023 and 1046–1047; sheets 15 & 16, Hattiesburg, MS, March, 1910, Sanborn; "Report on City Schools," March 22, 1909, box 167, folder 14, Hattiesburg Municipal Records; Teacher salaries taken from Noble, *Forty Years of the Public Schools in Mississippi,* 142; Smith, interview; Osceola McCarty, interviews by Shana Walton, Hattiesburg, MS, February 22 and 23, 1996, transcript, USM-OH; and Mrs. Mattie Lou Hardy, interview by Priscilla R. Walker, unspecified location, October 24, 1995, transcript, USM-OH.
10. Smith, interview.
11. Smith, interview; and McCarty, interviews.
12. Grace Elizabeth Hale, *Making Whiteness: The Culture of Segregation in the South,* 1890–1940 (New York: Random House, 1998), especially 121–197.
13. Constance Baker, interview by Kim Adams, Hattiesburg, MS, April 3, 1995, transcript, USM-OH; and Ariel Barnes interview by Sarah Rowe, April 1, 1993, transcript, USM-OH. For more on daily behavior and Jim Crow, see Stephen A. Berrey, *The Jim Crow Routine: Everyday Performances of Race, Civil Rights, and Segregation in Mississippi* (Chapel Hill: University of North Carolina Press, 2015).
14. Observations made at the gravesite of Ed Howell in the African American cemetery at the corner of Clark and Scott Streets in Hattiesburg on November 12, 2011; "Negro Banker Shot Down," *Indianapolis Freeman,* March 30, 1907, 4; "Hattiesburg, Miss.," *Indianapolis Freeman,* November 28, 1908, 4; "Banker Held for Murder," *New York Times,* March 24, 1907, 16; and "Negro Assassinated by His Own Race," *Louisville Courier-Journal,* March 22, 1907, 3.
15. David M. Oshinsky, *'Worse Than Slavery': Parchman Farm and the Ordeal of Jim Crow Justice* (New York: Free Press, 1996), especially 31–106; and Neil McMillen, *Dark Journey: Black Mississippians in the Age of Jim Crow* (Urbana: University of Illinois Press, 1990), especially 197–223. Local newspapers of the era are filled with countless examples of white crime. See the *Hattiesburg Daily Progress, Hattiesburg News,* and *Saturday Evening Eye* between 1903–1912.

16. "Swung . . ." quoted from "Two Negroes Lynched by Mob," *Saturday Evening Eye*, August 5, 1905, 1.
17. McMillen, *Dark Journey*, especially, 3–32; Leon L. Litwack, *Trouble in Mind: Black Southerners in the Age of Jim Crow* (New York: Vintage, 1998), especially 3–52; Nancy Krieger, Jarvis Chen, Brent Coull, Pamela Waterman, and Jason Beckfield, "The Unique Impact of Abolition of Jim Crow Laws on Reducing Inequalities in Infant Death Rates and Implications for Choice of Comparison Groups in Analyzing Societal Determinants of Health," *American Journal of Public Health* 103, no. 12 (2013): 2234–2244; Nancy Krieger, Jarvis Chen, Brent Coull, Jason Beckfield, Mathew Kiang, and Pamela Waterman, "Jim Crow and Premature Mortality among the US Black and White Population, 1960–2009," *Epidemiology* 25, no. 4 (2014): 494–504; and Kenneth Chay and Michael Greenstone, "The Convergence in Black-White Infant Mortality Rates During the 1960s," *American Economic Review* 90, no. 2 (2000): 326–332.
18. Smith, interview; sheets 1, 13, and 16, Hattiesburg, March, 1910, Sanborn; Mrs. Margaret Boutwell and Frances Griffith, "Assignment #26—Church History," May and September, 1937, box 10687, folder: Churches, Negro, Series 447: Historical Research Material, 1935–1942, WPA-Forrest; Patricia Blake, "St. Paul," in *The History of Forrest County, Mississippi*, 33; Otis Robinson, "Facts About Hattiesburg," box 3, folder 1, HHP, 75; and 1909 *Hattiesburg City Directory*.
19. Smith, interview; and US Bureau of the Census, *Negroes in the United States, 1920–1932* (Washington, DC: Government Printing Office, 1935), 544. Numbers are not available for all years, but the numbers of black Methodist churches in Mississippi were 528 MEC, 397 AME, and 370 CME. For more see, Daniel A. Payne, *History of the African Methodist Episcopal Church* (Nashville, TN: Publishing House of the A.M.E. Sunday School Union, 1891); James P. Campbell, *Songs of Zion: The African Methodist Episcopal Church in the United States and South Africa* (New York: Oxford University Press, 1995), especially 3–99; Peter C. Murray, *Methodists and the Crucible of Race, 1930–1975* (Columbia: University of Missouri Press, 2004), especially 8–26; and C. Eric Lincoln and Lawrence H. Mamiya, *The Black Church in the African American Experience* (Durham, NC: Duke University Press, 1990), especially 47–75.
20. Mrs. Margaret Boutwell and Frances Griffith, "Assignment #26—Church History," May and September, 1937, box 10687, folder: Churches, Negro, Series 447: Historical Research Material, 1935–1942, WPA-Forrest; *The History of Forrest County, Mississippi*, 28–36; sheets 1, 13, and 16, Hattiesburg, March, 1910, Sanborn; Charles Davis, interview by Anna Warren, Hattiesburg, MS, August 27, 2005, transcript, USM-OH; and 1909 *Hattiesburg City Directory*.

21. For more on African American church life and the "politics of respectability," see Evelyn Brooks Higginbotham, *Righteous Discontent: The Women's Movement in the Black Baptist Church, 1880–1920* (Cambridge, MA: Harvard University Press, 1993).
22. Examples taken from various issues of the *Indianapolis Freeman* between 1908 and 1912. For more, see Higginbotham, *Righteous Discontent;* Litwack, *Trouble in Mind,* especially 378–403; and Tera Hunter, *To 'Joy My Freedom: Southern Black Women's Lives and Labors after the Civil War* (Cambridge, MA: Harvard University Press, 1997), especially 68–73.
23. Smith, interview; "Hattiesburg, Miss.," *Indianapolis Freeman,* February 22, 1908, 8; "This club . . ." quoted in "Hattiesburg, Miss.," *Indianapolis Freeman,* March 7, 1908, 3; "Hattiesburg, Miss.," *Indianapolis Freeman,* March 14, 1908, 8; and "Hattiesburg, Miss.," *Indianapolis Freeman,* April 4, 1908, 2.
24. Julius E. Thompson, *The Black Press in Mississippi, 1865–1985* (Gainesville: University Press of Florida, 1993), 151–159; *Times* editorial reprinted in "Booker T. Washington," *Chicago Broad Ax,* October 12, 1907, 1; Monroe N. Work, ed., *Negro Year Book, 1914–1915* (Tuskegee, AL: The Negro Year Book Publishing Co., 1914), 385; "A List of Negro Banks of the United States," *Topeka Plaindealer,* January 24, 1913, 7; $13,000 taken from "Hattiesburg, Miss.," *Indianapolis Freeman,* October 17, 1908, 8; "Meridian, Miss.," *Indianapolis Freeman,* July 27, 1912, 2; sheets 15 & 16, Hattiesburg, MS, March, 1910, Sanborn; *1909 Hattiesburg City Directory*; and Mrs. Lillie McLaurin quoted in Department of Planning & Community Development Neighborhood Development Division, "Historic Hattiesburg," 6:2.
25. Examples taken from *1909 Hattiesburg City Directory,* USM; 1910 U.S. Census, Forrest County, Mississippi, Population Schedule, Hattiesburg, ward 4, beat 1, digital images, Ancestry.com, accessed May 13, 2014; various issues of the *Indianapolis Freeman* between 1908 and 1912; and Dr. Isaac Thomas interview by Jessie Flowers, Hattiesburg, MS, December 23, 1994, transcript, USM-OH.
26. 1900 U.S. Census, Perry County, Mississippi, Population Schedule, Hattiesburg, sheet 22B, dwelling 396, family 432, Gayther Hardaway, digital image, Ancestry.com, accessed May 13, 2014; 1900 US Census, Perry County, Mississippi, Population Schedule, Hattiesburg, sheet 25, dwelling 446, family 493, Shackelford, digital image, Ancestry.com, accessed May 20, 2013; 1900 US Census, Perry County, Mississippi, Population Schedule, Hattiesburg, sheet 17, dwelling 314, family 330, McBride, digital image, Ancestry.com, accessed May 20, 2013; Hattiesburg Daily Progress, *1905 Hattiesburg City Directory,* 45; *1909 Hattiesburg City Directory* lists Woods's occupation; and sheets 15 & 16, Hattiesburg, MS, March, 1910, Sanborn.
27. McKee, "The Residential Patterns of Blacks in Natchez and Hattiesburg and Other Mississippi Cities," especially 92; Smith, interview; sheets 15 & 16,

Hattiesburg, MS, March 1910, Sanborn; and 1909 *Hattiesburg City Directory*, USM.

28. "Negro Businessmen Organize at Hattiesburg for General Interest," *Indianapolis Freeman*, November 7, 1908, 1; Conner with Marszalek, *A Black Physician's Story: Bringing Hope in Mississippi* (Jackson: University Press of Mississippi, 1985); Theodore Kornweibel Jr., *Railroads in the African American Experience: A Photographic Journey* (Baltimore, MD: Johns Hopkins University Press, 2010), 113–130; and "Hattiesburg, Miss.," *Indianapolis Freeman*, May 25, 1912, 2. See Hunter, *To 'Joy My Freedom;* Larry Tye, *Rising From the Rails: Pullman Porters and the Making of the Black Middle Class* (New York: Owl Books, 2004); and Leslie Brown, *Upbuilding Black Durham: Gender, Class, and Black Community Development in the Jim Crow South* (Chapel Hill: University of North Carolina Press, 2008).
29. "'Railroad Day' Echoes," *Washington Bee*, July 18, 1914, 6. For more on early-twentieth-century black urban activism, see Tera Hunter, *To 'Joy My Freedom;* and Blair L. M. Kelley, *Right to Ride: Streetcar Boycotts and African American Citizenship in the Era of Plessy v. Ferguson* (Chapel Hill: University of North Carolina Press, 2010).
30. W. E. B. Du Bois, *The Souls of Black Folk* (New York: Cosimo, Inc., 2007, orig., 1903), quoted on 30. For more on Washington, his leadership, and his critics, see Booker T. Washington, *The Story of My Life and Work* (New York: Cosimo, Inc., 2007, orig., 1901); Louis R. Harlan, *Booker T. Washington: The Making of a Black Leader, 1856–1901* (New York: Oxford University Press, 1972); Louis R. Harlan, *Booker T. Washington: The Wizard of Tuskegee, 1901–1915* (New York: Oxford University Press, 1983); and August Meier, *Negro Thought in America, 1880–1915* (Ann Arbor: University of Michigan Press, 1966).
31. Frank Lincoln Mather, ed., *Who's Who of the Colored Race:* vol. 1, *1915* (Chicago, IL: Frank Lincoln Mather, 1915), 267. Thigpen editorials quoted in "Get In and Help," *Chicago Broad Ax*, September 21, 1907, 1; and "Booker T. Washington," *Chicago Broad Ax*, October 12, 1907, 1.
32. Sheet 15, Hattiesburg, MS, March 1910, Sanborn; Smith, interview; observations in the Hattiesburg Clark Street African American cemetery; "Hattiesburg, Miss.," *Indianapolis Freeman*, October 24, 1908, 1; "Hattiesburg, Miss.," *Indianapolis Freeman*, May 25, 1912, 2; and "one of . . ." and financial figures taken from "Among the Masons," *Savannah Tribune*, December 14, 1907, 8.
33. Sheet 15, Hattiesburg, MS, March 1910, Sanborn; Smith, interview; and Mather, ed., *Who's Who of the Colored Race*, 267. For more on the history and importance of black Masonic orders, see E. Franklin Frazier, *The Negro in the United States* (New York: Macmillan Co., 1957, orig., 1949), especially 367–286; W. E. B. Du Bois, *Economic Co-Operation Among Negro Americans* (Atlanta:

Atlanta University Press, 1907), especially 92–133; David T. Beito, *From Mutual Aid to the Welfare State: Fraternal Societies and Social Services, 1890–1967* (Chapel Hill: University of North Carolina Press, 2000); and Peter P. Hinks and Stephen Kantrowitz, eds., *All Men Free and Brethren: Essays on the History of African American Freemasonry* (Ithaca, NY: Cornell University Press, 2013).

34. Robin D. G. Kelley, "'We Are Not What We Seem': Rethinking Black Working-Class Opposition in the Jim Crow South," *Journal of American History* 80, no. 1 (1993): 75–112, quoted on 80.

35. "150 Men From Newman's Mill Walk Off Job," *Hattiesburg News*, December 7, 1916, 1; "Newman Strike Called Off," *Hattiesburg News*, December, 21, 1916, 1; "Strikers Back, Newman Mills Resume Work," *Hattiesburg News*, December 22, 1916, 1; and "Plants Close on Account of Heavy Exodus," *Chicago Defender*, December 23, 1916, 1.

36. "Labor Agents Take Many Negroes Away," *Hattiesburg American*, October 25, 1916, 6; "37 Negroes Leave for New Orleans," *Hattiesburg News*, December 12, 1916, 6; "Northern Invasion Starts," *Chicago Defender*, January 20, 1917, 1; "Hattiesburgers Arrive," *Chicago Defender*, March 10, 1917, 7; Charles S. Johnson, "Migration Study," box 86, folder: Migration Study Chicago Interviews, NUL; Johnson, Unnamed Document, box 86, folder: Migration Study Miscellany, NUL; and Johnson, "The Mississippi Colony," 29–31, box 86, folder: Migration Study Draft (Early), NUL.

37. James Grossman, *Land of Hope: Chicago, Black Southerners, and the Great Migration* (Chicago, IL: University of Chicago Press, 1989), especially 98–119; Johnson, "Migration Study," box 86, folder: Migration Study Chicago Interviews, NUL; Johnson, Unnamed Document; and Johnson, "The Mississippi Colony," 29–31, NUL.

38. Chicago Commission on Race relations, *The Negro in Chicago: A Study of Race Relations and a Race Riot* (Chicago, IL: University of Chicago Press, 1922), fifty thousand on 79. For more on the Great Migration, see James Grossman, *Land of Hope*; Isabel Wilkerson, *The Warmth of Other Suns: The Epic Story of America's Great Migration* (New York: Random House, 2010); and Nicholas Lehmann, *The Promised Land: The Great Black Migration and How It Changed America* (New York: Vintage, 1991).

39. Roi Ottley, *The Lonely Warrior: The Life and Times of Robert S. Abbott* (Chicago, IL: Henry Regnery Company, 1955), especially 81–139; The eighty thousand figure is from Emmett J. Scott, *Negro Migration during the War* (New York: Oxford University Press, 1920), 30; and James N. Gregory, *The Southern Diaspora: How the Great Migrations of Black and White Southerners Transformed America* (Chapel Hill: University of North Carolina Press, 2005), 50.

40. Johnson, "Migration Study," box 86, folder: Migration Study Chicago Interviews, NUL; "grab the . . ." and "simply because . . ." quoted in Scott, *Negro*

Migration during the War, 30 and 87, respectively; and "passed around . . ." quoted in Unnamed Document, box 86, folder: Migration Study Miscellany, NUL. For more on the *Defender,* railroads, and the Great Migration, see Kornweibel, *Railroads in the African American Experience,* especially 168–186.

41. Scott, *Negro Migration during the War,* especially 26–37; "semi-public . . ." and "ruining . . ." quoted in unnamed document, box 86, folder: Migration Study Miscellany; migrant quoted in Emmett J. Scott, "Letters of Negro Migrants of 1916–1918," *Journal of Negro History* 4, no. 3 (1919): 311; and "unquestionably . . ." quoted in "The Course of the Movement," box 86, folder: Migration Study Draft (Early), NUL.
42. Unnamed document, box 86, folder: Migration Study Miscellany; Scott, *Negro Migration During the War,* 34; and Johnson, "Migration Study," box 86, folder: Migration Study Chicago Interviews, NUL.
43. 1930 U.S. Census, Cook County, Illinois, Population Schedule, Chicago, sheet 9A, dwelling 48, family 227, Kinnard, digital image, Ancestry.com, accessed May 28, 2014; 1920 U.S. Census, Cook County, Illinois, Population Schedule, Chicago, sheet 6B, dwelling 72, family 139, McBride, digital image, Ancestry .com, accessed May 28, 2014; 1930 US Census, Cook County, Illinois, Population Schedule, Chicago, sheet 12A, dwelling 102, family, 221, Shackelford, digital image, Ancestry.com, accessed May 28, 2014; and 1920 US Census, Cook County, Illinois, Population Schedule, Chicago, sheet 6B, dwelling 78, family 97, Thigpen, digital image, Ancestry.com, accessed May 28, 2014. In his 1895 Atlanta Exposition address, Booker T. Washington borrowed the phrase "cast your bucket down" from educator Hugh M. Brown. For more, see Harlan, *Booker T. Washington,* 212. For a text of Washington's speech, see Lewis Copeland, Lawrence W. Lamb, and Stephen J. KcKenna, eds., *The World's Greatest Speeches* (Mineola, NY: Dover Publications, orig. published, Random House, 1942), 814–822.
44. "The Negro and the South," editorial, *Hattiesburg News,* December 7, 1916, 4; and "Big Wages Inveigle Negroes to Chicago," *Hattiesburg News,* October 9, 1916, 2.
45. "Oily-tongued . . ." quoted in "Negroes Find the Weather and People Cold Way Up North," *Hattiesburg News,* December 11, 1916, 1; "To Disperse Crowds of Negroes at Depot," *Hattiesburg News,* October 28, 1916, 1; "Officers Break Negro Loitering about Stations," *Hattiesburg News,* October 30, 1916, 1; Johnson, "Migration Study," box 86, folder: Migration Study Chicago Interviews, NUL; and Scott, *Negro Migration During the War,* 77–78.
46. "Negroes who . . ." quoted in "Negroes Find the Weather and People Cold Way Up North," *Hattiesburg News,* December 11, 1916, 1; "Chicago is not . . ." and "They are helpless . . ." quoted in "Chicago Yells for Influx of Blacks to Quit," *Hattiesburg News,* December 28, 1916, 1; "strong, healthy . . ." and "cold

climate . . ." quoted in "Southern Negroes Are Chill-Attached in North and Are Returning Home," *Hattiesburg News*, December 19, 1916, 6; "fading . . ."quoted in "200 Negro Wards of Labor Agents Get Home-Sickness Blues; Coming Back Home," *Hattiesburg News*, October 28, 1916, 1; and "will teach . . ." quoted in "The Negro and the South," editorial, *Hattiesburg News*, December 7, 1916, 4.

47. Johnson, "Migration Study Chicago Interviews," box 86, folder: Migration Study Chicago Interviews, NUL.
48. Frazier quoted in William P. Jones, *The Tribe of Black Ulysses: African American Lumber Workers in the Jim Crow South* (Urbana: University of Illinois Press, 2005), 45.
49. Johnson, "The Mississippi Colony," 29–31, box 86, folder: Migration Study Draft (Early), NUL; "Hattiesburgers Arrive," *Chicago Defender*, March 19, 1917, 7; McMillen, *Dark Journey*, migrant quoted on 264; and "for the first time . . ." in Johnson, "Migration Study Chicago Interviews," box 86, folder: Migration Study Chicago Interviews, NUL. None of this is to say that black life in Chicago was in any way idyllic. The African Americans who moved there experienced an onslaught of racially based discrimination and violence, most notably the 1919 Chicago Race Riot that resulted in thirty-eight deaths and more than five hundred injuries. For more on the experience of African Americans in Chicago, see Allan H. Spear, *Black Chicago: The Making of the Negro Ghetto, 1890–1920* (Chicago, IL: University of Chicago Press, 1967); E. Franklin Frazier, *The Negro Family in Chicago* (Chicago, IL: University of Chicago Press, 1932); Davarian L. Baldwin, *Chicago's New Negroes: Modernity, the Great Migration, and Black Urban Life* (Chapel Hill: University of North Carolina Press, 2007); Ira Katznelson, *Black Men, White Cities: Race, Politics, and Migration in the United States, 1900–1930, and Britain, 1948–68* (London: Oxford University Press, 1973); and Chicago Commission on Race Relations, *The Negro in Chicago*.
50. "Men who have . . . ," "Got the Northern fever . . . ," and "Chi" quoted in unnamed document, box 86, folder: Migration Study Miscellany, NUL; and "given away . . ." quoted in "Rumor of Many Passes to North Drawing Blacks," *Hattiesburg News*, December 6, 1916, 1.
51. Johnson, "Migration Study," box 86, folder: Migration Study Miscellany, NUL.
52. Johnson, "Migration Study Chicago Interviews," box 86, folder: Migration Study Chicago Interviews, NUL.
53. Johnson, "The Mississippi Colony," 29–31, box 86, folder: Migration Study Draft (Early), NUL.
54. Johnson, "The Mississippi Colony," 29–31, box 86, folder: Migration Study Draft (Early), NUL; 1907 *Hattiesburg Polk City Directory*, Microform Reading

Room at the Library of Congress; and Johnson, "Migration Study Chicago Interviews," box 86, folder: Migration Study Chicago Interviews, NUL.

55. Scott, *Negro Migration During the War,* 102; and Johnson, "Migration Study Chicago Interviews," box 86, folder: Migration Study Chicago Interviews, NUL.
56. Quoted in Scott, *Negro Migration during the War,* 30; Rev. S. W. White, "Colored Column," *Hattiesburg American,* May 3, 1919, 3; Rev. S. W. White, "Colored Column," *Hattiesburg American,* May 19, 1919, 7; Rev. S. W. White, "Colored Column," *Hattiesburg American,* April 5, 1919, 6; and Rev. S. W. White, "Colored Column," *Hattiesburg American,* June 28, 1919, 2.
57. Hattiesburg Chamber of Commerce Report on Negro Migration, May 2, 1923, box 73, folder 4, Tatum Papers; Scott, *Negro Migration during the War,* 87, for wage figures; Grossman, *Land of Hope,* especially 52–54; McMillen, *Dark Journey,* 85; and Alferdteen Harrison, *Black Exodus: The Great Migration from the South* (Jackson: University Press of Mississippi, 1991), 93.
58. See Chapter 6 for a more in-depth discussion of Eureka High School's extraordinary contribution to both the education of black students in Hattiesburg and the Hattiesburg community as a whole. "Negro School to be Ready on Day Studies Commence," *Hattiesburg American,* August 19, 1921, 7; "Former Eureka Principal Dies," *Hattiesburg American,* October 11, 1948, 9; "Mrs. Hathorn Critical of Expenditure," *Hattiesburg American,* July 15, 1922, 5; "Negro Education Makes Progress," *Chicago Broad Ax,* August 5, 1922, 3; Monroe N. Work, ed., *Negro Year Book,* 1921–1922 (Tuskegee, AL: Negro Year Book Publishing Company, 1922), 21; Smith, interview; Burger, interview; Mrs. Marie Washington Kent, interview by Jesse Flowers, Grenada, Mississippi, June 16,1995, transcript, USM-OH; Arthur M. Evans, "Schools Stop Negro Exodus," *Los Angeles Times,* September 14, 1923, 16. For more on the construction of the school in response to the Great Migration, see McMillen, *Dark Journey,* 85; and Charles C. Bolton, *The Hardest Deal of All: The Battle over School Integration in Mississippi,* 1870–1980 (Jackson: University Press of Mississippi, 2005), 17–18.
59. *Negroes in the United States,* 1920–1932, 60; Johnson, "The Mississippi Colony," 29–31, box 86, folder: Migration Study Draft (Early), NUL; and Greene and Woodson, *The Negro Wage Earner,* 210.

5. *Broken Promises*

Epigraph: Untitled article, *Hattiesburg Daily Progress,* July 17, 1902, 2.

1. "Tatum family History (1924)," box 464, folder 19, Tatum Papers; and quotes taken from "Mayor Tatum's Life Is Linked with Hub City's Past History," *Hattiesburg American,* January 7, 1929, 9.

2. "Tatum family History (1924)"; "Quiet Observance Marking Half Century of Happiness and Activities for Couple," *Hattiesburg American*, June 8, 1931, 5; and "W. S. F. Tatum," in Dunbar Rowland, *History of Mississippi*, vol. 4 (Chicago, IL: S. J. Clarke Publishing Co., 1925), 322–326.
3. "Tatum family History (1924)"; the 2,200-acre figure is taken from "Mayor Tatum's Life Is Linked With Hub City's Past History," *Hattiesburg American*, January 7, 1929, 9.
4. "Tatum family History (1924)"; forty thousand and four hundred figures and quotes taken from "Mayor Tatum's Life Is Linked with Hub City's Past History," *Hattiesburg American*, January 7, 1929, 9; "Lumber King Tells Story of Purchase," *Hattiesburg American*, January 7, 1924, 1; Jack Alan Smith, "A Study of Place-Names in Forrest County, Mississippi" (PhD diss., Auburn University, 1969); "robbissary" quoted from Earles, interview; "W. S. F. Tatum," in Rowland, *History of Mississippi*, vol. 4, 322–326; and "Estimated Worth of Tatum Lumber Co., Bonhomie, Forrest Co. Miss . . . (1916)," box 86, folder 2, Tatum Papers.
5. T. S. Jackson, "Glimpses of the Past: When I Was Twenty-One," *Hattiesburg American*, January 29, 1929, 4; personal observations made at T. S. Jackson gravesite in Hattiesburg's Oaklawn Cemetery on June 7, 2011; and 1900 U.S. Census, Amite County, Mississippi, Population Schedule, beat 2, sheet 1, dwelling 13, family 13, T. Smylie Jackson, digital image, Ancestry.com, accessed January 9, 2015.
6. T. S. Jackson, "Glimpses of the Past: When I Was Twenty-One," *Hattiesburg American*, January 29, 1929, 4; "Hub Wholesale Firm's Capital Stock is $500,000," *Hattiesburg American*, October 30, 1928, 4; "Merchants Company a Vital Local Factor for 50 Years," *Hattiesburg American*, January 29, 1959, 1; *Polk's Hattiesburg City Directory, 1918* (Memphis, TN: R. L. Polk & Co., 1918), 196; and 1920 U.S. Census, Forrest County, Mississippi, Population Schedule, Hattiesburg, sheet 17B, dwelling 306, family 366, Thomas S. Jackson, digital image, Ancestry.com, accessed January 9, 2015.
7. United States Selective Service System, World War I Selective Service System Draft Registration Cards, 1917–1918 (Washington, DC: National Archives and Records Administration), Registration State: Mississippi, Registration County: Forrest, Roll 1682920; Mississippi Genealogical Society, *Forrest County, Mississippi Tombstone Inscriptions* (Carrollton, MS: Pioneer Publishing Co., 1999, orig., 1986), 290; Edwin S. Coles to L. E. Faulkner, Mansfield, PA, July 16, 1928, box 1, folder 3, Faulkner Papers; and "L. E. Faulkner Dies," *Hattiesburg American*, January 16, 1961, 1.
8. Edwin S. Coles to L. E. Faulkner, Mansfield, PA, July 16, 1928, box 1, folder 3, Faulkner Papers; 1910 U.S. Census, Adams County, Mississippi, Population Schedule, Natchez, sheet 5A, dwelling 68, family 92, Louis Faulkner, digital image, Ancestry.com, accessed January 9, 2015; "L. E. Faulkner Services Set

for Wednesday," *Hattiesburg American*, January 17, 1961, 1; and "Final Tribute Paid to L. E. Faulkner," *Hattiesburg American*, January 19, 1961, 9A.

9. "Mayor Tatum's Life Is Linked with Hub City's Past History," *Hattiesburg American*, January 7, 1929, 9; "Rotary Club Gives Wilson Endorsement," *Hattiesburg American*, April 29, 1919, 8; "T. S. Jackson Will Lead Red Cross Drive," *Hattiesburg American*, November 9, 1928, 1; "Final Tribute to T. S. Jackson," *Hattiesburg American*, January 11, 1934, 8; and "Funeral for M'Millin Boy Here Tuesday," *Hattiesburg American*, October 20, 1924, 8.
10. 1906–1911 Commercial Club of Hattiesburg Record Book, box 1, folder 1, CoC.
11. T. S. Jackson, "Commerce Chamber Organized Here by Small Group in 1904," *Hattiesburg American*, October 30, 1928; Past Presidents, Commercial Club of Hattiesburg and Hattiesburg Area Chamber of Commerce, box 1, folder 1, CoC; and Hattiesburg Chamber of Commerce Constitution, box 73, folder 4, Tatum Papers.
12. T. S. Jackson, Hattiesburg Chamber of Commerce Report on Negro Migration, May 2, 1923, box 73, folder 4, Tatum Papers; and Benjamin Morris, *Hattiesburg, Mississippi: A History of the Hub City* (Charleston, SC: The History Press, 2014), especially 109–115.
13. US Census Bureau, *Census of the Population: 1920*, vol. 9, *Manufactures*, 1919, part 1 (Washington, DC: Government Printing Office, 1923), 759 and 769, respectively for Hattiesburg wage statistics; Buck Wells, interview with Lawrence Knight, Hattiesburg, MS, April 24 and 28, 1997, transcript, USM-OH; J. S. Finlayson, interview by Chester Morgan, Hattiesburg, MS, May 16, 1973, transcript, USM-OH. For more on wage labor and Mississippi consumerism, see Ted Ownby, *American Dreams in Mississippi: Consumers, Poverty, and Culture, 1830–1998* (Chapel Hill: University of North Carolina Press, 1999), especially 82–97.
14. "Newman's See Big Year for Pine Industry," *Hattiesburg American*, January 3, 1924, 8; and Journal Ledger, 1923–1925, box 8, Newman Lumber Company Records, USM.
15. Earles, interview.
16. Gulf & Ship Island Railroad vice president Thomas P. Hale quoted in "Gulf & Ship Island," *Wall Street Journal*, July 21, 1903, 5; McLeod and Pinchot quoted from "Plead Cause of Nation's Forests," *Chicago Tribune*, January 14, 1906, 5; "The Yellow Pine Timber of the South," *New York Times*, December 21, 1895, 16; and "Limiting Yellow Pine Output," *Washington Post*, April 9, 1900.
17. For more on the nature of lumber harvest, see Nollie W. Hickman, *Mississippi Harvest: Lumbering in the Longleaf Pinebelt, 1840–1915* (Jackson: University Press of Mississippi, 1962); and Gilbert H. Hoffman, *Steam Whistles in the Piney Woods: A History of the Sawmills and Logging Railroads of the Forrest and Lamar Counties, Mississippi*, vol. 1 (Hattiesburg: Longleaf Press, 1998).

18. Hickman, *Mississippi Harvest,* Newman figure on 181; and Henry B. Steer, compiling, *Lumber Production in the United States,* 1799–1946 (Washington, DC: U.S. Department of Agriculture, 1948), 12–15.
19. "Probable Yields from Fully Stocked Longleaf Pine Stands on University of Mississippi Land in South Mississippi," November 21, 1929, box 105, folder 2, Bilbo Papers, USM; and Earles, interview.
20. "A Study of the Effect of Fire on Longleaf Pine," box 105, folder 2, Bilbo (Theodore) Papers, USM; and Steer, *Lumber Production in the United States,* 15–16.
21. Wells, interview.
22. J. J. Newman Lumber Company Monthly Manufacturing States and Balance sheets, 1924–1929, Newman (J. J.) Lumber Company Records, USM; T. S. Jackson, "The Handwriting on the Wall," undated memo [most likely August/September 1929], box 3, folder 14, Faulkner Papers; "Newman's Mill Ends Work after 41 Consecutive Years," *Hattiesburg American,* November 16, 1935, 8; and Hoffman, *Steam Whistles,* 97–104.
23. This claim is based on 1903 Newman employment figures. Hoffman, *Steam Whistles,* quoted on 99; Howe (Tony) Railroad Map Collection, USM, for information on closing dates; Major-Sowers Company statistics taken from T. S. Jackson, "The Handwriting on the Wall," Hattiesburg, MS, undated memo, box 3, folder 14, Faulkner Papers; and Henry Watson, interview by Michael Vaughn, Piave, MS, June 4, 1997, transcript, USM-OH.
24. "G. & S. I. Costs I.C. $5,000,000," *Hattiesburg American,* January 3, 1925, 6; "Freight Carried during Year-Revenue," 510–511, MCRR Annual Report (1925), box 117, folder 23, sub-series J: Annual Reports, series 2, MCRR Collection; "Freight Carried during Year-Revenue," 512–519, MCRR Annual Report (1931), box 118, folder 3, sub-series J: Annual Reports, MCRR Collection; Henry B. Steer, comp., *Lumber Production in the United States,* 1799–1946 (Washington, DC: U.S. Department of Agriculture, 1948), 15–17; and veneer plant statistics taken from T. S. Jackson, "The Handwriting on the Wall," Hattiesburg, MS, undated memo, box 3, folder 14, Faulkner Papers.
25. Earles, interview; Hardy Roberts Stennis, interview by Charles Bolton, Macon, MS, September 22, 1999, transcript, USM-OH; "Three More Arrests in Connection with Money Theft at Hotel," *Hattiesburg American,* May 28, 1926, 8; "Hub City Hotel Will be Placed under Hammer," *Hattiesburg American,* January 28, 1929, 1; "Play Ball," editorial, *Hattiesburg American,* April 17, 1929, 4; "Toppers to Leave Hub City," *Hattiesburg American,* May 22, 1929, 1; and "Child's Body Is Discovered under Bridge," *Hattiesburg American,* November 30, 1928, 1.
26. T. S. Jackson, "The Handwriting on the Wall," Hattiesburg, MS, undated memo, box 3, folder 14, Faulkner Papers.

27. "There are . . ." quoted in F. W. Foote to Fenwick Peck, Hattiesburg, MS, January 4, 1929, box 3, folder 14, Faulkner Papers.
28. "Industries," box 10688, folder 3: Industry, series 447: Historical Research Material, 1935–1942, WPA-Forrest.
29. "Industries," box 10688, folder 3: Industry, series 447: Historical Research Material, 1935–1942, WPA-Forrest; and Davis Dyer and David B. Sicilia, *Labors of a Modern Hercules: The Evolution of a Chemical Company* (Boston, MA: Harvard Business School Press, 1990), quoted on 136.
30. US Census Bureau, *Census of the Population*: 1950, vol. 2, *Characteristics of the Population*: part 24, *Mississippi* (Washington, DC: Government Printing Office, 1952), 24–7.
31. Introducing Hattiesburg: "The Hub" of South Mississippi, distributed by the Hattiesburg Chamber of Commerce, Southern Tourism Collection, USM; and Minutes of March 18, 1930, Monthly Meeting of the Board of Directors, box 1, folder 2, CoC.
32. Examples taken from box 1, folders 2–15, Minutes of the Board of Directors, 1930–1943, CoC and Committees for 1928, box 3, folder 13, Faulkner Papers; "Activities of the Chamber of Commerce," box 4, folder 2, Faulkner Papers; and T. S. Jackson, "Commerce Chamber Organized Here by Small Group in 1904," *Hattiesburg American*, October 30, 1928, 3.
33. Examples taken from box 1, folders 2–15, Minutes of the Board of Directors, 1930–1943, CoC; and various correspondence in box 3, Faulkner Papers.
34. "Hub City Is Ready to Sign Pact with Nelson," *Hattiesburg American*, January 1, 1929, 1; F. W. Foote to Fenwick Peck, Hattiesburg, MS, January 4, 1929, box 3, folder 14, Faulkner Papers; L. E. Faulkner to F. W. Foote, Hattiesburg, MS, January 9, 1929, box 3, folder 14, Faulkner Papers; L. E. Faulkner to Fenwick Peck, Hattiesburg, MS, December 31, 1928, box 1, folder 5, Faulkner Papers; and Peck quoted in "Peck, Sawmill Veteran, Sees Bright Future," *Hattiesburg American*, January 21, 1930, 1.
35. T. S. Jackson to L. E. Faulkner, Hattiesburg, MS, August 23, 1928, box 3, folder 13, Faulkner Papers.
36. Club and Achievement Edition, *Hattiesburg American*, October 30, 1928, Jackson article on 3.
37. The Forrest Hotel Corporation Charter of Incorporation, September 21, 1928, box 137, folder 2, Tatum Papers; The Forrest Hotel Corporation Annual Report, December 31, 1930, box 137, folder 4, Tatum Papers; The Forrest Hotel Corporation Annual Report, December 31, 1932, box 137, folder 5, Tatum Papers; Audit Report of the Forrest Hotel Corporation, Year 1946, box 137, folder 18, Tatum Papers; T. S. Jackson, "Commerce Chamber Organized Here by Small Group in 1904," *Hattiesburg American*, October 30, 1928, 3; and Jody Cook, "Hub City Historic District National Register of Historic Places

Inventory—Nomination Form," 3, April 30, 1980, Hattiesburg, MS, U.S. Department of the Interior Heritage Conservation and Recreation Service. Building description drawn from personal observations made on June 15, 2011, and postcards of the Forrest Hotel found in box 1, Postcard Collection, USM.

38. "City Election Poll Officers Are Selected," *Hattiesburg American*, December 6, 1928, 8; and "Our Mayor—A Self-Made Man," editorial, *Hattiesburg American*, January 7, 1929, 16.

39. T. S. Jackson, Memo to Numerous Recipients, Hattiesburg, MS, June 6, 1928, box 3, folder 13, Faulkner Papers; T. S. Jackson, Memo, Hattiesburg, MS, December 12, 1928, box 3, folder 13, Faulkner Papers; Jackson quoted in T. S. Jackson, Memo to Industrial Affairs Committee, Hattiesburg, MS, July 17, 1928, box 3, folder 13, Faulkner Papers; and "Plant for Garment Factory Offered by Tatum," *Hattiesburg American*, December 15, 1928, 1.

40. "The Tuf-Nut Offer," *Hattiesburg American*, December 15, 1928, 1.

41. T. S. Jackson, Memo, Hattiesburg, MS, December 12, 1928, box 3, folder 13, Faulkner Papers; T. S. Jackson to Chamber of Commerce Board of Directors, Hattiesburg, MS, December 13, 1928, box 3, folder 13, Faulkner Papers; F. W. Foote to Fenwick Peck, Hattiesburg, MS, January 4, 1929, box 3, folder 14, Faulkner Papers; "The Tuf-Nut Offer," *Hattiesburg American*, December 15, 1928, 1; "Plant for Garment Factory Offered by Tatum," *Hattiesburg American*, December 15, 1928, 1; and "Garment Factory Stock Will Be Sold Tomorrow in Parcels of $125 Each," *Hattiesburg American*, December 17, 1928, 1.

42. "Garment Factory Stock Will be Sold Tomorrow in Parcels of $125 Each," *Hattiesburg American*, December 17, 1928, 1; and "Victory Seen by Factory Sales Force," *Hattiesburg American*, December 19, 1928, 1; and "Victory Seen by Factory Sales Force," *Hattiesburg American*, December 19, 1928, 1.

43. West Tatum, Memo, Hattiesburg, MS, December 24, 1928, box 3, folder 13, Faulkner Papers; "Factory Drive Postponed," *The Daily Herald*, December 22, 1928, 3; and "Victory Near in Drive for New Factory," *Hattiesburg American*, December 27, 1928, 1.

44. The description of this lynching is drawn from Special Session of Grand Jury Report, January 10, 1929, Forrest County Circuit Court Minute Books, vol. 9, 549–552, Hattiesburg, Mississippi; "Negro's Body, Half Clothed, Is Found on Richburg Hill," *Hattiesburg American*, December 27, 1928, 1; "Just Suppose," *Hattiesburg American*, December 29, 1928, 4; "Mississippi Ends Old Year by Lynching Two," *Chicago Defender*, January 4, 1929, 1; "Mass Meeting Asks Lynchers Be Arrested," *Pittsburgh Courier*, January 12, 1929, 5; "Man 'Hanged by Hands Unknown,' Jury Verdict," *Washington Post*, December 28, 1928; and "Inquiry into Another Lynching," *Washington Post*, January 1, 1929, 2.

45. 1900 U.S. Census, Perry County, Mississippi, Population Schedule, Township 5, 1A, dwelling 4, family 4, W. D. Easterling, digital image, Ancestry.com,

accessed January 9, 2015; US World War I Selective Service System Draft Registration Cards, 1917–1918, Mississippi, Lamar County, Roll 1682932, Ancestry.com, accessed January 9, 2015; Hattiesburg, sheet 3, May, 1925, Sanborn; and 1930 U.S. Census, Forrest County, Mississippi, Population Schedule, Hattiesburg, sheet 28A, dwelling 554, family 627, William Easterling, digital image, Ancestry.com, accessed January 9, 2015.

46. Special Session of Grand Jury Report, January 10, 1929, Forrest County Circuit Court Minute Books, vol. 9, 549–552, Hattiesburg, Mississippi; "Just Suppose," *Hattiesburg American*, December 29, 1928, 4; "Mississippi Ends Old Year by Lynching Two," *Chicago Defender*, January 4, 1929, 1; "Mass Meeting Asks Lynchers Be Arrested," *Pittsburgh Courier*, January 12, 1929, 5; "Man 'Hanged by Hands Unknown,' Jury Verdict," *Washington Post*, December 28, 1928; and "Inquiry into Another Lynching," *Washington Post*, January 1, 1929, 2.

47. The events surrounding McCallum's lynching were pieced together from the following sources: Special Session of Grand Jury Report, January 10, 1929, Forrest County Circuit Court Minute Books, vol. 9, 549–552, Hattiesburg, Mississippi; "Just Suppose," *Hattiesburg American*, December 29, 1928, 4; "Mississippi Ends Old Year by Lynching Two," *Chicago Defender*, January 4, 1929, 1; "Mass Meeting Asks Lynchers Be Arrested," *Pittsburgh Courier*, January 12, 1929, 5; "Man 'Hanged by Hands Unknown,' Jury Verdict," *Washington Post*, December 28, 1928; and "Inquiry into Another Lynching," *Washington Post*, January 1, 1929, 2.

48. "City Leaders in Vitriolic Words Condemn Killers and Call for Punishment," *Hattiesburg American*, December 29, 1928, 1, Smith quoted on 7.

49. "Mass Meeting Resolutions," *Hattiesburg American*, December 29, 1928, 1; "Money Needed for Burial Expenses of Mob's Victim," *Hattiesburg American*, December 29, 1928, 1; and "Mass Meetings Asks Lynchers Be Arrested," *Pittsburgh Courier*, January 12, 1929, 5.

50. "Dyer Bill Scares South into 'War' on Lynching," *Chicago Defender*, December 26, 1925, 1. For more on the Dyer Bill, see Walter White, *Rope and Faggot* (New York: Arno Press, 1969, orig., 1929), especially 109–113 and 178–181; Patricia Sullivan, *Lift Every Voice: The NAACP and the Making of the Civil Rights Movement* (New York: New Press, 2009), especially 61–101; Grace Elizabeth Hale, *Making Whiteness: The Culture of Segregation in the South, 1890–1940* (New York: Random House, 1998), 236–239; and Megan Ming Francis, "Crime and Citizenship: The NAACP's Campaign to End Racial Violence, 1909–1923" (PhD diss., Princeton University, 2008), especially 65–137.

51. "City Leaders in Vitriolic Words Condemn Killers and Call for Punishment," *Hattiesburg American*, December 29, 1928, 1 and 7, both quoted on 7; and "Real Civic Leadership," *Hattiesburg American*, December 29, 1928, 4.

52. Special Session of Grand Jury Report, January 10, 1929, Forrest County Circuit Court Minute Books, vol. 9, 549–552, Hattiesburg, Mississippi; and "Forrest County Starting Probe," *Jackson Clarion-Ledger*, January 8, 1929, 1.
53. "Topics of the Times," *New York Times*, February 10, 1929, 54; and "Light from Darkness," *Chicago Defender*, January 5, 1929, A2.
54. *Hattiesburg American*, January 10, 1929, 1; "A Worthy Successor to McLeod," editorial, *Hattiesburg American*, January 10, 1929, 4; and Hall and "The mass meeting . . ." quoted in "The Grand Jury Investigation," *Hattiesburg American*, January 11, 1929, 4.
55. Special Session of Grand Jury Report, January 10, 1929, Forrest County Circuit Court Minute Books, vol. 9, 549–552, Hattiesburg, Mississippi.
56. Special Session of Grand Jury Report, January 10, 1929, Forrest County Circuit Court Minute Books, vol. 9, 549–552, Hattiesburg, Mississippi; Hattiesburg Chamber of Commerce Finance Membership Committee, Memo to Members of the Chamber of Commerce, Hattiesburg, MS, March 26, 1928, box 3, folder 13, Faulkner Papers; Chamber of Commerce Financial Statement, January 1, 1929 to December 31, 1929, box 73, folder 4, Tatum Papers; "No Indictments Returned; Body May Meet Again," *Hattiesburg American*, January 10, 1929, 1; "Reward Mounts for Lynchers," *Los Angeles Times*, December 30, 1928, 6; and "Jury Fails to Indict in Lynch Case," *Chicago Defender*, January 19, 1929, 2.
57. "Shop Is Sold; Easterling to Quit Hub City," *Hattiesburg American*, January 17, 1929, 1; various Hattiesburg city directories, 1927–1956; and personal observations made at William Easterling gravesite in Hattiesburg, Mississippi's Highland Cemetery on June 7, 2011.
58. "Hub City Is Ready to Sign Pact with Nelson," *Hattiesburg American*, January 1, 1929, 1; "Nelson Here to Sign Pact for Factory," *Hattiesburg American*, January 15, 1929, 1; and "New Factory to be Ready in 3 Months," *Hattiesburg American*, January 16, 1929, 1.
59. "New Factory to be Ready in 3 Months," *Hattiesburg American*, January 16, 1929, 1; and "Factory Plan Is Postponed Indefinitely," *Hattiesburg American*, April 11, 1929, 1.
60. "A stain . . ." quoted in Special Session of Grand Jury Report, January 10, 1929, Forrest County Circuit Court Minute Books, vol. 9, 549–552, Hattiesburg, MS.
61. For more on the definition of lynching, see Christopher Waldrep, "War of Words: The Controversy over the Definition of Lynching, 1899–1940," *Journal of Southern History*, 66 (February 2000): 75–100.
62. Smith, interview; and fifty taken from Thompson, *Lynching in Mississippi*, 98.
63. State of Mississippi v. J. P. (Jay) Lee, Forrest County Circuit Court Minute Books, vol. 11, 118–162, Hattiesburg, Mississippi; "Pistol Ridge Stirred Anew by Shooting," *Hattiesburg American*, September 26, 1932, 1; "applauded his

manhood," quoted in "Pistol Ridge Murder Trial Near Close," *Hattiesburg American*, November 26, 1932, 1; and "Jury Returns Verdict, Out for 41 Hours," *Hattiesburg American*, November 28, 1932, 1.

64. State of Mississippi v. J. P. (Jay) Lee, Forrest County Circuit Court Minute Books, vol. 11, 118–162, Hattiesburg, Mississippi; and "Cause for Pride," editorial, *Hattiesburg American*, November 30, 1932, 4; "Dixie White Man Gets Life Sentence," *Pittsburgh Courier*, December 10, 1932, 5.
65. "Cause for Pride," editorial, *Hattiesburg American*, November 30, 1932, 4.
66. "Dixie White Man Gets Life Sentence," *Pittsburgh Courier*, December 10, 1932, 5.
67. "Convict White Man in Dixie Murder Case," *Chicago Defender*, December 10, 1932, 1; and "Dixie White Man Gets Life Sentence," *Pittsburgh Courier*, December 10, 1932, 5. For examples, see John O. Hodges, *Delta Fragments: The Recollections of a Sharecropper's Son* (Knoxville: University of Tennessee Press, 2013), 179; Renee C. Romano, *Racial Reckoning: Prosecuting America's Civil Rights Murders* (Cambridge, MA: Harvard University Press, 2014), 223; and James Meredith with William Doyle, *A Mission from God: A Memoir and Challenge for America* (New York: Simon & Schuster, 2012), 200.

6. *Those Who Stayed*

Epigraph: E. Hammond Smith, interview by Orley B. Caudill, Hattiesburg, MS, April 8, 1982, transcript, USM-OH.

1. Smith, interview; and Catalogue of the Officers and Students of Alcorn Agricultural & Mechanical College, 1914–1915, digital copy in author's possession, 44. It was Hammond himself who described his means of travel through the forest as a "wagon train."
2. Smith, interview.
3. Ibid.
4. Ibid.
5. Smith, interview; and 1923 and 1924 Meharry Commencement Catalogues, Meharry Medical College Archives, digital images, Meharry College, accessed April 8, 2015, http://diglib.mmc.edu/omeka/items/show/186. For more on Meharry Medical College, see Charles Johnson, *The Spirit of a Place Called Meharry: The Strength of Its Past to Shape the Future* (Franklin, TN: Hillsboro Press, 2000).
6. Smith, interview; sheet 10, Hattiesburg, MS, 1925, Sanborn; and *Polk's Hattiesburg City Directory: 1927* (Birmingham, AL: R. L. Polk & Co., 1927), 238–239.
7. Smith, interview; sheet 10, Hattiesburg, MS, 1925, Sanborn; 1930 U.S. Census, Forrest County, Mississippi, Population Schedule, Hattiesburg, sheets 17A and 18B, dwellings 382, 414, and 416, family 460, 493, 495, Smith, digital image,

Ancestry.com, accessed January 9, 2015; *Polk's Hattiesburg City Directory:* 1929 (Birmingham, AL: R. L. Polk & Co., 1929), 238–242; and "Dr. C. W. Smith Dies," *Hattiesburg American,* June 12, 1971, 1.

8. Smith, interview; and "Hattiesburg Group to Seat '65 Slate," *Hattiesburg American,* June 26, 1965, 19.
9. US Bureau of the Census, *Negroes in the United States, 1920–1932* (Washington, DC: Government Printing Office, 1935), 60.
10. US Bureau of the Census, *Census of the Population:* 1930, vol. 3, *Population,* part 1 (Washington, DC: Government Printing Office, 1932), 1301; and *Polk's Hattiesburg City Directory,* 1923 (Memphis, TN: R. L. Polk & Co., 1923).
11. *Census of the Population:* 1930, vol. 3, *Population,* part 1, 1301; *Polk's Hattiesburg City Directory,* 1923; Davis Dyer and David B. Sicilia, *Labors of a Modern Hercules: The Evolution of a Chemical Company* (Boston: Harvard Business School Press, 1990); and home ownership rates in *Negroes in the United States, 1920–1932,* 278.
12. *Negroes in the United States, 1920–1932,* 60 and 306; McKee, "The Residential Patterns of Blacks in Natchez and Hattiesburg and Other Mississippi Cities," especially 89–99; Douglas L. Conner with John F. Marszalek, *A Black Physician's Story: Bringing Hope in Mississippi* (Jackson: University Press of Mississippi, 1985), especially 1–18; sheet 16, Hattiesburg, May 1925, Sanborn; and May B. Everette, "Palmer, Forrest County," box 10687: Forrest County, folder 13: Forrest County: Early Settlements, WPA-Forrest.
13. McKee, "The Residential Patterns of Blacks in Natchez and Hattiesburg and Other Mississippi Cities," especially 89–99; "Anderson to Open Modern Show House," *Hattiesburg American,* September 16, 1926, 8; sheet 9, Hattiesburg, May 1925, Sanborn; *Polk's Hattiesburg City Directory,* 1923; Eberta Spinks, interview by Kim Adams, location unknown, spring 1995, transcript, USM-OH; and *Negroes in the United States, 1920–1932,* 292.
14. Sheet 10, Hattiesburg, May 1925, Sanborn; and "Mrs. Hathorn Critical of Expenditure," *Hattiesburg American,* July 15, 1922, 5.
15. Constance Baker, interview by Kim Adams, Hattiesburg, MS, April 3, 1995, transcript, USM-OH; Ariel Barnes interview by Sarah Rowe, April 1, 1993, transcript, USM-OH; N. R. Burger, interview by R. Wayne Pyle, Hattiesburg, MS, May 11, 1982, transcript, USM-OH; Marie Washington Kent, interview by M. L. Beard, Grenada, MS, June 16, 1995, transcript, USM-OH; and fourteen taken from "New School Board and Old Guests of Thames," *Hattiesburg American,* April 8, 1925, 2.
16. "'Black Billy' Will Talk on 'Devilution,'" *Hattiesburg American,* July 22, 1925, 8; "Negro Advises Race Brothers to Stay South," *Hattiesburg American,* July 21, 1923, 8; "Mississippi Association of Teachers, Colored Schools," *Hattiesburg American,* April 4, 1923, 8; "Full Week Is Promised for Colored Visitors," *Hatties-*

burg American, June 22, 1925, 6; "Afro-American Sons and Daughters Meet," *Chicago Defender,* August 23, 1930, 3; "Library Drive Great Success," *Hattiesburg American,* December 21, 1925, 6; "Eureka School to Have Movies," *Hattiesburg American,* September 23, 1926, 8; "Colored Singers Are to Be Here Monday Night," *Hattiesburg American,* May 6, 1922; "Famous Negro Singers Here," *Hattiesburg American,* November 22, 1926, 6; and "New School Board and Old Guests of Thames," *Hattiesburg American,* April 8, 1925, 2.

17. These conclusions are drawn from examining hundreds of issues of the *Hattiesburg American* between 1919 and 1930. In December of 1929, there was a brief column titled "Of Interest to Colored People" written by a local African American businessman that appeared on page two of the *Hattiesburg American.* Otherwise, almost all positive black news appeared on pages six or eight.
18. *Negroes in the United States, 1920–1932,* 60, 306, and 385; school budget details derived from "Mrs. Hathorn Critical of Expenditure," *Hattiesburg American,* July 15, 1922, 5; and Hattiesburg School Budget printed in *Hattiesburg American,* June 29, 1922, 1 and 7.
19. "Fatal Kiss Leads to Lyncher's Rope," *Chicago Defender,* March 26, 1921, 1; "Raid Jail, Hang Negro," *New York Times,* March 21, 1921, 13; "Negro Hanged by Mob," *Washington Post,* March 21, 1921, 4; "Negro Is Lynched by Mississippi Mob," *Nashville Tennessean,* March 21, 1921, 4; "Murdered Protecting Woman of His Race," *Chicago Defender,* September 29, 1923, 2; "Negro Lynched for Attack on Perry Citizen," *Hattiesburg American,* September 18, 1923, 1; "Seize and Slay Negro," *New York Times,* September 19, 1923, 3; and "Take Negro from Officers and Shoot Him to Death," *Chicago Daily Tribune,* September 19, 1923, 1.
20. Barnes, interview. For more on the history of racial violence and sexual assaults by whites on black women and girls during Jim Crow, see Leon F. Litwack, *Trouble in Mind: Black Southerners in the Age of Jim Crow* (New York: Vintage, 1998), especially 32–37; and Stephen A. Berrey, *The Jim Crow Routine: Everyday Performances of Race, Civil Rights, and Segregation in Mississippi* (Chapel Hill: University of North Carolina Press, 2015), especially 61–101.
21. See Nancy MacLean, *Behind the Mask of Chivalry: The Making of the Second Ku Klux Klan* (New York: Oxford University Press, 1994), statistic and quote on xi.
22. "The Birth of a Nation," editorial, *Hattiesburg News,* May 9, 1916, 4; Michael Newton, *The Ku Klux Klan in Mississippi* (Jefferson, NC: McFarland, 2010), especially 73–101; and Melvyn Stokes, *D. W. Griffith's The Birth of a Nation: A History of "The Most Controversial Motion Picture of All Time"* (New York: Oxford University Press, 2007).
23. The five hundred figure taken from "Hattiesburg Klansmen Will Dedicate Flag at Main Street School," *Hattiesburg American,* December 5, 1923, 1;

MacLean, *Behind the Mask of Chivalry*, especially 52–74; Newton, *The Ku Klux Klan in Mississippi*, 73–101; and Ben Earles, interview by R. Wayne Pyle, Hattiesburg, MS, June 28 and 29, 1979, transcript, USM-OH.

24. Stanton Hall, interview by Carl Willis, Hattiesburg, MS, April 14, 1972, transcript, USM-OH; "Murderer of Mrs. J. S. Mosley Pays for Crime at Hands of Masked Mob," *Hattiesburg American* July 23, 1921, 1; "Mississippi Mob Lynches Slayer," *Louisville Courier-Journal*, July 24, 1921, A7; "White Man Lynched by Mississippi Mob," *New York Times*, July 24, 1921, 16; "White Man Victim of Lynching Mob," *Atlanta Constitution*, July 24, 1921, 3; "Mississippians Hang White Man at Prison Door," *Chicago Defender*, July 30, 1921, 2; "Armed Preacher Alone Stops Mob on Lynching Bent," *Atlanta Constitution*, May 28, 1921, 14; and "Pastor, Armed, Saves Patient in Hospital from Masked Mob," *Louisville Courier-Journal*, May 28, 1921, 1. There is no direct evidence that the July 1921 lynching was the product of Klan activity, but the nature of the crime and attire of the assailants, who had tried to lynch the victim about six weeks earlier, suggests Klan involvement.

25. "Public Initiation" advertisement, *Hattiesburg American*, February 20, 1925, 8; "Former Ku Klux Head to Speak in City Sunday," *Hattiesburg American*, February 28, 1930, 12; "K.K.K. Submits, under Seal, Declaration of Its Principles, Objects," *Hattiesburg*, July 1, 1922, 2; "K.K.K. Gives Out Warning against Animal Cruelty," *Hattiesburg American*, July 15, 1922, 8; "Ku Klux in Battle on Glyn Film," *Hattiesburg American*, September 26, 1924, 1; "K.K.K. Chartered Train" advertisement appears in *Hattiesburg American*, July 22, 1925, 8; "Hattiesburg Klansmen Will Dedicate Flag at Main Street School," *Hattiesburg American*, December 5, 1923, 1; and "Ku Klux Aid in Hattiesburg Dry Raids," *Hattiesburg American*, February 13, 1924, 1. For more on Klansmen and prohibition enforcement, see Thomas R. Pegram, "Hoodwinked: The Anti-Saloon League and the Ku Klux Klan in 1920s Prohibition Enforcement," *Journal of the Gilded Age and Progressive Era* 7, no. 1 (2008): 89–119.

26. "History of National Negro Business League," *Atlanta Daily World*, August 18, 1937, 5; Louis R. Harlan, *Booker T. Washington: The Wizard of Tuskegee, 1901–1915* (New York: Oxford University Press, 1983), 538 and 229; and Louis Harlan, "Booker T. Washington and the National Negro Business League," in *Booker T. Washington in Perspective: Essays of Louis R. Harlan*, ed. Raymond W. Smock (Jackson: University of Mississippi Press, 1988), membership figures on 101.

27. The five thousand figure from "National Negro Business League Session a Success," *Philadelphia Tribune*, August 27, 1921, 1; Monroe N. Work, ed., *Negro Year Book, 1921–1922* (Tuskegee, AL: Negro Year Book Publishing Company, 1922), 347; "Chicago Host to National Business League," *Chicago Defender*,

August 16, 1924, 1; and "National Negro Business League to Present Great Program," *Pittsburgh Courier*, August 6, 1927, 11.

28. Gustavus Adolphus Steward, "Something New under the Sun," *Opportunity: A Journal of Negro Life*, January, 1925, 20–22; "most influential . . ." quoted in Willis Duke Weatherford, *Present Forces in Negro Progress* (New York: Association Press, 1912), 48; and "The National Negro Business League," *Philadelphia Tribune*, August 21, 1920, 9. For more on Charles Banks and the Mississippi Negro Business League, see David H. Jackson Jr., *A Chief Lieutenant of the Tuskegee Machine: Charles Banks of Mississippi* (Gainesville: University Press of Florida, 2002).

29. 1900 U.S. Census, Perry County, Mississippi, Population Schedule, Hattiesburg, sheet 22B, dwelling 396, family 432, Gaither Hardaway, digital image, Ancestry.com, accessed May 13, 2014; US, World War I Draft Registration Cards, 1917–1918, Gaither Hardaway, Serial Number 2555, digital image, Ancestry.com, accessed May 13, 2014; and Monroe N. Work, ed., *Negro Year Book, 1916–1917* (Tuskegee, AL: Negro Year Book Publishing Company, 1916), 322.

30. 1910 U.S. Census, Forrest County, Mississippi, Population Schedule, Hattiesburg, sheet 14B, dwelling 199, family 200, Gaither Hardaway, digital image, Ancestry.com, accessed May 13, 2014; 1909 *Hattiesburg City Directory*, USM, unpaginated; and US, World War I Draft Registration Cards, 1917–1918, Gaither Hardaway, Serial Number 2555, digital image, Ancestry.com, accessed May 13, 2014.

31. *Polk's Hattiesburg City Directory*, 1918; 1920 U.S. Census, Forrest County, Mississippi, Population Schedule, Hattiesburg, sheet 4B, dwelling 75, family 83, Gaither Hardaway, digital image, Ancestry.com, accessed May 13, 2014; "Groceryman" and delivery service taken from numerous advertisements in the *Hattiesburg American* between 1926 and 1928; and "G. Hardaway, Pioneer Negro Citizen, Dies at 76," *Hattiesburg American*, September 15, 1950, 7.

32. "G. Hardaway, Pioneer Negro Citizen, Dies at 76," *Hattiesburg American*, September 15, 1950, 7; "Services Tuesday for G. A. Hardaway," *Hattiesburg American*, September 18, 1950, 12; Louis Lautier, "Moton Again Heads Business League," *Pittsburgh Courier*, August 28, 1926, 2; "More Than 300 Persons at Annual Meeting of the Nat'l Negro Business League," *Philadelphia Tribune*, August 18, 1927, 9; "Average Race Business Lasts One Generation," *Baltimore Afro-American*, August 25, 1928, 1; "High Masons Hold Meet in Norfolk," *Pittsburgh Courier*, November 2, 1929, 4; "Red Cross Buttons Beginning to Make Appearance," *Hattiesburg American*, November 12, 1930, 1; "Colored Committee to Help in Drive by Salvation Army," *Hattiesburg American*, February 26, 1930, 14; "Mississippians in 'Race Uplift' Drive,"

Chicago Defender, September 14, 1929, 2; and Neil McMillen, *Dark Journey: Black Mississippians in the Age of Jim Crow* (Urbana, IL: University of Illinois Press, 1990), 308–312.

33. Smith, interview; "Doctors Urge Recognition," *Chicago Defender*, May 7, 1949, 26; "Funeral Directors Close Annual Meet in Mississippi," *Chicago Defender*, June 6, 1931, 11; and Charles C. Bolton, *The Hardest Deal of All: The Battle over School Integration in Mississippi, 1870–1980* (Jackson: University Press of Mississippi, 2005), 10–11.
34. These activities are derived from various issues of the *Hattiesburg American* and *Chicago Defender* between 1922 and 1932.
35. Donation amounts indicated in "Negro Charity Fund Is Growing," *Hattiesburg American*, December 20, 1927, 8; "Colored Club to Help Aged," *Hattiesburg American*, December 3, 1926, 6; J. C. Woodards, "Of Interest to Colored People," *Hattiesburg American*, December 20, 1929, 2; "Lion's Club Playing Santa Claus to Thousand Children of Hub," *Hattiesburg American*, December 26, 1930, 4; and "Y Sponsors Program for Negro Boys," *Hattiesburg American*, June 2, 1930, 7.
36. "Colored Group Seeks Support for New Home," *Hattiesburg American*, January 3, 1929, 8; "Contributions Requested for Colored Home," *Hattiesburg American*, January 16, 1929, 8; and "Employment Bureau Gets Complete Data from All Applicants," *Hattiesburg American*, February 11, 1929, 8.
37. 1909 *Hattiesburg City Directory*; "J. B. Woods, Negro Merchant, Dies," *Hattiesburg American*, May 25, 1944, 4; US World War I Draft Registration Cards, 1917–1918, John Bradley Woods, Serial Number 1954, digital image, Ancestry.com, accessed May 13, 2014; and *Polk's Hattiesburg City Directory, 1918*, 400.
38. Sheet 9, Hattiesburg, May 1925, Sanborn; and various Hattiesburg city directories between 1923 and 1962.
39. William White, "Demand G.O.P. Curb South," *Chicago Defender*, June 14, 1924, 1; "County G.O.P. to Hold Meet," *Hattiesburg American*, March 15, 1932, 6; "55 Alternates and Delegates at Chicago," *Baltimore Afro-American*, June 18, 1932, 1; "Colored Notables at Knox's Notification," *Atlanta Daily World*, August 11, 1936, 2; "Other Sidelights on Republican Convention," *Chicago Defender*, June 20, 1936, 4; and Cathi Carr, "Fire Destroys Historic Hotel; Memories Won't Die," *Hattiesburg American*, September 18, 1998, located in Woods Guest House Collection, USM.
40. "Xmas Seals' Sale Record is Reported," *Hattiesburg American*, February 27, 1922, 8; "Negro Will Work among Blacks in Xmas Seal Drive," *Hattiesburg American*, December 9, 1922, 8; "Committee Shows Christmas Seals Netted Good Sum," *Hattiesburg American*, February 8, 1923, 6; "Bishop Heard Will Dedicate Chapel Monday," *Hattiesburg American*, October 24, 1919, 8; "City

Negroes Pledged to Work for Victory," *Hattiesburg American*, June 29, 1918, 8; Minutes of the June 26, 1930 Hattiesburg Chamber of Commerce Board of Directors Meeting, box 1, folder 2, CoC; and "Many Seeking Relief Work," *Hattiesburg American*, November 30, 1932, 8.

41. "The Negro's Contribution," editorial, *Hattiesburg American*, March 26, 1929, 4.
42. Alcee Johnson, quoted in McMillen, *Dark Journey*, 310.
43. Reverend Ralph W. Woullard Jr., interview by Sadie Bailey, Hattiesburg, MS, February 20, 1995, transcript, USM-OH.
44. *Polk's Hattiesburg City Directory*, 1929, especially 350–351. For more on the historic role of women in black churches, see Bettye Collier-Thomas, *Jesus, Jobs, and Justice: African American Women and Religion* (New York: Knopf, 2010); Jerma A. Jackson, *Singing in My Soul: Black Gospel Music in a Secular Age* (Chapel Hill: University of North Carolina Press, 2004); and C. Eric Lincoln and Lawrence H. Mamiya, *The Black Church in the African American Experience* (Durham, NC: Duke University Press, 1990), especially 274–308.
45. "Negro Society Holds Meeting," *Hattiesburg American*, February 21, 1925, 7; "Colored Club Members Meet," *Hattiesburg American*, March 7, 1925, 6; "Colored Club Holds Meeting," *Hattiesburg American*, April 6, 1925, 2; February 28, 1925, 2; and "New Members for Colored Society," *Hattiesburg American*, April 30, 1925, 16.
46. These examples are taken from various issues of the *Chicago Defender* and *Baltimore Afro-American* between 1928 and 1933.
47. *Chicago Defender* circulation statistics taken from Paul K. Edwards, *The Southern Urban Negro as a Consumer* (New York: Negro University Press, 1969, orig., 1932), 174–177.
48. McGee, Brunson, and Mitchell are verified as regular correspondents in a number of reports. For examples, see "Hattiesburg, Miss.," *Chicago Defender*, August 17, 1929, 10; "Hattiesburg, Miss.," *Chicago Defender*, December 19, 1931, 17; and "Hattiesburg, Miss.," *Chicago Defender*, January 3, 1931, 17.
49. "Hattiesburg Social Service Club Entertains Visitors," *Chicago Defender*, September 27, 1930, 7; Hattiesburg Social Club Honors Guests of Member," *Chicago Defender*, August 22, 1931, 12; and "Hattiesburg Group to Seat '65 Slate," *Chicago Defender*, June 26, 1965, 19.
50. "Colored Club to Help Aged," *Hattiesburg American*, December 3, 1926, 6; "Hattiesburg, Miss.," *Chicago Defender*, January 21, 1928, A8; Negro Business League Advertisement, *Union Messenger*, November 29, 1934, 4; and "Negro Trade Survey Made in 33 Cities," *Hattiesburg American*, May 22, 1929, 4.
51. Smith, interview; Smith Drug Store advertisement printed in *Hattiesburg American*, February 2, 1928, 3; "Store Looted by Burglars," *Hattiesburg American*, January 30, 1933, 8; *Polk's Hattiesburg City Directory*, 1929;

52. Smith, interview; observations made at St. Paul Methodist Church on June 14, 2014; "Dr. C. W. Smith Dies," *Hattiesburg American*, June 21, 1971, 1; sheet 13, Hattiesburg, MS, April 1931 and August 1949, Sanborn; Mrs. Margaret Boutwell and Frances Griffith, "Assignment #26—Church History," May and September, 1937, box 10687, folder: Churches, Negro, Series 447: Historical Research Material, 1935–1942, WPA-Forrest; and "Negroes to Give Concert Wednesday Night at Eureka," *Hattiesburg American*, August 6, 1929, 2.
53. Charles Davis, interview by Anna Warren, Hattiesburg, MS, August 27, 2005, transcript, USM-OH; observations made at St. Paul Methodist Church on June 14, 2014; and *Polk's Hattiesburg City Directory*, 1929. When possible, these positions have also been corroborated with the 1930 US Census records.
54. Examples taken from *Chicago Defender* and *Baltimore Afro-American* between 1928 and 1933. Birthday party from "Pretty Party," *Chicago Defender*, October 7, 1933, 6.
55. "Hattiesburg," *Baltimore Afro-American*, September 3, 1932, 19; "Bride," *Chicago Defender*, November 12, 1932, 7; "Announce Engagement of Daughter at Pretty Party," *Chicago Defender*, August 20, 1932, 6; and "Hattiesburg," *Baltimore Afro-American*, October 1, 1932, 14.
56. "Bride," *Chicago Defender*, November 12, 1932, 7; "Announce Engagement of Daughter at Pretty Party," *Chicago Defender*, August 20, 1932, 6; "Hattiesburg," *Baltimore Afro-American*, October 1, 1932, 14; and 1940 U.S. Census, Coahoma County, Mississippi, Population Schedule, Clarksdale, sheet 11A, House Number 602, family 215, Gipson, digital image, Ancestry.com, accessed April 19, 2015.

7. *Reliance*

Epigraph: "Relief is Coming," editorial, *Hattiesburg American*, November 3, 1932, 6.

1. "Golden Jubilee Festival of Hattiesburg Will be Observed All Next Week," October 22, 1932, 1; "Rotary Holds Golden Jubilee Celebration At Its Weekly Meeting," *Hattiesburg American*, October 25, 1932, 1; "Shrine Hosts Will Invade Hattiesburg; Style Show and Big Frolic Tonight," *Hattiesburg American*, October 27, 1932, 1; "Parade Today to be Thrill for Throngs," *Hattiesburg American*, October 28, 1932, 1; "Hattiesburg Hails Governor Conner Today," *Hattiesburg American*, October 29, 1932, 1 & 7; and "Great Throng Sees Battle," *Hattiesburg American*, October 31, 1932, 7.
2. "New Foundation Laid for City's Expansion For Decades to Come," *Hattiesburg American*, October 26, 1932, 1.
3. Henry B. Steer, *Lumber Production in the United States, 1799–1946* (Washington, DC: US Government Printing Office, 1948), 11–16; Hickman, "Mississippi Forests," in Richard Aubrey McLemore, ed., *A History of Mississippi*, vol. 2

(Hattiesburg: University and College Press of Mississippi, 1973), 212–232; *The WPA Guide to the Magnolia State*, lumber figures on 109 and "scenery of . . ." quoted on 6; "Tatum Mill on Full Time Monday Morn," *Hattiesburg American*, July 30, 1932, 1; Gilbert H. Hoffman, *Steam Whistles in the Piney Woods: A History of the Sawmills and Logging Railroads of Forrest and Lamar Counties, Mississippi*, vol. 1 (Hattiesburg, MS: Longleaf Press, 1998) 106–178; *Polk's Hattiesburg City Directory*, 1923, 376–377; *Polk's Hattiesburg City Directory: 1929*, 371–372; "Where once . . ." quoted in "Numbered," Editorial, *Hattiesburg American*, November 8, 1932, 4; and "The Next Fifty," editorial, *Hattiesburg American*, October 26, 1932, 4.

4. J. Oliver Emmerich, "Collapse and Recovery," in McLemore, ed., *A History of Mississippi*, especially 97–119; cotton prices taken from William Lincoln Giles, "Agricultural Revolution, 1890–1970," in McLemore, ed., *A History of Mississippi*, vol. 2, 197; and state farm value taken from Donald B. Dodd, ed., *Historical Statistics of the States of the United States: Two Centuries of the Census, 1790–1990* (Westport, CT: Greenwood Press, 1993), 387. For more on global changes to cotton trade between 1860 and 1930, see Sven Beckert, *Empire of Cotton: A Global History* (New York: Knopf, 2015), especially 312–426.
5. State financial statistics taken from Emmerich, "Collapse and Recovery," in McLemore, ed., *A History of Mississippi*, 97 and 98; $2.3 million taken from "Financial Statement of the City of Hattiesburg for the Fiscal Year Beginning October 1st, 1931, and Ending September 30, 1932," *Hattiesburg American*, October 31, 1932, 6; and US Department of Commerce, *State Personal Income: 1929–1982* (Washington, DC: US Department of Commerce, Bureau of Economic Analysis, 1984), 8.
6. "Work on Road in this Area is Authorized," *Hattiesburg American*, October 27, 1932, 1; and US Bureau of the Census, *Census of the Population: 1940*, vol. 2, *Characteristics of the Population*, part 4, *Minnesota–New Mexico* (Washington, DC: Government Printing Office, 1943), 233.
7. This was also due to improved technology such as mechanical stokers that also made these positions much less difficult. "Attempt Made to Kill Negro," *Hattiesburg American*, August 9, 1932, 1; Eric Arnesen, *Brotherhoods of Color: Black Railroad Workers and the Struggle for Equality* (Cambridge, MA: Harvard University Press, 2001), especially 120–121; Theodore Kornweibel Jr., *Railroads in the African American Experience: A Photographic Journey* (Baltimore, MD: Johns Hopkins University Press, 2010), especially 62–80; and Howard W. Risher Jr., *The Racial Policies of American Industry, Report No 16: The Negro in the Railroad Industry* (Philadelphia, PA: University of Pennsylvania Press, 1971), 40–41.
8. *Polk's Hattiesburg City Directory, 1929* (Birmingham, AL: R. L. Polk & Co., 1929); *Polk's Hattiesburg City Directory, 1935* (Birmingham, AL: R. L. Polk &

Co., 1935); sheet 3, Hattiesburg, April, 1931+August, 1945, Sanborn; J. L. Langston and Lee R. Palmertree, "Lumber Industries—Past and Present," box #10688, folder: Industries, WPA-Forrest; Tatum wage statistics taken from a notice to employees, August 1, 1933, box 518, folder 5, Tatum Papers; and US Bureau of the Census, *Census of Partial Employment, Unemployment, and Occupations: 1937*, vol. 2 (Washington, DC: Government Printing Office, 1938), 382–383.

9. Ben Earles, interview by R. Wayne Pyle, Hattiesburg, MS, June 28 and 29, 1979, transcript, USM-OH; Dorothea Musgrove, interview by Cheri Adler, January 20, 2000, transcript, USM-OH; Buck Wells, interview with Lawrence Knight, Hattiesburg, MS, April 24 and 28, 1997, transcript, USM-OH; "Poverty Drives Out Drought Refugees," *Washington Post*, January 17, 1931, 3. For more on the precariat, see Guy Standing, *The Precariat: The New Dangerous Class* (London: Bloomsbury Academic, 2011).

10. These examples are taken from Minutes of the Hattiesburg Chamber of Commerce Board of Directors Meetings on various dates in 1930, box 4, folder 1, Faulkner Papers; Louis Faulkner to Fenwick Peck, Hattiesburg, MS, January 4, 1929, box 3, folder 14, Faulkner Papers; "Shall We Buy the Library," *Hattiesburg American*, January 28, 1929, 4; Display Ad—Improving Your I.Q., *Hattiesburg American*, November 2, 1935, 7; "Theatre Job is Let; Work Starts Soon," *Hattiesburg American*, January 29, 1929, 1; "Nearly 6,000 See Opening of Saenger," *Hattiesburg American*, November 29, 1929, 1; Donald Dana, "Library Vital to Civic Asset," *Hattiesburg American*, October 26, B4; Cook, "Hub City Historic District," item #7, pages 1–4; *Polk's Hattiesburg City Directory*, 1929 (Birmingham, AL: R. L. Polk & Co., 1929); 1935 *Polk's Hattiesburg City Directory*; sheet 3, Hattiesburg, April, 1931, and August, 1945, Sanborn; and Jackson quoted in undated memo summarizing activities of the Chamber of Commerce in 1930, box 4, folder 2, Faulkner Papers.

11. Personal observations of the tombstone at his gravesite in Hattiesburg's Oaklawn Cemetery on June 7, 2011; "T. S. Jackson Long Leader in City, Dies," *Hattiesburg American*, January 9, 1934, 1; various correspondence in box 4, folder 1, Faulkner Papers and box 1, folders 2–7 in CoC; "ill in bed . . ." quoted in Minutes of the October 11, 1932 Hattiesburg Chamber of Commerce Board of Directors Meeting, box 1, folder 4, CoC; and "Few . . ." quoted in "Good Citizen," editorial, *Hattiesburg American*, January 10, 1934, 2.

12. Donations and amounts taken from Dunbar Rowland, *History of Mississippi, The Heart of the South*, vol. 4 (Chicago: S. J. Clarke Publishing Co., 1925), 322–326, quoted on 322.

13. YMCA official J. Maury Gundy to Faulkner, Hattiesburg, MS, October 18, 1928, box 1, folder 4, Faulkner Papers. Dozens of letters and memos requesting

and acknowledging donations can be found in box 3, folders 6, 7, and 8, and box 5, folders 1 and 2, Faulkner Papers.

14. "Church and Charity Campaign," *Hattiesburg American*, October 19, 1932, 8; "Interest Shown for Campaign," *Hattiesburg American*, October 14, 1932, 3; Full Page Display Ad—Church and Charity Campaign, *Hattiesburg American*, October 22, 1932, 6, "open to . . ." quoted on 6; and Faulkner donations taken from correspondence found in box 5, folders 1 and 2, Faulkner Papers.
15. "Without . . ." quoted in "J. C. Fields Issues Appeal for Donations to Red Cross, Many Hundreds Immediately Need Help," *Hattiesburg American*, February 2, 1931, 10; and "No hungry . . ." quoted in "National Red Cross Takes Over Relief Here," *Hattiesburg American*, January 23, 1931, 1.
16. "'Nothing for Grafters and Spongers,' Red Cross Head Asserts," *Hattiesburg American*, February 3, 1931, 7; "Red Cross Head Scores Critics," *Hattiesburg American*, February 10, 1931, 7; and "Proportionate Giving," editorial, *Hattiesburg American*, January 28, 1931, 4.
17. "Red Cross Head Scores Critics," *Hattiesburg American*, February 10, 1931, 7; "Tatum Says Aid Seekers Hold Up Work," *Hattiesburg American*, February 12, 1931, 1; "White Supremacy," *Philadelphia Tribune*, March 19, 1931, 9; and "The droves . . ." quoted in "City Fathers Say Red Cross Action Hasty," *Hattiesburg American*, February 14, 1931, 1.
18. Bishop quoted in "Tatum Says Aid Seekers Hold Up Work," *Hattiesburg American*, February 12, 1931, 1.
19. "No nigger . . ." quoted in "The Red Cross Knows No Color," *New York Daily Mirror*, March 12, 1931, and Margaret Butler-Bishop to Robert E. Bondy, Hattiesburg, MS, February 12, 1931, both located in John H. Bracy and August Meier, eds., NAACP/mf, part 11, series A, reel 24, frame 0031; "Tatum Says Aid Seekers Hold Up Work," *Hattiesburg American*, February 12, 1931, 1; Mayor's Office statement included in "City Fathers Say Red Cross Action Hasty," *Hattiesburg American*, February 14, 1931, 1; "Mississippi Mayor 'Fires' Red Cross," *Chicago Defender*, February 21, 1931, 1; "White Supremacy," *Philadelphia Tribune*, March 19, 1931, 9; and "Inhumanity in Mississippi," *Wyandotte Echo*, April 10, 1931, 1.
20. "White Supremacy," *Philadelphia Tribune*, March 18, 1931, 9.
21. "Golden Jubilee to Fire All Citizens with New Hope and Zeal for Hub," *Hattiesburg American*, October 19, 1932, 1.
22. Minutes of the August 30, 1932, Hattiesburg Chamber of Commerce Meeting, box 1, folder 4, CoC; Minutes of the Hattiesburg Chamber of Commerce Board of Directors Meetings on August 30, 1932, September 23, 1932, October 17, 1932, and October 21, 1932, all located in box 1, folder 4, CoC; and Report of Special Committee on Reliance Manufacturing Company, box 1, folder 5,

CoC. For more on the Fantus Factory Locating Service, see James C. Cobb, *The Selling of the South: The Southern Crusade for Industrial Development* (Urbana: University of Illinois Press, 1993).

23. Advertisement—*Hattiesburg American*, October 26, 1932, 8–9.
24. "Hub Citizens Welcome Reliance Officials," *Hattiesburg American*, October 26, 1932, 1; "Rotary Holds Golden Jubilee Celebration at Its Annual Meeting," *Hattiesburg American*, October 25, 1932, 1; "Reliance Executives Return to Hub City for Further Factory Survey," *Hattiesburg American*, October 27, 1932, 1; Report of Special Committee on Reliance Manufacturing Company, box 1, folder 5, CoC; and Minutes of the October 11, 1932 Hattiesburg Chamber of Commerce Board of Directors Meeting, box 1, folder 4, CoC.
25. "Some folks will be embarrassed" quoted from "Cleanliness," editorial, *Hattiesburg American*, October 24, 1932, 4.
26. Minutes of Meeting of Special Committee for Reliance Manufacturing Project, September 23, 1932, box 1, folder 4, CoC; Minutes of Meeting of Special Committee for Reliance Manufacturing Project, October 17, 1932, box 1, folder 4, CoC; Minutes of Meeting of Special Committee for Reliance Manufacturing Project, October 21, 1932, box 1, folder 4, CoC; Minutes of Special Meeting of the Board of Directors of Hattiesburg Chamber of Commerce, August 15, 1933, box 1, folder 7, CoC; and "Total Expenditures for Reliance Factory Building," October 10, 1933, box 1, folder 7, CoC.
27. $2.3 million taken from "Financial Statement of the City of Hattiesburg for the Fiscal Year Beginning October 1st, 1931, and Ending September 30, 1932," *Hattiesburg American*, October 31, 1932, 6; Minutes of Meeting of Special Committee for Reliance Manufacturing Project, October 11, 1932, box 1, folder 4, CoC; Minutes of Meeting of Special Committee for Reliance Manufacturing Project, October 17, 1932, box 1, folder 4, CoC; Minutes of Meeting of Special Committee for Reliance Manufacturing Project, October 21, 1932, box 1, folder 4, CoC; Report of Special Committee on Reliance Manufacturing Company, box 1, folder 7, CoC; Contract between the Hattiesburg Chamber of Commerce and L. E. Faulkner, F. W. Foote, W. W. Crawford, and G. W. McWilliams, June 6, 1933, box 1, folder 7, CoC; Mortgage between the Hattiesburg Chamber of Commerce and the Hattiesburg First National Bank also found in box 1, folder 7, CoC; List of Contracts for Reliance Building, box 1, folder 7, CoC; "$80,000 is Sought by Saturday to Clinch Reliance Garment Factory for Hub City," *Hattiesburg American*, April 28, 1933, 1; and "More than $20,000 Still Needed for Factory," *Hattiesburg American*, April 29, 1933, 1.
28. "Factory Contract Made," *Hattiesburg American*, May 2, 1933, 1; and "This building . . ." quoted in "Citizens from Many Sections of State Here for Ceremony," *Hattiesburg American*, October 20, 1933, 1. Reliance also opened a new factory in Columbia, Mississippi, whose mayor, Hugh White, became

governor of Mississippi in 1936 and helped institute a program named Balance Agriculture With Industry (BAWI) that led to increased industrial development across the state beginning in the late 1930s and later influenced industrialization across the South. See Connie L. Lester, "Balancing Agriculture with Industry: Capital, Labor, and the Public Good in Mississippi's Home-Grown New Deal," *Journal of Mississippi History* 70 (Fall 2008): 235–263; and James C. Cobb, *The Selling of the South*, especially 5–34.

29. For a narrative of the 1912 presidential election, see James Chace, *1912: Wilson, Roosevelt, Taft and Debs—The Election That Changed the Country* (New York: Simon & Schuster, 2005).

30. See William E. Leuchtenburg, *Herbert Hoover: The American Presidents Series: The 31st President, 1929–1933* (New York: Times Books, 2009).

31. "Laying a Ghost," *Hattiesburg American*, October 21, 1932, 2; and *Congressional Record*, 72nd Cong., 1st sess., 1932, 75, pt. 8: 9190. For more on the Bonus Army, see Donald J. Lisio, *President and Protest: Hoover, Conspiracy and the Bonus Riot* (Columbia: University of Missouri Press, 1974); and Paul Dickson and Thomas B. Allen, *The Bonus Army: An American Epic* (New York: Walker and Company, 2006).

32. "Relief is Coming," editorial, *Hattiesburg American*, November 3, 1932, 6; "Hub City, Forrest and Neighbor Counties Give Roosevelt Great Total," *Hattiesburg American*, November 9, 1932, 1; and "Forrest County Vote," *Hattiesburg American*, November 10, 1932, 1. For more on the New Deal in Mississippi, see Chester M. Morgan, *Redneck Liberal: Theodore G. Bilbo and the New Deal* (Baton Rouge: Louisiana State University Press, 1985).

33. Wells, interview.

34. Ibid. "Every single issue" conclusion derived from examining thousands of issues of the *Hattiesburg American* between 1933 and 1940.

35. Ira Katznelson, *When Affirmative Action Was White: An Untold History of Racial Inequality in Twentieth Century America* (New York: Norton, 2005), especially 25–52.

36. See John A. Salmond, *The Civilian Conservation Corps, 1933–1942: A New Deal Study* (Durham, NC: Duke University Press, 1967), 570 million on 123.

37. Earles, interview. Examples include "18 Million Pine Seedlings to Be Planted," *Hattiesburg American*, November 26, 1935, 1; "Forest Fires," *Hattiesburg American*, January 29, 1936, 1; "Forestry," *Hattiesburg American*, March 14, 1936, 1; statistics reported and paper quoted in "Nearly 8 Million Pines Are Set Out," *Hattiesburg American*, March 24, 1937, 1; and "CCC To Hold Open House," *Forrest County News*, April 1, 1937, 1.

38. Salmond, *The Civilian Conservation Corps*, 84 for statistic on Mississippi CCC camps and 88–101 for more on African American workers and the CCC program.

39. For more on the NRA, see Robert F. Himmelberg, *The Origins of the National Recovery Administration: Business, Government, and the Trade Association Issue, 1921–1933* (New York: Fordham University Press, 1993).
40. Minutes of Special Meeting of the Board of Directors of Hattiesburg Chamber of Commerce, August 15, 1933, box 1, folder 7, CoC; "Reliance Manufacturing Quarter Sales Set Record," *Chicago Tribune*, April 29, 1934, A7; and Minutes of Special Meeting of the Board of Directors of Hattiesburg Chamber of Commerce, December 12, 1933, box 1, folder 7, CoC. The NRA was declared unconstitutional by the Supreme Court, which argued that the legislative branch had overstepped its authority by influencing consumer prices on intrastate goods.
41. Examples of Faulkner's political correspondence can be found in box 1, folders 1–15, Faulkner Papers; and Tatum examples can be found in various correspondence located in box 77, folder 15, Tatum Papers. Also see Hoffman, *Steam Whistles in the Piney Woods*, vol. 1, especially 133–178. Many Southern businessmen found New Deal measures such as the NRA and even the Social Security Act particularly troubling because of minimum wage requirements and employee benefits. See Bruce J. Schulman, *From Cotton Belt to Sunbelt: Federal Policy, Economic Development, and the Transformation of the South, 1938–1980* (New York: Oxford University Press, 1991), especially 21–31.
42. *Final Report on the WPA Program, 1935–1943* (Washington, DC: US Government Printing Offices, 1946), total spending on 99 and construction statistics on 131–133. For more on the WPA, see Donald S. Howard, *The WPA and Federal Relief Policy* (New York: Da Capo Press, 1973, orig., 1943), especially 70–101 for the WPA in the South.
43. Per capita WPA spending taken from Jason Scott Smith, *Building New Deal Liberalism: The Political Economy of Public Works, 1933–1956* (New York: Cambridge University Press, 2006), 116–117; and *Final Report on the WPA Program, 1935–1943*, 110–116.
44. Minutes of the May 28, 1935, Hattiesburg Chamber of Commerce Board of Directors Meeting, box 1, folder 9, CoC.
45. "WPA Projects: Many More Are Approved," *Hattiesburg American*, November 5, 1935, 7; "Immense City Paving Project Approved," *Hattiesburg American*, November 7, 1935, 1; "High School Gym Project Approved," *Hattiesburg American*, November 16, 1935, 1; "Hub City Gym Will Open Tuesday," *Hattiesburg American*, February 15, 1937, 1; "Open New Gym Tonight," *Hattiesburg American*, February 16, 1937, 1; "New Gymnasium Delights Crowd; Purvis and Hattiesburg Divide," *Hattiesburg American*, February 17, 1937, 1; WPA-related proposals and meetings can be found in box 1, folders 9 and 10, CoC; "Building in Hattiesburg and Vicinity Picks

Up Speed," *Hattiesburg American*, December 5, 1935, 6; and "C. of C. Banquet Ticket Deadline 9 a.m. Friday," *Hattiesburg American*, December 5, 1935, 12.

46. "Pine Street: Start Widening Work," *Hattiesburg American*, January 9, 1940, 8; Wells, interview; J. L. Langston, "Beautification Project—#1227 Forrest County," box 10687, folder: Forrest County Agriculture, WPA-Forrest; India Lou Bryant, "Assignment #16—Section 'C' Landscaping—College Grounds," box 10687, folder: The Arts, WPA-Forrest; and WPA-related proposals and meetings can be found in box 1, folders 9 and 10, CoC. "Building in Hattiesburg and Vicinity Picks Up Speed," *Hattiesburg American*, December 5, 1935, 6; Minutes of the May 28, 1935 Hattiesburg Chamber of Commerce Board of Directors Meeting, box 1, folder 9, CoC; Works Progress Administration, *Mississippi: The WPA Guide to the Magnolia State* (Jackson: University Press of Mississippi, 1938); "WPA Volume on Mississippi Ready to be Released," *Hattiesburg American*, May 5, 1938, 3; and Series 447: Historical Research Material, 1935–1942, MDAH.
47. T. S. Jackson, "Commerce Chamber Organized Here by Small Group in 1904," *Hattiesburg American*, October 30, 1928, 1; "Division Heads over Army Camps," *New York Times*, August 7, 1917, 3; "Select Last Sites for Guard Camps," *New York Times*, July 13, 1917, 4; Clara Rodgers Dunn, "Hattiesburg Merchants Busiest after Nightfall," *Trench and Camp*, October 31, 1917, 1; "Camp Shelby," *National Geographic Magazine*, November, 1917, 472; "Builders of Camp Shelby Ready to Leave for Home," *Trench and Camp* December 25, 1917, 1; "Tent Camps to be Abandoned," *Washington Post*, November 30, 1918, 6; and Mark Older and M &M Publishing, *The City of Hattiesburg, 1884–2009: Challenges and Growth, Historic Past and Brilliant Future* (Hattiesburg, MS: M & M Publishing, 2009), especially 30–31.
48. Minutes of the May 28, 1935 Hattiesburg Chamber of Commerce Board of Directors Meeting, box 1, folder 9, CoC; Memo from Lt. Col. H. J. Dalton, Jackson, MS, June 3, 1935, box 276, folder: WPA Camp Shelby Project 1940 Data, Mississippi Armed Forces Museum Archives, Camp Shelby, MS; Lt. Col. H. J. Dolton to Mr. G. M. McWilliams, Jackson, MS, December 2, 1936, box 276, folder: WPA Camp Shelby Project 1940 Data, Mississippi Armed Forces Museum Archives; Letter from Louis Faulkner, C. E. Fairley, and G. M. McWilliams to R. W. Dunn, President of Hattiesburg Chamber of Commerce, Hattiesburg, MS, August 2, 1937, box 1, folder 10, CoC; Letter from General Van Horn Moseley to Brigadier General John A. O'Keefe, Atlanta, GA, July 27, 1937; and Letter from Camp Shelby Committee to Hattiesburg Chamber of Commerce Board of Directors, November 26, 1937, box 1, folder 10, CoC.

49. "Work Begun at Camp Shelby," *Forrest County News*, December 10, 1936, 1; $80,000 taken from "Building Program Announced," *Hattiesburg American*, September 13, 1940, 13 (continued from 1); "2500 Troops Will Train at Shelby," *Forrest County News*, March 4, 1937, 1; and Francis Griffith, "Atlas Material on Cities and Towns-Forrest County," box 10687, folder: Forrest County: Early Settlements, WPA-Forrest.
50. "New Gymnasium Delights Crowd; Purvis and Hattiesburg Divide," *Hattiesburg American*, February 17, 1937, 1; "distended . . ." quoted in "Civic Pride," editorial, *Hattiesburg American*, February 17, 1937, 2; $50,000 taken from "Hub City Gym Will Open Tuesday," *Hattiesburg American*, February 15, 1937, 1; "Open New Gym Tonight," *Hattiesburg American*, February 16, 1937, 1; sheet 6, Hattiesburg, April, 1931, Sanborn; and "Forrest County," box: 10688, folder: Forrest County, Formation, WPA-Forrest.
51. These figures are taken from *Census of the Population: 1940*, vol. 2, part 4, 256 and 305; and *Negroes in the United States, 1920–1932*, 60.
52. *Census of the Population: 1940*, vol. 2, part 4, 256 and 305. The names and employment status of Forrest County WPA workers were cross-checked through the WPA Forrest County records available at MDAH and *Polk's Hattiesburg City Directory* for the years 1935 and 1937 available at USM.
53. Project descriptions taken from various issues of the *Hattiesburg American* between 1935 and 1940 and Series 447: Historical Research Material. 1935–1942, Work Projects Administration, Historical Records Survey, Forrest County, boxes 10687–10691, MDAH. For examples, the first announcement of a local WPA paving project included only streets in white neighborhoods. See "Immense City Paving Project Approved," *Hattiesburg American*, November 7, 1935, 1; and McKee, "The Residential Patterns of Blacks in Natchez and Hattiesburg and Other Mississippi Cities."
54. "Newman's Mill Ends Work after 41 Consecutive Years," *Hattiesburg American*, November 16, 1935, 8; Minutes of the January 4, 1937 Hattiesburg Chamber of Commerce Board of Directors Meeting, box 1, folder 10, CoC; "Industries," box 10688, folder: Industry, WPA-Forrest; $100,000 figure from William Weathersby, "Garment Plant, Silk Mill Workers Satisfied," *Hattiesburg American*, March 24, 1937, 1; Beulah Summers and Margaret Boutwell, "Forrest County's Most Important Industries," box 10688, folder: Industry, WPA-Forrest; and Beulah Summers, "The Reliance Manufacturing Company," March, 1937, box 10688, folder: Industry, WPA-Forrest.
55. Minutes of the February 11, 1935, Hattiesburg Chamber of Commerce Board of Directors Meeting, box 1, folder 9, CoC; "Silk Mill Construction Continues," *Hattiesburg American*, April 3, 1935, 8; "Seen and Heard Here and There about the City," *Hattiesburg American*, September 13, 1935, 10; "Silk Mill Investment

Wise One, Citizens Are Assured," *Hattiesburg American*, December 26, 1935, 8; Reliance Branch Plant Will Employ 350," *Hattiesburg American*, November 17, 1943, 7; Beulah Summers and Margaret Boutwell, "Forrest County's Most Important Industries," box 10688, folder: Industry, WPA-Forrest; $125,000 figure from William Weathersby, "Garment Plant, Silk Mill Workers Satisfied," *Hattiesburg American*, March 24, 1937, 1; and "Machines Come to Mississippi," *National Geographic Magazine*, September, 1937, 263–318, image of the Pioneer Silk Mill worker on 308.

56. Beulah Summers and Margaret Boutwell, "Forrest County's Most Important Industries," box 10688, folder: Industry, WPA-Forrest; and US Bureau of the Census, *Foreign Commerce and Navigation of the United States*, 1936, vol. 2 (Washington, DC: Government Printing Office, 1938), 42–43.
57. William Weathersby, "Garment Plant, Silk Mill Workers Satisfied," *Hattiesburg American*, March 24, 1937, 1; Frances W. Griffith, "District or Neighborhood Architecture and Housing," box 10687, folder: Antebellum Homes and Other Historic Buildings, WPA-Forrest; Beulah Summers, "The Reliance Manufacturing Company," March, 1937, box 10688, folder: Industry, WPA-Forrest; and "Benefit Dance at Dixie Club Tonight," *Hattiesburg American*, December 6, 1935, 12.
58. William Weathersby, "Garment Plant, Silk Mill Workers Satisfied," *Hattiesburg American*, March 24, 1937, 1; and "Form Club," *Hattiesburg American*, October 9, 1935, 8.
59. "Hercules Club One of the Most Modern Structures in State," *Hattiesburg American*, April 23, 1937, 1; and sheet 43, Hattiesburg, April 1931 and January 1945, Sanborn.
60. *Census of the Population:* 1940, vol. 2, part 4, 256. These metropolitan area figures are taken from *Polk's Hattiesburg City Directory*, 1929, 11; and *Polk's Hattiesburg City Directory*, 1939 (Birmingham, AL: R. L. Polk & Co., 1939), 7.
61. "Reliance Branch Plant Will Employ 350," *Hattiesburg American*, November 17, 1943, 7; "Exchange Club Hears Faulkner on New Industry," *Hattiesburg American*, August 17, 1938, 10; "City Affairs," *Hattiesburg American*, October 20, 1938, 10; "Tatum Company Closes Sawmill," *Hattiesburg American*, October 24, 1938, 1; 1937–1938 Tatum Lumber Company Payroll Ledgers, box 361, folders 5 and 6, Tatum Papers; Hoffman, *Steam Whistles in the Piney Woods*, vol. 1, especially 133–178; and "Strength in Unity," *Hattiesburg American*, October 26, 1938, 2.
62. *The WPA Guide to the Magnolia State*, quoted on 6; Ruth Gooch, "The Red Cross," *Hattiesburg American*, December 23, 1939, 2A; *Census of the Population:* 1940, vol. 2, part 4, 233; Wells, interview; William Weathersby, "Knights of the Rails Think New Deal Fails!" *Hattiesburg American*, November 6, 1935, 1;

Presley Davenport, interview by Tom Ward, Rawls Springs, MS, July 13, 1998, transcript, USM-OH; Musgrove, interview; Nezzie Jeanette Braswell, "The City," box #10687, folder: Forrest County, The Arts, WPA-Forrest; and William T. Schmidt, "The Middle Years," in McCarty, Jr., ed., *Hattiesburg: A Pictorial History*, 69–79.

63. Dodd, ed., *Historical Statistics of the States of the United* States, 387.
64. *Census of the Population:* 1940, vol. 2, part 4, 256 and 305; and 1937 *Census of Partial Employment, Unemployment, and Occupations*, vol. 2, 386 and 391.

8. *Community Children*

Epigraph: Dr. Isaac Thomas interview by Jessie Flowers, Hattiesburg, MS, December 23, 1994, transcript, USM-OH.

1. "Negroes Plan Fair for Park," *Hattiesburg American*, April 19, 1934, 4; "Negroes to Hold Fair Next Week to Raise Fund for New Park," *Hattiesburg American*, April 28, 1934, 8; "Worthy," editorial, *Hattiesburg American*, April 30, 1934, 2; and "Fair a Success," *Chicago Defender*, May 12, 1934, 4.
2. Minutes of the June 26, 1930 Hattiesburg Chamber of Commerce Board of Directors Meeting, box 1, folder 2, CoC; "Work on Park Starts Monday," *Hattiesburg American*, March 17, 1934, 8; and "Worthy," editorial, *Hattiesburg American*, April 30, 1934, 2. For more on the CWA, see Bonnie Fox Schwartz, *The Civil Works Administration, 1933–1934: The Business of Emergency Employment in the New Deal* (Princeton, NJ: Princeton University Press, 1984).
3. "Negroes Plan Fair for Park," *Hattiesburg American*, April 19, 1934, 4; "Local Weather," *Hattiesburg American*, May 2, 1934, 1; "Negroes to Hold Fair Next Week to Raise Fund for New Park," *Hattiesburg American*, April 28, 1934, 8; "Worthy," editorial, *Hattiesburg American*, April 30, 1934, 2; "Fair a Success," *Chicago Defender*, May 12, 1934, 4; "Parade Will Launch Fair," *Hattiesburg American*, April 30, 1934, 7; and "Negroes Raise $110 with Fair for Eureka School Equipment," *Hattiesburg American*, May 17, 1934, 7.
4. "Negroes to Hold Fair Next Week to Raise Fund for New Park," *Hattiesburg American*, April 28, 1934, 8; "worthy . . ." quoted in "Worthy," editorial, *Hattiesburg American*, April 30, 1934, 2; "Hub Negro Fair Proves Success," *Hattiesburg American*, May 2, 1934, 7; and "Fair a Success," *Chicago Defender*, May 12, 1934, 4.
5. "Negroes Raise $110 with Fair for Eureka School Equipment," *Hattiesburg American*, May 17, 1934, 7; "Fair a Success," *Chicago Defender*, May 12, 1934, 4; "Negroes Seek Funds for School Lavatory," *Hattiesburg American*, March 21, 1934, 8; "Plan Benefits for Playground," *Hattiesburg American*, June 1, 1935, 8; "Net $27 from Playground Rally," *Hattiesburg American*, July 5, 1935, 8; and

"Playground for Negroes Opens Tuesday," *Hattiesburg American*, June 1, 1936, 9.

6. "Plan Benefits for Playground," *Hattiesburg American*, June 1, 1935, 8; "Net $27 from Playground Rally," *Hattiesburg American*, July 5, 1935, 8; and "Playground for Negroes Opens Tuesday," *Hattiesburg American*, June 1, 1936, 9.
7. E. Hammond Smith, interview by Orley B. Caudill, Hattiesburg, MS, April 8, 1982, transcript, USM-OH; "Negro Business League Elects New Officers," *Hattiesburg American*, March 10, 1934, 8; "Negro League Elects Officers," *Hattiesburg American*, May 15, 1935, 8; and "Doctors Urge Recognition," *Chicago Defender*, May 7, 1949, 26.
8. Smith, interview; and 1935 *Polk's Hattiesburg City Directory*, 232 and 280.
9. Smith, interview; US Bureau of the Census, *Negroes in the United States, 1920–1932* (Washington, DC: Government Printing Office, 1935), 509; and "Store Looted by Burglars," *Hattiesburg American*, January 30, 1933, 8.
10. Smith, interview; "Hattiesburg," *Baltimore Afro-American*, July 30, 1932, 18; "Hattiesburg," *Baltimore Afro-American*, August 6, 1932, 9; "Hattiesburg," *Baltimore Afro-American*, November 4, 1933, 4; various Hattiesburg updates printed in the *Chicago Defender* between 1933 and 1937; and Hugh Sexton, "Graf Zeppelin Will Land at Chicago Today," *Chicago Tribune*, October 26, 1933, 1. For more on the 1933 Chicago World's Fair, see Cheryl R. Ganz, *The 1933 Chicago World's Fair: A Century of Progress* (Urbana: University of Illinois Press, 2008).
11. *Negroes in the United States, 1920–1932*, 306; *Census of Partial Employment, Unemployment, and Occupations: 1937*, vol. 2 (Washington, DC: Government Printing Office, 1938), 374, 386, and 391; and US Bureau of the Census, *Census of the Population: 1940*, vol. 2, part 4 (Washington, DC: Government Printing Office, 1943), 256 and 305. For more on black unemployment during the Great Depression, see William A. Sundstrum, "Last Hired, First Fired? Unemployment and Urban Black Workers during the Great Depression," *Journal of Economic History* 52, no. 2 (June, 1992): 415–429.
12. *Census of Partial Employment, Unemployment, and Occupations: 1937*, vol. 2, 374, 386, and 391; and *Census of the Population: 1940*, vol. 2, part 4, 256 and 305.
13. Ibid.; US Department of Commerce, *State Personal Income: 1929–1982*, 8; and Tatum wage statistics taken from a notice to employees, August 1, 1933, box 518, folder 5, Tatum Papers.
14. *Census of Partial Employment, Unemployment, and Occupations: 1937*, vol. 2, 374, 386, and 391; Richard Boyd, interview by Charles Bolton, Hattiesburg, MS, August 29, 1991, transcript, USM-OH; and *Census of the Population: 1940*, vol. 2, part 4, 256 and 305.
15. Osceola McCarty, interviews by Shana Walton, Hattiesburg, MS, February 22 and 23, 1996, transcript, USM-OH; *Negroes in the United States, 1920–1932*,

184; *Census of Partial Employment, Unemployment, and Occupations:* 1937, vol. 2, 383 and 391; and *Census of the Population:* 1940, vol. 2, part 4, 256 and 305. These observations are also derived from the 1930 and 1940 Forrest County Censuses and Hattiesburg City Directories between 1927 and 1941.

16. *Census of Partial Employment, Unemployment, and Occupations:* 1937, vol. 2, 386 and 391; *Census of the Population:* 1940, vol. 2, part 4, 256 and 305; and Richard Sterner, *The Negro's Share: A Study of Income, Consumption, Housing and Public Assistance* (New York: Harper & Brothers, 1943), especially 239–294; and Charles H. Wilson, *Education for Negroes in Mississippi since 1910* (Boston, MA: Meador Publishing Co., 1947), especially 55. For more on white Southern legislators and racially imbalanced New Deal policies, see Harvard Sitkoff, *A New Deal for Blacks: The Emergence of Civil Rights as a National Issue* (New York: Oxford University Press, 1978); and Ira Katznelson, *When Affirmative Action Was White: An Untold History of Racial Inequality in Twentieth Century America* (New York: Norton, 2005), especially 25–52.

17. Clearese Cook, interview by Kim Adams, Hattiesburg, MS, November, 1994, transcript, USM-OH; Douglas L. Conner with John F. Marszalek, *A Black Physician's Story: Bringing Hope in Mississippi* (Jackson: University Press of Mississippi, 1985), 6; Constance Baker, interview by Kim Adams, Hattiesburg, MS, April 3, 1995, transcript, USM-OH; and McCarty, interview.

18. "Robbers Steal $300 in Raid on Store," *Hattiesburg American,* September 4, 1928, 8; "Store Looted by Burglars," *Hattiesburg American,* January 30, 1933, 8; and Conner, *A Black Physician's Story,* 1–19, quoted on 10.

19. Rev. Ralph Woullard Jr., interview by Sadie Bailey, Hattiesburg, MS, February 20, 1995, transcript, USM-OH; Cook, interview; McCarty, interview; and Conner, *A Black Physician's Story,* 1–19, quoted on 6.

20. The names and activities of these organizations are drawn from various issues of the *Union Messenger, Hattiesburg American, Chicago Defender, Baltimore Afro-American,* and *Pittsburgh Courier* between 1931 and 1937.

21. 1935 *Polk's Hattiesburg City Directory,* 298–299.

22. Examples drawn from various issues of the *Hattiesburg American, Chicago Defender, Baltimore Afro-American,* and *Pittsburgh Courier* between 1929 and 1937. "Poor Folks Christmas Fund" quoted in "Of Interest to Colored People," *Hattiesburg American,* December 20, 1929, 2; "Colored Committee to Help in Drive by Salvation Army," *Hattiesburg American,* February 26, 1930, 14; "Colored Red Cross Group to Wind Up its Roll Call," *Hattiesburg American,* November 30, 1932, 8; "Negroes Rally to Red Cross," *Hattiesburg American,* October 22, 1932, 8; "we appreciate . . ." "Gatha Hardaway Will Head Red Cross Roll Call for Colored Here," *Hattiesburg American,* October 19, 1933, 9; and "Many Seeking Relief Work," *Hattiesburg American,* November 30, 1932, 8.

23. 1935 *Polk's Hattiesburg City Directory*, 334–335.
24. 1935 *Polk's Hattiesburg City Directory*, 334–335; *The Union Messenger*, November 29, 1934, available on microfilm at the University of Southern Mississippi Cook Library; Mrs. Margaret Boutwell and Frances Griffith, "Assignment #26—Church History," May and September, 1937, box 10687, folder: Churches, Negro, Series 447: Historical Research Material, 1935–1942, WPA-Forrest; Davis, interview; sheet 14, Hattiesburg, April, 1931, Sanborn; and "Mt. Carmel Will Be Dedicated Sunday," *Hattiesburg American*, April 25, 1953, 3.
25. 1935 *Polk's Hattiesburg City Directory*, 334–335; *The Union Messenger*, November 29, 1934; Davis, interview; sheet 14, Hattiesburg, April 1931, Sanborn; and various issues of the *Hattiesburg American* between 1932 and 1937. For more on the services of smaller black Southern churches, see C. Eric Lincoln and Lawrence H. Mamiya, *The Black Church in the African American Experience* (Durham, NC: Duke University Press, 1990), especially 92–163.
26. Woullard, interview. See Chapter 6 for more on the roles of Hammond and Charles Smith, J. B. Woods, and Gaither Hardaway in their respective churches.
27. The names and activities of these organizations are drawn from various issues of the *Union Messenger, Hattiesburg American, Chicago Defender, Baltimore Afro-American*, and *Pittsburgh Courier* between 1931 and 1937.
28. The information here was derived from the periodicals cited in the previous note. For more on the early activities of Christian missionaries in the United States, see Bettye Collier-Thomas, *Jesus, Jobs, and Justice: African American Women and Religion* (New York: Knopf, 2010), especially 120–187; and Derek Chang, *Citizens of a Christian Nation: Evangelical Missions and the Problem of Race in the Nineteenth Century* (Philadelphia: University of Pennsylvania Press, 2010).
29. *The Union Messenger*, November 29, 1934; "Union Choir Service Will Meet on Sunday Afternoon," *Hattiesburg American*, July 20, 1933, 11; "Union Choir Service Will Meet on Sunday," *Hattiesburg American*, November 23, 1933, 8; "Union Choir Service Will Assemble Sunday," *Hattiesburg American*, February 23, 1934, 7; "Union Choir Service," *Hattiesburg American*, May 26, 1934, 8; and 1935 *Polk's Hattiesburg City Directory*, 259.
30. "Our Aim," *The Union Messenger*, November 29, 1934, 1.
31. Ibid.; Ariel Barnes interview by Sarah Rowe, April 1, 1993, transcript, USM-OH; "Hattiesburg Group to Seat '65 Slate," *Chicago Defender*, June 26, 1965, 19; and "Program Tuesday," *Hattiesburg American*, December 31, 1934, 7.
32. For more on the black clubwomen's movement and black women's activism during Jim Crow, see Deborah Gray White, *Too Heavy a Load: Black Women in Defense of Themselves, 1894–1994* (New York: Norton, 1999), fifteen hundred

on 33; Linda Gordon, *Pitied but Not Entitled: Single Mothers and the History of Welfare, 1890–1935* (New York: Free Press, 1994), 111–143; Collier-Thomas, *Jesus, Jobs, and Justice*, especially 256–311; and Glenda Gilmore, *Gender and Jim Crow: Women and the Politics of White Supremacy in North Carolina, 1896–1920* (Chapel Hill: University of North Carolina Press, 1996), especially 147–224.

33. White, *Too Heavy a Load*; Collier-Thomas, *Jesus, Jobs, and Justice*, especially 256–311; and Gilmore, *Gender and Jim Crow*, especially 147–224. Examples of activities are drawn from various issues of the *Union Messenger, Hattiesburg American, Chicago Defender, Baltimore Afro-American*, and *Pittsburgh Courier* between 1931 and 1937.
34. A series of articles detailing the histories and activities of local white women's clubs can be found in the *Hattiesburg American*, June 26, 1932, 5.
35. Barnes, interview; and Thomas, interview. These examples of activities are drawn from various issues of the *Union Messenger, Hattiesburg American, Chicago Defender, Baltimore Afro-American*, and *Pittsburgh Courier* between 1931 and 1937.
36. Thomas, interview; and reporter quoted in "Other Republican Sidelights on Republican Convention," *Chicago Defender*, June 20, 1936, 4. During the 1930s, the *Baltimore Afro-American* and *Pittsburgh Courier* printed at least 250 updates from the Mobile Street District.
37. "Monthly Banquet of the Social Kings Club," *Chicago Defender*, May 20, 1933, 7; quoted in "Mah-Jong," *Chicago Defender*, July 29, 1933, 7; and 1937 *Polk's Hattiesburg City Directory*, 238 and 172.
38. Boyd, interview; Davis Dyer and David B. Sicilia, *Labors of a Modern Hercules: The Evolution of a Chemical Company* (Boston, MA: Harvard Business School Press, 1990), 183–220; 1937 *Polk's Hattiesburg City Directory*, 275; "Hattiesburg Nine Loses by Shutout," *Chicago Defender*, July 16, 1934, 17; and "Orchestra Will Jazz Up Ball Game," *Hattiesburg American*, April 26, 1935, 12. Hercules did for one season sponsor a local black baseball team that played other regional black ball clubs.
39. "Hattiesburg, Miss.," *Chicago Defender*, March 7, 1936, 22. These profiles were constructed using the 1930 and 1940 US Census Population Schedules from Forrest County, Hattiesburg city directories between 1935 and 1939, and the Digital Sanborn Map Collection.
40. 1935 *Polk's Hattiesburg City Directory*, 75; "Orchestra Will Jazz Up Ball Game," *Hattiesburg American*, April 26, 1935, 12; Stephen A. Berrey, *The Jim Crow Routine: Everyday Performances of Race, Civil Rights, and Segregation in Mississippi* (Chapel Hill: University of North Carolina Press, 2015), 27–28; Andrew English, *"All Off for Gordon's Station": A History of the Early Hattiesburg, Mississippi Area* (Baltimore, MD: Gateway Press, 2000), 88–95; "Draught

Beer Sold by Hotel," *Hattiesburg American*, March 1, 1934, 8; Gayle Dean Wardlow, *Chasin' That Devil Music: Searching for the Blues* (San Francisco, CA: Miller Freeman Books, 1998), 126–149; and Buck Wells, interview with Lawrence Knight, Hattiesburg, MS, April 24 and 28, 1997, transcript, USM-OH.

41. Alan Lomax, *Mister Jelly Roll: The Fortunes of Jelly Roll Morton, New Orleans Creole and "Inventor of Jazz"* (Berkeley: University of California Press, 2001, orig., 1950), 113; Lawrence Gushee, *Pioneers of Jazz: The Story of the Creole Band* (New York: Oxford University Press, 2005), especially 65–71; Wardlow, *Chasin' That Devil Music*, 126–140; English, *"All Off for Gordon's Station,"* 88–95; Gus Perryman, interview by Irene Cortinovis, St. Louis, MO, April 27, 1972, transcript, T-0106, State Historical Society of Missouri Oral History Collection, Columbia, MO; and Anthony DeCurtis and James Henke, eds., *The Rolling Stone Illustrated History of Rock and Roll*, 3rd ed. (New York: Random House, 1992), especially 3–16, quoted on 4.
42. Advertisement in the *Hattiesburg American*, October 23, 1936, 8; "Eureka High Wins Grid Championship in Miss.," *Chicago Defender*, January 2, 1937, 15; and sheet 18, Hattiesburg, April 1931, Sanborn.
43. "Everybody . . ." quoted in Thomas, interview; "Hattiesburg . . ." quoted in Baker, interview; W. A. Reed Jr., "special section" quoted in "Eureka Tigers Face Brookhaven Here Wednesday," *Hattiesburg American*, November 10, 1936, 9; and Ruby Cook, interview by Sarah Ramirez, Hattiesburg, MS, November 13, 1998, transcript, USM-OH.
44. "Eureka Wins Mississippi Grid Championship," *Chicago Defender*, December 25, 1937, 19; "Big Eight Football Title to Hattiesburg's Eureka," *Chicago Defender*, December 7, 1940; "Eureka Plays Haywood in Pine Bowl Wednesday," *Hattiesburg American*, December 24, 1940, 10; "Pine Bowl Classic for Prep Schools on Christmas Day," *Chicago Defender*, December 21, 1940, 22; and "Eureka Yields to Brownsville," *Hattiesburg American*, December 26, 1940, 8.
45. "Afro-American Sons and Daughters Meet," *Chicago Defender*, August 23, 1930, 3; "Big 8 Sports Body in First Meet for 1937," *Chicago Defender*, December 26, 1936, 15; "Big Eight Holds Athletic Confab," *Chicago Defender*, September 18, 1937, 20; and "Club Women Hold Meet at Hattiesburg," *Chicago Defender*, September 9, 1939, 19.
46. Charles C. Bolton, *The Hardest Deal of All: The Battle over School Integration in Mississippi, 1870–1980* (Jackson: University Press of Mississippi, 2005), especially 18–42, 1929–1930 statistic on 21; statewide and national averages taken from National Emergency Council, *Report on Economic Conditions of the South* (Washington, DC, 1938), 25–28; and Wilson, *Education for Negroes in Mississippi Since 1910*, statistics on 55.

47. Bolton, *The Hardest Deal of All*, 1940 expenditure statistic on 18; Wilson, *Education for Negroes in Mississippi Since 1910*, 52 for 1939 expenditure and high school number on 77; and EURO Alumni, *Euro Heritage House: Eureka, Royal Street, Rowan: Hattiesburg's Black High School System*, MDAH, call #: 373.76218/E89. For more on Forrest County schools compared with those in other Mississippi districts, see Bolton, *The Hardest Deal of All*, especially 16–24.
48. "822 Enrolled at Eureka," *Hattiesburg American*, September 18, 1937, 10; "Eureka High School Opens," *Hattiesburg American*, September 14, 1922, 8; and Thomas, interview. Teacher backgrounds were developed through the 1920, 1930, and 1940 US Census Population Schedules for Forrest County and Polk's Hattiesburg city directories from 1935, 1937, and 1939.
49. Wilson, *Education for Negroes in Mississippi since 1910*, 258–276; Thomas, interview; Conner, *A Black Physician's Story*, 15–17; and sheet 10, Hattiesburg, May 1925, Sanborn.
50. Martin L. Bartee, "Races and Nationalities of County," May 15, 1936, box #10689, folder: Negro, WPA-Forrest; Conner, *A Black Physician's Story*, quoted on 17; and Thomas, interview.
51. Woullard, interview; "The strap . . ." quoted in Baker, interview; "He came in . . ." quoted in Barnes, interview; "Miss Cora . . ." quoted in Conner, *A Black Physician's Story*, 17; Thomas, interview; and Sarah Harris Ruffin, interview by Fannie Cole Dickerson, Brooklyn, NY, November 23, 1995, transcript, USM-OH.
52. "Colored Youth Is Organized," *Hattiesburg American*, February 2, 1931, 7; "Speaks Sunday," *Hattiesburg American*, February 6, 1931, 10; "Musical Will Be Given at Eureka High," *Hattiesburg American*, March 30, 1931, 10; and "Hattiesburg, Miss.," *Chicago Defender*, February 16, 1935, 24.
53. "Negro Boys and Girls Return from Conference Sponsored by State Y," *Hattiesburg American*, May 3, 1934, 3; "Luxis Club," *Hattiesburg American*, April 18, 1935, 3; "Building Boys Is Big Business," *Hattiesburg American*, October 5, 1934, 1 and 4; Anselm Joseph Finch, "Mississippi Snaps," *Pittsburgh Courier*, March 21, 1936, A9; "Negro Clubs," *Hattiesburg American*, March 26, 1936, 12; and Gladys Noel, who later became Gladys Noel Bates, is listed as an attendee in "Luxis Clubs," *Hattiesburg American*, March 27, 1936, 7. For more on the 1948 Bates suit, see Bolton, *The Hardest Deal of All*, 45–51.
54. Conner, *A Black Physician's Story*, 13–17; Thomas, interview; Woullard, interview; Veola Chase, interview by Annie Pope, location unknown, December 22, 1995, transcript, USM-OH; Barnes, interviews; and Baker, interview.
55. Woullard, interview; and Jobie Martin, interview by Martin Beard, Hattiesburg, MS, August 10, 1995, transcript, USM-OH. For a detailed study on the

communal roles of black teachers in the Jim Crow South, see Vanessa Siddle Walker, *Their Highest Potential: An African American School Community in the Segregated South* (Chapel Hill: University of North Carolina Press, 1996).

56. List of PTA captains is taken from "Hattiesburg, Miss.," *Chicago Defender*, December 25, 1937, 23. Individual descriptions constructed from 1920, 1930, and 1940 US Census Population Schedules for Forrest County and Polk's Hattiesburg city directories from 1935, 1937, and 1939. "Eureka P.T.A. Reports on Drive for Funds," *Hattiesburg American*, December 13, 1937, 8; "Baskets," *Hattiesburg American*, December 29, 1939, 3; "Singers at Eureka Sunday," *Hattiesburg American*, November 19, 1938, 3; "Eureka: School Strives for Brass Band," *Hattiesburg American*, January 14, 1938, 5; and "Eureka P.T.A. Asks Help in Band Campaign," *Hattiesburg American*, October 19, 1938, 9.
57. Barnes, interview; Ruffin, interview; "Movie Program Friday Night at Eureka School," *Hattiesburg American*, April 21, 1938, 11; "Colored Youth Forum Debate Tonight," *Hattiesburg American*, April 6, 1939, 12; "Pageant Sunday at Eureka School," *Hattiesburg American*, January 28, 1938, 9; Thomas, interview; and "Negro Children Win Prizes at Club Exhibit," *Hattiesburg American*, October 23, 1935, 6.
58. Chase, interview.
59. Conner, *A Black Physician's Story*, 12.
60. Ibid., 15, 86.
61. Thomas, interview.
62. Arvarh E. Strickland, "Remembering Hattiesburg: Growing Up Black in Wartime Mississippi," in *Remaking Dixie: The Impact of Work War II on the American South*, ed. Neil McMillen (Jackson: University Press of Mississippi, 1997), quoted on 149.
63. Ibid., quoted on 158.

9. *Salvation*

Epigraph: Cameron quoted in "South Mississippians Form Camp Shelby Association," *Hattiesburg American*, November 12, 1940, 9. Cameron in 1940 was the president of the Merchants Grocery Company, the wholesaler grocery founded by T. S. Jackson and others in the early twentieth century.

1. "The Weather," *Hattiesburg American*, September 16, 1940, 1; "Camp Shelby Work Begins: Job-Hunters Swarm into Hattiesburg," *Hattiesburg American*, September 16, 1940, 1; "Shelby Briefs," *Hattiesburg American*, September 16, 1940, 1 and 8; quotations taken from John Frasca, "Army of Job-Seekers Lay Siege to Shelby," *Hattiesburg American*, September 17, 1940, 1; Henry Watson, interview by Michael Vaughn, Piave, MS, June 4, 1997, transcript, USM-OH; Bobby Chain, interview by Blain Fandrich, Hattiesburg, MS, November 17,

1999, transcript, USM-OH; and Jimmy Mordica, interview by Elizabeth Bice, Hattiesburg, MS, August 8, 1998, transcript, USM-OH.

2. Quotations taken from John Frasca, "Army of Job-Seekers Lay Siege to Shelby," *Hattiesburg American,* September 17, 1940, 1.
3. US Public Law 783, 76th Cong., 3d sess. (September 16, 1940), 885–897; SR 4119, 76th Cong., 3rd sess., *Congressional Record,* vol. 86, part 9 (July 11, 1940), 9540; John Ray Skates Jr., "World War II and Its Effects, 1940–1948," in McLemore, ed., *A History of Mississippi:* vol. 2, 120–139; William T. Schmidt, "The Middle Years," in Kenneth G. McCarty Jr., ed., *Hattiesburg: A Pictorial History* (Jackson: University Press of Mississippi, 1982), 69–128; Sandra K. Behel, "The Mississippi Home Front during World War II: Tradition and Change" (PhD diss., Mississippi State University, 1989); and "the most . . ." quoted in William Theodore Schmidt, "The Impact of Camp Shelby on Hattiesburg, Mississippi, 1940–1946" (PhD diss., University of Southern Mississippi, 1972), 9. For more on World War II–era mobilization, see Paul A. C. Koistinen, *Arsenal of World War II: The Political Economy of American Warfare, 1940–1945* (Lawrence: University Press of Kansas, 2004); and James T. Sparrow, *Warfare State: World War II Americans and the Age of Big Government* (New York: Oxford University Press, 2011).
4. "Need 5,000 to Work at Camp Shelby," *Hattiesburg American,* September 13, 1940, 1 and 13; "Building Program Announced," *Hattiesburg American,* September 13, 1940, 1; *A Serviceman's Guide to Hattiesburg,* compiled by Service Division Works Project Administration for the State of Mississippi, June 1942, box 10688, folder: Hattiesburg, History of, WPA-Forrest; and $22 million taken from "Report of Chamber of Commerce President of 1940," box 1, folder 15, CoC.
5. "Announce Shelby Wage Scale," *Hattiesburg American,* September 14, 1940, 1; US Department of Commerce, *State Personal Income: 1929–1982,* 8; and "Need 5,000 to Work at Camp Shelby," *Hattiesburg American,* September 13, 1940, 1.
6. "52,000 Men for Camp Shelby," *Hattiesburg American,* September 19, 1940, 1; "5,876 Working at Camp Shelby," *Hattiesburg American,* October 1, 1940, 1; "Shelby Crews Exceed 10,000," *Hattiesburg American,* October 16, 1940, 1; "Van of Ohio Guard Enters Camp Shelby," *New York Times,* October 21, 1940, 25; and "Shelby Payroll over a Million," *Hattiesburg American,* October 30, 1940, 1.
7. "Shelby Briefs," *Hattiesburg American,* September 16, 1940, 1 and 8; "Camp 'Problem' Meeting at City Hall Tonight," *Hattiesburg American,* September 17, 1940, 1; and Minutes of Meeting of Directors of Chamber of Commerce and Business Leaders and Officials Regarding Camp Shelby, September 17, 1940, box 1, folder 13, CoC.

8. "Hattiesburg Stores to Open at Night," *Hattiesburg American*, October 12, 1940, 1; "Part-Time Jobs for College Students Planned," *Hattiesburg American*, September 25, 1940, 5; "Shelby Briefs," *Hattiesburg American*, December 19, 1940, 1; "Syndicate Announces Enterprise," *Hattiesburg American*, October 12, 1940, 1; "M.C Trains Run to Shelby Again," *Hattiesburg American*, October 17, 1940, 1; "New Paving for 2 Roads," *Hattiesburg American*, October 28, 1940, 1; "Aviation Base Here Assured," *Hattiesburg American*, October 28, 1940, 1; "Report of Chamber of Commerce President of 1940," box 1, folder 15, CoC; "Modern Water, Sewer Systems to Serve Camp," *Hattiesburg American*, September 24, 1940, 8; "Camp Shelby Boom Ups Utilities' Vol.," *Hattiesburg American*, September 25, 1940, 12; Schmidt, "The Impact of Camp Shelby on Hattiesburg, Mississippi," 9–19; and Benjamin Morris, *Hattiesburg, Mississippi: A History of the Hub City* (Charleston, SC: The History Press, 2014), 129–160.
9. "Girls Needed for Newsreels," *Hattiesburg American*, December 20, 1940, 1.
10. "Tigers," *Hattiesburg American*, August 15, 1940, 10; "Tigers May Lose Three Men," *Hattiesburg American*, September 17, 1940, 3; "Tigers Taper Off for Opener," *Hattiesburg American*, September 18, 1940, 14; and "Tigers," *Hattiesburg American*, September 27, 1940, 8.
11. "South Mississippians Form Camp Shelby Association," *Hattiesburg American*, November 12, 1940, 1; D. P. Cameron to W. O. Tatum, Hattiesburg, MS, November 26, 1940, box 234, folder 4, Tatum Papers; Minutes of the Meeting of the Mississippi Camp Shelby Cooperative Association, November 27, 1940, box 11, folder 2, CoC; Charter of Incorporation of Mississippi Camp Shelby Cooperative Association, box 11, folder 2, CoC; and By-Laws of Mississippi Camp Shelby Cooperative Association, box 11, folder 2, CoC.
12. "Housing: Loan Contract Approved," *Hattiesburg American*, August 1, 1939, 1; "Housing Project Sites Announced," *Hattiesburg American*, September 28, 1939, 1; $744,000 taken from National Association of Housing Officials, *Housing Year Book, 1941* (Chicago, IL: 1941), 110; Travis Boykin to William Colmer, Hattiesburg, MS, April 17, 1939, box 164, folder 15, Colmer (William M.) Papers, USM; Nathan Straus to Congressman Colmer, Washington, DC, June 24, 1939, box 164, folder 15, Colmer Papers; and A. M. Smith to William Colmer, Hattiesburg, MS, June 29, 1939, box 164, folder 15, Colmer Papers. Colmer's correspondence regarding the 1939 housing loan can be found in box 164, folder 15, Colmer Papers.
13. Public Law 412, 75th Cong., 1st sess. (September 1, 1937), 888; and A. M. Smith, "Housing Discussion," *Hattiesburg American*, January 31, 1940, 1 and 3. For more on the Wagner-Steagall Housing Act, see Timothy L. McDonnell, *The Wagner Housing Act: A Case Study of the Legislative Process* (Chicago, IL: Loyola University Press, 1957); Harvard Sitkoff, *A New Deal for Blacks: The*

Emergence of Civil Rights as a National Issue (New York: Oxford University Press, 1978), 51; Kenneth T. Jackson, *Crabgrass Frontier: The Suburbanization of the United States* (New York: Oxford University Press, 1985), especially 222–226; and Richard Sterner et al., *The Negro's Share: A Study of Income, Consumption, Housing and Public Assistance* (New York: Harper & Brothers, 1943), 316–318 for the USHA and African Americans.

14. "Housing," *Hattiesburg American*, December 29, 1939, 7; N. R. Burger, interview by R. Wayne Pyle, Hattiesburg, MS, May 11, 1982, transcript, USM-OH; rent figures taken from "Housing," *Hattiesburg American*, March 3, 1941, 7; and Arvarh E. Strickland, "Remembering Hattiesburg: Growing Up Black in Wartime Mississippi," in *Remaking Dixie: The Impact of Work War II on the American South*, ed. Neil McMillen (Jackson: University Press of Mississippi, 1997), 146–158. See Chapter 6 for more on the Royal Street Neighborhood.
15. $398,000 taken from "Housing," *Hattiesburg American*, December 29, 1939, 7; "Housing: Loan Contract Approved," *Hattiesburg American*, August 1, 1939, 1; $744,000 taken from *Housing Year Book, 1941*, 110; $100 and $840 taken from "Chancery Court," *Hattiesburg American*, January 29, 1940, 8; "Chancery Court," *Hattiesburg American*, April 3, 1940, 9; and rental rates taken from 1940 U.S. Census, Forrest County, Mississippi, Population Schedule, sheets 8A, 8B, and 9A, various dwellings, digital image, Ancestry.com, accessed June 14, 2016.
16. "Brown Named Chairman of Housing Authority," *Hattiesburg American*, February 29, 1940, 5; "Housing," *Hattiesburg American*, March 6, 1940, 12; "Housing," *Hattiesburg American*, April 24, 1940, 12; "City Affairs," *Hattiesburg American*, August 30, 1940, 12; and wage figures taken from "Housing Project Payroll Totals Nearly $50,000," *Hattiesburg American*, September 5, 1940, 9.
17. "Housing Project Payroll Totals Nearly $50,000," *Hattiesburg American*, September 5, 1940, 9.
18. "Camp 'Problem' Meeting at City Hall Tonight," *Hattiesburg American*, September 17, 1940, 1 and 9; "City, County Organize to Handle Camp Problems," *Hattiesburg American*, September 18, 1940, 1; and "Rotary Club," *Hattiesburg American*, December 3, 1940, 8. The arrival of black troops was announced as early as September 25, 1940. "Announce Camp Shelby Mobilization Schedule," *Hattiesburg American*, September 25, 1940, 1.
19. W. O. Tatum to Federal Housing Authority of the City of Hattiesburg, Hattiesburg, MS, December 14, 1940, box 234, folder 4, Tatum Papers; and William Colmer to Frank Knox, Washington, DC, January 8, 1941, box 165, folder 1, Colmer Papers.
20. Minutes of the Meeting of the Executive Committee of the Mississippi Camp Shelby Cooperative Association, January 24, 1941, box 11, folder 2, CoC;

Minutes of the Meeting of the Executive Committee of the Mississippi Camp Shelby Cooperative Association, January 31, 1941, box 11, folder 2, CoC; Henry Stimson to William Colmer, Location Unknown, February 3, 1941, box 165, folder 1, Colmer Papers; Burger, interview; Minutes of the Meeting of the Executive Committee of the Mississippi Camp Shelby Cooperative Association, February 8, 1941, box 11, folder 2, CoC; "Housing," *Hattiesburg American*, March 3, 1941, 7; and "Housing," *Hattiesburg American*, March 15, 1941, 10.

21. "120 Happy Families at Briarfield Homes," *Hattiesburg American*, December 24, 1941, 2.
22. "Only 141 Civilian Workers at Camp," *Hattiesburg American*, February 28, 1941, 11; James K. Hutsell, "Buildings Rise, Paved Roads Appear Overnight at Shelby," *Hattiesburg American*, Camp Shelby Edition, vol. 45, no. 46, February 22, 1941, 9; and "Camp Shelby Sets Building Record," *New York Times*, March 16, 1941, 33.
23. "Biggest boom . . ." quoted in "Business Boom," *Hattiesburg American*, February 22, 1941, vol. 45, no. 46, Camp Shelby Edition, 1; "Hattiesburg's Business Surge Analyzed," *Hattiesburg American*, January 15, 1941, 1; "Hattiesburg Leads in Business Gains," *Hattiesburg American*, March 5, 1941, 1; "Camp Expansion Program Adds to Bright Outlook," *Hattiesburg American*, February 22, 1941, 10; and G. M. McWilliams, "Camp Shelby Brings Economic Benefits," *Hattiesburg American*, Camp Shelby Edition, vol. 45, no. 46, February 22, 1941, 9.
24. "Camp Shelby Sets Building Record," *New York Times*, March 16, 1941, 33; and "Camp Shelby," *New York Times*, August 23, 1941, 28.
25. Robert Loftus, "Camp Shelby Goes Out of Business," *Hattiesburg American*, October 1, 1946, 1 and 6; Chad Daniels, "Military Pastimes: Entertaining the Troops at Camp Shelby, 1918–1945," *Southern Quarterly* 50, no. 1 (2012): 131–151; Schmidt, "The Impact of Camp Shelby on Hattiesburg, Mississippi," 9–19; Morris, *Hattiesburg, Mississippi*, 129–139; and US Bureau of the Census, *Census of the Population*: 1950, vol. 2, part 24, *Mississippi* (Washington, DC: Government Printing Office, 1952), 24–27.
26. "Hub City Tax Rate Increased 5 Mills," *Hattiesburg American*, November 1, 1940, 1; Schmidt, "The Impact of Camp Shelby on Hattiesburg, Mississippi," especially 20–45 and 96–99, quoted on 21–22; Jack Thompson, "Shelby Troops Hope for Rain to End Blackouts," *Chicago Tribune*, June 19, 1941, 8; and "Prostitutes a Problem," *Hattiesburg American*, December 7, 1940, 1.
27. "Military, Civil Leaders Fan Friendship Fires," *Hattiesburg American*, November 2, 1940, 1 and 7; *Serviceman's Guide to Hattiesburg*; and "Report of the Chamber of Commerce President of 1940," box 1, folder 15, CoC.
28. Schmidt, "The Impact of Camp Shelby on Hattiesburg, Mississippi," 46–63; Morris, *Hattiesburg, Mississippi*, 145; Donald Cooley to Eleanor, Camp

Shelby, MS, June 15, 1942, box 572, folder 1, Donald Cooley Collection, Mississippi Armed Forced Museum Archives, Camp Shelby, MS; "Start Work on New 49 Lane to Camp," *Hattiesburg American*, February 21, 1941, 8; and Ben Earles, interview by R. Wayne Pyle, Hattiesburg, MS, June 28 and 29, 1979, transcript, USM-OH.

29. Earles, interview; J. S. Finlayson, interview by Chester Morgan, Hattiesburg, MS, May 16, 1973, transcript, USM-OH; Herb Sasaki, interview by Elizabeth Bice, Hattiesburg, MS, October 23, 1998, transcript, USM-OH; and Musgrove, interview.
30. Schmidt, "The Impact of Camp Shelby on Hattiesburg, Mississippi," 16–19; Lorene Mandina, interview by Elizabeth Bice, location unknown, October 17, 1998, transcript, USM-OH; Gloria and Jeanette Coleman, interview by Jana Hudson, Hattiesburg, MS, February 25, 2002, transcript, USM-OH; Bernard and Rachel Walton, interview by Elizabeth Bice, Hattiesburg, MS, October 25, 1998, transcript, USM-OH; Ewetha Royse, interview by Elizabeth Bice, location unknown, November 18, 1998, transcript, USM-OH; and Betty Cooley, interview by Elizabeth Bice, Hattiesburg, MS, October 15, 1998, transcript, USM-OH. For more on Mississippi women and labor during World War II, see Behel, "The Mississippi Home Front during World War II," 68–89.
31. Presley Davenport, interview by Tom Ward, Rawls Springs, MS, July 13, 1998, transcript, USM-OH; Chain, interview; and Mordica, interview.
32. Forrest Hotel Corporation Charter of Incorporation, September 21, 1928, box 137, folder 2; Forrest Hotel Corporation Preferred and Common Stockholders of Record, December 31, 1945, box 137, folder 3; Forrest Hotel Corporation Annual Report, December 31, 1932, box 137, folder 5; and Audit Report of the Forrest Hotel Corporation, Year 1946, box 127, folder 18, all located in Tatum Papers.
33. Wilmut Gas and Oil Co.: History, box 603, folder 11, Tatum Papers. Monthly revenue figures for Wilmut gas are available in boxes 601–612, Tatum Papers. These examples were taken from box 604, folder 9; box 605, folder 8; box 602, folder 12; and box 603, folder 1, respectively.
34. "Faulkner Concrete Company," box 10688, folder: Industry, WPA-Forrest; "New Faulkner Pipe Plant Now in Full Production," *Hattiesburg American*, July 21, 1966, 6; Faulkner Concrete Pipe history printed in *Hattiesburg American*, November 21, 1969, 29; and "Faulkner Concrete Pipe Co. Expanding," *Hattiesburg American*, June 24, 1967, 1B.
35. Letter from L. E. Faulkner, C. E. Fairley, and G. M. Williams to R. W. Dunn, Hattiesburg, MS, August 2, 1937, box 1, folder 10, CoC; and Lt. Col. George H. Schumacher to Lt. Col. H. J. Dolton, Atlanta, GA, September 6, 1940, box 276, folder: WPA Camp Shelby Project 1940 Data, Mississippi Armed Forces Museum Archives.

36. F. M. Tatum to William Colmer, Hattiesburg, MS, July 14, 1944, box 77, folder 15, Tatum Papers; and Gilbert H. Hoffman, *Steam Whistles in the Piney Woods: A History of the Sawmills and Logging Railroads of the Forrest and Lamar Counties, Mississippi*, vol. 1 (Hattiesburg, MS: Longleaf Press, 1998), 106–178.
37. Chain, interview; Coleman, interview; Yvonne Arnold, interview by Charles Bolton, Hattiesburg, MS, October 6, 1998, transcript, USM-OH; and number of units taken from "Rent Income Here Nearly $4,000,000 a Year," *Hattiesburg American*, October 19, 1944, 1.
38. Chain, interview; Arnold, interview; "High Rent Hurts," *Hattiesburg American*, October 12, 1940, 8; Mrs. Joseph Sherman Hammond Bride's Book, box 536, folder 3, Hammond Collection, Mississippi Armed Forces Museum; and Coleman, interview.
39. Coleman, interview; Chain, interview; rates taken from "High Rent Hurts," *Hattiesburg American*, October 12, 1940, 8; and Jay Piccinati, interview by Blain Fandrich, location unknown, November 12, 1999, transcript, USM-OH.
40. Total rental income and 150 taken from "Rent Income Here Nearly $4,000,000 a Year," *Hattiesburg American*, October 19, 1944, 1; "Landlords . . ." quoted in "Don't Chisel," *Hattiesburg American*, September 19, 1940, 1; "defense rental areas . . ." quoted in "Hattiesburg One of 60 Areas Named," *Hattiesburg American*, June 23, 1942, 1; and example taken from Schmidt, "The Impact of Camp Shelby on Hattiesburg, Mississippi," 37–41.
41. *Serviceman's Guide to Hattiesburg*; and Schmidt, "The Impact of Camp Shelby on Hattiesburg, Mississippi," 64–77.
42. Schmidt, "The Impact of Camp Shelby on Hattiesburg, Mississippi," 64–77.
43. *Serviceman's Guide to Hattiesburg*; Schmidt, "The Impact of Camp Shelby on Hattiesburg, Mississippi," 64–77, statistic taken from 74.
44. *Serviceman's Guide to Hattiesburg*; Coleman, interview; Cooley, interview; Schmidt, "The Impact of Camp Shelby on Hattiesburg, Mississippi," 78–95; Daniels, "Military Pastimes," 137–149; Morris, *Hattiesburg, Mississippi*, 129–160; "dates will be . . ." quoted in Letter from Program Committee of the Halloween Party for Camp Exchange Office Employees to Miss Anne Sherman, Camp Shelby, October 14, 1942, box 562, folder 9, Mississippi Armed Forces Museum Collection, Mississippi Armed Forces Museum; and various examples of social programs found in box 562, Mississippi Armed Forces Museum Collection, Mississippi Armed Forces Museum.
45. Daniels, "Military Pastimes," 137–149; "Bond Buying 'In High,'" *Hattiesburg American*, February 9, 1943, 1; Chain, interview; "I had never . . ." quoted in Coleman, interview; and Morris, *Hattiesburg, Mississippi*, 129–160.

46. Dorothea Musgrove, interview by Cheri Adler, January 20, 2000, transcript, USM-OH; Harmon and Elizabeth Strickland, Hattiesburg, MS, May 16, 2000, transcript, USM-OH; Earles, interview; and William T. Schmidt, "The Middle Years," in McCarty, ed., *Hattiesburg*, 79.
47. "Airline Petition Reveals Community Statistics," *Hattiesburg American*, May 9, 1946, 1 and 10; and Schmidt, "The Impact of Camp Shelby on Hattiesburg, Mississippi," 63.
48. James Kittrell, interview by Michael Vaughn, Richton, MS, October 6, 1998, transcript, USM-OH; manufacturing statistics taken from Donald B. Dodd, ed., *Historical Statistics of the States of the United States: Two Centuries of the Census, 1790–1990* (Westport, CT: Greenwood Press, 1993), 387–388; and Behel, "The Mississippi Home Front during World War II," 20–67. As James T. Sparrow has argued, Southern incomes were transformed by expanded military spending that increased the region's "share of total federal investment . . . by a third." See James T. Sparrow, "A Nation in Motion: Norfolk, the Pentagon, and the Nationalization of the Metropolitan South, 1941–1953," in *The Myth of Southern Exceptionalism*, eds. Matthew D. Lassiter and Joseph Crespino (New York: Oxford University Press, 2012), 167–189, quoted on 169.
49. "Forrest County Votes 93 Percent for Ticket," *Hattiesburg American*, November 6, 1940, 13; Strickland, interview; Buck Wells, interview with Lawrence Knight, Hattiesburg, MS, April 24 and 28, 1997, transcript, USM-OH; and "Forrest County," and "Mississippi," *Hattiesburg American*, November 8, 1944, 1.
50. See Daniel Kryder, *Divided Arsenal: Race and the American State during World War II* (New York: Cambridge University Press, 2000), 25–87; Robin D. G. Kelley, *Hammer and Hoe: Alabama Communists during the Great Depression* (Chapel Hill: University of North Carolina Press, 1990); Sitkoff, *A New Deal for Blacks*; Patricia Sullivan, *Days of Hope: Race and Democracy in the New Deal Era* (Chapel Hill: University of North Carolina Press, 1996); George B. Tindall, *The Emergence of the New South, 1913–1945* (Baton Rouge: Louisiana State University Press, 1967), 505–539; Robert Korstad, *Civil Rights Unionism: Tobacco Workers and the Struggle for Democracy in the Mid-Twentieth-Century South* (Chapel Hill: University of North Carolina Press, 2007); Eric Arnesen, *Brotherhoods of Color: Black Railroad Workers and the Struggle for Equality* (Cambridge, MA: Harvard University Press, 2001), 84–150; Erik Gellman, *Death Blow to Jim Crow: The National Negro Congress and the Rise of Militant Civil Rights* (Chapel Hill: University of North Carolina Press, 2012); Robert H. Ziegler, *The CIO, 1935–1955* (Chapel Hill: University of North Carolina Press, 1995), especially 66–89; John Egerton, *Speak Now Against the Day: The Generation before the Civil Rights Movement in the South* (New York: Knopf, 1994), especially 15–330; and Robert Korstad

and Nelson Lichtenstein, "Opportunities Found and Lost: Labor, Radicals, and the Early Civil Rights Movement," *Journal of American History*, vol. 75, no. 3 (1988), 786–811.

51. Dodd, ed., *Historical Statistics of the States of the United* States, 2–104; Doris Kearns Goodwin, *No Ordinary Time: Franklin and Eleanor Roosevelt: The Home Front in World War II* (New York: Simon & Schuster, 1994), especially 161–189; "Brotherhood Ends Confab," *New York Amsterdam News*, September 28, 1940, 4; "Porters Vote Curb on Reds in Union," *New York Times*, September 15, 1940, 14; "Mrs. Roosevelt to Address Pullman Porters," *Chicago Defender*, September 14, 1940, 3; and "Platform Adopted by Democratic Convention at Philadelphia," *Washington Post*, July 14, 1948, 16. For more on the growing political power of Northern black migrants in the mid-to-late 1940s, see Henry Lee Moon, *Balance of Power: The Negro Vote* (Garden City, NY: Doubleday & Co., 1948); and Steven F. Lawson, *Black Ballots: Voting Rights in the South, 1944–1969* (New York: Columbia University Press, 1976), especially 55–85.

52. Ira Katznelson, *Fear Itself: The New Deal and the Origins of Our Time* (New York: Liveright, 2013), especially 58–95, 148–182; Ira Katznelson, *When Affirmative Action Was White: An Untold History of Racial Inequality in Twentieth Century America* (New York: Norton, 2005), especially 25–52; William F. Winter, "New Directions in Politics, 1948–1956," in McLemore, ed., *A History of Mississippi*, vol. 2, 140–153; Tindall, *The Emergence of the New South*, 687–731; and see Chester M. Morgan, *Redneck Liberal: Theodore G. Bilbo and the New Deal* (Baton Rouge: Louisiana State University Press, 1985), for an analysis of the racially based New Deal politics of Mississippi senator Theodore G. Bilbo.

53. Bilbo quoted in Benjamin E. Mays, "Veterans: It Need Not Happen Again," *Phylon* 6, no. 3 (1945), 208; Eastland quoted in Chris Myers Asch, *The Senator and the Sharecropper: The Freedom Struggles of James O. Eastland and Fannie Lou Hamer* (New York: New Press, 2008), 117; John E. Rankin, "Political Address" (October 7, 1947), MDAH Digital Archives, transcript, www.mdah.ms.gov/arrec/digital_archives/vault/projects/OHtranscripts/AU_1009_117289.pdf, accessed June 26, 2016; Colmer quoted in "Colmer to Continue Fight for South at Special Session," *Hattiesburg American*, July 24, 1948, 1 and 9; "Nature of the Beast," *Hattiesburg American*, January 29, 1946, 2; and "Evils of FEPC," *Hattiesburg American*, February 10, 1949, 2; Charles Smith Pope, "Theodore G. Bilbo's Senatorial Career: The Final Years: 1941–1947" (PhD diss., University of Southern Mississippi, 1983), especially 132–177; and Jason Morgan Ward, *Defending White Democracy: The Making of a Segregationist Movement and the Remaking of Racial*

Politics, 1936–1965 (Chapel Hill: University of North Carolina Press, 2011), especially 67–91.

54. Pope, "Theodore G. Bilbo's Senatorial Career," 178–208; Bilbo quoted in "Bilbo Screams Mob Violence," *Chicago Defender*, June 29, 1946, 1; "He Holds 3400-Vote Majority over Field," *Hattiesburg American*, July 3, 1946, 1; and "Forrest County Complete and Official," *Hattiesburg American*, July 3, 1946, 1.
55. Pope, "Theodore G. Bilbo's Senatorial Career," 209–248; and "Bilbo Dead at 69 of Heart Ailment," *New York Times*, August 22, 1947, 1.
56. "Stennis Elected," *Hattiesburg American*, November 5, 1947, 1; and Jessie Curtis, "Awakening the Nation: Mississippi Senator John C. Stennis, the White Countermovement, and the Rise of Colorblind Conservatism, 1947–1964" (master's thesis, Kent State University, 2014). For more on internal divisions within Mississippi's Democratic Party, see V. O. Key, *Southern Politics: In State and Nation* (New York: Knopf, 1949), 229–253.
57. John E. Rankin, "Political Address" (October 7, 1947).

10. *A Rising*

Epigraph: Victoria Adams, "Autobiography," November 28, 1945, box 7, folder 1, Adams (Victoria Gray) Papers, 1938–2006, USM.

1. Smith, interview; and "Building Permits," *Hattiesburg American*, April 15, 1942, 12.
2. Smith, interview; James Cohen, interview by Mike Garvey, Hattiesburg, MS, February 2, 1976, transcript, USM-OH; Iola Williams, interview by Patricia Buzard, Hattiesburg, MS, November 6, 2006, transcript, USM-OH; Raylawni Branch, interview by Kim Adams, Hattiesburg, MS, October 25, 1993, transcript, USM-OH; and Brad J. Kavan, "The Rise and Decline of Mobile Street: Race and the Impact of Camp Shelby on African-American Hattiesburg" (master's thesis, University of Southern Mississippi, 2004), 56.
3. Ulysses Lee, *The Employment of Negro Troops* (Washington, DC: Center of Military History, 1994, orig., 1966), especially 88–178, 10 percent figure taken from 134, Georgia Selective Service director quoted on 411; Morris J. MacGregor Jr., *Integration of the Armed Forces, 1940–1965* (Washington, DC: Center of Military History, 1981), especially 17–57; "Senator Asks Army to Keep Northern Negroes in North," *Washington Post*, August 3, 1942, 1; and Jason Morgan Ward, *Defending White Democracy: The Making of a Segregationist Movement and the Remaking of Racial Politics, 1936–1965* (Chapel Hill: University of North Carolina Press, 2011), especially 38–66.

4. "Shelby Briefs," *Hattiesburg American*, July 1, 1941, 10; Ollie Stewart, "Shelby Men Want to Be Transferred," *Baltimore Afro-American*, August 2, 1941, 1; N. R. Burger, interview by R. Wayne Pyle, Hattiesburg, MS, May 11, 1982, transcript, USM-OH; and Kenneth H. Paul, "East Sixth Street U.S.O. Building," National Register of Historic Places Registration Form, U.S. Department of the Interior National Park Service.
5. *A Serviceman's Guide to Hattiesburg*, box 10688, folder: Hattiesburg, History of, WPA-Forrest.
6. Kavan, "The Rise and Decline of Mobile Street," Williams and Hopkins quoted on 62 and 52, respectively.
7. Smith, interview; *Polk's Hattiesburg City Directory: 1939* (Birmingham, AL: R. L. Polk & Co., 1939), 358–360 and 374–375; *Polk's Hattiesburg City Directory: 1946* (Richmond, VA: R. L. Polk & Co., 1946), 571–573, 544–546, and 516; Williams, interview; and Charles Brown, interview by Vincent Clark, Hattiesburg, MS, March 26, 1997, transcript, USM-OH.
8. Vernon Dahmer Jr., interview with ReTina D. Gray, Kelly Settlement, Hattiesburg, MS, April 2, 2001, transcript, USM-OH; Ellie Dahmer, interview with Orley B. Caudill, Kelly Settlement, Hattiesburg, MS, July 2, 1974, transcript, USM-OH; Dahmer listed as a participant in "Sales Force Will Meet at the U.S.O.," *Hattiesburg American*, June 12, 1944, 1 and 9; and "Negroes to Plan Victory Loan Drive," *Hattiesburg American*, November 8, 1945, 11.
9. "Hattiesburg, Miss.," *Chicago Defender*, March 7, 1936, 22; and James Brown with Nathan Whitaker, *Role of a Lifetime: Reflections on Faith, Family, and Significant Living* (New York: Faith Words, 2009), 24–27. James Brown, a well-known sportscaster, is the grandson of Milton Barnes. The rest of Barnes's background was developed through the 1920, 1930, and 1940 US Census Population Schedules for Jefferson Davis and Forrest Counties; and the 1935 and 1937 *Polk's Hattiesburg City Directory*.
10. Brown with Whitaker, *Role of a Lifetime*, chap. 2; Kavan, "The Rise and Decline of Mobile Street," 66–70; Preston Lauterbach, *The Chitlin' Circuit: And the Road to Rock 'n' Roll* (New York: Norton, 2011), 222–231; Emily D. Edwards, *Bars, Blues, and Booze: Stories from the Drink House* (Jackson: University Press of Mississippi, 2016), 68–71; "Embassy Club at Palmer's Burns," *Hattiesburg American*, February 4, 1958, 3A; "Negro Veterans Asked to Meet Friday Night," *Hattiesburg American*, May 23, 1946, 14; and "More than $300 Donated So Far for Negro Scout Camp," *Hattiesburg American*, March 22, 1951, 12. Also see the Mississippi Blues Trail Hi-Hat Club Historical Marker, which can be accessed at: www.msbluestrail.org/blues-trail-markers/hi-hat-club.
11. "Hattiesburg Negro Wins Navy Rating," *Hattiesburg American*, October 21, 1948, 5; "Native Mississippian Gets Naval Aviator Commission," *Atlanta Daily*

World, April 28, 1949, 1; "Navy's Negro Pilot Dies in Flames," *Cleveland Call and Post*, December 16, 1950, 1A; "Negro Navy Pilot Killed in Korea," *Hattiesburg American*, December 9, 1950, 1; Theodore Taylor, *The Flight of Jesse Leroy Brown* (New York: Avon Books, 1998), 59–75; and Adam Makos, *Devotion: An Epic Story of Heroism, Friendship, and Sacrifice* (New York: Ballantine Books, 2015), 18–37.

12. J. C. Fairley, interview with Mike Garvey, Hattiesburg, MS, January 31 and February 4, 1977, transcript, USM-OH; Lee Owens Jr., interview by William Henderson, Biloxi, MS, April 26, 2000, transcript, USM-OH; Isaac Grey, interview by Allysha Michelle Patrick and Joseph T. Tenney, Hattiesburg, MS, November 18, 2008, transcript, USM-OH; and Clearese Cook, interview by Kim Adams, Hattiesburg, MS, November, 1994, transcript, USM-OH.
13. Osceola McCarty, interviews by Shana Walton, Hattiesburg, MS, February 22 and 23, 1996, transcript, USM-OH; and "Laundry Near Camp Enjoys Business Boom," *Baltimore Afro-American*, August 2, 1941, 3.
14. 1939 *Polk's Hattiesburg City Directory*, 349–350; 1946 *Polk's Hattiesburg City Directory*, 527; wages indicated in "Laundry Near Camp Enjoys Business Boom," *Baltimore Afro-American*, August 2, 1941, 3; Osceola McCarty, interviews by Shana Walton, Hattiesburg, MS, February 22 and 23, 1996, transcript, USM-OH; and Richard Boyd, interview by Charles Bolton, Hattiesburg, MS, August 29, 1991, transcript, USM-OH.
15. Boyd, interview; McCarty, interview; and Cook, interview.
16. Victoria Gray Adams, interview by Katherine Mellen Charron, Petersburg, VA, April 22, 2002, transcript, in author's possession; and "Dedicate Colored Health Center Sunday," *Hattiesburg American*, May 29, 1942, 3.
17. Three thousand taken from Rachel Leifer Norman, "Shelby Home to 3,000 POWs in WWII," *Hattiesburg American*, July 15, 2007, 5; John Rankin to Frank Tatum, Washington, DC, June 7, 1944, box 77, folder 15, Tatum Papers; and Boyd, interview. White anxiety over the loss of black labor was common across the South. For more, see Sandra K. Behel, "The Mississippi Home Front during World War II: Tradition and Change" (PhD diss., Mississippi State University, 1989), especially 128–130; and James T. Sparrow, *Warfare State: World War II Americans and the Age of Big Government* (New York: Oxford University Press, 2011), 95–100.
18. Kavan, "The Rise and Decline of Mobile Street," 53–75; ten thousand taken from Paul, "East Sixth Street U.S.O. Building"; and Arvarh E. Strickland, "Remembering Hattiesburg: Growing Up Black in Wartime Mississippi," in *Remaking Dixie: The Impact of Work War II on the American South*, ed. Neil McMillen (Jackson: University Press of Mississippi, 1997), 152–153.
19. Burger, interview; Carl Corbin, "School Survey Points Up Problems," *Hattiesburg American*, November 15, 1945, 1 and 14; and William Theodore Schmidt,

"The Impact of Camp Shelby on Hattiesburg, Mississippi, 1940–1946" (PhD diss., University of Southern Mississippi, 1972), 96–110.

20. "School Survey Points Up Problems," *Hattiesburg American*, November 15, 1945, 1 and 14; and Charles C. Bolton, *The Hardest Deal of All: The Battle Over School Integration in Mississippi, 1870–1980* (Jackson: University Press of Mississippi, 2005), per capita statistic on 21.
21. Burger, interview; and Williams, interview.
22. "Two Negro Soldiers Shot," *Hattiesburg American*, December 10, 1940, 1; "Half of New Base Hospital Opened," *Hattiesburg American*, December 11, 1940, 8; and Strickland, "Remembering Hattiesburg,"152–155.
23. Smith, interview; Strickland, "Remembering Hattiesburg," 152–153; Jake Chambliss, "Letters to Editor," *Hattiesburg American*, January 31, 1941, 4; "Soldiers and Civilians 'Burned Up' about Busses," *Hattiesburg American*, May 21, 1942, 1 and 11; and "Police Order Bus Passenger Segregation," *Hattiesburg American*, February 22, 1941, 1 and 14.
24. "All Not Well at Camp Shelby, Miss.," *Baltimore Afro-American*, July 5, 1941, 1; police chief quoted in "Negro Soldiers Warned to Watch Step in Town," *Hattiesburg American*, June 9, 1941, 3; Brown quoted in "'It's Hell in the South,' States Vet Army Man," *Baltimore Afro-American*, October 25, 1941, 5; Owens, interview; and "Mississippi Bans Sales of Northern Colored Weeklies," *Baltimore Afro-American*, July 24, 1943, 20. For more on the experiences of black Mississippi soldiers during World War II, see Neil McMillen, "Fighting for What We Didn't Have: How Mississippi's Black Veterans Remember World War II," in *Remaking Dixie: The Impact of World War II on the American South*, ed. Neil McMillen (Jackson: University Press of Mississippi, 1997), 93–110.
25. Williams, interview; Jason Morgan Ward, *Hanging Bridge: Racial Violence and America's Civil Rights Century* (New York: Oxford University Press, 2016), 91–164 for the 1942 Shubuta double lynching; see Patricia Michelle Boyett, *Right to Revolt: The Crusade for Racial Justice in Mississippi's Central Piney Woods* (Jackson: University Press of Mississippi, 2015), 21–31 for Howard Wash; "Army Race Riots Spread," *Chicago Defender*, June 19, 1943, 1; Lee, *The Employment of Negro Troops*, 348–379; Mary Penick Motley, ed., *The Invisible Soldier: The Experience of the Black Soldier, World War II* (Detroit, MI: Wayne State University Press, 1975), especially 39–72 for more on black soldiers' domestic experiences; and Marilynn S. Johnson, "Gender, Race, and Rumours: Re-examining the 1943 Race Riots," *Gender and History* 10, no. 2 (1998), 252–277.
26. See Lee, *The Employment of Negro Troops*, 100–110.
27. *Serviceman's Guide to Hattiesburg*, 19; Strickland, "Remembering Hattiesburg," quoted on 154; "Miss. Teacher Institutes Novel Plan for Soldiers," *Pittsburgh Courier*, May 16, 1942, 7; "Draftees," *Hattiesburg American*, May 25,

1942, 10; Paul, "East Sixth Street U.S.O. Building"; "Negro Employment Office Established," *Hattiesburg American*, September 16, 1940, 10; "Improve Camp Bus Service," *Hattiesburg American*, May 26, 1942, 1; "Draftees," *Hattiesburg American*, May 25, 1942, 10; "Health Conference Friday for Negroes," *Hattiesburg American*, November 8, 1944, 4; and "Notes from Camp Shelby," *Baltimore Afro-American*, February 7, 1942, 5.

28. "Negro Air Raid Wardens Appointed," *Hattiesburg American*, May 2, 1942, 5; "Negroes Give to Red Cross War Fund," *Hattiesburg American*, January 17, 1942, 5; "Colored People Prepare for Red Cross Drive," *Hattiesburg American*, March 11, 1944, 5; "Colored War Loan Committee Meets Thursday," *Hattiesburg American*, January 19, 1944, 8; "Negro Committees Named in 5th War Loan," *Hattiesburg American*, May 27, 1944, 5; and "Colored business . . ." quoted in "Colored People Put Bond Money on 'Barrel-Head,'" *Hattiesburg American*, January 31, 1944, 1.

29. "Colored Workers Meet," *Hattiesburg American*, October 22, 1943, 4; "Negroes Will Organize Monday for Bond Drive," *Hattiesburg American*, January 15, 1944, 7; "Colored War Loan Committee Meets Thursday," *Hattiesburg American*, January 19, 1944, 8; and $18,000 and quotations taken from "Colored People Put Bond Money on 'Barrel-Head,'" *Hattiesburg American*, January 31, 1944, 1.

30. "Negro Committees Named in 5th War Loan," *Hattiesburg American*, May 27, 1944, 5; "Fifth War Loan Campaign Begins Tonight," *Hattiesburg American*, June 12, 1944, 1 and 9; quotations taken from "Negroes Organize for 6th War Loan," *Hattiesburg American*, November 18, 1944, 1; "Negroes to Plan Victory Loan Drive," *Hattiesburg American*, November 8, 1945, 11; and "Negroes Are Ready for Bond Drive," *Hattiesburg American*, May 14, 1945, 11.

31. Colored Health Committee of Hattiesburg Announcement, *Hattiesburg American*, April 7, 1945, 2; "Colored War Loan Committee Meets Thursday," *Hattiesburg American*, January 19, 1944, 8; William T. Schmidt, "The Middle Years," in Kenneth G. McCarty Jr., ed., *Hattiesburg: A Pictorial History* (Jackson: University Press of Mississippi, 1982), 122–123; "Improvements in Negro Areas of City South," *Hattiesburg American*, October 8, 1941, 12; and "County's U.S.O. Quota is Over-Subscribed," *Hattiesburg American*, May 26, 1942, 1.

32. Quotation taken from "Continue Clean-up on Mobile Street," *Hattiesburg American*, December 5, 1941, 1 and 15; "Negro Welfare Body Names Chairmen," *Hattiesburg American*, January 23, 1942, 11; "Negro Civic Welfare Meeting," *Hattiesburg American*, July 22, 1943, 4; "Negro Welfare Group to Help Fight VD," *Hattiesburg American*, March 22, 1945, 11; "Famed Colored Quartet Sings Here Nov. 23," *Hattiesburg American*, November 16, 1943, 7; "Vesper Services at 6 p.m. Sunday at Negro U.S.O.," *Hattiesburg American*,

November 13, 1943, 3; and "Delinquency Conference Tonight," *Hattiesburg American*, February 12, 1941, 4.

33. "Continue Clean-up on Mobile Street," *Hattiesburg American*, December 5, 1941, 1 and 15; "Negro Welfare Body Names Chairmen," *Hattiesburg American*, January 23, 1942, 11; "Negro Civic Welfare Meeting," *Hattiesburg American*, July 22, 1943, 4; and "Negro Welfare Group to Help Fight VD," *Hattiesburg American*, March 22, 1945, 11.
34. "Negroes Elated over New U.S.O. Building," *Hattiesburg American*, March 23, 1942, 7; East Sixth Street U.S.O. Souvenir Booklet, box 2, folder 11, Wade (Daisy Harris) Papers, USM; Paul, "East Sixth Street U.S.O. Building"; sheet 29, Hattiesburg, April, 1931 and August, 1949, Sanborn; "Mobile U.S.O. Club Dedicated," *Atlanta Daily World*, April 26, 1945, 2; "Hattiesburg Gets $50,000 U.S.O. Unit," *Atlanta Daily World*, April 3, 1942, 2; "Camp Shelby Soldiers Get a U.S.O. Center," *Chicago Defender*, March 21, 1942, 5; and "Camp Shelby Gets Center," *Philadelphia Tribune*, March 28, 1942, 2.
35. "Deadline for New Buildings," *Hattiesburg American*, October 11, 1941, 1; "Fund Approved for Negro Center," *Hattiesburg American*, September 18, 1941, 9; "U.S.O. Building for Negroes Opens March 22," *Hattiesburg American*, March 11, 1942, 4; and 300 taken from Paul, "East Sixth Street U.S.O. Building." For more on the FWA, see Smith, *Building New Deal Liberalism*, 190–231.
36. "County's U.S.O. Quota is Over-Subscribed," *Hattiesburg American*, May 26, 1942, 1; "Need for U.S.O.'s Services Mounting," *Hattiesburg American*, May 15, 1942, 1 and 11; "More Donors to U.S.O. Fund Announced," *Hattiesburg American*, June 4, 1942, 12; "Negroes Go over Top in U.S.O. Drive," *Hattiesburg American*, June 16, 1942, 4; "Negro Program to Be Held Sunday Afternoon," *Hattiesburg American*, June 27, 1942, 4; and "Start Work on Center for Negro Soldiers," *Hattiesburg American*, October 18, 1941, 5.
37. "Agreement for the Operation of the Negro U.S.O. Club in the City of Hattiesburg, Miss.," box 584, folder 1; John Tally to Frank Tatum, Hattiesburg, MS, April 15, 1943, box 584, folder 30; Luther Smith to Frank Tatum, Hattiesburg, MS, April 19, 1943; and quotation from Frank Tatum to George Calhoun, Hattiesburg, MS, April 13, 1943, box 584, folder 30, all located in Tatum Papers.
38. "Former Instructor Director at Center," *Chicago Defender*, June 6, 1942, 17; East Sixth Street U.S.O. Souvenir Booklet, box 2, folder 11, Wade Papers; Paul, "East Sixth Street U.S.O. Building"; and Program of the First Anniversary East Sixth Street USO, March 19 and 21, 1943, box 584, folder 8, Tatum Papers.
39. East Sixth Street USO Souvenir Booklet, box 2, folder 11, Wade Papers; 40,261 hours taken from Paul, "East Sixth Street U.S.O. Building"; "Ceremony Tonight Marks Closing of Sixth St. USO," *Hattiesburg American*, August 15,

1946, 10; "Church Activities," *Hattiesburg American*, October 16, 1943, 5; J. R. Jenkins to Rainbow Sewing Circle, Hattiesburg, MS, April 11, 1944, box 584, folder 9, Tatum Papers; December,1943 Program of Activities, at the East 6th Street USO., box 584, folder 9, Tatum Papers; Undated East Sixth Street U.S.O. Program Report, box 584, folder 8, Tatum Papers; Narrative Report, December 1943, box 584, folder 9, Tatum Papers; and East Sixth Street U.S.O. Souvenir Booklet, box 2, folder 11, Wade Papers.

40. Examples of activities taken from East Sixth Street U.S.O. Weekly Bulletins from 1942 and 1943 found in box 584, folder 8 and 14, Tatum Papers; 16,090 taken from U.S.O. Club East 6 Street Program Report, Undated, box 584, folder 8, Tatum Papers; 386,676 taken from Paul, "East Sixth Street U.S.O. Building"; and Daniels, "Military Pastimes," 137–149.

41. "Educator Will Speak at Negro U.S.O. Center," *Hattiesburg American*, July 8, 1942, 10; "Negro Educator Speaks Tonight at Colored U.S.O." *Hattiesburg American*, July 13, 1942, 5; Bethune quoted in "Camp Shelby, Miss.," *Chicago Defender*, August 8, 1942, 9; and "Jesse Owens Surveys Recreation Facilities Here," *Hattiesburg American*, July 27, 1942, 5.

42. "Joe Louis at Shelby December 22," *Hattiesburg American*, December 16, 1943, 6; Saenger Theatre Performance Schedule, *Hattiesburg American*, April 21, 1944, 6; Richard Kostelanetz, ed., *The B. B. King Reader: 6 Decades of Commentary* (Milwaukee, WI: Hal Leonard, 2005), 146; Kavan, "The Rise and Decline of Mobile Street," Hopkins quoted on 54; "Shelby Soldiers to Play Champs," *Atlanta Daily World*, December 8, 1943, 5; and Daniels, "Military Pastimes," 137–149.

43. Summary Program Activities for the Month of January 1943, box 584, folder 28, Tatum Papers; and Brief Summary Program Activities for the Month of February 1943, box 584, folder 28, Tatum Papers.

44. Ariel Barnes interview by Sarah Rowe, April 1, 1993, transcript, USM-OH; "Ceremony Tonight Marks Closing of Sixth St. USO," *Hattiesburg American*, August 15, 1946, 10; and Paul, "East Sixth Street U.S.O. Building." The website for the current Hattiesburg African American Military History Museum can be found at www.hattiesburguso.com/.

45. "Funeral Rites Wednesday for Aged Negro," *Hattiesburg American*, May 9, 1944, 10; Smith, interview; and observations made at the gravesite of Turner Roger Smith, River View Cemetery, Hattiesburg, MS on June 25, 2014.

46. Smith, interview.

47. Ibid.

48. Smith, interview; "Colored People Praise New Health Centers," *Hattiesburg American*, July 9, 1942, 5; "County's U.S.O. Quota is Over-Subscribed," *Hattiesburg American*, May 26, 1942, 1; "Negroes Organize Defense Savings

Drive," *Hattiesburg American*, February 21, 1942, 9; "Negroes to Receive United Drive Instructions," *Hattiesburg American*, September 27, 1945, 4; "Red Cross," *Hattiesburg American*, March 15, 1944, 7; and "Colored War Loan Committee Meets Thursday," *Hattiesburg American*, January 19, 1944, 8.

49. "Health Week Program Will Begin Monday," *Hattiesburg American*, April 1, 1944, 8; William T. Schmidt, "The Middle Years," 122–123; Sharon Wertz, "The Birth of Civil Rights," *Hattiesburg American*, May 30, 1982, 7E; Dr. Isaac Thomas interview by Jessie Flowers, Hattiesburg, MS, December 23, 1994, transcript, USM-OH; Cohen, interview; Williams, interview; and Barnes, interview.

50. *The History of Forrest County, Mississippi*, Hattiesburg Area Historical Society Volunteers (Hattiesburg, MS: Hattiesburg Historical Society, 2000), 36; Gordon A. Martin, Jr., *Count Them One by One: Black Mississippians Fighting for the Right to Vote* (Jackson: University Press of Mississippi, 2010), 9 and 10; and Patricia Michelle Buzard-Boyett, "Race and Justice in Mississippi's Central Piney Woods, 1940–2010" (PhD diss., University of Southern Mississippi, 2011), 122–123. For more on the history of the Forrest County NAACP, see Boyett, *Right to Revolt*.

51. Membership figures taken from Richard M. Dalfiume, "The 'Forgotten Years' of the Negro Revolution," *Journal of American History* 55, no. 1 (1968), 99–100. For more on the extensive NAACP campaigns of the postwar era, see Patricia Sullivan, *Lift Every Voice: The NAACP and the Making of the Civil Rights Movement* (New York: New Press, 2009); Jeffrey D. Gonda, *Unjust Deeds: The Restrictive Covenant Cases and the Making of the Civil Rights Movement* (Chapel Hill: University of North Carolina Press, 2015); Mark V. Tushnet, *The NAACP's Legal Strategy against Segregated Education, 1925–1950* (Chapel Hill: University of North Carolina Press, 1987); and Gilbert King, *Devil in the Grove: Thurgood Marshall, the Groveland Boys, and the Dawn of a New America* (New York: Harper Perennial, 2012).

52. Edgar T. Rouzeau, "Black America Wars on Double Front for High Stakes," *Pittsburgh Courier*, February 7, 1942, 5; "The Courier's Double 'V' For a Double Victory Campaign Gets Country-Wide Support," *Pittsburgh Courier*, February 14, 1942, 1; Rayford W. Logan, ed., *What the Negro Wants* (Chapel Hill: University of North Carolina Press, 1944); Kevin Kruse and Stephen Tuck, eds., *Fog of War: The Second World War and the Civil Rights Movement* (New York: Oxford University Press, 2012); Gunnar Myrdal, *An American Dilemma: The Negro Problem and Modern Democracy* (New York: Harper, 1944); Carol Anderson, *Eyes off the Prize: The United Nations and the African American Struggle for Human Rights, 1944–1955* (New York: Cambridge University Press, 2003); Lee, *The Employment of Negro Troops*; Neil McMillen,

ed., *Remaking Dixie*; and John Dittmer, *Local People: The Struggle for Civil Rights in Mississippi* (Urbana: University of Illinois Press, 1994).

53. *Smith v. Allwright*, 321 US 649 (1944); Darlene Clark Hine, *Black Victory: The Rise and Fall of the White Primary in Texas* (Columbia: University of Missouri Press, 2003, orig., 1979); Bilbo quoted in "Bilbo Screams Mob Violence," *Chicago Defender*, June 29, 1946, 1; and "No Disorders Reported as Negroes Vote," *Hattiesburg American*, July 2, 1946, 1 and 12. For more on the immediate impact of *Smith v. Allwright* in Mississippi, see Robert Mickey, *Paths Out of Dixie: The Democratization of Authoritarian Enclaves in America's Deep South, 1944–1972* (Princeton, NJ: Princeton University Press, 2015), 95–119.
54. Barnes, interview; and *United States v. Lynd*, 349 F.2d 790 (1965), Brief for Petitioner, box 1, folder 13, Martin Papers.
55. *United States v. Lynd*, 349 F.2d 790 (1965), Brief for Petitioner, box 1, folder 13, Martin Papers; "Land sales . . ." taken from Smith, interview; "Elected," *Hattiesburg American*, August 28, 1935, 8; *Polk's Hattiesburg City Directory: 1946* (Richmond, VA: R. L. Polk & Co., 1946), 93; "Use Silly Quiz to Deny Vote," *Chicago Defender*, May 10, 1952; and *Peay et al. v. Cox*, 190 F.2d 123 (5th Cir. 1951).
56. *Peay et al. v. Cox*, 190 F.2d 123 (5th Cir. 1951); and Martin, *Count Them One by One*, 6–14. See Chapter 2 for more on the 1890 Constitution and the "understanding clause."
57. *Peay et al. v. Cox*, 190 F.2d 123 (1951); Cohen, interview; Smith, interview; "Negroes Sue for Voting Registration Rights," *Hattiesburg American*, April 14, 1950, 1; and "Negroes' Suit Against Cox Is Dismissed," *Hattiesburg American*, October 12, 1950, 1. The backgrounds of the plaintiffs were developed using the 1910, 1920, 1930, and 1940 US Census Population Schedules for Forrest County and Polk's Hattiesburg city directories between 1918 and 1958.
58. *Peay et al. v. Cox*, 190 F.2d 123 (5th Cir. 1951), quotations taken from decision; and "Negroes' Suit against Cox Is Dismissed," *Hattiesburg American*, October 12, 1950, 1.
59. *United States v. Lynd*, 349 F.2d 790 (1965), Brief for Petitioner, box 1, folder 13, Martin Papers; "15 Sue to Vote in Mississippi," *Chicago Defender*, April 22, 1950, 2; $100 and $500 taken from "Discrimination Charged in Case against Registrar," *Atlanta Daily World*, September 23, 1951, 1; "Use Silly Quiz to Deny Vote," *Chicago Defender*, May 10, 1952, 1; Marshall quoted in "How Many Bubbles in Soap Bar," *Philadelphia Tribune*, May 10, 1952, 9; "NAACP Asks Probe of Mississippi Registrar," *Cleveland Call and Post*, May 17, 1952, 4_B; "No More 'Soap Bubbles' Queries for Negro Voters," *Arkansas State Press*, February 27, 1953, 1 and 8; Martin, *Count Them One by One*, 6–23; and Brian K. Landsberg, *Enforcing Civil Rights: Race Discrimination and the*

Department of Justice (Lawrence: University Press of Kansas, 1997), 104–106.

60. *United States v. Lynd*, 349 F.2d 790 (1965), Brief for Petitioner, box 1, folder 13, Martin Papers; "How Many Bubbles in Soap Bar," *Philadelphia Tribune*, May 10, 1952, 9; "NAACP Asks Probe of Mississippi Registrar," *Cleveland Call and Post*, May 17, 1952, 4_B; "No More 'Soap Bubbles' Queries for Negro Voters," *Arkansas State Press*, February 27, 1953, 1 and 8; and Martin, *Count Them One by One*, 6–23.
61. Martin, *Count Them One by One*, 6–23; and voter registration figures taken from James Franklin Barnes, "Negro Voting in Mississippi" (master's thesis, Mississippi College, 1955), 40–43.
62. *Polk's Hattiesburg City Directory*, 1950 (Richmond, VA: R. L. Polk & Co., 1950), 165; and Cohen, interview.
63. "Smith Drug Co. Formally Opens New Store Thursday," *Hattiesburg American*, October 13, 1954, 4B; observations made at St. Paul Methodist Church, Hattiesburg, MS on June 25, 2014; and "Ceremony Set Sunday at St. Paul," *Hattiesburg American*, September 28, 1962, 1B.
64. Smith, interview; Cohen, interview; Barnes, interview; Charles Davis, interview by Anna Warren, Hattiesburg, MS, August 27, 2005, transcript, USM-OH; "Cite Mississippi Medic," *Chicago Defender*, May 10, 1952, 13; Medgar Evers, 1955 Annual Report MS State Office NAACP, box 1, folder 39, Evers Papers; Myrlie Evers with William Peters, *For Us, the Living* (Jackson: University Press of Mississippi, 1996, 2nd edition, orig., 1967), especially 7–160; and Michael Vinson Williams, *Medgar Evers: Mississippi Martyr* (Fayetteville: University of Arkansas Press, 2011), especially 13–116.
65. Smith, interview; Cohen, interview; Barnes, interview; Davis, interview; Clyde Kennard Affidavit in box 2, folder 4, Evers Papers; and Statement of Reverend W. D. Ridgeway, box 2, folder 21, Evers Papers.

11. *Crying in the Wilderness*

Epigraph: Tom P. Brady to Louis Faulkner, Brookhaven, MS, July 18, 1955, box 23, folder 2, Faulkner Papers.

1. "Weather," *Hattiesburg American*, October 8, 1949, 1; "Looking for . . . ," quoted in "W. S. F. Tatum Dies; Funeral Saturday," *Hattiesburg American*, October 7, 1949, 1 & 11; and "Mayor Proclaims Day of Mourning," *Hattiesburg American*, October 7, 1949, 1.
2. "Southern Prepares for Big Day," *Hattiesburg American*, October 7, 1949, 1; "MSC Homecoming Parade a Honey," *Hattiesburg American*, October 8, 1949, 1; "Plan of the Day," *Student Printz*, October 7, 1949, 1; and "Governor Leads MSC Parade," *Student Printz*, October 14, 1949, 1.

3. "Southern Prepares for Big Day"; "MSC Homecoming Parade a Honey"; "Plan of the Day"; and "Southerners Hit Road For First G.S.C. Game This Week," *Hattiesburg American*, October 10, 1949, 6.
4. V. O. Key, *Southern Politics: In State and Nation* (New York: Knopf, 1949), 230–238; "Gov. Wright Tosses Hat in the Ring," *Hattiesburg American*, January 27, 1947, 1; and Election Results taken from *Hattiesburg American*, August 6, 1947, 1.
5. Wright quoted in Rod Sparrow, "Wright Asks South to Bolt Party if Democrats Continue Radicalism," *Hattiesburg American*, January 20, 1948, 1.
6. The full text of those remarks can be found in "The Text of President Truman's Message on Civil Rights," *New York Times*, February 3, 1948, 22; and 1948 Republican Party Platform taken from "Here's the Republican Platform for 1948," *Chicago Tribune*, June 23, 1948, 4. For more on the Republican Party and the 1948 election, see Timothy N. Thurber, *Republicans and Race: The GOP's Frayed Relationship with African Americans, 1945–1974* (Lawrence: University Press of Kansas, 2013), especially 24–35.
7. Three hundred thousand figure taken from John Dittmer, *Local People: The Civil Rights Struggle in Mississippi* (Urbana: University of Illinois Press, 1994), 14. For more on the growing political power of Northern black migrants in the mid-to-late 1940s, see Henry Lee Moon, *Balance of Power: The Negro Vote* (Garden City, NY: Doubleday & Co., 1948); and Martha Biondi, *To Stand and Fight: The Struggle for Civil Rights in Postwar New York City* (Cambridge, MA: Harvard University Press, 2003).
8. For more on the relationship between the Cold War and civil rights, see Mary Dudziak, *Cold War Civil Rights: Race and the Image of American Democracy* (Princeton, NJ: Princeton University Press, 2000).
9. Patricia Sullivan, *Days of Hope: Race and Democracy in the New Deal Era* (Chapel Hill: University of North Carolina Press, 1996), especially 133–247; and Harvard Sitkoff, *A New Deal for Blacks: The Emergence of Civil Rights as a National Issue* (New York: Oxford University Press, 1978), 44–104.
10. All quotes taken from "Sen. Byrd Is Sought as Party Revolt Leader," *Hattiesburg American*, February 13, 1948, 1.
11. "Declared war . . ." quoted in "Dixie Congressmen Hold 'War' Council," *Hattiesburg American*, February 20, 1948, 1; "Invasion . . ." quoted in "Southern Congressmen Prepare for War on Civil Rights Bills," *Atlanta Daily World*, February 21, 1948, 1; "Dixie Party Leaders to Meet in Jackson," *Hattiesburg American*, February 21, 1948, 1; and William F. Winter, "New Directions in Politics, 1948–1956," in Richard Aubrey McLemore, ed., *A History of Mississippi*, vol. 2 (Hattiesburg: University & College Press of Mississippi, 1973), 140–147.
12. Wright quoted in Rod Sparrow, "Wright Asks South to Bolt Party if Democrats Continue Radicalism," *Hattiesburg American*, January 20, 1948, 1; and John

Ray Skates Jr., "World War II and Its Effects, 1940–1948," in McLemore, ed., A *History of Mississippi*, vol. 2, per capita income taken from 125.

13. Wright quoted in Rod Sparrow, "Wright Asks South to Bolt Party if Democrats Continue Radicalism," *Hattiesburg American*, January 20, 1948, 1.
14. For more on Strom Thurmond and the Dixiecrats, see Joseph Crespino, *Strom Thurmond's America* (New York: Hill and Wang, 2012), especially 34–84.
15. The figure of 87 percent taken from Winter, "New Directions in Politics, 1948–1956," 144; "Vote Tuesday," *Hattiesburg American*, November 1, 1948, 2; "Maximum Vote Sought in Next Tuesday's Election," *Hattiesburg American*, October 27, 1948, 1; "Vote Tuesday," editorial, *Hattiesburg American*, November 1, 1948, 2. Advertisement offering transportation to the polls found on 1; and "Huge Vote for Thurmond Here," *Hattiesburg American*, November 3, 1948, 1.
16. Kari Frederickson, *The Dixiecrat Revolt and the End of the Solid South, 1932–1968* (Chapel Hill: University of North Carolina Press, 2001), especially 69–76 for Mississippians' reaction to Truman, one-fifth statistic taken from 184; and Winter, "New Directions in Politics, 1948–1956," 140–153.
17. Frederickson, *The Dixiecrat Revolt and the End of the Solid South*; and Winter, "New Directions in Politics, 1948–1956," 140–153.
18. "Drastic Adjustment," editorial, *Hattiesburg American*, September 13, 1945, 1; "Seek $75,000 to Thwart Slump," *Hattiesburg American*, September 13, 1945, 1; Post-War Development Fund Ledger, 1945, box 11, folders 3–6, CoC; and "Post-War Development Fund," box 11, folder 7, CoC.
19. Rod Sparrow, "Mississippi Bids for More Industries," *Hattiesburg American*, August 24, 1945, 3; Ralph Rogers, "The Effort to Industrialize," in McLemore, ed., A *History of Mississippi*, vol. 2: 233–249; and Donald B. Dodd, ed., *Historical Statistics of the States of the United States: Two Centuries of the Census*, 1790–1990 (Westport, CT: Greenwood Press, 1993), 387–388.
20. James C. Cobb, *The Selling of the South: The Southern Crusade for Industrial Development* (Urbana: University of Illinois Press, 1993), 35–63; Bruce J. Schulman, *From Cotton Belt to Sunbelt: Federal Policy, Economic Development, and the Transformation of the South*, 1938–1980 (New York: Oxford University Press, 1991), 63–111; and Dodd, ed., *Historical Statistics of the States of the United States*, 339–442.
21. "Appropriate . . ." and "to be used . . ." quoted in J. P. Cameron to Rotary Club, August 20, 1946, box 171, folder 5, transcript, Tatum Papers; and Post-War Development Fund Ledger, 1945, box 11, folders 3–7, CoC. This range excludes the donation of the Forrest County Board of Supervisors, which contributed $5,000 from tax revenues.
22. "Report of the Chamber of Commerce President of 1940," box 1, folder 14, CoC.

23. "Broke . . . ," quoted in "Drastic Adjustment," editorial, *Hattiesburg American*, September 13, 1945, 1.
24. Post-War Development Fund, box 11, folder 7, CoC; and J. P. Cameron to Rotary Club, August 20, 1946, box 171, folder 5, transcript, Tatum Papers.
25. Robert Loftus, "Camp Shelby Goes Out of Business," *Hattiesburg American*, October 1, 1946, 1; Janet Braswell, "Doctor Key in Bringing Shelby to City," *Hattiesburg American*, July 15, 2007, 3 and 15; and Emma James, "Shelby Brings $100M Payroll to Pine Belt," *Hattiesburg American*, July 15, 2007, 14. For more on Camp Shelby, see the Mississippi National Guard website: http://ms.ng.mil/installations/shelby/Pages/default.aspx. This was not the case for all Southern military installations, since the South's share of defense-related contracts rapidly expanded throughout the 1950s and 1960s. See Schulman, *From Cotton Belt to Sunbelt*, 135–173.
26. Memo from J. O. Barron to Members of the Hattiesburg Chamber of Commerce, Hattiesburg, MS, July 2, 1947, box 170, folder 19, Tatum Papers; and "Industries Interested in Locating Here," *Hattiesburg American*, August 20, 1946, 1.
27. Memo from J. O. Barron to Members of the Hattiesburg Chamber of Commerce, Hattiesburg, MS, July 2, 1947, box 170, folder 19, Tatum Papers; and "Industries Interested in Locating Here," *Hattiesburg American*, August 20, 1946, 1.
28. Post-War Development Fund, box 11, folder 7, CoC.
29. Minutes of a Special Meeting of the Industrial Affairs Committee and the Executive Committee of the Hattiesburg Chamber of Commerce, September 5, 1947; Minutes of a Special Joint Meeting of the Industrial Affairs Committee and the Executive Committee of the Hattiesburg Chamber of Commerce, September 12, 1947; Minutes of a Special Joint Meeting of the Industrial Affairs Committee and the Executive Committee of the Hattiesburg Chamber of Commerce, September 15, 1947; Minutes of a Special Meeting of the Industrial Affairs Committee and the Executive Committee of the Hattiesburg Chamber of Commerce, October 2, 1947; Minutes of a Special Joint Meeting of the Board of Directors, Executive Committee, Industrial Committee of the Hattiesburg Chamber of Commerce and Special Invited Guests, October 2, 1947, all located in box 2, folder 5, CoC; Minutes of the Regular Monthly Meeting of the Board of Directors of Hattiesburg Chamber of Commerce, May 28, 1948, box 2, folder 6, CoC; and City of Hattiesburg, Financial Statement, October 1, 1945, to September 30, 1946, *Hattiesburg American*, October 29, 1946, 8.
30. "C of C Announces Farm-Help Program," *Hattiesburg American*, December 10, 1946, 1; "Factory Farming Plant Site Will Be Chosen Soon,"

Hattiesburg American, March 6, 1947, 4; "New Concrete Products Plant Located Here," *Hattiesburg American*, May 13, 1946, 1; Samples taken from 1950 *Polk's Hattiesburg City Directory*, 347–428; and US Bureau of the Census, *Census of the Population:* 1950, vol. 2, part 24, *Mississippi* (Washington, DC: Government Printing Office, 1952), 24–46.

31. World War II figures taken from "Rotary Club," *Hattiesburg American*, April 9, 1946, 4; and "Reliance Anniversary Day Here Thursday," *Hattiesburg American*, May 26, 1948, 1.

32. "Employment Booths Set Up for Reliance," *Hattiesburg American*, October 26, 1946, 4; "Reliance Plants Need 225 Women Workers," *Hattiesburg American*, October 23, 1945, 1; "Rotary Club," *Hattiesburg American*, April 9, 1946, 4; "The Reliance Plants," editorial, *Hattiesburg American*, May 27, 1948, 2; "Reliance Anniversary Day Here Thursday," *Hattiesburg American*, May 26, 1948, 1; Yvonne Arnold, interview by Charles Bolton, Hattiesburg, MS, October 6, 1998, transcript, USM-OH; and Raylawni Branch, interview by Kim Adams, Hattiesburg, MS, October 23, 1993, transcript, USM-OH.

33. "Hercules Powder Plans New Insecticide Plant," *Wall Street Journal*, September 5, 1950, 5; Davis Dyer and David B. Sicilia, *Labors of a Modern Hercules: The Evolution of a Chemical Company* (Boston, MA: Harvard Business School Press, 1990), 221–290, especially 268 and 270 for expansion plans at the Hattiesburg plant; 1950 *US Census:* 1950, vol. 2, part 24, 24–46; and US Census Bureau, *Census of the Population:* 1960, vol. 1, *Characteristics of the Population*, part 26, *Mississippi* (Washington, DC: Government Printing Office, 1963), 26–154.

34. "Union & Company May Confer Today," *Hattiesburg American*, June 8, 1946, 1; "Company Discusses Union's Demands," *Hattiesburg American*, June 10, 1946, 1 and 8; "Hercules-Union Contract Announced," *Hattiesburg American*, July 1, 1946, 1; and Daisy Harris Wade, interview by author, Hattiesburg, MS, October 6, 2011, recording in author's possession.

35. Richard Boyd, interview by Charles Bolton, Hattiesburg, MS, August 29, 1991, transcript, USM-OH; William M. Conner, interview by Felisha Simmons and Kimberly Wadley, November 17, 2009, transcript, USM-OH; and Gordon A. Martin, Jr., *Count Them One by One: Black Mississippians Fighting for the Right to Vote* (Jackson: University Press of Mississippi, 2010), 116–129.

36. Dunagin quoted in Martin, *Count Them*, 124; "Hercules-Union Contract Announced," *Hattiesburg American*, July 1, 1946, 1 and 15; Conner, interview; Boyd, interview; and US Department of Commerce, *State Personal Income: 1929–1982*, 8–10.

37. Chester M. Morgan, *Dearly Bought, Deeply Treasured: The University of Southern Mississippi, 1912–1987* (Jackson: University Press of Mississippi, 1987), 72–104; Richard Aubrey McLemore, "Higher Education in the Twentieth Century," in McLemore, ed., *A History of Mississippi*, vol. 2: 415–445; State Teachers College Silver Jubilee Issue, *Hattiesburg American*, May 22, 1937; Mabel Donavan, "Southern 50 Years Old," *Hattiesburg American*, March 30, 1960, 1 and 4B; "Enrollment Struts toward Fascinating 5G," *Hattiesburg American*, October 23, 1959, 2C; and Robert Cecil Cook, interview by Claude Fike and John Gonzales, Hattiesburg, MS, February 1, 1972, transcript, USM-OH.
38. Kathleen J. Frydl, *The GI Bill* (New York: Cambridge University Press, 2009), $700 million figure on 311; and Keith W. Olson, "The Astonishing Story: Veterans Make Good on the Nation's Promise," *Educational Record* 75, 4 (1994), 16–26.
39. Enrollment figures taken from *Hattiesburg American*, May 22, 1937, 2; "Enrollment Struts toward Fascinating 5G," *Hattiesburg American*, October 23, 1959, 2-C; and Cook, interview.
40. Cook, interview; Bernard Green, interview by Orley Caudill, Hattiesburg, MS, February 23, 1977, transcript, USM-OH; Morgan, *Dearly Bought, Deeply Treasured*, 72–104; and Chester M. Morgan, *Treasured Past, Golden Future: The University of Southern Mississippi* (Jackson: University Press of Mississippi, 2010), especially 64–97.
41. Anna Margaret Roberts, interview by Carl Willis, Hattiesburg, MS, April 28, 1972, transcript, USM-OH; Morgan, *Dearly Bought, Deeply Treasured*, 50–53; Mississippi Southern College to Louis Faulkner, Hattiesburg, MS, November 28, 1953; Louis Faulkner to Dr. R. C. Cook, Hattiesburg, MS, December 15, 1953; Dr. R. C. Cook to Louis Faulkner, Hattiesburg, MS, December 18, 1953; and William McCain to Louis Faulkner, Hattiesburg, MS, October 18, 1955, all located in box 1, folder 15, Faulkner Papers.
42. *1950 US Census: 1950*, vol. 2, part 24, 24–19, 24–44, 24–46, and 24–97; *1960 US Census*, vol. 1, part 26, 26–118.
43. *1950 US Census: 1950*, vol. 2, part 24, 24–7; *County Business Patterns, First Quarter 1953: Part 7 East South Central States* (Washington, DC: United States Department of Commerce, 1953), 78; and "Hattiesburg Area Leads in State Business Boom," *Hattiesburg American*, April 5, 1956, 1.
44. "Faulkner Speaks against Federal Council of Churches," *Hattiesburg American*, August 12, 1947, 2; and Louis Faulkner to Frank M. Tatum, Hattiesburg, MS, May 5, 1950, box 5, folder 6, Faulkner Papers. Faulkner's anti-FCC and NCC correspondence can be found in boxes 31–51. The bulk of Faulkner's anti-NCC editorials can be found in the *Hattiesburg American* between

February 10 and March 10, 1951. For more about the effects of race on the relationships between Mississippi congregations and national religious organizations, see Carolyn Renee Dupont, *Mississippi Praying: Southern White Evangelicals and the Civil Rights Movement, 1945–1975* (New York: New York University Press, 2013), especially 39–62; and James F. Findlay Jr., *Church People in the Struggle: The National Council of Churches and the Black Freedom Movement, 1950–1970* (New York: Oxford University Press, 1993).

45. L. E. Faulkner to Charles Williams, Hattiesburg, MS, July 12, 1954, box 23, folder 1, Faulkner Papers. Faulkner's extensive correspondence related to the *Brown* case is located in box 23 of his personal collection.

46. Winstead and Williams quoted in "Mississippi Representative Hopes for Calm, but Eastland Sees Strife," the *New York Times*, May 18, 1954, 19; and Eastland quoted in William S. White, "Eastland Scores Supreme Court," *New York Times*, May 28, 1954, 16. Michael Klarman has termed this reaction the "backlash thesis." For more, see Michael Klarman, "How *Brown* Changed Race Relations: The Backlash Thesis," *Journal of American History* 81, no. 1 (1994): 81–118.

47. Correspondence found in box 23 of Faulkner Papers; and James Eastland to Louis Faulkner, Ruleville, MS, September 6, 1955, box 23, folder 2, Faulkner Papers.

48. Faulkner's term on the board of directors expired at the end of 1948. List of directors of the Hattiesburg Chamber of Commerce for 1947, box 11, folder 5, CoC; and Faulkner Concrete Pipe Company Statement of Earnings, 1/1/46–11/30/46, box 5, folder 9, Faulkner Papers. Family details constructed using the 1930 and 1940 US Census Population Schedules from Forrest County and Hattiesburg city directories between 1937 and 1954. See Chapter 9 for more on the effects of the wartime economy on Louis Faulkner's business interests.

49. EURO Alumni, *Euro Heritage House: Eureka, Royal Street, Rowan: Hattiesburg's Black High School System*, MDAH, call #: 373.76218 / E89; "Work to Begin Immediately on New Negro Schools Here," *Hattiesburg American*, March 25, 1949, 14; "Camp and Jeff Davis School Remodeling Project Okayed," *Hattiesburg American*, June 7, 1950, 1; N. R. Burger, interview by R. Wayne Pyle, Hattiesburg, MS, May 11, 1982, transcript, USM-OH; "Hattiesburg, Mississippi, 1884–1964: 80 Years of Progress," A Report to the Citizens of Hattiesburg from the Mayor and Commissioners," box 10, folder 10, Southern Tourism Collection, USM; and Charles C. Bolton, *The Hardest Deal of All: The Battle Over School Integration in Mississippi, 1870–1980* (Jackson: University Press of Mississippi, 2005), 33–95, school spending figures on 49.

50. Bolton, *The Hardest Deal of All*, 33–95, school spending figures on 49.

51. Michael J. Klarman, *From Jim Crow to Civil Rights: The Supreme Court and the Struggle for Racial Equality* (New York: Oxford University Press, 2004), 312–320 for *Brown II*; and Bolton, *The Hardest Deal of All*, 61–95, four times figure on 87.
52. Yasuhiro Katagiri, *The Mississippi State Sovereignty Commission: Civil Rights and States' Rights* (Jackson: University Press of Mississippi, 2001), quoted on 6; and "Segregation Commission Waits Senate OK," *Hattiesburg American*, March 22, 1956, 1.
53. Patterson quoted in McMillen, *The Citizens' Council: Organized Resistance to the Second Reconstruction, 1954–64* (Urbana: University of Illinois Press, 1994 edition, orig., 1971), 17; Attorney Arthur Clark quoted in "Integration Foes Arise in the South," *New York Times*, November 21, 1954, 52; and "The Citizens' Council: A History," address by Robert P. Patterson to the Annual Leadership Conference of the Citizens' Councils of America, Jackson, MS, October 26, 1963, folder 1, Steven Bingham Papers, 1965, transcript, WHS.
54. "Organize Citizens Council Tonight," *Hattiesburg American*, March 22, 1956, 1; "Citizens Council Will Elect Officers April 3," *Hattiesburg American*, March 23, 1956, 1; and M. W. Hamilton, interview by Orley B. Caudill, Petal, MS, February 13, 1978, transcript, USM-OH.
55. "Organize Citizens Council Tonight," *Hattiesburg American*, March 22, 1956, 1; "Citizens Council Will Elect Officers April 3," *Hattiesburg American*, March 23, 1956, 1; and *Polk's Hattiesburg City Directory: 1958* (Richmond, VA: R. L. Polk & Co., 1958), 98, 136, and 326.
56. Correspondence with Patterson and Brady found in box 23, Faulkner Papers; *Time*, October 22, 1965, 94; "Thomas P. Brady, Mississippi Judge," *New York Times*, February 1, 1973, 38; Tom Brady to Louis Faulkner, Brookhaven, MS, October 17, 1928, box 1, folder 4, Faulkner Papers; and Louis Faulkner to Tom Brady, October 22, 1928, box 1, folder 4, Faulkner Papers.
57. "Mississippi Gunmen Take Life," *Jet*, May 26, 1955, 8–11; "Lynching in Mississippi: Minister Shotgunned to Death Gang Style," *Chicago Defender*, May 21, 1955, 1; Dittmer, *Local People*, 53–54; "Three White Men Charged with Assassination of Political Leader," *Philadelphia Tribune*, August 23, 1955, 2; Alex Wilson, "Belzoni Grocer Describes Attack," *Chicago Defender*, December 3, 1955, 1; Medgar Evers, "1955 Annual Report Mississippi State Office NAACP," 7, box 2, folder 39, Evers Papers; David T. Beito and Linda Royster Beito, *Black Maverick: T. R. M. Howard's Fight for Civil Rights and Economic Power* (Urbana: University of Illinois Press, 2009), 69–114; and for "death lists," see Myrlie Evers with William Peters, *For Us, the Living* (Jackson: University Press of Mississippi, 1996, 2nd edition, orig., 1967), 160.
58. McMillen, *The Citizens' Council*, 207–234; correspondence in box 23, Faulkner Papers; Louis Faulkner to Hugh L. White, Hattiesburg, June 6, 1955,

box 23, folder 2, Faulkner Papers; *The Eagle Eye*, March 31, 1956, found in box 23, folder 7, Faulkner Papers; "Arrington High as Told to Marc Crawford, *Jet* Exclusive: I Escaped Mississippi in a Casket," *Jet*, February 27, 1958, 10–15; and "Crusading Publisher Who Fled Mississippi in Casket Dies; Returns for Burial," *Jet*, May 16, 1988, 64–65; T. R. M. Howard to Amzie Moore, undated, box 1, folder 3, Moore Papers; and Citizens' Council Report, Bolivar County, 9/30/1955, box 2 folder 3, Evers Papers.

59. 1956 Membership and Freedom Fund Contributions Received from Mississippi Branches, January 1–December 12, 1956, box 2, folder 47, Evers Papers; Total 1956 Memberships and Freedom Fund Contributions Received, January 1–August 23, 1957, box 2, folder 47 Evers Papers; Total 1957 Memberships and Freedom Fund Contributions Received box 2, folder 47 Evers Papers; and Burger, interview.

60. James Cohen, interview by Mike Garvey, Hattiesburg, MS, February 2, 1976, transcript, USM-OH; Burger, interview; "Forrest County," Date Unknown, 2-5-1-53-8-1-1, MSSC; and Zack J. Van Landingham to Director, State Sovereignty Commission, no location given, December 17, 1958, 2-3-0-10-1-1-1 to 2-3-0-10-4-1-1, MSSC.

61. Zack J. Van Landingham to Director, State Sovereignty Commission, no location given, December 17, 1958, 2-3-0-10-1-1-1 to 2-3-0-10-4-1-1, Sovereignty Commission; "Mt. Carmel Church Will Be Dedicated Sunday," *Hattiesburg American*, April 25, 1953, 3; and Cohen, interview.

62. Statement of Reverend W. D. Ridgeway, Pastor of the Truelight Baptist Church in Hattiesburg, Mississippi, Before Senate Subcommittee on Constitutional Rights, February 28, 1957, box 2, folder 21, Evers Papers; Michael Vinson Williams, *Medgar Evers: Mississippi Martyr* (Fayetteville: University of Arkansas Press, 2011), 149; "Beer-Selling Permit Revoked," *Hattiesburg American*, March 27, 1957, 2; and "Embassy Club at Palmer's Burns," *Hattiesburg American*, February 4, 1958, 3-A.

63. P. D. East, *The Magnolia Jungle: The Life, Times and Education of a Southern Editor* (New York City: Simon & Schuster, 1960); and Gary Huey, *Rebel with A Cause: P. D. East, Southern Liberalism, and the Civil Rights Movement*, 1953–1971 (Wilmington, DE: Scholarly Resources, Inc., 1985).

64. East, *The Magnolia Jungle*, quoted on 121 and 122, respectively, 2,000 and 39 taken from x and 121, respectively.

65. "School Amendment's Fate in Hands of Voters," *Hattiesburg American*, December 21, 1954, 1; Bolton, *The Hardest Deal of All*, 61–73; and East, *The Magnolia Jungle*, quoted on 130 and 131.

66. East, *The Magnolia Jungle*, 124, 159, 165–167; and P. D. East, editorial: "A Letter to a Friend," February 16, 1956, *Editorial Reprints from The Petal Paper*, box 1, folder 3, East Collection, USM. For more on the murder of Emmett Till, see

John Dittmer, *Local People: The Civil Rights Struggle in Mississippi* (Urbana: University of Illinois Press, 1994), 55–58

67. East, *The Magnolia Jungle,* 175–181; and P. D. East, editorial: "The Bigger and Better Bigots Bureau," June 7, 1956, *Editorial Reprints from The Petal Paper,* box 1, folder 3, East Collection.
68. East, *The Magnolia Jungle,* 175–243; "they're going to kill you . . ." quoted in P. D. East, Letter to Friends, Hattiesburg, MS, undated, box 1, folder 1, East Collection; McMillen, *The Citizens' Council,* 256–258; Huey, *Rebel with A Cause,* 165–201; and Zack J. Van Landingham, Memo to Director, State Sovereignty Commission, August 25, 1959, 1-62-0-1-1-1-1, Sovereignty Commission. A Citizens' Council report to the State Sovereignty Commission indicated, "We have a full file on East's activities." Unknown Author, to Director, State Sovereignty Commission, location unknown, August 17, 1960, 7-0-2-86-1-1-1, Sovereignty Commission.
69. Zack J. Van Landingham, Clyde Kennard Report, December 17, 1958, 1-27-0-6-1-1-1 to 1-27-0-6-37-1-1, Sovereignty Commission; 1940 US Census, Forrest County, Mississippi, Population Schedule, beat 2, sheet 13B, House 239, Grant family, digital images, Ancestry.com, accessed May 12, 2017; and Timothy J. Minchin and John A. Salmond, "'The Saddest Story of the Whole Movement': The Clyde Kennard Case and the Search for Racial Reconciliation in Mississippi 1955–2007," *Journal of Mississippi History* 81, no. 3 (2009): 191–234.
70. Zack J. Van Landingham, Clyde Kennard Report, December 17, 1958, 1-27-0-6-1-1-1 to 1-27-0-6-37-1-1, Sovereignty Commission; and Clyde Kennard, "Letter to the Editor," *Hattiesburg American,* December 6, 1958, 2A.
71. Morgan, *Dearly Bought, Deeply Treasured,* 82–104; Boyett, *Right to Revolt,* 57; McCain quoted in *The History of Forrest County, Mississippi,* Hattiesburg Area Historical Society Volunteers (Hattiesburg, MS: Hattiesburg Historical Society, 2000), 14; and Bradley G. Bond, "'Unmitigated Thievery': The Case against William David McCain," *Journal of Mississippi History* 72, no. 2 (2010): 163–197.
72. Zack J. Van Landingham, Clyde Kennard Report, December 17, 1958, 1-27-0-6-1-1-1 to 1-27-0-6-37-1-1, MSSC; Dorie Ann Ladner and Joyce Ladner, interview by Joseph Mosnier, Washington, DC, transcript, Library of Congress; Joyce Ladner to Medgar Evers, Palmer's Crossing, MS, October 12, 1959, box 2, folder 9, Evers Papers; and Clyde Kennard Affidavit, box 2, folder 4, Evers Papers.
73. Zack J. Van Landingham, Clyde Kennard Report, December 17, 1958, 1-27-0-6-1-1-1 to 1-27-0-6-37-1-1, MSSC.
74. Van Landingham, Clyde Kennard Report; and "Negro Threatens Suit against Miss. College," *Chicago Defender,* December 20, 1958, 2.

75. Zack J. Van Landingham, Memo to Director, State Sovereignty Commission, May 4, 1959, 5-3-1-19-1-1-1, MSSC; and Zack J. Van Landingham, Memo to Governor J. P. Coleman, September 15, 1959, 1-27-0-40-5-1-1, MSSC.
76. Van Landingham, Memo to Director, State Sovereignty Commission, May 4, 1959; Van Landingham, Memo to Coleman, September 15, 1959; and Kennard quoted in "Drops School Fight Plan," *Chicago Defender*, January 7, 1959, A2.
77. Zack J. Van Landingham, Memo to Governor J. P. Coleman, August 27, 1959, 1-27-0-26-1-1-1, MSSC; and Clyde Kennard to Aubrey Lucas, Hattiesburg, MS, September 2, 1959, 1-27-0-29-1-1-1 to 1-27-0-29-7-1-1, MSSC.
78. Zack J. Van Landingham, Memo to Governor J. P. Coleman, September 14, 1959, 1-27-0-36-1-1-1 to 1-27-0-36-6-1-1, MSSC.
79. Zack J. Van Landingham, Memo to Governor J. P. Coleman, September 15, 1959, 1-27-0-40-1-1-1 to 1-27-0-40-6-1-1, MSSC; "Negro Refused Admittance at MSC, Then Arrested," *Hattiesburg American*, September 15, 1959, 1; and "Nabbed as He Tries to End Miss. Race Ban," *Chicago Defender*, September 26, 1959, 2.
80. Zack J. Van Landingham, Memo to Governor J. P. Coleman, September 15, 1959, 1-27-0-40-5-1-1, MSSC; Clyde Kennard, "Letter to the Editor," *Hattiesburg American*, September 25, 1959, 6A; Clyde Kennard, "Letter to the Editor," *Hattiesburg American*, January 26, 1960, 10; and Dorie Ladner, interview by author, recording, Jackson, MS, March 22, 2012.
81. *Kennard v. State*, 246 Miss. 209 (Miss., 1963); "New Charges Are Filed against Kennard," *Hattiesburg American*, September 26, 1960, 1; Branch, interview; Jerry Mitchell, "The Clyde Kennard Story," *Jackson Clarion-Ledger*, December 31, 2005, 1A; "Kennard Convicted, Sentenced to Seven Years," *Hattiesburg American*, November 22, 1960, 1; and Minchin and Salmond, "'The Saddest Story of the Whole Movement.'"
82. Copy of Patient Discharge Summaries, University Hospital, Jackson, MS; Report of Mary Senter, Medical Record Librarian, June 21, 1962; and R. Jess Brown to C. E. Breaseale, location unknown, January 19, 1963, all in box 2, folder 10, Evers Papers; "Clyde Kennard Begins New Fight," *Chicago Defender*, February 2, 1963, 1; and Minchin and Salmond, "'The Saddest Story of the Whole Movement.'"
83. Clyde Kennard, "Letter to Editor," *Hattiesburg American*, December 6, 1958, 2A; and Bond, "'Unmitigated Thievery.'"
84. "L. E. Faulkner Dies," *Hattiesburg American*, January 16, 1961, 1; J. Edgar Hoover to Louis Faulkner, Washington, DC, September 15, 1955, box 23, folder 2; and "not within . . ." quoted in J. Edgar Hoover to Louis Faulkner, Washington, DC, January 30, 1956, box 23, folder 5, Faulkner Papers.
85. Zack J. Van Landingham, Memo to File, February 4, 1960, 1-27-0-62-1-1-1, MSSC.

12. *When the Movement Came*

Epigraph: Daisy Harris Wade, interview by Dick Conville, Hattiesburg, MS, July 12, 2001, transcript, USM-OH.

1. Hollis Watkins, interview by author, Jackson, MS, December 18, 2009, recording in author's possession; Victoria Gray Adams, interview by Taylor Branch, May 14, 1991, box 148, folder 1051, transcript, Taylor Branch Papers (hereafter, Branch Papers), Southern Historical Collection, Wilson Library, University of North Carolina at Chapel Hill, NC; Joyce Ladner, interview by Taylor Branch, February 22, 1991, box 149, folder 1081, transcript, Branch Papers; Hollis Watkins with C. Liegh McInnis, *Brother Hollis: The Sankofa of a Movement Man* (Clinton, MS: Sankofa Southern Publishing, 2015), 93–105; and Curtis Hayes, Forrest County Report, SNCC-M, reel 38, no. 104.
2. Watkins, interview; Bob Moses, interview by author, Jackson, MS, March 27, 2010, recording in author's possession; Watkins, *Brother Hollis*, 58–91; John Dittmer, *Local People: The Civil Rights Struggle in Mississippi* (Champagne: University of Illinois Press, 1994), 90–115; Clayborne Carson, *In Struggle: SNCC and the Black Awakening of the 1960s* (Cambridge, MA: Harvard University Press, 1995, orig., 1981), 45–55; and James Silver, *Mississippi: The Closed Society* (New York: Harcourt, Brace, & World, 1964), quoted on 151.
3. Watkins, interview.
4. Brad J. Kavan, "The Rise and Decline of Mobile Street: Race and the Impact of Camp Shelby on African-American Hattiesburg" (master's thesis, University of Southern Mississippi, 2004); and *Polk's Hattiesburg City Directory: 1959* (Richmond, VA: R. L. Polk & Co., 1959), Street and Avenue Guide, 1–140.
5. US Bureau of the Census, *Census of the Population: 1960*, vol. 1, part 26 (Washington DC: Government Printing Office, 1963), 26–42 and 26–25.
6. *Census of the Population: 1960*, vol. 1, part 26, 26–25 and 26–132; US Bureau of the Census, *Census of the Population: 1950*, vol. 2, part 24 (Washington DC: Government Printing Office, 1952), 24–41; and Donald B. Dodd, ed., *Historical Statistics of the States of the United States: Two Centuries of the Census, 1790–1990* (Westport, CT: Greenwood Press, 1993), 50.
7. *Census of the Population: 1960*, vol. 1, part 26, 26–158 and 26–160.
8. *Census of the Population: 1960*, vol. 1, part 26, 26–54; *Polk's Hattiesburg City Directory: 1959*; William M. Conner, interview by Felisha Simmons and Kimberly Wadley, November 17, 2009, transcript, USM-OH; and Anthony Harris, interview by William Sturkey, Hattiesburg, MS, October 22, 2010, recording in author's possession.
9. *Census of the Population: 1960*, vol. 1, part 26, 26–154; and *Polk's Hattiesburg City Directory: 1959*.

10. Raylawni Branch, interview by Kim Adams, Hattiesburg, MS, October 23, 1993, transcript, USM-OH; and "Rotary Club Hears Address on Reliance Co.," *Hattiesburg American*, April 9, 1946, 4.
11. *Census of the Population: 1960*, vol. 1, part 26, 26–160 and 26–142.
12. 1959 *Polk's Hattiesburg City Directory*, 121–122.
13. Claude Sitton, "Flood Gave Unity to Mississippi City," *New York Times*, March 19, 1961, 67; and Charles Davis, interview by Anna Warren, Hattiesburg, MS, August 27, 2005, transcript, USM-OH.
14. "Negro Deaths—Wendell P. Smith," *Hattiesburg American*, November 4, 1954, 13A; and observations made at River View Cemetery, Hattiesburg, MS on June 25, 2014.
15. Observations made at St. Paul Methodist Church, Hattiesburg, MS on June 25, 2014; and "Ceremony Set Sunday at St. Paul," *Hattiesburg American*, September 28, 1962, 1B.
16. N. R. Burger, interview by R. Wayne Pyle, Hattiesburg, MS, May 11, 1982, transcript, USM-OH; and EURO Alumni, *Euro Heritage House: Eureka, Royal Street, Rowan: Hattiesburg's Black High School System*, MDAH, call #: 373.76218/E89.
17. Burger, interview.
18. Burger, interview; EURO Alumni, *Euro Heritage House*; and "Royal Street High Graduation Exercises Wednesday Night," *Hattiesburg American*, May 27, 1952, 13.
19. Teacher pay taken from Mississippi State Department of Education, *Statistical Data School Session, 1961–1962*, 42, cited in Civil Action 3312: *U.S. v. State of Mississippi et al.*, 256 F. sup. 344 (1966), Plaintiff's list of exhibits, Comparison of Education for Negroes and White Persons 1890–1963, box 2, folder 1, Martin Papers; Burger, interview; EURO Alumni, *Euro Heritage House*; N. R. Burger, "Rowan High," *Hattiesburg American*, January 1, 1959, 4A; "Rowan Dedication and Open House Sunday," *Hattiesburg American*, April 22, 1960, 2; and "Eureka School Will Be Occupied Soon," *Hattiesburg American*, February 3, 1960, 4A.
20. Teacher pay taken from Mississippi State Department of Education, *Statistical Data School Session, 1961–1962*, 42.
21. Burger, interview; and *United States v. Lynd*, 349 F.2d 790 (1965), Brief for Petitioner, box 1, folder 13, Martin Papers.
22. Burger, interview; EURO Alumni, *Euro Heritage House*; N. R. Burger, "Rowan High," *Hattiesburg American*, January 1, 1959, 4A; "Rowan Dedication and Open House Sunday," *Hattiesburg American*, April 22, 1960, 2; "Eureka School Will Be Occupied Soon," *Hattiesburg American*, February 3, 1960, 4A.
23. Howard Zinn, *SNCC: The New Abolitionists* (Chicago, IL: Haymarket Books, 2013, orig., 1964), quoted on 103.

24. Charles Evers and Andrew Szanton, *Have No Fear: The Charles Evers Story* (New York: John Wiley & Sons, 1997), 60–64.
25. Prospectus of the First Annual Meeting of the Mississippi Regional Council of Negro Leadership, box 1, folder 62, Howard Papers; "Mississippi Leadership Meeting Set," *Chicago Defender*, April 12, 1952, 5; Myrlie Evers with William Peters, *For Us, the Living* (Jackson: University Press of Mississippi, 1996, 2nd edition, orig., 1967), 75–97; and David Beito and Linda Beito, *Black Maverick: T. R. M. Howard's Fight for Civil Rights and Economic Power* (Champaign: University of Illinois Press, 2009).
26. Evers, *For Us*, 98–119 and 133–143; and Gloster Current to Medgar Evers, New York City, December 15, 1954, box 2, folder 6, Evers Papers.
27. Medgar Evers, "1955 Annual Report Mississippi State Office NAACP," box 2, folder 39, Evers Papers; Medgar Evers, "1957 Annual Report Mississippi State Office NAACP," box 2, folder 47, Evers Papers; Southern NAACP figures cited from Charles Payne, *I've Got the Light of Freedom: The Organizing Tradition and the Mississippi Freedom Struggle* (Berkeley: University of California Press, 1995), 43; and Michael Vinson Williams, *Medgar Evers: Mississippi Martyr* (Fayetteville: University of Arkansas Press, 2011), 85–116, Evers quoted on 144.
28. Evers, *For Us*, 154–159 and 180–183, quoted on 224; Colia Clark, interview by author, recording, New York City, July 7, 2010, in author's possession; correspondence relating to Citizens' Council activities can be found throughout box 2 of the Evers Papers; material related to the Clyde Kennard case found in box 2, folder 10, Evers Papers; "Cite Mississippi NAACP Official for Contempt," *Atlanta Daily World*, December 8, 1960, 2; and Myrlie Evers-Williams and Manning Marable, eds., *The Autobiography of Medgar Evers: A Hero's Life and Legacy Revealed through His Writings, Letters, and Speeches* (New York: Basic Books, 2005), 1–46.
29. Medgar Evers, "1955 Annual Report Mississippi State Office NAACP," "1956 Annual Report Mississippi State Office NAACP," and "1957 Annual Report Mississippi State Office NAACP," all in box 2, folder 39, Evers Papers; Evers, *For Us*; and Aaron Henry with Constance Curry, *Aaron Henry: The Fire Ever Burning* (Jackson: University Press of Mississippi, 2000), quoted on 110.
30. Medgar Evers, "1955 Annual Report Mississippi State Office NAACP," "1956 Annual Report Mississippi State Office NAACP," and "1957 Annual Report Mississippi State Office NAACP," all in box 2, folder 39, Evers Papers; and Clark, interview.
31. Medgar Evers, "1955 Annual Report Mississippi State Office NAACP," box 2, folder 39, Evers Papers; and Davis, interview. Evers quoted in 1955 report.
32. W. G. Gray to L. C. Hicks, Hattiesburg, MS, February 14, 1958, 2-3-0-5-1-1-1, MSSC.

33. Ed King interview by author, recording, Jackson, MS, March 27, 2010, in author's possession; Henry with Curry, *Aaron Henry*; and regional and statewide meeting correspondence found in box 5, folder 1, Moore Papers.
34. Bob Moses, interview by author, recording, Jackson, MS, March 27, 2010, recording in author's possession; and fifty thousand statistic taken from Clayborne Carson, *In Struggle: SNCC and the Black Awakening of the 1960s* (Cambridge, MA: Harvard University Press, 1982), 11.
35. "I could feel how they felt . . ." quoted in Dittmer, *Local People*, 102; Eric Burner, *And Gently He Shall Lead Them: Robert Parris Moses and Civil Rights in Mississippi* (New York: NYU Press, 1994), especially 9–31 for Moses's early background; and Laura Visser-Maessen, *Robert Parris Moses: A Life in Civil Rights and Leadership at the Grassroots* (Chapel Hill: University of North Carolina Press, 2016), 10–60. For more on the origins of SNCC, see Wesley Hogan, *Many Minds, One Heart: SNCC's Dream for a New America* (Chapel Hill: University of North Carolina Press, 2007), 13–44.
36. Moses, interview; Visser-Maessen, *Robert Parris Moses*, 37–60; and Burner, *And Gently He Shall Lead Them*, especially 9–31. For more on Ella Baker, see Barbara Ransby, *Ella Baker and the Black Freedom Movement: A Radical Democratic Vision* (Chapel Hill: University of North Carolina Press, 2002).
37. Amzie Moore, interview by Mike Garvey, Cleveland, MS, March 29, 1977, transcript, USM-OH; Amzie Moore to Bob Moses, Cleveland, MS, December 22, 1960, box 1, folder 4, Moore Papers; Moses, interview; and Moore quoted in Howell Raines, ed., *My Soul is Rested: Movement Days in the Deep South Remembered* (New York: Penguin, 1977), 235.
38. Moses, interview.
39. Moses, interview; Watkins, interview; C. C. Bryant, interview by Jimmy Dykes, McComb, MS, November 11, 1995, transcript, USM-OH; Hayes, Forrest County Report, reel 38, no. 104, SNCC-M; Watkins and McInnis, *Brother Hollis*, 93–105; Taylor Branch, *Pillar of Fire: America in the King Years, 1963–1965* (New York: Simon & Schuster, 1998), 50–63; and Patricia Michelle Boyett, *Right to Revolt: The Crusade for Racial Justice in Mississippi's Central Piney Woods* (Jackson: University Press of Mississippi, 2015), 67–69.
40. Zack J. Van Landingham, Memo to File, February 4, 1960, 1-27-0-62-1-1-1, MSSC; Report by Robert C. Thomas, July 12, 1960, 2-70-0-27-1-1-1 to 2-70-0-27-3-1-1, MSSC; Lynd background developed through US Census records and Hattiesburg city directories between 1920 and 1958; "Circuit Clerk," *Hattiesburg American*, August 24, 1955, 1; and "Theron Lynd Elected," *Hattiesburg American*, February 25, 1959, 1.
41. "Theron Lynd Elected," *Hattiesburg American*, February 25, 1959, 1.
42. CBS Reports, "Mississippi and the 15th Amendment," original air date September 26, 1962; Report by Robert C. Thomas, July 12, 1960, 2-70-0-27-1-1-1

to 2-70-0-27-3-1-1, MSSC; and Aniko Bodroghkozy, *Equal Time: Television and the Civil Rights Movement* (Champaign: University of Illinois Press, 2012), 46–51.

43. *United States v. Lynd*, 349 F.2d 790 (1965), Brief for Petitioner, box 1, folder 13, Martin Papers, "to promote . . ." quoted on 13; Burger, interview; Report by Robert C. Thomas, July 12, 1960, 2-70-0-27-1-1-1 to 2-70-0-27-3-1-1, MSSC; and Franklin Barnes, "Negro Voting in Mississippi" (master's thesis, Mississippi College, 1955), 40–43.
44. US Senate, *Civil Rights—1957: Hearings before the Subcommittee on Constitutional Rights of the Senate Committee on the Judiciary*, 85th Cong., 1st sess. (Washington, DC: Government Printing Office, 1957), 564–565; Kennard affidavit located in box 2, folder 4, Evers Papers; Lloyd and Bourn affidavits located in box 2, folder 22, Evers Papers; US Senate, *Civil Rights—1959: Hearings before the Subcommittee on Constitutional Rights of the Senate Committee on the Judiciary*, part 2, 86th Cong., 1st sess. (Washington, DC: Government Printing Office, 1959), Barnes quoted on 1075; J. C. Fairley, interview with Mike Garvey, Hattiesburg, MS, January 31 and February 4, 1977, transcript, USM-OH; and Comments on Barnes quoted from Report by Robert C. Thomas, July 12, 1960, 2-70-0-27-1-1-1 to 2-70-0-27-3-1-1, MSSC.
45. For more on the Hercules workers, see Gordon A. Martin Jr., *Count Them One by One: Black Mississippians Fighting for the Right to Vote* (Jackson: University Press of Mississippi, 2010), 130–153.
46. Ibid.
47. Statement of Reverend W. D. Ridgeway, box 2, folder 21, Evers Papers; Senate Subcommittee, *Civil Rights—1957*, 564–565; Ralph Matthews, "Horrors of South told to Senate," *Baltimore Afro-American*, March 9, 1957, 2; Williams, *Medgar Evers*, 148–151; Senate Subcommittee, *Civil Rights—1959*, 1075; "Local Negroes Tell of Vote Troubles," *Hattiesburg American*, April 25, 1959, 1; and "'No Justice' in Miss. Leader Tells Group," *Chicago Defender*, April 27, 1959, 2.
48. Senate Subcommittee, *Civil Rights—1957*; and Senate Subcommittee, *Civil Rights—1959*, 1075.
49. Barnes, "Negro Voting in Mississippi," 40–43; and Ralph Matthews, "Horrors of South Told to Senate," *Chicago Defender*, March 9, 1957, 2.
50. Johnson quoted in Robert A. Caro, *Master of the Senate: The Years of Lyndon B. Johnson* (New York: Vintage, 2002), 1003; Roy Wilkins and Tom Mathews, *Standing Fast: The Autobiography of Roy Wilkins* (New York: Viking, 1982), 221–246 (the chapter is named "A Small Crumb from Congress"); and "Our Opinions: Our Crippled Civil Rights Bill," *Chicago Defender*, September 28, 1957, 10. For more on the passage of the 1957 and 1960 Civil Rights Acts, see Caro, *Master of the Senate*, especially 886–1034, quoted on 1033;

Charles V. Hamilton, *The Bench and the Ballot: Southern Federal Judges and Black Voters* (New York: Oxford University Press, 1973), 41–69; Steven F. Lawson, *Black Ballots: Voting Rights in the South, 1944–1969* (New York: Columbia University Press, 1976), 140–249; David Nichols, *A Matter of Justice: Eisenhower and the Beginning of the Civil Rights Revolution* (New York: Simon & Schuster, 2007), especially 143–168 and 235–263; and J. W. Anderson, *Eisenhower, Brownell, and the Congress: The Tangled Origins of the Civil Rights Bill of 1956–1957* (Tuscaloosa: University of Alabama Press, 1964).

51. *Civil Rights Act of 1957*, Public Law 85-315, *United States Statutes at Large* 71 (1957): 634–638.
52. "NAACP Rates Civil Rights Act as Best Achievement of 1957," *Philadelphia Tribune*, July 8, 1958, 3; Evers quoted in "Right to Vote Primary Goal of Negroes," *Hattiesburg American*, October 7, 1957, 3A; The United States Commission on Civil Rights, *Civil Rights '63: 1963 Report of the United States Commission on Civil Rights* (Washington, DC: Government Printing Office, 1963), 11–31; and John Doar, "The Work of the Civil Rights Division in Enforcing Voting Rights under the Civil Rights Acts of 1957 and 1960," *Florida State University Law Review* 24, no. 1 (1997): 1–17.
53. Senate Subcommittee, *Civil Rights—1959; Civil Rights Act of 1960*, Public Law 86-449, *United States Statutes at Large* 74 (1960): 86–92; *United States v. Lynd*, 349 F.2d 790 (1965), Brief for Petitioner, box 1, folder 13, Martin Papers; and United States Commission on Civil Rights, *Excerpts from the 1961 Commission on Civil Rights Report* (Washington, DC: Government Printing Office, 1961), especially 17–24.
54. *United States v. Lynd*, 301 F.2d 818 (5th Cir., 1962); *Kennedy v. Lynd*, 306 F.2d 222 (5th Cir., 1962); *United States v. Lynd*, 349 F.2d 785 (5th Cir., 1965); Hamilton, *The Bench and the Ballot*, 41–69; and Martin, *Count Them One by One*, 77–85.
55. The United States Commission on Civil Rights, *Civil Rights '63*, 37–46; and Neil McMillen, "Black Enfranchisement in Mississippi: Federal Enforcement and Black Protest in the 1960s," *Journal of Southern History* 43, no. 3 (1977): 351–372.
56. *United States v. Lynd*, 349 F.2d 790 (1965), Brief for Petitioner, box 1, folder 13, Martin Papers. For more details on the Lynd case, see Martin, *Count Them One by One*; and Boyette, *Right to Revolt*, especially 51–97.
57. *United States v. Lynd*, 349 F.2d 790 (1965), Brief for Petitioner, box 1, folder 13, Martin Papers; and US Senate, *Voting Rights: Hearings before Subcommittee No. 5 of the Committee on the Judiciary House of Representatives*, 89th Cong., 1st sess. (Washington, DC: Government Printing Office, 1965), Forrest County references on 36, 37, 307, 310, and 311.

58. Hayes, Forrest County Report, SNCC-M, reel 38, no. 104; Watkins, interview; and Ladner, interview.
59. Watkins, interview.
60. Ibid.
61. *United States v. Lynd*, 349 F.2d 790 (1965), Brief for Petitioner, appendix A, box 1, folder 13, Martin Papers; Hayes, Forrest County Report, reel 38, no. 104, SNCC-M; Watkins, interview; and *Congressional Record*, 88th Cong., 2d sess., 1964, 110, pt. 5: 6744–6746.
62. *Congressional Record*, 88th Cong., 2d sess., 1964, 110, pt. 5: 6744–6746.
63. Previously known as Victoria Jackson and later known as Victoria Adams, Victoria Gray is referred to here as she was known in the early 1960s. Victoria Jackson, "Autobiography," November 28, 1945, box 7 folder 1, Adams Papers, USM; Branch / Adams, interview; "committed," quoted in Victoria Gray Adams, interview by Katherine Mellen Charron, Petersburg, VA, April 22, 2002, transcript, in author's possession; Victoria Gray Adams, "They Didn't Know the Power of Women," in Faith S. Holsaert, et al., eds., *Hands on the Freedom Plow: Personal Accounts by Women in SNCC* (Champaign: University of Illinois Press, 2010), 230–239; and 1959 *Polk's Hattiesburg City Directory*, 101.
64. Charron / Adams, interview; and Watkins, interview.
65. Branch / Adams, interview; Charron / Adams, interview; Watkins, interview; and Gray Adams, "They Didn't Know the Power of Women," quoted on 232. Sociologist Belinda Robnett has labeled such women "Bridge Leaders." For more, see Belinda Robnett, *How Long? How Long?: African-American Women in the Struggle for Civil Rights* (New York: Oxford University Press, 1997), especially 140–156 for the relationship between SNCC organizers and local black Mississippi women.
66. *United States v. Lynd*, 349 F.2d 790 (1965), Brief for Petitioner, Gray Testimony, 373–395.
67. Charron / Adams, interview. For more on Citizenship Schools, see Katherine Mellen Charron, *Freedom's Teacher: The Life of Septima Clark* (Chapel Hill: University of North Carolina Press, 2009).
68. Charron / Adams, interview.
69. Gray Adams, "They Didn't Know the Power of Women," quoted on 230; and Charron / Adams, interview.
70. Gene Roberts and Hank Klibanoff, *The Race Beat: The Press, the Civil Rights Struggle, and the Awakening of a Nation* (New York: Vintage, 2007). For more on how the Mississippi press responded to local and national civil rights stories, see David Davies, ed., *The Press and Race: Mississippi Journalists Confront the Movement* (Jackson: University Press of Mississippi, 2001); and Steven Classen, *Watching Jim Crow: The Struggles over Mississippi TV, 1955–1969* (Durham, NC: Duke University Press, 2004).

71. CBS Reports, "Mississippi and the 15th Amendment," original Air Date September 26, 1962. Examples taken from each of these newspapers between 1962 and 1963.
72. Joyce Ladner, "Standing Up for Our Beliefs," in Holsaert et al., eds., *Hands on the Freedom Plow*, 217–223, quoted on 219; Ladner, interview; Medgar Evers, Memo, Mississippi NAACP State Conference of Branches, January 21, 1962, box 2, folder 10, Evers Papers; and "NAACP holds 'Kennard Day' Meeting Here," *Hattiesburg American*, January 29, 1962, 2. Kennard's death was covered in the *Chicago Defender, Baltimore Afro-American, Pittsburgh Courier, Atlanta Daily World, Washington Post, Chicago Tribune,* and *New York Times*, among others.
73. Connor quoted in transcript of 1999 "Freedom Summer Roundtable Symposium," Hattiesburg, MS, June 7, 1999, transcript, USM-OH.
74. Connor quoted in transcript of 1999 "Freedom Summer Roundtable Symposium"; Peggy Jean Connor, "A Commentary on the Civil Rights Movement in Mississippi," box 1, folder 1, Connor (Peggy Jean) Papers, USM; Peggy Jean Connor, interview by Dick Conville, Hattiesburg, MS, September 11, 2001, transcript, USM-OH; and Frank Parker, *Black Votes Count: Political Empowerment in Mississippi after 1965* (Chapel Hill: University of North Carolina Press, 1990), 104–129 for *Connor v. Johnson.*
75. *United States v. Lynd*, 349 F.2d 790 (1965), Brief for Petitioner, box 1, folder 13, Martin Papers; "Dixie Vote Registrar Is Found in Contempt," *Washington Post*, July 16, 1963, A6; Gordon, *Count Them One by One*, 199–212; Boyett, *Right to Revolt*, 71–74; and Connor, interview.
76. "Fact Sheet: Hattiesburg" and *Voice of the Movement*, vol. 1, no. 1, box 98, folder 24, SNCC Papers; Lawrence Guyot, interviews by author, Jackson, MS, May 25, 2010 and March 22, 2010, recordings in author's possession; various Hattiesburg-related SNCC reports contained in reel 39, no. 169, SNCC-M; Conner, interview; Zinn, *SNCC*, 102–122; and Dittmer, *Local People*, 178–184.
77. Hattiesburg Freedom Day, reel 39, no. 169, SNCC-M; Smith, interview; Elliott Chase, "Voter Registration Drive Begins Here," *Hattiesburg American*, January 22, 1964, 1; Branch, *Pillar of Fire*, 214–224; and Zinn, *SNCC*, 102–122.
78. Evers quoted in Elliott Chase, "Voter Registration Drive Begins Here," *Hattiesburg American*, January 22, 1964, 1; Baker and other dialogue quoted in Zinn, *SNCC*, 106; and Branch, *Pillar of Fire*, 214–224.
79. Smith, interview.
80. Various images of Freedom Day found in the Moncrief Photograph Collection, MDAH; "Hattiesburg Freedom Day," SNCC Press Release, January 13, 1964, reel 39, no. 169, SNCC-M; Harris, interview; Elliott Chase, "Voter Registration Drive Begins Here," *Hattiesburg American*, January 23, 1964, 1;

"Pickets Resume Damp Tramp," *Hattiesburg American*, January 23, 1964, 1; "Negroes Start Mississippi Voter Drive," *Washington Post*, January 23, 1964, A7; Branch, *Pillar of Fire*, 214–224; Zinn, *SNCC*, 102–122; and Boyett, *Right to Revolt*, 75–97.

81. "Hattiesburg Freedom Day," SNCC Press Release, January 13, 1964, reel 39, no. 169, SNCC-M; Branch, *Pillar of Fire*, 214–224; Zinn, *SNCC*, 102–122; and Boyett, *Right to Revolt*, 75–97.

82. "Ignore Agitators," editorial, *Hattiesburg American*, January 21, 1964, 2; and "No Place for Ministers," *Hattiesburg American*, January 25, 1964, 2.

83. Clergy Participation, Hattiesburg Freedom Day, reel 39, no. 169, SNCC-M; James F. Findlay Jr., *Church People in the Struggle: The National Council of Churches and the Black Freedom Movement, 1950–1970* (New York: Oxford University Press, 1993), 3–47 and 82–85 for Hattiesburg Freedom Day; and Mark Newman, *Divine Agitators: The Delta Ministry and Civil Rights in Mississippi* (Athens: University of Georgia Press, 2004), especially 46–67.

84. Elliott Chase, "Voter Registration Drive Begins Here," *Hattiesburg American*, January 22, 1964, 1; "Law Enforcement," *Hattiesburg American*, January 23, 1964, 12; and "Bud" Gray, interview by Charles Bolton, Hattiesburg, MS, March 19, 1999, transcript, USM-OH.

85. Daisy Harris Wade, interview by author, Hattiesburg, MS, October 6, 2011, recording in author's possession; Daisy Harris Wade, interview by Misty Lambert, Hattiesburg, MS, February 11, 2000, transcript, USM-OH; Wade / Conville, interview; Daisy Harris Wade, interview by Tonya Blair, Hattiesburg, MS, July 20, 2001, transcript, USM-OH; and Anthony Harris, interview by Charles Bolton, Hattiesburg, MS, June 6, 2001, transcript, USM-OH; Howard Zinn, "Incident in Hattiesburg," *The Nation*, May 18, 1964; and quotation taken from Branch, *Pillar of Fire*, 217.

86. "Rights Demonstrators Enjoined in Hattiesburg Vote Drive," SNCC Press Release, February 1, 1964, reel 39, no. 169, SNCC-M; Clergy Participation, Hattiesburg Freedom Day, reel 39, no. 169, SNCC-M; COFO Memo, Jackson, MS, April 14, 1964, reel 39, no. 169, SNCC-M; "Ministers in Hattiesburg, Mississippi, January–May, 1964," box 5, folder 1, Beech Papers; Boyette, *Right to Revolt*, 75–97; Branch, *Pillar of Fire*, 214–224; and "Hattiesburg, Miss. Vote Push Continues," SNCC Press Release, undated, reel 39, no. 169, SNCC-M.

87. Branch, interview; Fairley, interview; Smith, interview; and Herbert Randall and Bobs M. Tusa, *Faces of Freedom Summer* (Tuscaloosa: University of Alabama Press, 2001), 1–28.

88. Burger, interview.

89. McMillen, "Black Enfranchisement in Mississippi," quoted on 367; Hattiesburg Summer Project Workers, box 2, folder 1, Ellin (Joseph and Nancy)

Freedom Summer Collection (hereafter, Ellin Papers), USM. For more on Freedom Summer in Hattiesburg and Mississippi, see Tusa, *Faces of Freedom Summer*, 1–28; Dittmer, *Local People*, 242–271; Payne, *I've Got the Light of Freedom*, 284–316; and Bruce Watson, *Freedom Summer: The Savage Season That Made Mississippi Burn and Made America a Democracy* (New York: Viking, 2010).

90. Three thousand statistic taken from Randall and Tusa, *Faces of Freedom Summer*, 7; Herbert Randall, interview by author, Shinnecock Indian Reservation, Long Island, New York, July 6, 2010; Sandra Adickes, interview by author, New Brunswick, NJ, July 5, 2010; and Sheila Michaels, interview by author, Columbus, OH, June 18, 2010, recording in author's possession.

91. Bulletin, July 3, 1963, box 1, folder 4, Freedom Information Service Records, 1962–1979, WHS; Arthur Reese, "Freedom Schools—Summer 1964," *The Detroit Teacher*, December, 1964, 4; and elderly man quoted in "COFO Worker Explains Summer Project Aims," *Hattiesburg American*, July 7, 1964, 5.

92. John Wesley D., "Freedom and What It Means to Me," *Student Voice of True Light*, July 24, 1964, 4, box 2, folder 3, Ellin Papers; Albert Evans, "Why I Deserve Freedom," *Student Voice of True Light*, July 20, 1964, 2, box 2, folder 3, Ellin Papers; Barbara Schwartzbaum, interview by author, July 9, 2010, New York, NY; Joseph Ellin, interview by author, August 13, 2010, Kalamazoo, MI; and Paula Pace interview by author, July 7, 2010, New York City, NY. All interview recordings are in the author's possession.

93. Larry B., "What I Don't Like about Hattiesburg," *Student Voice of True Light*, July 20, 1964, 2; Mattie Jean Wilson, "My Brother on a Bus," *Student Voice of True Light*, July 20, 1964, 6; Lilly, "The Town Nobody Loved," *Freedom Press*; and Lynette Y., "Dear Gov. Johnson," *Freedom Press*, all found in box 2, folder 3, Ellin Papers.

94. Thousand number cited from Reese, "Freedom Schools—Summer 1964," *The Detroit Teacher*, December, 1964, 4; Randall, interview; Michaels, interview; Adickes, interview; and Stanley Zibulsky, interview by author, Queens, New York, July 9, 2010; Ellin, interview; Sandra Adickes, *Legacy of a Freedom School* (New York: Palgrave, 2005), 55–100.

95. Glenda Funchess, interview by author, December 16, 2009, Hattiesburg, MS, recording in author's possession.

96. "Three Civil Rights Workers Attacked," *Hattiesburg American*, July 10, 1964, 1; David Halberstam, "Rabbi and 2 Rights Aides Attacked in Mississippi," *New York Times*, July 11, 1964, 22; and Summer Project Workers—Hattiesburg, box 2, folder 1, Ellin Papers.

97. Statement by Lawrence D. Spears to the FBI, July 16, 1964, box 1, folder 2, Spears (Lawrence D.) Civil Rights Collection, USM; Memo of the report to

the FBI of the attack on three civil rights workers in Hattiesburg, Mississippi, July 10, 1964, box 1, folder 2, Spears Papers, USM; Herbert Randall, "Lelyveld Beating" and "Owen Injury," July, 1964, box 2, folder 2, Randall Photos, USM; "Three Civil Rights Workers Attacked," *Hattiesburg American*, July 10, 1964, 1; "Rabbi, Rights Workers Beaten by Iron Pipes," *Los Angeles Times*, July 11, 1964, 7; David Halberstam, "Rabbi and 2 Rights Aides Attacked in Mississippi," *New York Times*, July 11, 1964, 22; and "Mississippian Held in Attack on Rabbi and 2 Students," *New York Times*, July 19, 1964, 43.

98. Statement by Lawrence D. Spears to the FBI, box 1, folder 2, Spears Papers; and Herbert Randall, "Lelyveld Beating," box 2, folder 2, Randall Photos.
99. Randall, interview; and Herbert Randall, "Lelyveld Beating," box 2, folder 2, Randall Photos.
100. Randall, interview; "Rabbi, Rights Workers Beaten by Iron Pipes," *Los Angeles Times*, July 11, 1964, 7; "Rabbi, 2 Other Workers Beaten in Mississippi," *Washington Post*, July 11, 1964, A2; "FBI Chief Believes Rights Aids Are Dead," *Chicago Tribune*, July 11, 1964, 1; David Halberstam, "Rabbi and 2 Rights Aides Attacked in Mississippi," *New York Times*, July 11, 1964, 22; "Two Men Charged with Beating Rights Workers," *Los Angeles Times*, July 19, 1964, D2; and Memo from FBI Special Agent New Orleans, July 23, 1964, box 1, folder 2, Spears Papers. The attackers were reportedly from Collins, Mississippi, a community located about twenty-eight miles northwest of Hattiesburg.

Conclusion

Epigraph: Daisy Harris Wade, interview by Misty Lambert, Hattiesburg, MS, February 11, 2000, transcript, USM-OH.

1. Patricia Michelle Boyett, *Right to Revolt: The Crusade for Racial Justice in Mississippi's Central Piney Woods* (Jackson: University Press of Mississippi, 2015); Herbert Randall and Bobs M. Tusa, *Faces of Freedom Summer* (Tuscaloosa: University of Alabama Press, 2001); bailiff quoted in Jack Nelson, "South Finds 'Sensed of Somebodiness,'" *Los Angeles Times*, November 21, 1965, K3; "Cannon Found Guilty of Rape," *Hattiesburg American*, November 11, 1965, 1; Danielle L. McGuire, *At the Dark End of the Street: Black Women, Rape, and Resistance—A New History of the Civil Rights Movement from Rosa Parks to the Rise of Black Power* (New York: Knopf, 2011), 189–195; Raylawni Branch, interview by Kim Adams; and Chester M. Morgan, *Dearly Bought, Deeply Treasured: The University of Southern Mississippi, 1912–1987* (Jackson: University Press of Mississippi, 1987), 128–131.
2. Daisy Harris Wade, interview by author, Hattiesburg, MS, October 6, 2011, recording in author's possession; Wade/Lambert, interview; Daisy Harris Wade, interview by Dick Conville, Hattiesburg, MS, July 12, 2001, transcript,

USM-OH; Daisy Harris Wade, interview by Tonya Blair, Hattiesburg, MS, July 20, 2001, transcript, USM-OH; Anthony Harris, interview by Charles Bolton, Hattiesburg, MS, June 6, 2001, transcript, USM-OH; and Victoria Gray Adams, interview by Katherine Mellen Charron, Petersburg, VA, April 22, 2002, transcript, in author's possession.

3. These examples are taken from Charron/Adams, interview; Wade, interviews; and Victoria Adams, "Autobiography," November 28, 1945, box 7, folder 1, Adams Papers, USM.
4. Senate Subcommittee, *Civil Rights—1959*, 1075.
5. US Senate, Hearings Before the Committee on the Judiciary, 84th Congress, 2nd sess. (Washington, DC: Government Printing Office, 1956), 77–106, quotation on 81. For more on the influence of the Northern black vote, see Henry Lee Moon, *Balance of Power: The Negro Vote* (Garden City, NY: Doubleday & Co., 1948); Steven F. Lawson, *Black Ballots: Voting Rights in the South, 1944–1969* (New York: Columbia University Press, 1976); and Doug McAdam, *Political Process and the Development of Black Insurgency, 1930–1970* (Chicago: University of Chicago Press, 1982), 157–158.
6. For more on freedom-of-choice, see Charles C. Bolton, *The Hardest Deal of All: The Battle over School Integration in Mississippi, 1870–1980* (Jackson: University Press of Mississippi, 2005), 117–166; and Joseph Crespino, *In Search of Another Country: Mississippi and the Conservative Counterrevolution* (Princeton, NJ: Princeton University Press, 2007), 173–204 and 240–266.
7. Harris, interview; and Anthony Harris, *Ain't Gonna Let Nobody Turn Me 'Round: A Coming of Age Story and a Personal Account of the Civil Rights Movement in Hattiesburg, Mississippi* (CreateSpace Independent Publishing Platform, 2013).
8. Glenda Funchess, interview by author, December 16, 2009, Hattiesburg, MS, recording in author's possession; Compliance Plans Approved by US Office of Education and State Department of Education, Jackson, Mississippi, Counties and Municipal Separate School Districts, page no. 2, both located in box 57, folder 1767b, Tubb (J. M.) Papers, 1943–1974, MDAH; Boyette, *Right to Revolt*, 199–222 for Hattiesburg school desegregation; and Bolton, *The Hardest Deal of All*, 1966 statistic on 140.
9. Bolton, *The Hardest Deal of All*, 117–192; Crespino, *In Search of Another Country*, 173–204 and 240–266; *Alexander v. Holmes County Board of Education*, 396 US 19 (1969); and "Plan Private White School Here," *Hattiesburg American*, June 22, 1965, 10. For more on the concept of "white flight" and white Southern conservative responses to the civil rights movement, see Kevin Kruse, *White Flight: Atlanta and the Making of Modern Conservatism* (Princeton, NJ: Princeton University Press, 2005).

10. Sharon Lerner, "A School District That Was Never Desegregated," *Atlantic*, February 5, 2015, www.theatlantic.com/education/archive/2015/02/a-school-district-that-was-never-desegregated/385184/, accessed August 25, 2017; Bolton, *The Hardest Deal of All*, 221; Mississippi Department of Education Public Reports, http://reports.mde.k12.ms.us/data/, accessed July 9, 2018; and US Bureau of the Census, *Census of the Population: 2010, Summary Population and Housing Characteristics* (Washington, DC: Government Printing Office, 2013), 170.
11. SNCC Press Release, "Negro Woman Qualifies for Mississippi Senate Seat," April 10, 1964, reel 39, no. 169, SNCC-M; and "Negro Runs Close 4th in Mississippi Primary," *Chicago Defender*, June 4, 1964, 4.
12. Robert G. Spivack, "Will Miss. Voting Drive Cause Breakdown or Breakthrough?" *Philadelphia Tribune*, June 23, 1964, 5; and Crespino, *In Search of Another Country*, 75–107. For more on partisan shifts in Mississippi after 1964, see Chris Danielson, *After Freedom Summer: How Race Realigned Mississippi Politics, 1965–1986* (Gainesville: University of Press of Florida, 2011); and Frank Parker, *Black Votes Count: Political Empowerment in Mississippi after 1965* (Chapel Hill: University of North Carolina Press, 1990).
13. Conville/Wade, interview.
14. *United States v. Lynd*, 349 F.2d 785 (5th Cir. 1965); *Voting Rights Act of 1965*, Public Law 89–111, *United States Statutes at Large* 79 (1965): 437–446; Parker, *Black Votes Count; United States v. Lynd*, 349 F.2d 790 (1965), Brief for Petitioner, box 1, folder 13, Martin Papers; and Mark Newman, *Divine Agitators: The Delta Ministry and Civil Rights in Mississippi* (Athens: University of Georgia Press, 2004), Hattiesburg figure on 66.
15. Copies of these newspapers from multiple dates are located in box 1, folder 3, Kwanguvu (Umoja) Freedom Summer Collection, 1964, 1999, USM; box 2, folder 6, Ellin Papers; box 98, folder 24, SNCC; and box 5, folders 4 and 7; and Freedom of Information Service, "The Time Has Come to Get that Power," box 5, folder 7, Beech Papers.
16. Parker, *Black Votes Count*, quoted on 37; Chris Danielson, "'Lily White and Hard Right': The Mississippi Republican Party and Black Voting," *Journal of Southern History* 75, no. 1 (2009): 83–118; and Crespino, *In Search of Another Country*. For more on modern Southern repression of black votes, see Ari Berman, *Give Us the Ballot: The Modern Struggle for Voting Rights in America* (New York: Farrar, Straus and Giroux, 2015), 245–314.
17. For more on these court battles, see Parker, *Black Votes Count*, especially 78–129, election statistics taken from 70 and 2; *Connor v. Johnson*, 402 US 690 (1971); Edward Grobow Redlich, "Toward Equal Representation: The *Connor* Case and the Struggle for Reapportionment of the Mississippi Legislature"

(bachelor's thesis, Harvard College, 1981); and *Fairley v. Patterson*, 493 F.2d 598 (5th Cir. 1974).

18. "The Weather," *Hattiesburg American*, August 13, 1964, 1; "Negroes Leave City Bus after Seating Incident," *Hattiesburg American*, August 12, 1964, 14; "Library Closed after Integration Attempt," *Hattiesburg American*, August 14, 1964, 1; "Library Is Closed Again," *Hattiesburg American*, August 17, 1964, 1; and Sandra Adickes, *Legacy of a Freedom School* (New York: Palgrave, 2005), 81–100.
19. Adickes, *Legacy of a Freedom School*, 81–100 and 137–154; Sandra Adickes, Freedom Summer Journal, box 1, folders 1–4, USM; Sandra Adickes, "History Lessons in Hattiesburg," box 1, folder 7, USM; and Report from Hattiesburg, August 1–14, 1965, box 5, folder 4, Beech Papers.
20. "Call It Off," *Hattiesburg American*, editorial, June 23, 1964, 4; M. W. Hamilton, interview by Orley B. Caudill, Petal, MS, February 13, 1978, transcript, USM-OH; COFO News Release, box 4, folder 5, Beech Papers; "Beatings, Harassment, Injustice, Violence," *The Voice of the Movement*, February 1, 1965, box 4, folder 5, Beech Papers.
21. COFO News Release; "Beatings, Harassment, Injustice, Violence"; copies of affidavits located in box 5, folder 2, Beech Papers; and Commission on the Delta Ministry Budget, box 5, folder 3, Beech Papers.
22. Report from Hattiesburg, August 1–14, 1965, box 5, folder 4, Beech Papers.
23. Ellie Dahmer, interview; "Negro's Home and Store Burned by Nightriders," *Hattiesburg American*, January 10, 1966, 1; Elliot Chaze, "Push Probe of Fire Bomb Death," *Hattiesburg American*, January 11, 1966, 1; Don Whitehead, *Attack on Terror: The FBI against the Ku Klux Klan in Mississippi* (New York: Funk & Wagnalls, 1970), 233–245; and Boyette, *Right to Revolt*, 143–145.
24. "Chamber of Commerce Adopts Statement," *Hattiesburg American*, January 12, 1966, 1; "Dahmer Family Fund Created," *Hattiesburg American*, January 11, 1966, 1; and "A Tragedy for Everybody," *Hattiesburg American*, January 11, 1966, 2.
25. "Applicants for Registration, Forrest County, Mississippi," *Hattiesburg American*, September 4, 1964, 14.
26. J. C. Fairley, interview with Mike Garvey, Hattiesburg, MS, January 31 and February 4, 1977, transcript, USM-OH; Elliot Chaze, "15 Requests to Be Made by CR Leaders," *Hattiesburg American*, January 12, 1966, 1; Elliot Chaze, "NAACP Revises Its 'Grievance List,'" *Hattiesburg American*, January 13, 1966, 1; and the following all from box 4, folder 2, CoC: Minutes of the January 12, 1966 Hattiesburg Chamber of Commerce Board of Directors Meeting; Untitled Statement related to Vernon Dahmer murders, January 12, 1966; "Grievance List and Responses"; Untitled News Release, January 27, 1966; "Report on the Forrest County Branch of the National Association for the Advancement of Colored People," January 28, 1966.

27. Conville / Wade, interview; Fairley, interview; James Nix, interview by Sarah Rowe, Hattiesburg, MS, March 7, 1993, transcript, USM-OH; and Bob Beech to Howard, Hattiesburg, MS, March 3, 1966, box 3, folder 4, WHS.
28. Wade, interviews; Fairley, interview; and Nix, interview. For more on Head Start in Mississippi, see Crystal R. Sanders, *A Chance for Change: Head Start and Mississippi's Black Freedom Struggle* (Chapel Hill: University of North Carolina Press, 2016), especially 72–106.
29. Nix, interview; Wade, interviews; Fairley, interviews; Beech correspondence between 2/66 and 4/66 related to NAACP internal division contained in box 1, folder 4, Beech Papers; and Boyett, *Right to Revolt*, 146–175.
30. Boyett, *Right to Revolt*, 146–198; Michael Newton, *The Ku Klux Klan in Mississippi* (Jefferson, NC: McFarland & Co., 2010), 127–182; Whitehead, *Attack on Terror*, Bowers quoted on 5; and Seth Cagin and Philip Dray, *We Are Not Afraid: The Story of Goodman, Schwerner, and Chaney, and the Civil Rights Campaign for Mississippi* (New York: Scribner, 1988).
31. Boyett, *Right to Revolt*, 146–198; Newton, *Ku Klux Klan in Mississippi*, 127–182; Whitehead, *Attack on Terror*, Bowers quoted on 5; and Cagin and Dray, *We Are Not Afraid*.
32. Elliot Chaze, "11 Charged with Murder and Arson," *Hattiesburg American*, January 25, 1968, 1 and quoted on 9.
33. Samuel Holloway Bowers, interview by Debra Spencer, recording, October 24, 1983, Jackson, MS, MDAH; and Patricia Michelle Buzard-Boyett, "Race and Justice in Mississippi's Central Piney Woods, 1940–2010" (PhD diss., University of Southern Mississippi, 2011), 284–297, quoted on 284.
34. Whitehead, *Attack on Terror*, 246–259.
35. Buzard-Boyett, "Race and Justice," 523–670; Elliot Chaze, "Hung Jury Results in Bowers Mistrial," *Hattiesburg American*, May 18, 1968, 1 and 6; Sharon Wertz, "Fire-Bombing Death of Vernon Dahmer 'Changed Everything,'" *Hattiesburg American*, May 30, 1982, 6E; Nikki Davis Maute, "Prayer, Tears Entered into Jury's Vote," *Hattiesburg American*, August 23, 1998, 1; and Monica Carter, "Verdict Bodes Well for Mississippi," *Hattiesburg American*, August 22, 1998, Funchess quoted on 5A.
36. Buzard-Boyett, "Race and Justice," 740–748; www.hattiesburguso.com/uso/; and observations made by author.
37. Observations made by author on various occasions.
38. Observations made at the gravesite of Hammond Smith, Highland Cemetery, Hattiesburg, MS on June 26, 2014; and "Dr. C. W. Smith Dies," *Hattiesburg American*, June 21, 1971, 1.
39. For more on Southern suburbanization in the wake of the Civil Rights Movement, see Matthew D. Lassiter, *The Silent Majority: Suburban Politics in the Sunbelt South* (Princeton, NJ: Princeton University Press, 2006).

40. Patrick Magee, "Southern Miss Removes Confederate Flag from All Campuses," *Gulfport Sun Herald*, October 28, 2015, www.sunherald.com/news/article41689311.html; and William Scarborough, "Heritage, Not Hate. Let's Keep the State Flag," *Jackson Clarion Ledger*, July 28, 2017, www.clarionledger.com/story/opinion/columnists/2017/07/28/heritage-not-hate-lets-keep-state-flag/518740001/.

Acknowledgments

First and foremost, I would like to thank my mother for her love and support over the years. The origins of my academic and intellectual journeys are deeply rooted in the examples and encouragement she has provided throughout my life. Because we are close, she has also lived with this project for many years and has always been willing to listen to me speak about archival discoveries and new revelations that at the time mattered to no one but me. Her time and patience have made this process less isolating.

Thank you also to my family—Dave, Jess, and Dad—for your constant encouragement and support. You have all been sources of joy and reality at times when I was obsessive in my thinking. Thank you as well to Janet, Derek, Grandma, Flo, Linda, Paul, Bob, Ed, and all members of my extended family for your support.

I began this project while in the Department of History at Ohio State University. Hasan Jeffries was terrific to work with; his wisdom and advice profoundly shaped this book and my intellectual growth; all those softball games (OSU intramural champs 2011) were a fun respite, even though we usually just talked about work. Kevin Boyle is the best teacher I have ever seen. Working with him during those years was essential to the development of this book and to many other components of my career. Ken Goings provided wonderful feedback on every single page of an early draft. His influence remains omnipresent every time I teach "The History of the Civil Rights Movement."

I first realized what this book could be while talking to Joe Arena outside a bar on High Street in Columbus, Ohio. Joe influenced this book as much as anyone else, telling me not to "sell it short" and correctly insisting on a new opening chapter. Christopher Elias, the third member of my writing group during the early stages of this book, helped me think differently about prose and art. Our group was connected by a profound love of storytelling, history, and writing. Although we never did adopt a name, our writing group meetings had a great impact on me, and I will always cherish those memories.

Others at OSU helped provide a rich intellectual environment and supportive atmosphere that incubated this work and my career. Thank you to Judy Wu, Stephanie Shaw, Leslie Alexander, Paula Baker, Tiyi Morris, Harvey Graff, Robin Judd, Randy Roth, David Staley, Tyran Steward, Jessica Pliley, Robert Bennett III, Giselle Jeter, Matt Yates, Lindsey Parker, Tony Gass, Jason Perkins, Nicole Jackson, Noel Voltz, and dozens of other graduate students. Great friends in and around Columbus—including Lou Tobin, Bill and Kari

Warfield, Jason Gibson, the CFFL, the Grinders, Chi Nguyen, Anne McDaniel, and Ashley Bowerman—helped provide much-needed breaks from an otherwise all-consuming academic experience. I realize that I was lucky to be surrounded by the right people at the right time and place. My life and work would otherwise have been quite different.

The year I spent in Hattiesburg teaching at the University of Southern Mississippi was the most valuable professional experience of my life. I am so grateful to Southern Miss, the Department of History, and all of my colleagues from that year, especially Curtis Austin, Max Grivno, Phyllis Jestice, Andy and Jill Weist, Doug Bristol, Heather Stur, Andrew Haley, Kyle Zelner, Doug Chambers, Bo Morgan, Susannah Ural, and Christian Pinnen—all of whom helped shape this book. Not only did Max Grivno introduce me to two types of sources that proved invaluable, but he also provided a ride to the archives in Jackson. Thanks also to Charles Bolton and Louis Kyriakoudes for their contributions to the USM Oral History collection. People often ask me, "Why Hattiesburg?" The truth is that this book, especially the sections about African Americans, could not have been written without the incredible oral histories USM began collecting in the 1970s. My approach would not have been possible in other cities with less rich collections. Others in the USM community helped shape this work and enrich my experiences there, especially Kevin Greene, Dave Davies, Jennifer Marquardt, Don Holmes, and Sherita L. Johnson.

The archivists at Southern Miss, especially Jennifer Brannock, Andrew Rhodes, Cindy Lawler, and Leah Rials, have been incredibly supportive. I know all archivists are helpful, but these folks have truly gone far beyond their normal duties to aid my research. They processed special orders, scanned and emailed documents, and even took the time to speak with me at parties and social events about document collections (sorry for that). Other archivists who provided valuable research assistance include Michael Edwards at the Wisconsin Historical Society, Anne Webster at the Mississippi Department of Archives and History, Chris Harter at the Amistad Research Center, and Elaine Hall at the King Center. Thank you to all the countless librarians and archivists who helped make this research possible. Thank you also to Alice Thiede who produced a map for this book.

This book has also been shaped by conversations and interviews with several legendary civil rights activists who have helped me gain a much better understanding of the civil rights movement and life in the Jim Crow South: Staughton Lynd, Bob Moses, Hollis Watkins, Charlie Cobb, Mark Levy, Roscoe Jones, Ed King, Lawrence Guyot, Joseph Ellin, Sandra Adickes, Jan Hillegas, Julian Bond, Margaret Kibbee, Marilyn Lowen, Colia Clark, Herbert Randall, Heather Booth, Ira Landess, Paula Pace, Sheila Michaels, Stanley Zibulsky, Frank Figgers, Glenda Funchess, Peggy Jean Connor, Anthony Harris, Daisy Harris Wade, Jessie Morris, Raylawni Branch, Dorie and Joyce Ladner.

Dozens more historians and scholars have also shaped this work. There are too many to list, but those with whom I have most directly engaged include Robin D. G. Kelley,

Jason Ward, Crystal Sanders, Nan Woodruff, William Van Deburg, Emilye Crosby, Nishani Frazier, Françoise Hamlin, Charles Payne, John Dittmer, Danielle McGuire, Antwain Hunter, Ariane Cruz, Sabrina Strings, Jessie Dunbar, Shannen Dee Williams, Grace Hale, Jon Hale, Davarian Baldwin, Daphne Chamberlain, Scott Nelson, Kevin Greene, Ted Ownby, Nan Woodruff, Tony Kaye, Jessica Johnson, Deidre Cooper Owens, Glenda Gilmore, Kidada Williams, Becca Walton, Nishani Frazier, Treva Lindsey, Charles Hughes, Keme Hawkins, Tanisha Ford, Keisha Blain, Ashley Farmer, Christina Greene, Brenda Gayle Plummer, Craig Werner, Charles Reagan Wilson, Louis Ferleger, Linda Heywood, Bruce Schulman, Adrian Pettey, and Michael Vinson Williams. There are many hundreds more whose work has in some way shaped this book. Thank you. I apologize for any omissions.

At my current home institution, the University of North Carolina at Chapel Hill, I have enjoyed an exceptional level of support and access to a phenomenal intellectual environment. My work has truly been elevated by tremendous colleagues. Thank you to everyone in the Department of History, especially Karen Auerbach, Fitz Brundage, Claude Clegg, Lloyd Kramer, Kathleen DuVal, Matt Andrews, Lauren Jarvis, Bill Ferris, Marcie Ferris, Joseph T. Glatthaar, Jerma Jackson, Jacquelyn Dowd Hall, Miguel La Serna, Jim Leloudis, Lisa Lindsay, Heather Williams, Kenneth Janken, Malinda Lowery, Genna Rae McNeil, Michael Morgan, Molly Worthen, Susan Dabney Pennybacker, Louis A. Pérez, Jr., Katie Turk, Erik Gellman, Ben Waterhouse, and Harry Watson. These people have helped shape my work the most profoundly, but this book is the product of a broader supporting community in Chapel Hill. Thanks also to Joyce Loftin, Sharon Anderson, Adam Kent, Michael Williams, and Jennifer Parker for helping facilitate research and other logistics.

The intellectual community at UNC-Chapel Hill and in central North Carolina's Research Triangle makes this the best place in the world to study Southern history. Outside of my own department, I am also grateful to Sibby Anderson-Thompkins, Jennifer Pruitt, Ron Williams, Brandon Proia, Tim Tyson, Kat Charron, Elizabeth Engelhardt, Gabrielle Berlinger, Joey Fink, Ben Frey, Elizabeth Manekin, Bernie Herman, Anna Krome-Lukens, Bob Korstad, Wesley Hogan, Sean Zeigler, Lindsay Ayling, Maya Little, Brendon Thornton, Adriane Lentz-Smith, Christian Lentz, Jennifer Ho, Ariana Vigil, Danielle Christmas, Patrick Horn, Rachel Seidman, Jennifer Standish, Seth Kotch, Mosi Ifatunji, Rob Shapard, Mishio Yamanaka, T. Evan Faulkenbury, Laura Edwards, Jarvis McInnis, Blair Kelley, Thavolia Glymph, Nancy MacLean, Reginald Hildebrand, Susanna Michele Lee, Watson Jennison, Lisa Levenstein, and everyone affiliated with the Center for the Study of the American South. Thank you also to close friends Alyson Bancroft, Lindsay Starck, Brett Currier, Andrew Erickson, Mike Kelly, Kelly Pearson, and Beth Doran.

It has been a joy to work with Harvard University Press. Thank you in particular to my editor, Andrew Kinney, who helped navigate this manuscript to publication. Thanks also to all the others at HUP who have helped make possible the production of this book, especially Brian Distelberg, Olivia Woods, Stephanie Vyce, Louise E. Robbins, Michael Higgins, and Joyce Seltzer. Richard Feit provided tremendous copyediting services that greatly improved this book. Thanks, as well, to Wendy Muto at Westchester Publishing Services. Additional thanks to the anonymous reviewers who took the time to read and engage with my work.

Index

Note: *Italicized* page numbers indicate photographs. Page numbers followed by n or *t* indicate notes or tables.

Index